THE RECORD OF AMERICAN HISTORY: INTERPRETIVE READINGS

VOLUME I   1607-1877

EDITED BY

IRWIN UNGER
New York University

DAVID BRODY
University of California, Davis

PAUL GOODMAN
University of California, Davis

XEROX COLLEGE PUBLISHING

Waltham, Massachusetts / Toronto

The Record of American History: Interpretive Readings

VOLUME I   1607–1877

Copyright © 1971 by Xerox Corporation.
All rights reserved. No part of the material
covered by this copyright may be produced
in any form or by any means of reproduction.
Library of Congress Catalog Number: 77-141259
Printed in the United States of America.

ACKNOWLEDGMENTS

Footnotes have been omitted except where they are necessary for an understanding of the text.

DOUGLASS G. ADAIR, " 'Experience Must Be Our Only Guide': History, Democratic Theory, and the United States Constitution." Reprinted with permission of the Henry E. Huntington Library and Art Gallery.

BERNARD BAILYN, from *The Ideological Origins of the American Revolution*. Excerpted by permission of the publishers. Cambridge, Mass.: The Belknap Press of Harvard University Press. Copyright, 1967, by the President and Fellows of Harvard College.

THOMAS C. BARROW, "The American Revolution as a Colonial War for Independence." Reprinted by permission of the author.

ARTHUR BESTOR, "The American Civil War as a Constitutional Crisis." Reprinted by permission of the author.

RAY ALLEN BILLINGTON, "Frontier Democracy: Social Aspects" from *America's Frontier Heritage* by Ray Allen Billington. Copyright © 1966 by Ray Allen Billington. Reprinted by permission of Holt, Rinehart and Winston, Inc.

W. R. BROCK, "Policies and Possibilities." Reprinted by permission of St. Martin's Press, Inc., Macmillan & Co., Ltd.

MILDRED CAMPBELL, "Social Origins of Some Early Americans" from *Seventeenth-Century America* by James Smith. Reprinted by permission of the University of North Carolina Press. Copyright © 1959 by the Institute of Early American History and Culture.

WILLIAM N. CHAMBERS, "Parties and Nation-Building in America" from *Political Parties and Political Development*, eds. J. LaPalombara and Myron Weiner, Social Science Research Council (copyright © 1966 by Princeton University Press; Princeton Paperback, 1968).

DAVID DONALD, "A. Lincoln, Politician" from *Lincoln Reconsidered,* by David Donald. Copyright © 1956 by David Donald. Reprinted by permission of Alfred A. Knopf, Inc.

OSCAR HANDLIN, "The Significance of the Seventeenth Century" from *Seventeenth-Century America* by James Smith. Reprinted by permission of the University of North Carolina Press. Copyright © 1959 by the Institute of Early American History and Culture.

JAMES A. HENRETTA, "Economic Development and Social Structure in Colonial Boston." First published in the *William and Mary Quarterly,* 3rd ser., vol. 22 (1965). Reprinted by permission of the author.

RICHARD HOFSTADTER, "Thomas Jefferson: The Aristocrat as Democrat" from *American Political Tradition,* by Richard Hofstadter. Copyright 1948 by Alfred A. Knopf, Inc. Reprinted by permission of the publisher.

MILTON M. KLEIN, "Democracy and Politics in Colonial New York." Reprinted by permission of the author and *New York History.*

AUBREY C. LAND, "Economic Base and Social Structure: The Northern Chesapeake in the Eighteenth Century." Reprinted by permission of *The Journal of Economic History.*

RICHARD P. MCCORMICK, "Political Development and the Second Party System" from *The American Party Systems: Stages of Political Development,* edited by William Nisbet Chambers and Walter Dean Burnham. Copyright © 1967 by Oxford University Press, Inc. Reprinted by permission.

FREDERICK MERK, "Manifest Destiny" from *Manifest Destiny and Mission in American History,* by Frederick Merk. Copyright © 1963 by Frederick Merk. Reprinted by permission of Alfred A. Knopf, Inc.

PERRY MILLER, "The Contribution of the Protestant Churches to Religious Liberty in Colonial America." Reprinted by permission of the estate of Perry Miller and *Church History.*

DAVID MONTGOMERY, "The Working Classes of the Pre-Industrial American City, 1780–1830." Reprinted by permission of *Labor History.*

ROBERT R. PALMER, "The People as Constituent Power" from *The Age of Democratic Revolution: A Political History of Europe and America, 1760–1800,* vol. 1, *The Challenge* (copyright © 1959 by Princeton University Press; Princeton Paperback, 1969). Reprinted by permission of Princeton University Press.

ROY HARVEY PEARCE, "The 'Ruines of Mankind': The Indian and the Puritan Mind." Reprinted by permission of the *Journal of the History of Ideas.*

NORMAN K. RISJORD, "1812: Conservatives, War Hawks, and the Nation's Honor." Reprinted by permission of the author.

A. L. ROWSE, "Tudor Expansion." Reprinted by permission of Curtis Brown, Ltd. Copyright © 1957 by the Institute of Early American History and Culture.

ALAN SIMPSON, "The Covenanted Community" from *Puritanism in Old and New England.* Reprinted by permission of The University of Chicago Press. Copyright © 1955 by The University of Chicago. Copyright under the International Copyright Union, 1955.

KENNETH M. STAMPP, "From Day Clean to First Dark" from *The Peculiar Institution,* by Kenneth M. Stampp. Copyright © 1956 by Kenneth M. Stampp. Reprinted by permission of Alfred A. Knopf, Inc.

THAD W. TATE, JR., from *The Negro in Eighteenth-Century Williamsburg.* Reprinted by permission of Colonial Williamsburg, Inc., and the University Press of Virginia.

JOHN L. THOMAS, "Romantic Reform in America, 1815–1865." Reprinted by permission of the author and the *American Quarterly* of the University of Pennsylvania. Copyright, 1965, Trustees of the University of Pennsylvania.

BARBARA WELTER, "The Cult of True Womanhood, 1820–1860." Reprinted by permission of the author and the *American Quarterly* of the University of Pennsylvania. Copyright, 1965, Trustees of the University of Pennsylvania.

JOEL WILLIAMSON, "New Patterns in Economics." Reprinted by permission of the University of North Carolina Press.

Contents

Introduction   xi

PART 1
The American Colonial Experience 1607–1763

Roots of English Colonization   3
 Tudor Expansion: The Transition from Medieval to Modern History   **A. L. Rowse**   4

The Transit of Civilization from the Old World to the New   10
 The Significance of the Seventeenth Century   **Oscar Handlin**   11

The Red Man as the White Man's Burden   19
 The "Ruines of Mankind": The Indian and the Puritan Mind   **Roy Harvey Pearce**   20

The New England Way: Puritan Quest for Utopia   32
 The Covenanted Community   **Alan Simpson**   33

Peopling the Colonies   42
 Social Origins of Some Early Americans   **Mildred Campbell**   43

The Beginnings of Slavery   60
 From *The Negro in Eighteenth-Century Williamsburg*   **Thad W. Tate, Jr.**   61

The Plantation South   75
 Economic Base and Social Structure: The Northern Chesapeake in the Eighteenth Century   **Aubrey C. Land**   76

Colonial Roots of Popular Government   87
 Democracy and Politics in Colonial New York   **Milton M. Klein**   88

Religion in the New World   100
 The Contribution of the Protestant Churches to Religious Liberty in Colonial America   **Perry Miller**   101

Class and Status in the New World   107
 Economic Development and Social Structure in Colonial Boston   **James A. Henretta**   108

PART 2
The Birth of the Republic 1763–1815

Roots of the American Revolution   121
   From *The Ideological Origins of the American Revolution*   Bernard Bailyn   122

The Nature of the American Revolution   135
   The American Revolution as a Colonial War for Independence   Thomas C. Barrow   136

Nation-Building, American Style   144
   The American Revolution: The People as Constituent Power   Robert R. Palmer   145

The Founding Fathers: Democrats or Aristocrats?   160
   "Experience Must Be Our Only Guide": History, Democratic Theory, and the United States Constitution   Douglass G. Adair   161

The First American Party System, 1790–1820   172
   Parties and Nation-Building in America   William N. Chambers   173

The Enigma of Thomas Jefferson   191
   Thomas Jefferson: The Aristocrat as Democrat   Richard Hofstadter   192

The Perils of a Young Republic   208
   1812: Conservatives, War Hawks, and the Nation's Honor   Norman K. Risjord   209

The State of the Union: 1800   218
   From *History of the United States During the Administrations of Jefferson and Madison*   Henry Adams   219

PART 3
The Middle Years 1815–1877

The Urban Wage Earner in the Early Republic   233
   The Working Classes of the Pre-Industrial American City, 1780–1830   David Montgomery   234

The Frontier and American Society   245
   Frontier Democracy: Social Aspects   Ray Allen Billington   246

The Second Party System   259
   Political Development and the Second Party System   Richard P. McCormick   260

Women in Ante-Bellum America   279
   The Cult of True Womanhood, 1820–1860   Barbara Welter   280

The Black Slave   298
    From Day Clean to First Dark   **Kenneth M. Stampp**   299

Ante-Bellum Reform   321
    Romantic Reform in America, 1815–1865   **John L. Thomas**   322

Ante-Bellum Expansionism   341
    Manifest Destiny   **Frederick Merk**   342

The Causes of the Civil War   364
    The American Civil War as a Constitutional Crisis   **Arthur Bestor**   365

Lincoln and the Civil War   385
    A. Lincoln, Politician   **David Donald**   386

Constitutional Reconstruction   396
    Policies and Possibilities   **W. R. Brock**   397

Black Reconstruction in the South   416
    New Patterns in Economics   **Joel Williamson**   417

Introduction

This collection is designed principally to meet the needs of the introductory survey of United States history. This course is currently undergoing considerable change on college campuses around the country. At one time the typical beginning survey strongly emphasized political history—but political history conceived in the narrowest way as the succession of presidential administrations. Though this approach may survive here and there, it is rapidly being replaced by classes stressing the social and intellectual dimensions of the American past. It seems less important to students and faculty today to talk about Jackson's Kitchen Cabinet than about the condition of women in Jacksonian times; it seems less interesting to focus on the details of the Kansas–Nebraska Act than on the plight of blacks under slavery; it appears pointless to deal with scandals in the Truman regime when we all want to know more about the roots of the cold war.

Recognizing the new concerns of both teachers and students, we have sought to devote half our space to articles on society and social events. We have not, however, neglected politics. Instead we have attempted to include important synthesizing articles that bring together material on an entire political epoch. Our purpose has been to provide the student with a liberal sampling of the very best of the new American history while at the same time furnishing readable and provocative special studies to supplement the narratives of paperback books and standard texts.

IRWIN UNGER
DAVID BRODY
PAUL GOODMAN

PART 1

*The American Colonial Experience
1607-1783*

Roots of English Colonization

The first permanent English settlement in North America was established at Virginia in 1607, a century after Spain had laid the foundations of a great empire in the Western Hemisphere. England's late entry into the scramble for overseas colonies resulted from the unsettled and turbulent conditions within sixteenth-century Britain, conditions that were transforming the island from a feudal kingdom into a modern nation. In the following essay, A. L. Rowse describes the internal changes that prepared England to become Europe's leading colonial power in the next three centuries.

The preconditions of overseas expansion were territorial and political unification, economic development, and an adventurous spirit, willing to take risks in distant and dangerous enterprises. By 1600, England had satisfied all three. Political centralization came through the efforts of Henry VIII, Queen Elizabeth, and other members of the Tudor dynasty (1485–1603) who occupied the English throne for over a century. They subdued the powerful aristocratic landowning families, they placed the authority, wealth, and power of the church under royal control by breaking with the Papacy in Rome, and they encouraged the development of new, middle-class men who prospered through Crown favor and were loyal in return. Acting through Parliament, the Tudors gave greater legitimacy to their rule by granting some of their subjects limited opportunity to participate in governing the realm.

Equally important in the modernization of England were developments in the English economy which increased the nation's wealth. The key was the growing commercialization and efficiency of agriculture. Increased production of wool, England's staple product, only stimulated a vigorous export trade with Europe in both raw materials and manufactured cloth. By the middle of the sixteenth century, overseas trading companies, building on precedents set by the wool trade, sought new opportunities for profit in Russia, India, and eventually North America. Tapping accumulated capital and enjoying corporate privileges granted by the Crown, the Virginia Company was the first of more than a dozen that planted the English flag in the New World during the early seventeenth century. Politically unified, its wealth growing, Elizabethan England was poised for the leap across the Atlantic, emboldened by the victory over the Spanish Armada in 1588. Its self-confidence and vigor found an outlet overseas, just as it found a voice in William Shakespeare who set his last play in a distant, unknown, and remarkable land —

> O, wonder!
> How many goodly creatures are there here!
> How beauteous mankind is! O brave new world,
> That has such people in't.

FOR FURTHER READING:

Jones, Howard M. *O Strange New World.* New York: The Viking Press, Compass Books, 1967.*
Notestein, Wallace. *The English People on the Eve of Colonization.* Harper & Row, Publishers, Torchbooks, 1954.*
Parry, J. H. *The Age of Reconnaissance.* New American Library, Mentor Books, 1963.*

Asterisk denotes paperback edition.

Tudor Expansion: The Transition from Medieval to Modern History   A. L. ROWSE

"How much the greatest event it is that ever happened in the world! and how much the best!" said Charles James Fox of the French Revolution. Charles Fox was a man of notoriously bad judgment — and I am not sure that we historians are not too generous in our estimate of the importance of revolutions. I am not speaking of their value or their merits, where bad is mixed with good, the destructive with the constructive, losses with gains. I am speaking of the *importance* of revolutions as a factor in history and wondering whether we do not overrate it. I suppose that their chief contribution lies in the release they give to forces in society that have been withheld or restrained — though not all is for the good when the safety valve is blown off.

We historians attach much significance to the Puritan Revolution in England, the Revolution of 1688, the French, the American, the Russian revolutions — many books, whole libraries, have been written about them. Yet I wonder whether there are not quieter, underlying movements, that attract less spectacular notice — the movements of peoples, the internal movements of population — which are more fundamental and achieve more durable results in the history of mankind. We in the twentieth century lie under the sinister shadow of the Russian Revolution: we are not likely to underestimate it. Yet it may well be that before long we shall come to think of the Russian colonization of Siberia, her expansion into the vast spaces of Northern Asia, as a matter of more solid and insurmountable importance for the world.

The fact is that people's attention is arrested by the drama of the revolutionary break in society: they are rather mesmerized by the cross section that is revealed and are apt not to grasp the long process in which revolution is a jolt, a disturbance, sometimes hurrying things up, sometimes obstructing or deflecting the current.

How many people have the historic imagination to realize that the making of the American nation must be the greatest single, homogeneous achievement of modern history?

Its appeal is epic rather than dramatic: a slower moving, in some ways a more subtle, appeal to the imagination. But one feels it no less strongly — and perhaps it is a deeper level of experience of life, of realization of the heroism and the pathos that it speaks to — as one moves across the prairies, down the Ohio and across the Mississippi, or out of the Cumberland Gap from Kentucky into southern Illinois

---

Source: A. L. Rowse, "Tudor Expansion: The Transition from Medieval to Modern History," *William and Mary Quarterly,* 3d ser., vol. 14 (1957), pp. 309–316.

and spreading fanwise across the Middle West, or along the trails from St. Louis to Oregon, to Santa Fé and across the passes into California. Again, to go back to an earlier phase, as one approaches the coast of America, one is touched to tears to think of all the effort and endurance, the sacrifice of men's lives that went into it, the hundreds and thousands of forgotten simple men along with the unforgotten — a Thomas Cavendish, most gifted young captain, second circumnavigator of the globe after Drake; a Stephen Parmenius, the Hungarian geographer, bedfellow of Hakluyt's in Oxford days, no less than a Humphrey Gilbert or a Henry Hudson, coming to his end in the ice floes of the bay now named after him. Or we remember how Gilbert beggared himself, spent his own fortune and his wife's, on his dream of the English colonization of North America; how Walter Raleigh spent similarly all that he won from the favor of the Queen upon the same great enterprise, and how, in circumstances of defeat, discouragement, disgrace, he wrote: "I shall yet live to see it an English nation."

We may regard the peopling of North America as an extension across the Atlantic of the process a thousand years before, in the time of the *Völkerwanderungen,* by which Britain was colonized by the original Anglo-Saxon stocks: a comparable process on a much smaller scale, occupying a much longer tract of time, by which forest was felled, the frontier extended, the nation took shape out of a creative mixing, a fusion of stocks. (It would be a fine subject for a book, to have a comparative study of these parallel processes, the naming of places and similar matters separated by a thousand years.) I am to speak of the beginnings of that second process, of which the twentieth century has seen the consolidation, the fulfillment, rather than the end.

My story may be said to be concerned with the junction between the two processes, the transition from the medieval to the modern world. For, surely, this is where the transition comes between the Middle Ages and modern history, this is the factor that in the long run made the greatest difference: the discovery of the new world. We are all aware of the long and fruitful discussion as to what constituted the Renaissance — nowhere better summed up than in Wallace K. Ferguson's admirable and discriminating book, *The Renaissance in Historical Thought* — what were the factors out of which came the modern world and its characteristic experience. Whatever we may think, however much we may disagree, about the rediscovery of antiquity, the importance of the study of Greek, the new standards of criticism and scholarship, the significance of humanism, of Renaissance state and new monarchy, here is a *differentia* that is indisputable, the significance of which grows with the expanding world, with which the Middle Ages come to an end.

I often think how vividly it is brought home by that letter of a fourteenth-century bishop of Exeter, John Grandison, to a friend at the papal court at Avignon, describing the state of his remote diocese in the west: where in farthest Cornwall the people speak a language that is not even English or understood by the English, and beyond the Land's End is nothing but the great sundering flood. It is the end of the known world.

A couple of centuries later, how all that has changed! The West Country now, from being a remote backwater, is in the front line of all the maritime activity launching out across the oceans: to the Canaries and the Guinea Coast, into the South Atlantic to Brazil; from Guinea across to the Caribbean and out by the Florida Channel; to Labrador and Hudson's Bay up into the gap between Greenland and North America searching for a northwest passage to the Far East; to Newfoundland and down the coast of New England into the unknown; to the West Indies and up the coast to plant the Virginia colonies; at length direct to the coast to plant the New England colonies; into the South Atlantic with Drake and Cavendish, to penetrate the Pacific and establish contact with the Far East. All these voyages took wing from Plymouth, in Bishop Grandison's diocese: in his days a very inconsiderable place, confined to the small change of cross-channel trade and tit-for-tat raiding, which has left its memento in the name of Bretonside by Sutton Pool. These voyages made the name and fortune of Plymouth, under the guidance of the remarkable Hawkins family and their brilliant poor relation, Francis Drake. (He did not remain a poor relation for long.) The transition from the medieval to the modern world stands well expressed in the change of name of the fortified island off Plymouth Hoe: known to the medieval people as St. Nicholas's island, to the moderns it is Drake's Island.

I realize that this is looking at the matter simply from an English perspective. But a wider one makes my point all the stronger, when one considers that by this time Portuguese and Spaniards had discovered half the world's coasts, were in occupation of much of Central and South America, and had established a regular route across the Pacific to the Far East. That brings home more powerfully than ever the difference between the Middle Ages, in this sense circumscribed and rather static, and the modern world, expansive and essentially dynamic.

The end of the Middle Ages in England was marked by contraction rather than expansion: withdrawal from the long dream of conquest in France, and, what is particularly significant, a marked shrinkage in the area of English control, of English language and civilization, in Ireland. Gaeldom came once more lapping like lake water up to the walls of the towns — Dublin, Waterford, Cork, Galway, last outposts of earlier Anglo-Irish. In the early fifteenth century, with Owen Glendower's rebellion, Wales achieved a temporary quasi independence; though it was defeated and crushed, Wales remained resentfully aloof, unabsorbed. Nor was any real progress made with the integration of Cornwall or the Scottish Borders, where they "knew no king but a Percy," into the fabric of the state. The fact was that the central institutions of the state were giving way under the strain of royal minorities, dynastic conflict, unsuccessful foreign war. The state's hold was contracting, government ineffectual, society itself inefficient and showing some signs of arrested development and decline.

The dynamic movement that initiates and motivates modern history reversed all that. The beginnings of this process form the subject of my book, *The Expansion of Elizabethan England*, and I have no wish to impose a summary of it here, apart from the unprofitability of such a procedure. But perhaps I may draw one or two conclusions from the detailed study made there.

By far the most important, and one that I had not realized before going into it, was the continuity of the process of expansion within the islands with that across the oceans, especially the phase of it which is crucial for modern history — Bismarck called it "the decisive fact in the modern world" — that across the Atlantic to the peopling of North America. These were two phases of the same movement, the second gathering momentum as it went forward, until it became the greatest single influence upon the home country in turn, a chief factor in transforming its society, making its fortune; today — it is not too much to say — constituting its fate. Without America the islands would have gone down to defeat and destruction twice in this century; without America I see no viable future for them.

The English state gathered its resources together under the Tudors and achieved an effective relation with society, particularly the leading middle elements in it — country gentry and town middle class — that enabled it to go forward with the work of expansion and internal integration.

We may see the process vividly brought home to us in the history of my native Cornwall. Small as it is, it was a little country on its own, with its own life, language, and culture. The Cornish were content with their Celtic ways — the remote people, who did not speak English, of Bishop Grandison's letter, wrapped up in their cult of the saints, their holy wells and wayside crosses, their feasts and pilgrimages, dreaming their dream of King Arthur and his return someday to the land. That self-regarding life was rudely shaken by the demand of Henry VII's government in 1497 for taxation for the defense of the Scottish Border. The Scottish Border was nothing to do with them, said the Cornish, and proceeded to raise a formidable rebellion which was only arrested outside of London, on Blackheath field. We see that the Cornish had an inadequate comprehension of the modern state, with its characteristic feature of central taxation for over-all state purposes. The Cornish were still living in the Middle Ages.

Nor were they any more reconciled half a century later when the central state imposed in 1549 a new religious uniformity upon the country with a prayer book in *English.* The English service was no better than a Christmas mumming, said the Cornish, and joined with the men of Devon in a rebellion that paralyzed government for several months in the summer of 1549, until it was crushed with some bloodshed. This time the repression was severe and the Cornish were taught a lesson they did not have to learn again. Indeed, the change of sentiment and of power within Cornwall was most marked, from the old inland families of Catholic sympathies to the newer coastal families, seafaring and Protestant, closely concerned in the ports and harbors engaged in the multifarious activities of oceanic expansion and sea warfare, their mouths open to the new world. It is surely very significant that all these families were to the fore in the voyages to America and the colonizing expeditions: one meets their names again and again in the records, Grenvilles, Killigrews, Tremaynes, Gilberts, Kendalls, Prideaux, Rouses.

Wales offers an example of integration with the state on a bigger scale, a much large undertaking. Here the process was greatly helped and made much smoother by the Welsh capture of the throne in the person of Henry Tudor. Never the breath of a rebellion was raised against the dynasty that was Welsh — even when the representative of the central government, Bishop Rowland Lee, was repressing the agelong delights of Welsh society, thieving and cattle stealing, stringing up thieves in hundreds, stamping out blood feuds and affrays, reducing the Welsh to English ideas of law and order.

We do not find the Welsh so much to the fore as the West Country in the American voyages. All the same we come across their names on them — Morgans and Vaughans, Floyds and Trevors. And we remember that the Welsh Captain Middleton, who bore the news of the approaching Spanish fleet to Grenville in the Azores, finished his translation of the Psalms into Welsh *apud Scutum, insulam occidentalium Indorum.* The chief field for Welsh expansionist activity — after England, where they virtually bore rule with the Tudors and the Cecils — was Ireland, to which they sent captains and soldiers for the wars, undertakers and colonists, administrators, lawyers, a Lord Deputy, and even bishops.

Ireland was a far tougher proposition for the Tudor state with its exiguous resources. It seems that historians have not even yet realized how deep was the chasm between Tudor England, in essence a modern society, and the Celtic civilization of Ireland, in many parts not even a medieval society, but pre-medieval, nomadic and pastoral, with its tribal chieftains and their endemic warfare — a culture arrested in development and run down, closer to the England of the Anglo-Saxon heptarchy than it was to the England of Elizabeth. No doubt the subjugation of Ireland could have been effected by the Tudor state earlier — if that had been its intention; or with far less difficulty in the end, if it had been able to concentrate on the objective, instead of having to regard it as one sector of a continental and oceanic struggle with Spain.

However, in the end Ireland was subjugated and a basis laid for a fruitful intermixture of the two peoples which — in spite of disappointments and the subsequent frustrations of Irish history — has led to a distinguished contribution to the world in the shape of Anglo-Irish culture. Whatever anyone may say, the basis of modern Irish society, on the land, in its property system, in law and language, is not Celtic but English. The foundation was not laid until the accession of a Scottish king came to complete the lifework of an Anglo-Welsh queen: with the union of the two kingdoms, the settlement of Ulster could go forward along with the transformation of the Scottish Borders into the middle shires of a joint kingdom. It fell to a Scottish king to proclaim the union of Britain:

> the Isle within itself hath almost none but imaginary bounds of separation, without but one common limit or rather guard of the Ocean sea, making the whole a little world within itself, the nations an uniformity of constitutions both of body and mind, especially in martial processes, a community of language (the principal means of civil society), an unity of religion (the deepest bond of hearty union and the surest knot of lasting peace).

The unification of the islands gave the basis for the great lunge forward across the Atlantic, the exodus of stocks to North America, the open door for which the Elizabethans had fought. We are all aware of the part played by the West Country, the Plymouth Company and its promoters — such men as Sir Ferdinando Gorges, John Trelawny, and John White of Dorchester — in the later beginnings of New England. But observe, what has been very little observed by historians, that it was the very people who were most deeply concerned with the plantation and colonization of Southern Ireland — Humphrey Gilbert, Walter Raleigh, Richard Grenville — who took the leading part in planting the first colonies in Virginia. It is as if Ireland were the blueprint for America.

The question of North America became one of national concern; that is to say, so many of the leading spirits of the age were interested, not a few of them engaged by it. The leading figures at Court were closely concerned — Leicester and Walsingham, Sir Christopher Hatton and Sir Philip Sidney, even Burghley in a watchful, conservative way; the Queen herself was less conservative, and she was interested in everything that affected America. She invested in at least two of Hawkins' voyages to the Caribbean, and one of Frobisher's towards the Northwest Passage. Unbeknown to her sage Lord Treasurer, she planned Drake's great voyage with him: in that she was the principal investor and the principal recipient of the booty. It was she who granted Humphrey Gilbert the patent to settle and colonize North America; on his death she passed it on to Walter Raleigh, to whom she permitted the land to be called Virginia after her. She would never make peace with Spain without security for the liberties of the Netherlands or the open door for English settlement in North America.

On the side of action, names are legion, so many of the most famous Elizabethans took part or were involved: Drake, Raleigh, the Gilberts, Grenville, Thomas Cavendish, Frobisher, the Hawkinses. On the side of science and intellect: John Dee, the leading mathematician and cosmographer of the early part of the reign; Thomas Hariot, first mathematician of the age; Richard Hakluyt, whose lifework it was to focus their minds upon America — the priority that the American school of thought and action came to have was due to a lifetime of concentrated, educated propaganda from his brain and pen. It has been given to few men to fertilize the history of their country so prodigiously. To him we owe the survival of nearly everything we know of the American voyages. His long life proved the one continuing figure that linked the two waves of Virginia enterprise, the successive attempts of the 1580's and those that gained a permanent foothold after the Queen's death. In literature, before Shakespeare died, the impact of America upon the English imagination is already rich and evident, in Spenser and Drayton, in Raleigh and Chapman and Donne, never more beautifully than in *The Tempest*.

Perhaps then we may leave the last word to a poet, Samuel Daniel — one of Sidney's circle and a West Countryman — who glimpsed something of the limitless possibilities to come out of the unimaginable future, in that process of which we have indicated the beginnings:

> And who in time knows whither we may vent
> The treasure of our tongue, to what strange shores
> This gain of our best glory shall be sent,
> To enrich unknowing nations with our stores?
> What worlds in the yet unformèd Occident
> May come refined with the accents that are ours?

But what a difference from the accent of the Middle Ages, what a world we are away now from the medieval world!

The Transit of Civilization from the Old World to the New

Englishmen crossing the ocean to America expected to transfer to the new colonies the familiar institutions and arrangements under which men lived in the Old World. The forms of government, religious worship, economic activity, and family relationships that people knew at home became the basis for establishing new societies in a wilderness. But according to Oscar Handlin in the following selection, Englishmen failed to transfer intact the structure of society they left behind.

Establishing settlements proved to be full of surprises. The migration of people and institutions was selective. Few English aristocrats, for instance, were willing to migrate to an empty wilderness. Hence, the class structure in America lacked a hereditary aristocracy, such as occupied the top of the social pyramid in England. Similarly, colonists did not reproduce English political patterns. The Crown, which played a dominant role in English politics during the seventeenth century and was still a major force in the eighteenth century, was a remote and much weaker institution in the colonies. At a time when the tendency in England was for political authority to gravitate to London, in the colonies power became fragmented, dispersed among the gentry of dozens of towns and counties. Nor did Englishmen plant in America a productive system like that in England. There, most arable land was under cultivation and falling into the hands of fewer and fewer landowners as the wealthier, more progressive landlords pushed unneeded peasants off their estates. In America, a virgin continent awaited the axmen to clear the trees, and abundant lands made possible an ever-growing army of small freeholders who chiefly populated British North America. Religious institutions, no less than political and economic institutions, underwent alteration in America. Instead of supporting a state church, embodiment of the one true faith, the colonists spawned a dozen competing churches, none of which enjoyed the monopoly possessed by the Church of England. The result was that, though few came to America with the purpose of creating a new society, well before the American Revolution discerning observers realized a new society was emerging in the colonies inhabited by what one Frenchman described as "a new race of men."

FOR FURTHER READING:

BOORSTIN, DANIEL. *The Americans: The Colonial Experience.* New York: Random House, Vintage Books, 1958.*

HANDLIN, OSCAR. *The Americans: A History of the People of the United States.* Boston : Little, Brown & Company, 1963.*

VER STEEG, CLARENCE. *The Formative Years.* New York: Hill & Wang, Making of America Series, 1964.*

Asterisk denotes paperback edition.

The Significance of the Seventeenth Century   OSCAR HANDLIN

The historian is trained to see the past in its own terms. He studies the seventeenth century as the product of that which had gone before it, and he attempts to reconstruct the culture and society of the American colonies as those might have seemed to the men who lived in them.

This is the necessary perspective for an understanding of the period. An impressive body of recent studies has shown that the settlements along the coast of North America were elements of imperial systems that had their counterparts in many other regions of the world. We have learned that the institutional life of the colonies can only be understood against a background that reaches back to the medieval past. The labor system, the forms of government, even the modes of thought of the seventeenth century extended patterns that had long before been developing in Europe. To see in them the forerunners or prototypes of what would emerge in the eighteenth or nineteenth century is grievously to misinterpret them.

But our purpose in celebrating the 350th anniversary of the settlement of the Jamestown colony must be somewhat different. The seventeenth century should have general meaning, for we — and the historians along with the rest of us — live, after all, in the twentieth century; and we expect somehow that the experiences of the men who began to come off the ships at Jamestown have also a meaning for us in the twentieth century. A commemorative occasion is a time for retrospection — for looking backward from the present to take account of the way we have come. It has its picturesque and interesting aspects, of course. But its true value arises from the opportunity it offers us to acquire perspective on the present and the future. From that point of view, it is our obligation to look back to the seventeenth century for what it can reveal of the antecedents of our own culture.

In that respect the seventeenth century was immensely significant. In the decades after the settlement at Jamestown, three generations of Americans — the first Americans — began to shape the social order, the way of life, and an interpretation of their own experience that would influence much of subsequent American history. Pick up the story where you will — in the eighteenth or nineteenth century or in our own times — and invariably in these matters the threads lead back to the seventeenth century. It will be worth while to discuss each of these developments briefly.

The colonists who settled at Jamestown and elsewhere along the coast after 1607 brought with them fixed conceptions of what a social order should be like. Their whole effort thereafter was devoted to recreating the forms they had known at home. Yet in practice their experience persistently led them away from the patterns they judged desirable. The American social order that finally emerged was abnormal. That is, it not only diverged from the experience of the European society from which the newcomers emigrated, but it was also contrary to their own expectations of what a social order should be.

The settlers were loyal to the governments from which they emigrated, and they were conservative in their attitudes toward existing institutions. Repeatedly they ex-

---

Source: Oscar Handlin, "The Significance of the Seventeenth Century," in *Seventeenth-Century America*, ed. James M. Smith (Chapel Hill: University of North Carolina Press, 1959), pp. 3–12.

plained that their emigration was not intended to disrupt but rather to preserve and improve the society they left. Nevertheless they were constantly moving off on tangents through the force of circumstance and the pressure of the environment. A number of examples will clarify this point.

The forms of colonial government developed slowly and erratically. The first settlers transplanted two forms commonplace in the practice of Europeans in this period. The chartered commercial companies, as in Virginia and Plymouth, carried across to their plantations institutions that went back to the medieval boroughs. The proprietary colonies rested on old feudal precedents. Both efforts at imitation quickly proved unstable, however, and the colonies of either sort passed through a period of rapid change.

The problem of changing political forms was, of course, also troubling Europe in the seventeenth century. But in the Old World this era witnessed the emergence of the centralized bureaucratic state. Theory and practice moved in the same direction, toward the derivation of all authority from a single source, such as the Crown, however defined.

The colonies accepted the theory. Their most prominent men were surprisingly legalistic and had no inclination to dispute the authority under which their government functioned. But practice took another direction. Power tended to devolve to its local sources. Whether that involved the town, as in New England, or the local powers sitting in the vestry, as in Virginia, the characteristic political organization was decentralized. Whatever acknowledgment might be given to the authority of the Crown, political institutions were decisively shaped by the necessity of defining connections to local power. Significantly, the most stable colonies of this period were Connecticut and Rhode Island, where the organization of local government in the towns preceded and remained basic to the organization of central political institutions.

The dispersal of power to local sources was, however, characteristic of other, nonpolitical institutions also. The churches developed a *de facto* congregational form, despite the fact that their communicants theoretically held to a belief in centralized authority. Apart from the Plymouth Separatists, there was no disposition to challenge the traditional hierarchical and centralized structure of the church. Yet, the New England Puritans, once here, found themselves closer to the Separatists than to the Church of England of which they had expected to remain adherents. Most strikingly, the members of the Church of England throughout the colonies continued to acknowledge that a bishop was essential to the full practice of their religious duties. Yet in practice, delays, obstructions, and evasions prevented the emergence of an episcopate before the Revolution. Religious functions too seemed to devolve to their local sources.

These developments were related to the structure of the population, which was also anomalous in the sense that it ran contrary to the expectations of those who planted the colonies. The founders expected that their societies would consist of functionaries and peasants. The companies anticipated plantations populated by servants, that is, by soldiers and clerks, who would carry forth the business of trade and defense. The proprietors looked forward to a population of native or imported peasants who would reconstruct some sort of manorial system in the New World. This was evident, even toward the end of the seventeenth century, in the plans of the Carolina proprietors.

Instead, surprisingly, all the colonies developed a society of yeomen and artisans

— not by plan, and often, it seemed, simply through the want of an alternative. Yet the consequences were radical. There developed in the mainland colonies of the seventeenth century a wide variety of social types, a microcosm of the Old World as it were, ranging from slaves and servants at the bottom through yeoman farmers and artisans, to a gentry at the top. Within this variety of types there were both the recognition of actual stratification and a high degree of mobility. The fact that a servant was different from a yeoman and yet that a servant could become a yeoman led to the definition of a new concept of freedom and to the development of distinctive social institutions.

In the structure of the population, therefore, as in the evolution of governmental and other institutions, the seventeenth-century colonies followed an abnormal path, one which was different from the experience of Europeans at home or in other parts of the world and one which was contrary to their own expectations. The causes of this abnormality were complex. In part it was due to the extensive quality of the land to which these settlers came. They had pitched upon the edge of an almost empty continent; and the existence of open space to which men could withdraw remained a constant condition of their life. That in itself was an element tending toward looseness of social structure.

Furthermore, they encountered no going society with fixed institutions of its own. The Indians who inhabited the region had a culture, of course. But they were so few in number and so little prepared to resist as to have relatively little effect upon the whites. The Europeans of the same period in India or even in Africa were significantly influenced by the institutions they encountered there; those in America, hardly at all. Indeed the American colonists were often disappointed in their natives. The continued inclination to refer to the Indian kings, queens, and nobility reflected an eagerness to discover in the red men a fixity of forms that did not exist. Its absence was a further source of instability.

But most important, the institutional looseness of the seventeenth century was related to the way of life that developed in the colonies. The American seventeenth-century social order was disorderly by the expectations of normal men. But the settlers were not normal men. The terms of American existence compelled frequent and serious deviations from the norms of behavior accepted by the men who peopled the colonies. Every aspect of their existence combined to produce disorder.

The century was occupied by a succession of waves of immigration, so that the experience of transplantation was not limited to one group or to one moment, but was repeated again and again. And that experience caused enormous shocks in the personal and social relationships of those involved in it. The circumstances of the crossing at once threw these men and women into disorder. It takes an effort of the imagination to conceive of the conditions of life on the three ships which came to Jamestown in 1607. These vessels of 100, 40, and 20 tons, respectively, were laden with the gear and the supplies and provisions for the voyage and also with all that the plantations would at first require. Yet, there was also room on these tiny craft for 140 people. The settlers were almost five months in transit, at the mercy of the winds and weather and of the unknown sea. Later voyages involved larger ships — but not much larger; and the time spent in crossing shrank, although not dependably. But accommodations were never commodious and the experience was never pleasant. Few immigrants recovered quickly from the difficulties of crowded and uncomfortable weeks at sea in tiny ships that carried them to their strange destinations.

Many of those who made the crossing were people whose life was already in disorder. Often, they had already been displaced and compelled to move once; their stamina had already been tried. The residents of London who came to the colonies had, as likely as not, been born in the country and had drifted to the city. Others among the newcomers, like the Pilgrims, like the Finns who settled on the Delaware, like the German sectarians, were already uprooted and had already deviated from the settled life of stable societies.

Hard conditions of life compounded the disorder for a greater or lesser time in each of the colonies. Everywhere the settlers who survived could look back upon a starving time, a period when the margin between life and death narrowed perilously and when the very existence of the feeble societies hung by a thread. So, in retrospect, the Virginia burgesses looked back to the administration of Sir Thomas Smith and recalled:

> The allowance in those tymes for a man was only eight ounces of meale and half a pinte of pease for a daye the one & the other mouldy, rotten, full of Cobwebs and Maggots loathsome to man and not fytt for beasts; which forced many to flee for reliefe to the Savage Enemy, who being taken againe were putt to sundry deaths as by hanginge, shootinge and breakinge upon the wheele; & others were forced by famine to filch for their bellies, of whom one for steelinge 2 or 3 pints of oatmeale had a bodkinge thrust through his tongue and was tyed with a chaine to a tree untill he starved. Yf a man through his sickness had not been able tow worke, he had no allowance at all, and so consequently perished. Many through these extremities, being weery of life digged holes in the earth and hidd themselues till they famished. . . . So lamentable was our scarsitie that we were constrained to eat Doggs, Catts, ratts, Snakes, Toad-Stooles, horsehides and wt nott; one man out of the mysery he endured, killinge his wiefe powdered her upp to eate here, for wch he was burned. Many besides fedd on the Corps of dead men, and one who had gotten unsatiable, out of custome to that foode could not be restrayned, until such tyme as he was executed for it, and indeed soe miserable was our estate that the happyest day that eyer some of them hoped to see, was when the Indyands had killed a mare they wishing whilst she was boyling that St *Tho: Smith* [the Governor] was uppon her backe in the kettle.

Later prosperity never dimmed the memory of the early difficulties; and there remained always areas where the trying experience of survival was being repeated. As settlement spread, there was always at its edge a brutal and disorderly struggle for existence.

Some of the harsh features of pioneer life disappeared with the development of settled communities. But others endured for a long time. A high death rate remained constant and throughout the century embittered the personal relationships of the colonists. In the first winter at Plymouth, one-half the Pilgrims died. Between 1606 and 1623 about five thousand immigrants came to Virginia. They had children and raised families. Yet at the end of that period there were only one thousand left.

Nor was this cruel mortality simply a condition of initial settlement. It remained characteristic of seventeenth-century life. Infant mortality was murderous; and although many children were born, the number of survivors was distressingly low. It was rare in this century that a husband and wife should live into old age together. The frequency of remarriages by widowers and widows showed how familiar a factor in life was death.

More generally, constant nagging difficulties intruded in the management of the details of home or farm or shop. Old habits did not apply to new circumstances; and it was hard for individuals to fulfill the personal, family, religious, or communal roles they were expected to play. This, perhaps, explains the harsh judgments that the colonists were always making of one another. The lack of stability or orderliness even in the home was particularly troublesome. In the tight quarters of the seventeenth-century houses, large families had to learn to live with one another, and also with the Negroes and other strange servants. Emotional strains were inevitable and weak community discipline sometimes led to violence, desertion, or criminality. The lack of permanence, the constant mobility that shifted individuals and families about through the continent exacerbated all these tensions. By contrast, the old homes of the Old World in retrospect came to embody orderliness. Often, in thinking of what they had left in Europe, the colonists expressed a poignant sense of separation from the source of stability and culture.

Finally, their life was rendered harsh by the apparent hostility of the elements. The wilderness itself created problems for men accustomed to open spaces. In the folk literature of Europe the forests were peopled by wild, inhuman creatures often hostile to man. In America even the climate and the changes of the seasons were unfamiliar. Most important, the denizens of the wilderness were a constant threat to the flimsy structure of civilization. The Indians grew more and more fearsome as the century advanced; and on the borders French and Spanish Papists were a continuing threat. In the face of all these dangers, there was no security in the settlements. The precariousness of existence was at the root of the disorder that overwhelmed them. Everywhere from the moment they boarded ship the first Americans found risks of the greatest order inseparable from the conduct of their lives.

The native-born, that is, the second and third generations, were more at home in the wilderness and, never having known Europe, were less pressed by the necessity of making comparisons with that which had been left across the ocean. They had sources of instability of their own, in their heightened rootlessness and mobility. But they were likely to accept the disorder and precariousness that troubled their immigrant parents or grandparents as a way of life and to adjust to its conditions.

The men subject to so many elements of abnormality and disorder necessarily interpreted their own experiences in a distinctive way. They were constantly driven to ask questions that other men had no need to raise. People whose families had lived generations without end in the same village had no cause to wonder why they were where they were or to speculate on the significance of having been placed where they were. But the immigrants whose conditions of life and whose institutions had been driven so far from every ordinary course necessarily had to seek answers to such questions.

The necessity was particularly urgent in the seventeenth century when men ascribed to every event a deep meaning. Nothing that occurred was taken as simply random. Everything was the product of the intent of some mover. A tree did not fall; it was felled. If a monstrous child was born or a school of porpoises seen, that was a sign of something. In the same way, there was necessarily a significance to the painful shift of population that created colonial society. In an era in which men believed literally in signs, portents, curses, spells, and imprecations, to say nothing of witches, they had to seek a meaning to their own unusual experiences.

The first Americans continued the habit of explaining every occurrence in terms of a familiar dichotomy. On the one hand, they could see in some events good impulses, derived from God and reflecting a divine intent. But they also found abundant evidence of evil impulses or dark desires emanating from satanic intentions.

The fearful men who lived with risk and disorder were constantly on the lookout for the means of identifying and interpreting what happened to them. As a simple matter of a guide to personal life, it was essential to know whether an incident was the product of divine or devilish interference.

The same confrontation of good and evil could be seen in the social world that surrounded the individual. There in the external wilderness, in the savagery of life without reliable guides, were the sources of corruption. Were not the Indians imps of Satan, and the Papists, creatures of the Devil, and was not therefore the whole American experience one which endangered man's salvation? On the other hand, was it not possible to identify that which lay across the ocean with that which was good and conducive to man's salvation? Europe, from the American perspective, was the source of morality, of law, of order, and of Christianity. But in that event, how was the colonist to explain his migration, away from order to disorder, away from law to savagery, away from Christianity to the spiritual perils of the New World?

The question thus raised could be answered on both the personal and the social level; and the answer on the one offers an analogy to the answer on the other. The character of this response may be discerned in the poem that a grieving grandmother wrote in the 1660's to explain to herself the death of three grandchildren within four years. All were under the age of four. Surely these tender innocents had been stricken down through no fault, no evil deed, of their own. There was, however, a reason. Anne Bradstreet explained:

> By nature Trees do rot when they are grown.
> And Plumbs and Apples thoroughly ripe do fall,
> And corn and grass are in their season mown,
> And time brings down what is both strong and tall.
> But plants new set to be eradicate,
> And buds new blown, to have so short a date,
> Is by his hand alone that guides nature and fate.

An unnatural misfortune of this sort was thus in itself evidence of a particular divine concern. While the nature of God's intentions might be inscrutable to men and closed to fallible human understanding, the event itself nevertheless was a sure indication of some particular purpose. It could even supply a kind of assurance of divine interest and oversight.

It was also true that a way of life out of the usual course was evidence of some particular design. The whole character of the plantation of these settlements, by its very abnormality, indicated that there had been some special purpose to the coming to America. The fact that this whole area had been withheld from previous human habitation indicated that there was some special intention for its use. The fact that their institutions and their course of life did not follow any usual pattern was itself a sign that these settlements had an unusual destiny.

As the immigrants examined their own coming, they could see evidence of a larger will in their own careers. Their migration was largely the product of their own helplessness, of social forces over which they had no control — persecution by the Established Church, changes in agriculture and the unavailability of land, the disruption of the wool trade and the growth in the number of men without employment. But on the other hand, the migration was also the product of their own choice. Not all those who were persecuted or displaced or unemployed had come. Migration stemmed from a compulsion that forced the emigrant to leave and also the positive act of will by which he decided to go. The emigrant might thus be compared to a legate dispatched on a mission by a potentate, a legate who accepted the errand voluntarily. The fact, too, that not all those who went arrived reflected a process of survival and seemed to imply a kind of selection of some from among the rest.

In no other way could these people account for the experience but by the conclusion that somehow they had been chosen to depart from the ways of ordinary men and to become in their own lives extraordinary for some special purpose.

Among some of the colonists this intention was spelled out with considerable sophistication. New England Puritans thought of themselves as led by Divine Providence to a new Canaan where they were to create a new kind of society that would be a model for the whole world. Their city upon a hill would ultimately be emulated by all other men. It was a part of the scheme of divine redemption, occupying the stage at a critical turn in the cosmic drama that had begun with the Creation, that had been continued in the Reformation, and that would end in the Second Coming.

Elsewhere the explanation was less sophisticated, less explicit, and less literate. But there nonetheless emerged again and again expressions of conviction in a sense of mission — to convert the Indians or to civilize the wilderness. The newness of a New World reserved for some ultimate purpose and waiting for those who would bring it under cultivation or use it as the setting for their own experiments in salvation confirmed the successive groups of immigrants, in the seventeenth century and later, in the belief that there was a profound importance to their coming.

The second and third generations were different in this respect also. They were natives, not subject to the strains of the decisions that had burdened their parents or grandparents. Indeed, in the eyes of the immigrants, the second generation seemed a ruder, less cultivated, and wilder people. That accounts for the complaints about declension and about the loss of the sense of mission that began to be sounded in the last quarter of the century.

But the second generation had actually not lost the sense of mission so much as transformed it beyond the recognition of their predecessors. The very fact that they were a wilderness people, at home in the New World, gave them a sense of power. They could deal with the forest and the savage as their parents could not. Out of contact with the standards of the Old World, they developed their own, and their ability to do so generated confidence in their own capacity for achievement.

Therefore they too, although in a different form, were moved by a conviction of the grandeur of their destiny; and they could link that conviction to the potentialities of the land, which was not alien to them as it had been to their parents. Pride in their own power and in the future greatness of their homes created for them a picture of themselves as a people destined to conquer, an idea to be eloquently expressed just after the turn of the century by Robert Beverley.

In a variety of forms, the sense of mission has remained a continuing theme in American life. In the eighteenth century Jefferson's generation gave it secularized liberal expression. The nineteenth century imbued it with the spirit of liberal reform. And at the opening of the twentieth century, it was woven into the ideology of imperialism. So, too, social disorder, the acceptance of risk, and the precariousness of life that developed in the seventeenth century long remained characteristic of America. It was the significance of the seventeenth century to bring into being peculiarities of character and institutions, the influence of which was long thereafter felt in the history of the United States.

The Red Man as the White Man's Burden

From a population of between 1 and 2 million, when white men first encountered them in North America, the Indians steadily declined for almost three centuries until there were only little more than 200,000 left in 1900. This tragic event had its roots in the pattern of relationships between the natives and the Europeans that took shape in the colonial period. In the following essay, Roy Harvey Pearce describes how New England Puritans regarded Indians either as their instruments or as an obstacle to achieving their goals.

The grim choice facing the Indians was "civilization or death." By "civilization," however, Americans meant *their* version; but even the most receptive Indians, subject to untiring missionary efforts, proved unable to adjust. "For, take a young Indian lad," a French traveler in the colonies observed, "give him the best education you possibly can, load him with your bounty, with presents, nay with riches; yet he will secretly long for his native woods . . . and on the first opportunity he can possibly find, you will see him voluntarily leave behind him all you have given him, and return with expressible joy to lie on the mats of his fathers."

At first, Europeans and Indians lived in peace. Indians welcomed the artifacts whites brought and had little fear of such fledgling settlements as those at Jamestown, Virginia, or at Plymouth, Massachusetts. And whites patronizingly regarded Indians as "noble savages," or one of the ten lost tribes of Israel, or primitive but brave and resourceful people. Being outnumbered, whites could not risk conflict until they had grown stronger. As the European population grew and spread more deeply into the forests, Indians became alarmed. Warfare followed until the Europeans subdued the Indians and restored peace temporarily. A thousand times on a thousand frontiers this process repeated itself. For though the Indians never stood much chance against the whites in the long run, the Americans had to subdue each tribe they encountered separately, because the Indians were divided into a hundred innumerable tribes and the defeat of one did not reduce the others. Though warfare killed many Indians, the white man's disease, against which the red man had little or no immunity, killed many more.

Troubled by the Indians' tragic fate, Americans rationalized it as the just reward of a race many regarded as "a set of miserable, dirty, lousy, blanketed, thieving, lying, sneaking, murdering, graceless, faithless, gut-eating skunks whose immediate and final extermination all men . . . should pray for." Those whose troubled consciences could not be stilled by dehumanizing the Indians found comfort in the thought that the Indians' decline was the price one had to pay for the advance of civilization. Two centuries after the Puritans defined the Indians in terms of their own needs, an American novelist updated their explanation of the red man's historic role: "He hath a pioneer mission, to prepare the wilds for the superior race; and, this done, he departs; and, even as one growth of the forest, when hewn down, makes way for quite another growth of trees, so will he give place to another people. Verily, the mysteries of Providence are passing wonderful."

FOR FURTHER READING:

HAGAN, WILLIAM T. *American Indians.* Chicago: University of Chicago Press, 1961.*
PEARCE, ROY H. *Savagism and Civilization.* Original title: *Savages and America: A Study of the Indian and the Idea of Civilization.* Baltimore: The Johns Hopkins Press, 1967.*
VAUGHAN, ALDEN T. *New England Frontier: Indians and Puritanism.* Boston: Little, Brown & Company, 1965.*

Asterisk denotes paperback edition.

The "Ruines of Mankind": The Indian and the Puritan Mind   ROY HARVEY PEARCE

The Indian whom colonial Americans everywhere encountered was, above all, an obstacle to civilization. And he was an obstacle not only to overcome, but also to understand and then perhaps to civilize in the overcoming. For in his very nature, in what was taken to be his essential humanity, the Indian seemed to be capable of that civil state which the colonizers had achieved, yet seemed somehow not to be inclined toward that state. The problem for those Americans who wanted to understand him was to define the nature of his savage society — what in the eighteenth century came to be called his "savagism" — in such a way as to relate it to the nature of the high civilization which they were bringing to the new world. Thus, in the perspective of our cultural history, a colonial understanding of savagism is really a colonial understanding of civilization — of the good life as the Indian did and did not share in it. And colonial definitions of savage life are really re-definitions of civilized life, *apologia* for that life, expressions and applications of theories of civilization.

So it is that we may comprehend our colonial civilization concretely and particularly as it realizes itself in working out its ideas of the savage. So it is that the New England Puritan obsession with the savage is a significant aspect of the New England Puritan obsession with the civilized. This essay, then, is offered as a study in the history of colonial New England civilization — a history in terms of the Puritan idea of the savage, as that idea came to be worked out in the context of Puritan experience with the Indian and his society.

For the Englishman going to New England in the 1620's and 30's, the destiny of the Indians could be understood only as it related to the destiny of the whole colonial enterprise. In Plymouth the Pilgrim rejoiced to find that it had pleased God so to possess the Indians with a fear and love of the English that they would forthwith submit themselves as loyal and dutiful subjects. Moreover, it was to be observed that God had lately sent a "wonderful plague" among the savages and had so destroyed them and left most of their lands free for civilized occupation. The Indians whom the Pilgrims found were amenable enough; watched closely, dealt with fairly,

Source: Roy Harvey Pearce, "The 'Ruines of Mankind': The Indian and the Puritan Mind," *Journal of the History of Ideas,* vol. 13 (1952), pp. 200–217.

punished occasionally, they gave little trouble. But then, God had already shown them the way with His plague.

For Puritans in the Massachusetts Bay Colony and what came to be Connecticut, matters were somewhat more difficult. Although in 1634 John Winthrop could write to an English friend, "[the natives] are neere all dead of the small Poxe, so as the Lord hathe cleared our title to what we possess," yet Indians to the south and north, who were plagued mainly by the English themselves, were relatively strong and independent. Twice in the century formal frontier war was waged: in 1637, against the Pequots, who were easily slaughtered at Mystic by Mason's expedition; and in 1675–1676, against the Wampanoags and their leader King Philip, who were destroyed in their turn, though not quite so easily as had been the Pequots. And continually there was trouble on a small scale; the problem was to keep various tribal groups split up and thus weak in striking power, to protect frontier settlements from marauding bands of Indians, somehow to combat papist French influence on the northern Indians, and gradually to take over lands as the proper time came. Steadily, as the colonies developed in holdings and in power, the English moved further inland from their coastal settlements and took over more Indian land. Warfare resulted. But this too was part of God's Way with New England.

For, and Puritans took this as the meaning of their own history, God had meant the savage Indians' land for the civilized English, and, moreover, had meant the savage state itself as a sign of Satan's power and savage warfare as a sign of earthly struggle and sin. The colonial enterprise was in all ways a religious enterprise. Demonstrating land tenure from theology had been simple even for Pilgrim precursors of the Puritans. Robert Cushman, if it was he who in 1622 contributed the concluding section to the Pilgrim *Mourt's Relation,* argued merely that the Indians were heathens and thus in need of conversion; that Indians' lands were empty, English lands full, and the English therefore bound to go to the Indians and fill their lands:

> Their land is spacious and void, and there are few, and do but run over the grass, as do also the foxes and the wild beasts. They are not industrious, neither have art, science, skill or faculty to use either the land or the commodities of it; but all spoils, rots, and is marred for want of manuring, gathering, ordering, &c. As the ancient patriarchs, therefore, removed from straiter places into more roomy, where the land lay idle and waste, and none used it, though there dwelt inhabitants by them, as Gen. xiii, 6, 11, 12, and xxxiv, 21, and xli, 20, so it is lawful now to take a land which none useth, and make use of it.

This argument was at the center of the New England understanding of the Indian in the seventeenth century as, in fact, it was in some version to be at the center of American understanding of the Indian until the middle of the nineteenth century. For the Pilgrim as for the Puritan, religion and empire, christianization and civilization, divine order and natural order, were known to be one. So Cushman concluded,

> Yea, and as the enterprise is weighty and difficult, so the honor is more worthy, to plant a rude wilderness, to enlarge the honor and fame of our dread sovereign, but chiefly to display the efficacy and power of the Gospel, both in zealous preaching, professing, and wise walking under it, before the faces of these poor blind infidels.

Such statements on this problem of land tenure as came some seven years later from Massachusetts authorities were characteristically more legal in tone and concern than Cushman's but were pointed towards the same conclusions. Indian lands were to be bought if local savages should pretend to ownership, but to be bought only as a means of keeping peace with those savages. For, in truth, the Indians possessed their lands only as a natural right, since that possession existed anterior to and outside of a properly civilized state and since that possession was not in accordance with God's commandment to men to occupy the earth, increase, and multiply; what followed, then, was that the land was technically *vacuum domicilium*, and that the English, who would farm the land and make it fructify, who would give it order, were obliged to take over. If the Indians were ever to be civilized, if they were ever to know the true God, they would be obliged to let God's chosen people lead them to God's chosen civilization; specifically, the way to God was through His chosen civilization. This is perhaps essentially what we call the Protestant-capitalistic ethic; but it is also, and more particularly, a late Renaissance ethic — a solemn and brave, even desperate, determination to hold on to the idea of a received, assured order which would give meaning and direction to all life. For John Winthrop, in 1629, it was a matter of such divine logic:

> . . . the whole earth is the Lord's garden, and he hath given it to the sons of Adam to be tilled and improved by them. Why then should we stand starving here for the places of habitation, (many men spending as much labor and cost to recover or keep sometimes an acre or two of lands as would procure him many many hundreds of acres, as good or better, in another place), and in the mean time suffer whole countries, as profitable for the use of man, to lie waste without any improvement.

Convinced thus of his divine right to Indian lands, the Puritan discovered in the Indians themselves evidence of a satanic opposition to the very principle of divinity. In a world in which the divine plan was so clear, in a world through which the Bible would guide all men in all things, in a world in which civilization and the divinely illuminated human reason had to count for everything, the Indian might well be a terrifying anomaly, at best a symbol of what men might become if they lived far from God's Word. Yet these savages were essentially men; and so they had to be brought to manhood and the civilized responsibilities of manhood. And this was to be achieved through bringing them eventually to God. As the wild lands of New England were to be improved, so were the wild men. For the Puritan there could be no half-way measures in his own life or in the lives of the savages about him. It was never a question of understanding the savage as he was, of knowing him in his low state. Rather it was a question — a driving necessity, really — first, of finding the savage's place in a Puritan world, and then, of making the savage over into a Puritan. If one looked closely at the savage, it was to look closely at a similitude to God's Way with the world — as one would look closely at a storm, or an illness, or a death, or a birth, or a quarrel among one's children — and so to discover evidence of that Way.

Wherever the Indian opposed the Puritan, there Satan opposed God. Satan had possessed the Indian until he had become virtually a beast. Indian worship was devil worship. The faintly optimistic (and propagandistic?) reports about Indian religion which were published in London early in the seventeenth century soon were drowned out in the general recounting of the evil religious state of the savages. Typically, when Dr. John Stoughton, Rector of St. Mary Aldermanbury, London, wanted to encourage the erection of a college in which Indians, among others, should be trained, he felt constrained to argue the great necessity for the college from the fact that ". . . the Divell is not unlike to stire them up to[o] for the disturbance of this worke intended for the overthrow of his Kingdome in them. . . ." Satanism, it was abundantly evident, was at the very core of savage life. And it was not hard to associate the physical state of the Indian, his living a cold hard life, with his spiritual state; hence, everywhere one might see in the flesh what it meant to be a devil-worshipper. So racial and cultural tension mounted throughout the century, until, in the 1690's, the very presence of evil Indian devil-worshippers was taken as part of the evidence of that great visitation of witches to New England, which we call the Witchcraft Craze. Indian witch doctors clearly were sharing diabolically in the wonders of the invisible world. At the end of the century, when Cotton Mather interpreted the continuing (now French-inspired) Indian skirmishes after King Philip's War as the direct result of God's harrowing sinful and weakening New England through Satan, he too was sure that New England witchcraft and Indian witchcraft were all of a piece:

> The Story of the Prodigious War, made by the Spirits of the Invisible World upon the People of New-England, in the year, 1692, hath Entertain'd a great part of the English World, with a just Astonishment: and I have met with some Strange Things, not here to be mentioned, which have made me often think, that this inexplicable War might have some of its Original among the Indians, whose chief Sagamores are well known unto some of our Captives, to have been horrid Sorcerers, and hellish Conjurers and such as conversed with Daemons.

Practical experience seemed to bear all this out. Fighting to hold on to their lands and their culture, the Indians would properly be savage. Inevitably New Englanders living on the frontier settlements suffered raids, destruction, sometimes captivity, and inevitably they interpreted each as God's warning to New England through Satan. Of the hard captivity of Mary Rowlandson in 1676, the contemporary editor of her narrative concluded:

> I must say, that as none knows what it is to fight and pursue such an enemy as this, but they that have fought and pursued them: so none can imagine what it is to be captivated, and enslaved to such atheisticall, proud, wild, cruel, barbarous, brutish (in one word) diabolicall creatures as these, the worst of the heathen. . . .

In the frontier settlements to the west and south and to the north in Maine, it was destroy or be destroyed. And it seemed everywhere continuingly evident that this frontier fight for survival was but another skirmish in man's Holy War against Satan, now on a new-world battlefield. When, as late as 1703, Solomon Stoddard recommended to Governor Joseph Dudley that troublesome Indians be hunted down with dogs, he was arguing as John Underhill (second in command to Mason at the proceedings at Mystic) had argued some sixty-five years before in defense of the massacre of the Pequots:

> It may be demanded, Why should you be so furious? (as some have said). Should not Christians have more mercy and compassion? But I would refer you to David's war. When a people is grown to such a height of blood, and sin against God and man, and all confederates in the action, then he hath no respect to persons, but harrows them, and saws them, and puts them to the sword, and the most terriblest death that may be. Sometimes the Scripture declareth women and children must perish with their parents. Sometimes the case alters; but we will not dispute it now. We had sufficient light from the Word of God for our proceedings.

Thus it was that the whole history of the relations with the Indians, which was part of the whole history of the Puritan enterprise, was read in light from the Word of God. Edward Johnson's *Wonder-Working Providence of Sion's Saviour in New England* (1654) deals characteristically with that history. Now, Johnson's account is generally concerned with the whole history of New England seen properly *sub specie aeternitatis;* as a result, he is able to find the right place and the right amount of space for each of the important events in the course of colonial relations with the Indians. Devoting large parts of some seven of his eighty-three chapters to the discussion of Indian affairs, he tells how God had sent a plague in 1619 (the correct date is, of course, 1616–1617) to clear the way for the settlers at Plymouth and how the Indians had been thus disposed to receive those settlers peacefully; he tells how a plague among the Massachusetts Indians likewise saved the Bay Colony in 1631 ("Thus did the Lord allay their quarrelsome spirits, and made roome for the following part of his army."); he recounts the history of the Pequot War in some detail, pointing out, as had many another, how this war and the Antinomian troubles of the 1630's were equally Satanic trials for men establishing a Holy Commonwealth; he recounts further God's intervention in a possible Indian war in 1645; and finally, he insists that by the 1650's missionary work to the Satanic heathen is going well. In every event he can find evidence that God, through Satan, has been showing the colonists at once their own sinfulness and the promise of their great undertaking.

Later Puritan historians deal more specifically with Indian troubles, and, of course, they recount later troubles — King Philip's War and the continuing skirmishes in the northeast throughout the seventeenth century and into the eighteenth. Yet in tone and orientation their work simply duplicates Johnson's *Wonder-Working Providence* and reflects equally the integrative orthodoxy of Puritan culture. Often writing more in detail and from broader and more immediate experience than does Johnson, they emphasize even more than he the brutish, diabolical quality of the Indian enemy. To this end, Captain John Mason appends to his *Brief History of the Pequot War* (first printed separately in 1736) a list of "special providences" by means of which the English have won their victory. In his three-part report (1675–1676) of King Philip's War, Nathaniel Saltonstall insists that however heavily the hand of the Lord lies upon his Puritan sinners, still He "hath Commission to the Sword" to destroy the crafty, bestial, diabolical creatures who oppose those sinners. William Hubbard, in his *Narrative of the Indian Wars in New England* (1677), is sure that King Philip's War in particular is nothing less than a Satanic plot against God's Chosen People: The war could not possibly have occurred because of anything the English have done to the Indians.

> What can be imagined, therefore, [he says] besides the instigation of Satan, that envied at the prosperity of the church of God here seated, or else fearing lest the power of the Lord Jesus, that had overthrown his kingdom in other parts of the world, should do the like here, and so the stone taken out of the mountain without hands, should become a great mountain itself, and fill the whole earth: no cause of provocation being given by the English.

Thus through the century and beyond, the Puritans wrote down their history and discovered and rediscovered the Indians' place in that history. In such a vein, in such a manner — to note only the full-fledged histories — Increase Mather wrote his *Brief History of the Warr with the Indians* [i.e., King Philip's War] (1676) and his *Relation of the Troubles which have hapned in New England, By reason of the Indians there: From the Year 1614 to the Year 1675* (1677); his son Cotton wrote his *Decennium Luctuosum* (1699), which was included, somewhat expanded, in the *Magnalia Christi Americana* (1702); and Samuel Penhallow wrote his survey of troubles with the northeast Indians early in the seventeenth century, *The History of the Wars of New-England with the Eastern Indians, or a Narrative of their continued Perfidy and Cruelty* (1726). History was everywhere cosmically and eternally meaningful. A Satanic principle was part of that meaningfulness; and the New England Indians somehow embodied that principle. The Indian was significant precisely as history was significant.

Out of such an understanding of the nature and destiny of civilized man in New England, here rose the Puritan understanding of the nature and destiny of savage man. There was, at the outset, no difficulty in accounting for the origin and genesis of the savage: Universally it was agreed that the Indians were of the race of men — descendants, in order, of Adam, Noah, and those Asiatic Tartars who had come to America by a land-bridge from northern Asia. This was orthodox seventeenth-century opinion. And it allowed Puritans to account simply for the savage, heathenish state of the Indian. Was he not perhaps the farthest of all God's human creatures from God Himself? Descended from wanderers, had he not lost his sense of civilization and law and order? Had he not lost — except for a dim recollection — God Himself? And wasn't he, as a direct result of this loss, in the power of Satan? Seen thus — and only thus — as one item in a God-centered course of experience, the Indian took on an awful meaning for the Puritan mind.

The Puritan writer on the Indian was, therefore, less interested in the Indian's culture than in the Indian's fallen spiritual condition as it was to be seen everywhere about him. Such early accounts of the Indians as those contained in Edward Winslow's *Good Newes from New England* (1624), Francis Higginson's *New-England's Plantation* (1630), and William Wood's *New England's Prospect* (1634) describe the appearance, social organization, and customs of the local Indians sketchily and, considering the tone of later accounts, somewhat optimistically: The heathen Indians, almost wiped out by the plague, living without the benefits of civilization, fearing their enemies, will certainly welcome the English; and it will be, presumably, no great task to civilize them and so to bring them to Christianity. But as the century wore on, as more distant Indians became better known, and as all the Indians seemed more and more to be setting themselves against civilization and Christianity, as disputes and warfare broke out, it seemed clearer and clearer that all Indians were inextricably involved in their low state and so not worth discussing in great detail. By the 1680's even Daniel Gookin, in charge of Christian Indian settlements for the United Colonies and so known to be soft toward the savages, could give only a despairing account of Indian culture. His account of the Indians in his "Of the Language, Customs, Manners, and Religion of the Indians" is straightforward and gloomy. The Indians have been and continue to be — with a few Christianized exceptions — brutish and barbarous; they indulge in polygamy; they are revengeful; the men only hunt and fish and fight while the women cook and do a little planting; they are all thieves and liars and by now they have virtually all become drunkards. True enough, they are hospitable and have some faintly systematic way of government. Yet their worship of the sun, moon, and the earth and of both a supreme doer of good and a supreme doer of evil and their submitting to their powwows, who are nothing but witches and wizards holding familiarity with Satan, damn them forever. Gookin might have held out a hope for missionary efforts with the Indians; but his evidence is not far from that which caused William Hubbard, in 1677, fiercely to denounce an Englishman who had turned Indian during King Philip's War, married a squaw, "renounced his religion, nation, and natural parents, all at once fighting against them." Captured, this man had been examined and condemned to die. And Hubbard had been obliged to comment:

> As to his religion he was found as ignorant as an heathen, which no doubt caused the fewer tears to be shed at his funeral, by, being unwilling to lavish pity upon him that had divested himself of nature itself, as well as religion, in a time when so much pity was needed elsewhere.

Savage life, then, could be only a life against nature and against religion.

What mattered, therefore, was not the intrinsic character of the New England Indians, but rather the meaning that that character might have the whole of New England life. Thus we must note in passing that the account of tarnished noble savages in Thomas Morton's *New English Canaan* (1632), of hypercholeric warriors in Philip Vincent's *True Relation* (1638), of natural men in Thomas Lechford's *Plain Dealing* (1643) and in John Josselyn's *Account of Two Voyages* (1674) — each of these attempts by non-Puritans to describe New England Indians "disinterestedly" would have seemed to Puritans mistaken in its very disinterestedness. Precisely because the Puritan was so deeply concerned with the meaning of the Indian for the whole of his culture, he hardly could conceive of describing that Indian disinterestedly. The Puritan understanding of the nature and destiny of savage man is to be found, as we have seen, in the record of Puritan-Indian relations, in Puritan accounts of God's Way with New England, and finally, as we shall see, in the history of the bitter failure of Puritans to bring the Indians to civilization and to God.

From the first, the Puritans, like most other seventeenth-century colonizers, firmly intended to convert the heathen. This indeed was an essential part of their mission on earth as they understood it. They were justified in taking Indian lands because they could use those lands as God had intended them to be used; yet God had also intended that His colonizers give civil and spiritual form to aboriginal dwellers in those lands. Practically, then, Indians were to be made into Puritans. Now, this was to be merely the peculiarly Puritan form of the Renaissance obsession with order and rationality; the Puritan mind, however, was to be so intense, so very fierce in its seizing upon ultimately supernaturalistic and absolutistic sanctions for a particular and local notion of order and rationality, that, unable to face the fact of cultural change and human variance, it was virtually blind to such alien forms of order and rationality as existed in aboriginal New England cultures. Equally, there is little evidence that Puritan order and Puritan reason, with their special scriptural ground, ever meant very much to the New England aborigines who were to be saved by that order and that reason.

". . . the glory of God, the propagation of the Gospel of Christ, the conversion of the Indians, and the enlargement of the King's Majesty's dominions in America . . ." — so go the expressed aims of the Massachusetts Bay enterprise. And chiefest of these aims was to be conversion. Yet the record of individual New England missionary efforts is relatively scattered, involving, as it does, almost as many organizations as men. Apparently money was first sent to New England for missionary work in the 1630's. During the 1630's, too, Roger Williams and perhaps John Eliot were active among the Indians. In 1636 Plymouth Colony enacted laws to provide for the preaching of the Gospel among the Indians, and in 1643 Thomas Mayhew began to carry on missionary work on Martha's Vineyard and Nantucket. Little or nothing was achieved, however, until November 1644 when the Massachusetts General Court asked the ministers to recommend measures for converting the Indians; two years later the General Court directed the ministers to elect two of their number every year to engage in gospel work among the heathen; and in 1646 John Eliot, having learned a local Indian dialect, began systematically to preach to them. Then, in 1649, Edward Winslow, acting as London agent for the United Colonies, managed to get Parliament to authorize the incorporation of "The President and Society for the Propagation of the Gospel in New England." It was this organization, poorly administered, which financed missionary work in New England until the Restoration. When, with the Restoration, the charter of "The President and Society" was declared legally invalid, a royal Charter was granted, in February 1662, to the "Company for Propagacion of the Gospell in New England, and parts adjacent, in America." It was this Company which carried on most of the financing of missionary work in New England until 1779, when the Revolutionary War caused remittances to America to be cut off. A "Society for Promotion of Christian Knowledge," formed in England in 1698, the "Society in Scotland for Propagating Christian Knowledge," formed in 1709, and an abortive "Society for Propagating Christian Knowledge," incorporated in Massachusetts in 1762, also variously contributed to the holy cause. (The "Society for the Propagation of the Gospel in Foreign Parts" was an Anglican corporation founded in 1701, which sent its missionaries mainly to the Indians in the middle colonies and which gave up work with the Indians late in the eighteenth century.) All these organizations issued, finally, in "The Society for Propagating the Gospel among the Indians, and Others, in North America," founded in 1787. A great number of intentions and organizations certainly — but few practical results. Only with such self-consciously dedicated souls as Eliot and the Mayhews in the later seventeenth century and with various evangelical missionaries such as Sargeant and Brainerd in the earlier eighteenth century, did the Gospel reach the heathen. There were, it seemed, only a few workers for this vast, wild vineyard.

For all his assurances that it was his holy mission to convert the heathen, to the Puritan in the middle of the seventeenth century, the business seemed to be proceeding with agonizing delay. Why, he wondered. And, as always, he had answers from scripture and from reasoned interpretation of scripture. As we have seen, Indian troubles, Indian opposition, and Indian recalcitrance were taken to be God-ordained reminders to the Puritan that his way on this earth was a hard way; and so the Indian was to be literally and continually the devil's advocate for a people who needed such to remind them of their own sinfulness and the agonizing hope of regeneration and election. Moreover, in the 1640's it seemed that there was specific scriptural authority for the delay in Indian conversion. The wild prophecy of Revelation 15 was interpreted as meaning that there could be no large-scale conversion of the heathen until the Jews themselves had been converted and until the Anti-Christ had been destroyed. The notion still persisted in the 1670's, during King Philip's War, when Increase Mather — in a history of that war — tried to erase it by pointing out that, in spite of the troubles which had resulted in the war, there nevertheless was a "glorious Sprinkling" of Indian converts in New England.

It was indeed a "Sprinkling," and as such the result of work carried on by a few men who felt a deep personal need to go to the Indians directly — yet the great majority of whom were so sure of their Puritan way that they could not see the Indians as anything but imperfect copies of themselves. John Eliot, for example, worked for the Indians from 1634 on, was able in the 1640's to preach to them in their own language, translated the Old and the New Testaments into the local Massachusetts dialect, founded a Christian Indian town in 1651 and saw thirteen others founded by 1674, even ventured in 1659 to suggest that it would be possible to form the purest of Christian Commonwealths on the basis of his experiments in organizing Indian towns. Yet the evidence of the various accounts of his work he sent to the Society for the Propagation of the Gospel shows that he viewed savage life as one of satanic degradation and that he knew the Indians to be, as Cotton Mather pointed out in his biography of Eliot, "doleful creatures who were the veriest *ruines of mankind,* which were to be found any where on the face of the earth." Even a man like Roger Williams, who strove for savage as well as for civilized rights, was appalled by the Indians in their "hideous *worships* of *creatures* and *devils.*" The Indians needed a Christian God; and the missionaries devoted themselves to bringing that God to the Indians. Their faith was simple: If they could go to the Indians, first organize their living into some civil pattern, and then teach them the Word, they might be pulled from the embrace of Satan. An ordered civil life was the basic condition of an holy life; civilization was properly a means to holiness. The Civil and the Holy Covenants of man with God were parts of a cosmically great principle of order. And civil order was a prerequisite of holy order.

Yet for all their faith in themselves, their society, and savage potentialities for civilization and God, the few missionaries who worked with the Indians were bound to fail. The Indian wars of the 1630's and 70's, the expansion of New England, the very clash of civilized and primitive cultures — these spelled the doom of the New England Indian, in spite of the effort of a "Sprinkling" of missionaries; for, as we know now, the missionaries themselves carried an alien and destructive culture to the Indians. Actually, by the end of the seventeenth century, it seemed very clear to all concerned that the New England missionary enterprise was likely to fail. The trials of King Philip's War had hardened Puritan hearts; even the Christian Indians, well on the way to salvation, were mistreated. A list drawn up in 1698 gives 2500 as the number of converts in the Indian towns, and points out that most of these are dying off rapidly. For this Cotton Mather blamed not the citizens of the Holy Commonwealth but the English traders who were bringing liquor and vice to the Indians. His father, seeing the Puritan faith weakening everywhere about him went further and instanced both the failure of the missions and the successes of the corrupt traders as partial proof of that weakening. Instead of being converted, he sermonized, the Indians are being perverted; for there are no more goodly Eliots among us; and now God has sent disease among the Indians as a final warning to us to mend our ways before he withdraws his Glory from us as he has from the Jews and from the Spanish and even from those in old England. Indian drunkenness, which had been sadly remarked before, came regularly to be denounced in a kind of ritualistic Puritan breastbeating. Yet we can see that the cause of failure went deeper than the introduction of disease and drunkenness and vice. It stemmed from the very quality of Puritan understanding of the Indian, necessarily from high Puritanism itself —

from the desperate need of those who had settled New England to hold on to their special beliefs about the nature and destiny of man if they were to hold on to their God-ordained way of life. They had to assume that the Indian's nature was essentially and absolutely one and the same with their nature; for the very integrative orthodoxy of their society demanded such an absolute. Herein they might very well fool themselves. Or so a Royal Commission noted in 1665 — reporting first that in Rhode Island "is the greatest number of Indians yet they never had any thing allowed towards the civilizing and converting of the Indians," and then that in Massachusetts:

> They convert Indians by hiring them to come & heare Sermons: by teaching them not to obey their Heathen Sachims, & by appointing Rulers amongst them over tenns, twenties, fifties, &c. The lives, Manners, & habits of those, whom they say are converted, cannot be distinguished from those who are not, except it be by being hyred to heare Sermons, which the more generous natives scorne.

This is perhaps unfair, certainly antagonistic. Yet it points, however obliquely, to the essential fact: that the seventeenth-century Puritan, in trying to recover for the Indian a civil and religious purity which he was sure he had already recovered for himself, was simply defining one reality in terms of another, the primitive in terms of the civilized, the Indian in terms of the Puritan. And, in the nature of things, he was bound to be wrong — and so to fail in his holy enterprise.

However, there was yet, and anticlimactically, to be hope. It was to be essentially an evangelical hope, a hope of saving the Indian not so much for civilization but for God, and this just before he should die. It was a hope which rose as part of the last ditch efforts of Puritans to hold on to their covenant theology and polity in the face of the rationalistic theology, material prosperity, and general enlightenment which had been making men discount the sense of sin since the last quarter of the seventeenth century.

During the first quarter of the eighteenth century, reports to the English missionary societies which were financing missionary work recounted, proposed, and promised great things — increased use of native missionaries, a kind of reservation system, some thirty congregations newly established in southern New England, more attempts to get to the eastern Indians whom the French papists had debauched, coöperation with Dutch missionaries working among the Five Nations, and attempts to combat the effects of liquor, dishonest traders, and disease. Yet God was angry with New England for her failure to Christianize the heathen when He had clearly indicated in Scripture that it was to be done. Thus Solomon Stoddard, he who had recommended in 1703 that Indians be hunted down with dogs, could conclude by 1723:

> And as we dread to go to Hell our selves, it should be awful to us to consider their Damnation. Love and Pity calls for it, that we should help them out of their Danger. We should pity *Beasts* in Misery, much more *Men:* Tho, they be Brutish Persons; yet, they are of Mankind, and so objects of Compassion. It is an act of Love to our own nature to seek their Salvation. . . .

Who were the Indians who were thus to be saved? There was, for example, Joseph Quasson who had been bound to a white man when his father died in debt, who in his servitude had learned how to read and had come to know God. Freed, however, he had become a roisterer and a drunkard, and so by 1726 a condemned murderer. The account of Quasson which we have was written from his death-cell by a friendly minister. And the point that the minister makes is this: the fact that Quasson had been bound to a white man; that his trial was delayed three years after the murder; that he was given seven weeks to live after being condemned; that liquor was taken away from him — all this shows how hard the Lord has been working for his salvation. And there was Sarah Coomes, the dying six-year-old of whom Experience Mayhew wrote in 1727:

> She lay sick a considerable while before she died; and in that time continued to crave Instructions in things of God and the eternal World, and to express her Assent to, and acquiesce in them. She in particular expressed her steadfast Belief of the Doctrines of Christ's Person, Suffering, and Intercession for Sinners; and when she prayed, she called upon God to have Mercy upon her for his sake.

This is the Puritan sense of sin *in extremis.*

And in the context of the general failure of the sense of sin, there is to be understood, along with the neo-Calvinism of the Great Awakening, the final revivalistic interest in Indian conversion. The work of New-England born and trained Congregationalist missionaries had shifted by 1725 to the western parts of the middle colonies, where they were joined by and so worked with Scotch-Irish Presbyterian missionaries from the middle colonies. Here began that union of Congregationalist and Presbyterian missionary efforts which was to become official at the end of the century. The infusion of Presbyterian Calvinism must have done much to hearten the Congregationalist ministers. For the ministers herein involved, John Sargeant, David Brainerd, Charles Beatty, and Jonathan Edwards chief among them, conversion was everything and civilization nothing; the high Puritan faith in the uses of civilization as a means to conversion had gone almost entirely. So, in a report prepared for the Society in Scotland for the Propagation of Christian Knowledge, Brainerd is primarily concerned with "experimental [*i.e.,* experiential] religion" — which is to say, religious conversion as it relates to overt emotional tension and crisis. He tells, for example, of his violent preaching to Indians, 8 August 1745, in Crosweeksung, New Jersey; he was pleased that the Indians were not able to "withstand the shock of this surprising operation. . . . They were almost universally praying and crying for mercy in every part of the house, and many out of doors, and numbers could neither go nor stand." He was thus living up to the precepts of Ebenezer Pemberton who had preached at his ordination, insisting that conversion was to be achieved only by powerful preaching: "They [the preachers] are to 'compel sinners to come in' by a living representation of the power and grace of an almighty Redeemer. And in his own short life, so his editor, biographer, and intended father-in-law, Jonathan Edwards, was pleased to note, the desperately consumptive Brainerd showed evidence, above all, of those authentic religious affections only through which men are surely and truly saved. In an edition of the *Life of Brainerd,* published after Edwards' death, there was included further contemporary evidence of the need for violent conversion of the heathen — this in Charles Beatty's "Further remarks respecting Indian affairs." Beatty argues in so many words that the conversion of the Indians must precede their being civilized; for the Indians hate civilization and Christianity equally and must be convinced of the misery of their spiritual state before they can realize the misery of their civil state. Only "gospellizing" will succeed where civilizing has failed. Thus the continuing miserable state of the savage heathen was taken as additional evidence not only of the failure of earlier missionary methods but also of the need of direct and violent religious experience as an absolute prerequisite to civil and social improvement. Having virtually destroyed the Indian by trying to bring a new, civil life to him, the New England missionaries, encouraged by their Scotch-Irish Presbyterian brethren, were now to call the Holy Spirit directly to the Indian in order that they might give him that new life immediately. Certainly, a miracle was needed.

Always deriving its meaning from the Puritan view of man and his nature, inevitably the Puritan understanding of the Indian issued, towards the middle of the eighteenth century, into a particular form of the revivalism and anti-rationalism into which the Puritan view in general had issued. And so, this final Puritan understanding of the Indian is to be comprehended essentially as it relates to the Edwardean neo-Calvinism of the Great Awakening. Always the Puritan mind had worked from the inside out, from God and Scripture and reason to man and nature. Whatever he saw outside, the Puritan had somehow already seen inside. Understanding the Indian as he was related to man and nature, the Puritan thus succeeded — if he did succeed — only in knowing a little more about God and Scripture and reason, and in understanding himself. There is a simple explanation, perhaps: In order to make his new society in a new world, the Puritan could not afford to understand anyone but himself.

The New England Way: Puritan Quest for Utopia

Most of those who left Europe for America came to improve their lot by acquiring a larger share of the world's goods. Settlers in colonial New England were no exception, but the Puritans who established the Massachusetts Bay Colony were also driven by a vision of recreating an archaic Christian commonwealth that had once existed when the Christian faith was young and uncorrupted. In the following selection, Alan Simpson explores the Puritan quest, explaining how the vision of establishing "a city upon a hill" in a wilderness shaped the settlement of New England and why that adventure ended in failure.

Puritans came to America to escape, not simply from persecution by English authorities, but because they had lost hope of purifying the church in England. This was a cause they regarded as the first step in the struggle to regain control over forces that were transforming England from a more stable, placid, and secure place in which to live into an unpredictable, rapidly changing modern society in which no one's position was secure, especially no one in middle classes. Neither the nobility, whose positions were fairly fixed, nor the poor peasantry, who pessimistically accepted as fixed their lowly position, proved as receptive to the voices spreading the gospel of the Protestant Reformation in Britain. But to middle-class folk, Protestantism was a compelling new vision.

Protestantism switched the burden of Christian salvation from the shoulders of the church, and placed it directly on those of the sinners. Since neither priest nor Pope could intercede with God, each man must be his own priest. Moreover, it insisted that God preordained each person's spiritual fate, yet no one could know for certain what that fate was — Heaven or Hell. The result was that the Christian pilgrimage was redefined as an endless search for signs of God's grace, for indications that one was among the saved, and evidence for this was man's capacity to resist temptation. Puritans could not rely on a merciful God who would forgive; they lived in awe of a stern God who demanded that men actively struggle, not only against sin in their personal lives, but in their society.

With such convictions, Puritans attempted to establish a Christian commonwealth in Massachusetts which made the welfare of the community superior to the wishes of the individual. By imposing communal constraints on settlement patterns and on all forms of individual enterprise, Puritans hoped to create a stable and just society modeled on their notions of God's design. Such an experiment could only be attempted in a wilderness where no kings or bishops could interfere, yet the empty spaces, the limitless abundance, and the weakness of authority spelled ultimate failure. The Puritans learned that even in America man could not escape the physical world.

FOR FURTHER READING:

HALL, DAVID, ed. *Puritanism in Seventeenth-Century Massachusetts.* New York: Holt, Rinehart & Winston, 1956.*
MILLER, PERRY. *Errand into the Wilderness.* New York: Harper & Row, Publishers, Torchbooks, 1956.*
MORGAN, EDMUND S. *The Puritan Dilemma: The Story of John Winthrop.* Boston: Little, Brown & Company, 1958.*

Asterisk denotes paperback edition.

The Covenanted Community

ALAN SIMPSON

The first chance to see what the Puritan saint would make of life, if he had the freedom to experiment, came in America. The early history of Massachusetts (together with that of Plymouth, Connecticut, and New Haven, for the differences are unimportant from our point of view) is the story of men who shared an ideal, left the Old World to realize it in the New, only to discover when the work of planting was done that the spirit had evaporated. Frustration was the fate which awaited every Puritan. In England, where the defeat came in war, it has all the features of tragedy; here, where there was no defeat but apparent success, it becomes a kind of ironic tale.

The Puritans who came to America continued to have much in common with those who stayed at home. Take, for instance, that apocalyptic view of their place in history which all Puritans shared and which can hardly be overemphasized if we want to understand the quality of their enthusiasm. We are all familiar today with the Communist's conviction that he is moving toward a preordained victory. His science tells him that the historical process is obeying a determinate logic, and, so far from the inevitability of this process slowing down his efforts, it acts as an enormous spur to them. The Puritan has a similar theory of history and the same sort of compulsion to cooperate with destiny. Admittedly, Divine Providence is a good deal more mysterious than dialectical materialism. But this unpredictability, if an argument in some situations for more patience than a Communist could admit in his timetable, always offers the possibility of a miraculous delivery. The winters of the church may be cruelly long; but when that frozen world thaws, as in the springtime of the Reformation, the whole earth seems to rush toward its harvest.

The Puritan thought of human history as the field in which God gathered his saints, saving the few from the fate which all had deserved and imparting to that few some knowledge of his Will. For reasons known only to himself, God had permitted ignorance of his Will to envelop the visible church between the age of the apostles and the age of the Reformation. These thirteen or fourteen centuries had seen a downward swing to the lowest depths of depravity; then a slow ascent had begun as God chose to reveal more and more of himself. Wave after wave of witnesses had been summoned to testify; country after country seemed likely to be the scene in which the destiny of the age would be fulfilled. On the crest of that movement stood the Puritan, with his "panting, longing, eager" desire to find the revelation com-

---

Source: Alan Simpson, *Puritanism in Old and New England* (Chicago: University of Chicago Press, 1955), chap. 2, "The Covenanted Community," pp. 19–38.

pleted in himself. These adjectives are not mine, nor are they those of some simple enthusiast. They might be Oliver Cromwell's or John Milton's. They are, in fact, the words of John Cotton, the leading intellectual among the founders of the New England Way.

Incidentally, the intellectual quality in the Puritan's piety can easily be overstated. When every compliment has been paid to Professor Miller's studies of Puritanism — and I yield to no one in my admiration for those ingenious works — at least one gentle criticism may be made. He has told us too much about the Puritan mind and not enough about the Puritan's feelings. If the seventeenth-century Puritan, with his formal training in scholasticism, usually tries to give a rational account of his faith, it is the stretched passion which makes him what he is. They are people who suffered and yearned and strived with an unbelievable intensity; and no superstructure of logic ought to be allowed to mask that turmoil of feeling.

It may be said, of course, that the Puritan was better prepared for disappointment than most men and therefore less disposed to commit himself to a utopian dream. It was some such thought as this that led Professor Miller to say that a disillusioned Puritan is impossible to conceive. Was it not the Puritan who had preached the arbitrariness of God and the depravity of man? Who was he to falter if the age missed what in his foolish pride he had allowed himself to believe was its destiny? I can only say this was not the mood of 1630, when the Pilgrims left England to build their Zion in the wilderness. It was not the mood of Oliver Cromwell when he told a Parliament of Puritan saints that they stood on the edge of the promises and the prophecies. It was the Puritan's compromise with defeat, and when he finally made it — either in the despairing cry of the English Puritan, "God has spit in our faces," or in the melancholy dirge of the American Puritan at the end of the century — the crusade was finished.

The founders of New England not only shared the apocalyptic view of history with the Puritans whom they left behind. Their confession of faith, their search for regeneration and sanctification, their techniques of self-trial and self-denial, all spring from the same community of experience. A series of New England sermons explaining how God calls, justifies, and sanctifies his elect; a New England diary recording an agonizing search for the evidence of this work in the diarist's soul; New England's advice to educators on the education of a saint or to businessmen on the duty of combining "diligence in business with deadness to the world"; New England's conviction that every man is his brother's keeper; New England's persuasion that a good joke ought to be balanced with some savory morsel to keep merriment in its proper bounds; New England's cultivation of the Puritan art forms: the biography of the saint, the record of divine judgments, the history which weaves both into a narrative of God's blessings and punishments — all this, and much else, can be matched on both sides of the water. Behind it shines that vision which a tinker living on the ecstatic fringe of the movement described for all Puritans in the *Pilgrim's Progress.*

The specialty of the New England Way only emerged as its founders came to grips with the problems of embodying the vision in institutions. It is suggested by that analogy which was not confined to them but which acquired a more concrete and durable form in their experience than elsewhere: the analogy between themselves and the first people who were admitted into a covenant of grace with God. New England was to be a New Israel — a covenanted community. Its founders, who had already experienced in their own lives the sensation of being offered, and of accepting, the covenant of grace, were to form themselves into a community of saints for the enjoyment of God's ordinances and the elevation of their colony into the status of a chosen people. Such seemed to be the opportunity which God, working through the secondary causes which made colonization possible at this juncture of history, was offering to the regenerate. The labor of explorers, the greed of merchants, the ambition of kings, the pressure of persecution, the incidence of economic hardship, every motive and every capacity for colonization was but a web of contrivance designed by invisible hands for ends which only the elect could fathom. The interpretation of those ends in terms of a covenanted community begins with the famous sermon by Governor Winthrop in mid-ocean and only ends among the disenchantments of the late seventeenth century after desperate efforts to recall the wandering pilgrims to a proper sense of their destiny.

Let me quote Governor Winthrop's own words. They are taken from the sermon called "A Modell of Christian Charity," which was delivered on board the *Arabella:*

> Thus stands the cause between God and us; we are entered into Covenant with him for this work; we have taken out a Commission; the Lord hath given us leave to draw our own Articles; we have professed to enterprise these actions upon these and these ends; we have hereupon besought him of favor and blessing. Now if the Lord shall please to hear us, and bring us in peace to the place we desire, then hath he ratified this Covenant and sealed our Commission, and will expect a strict performance of the Articles contained in it, but if we shall neglect the observation of these Articles which are the ends we have propounded, and dissembling with our God, shall fall to embrace this present world and prosecute our carnal intentions, seeking great things for our selves and our posterity, the Lord will surely break out in wrath against us, be revenged of such a perjured people, and make us know the price of the breach of such a Covenant.

What this decision came to mean was the tribalization of the Puritan spirit. The goals of regeneration and sanctification, common to Puritans everywhere, were to be sought within a tribal community. Let me sketch some of the implications of this conception as it appeared to its authors.

First, no diversity of opinion in fundamentals would be permitted within the tribe. Regenerate men, using that faculty of reason which grace had restored, and applying it to the Word of God as revealed in Scripture, could come to only one conclusion. Rightly informed consciences do not judge differently; they concur. What they perceive is that regenerate men must form their lives within an external discipline and cooperate in enforcing that discipline on the unregenerate. The mission of the elect is to uphold an orthodoxy.

The external discipline of the tribe would involve, in Winthrop's words, "a due form of ecclesiastical and civil government." So far as the first was concerned, all Puritans believed that the true form of ecclesiastical government had been prescribed in Scripture, and what these Puritans found in Scripture was authority for confining church membership to "visible saints." Churches would be composed of groups of converted souls who formed a covenant among themselves to create a church and who looked forward to a perpetual succession of saints who would enter the church covenant as the work of conversion continued. The orthodox idea of a church, whether in Anglican England or Presbyterian Scotland, was a body coextensive with the community, admission to which depended on baptism, subsequently confirmed by a profession of faith. But this New England church is going to be built out of the conversion experience, and it is assumed that a subjective experience can be detected by objective tests. However, there is one other class of members attached to the church besides the converted. God's covenant with Abraham had included not only Abraham but his seed. The children of the converted will be admitted to baptism, in the expectation that they will eventually be able to attest the conversion experience and qualify for full membership.

These churches, around which the New England towns will be built, are autonomous congregations. The powers of church government were not given by God to bishops, or to Presbyterian assemblies, but to them. However, no anarchic consequences need be feared from their autonomy. Rightly informed consciences reach the same conclusions; that is the essence of the promise. Congregations are expected to consult if they encounter difficulties, and erroneous consciences, persisting in their errors, will find themselves opposed by the massed forces of orthodoxy.

So much for the ecclesiastical discipline. But in a convenanted community the discipline of the state must also be directed by saints. It is true that all Puritans talk about the separation of church and state, and this is one of the things that distinguish them from all Anglicans. But nine out of ten Puritans only want to separate church and state in order to bind them together again. In other words, they have to break the indissoluble unity of church and state in Anglican England so as to get the church on its scriptural basis, Presbyterian or Congregational, as the case may be; but, once on that basis, they expect the state to uphold it, to be "the nursing father" of the church. Separation of church and state, in such a context, meant simply a division of functions between two partners with a tendency to reduce the state to a junior partner where the clergy claimed a superior insight into the Divine Will. In New England it was expected to be a partnership in unison, for church and state alike were to be dominated by saints.

The same compact among saints would underlie the civil government as it underlay the ecclesiastical government. The idea that political authority, while authorized by God, derives from the consent of the people was a familiar one in the English tradition, and Puritans invoked it to suit their purposes. The founders of Massachusetts were prepared to interpret their charter as a social covenant, and the communities which hived off from Massachusetts used the covenant device to launch their plantations. But the consent which is expressed in these compacts is not to be confused with any notion of popular sovereignty. Popular sovereignty is the grossest atheism in a Puritan universe governed by God. It is a consent to be governed according to the ordinances of God: an acceptance by saints of the political obligations of a chosen people.

These compacts do not commit them to any particular form of government. Forms of civil government, unlike forms of ecclesiastical government, are not prescribed in Scripture, and there is no reason why English representative institutions and English common-law principles should not be admitted into the holy community provided they do not prevent saints from governing that community, from protecting its church, and from making such changes as are necessary to bring English legal custom in line with the laws of God. However, this is some proviso. It means that in a remote corner of His Majesty's realm there will be a group of one-party states, where access to power depends on evidence of conversion. Party politicians will uphold the party preacher; laws will be modified to suit the party ethic; the administration of law will not be embarrassed by procedural safeguards; and all deviationists will either repent or suffer expulsion.

So much for "the due form of ecclesiastical and civil government." One further decision will be necessary to underpin the stability of the whole enterprise: a crucial decision about the qualifications of the prophet in the chosen community. The Puritan way of life had been worked out by a learned clergy, and learning — the learning of the schools — had been regarded as an indispensable means for the discovery and the application of the Divine Will in the lives of the regenerate. However, Puritanism had preached that without grace reason was helpless, that the pilgrim must await the miracle which no merit on his part could produce, and that, once this miracle had been bestowed, Christ was "ingrafted" in his heart. Could these regenerate spirits be held within any bounds? Could reason, which had begun by abdicating its authority, reassert itself so as to insure that one true discipline which was God's design for men — or even to insure any society at all? The whole history of Puritanism is a commentary on its failure to satisfy the cravings which its preaching had aroused. It was forever producing rebellions against its own teachers: rebellions within the learned camp and rebellions from outside that camp against the assertion that learned reason had anything to teach the illuminated spirit.

How much of this the founders of the covenanted community foresaw is open to question. The history of the Reformation had been full of it, and they were always being reminded by their enemies of the risks they ran; but in the nature of things these risks would not be fully revealed until the opportunity came for the saint to claim his privileges — the opportunity so delightfully expressed by that admirer of Anne Hutchinson who said to Edward Johnson: "I'll bring you to a woman that preaches better gospel than any of your black-coats that have been at the Ninneversity." However, whether they foresaw it or not, it is certain that they carried with them the ideal of a learned clergy, and everyone knows of their determination to reproduce on the frontier the basic intellectual institutions of the Old World: the school, the college, the library, and the press. What is less clear, perhaps, since Professor Morison wrote his history of Harvard, is the purpose of these institutions. The merits of that great work speak for themselves, but it has one small flaw. The author has tried, in devious ways, to redeem his alma mater from the suspicion of being too much troubled by sin. But the founders of Harvard College would hardly have thanked him for this carnal enterprise. What they aimed at producing was not Christian gentlemen with a liberal education but saints with a saving knowledge. The college was to be a school of prophets — learned prophets, certainly, but emphatically prophets. What else would a chosen people expect from its educational institutions?

I have tried to sketch the lines along which the vision would be embodied in these communities. Between 1630 and the mid-forties the work of planting and consolidating went on, until at last one species of Puritanism had been stabilized. Viewed simply as an achievement of order in the wilderness, out of human beings as potentially explosive as Puritans, this was certainly impressive. But it is no slight to the leadership to suggest that the problem of welding communities out of Puritan material was somewhat simplified for them.

The most obvious simplification was the opportunity to create a new community without having to tear an old one to pieces and to go on creating new communities if the first proved disappointing. These Puritans leave all their opponents behind them. They pass straight from settled life to the tasks of creating a new life without any disorderly interlude. When they reach the wilderness, work crowds in and danger binds them. If the worse comes to the worst, there is always the frontier. The deviationists can take their chances in Rhode Island. Thomas Hooker, who is no deviationist, but who may have felt that Massachusetts was too small for two such redoubtable saints as himself and Mr. Cotton, can become the founder of Connecticut. The saints in England must often have sighed for some such *Lebensraum.*

The other great advantage might seem to be the preagreement about ecclesiastical policy. Puritans had little difficulty in agreeing about doctrine. What they usually disagreed about was the form of church government within which the elect should fulfil their mission. When the Puritans came into power in England, they were prepared to fight a civil war over the rival merits of Presbyterianism, Nonseparating Congregationalism, and Separatism. New England, although it shares part of this experience in its contests with separatists like Roger Williams, rallies with surprising ease around the principle of Nonseparating Congregationalism and has relatively little difficulty with Presbyterianism. How did this happen?

It used to be thought that the adoption of Congregationalism was suggested by the example of Plymouth which the main body of the colonists found when they got there. It is now assumed that Professor Miller has conclusively demonstrated a preengagement among the majority of the clergymen which can be traced back through their Dutch experience to the original advocates of Nonseparating Congregationalism as a middle way between Presbyterianism and Separatism. However, Professor Miller has to admit that some ministers were Presbyterians; that others, who had not gone through the Dutch experience, might have been uncommitted, and that the views of the secular leaders, at the time of their arrival, are largely unknown.

Doubtless the Congregationalists were in a position to take the initiative. But the acquiescence in that initiative must certainly have been helped by the composition of the Puritan population that came over here and by the frontier situation. Congregationalism aroused objections in England as an unsuitable organization for a community which was both hierarchical and centralized. It deprived the great Puritan magnate of his power to appoint ministers. It seemed to place hereditary influence at the mercy of the conversion experience, for, unless his children could attest it, they would presumably find themselves deprived of both church membership and political power. Worst of all, it looked like a dangerous loosening of the social bonds to substitute a church of autonomous congregations for the corporate and centrally controlled church of tradition. Just how dangerous was to become clear enough in the Civil Wars when Congregationalism, in its separatist form, became the medium through which every kind of radicalism found expression. But few of these fears were realistic in New England. Puritan peers and very rich Puritans, the backbone of English Presbyterianism, were conspicuous by their absence. The lesser leaders who came over were reasonably insured against social, as distinct from theological, unrest by their monopoly of talent and by the frontier opportunities which took the sting out of class bitterness. And the communities to be administered were, after all, a handful of decentralized settlements as compared with a highly integrated England. Congregationalism commended itself to clerical specialists like Cotton and Hooker as the one form of church government prescribed by God for his saints; but, if the local situation had not made it a safe enough proposition, the Word would doubtless have seemed less clear.

So much for the New England Way viewed simply as an achievement of order. But how far did it fulfil the expectations of its founders: that this covenanted people would represent the ideal toward which all history was converging; that there would be a succession of saints with the same intense piety as themselves; and that under the rule of these saints the whole community would be held to the obligations of the covenant and sanctified by its blessings?

Much of the frustration which follows is common to Puritans everywhere. They had dreamed of themselves as a united army forming the vanguard of history; but the army splinters into columns, battalions, and platoons, while history seems to be marching on. They had thought that conversion could become an institution, but they find themselves with church members where they had hoped for saints. They had devised one of the most formidable disciplines ever seen for keeping sin within bounds, but there seemed to be as much of it inside the covenant as outside. They had demanded an impossible tension from the elect and an impossible submission from the mass. Everywhere the taut springs relax, the mass rebels, and compromises eat away at a distinction on which the whole system was based.

The history of the New England Way is the history of a losing struggle to preserve the intensity of the experience of the saint and his authority over society. On the one hand, a church of visible saints, each of whom could attest the miracle of conversion, is gradually transformed into a church where membership depends on a profession of faith and a standard of Puritan morality. On the other hand, the church, thus formalized, is deprived of its organic control of political power and forced to depend for its control over society on the opportunity its clergy have had to make themselves a ruling class and the allies of ruling families.

The decay of spiritual intensity is the theme of almost all the founders as they survey the tribal community in their declining years. Few things are more moving than the comparisons drawn by a Bradford, a Winthrop, or a Shephard between the spirit that sustained them and the spirit they find around them.

Let me quote from Bradford — that simple hero who never forgot, in all the labor of planting a colony, that his true home was elsewhere. He had copied into his journal the claim which the leaders of their little church had made when they applied in 1617 for permission to settle in the New World:

> We are knit together as a body in a most strict and sacred bond and covenant of the Lord, of the violation whereof we make great conscience, and by virtue whereof we do hold ourselves straightly tied to all care of each other's good, and of the whole by every one, and so mutually.

When he read that entry in his old age, he wrote this confession on the back of the page:

> O sacred bond, whilst inviolably preserved! How sweet and precious were the fruits that flowed from the same, but when this fidelity decayed, then their ruin approached. O that these ancient members had not died or been dissipated (if it had been the will of God) or else that this holy care and constant faithfulness had still lived, and remained with those that survived, and were in times afterward added unto them. But (alas) that subtle serpent hath slyly wound in himself under fair pretenses of necessity and the like to untwist these sacred bonds and ties, and as it were insensibly, by degrees, to dissolve or in a great measure to weaken, the same. I have been happy, in my first times, to see, and with much comfort to enjoy, the blessed fruits of this sweet communion, but it is now a part of my misery in old age, to find and feel the decay and want thereof (in a great measure), and with grief and sorrow of heart to lament and bewail the same. And for others warning and admonition, and my own humiliation, do I here note the same.

What had happened to them is part of the common experience of all creative revivals, when the first generation hands over to the second, when the organizer follows the visionary, and habit replaces direct experience as the source of guidance. But, of course, it is colored by their own circumstances. There is little to keep alive their memories of persecution. There is less and less to sustain their sense of the

New World as a beacon for the Old when the progress of events in England reduces the New England Way first to a backwater of the Puritan spirit and later to a provincial anachronism. There is plenty of evidence that, in spite of all their precautions, worldliness is still with them and that saints who struggle to rule the world may find themselves ruled by it — especially the Puritan, who develops for religious purposes a type of character which can hardly fail to be a worldly success.

All this they see. What they fail to see is that the very work to which they have set their hands with so much resolution — the tribalization of the Puritan experience — is stifling its free spirit. Every repression of dissent, every insistence on the subordination of subjective experience to the judgment of the church, makes the work of enlisting zeal so much harder. They were probably right in thinking that order was possible on no other terms; but so was Anne Hutchinson when she accused them of substituting a covenant of works for a covenant of grace. Obedience to an external order, rather than immediate confrontation of God, was becoming, in spite of its formal theology, the criterion of New England Puritanism.

Before this first generation had passed away, it was obvious that the second generation would not be able to attest the conversion experience in sufficient numbers to perpetuate the succession of saints. It is some testimony to the severity of their standards that the fact was faced: that the second generation was held to be, and admitted itself to be, deficient in grace, though it was willing to support the church and to conform itself to its discipline. However, the sincerity of all parties only heightens the irony of a situation in which a chosen people cannot find enough chosen people to prolong its existence. Everything depended on saints. They composed the church and ruled the state. What would happen if the supply ran out? The escape was found through the famous halfway covenant, a device whereby the second generation was admitted to church membership, after making a profession of obedience, and so enabled to have its children baptized. The return to tradition had begun. Of course the effort to produce conversions among the children and grandchildren was not abandoned. The preachers kept reminding themselves, and the clans, that the covenant had included Abraham's seed. But somehow, in spite of all their struggles, the religious experiences of the first generation refused to become a hereditary endowment. "Doth not a careless, remiss, flat, dry, cold, dead frame of spirit, grow in upon us secretly, strangely, prodigiously?" We are hardly surprised to learn that the halfway covenant was in most cases just a halfway house between a church from which all but the saint had been excluded and one in which all but the flagrant sinner was admitted.

It was inevitable that this subsidence of the saints into a company of conformists should be reflected in the deterioration of Puritan piety. The congregations are not, of course, to be judged by the condemnations which the preachers heaped on them as part of the Puritan ritual during that prolonged jeremiad known to history as "God's controversy with New England." The deterioration is not a matter of crimes or misdemeanors. It is entirely compatible with the most persevering virtues. But it means contracted sensibility; gestures replacing feelings; taste subduing zeal; pride elbowing out humility; intellect playing a game; divided souls acting a part their ancestors have forced on them. It is the well-meant mimicries of Samuel Sewall which produce such farcical effects when compared with the old, high seriousness. The diarist who finds it "an awful yet pleasing treat" to review the coffins in his family vault has traveled a long way from Bradford or Winthrop. Equally far is the distance between the Puritan who knew the difference between spiritual and financial success and his descendant who sometimes confused them. The old Puritans had a grim description for this compromise with the covenant: they called it "the forms of godliness without the power."

Meanwhile, as a utopian church subsides into an established church, its grip over political power also relaxes. An early symptom was that pressure for a rule of law as opposed to a rule of discretion which distinguished the politics of Englishmen everywhere in the seventeenth century. Saints in power were always tempted to demand as free a hand for themselves as possible. A life-tenure for the trusted saint seemed to Cotton, as it later seemed to Milton, the best security for the holy commonwealth, and Winthrop's effort to keep a wide discretion in the hands of a chosen few has its counterpart in Cromwell's practice. But on both sides of the water the parliamentary tradition refused to be ousted by the theocrats. In Old England it was temporarily swept aside and then vindicated at the expense of the saints. In New England the saints discovered early that they would have to compromise with it if they hoped to control it. They were not even able to establish the system in Massachusetts without concessions to the principles of limited government which were extracted by the freemen in their struggles with the magistrates.

The intention, notwithstanding these concessions, was to maintain a theocracy within the forms of representative government, and the essence of the system was the restriction of political power to church members. In Massachusetts and New Haven this was achieved by confining the franchise to the elite. In Connecticut the same result could be expected without a formal restriction. But in the long run this monopoly of power was bound to be weakened by combined pressure from inside and outside: the pressure of expanding communities for a relaxation of religious tests and the pressure of imperial authority on a colonial theocracy. New Haven, the purest theocracy of the original settlements, had already suffered from its restrictive practices before its enforced absorption in Connecticut in 1662. Massachusetts, under pressure from England, went through the motions of liberalizing its religious tests at the same time. Finally, with the loss of the old charter in 1684, and the issue of a new one in 1691, the custodians of the Puritan ideal in Massachusetts were obliged to defend it under increasingly difficult conditions.

The power to choose their governor had passed to the Crown. Synods no longer advised legislatures. Boston flaunted the corruptions of a colonial court, the heresies of enforced toleration, and the sins of a thriving seaport before the eyes of the faithful, while the secularized culture of western Europe seeped in through a hundred different channels. No doubt all was far from lost. Preachers might keep their hold on rural communities by the combined force of personality and tradition. Conversions would certainly come back again; and the notion of a chosen people, still maintained in the pulpit, was only beginning its career in the world. But none of this should obscure the fact that an effort to escape from history into a utopia ruled by saints had suffered its usual failure.

Peopling the Colonies

Except for sparse numbers of intractable Indians, the English found an uninhabited continent with which nothing could be done without a sizable labor force with the right skills. Recruiting people, therefore, became one of the principal problems facing colony-builders. For 300 years, a steady stream of Europeans migrated to America, pushed by poverty and oppressed at home, pulled by freedom and opportunity in America. In all, some 60 million people left Europe in the years following 1700, most headed for America. This movement was one of the great folk migrations in history. In the following selection, Mildred Campbell closely examines groups of seventeenth-century immigrants to illuminate who they were and what forces propelled them.

Though North America drew on all parts of the world for its population, England supplied most of those who came during the first two centuries. At that time, England was unable to fully employ willing workers on the farms and in the towns. An agricultural revolution forced tens of thousands off the land, as enterprising large landholders discovered that it was more profitable to consolidate many fragmented plots into large, but well-managed estates. The displaced peasantry, however, had no place to go in this preindustrial era. Many became public charges and drifted into the towns, especially London which was fast becoming a metropolis. At the same time, many urban craft guilds encountered tough competition from new, more efficient modes of production, and they, too, suffered eclipse. The result was large-scale technological unemployment, until the Industrial Revolution in the latter half of the eighteenth century created new jobs.

Until then, however, those people who could no longer continue at old jobs, either accepted inferior ones, sank into pauperdom, or migrated. According to Mildred Campbell, the migration was a highly selective process that appealed more to the young than to the old, and to the not-so-poor more than to the impoverished. Young people, hoping to inherit a family plot or trade, experienced the pangs of economic dislocation most acutely, and were most prone to seek alternatives. And those who descended from yeoman farming and skilled artisan families, in contrast to the poorer peasantry and unskilled laborers, had more to lose by staying in England where opportunities were shrinking. Rather than suffer a decline in status, some came to America where they could become landowning farmers and prosperous craftsmen as their forebears had been.

The breakup of medieval patterns of agricultural and industrial organization, a process that occurred first and most extensively in England, later spread to the rest of Europe, and in the nineteenth century sent millions of Europe's landless and homeless to the New World.

FOR FURTHER READING:

HANDLIN, OSCAR. *The Uprooted.* New York: Grosset & Dunlap, 1957.*
HANSEN, MARCUS LEE. *The Atlantic Migration.* Magnolia, Mass.: Peter Smith, 1940.*
SMITH, ABBOTT E. *Colonists in Bondage: White Servitude and Convict Labor in America.* Magnolia, Mass.: Peter Smith, 1947.*

Asterisk denotes paperback edition.

Social Origins of Some Early Americans   MILDRED CAMPBELL

A study of American origins must eventually lead to the structure and functioning of many Old World societies, for the national fabric is woven of many threads. But the people who came first in their sturdy ships of fifty to a hundred tons, who kept coming throughout the seventeenth century until the small seaboard settlements had moved out of their first precarious existence to a more certain future — these have a special claim upon us. Indeed, one wonders whether individuals ever meant as much to any enterprise as did those who filled the emigrant ships in that first century of colonization. Emigration across the Atlantic has never ceased from their day to ours, but only then did actual survival depend on the arrival of a relatively few people.

It was also only in the first century that those who came were a fairly homogeneous group in terms of national origins. For despite the Dutch on the Hudson, and small groups of Swiss, Swedes, Finns, and French Huguenots pocketed along the coast, the small vessels which set out on the American voyage were chiefly English built and English manned. Their cargoes, moreover, consisted largely of Englishmen and, later and in smaller numbers, Englishwomen. Even the Scots and Irish, who in the next century would crowd the harbors of the New World, were a minority in the first century.

We have long been accumulating a vast amount of information about these early settlers, and able historians have exploited the material with skill and insight. Only in more recent years, however, have serious attempts been made to push the story further back. We now try to discover their social origins. We want to know more about what they brought with them; not their material possessions — the *Susan Constant* and her sister ships provided space for only the barest minimum of necessities — but that other luggage which every individual perforce carries about with him, his heritage. That heritage was the sum total of his own experiences and the environment in which he grew up; it had made him what he was and determined, to an extent, what he would become. The impact of the New World might, and we know often did, produce marked changes in a settler which, for good or ill, would affect his whole future. It could never entirely obliterate his past.

Let us admit at the outset that we shall never know the past of these first Americans, still English in their own eyes and in the eyes of others, as well as we should like to know it; nor shall we be able to answer half the questions about them that can be asked. An appallingly large number of them never lived to play their part in

---

Source: Mildred Campbell, "Social Origins of Some Early Americans," in *Seventeenth-Century America,* ed. James M. Smith (Chapel Hill: University of North Carolina Press, 1959), pp. 63–89.

the enterprise to which they were so important. Thousands either died on the voyage or during the first year after their arrival. Most of those who came never kept personal records and no records were kept about them. Except for the concern of a ship captain or his agent that there be a profitable cargo for the outgoing voyage, their homeland in most cases took little note of their leaving. And the New World soon made it clear that their past mattered less than what they could do in the "needful" present. But the search is worth while if one can know even a little more about the lives of these people in their native England: the social strata from which they sprang, the fabric of life in their home communities, the reasons why the New World made its appeal — all matters about which we have thus far little concrete information.

The scene of the search is England under the Stuarts and in the Cromwellian interlude. Recent decades have taught us much about the entire social background of this period. Professors Trevelyan and Rowse paint the larger canvas in the bold strokes they use so effectively. Wallace Notestein perhaps comes nearer than anyone else to taking up residence among seventeenth-century Englishmen and learns from his close acquaintance both big and little things about them that are revealing. Others have dealt more narrowly with special segments of society, or have done what the English scholars do so well — shown what life was like in specific localities. The Tawney-Trevor Roper controversy over the gentry has also added light as well as heat. Such studies have enabled us to read a broadside addressed to "earls, lords, knights, gentlemen, and yeomen," with a better knowledge of what those terms mean. There remains, however, a multitude of shadings to vex us, especially in the lower groups and in the more mobile and intricate relationships of urban society.

In searching for the origins of American settlers we shall not be concerned equally with all of the social strata. Yet two basic aspects of seventeenth-century social philosophy which affected everyone must be kept in mind: first, the universal acceptance of the concept of social gradation and a complete belief in its rightness; and second, the belief, held simultaneously, that differences in rank, although normally to be observed, were not unalterable. One will not, of course, forget that the period of the Civil Wars produced a handful of Diggers on St. George's Hill who espoused a doctrine of communistic living, or that John Lilburne and his fellow-soldiers turned a part of the Cromwellian army into a debating society on political democracy. The issues of these debates would one day assume great importance; but they are probably remembered more for their later significance than because of any immediate effect they had on social structure. Degree, priority, and place, as Shakespeare described it, as the clergy taught and preached it, and as the people of all ranks lived it, was the accepted social philosophy of the day. "For that infinite wisdom of God which hath distinguished his angels by degrees . . . hath also ordained kings, dukes . . . and other degrees among men."

The normal expectation of the members of every class was to see their children settled and married within their own social group. On the other hand, if a man came to a position of substance and outlook more in keeping with another class above or below him, he eventually moved into its ranks. This practice had long lent a freshness and toughness to the fiber of English society. Now in the fast changing and more competitive conditions of the Tudor and Stuart era, social fluidity was greater than it had ever been. Some deplored the current development in which "Joan is as good as My Lady," where "Citizen's wives have of late growne Gallants," and "the yeoman doth gentilize it." But most people considered it a source of national strength that "in England the temple of honour is bolted against none."

It worked both ways though. A man could go down as well as up. Inflationary prices, a fluctuating land market, defective land titles, precarious investments, and bad debts created a milieu which gave some men their opportunity and brought dismal failure to others. Every social category had its crop of new men. Increased competition placed a higher premium on personal initiative than had been known in an earlier England. In emphasizing the manner in which pioneer colonial life developed individual initiative, it may be that we have not sufficiently recognized that much initiative was already present in the society from which the early settlers came, that indeed this may partially explain their coming.

In England tales of discovery and exploration had enlisted the interest and stretched the imagination of people of every class. But those at the top of the social hierarchy rarely were concerned with actual settlement. In terms of patronage and investment, however, many of them were active. Lord Baltimore had able friends among his own associates to aid in the Maryland enterprise; and no fewer than eight earls, one viscount, and a bishop helped to launch the Virginia Company under its second charter in 1609. Interest in colonial schemes became a favorite hobby, more than a hobby in some cases, with noblemen at the court of Charles II. But in answer to the query, "Who would venture their persons and who their purses?" the noblemen usually answered in favor of the latter, and few members of the nobility actually emigrated with the intention of remaining in the colonies.

Below the nobility came the knights and country gentry: "gentlemen of the blood," of ancient lineage. But with them also were newly landed men, office holders, members of the professions, university men, and many with business and mercantile interests — these too were known as "gentlemen." Dozens of such men became involved in colonial activities. Indeed, one wonders if seventeenth-century America would have advanced much beyond the trading-post stage had it not been for their money, vision, and perseverance. They were the men who instituted, to a great extent financed, and almost wholly ran the great companies under which the first colonies were started. The wealthier and more important men like Sir Ferdinand Gorges, Sir John Popham, Matthew Cradock, Sir Thomas Smith, carried on their work from England. But others came in person to lead the new plantations: younger sons of the financial backers, gentry of lesser pretensions, clergymen, and merchants. This was especially true in the earlier years, partly because leadership from below had not yet had time to develop, and partly because it seems to have been the original intent that the colonies should be led by individuals of the upper classes, a policy in keeping with the philosophy of the time. It is also apparent that in the beginning such men had little idea that the demands made upon them by the New World would be so different from those to which they had been accustomed at home.

More is known about these leaders than about any of the other settlers and for obvious reasons. They were the articulate ones. They themselves wrote and kept records, though not perhaps as many records as we should like, and others wrote about them. They were the clergymen about whom Perry Miller, Alan Simpson, and a host of writers tell us, those who preached *Puritanism in Old and New England* and made frequent journeys back and forth. Among them are some of Louis Wright's *First Gentlemen of Virginia* and some of John Pomfret's proprietors of *The Province of West New Jersey*. They wander through the pages of Bernard Bailyn's *New England Merchants in the Seventeenth Century*. In terms of social origins, less illustrious people also belong in this group: bankrupt businessmen; ill-starred younger sons and brothers of the gentry; proverbial ne'er-do-wells whose families hoped that a change of scene would set them on a better path, youths like Lady Finch's unruly son, "whom she sent to Virginia to be tamed." Sometimes family hopes for reformation were realized. Often enough, however, parents had to face the fact that the voyage across the Atlantic was not sufficient to bring about the moral transformation desired. Despite this unpromising contingent, men of the rank of knight or gentleman (whether that rank came by birth or acquisition) played a role in colonial society out of proportion to their numbers. And the more we know about them, the better off we shall be. They are recognized by the title "Sir" if they were knights, or merely by "Mr.," a term not applied below the gentry. In many colonial narratives they are spoken of as "the better sort" and in lists of ships' passengers are usually identified as the "men of quality." Thus one ship carried "eighteen men of quality and eighty-seven others." Another speaks of "seven gentlemen and sixty-four others." And again, we read of "about a score of men of quality and a hundred and four others." One becomes familiar with the pattern.

But who were "the others"? Practically nothing is known about them, although the passenger lists make it perfectly clear that they account for the overwhelming numbers in the emigrant ships. "How to people His Majesty's dominions with people?" becomes a kind of recurrent refrain in the plantation literature of the seventeenth century. It was "the others" who chiefly furnished the answer to that query. Because there were so many of them and because our information about them is so woefully scant they have perhaps a special claim to attention. Who actually were they? Did they belong chiefly to the "middling people" — yeomen and artisans? Were they largely the poor agricultural laborers whose sorry plight in this period is well known? Or were they mostly riffraff from the streets of London and Bristol, the poor who had so increased under the Tudors as to demand state action; or beggars, and condemned persons who filled the prisons? We know that all of these were represented among the early colonists. But beyond that we have had little concrete information about them, and slight knowledge of the relative degree with which the various groups responded to the appeals from the New World for settlers.

Two sets of seventeenth-century manuscripts merit attention for what they have to offer about the identity of "the others." They record the departure of slightly more than 11,000 emigrants from Bristol and London in the second half of the seventeenth century. The Bristol record, the more important of the two, contains the names of some 10,000 people who shipped from that port between 1654 and 1685. It provides a small amount of data for the entire group over the whole period; but the fuller part of the record, and that part which contains information pertinent to the subject of social origins, covers approximately the first 7 years and deals with upwards of 3,000 people. The London record includes approximately 750 men and women who left for the New World in the year 1683-84. Although a smaller sample, it contains the same type of information (including several additional items) as found in the Bristol record, thus providing comparative material from another area. The London and Bristol records list only a few of the many thousands of men and women who made their beginning in the New World as indentured servants before the American Revolution. But they originated in a period for which data are scarce; hence, though neither record is statistically perfect, both deserve careful consideration.

The first significant fact about both records is that they deal entirely with people who were coming to America as indentured servants. This is perhaps fortunate; for studies made in the last two decades have demonstrated that a far larger percentage of our colonial population entered the country under indenture than was formerly thought. One-half of the total is held to be a conservative estimate. On the question of their social origins, moreover, almost no concrete information is available.

The plan of indenture has been so fully treated by scholars that only a brief definition is required here. Under the indenture terms, a prospective settler agreed to serve a master in one of the colonies for a period of years (usually four or five), in return for free passage across the Atlantic and certain "Freedom dues" when his term of service was over. One aspect of indenture, however, has not been sufficiently considered: the fact that within the framework of English society, as it actually functioned in the seventeenth century, such a practice would be considered not only natural but salutary. This is of great importance if we look at the New World from the point of view of the prospective emigrant still in England, or of the family of a young person contemplating settlement. The whole idea of service and services in return for land, training, protection — in short, for social and economic security — was an idea basic to medieval thinking and practice and one that had by no means disappeared. The practice of apprenticeship, for example, was not legalized and specifically defined until 1563, but it had been the general practice for generations.

The same mental and social outlook that found positive values in the seven-year apprenticeship for young children would see social values in a four- or five-year indenture for a young man — and even more for a young woman — who was preparing to set out on a journey of three thousand miles in the hope of eventually establishing himself. Promotion literature advised young single men — particularly those with small means — to go into service for a few years and especially recommended indenture for young women. Some tales that came back across the water about the life of an indentured servant in the American colonies made it clear that it was often very different from the version presented in the promotion literature. But stories of those settlers who had been fortunate circulated in England as well; and the practice of indenture, which was based on the long-accepted principle of service, could weather reports of abuse and failure.

Historians have long been interested in the social status of the colonists who came under indenture; but throughout the first third of the twentieth century it remained a subject of the widest conjecture, despite the tremendous amount of excellent work done in the colonial field. Professor Andrews, who often deplored our lack of sufficient knowledge on the subject, said of the indentured servants in Virginia: "Some of them, perhaps many, seem to have been in origin above the level of menials, to have good family connections in England, and in a few instances to have been even of gentle birth." Marcus Jernegan believed they came chiefly from the undesirables and the agricultural class who under conditions in England had no chance to better themselves. In his *First Americans,* Professor Wertenbaker shared this view. The bulk of the indentured servants were, he said, "poor laborers who were no longer content to work in misery and rags in England while opportunity beckoned them across the Atlantic." Fifteen years later he had accepted what Abbot Smith, Richard Morris, and others were saying, namely, that "all kinds came." An analysis of the Bristol and London records helps to define that phrase and to show in what proportions different social groups were represented.

It is a matter of considerable interest that approximately twenty-five percent of the Bristol group are women. We shall have something more to say of them later. Among the men, yeomen and husbandmen are in the majority; they account for about thirty-six percent, with the yeomen outnumbering the husbandmen. Artisans and tradesmen number approximately twenty-two percent; laborers account for about ten percent; gentlemen and professional men make up a little less than one percent. Thus the farmers outnumber the skilled workers almost two to one, and the combined farmers and skilled workers outnumber the laborers more than five to one.

In the smaller London sampling, the women are somewhat under the twenty-five percent of the Bristol records. The skilled workers outnumber the yeomen and husbandmen in almost the reverse proportion to the Bristol record: approximately two to one. This difference is, of course, to be expected in the records of an urban center. The husbandmen are also more numerous than the yeomen. But as in the case of the Bristol servants, the number of farmers and skilled workers in comparison with the laborers is in a ratio of about five to one.

A question may be raised concerning the authenticity of the status terms. Would not an ordinary laborer, knowing that masons, bricklayers, and carpenters were in great demand in the colonies at high wages, possibly try to assume a skill for which he had no training? Some may have tried this deception, and it is possible that the number of artisans should be slightly lowered to take care of self-styled craftsmen. But two factors weigh in favor of the general validity of the terms. First, the number and variety of the skills listed in the records suggest accuracy: there are ninety-eight trades, many of which, such as the tuckers, fullers, and button makers, were not those most sought after by the colonial agents. Secondly, men in the seventeenth century were still accustomed to being recorded in terms of their status or occupation. They were so listed in court records, wills, deeds, leases, and business transactions of all kinds. It would have seemed natural and prudent to give the same information for this record as for all others. Hence, allowing for a certain margin of error and even some false reporting, the evidence still points to a large majority of farmers and tradesmen over laborers.

The relatively low number of laborers was at first puzzling. According to writers of the period, the laborers' status was the lowest in the social hierarchy. They were the most numerous and poorest members of England's working population. Although their wages rose slightly during the first half of the century, they tended to remain constant, even in some places to drop a little, from then until the end of the century. Those who worked by the year for an annual wage ranging from three to five pounds were perhaps the most fortunate. They had a roof over their heads and something to eat. We think it a hardship that the medieval serf could not escape the land, but neither, it may be well to remember, could the land get away from him. His life was meager, often harsh, but economically it was more secure than that of his successor, the landless laborer.

In the comments of some of their contemporaries may lie a partial explanation of the laborers' lack of enthusiasm for emigration. Thomas Ludwell, a Somerset man, received a request for servants from his brother in Virginia. He answered that there were workmen in his neighborhood to spare, but "they will live meanly and send their families to the parish to be relieved rather than hear of such a long journey to mend their condition." Robert Southwell, who had had poor luck in his attempt to recruit laborers in 1669, said of them: "They are loth to leave the smoke of their own cabin if they can but beg neere it." There are other comments in the same vein. The laborers were accustomed to little; they could do with little. In times of dearth they would be hungry; but they had rarely had full stomachs, and while they might come close to starvation, the parish would not let them die. In addition, they were a superstitious lot and quite possibly would have been frightened by the tales about the dangers of the long voyage over strange waters.

If the London and Bristol records can be taken as a fair sample (and they are in accord with other recent studies), it is clearly a mistaken assumption to think that the laborers formed the large part of those who came to America as indentured servants. The majority were farmers and skilled workers.

Most of the women in the list were not classified according to status except as "singlewoman" or "spinster," the latter term being used at this period to describe either a married or an unmarried woman. A number of "widows" were listed, and a few women were classified according to the skill or occupation which they hoped to have in the homes of their new masters — "dairy maid," "lady's maid," and the like. Young women often went in twos and threes from the same village, and now and then the lists show members of the same family. It is quite possible that a larger percentage of women than men came from among the laborers. Country folk had their own measuring rods in terms of social codes and behavior patterns; a yeoman or tradesman of some standing would feel more reluctant to see his daughter set off on such a journey than would a laborer. Yeomen and husbandmen worked alongside farm laborers getting in the crops and mingled with them in the village alehouse. Yet it was not considered the proper thing for the daughters of yeomen to work in the fields, although the wives and daughters of laborers did so as a matter of course. Daughters of yeomen and tradesmen, however, often went into the service of families in their neighborhoods, and in certain industries such as lacemaking, girls were apprenticed in the usual way.

There are women listed in both these records who were going in answer to personal requests from planters in Maryland and Virginia for servants of various skills. Charles Peck of London was sending one to his brother Tom in Virginia at the latter's request. She was to serve in his own home, and "not be soulde unless to some planter for a wife." It was commonly accepted that a husband was the chief inducement the New World had to offer a young girl. Nor would she have much trouble getting one, although the match was not always with the wealthy planter that the promotion literature promised. It is interesting that promoters were becoming a bit more discriminating in their advice respecting the women who were wanted. They were somewhat on the defensive about the women who had been sent over from the houses of correction: "But if they come of honest stock, and have good repute they may pick their husbands out of the better sort of people." Three months, one of them thought, was as long as one could hope to keep a good maid before "some proper young fellow" would come after her.

Servants sought as wives were purchased either in pounds sterling or tobacco. This businesslike way of approaching marriage strikes a wrong note in our generation. But it would have seemed quite normal to the seventeenth century, where every girl (except those of the very lowest groups, who were not too particular about such things) was accustomed to a marriage that was largely a business arrangement. Women who went to the colonies, however, may not always have accepted husbands immediately, even if they were not under indenture; there was plenty of work at good pay for them until such time as they did marry. Later in the century when many servants were going to Pennsylvania, Gabriel Thomas lamented about the exorbitant wages women could command: "They are not as yet very numerous which makes them stand on high terms for their several services." He added, however, "They are usually marry'd before they are twenty years of age."

Practically all of the servants were young. Indeed, it is clear that the whole plan for indentured service was designed for the young unmarried man and woman. It is easier for the young to be uprooted, and a new-found land across the sea would beckon to twenty-one as it would not to fifty. The Bristol record does not give ages, but they are given in the London group. The majority were between the ages of eighteen and twenty-four, with twenty-one and twenty-two predominating — just the age when the young tradesmen were finishing their apprenticeship. The large number of farmers and skilled workers going under indenture demonstrates the appeal which this method of emigration made to single young men of small means and even to those whose parents could perhaps have managed the passage money.

A young man just out of his apprenticeship would not, if he remained in England, set up for himself at once. Likewise, a yeoman's son, unless he were the eldest or his father were able to buy land for him, would work at home or for a neighboring yeoman or gentleman through his earlier years while he accumulated piecemeal holdings of his own. English yeomen were a canny lot. Perhaps farmers everywhere are. To be able to get to America without any expense to himself or his family would appeal to a lad brought up as these had been. Besides if a young man went to America alone without enough money to buy labor, reputed to be both high and scarce, what could he do with the fifty or a hundred acres of land that he hoped to get? Nobody knew better than a farmer's son that it took more than one pair of hands to get crops in the ground and to harvest them. These were some of the facts that would have been in the minds of the yeomen and husbandmen, carpenters, tilemakers, and weavers whose names are enrolled in the Bristol and London lists.

A few married men went without their wives, leaving them sometimes provided for, sometimes not. And there were a few married couples going together, but not many, for this practice was discouraged because of complications likely to arise on the other side. Finally in 1682 an order prohibiting a married man from going as an indentured servant went into effect. But it is doubtful if recruiting agents looked into the matter too closely. There are examples in other records of groups of married people who paid their own passage, but were apparently somewhat older and better established. They took along with them single young men and women under indenture — their neighbors, friends, and kinspeople. They would thereby get the "headright" lands for having brought them over, and the young people coming as servants were with friends and kinsfolk during their early years in a strange country. Hundreds who were not so fortunate left it to chance to place them in the hands of a good master or a poor one when the ship docked.

It is significant that the married people referred to above who took their families and paid their own passage were for the most part farmers and tradesmen of the same social rank as the servants they took with them. This was, I believe, generally the case. For one of the gratifying by-products of the information concerning status that comes from these records is that through them we are also able indirectly to determine the status of the remainder of "the others" who filled the emigrant ships. If the laborers at the bottom of the economic scale account for a relatively small number of those coming under indenture, it is certain that they were not widely represented among those who paid their own passage. The reluctance of the laborers to go as servants has already been shown. If one adds to that the crucial fact that they simply would not have had the five or six pounds required to pay their own passage, it is clear that there would be few of them in that group. Individuals or small groups sometimes came over in the personal service of men of better substance, but this would not account for many. If, therefore, the laborers at the bottom of the social and economic hierarchy were a minority, as were also the "men of quality" at the other extreme, we can but conclude that "the others," both those who came under indenture and those who paid their own fare, were drawn from the middling classes: farmers and skilled workers, the productive groups in England's working population. The difference between those who came as servants and those who paid their own fare was partly economic, with the poorer farmers and "decayed" tradesmen coming under indenture; and partly, as we have seen, it was a matter of age, experience, and marital position.

Status is basic to the quest for social origins. But before attempting further to spell out its meaning in terms of actual living conditions, we must pay our respects to one other relatively small group among the Bristol servants, the children. The term of service set down in the indenture provides the key for determining their numbers. The vast majority of adult terms are for four or five years, the four-year term slightly predominating, although now and then a servant went for two or three years, or more rarely, even for one. Children, however, were sent for longer terms in order that they should reach adulthood by the time their service was over. Their average term was seven years, as was that of the ordinary apprentice in England; but in both cases it might be as high as ten or twelve years, depending on the child's age.

About eight percent of the Bristol group went for a term of six years or more, chiefly seven. But seven years or longer is also the term assigned to those recalcitrants whom the justices of the peace sent to the colonies for the punishment of minor crimes. How can we know that the emigrants with terms of seven years or more were not these delinquents rather than minors? It is likely that some of them were, for delinquents of this type were sent along with other servants and we know of some who were in this group. Fortunately, the London indentures containing the actual ages for everyone are of assistance in this problem. For they show that almost all of the indentures for long terms (about six percent in this record) apply to children under fifteen. Only occasionally is an older person given a longer term. An examination of Quarter Sessions court records, where instances of forced emigration for minor crimes were documented, offers supporting evidence during the years in question that this type of punishment was apparently used sparingly by the county officials. Hence, unless there was a larger percentage of delinquents in the Bristol group than among those going from London, which hardly seems likely, we may assume that the majority of Bristol's eight percent assigned to long terms were also minors.

Not infrequently, of course, some of the individuals deported for misdemeanors were likewise minors; often the children who went as servants were orphans or problem children whom someone wished to dispose of. We glimpse them now and again in the records. John Morgan, a Bristol upholsterer, appeared in July, 1659, with an uncancelled indenture that had been made out for David Thomas, a Glamorgan boy who was bound to him. He should have been registered earlier: "But in regard he was on shipboard, and could not be brought up for fear of his running away, he was not enrolled in the middle of the book." A fourteen-year-old girl in

London was taken out of White Chapel jail to which she had been committed for "pilfering lace" and with the consent of her father and mother was indentured for service in America. A stray letter among the London indentures tells the story of Robert Redman. An uncle in Cambridge had sent him up to London to be put aboard *The Hopewell*. He writes that in the boy's trunk "is his best and worst cloathes, an extra shirt, 2 pr. stockins, 6 neck cloathes, 6 handkerchers, 2 caps, 1 hatt, 1 pr. shoes." Instructions are given that anything else needful is to be provided. "If 9 years or tenn yeares service be required," the uncle writes, "I am contented provided he have his bellefull of food, with cloathes to keep him warm and warm lodgin at night." He asks to be told when the boy is "disposed of" and to whom and "how to rit a letter to his master and to him." It is apparent that things have not gone well. Young Redman is not to be given the keys to his trunk for fear he will either sell or give away his belongings. "I could keep him no longer," the uncle says; yet he hopes he will have a good voyage, and has sent along "Balsome and salve" for the ship's surgeon to use in treating an injury on the boy's leg. After a somewhat formal ending according to the fashion of the day, a postscript adds that "Thers a Rage to dress his wounded leg with."

Aside from the delinquents, both minor and adult, sent by the justices, two groups of indentured servants entered into their contracts under compulsion: convicts and, during both the Commonwealth and Restoration period, political prisoners. Neither group will be considered here; for with the few possible exceptions which have been considered among those holding long terms, it seems clear that these records deal with the ordinary men and women who went to America under indenture of their own volition. Therefore, we turn again to the two basic records for additional clues which will make possible at least a fragmentary reconstruction of the environment they were leaving behind them.

Next in importance to the status term is that part of the record which gives the emigrant's place of origin; for without this information, it would be impossible to enlarge our understanding of the American settler's background. Both records show how widely the New World ventures were known in England. The Bristol names include representatives from every English county except Rutland, and many from Wales. An overwhelming majority are from the West, with Somerset, Gloucestershire, and Wiltshire taking the lead among the English counties and Monmouthshire first among the Welsh. Proximity to Bristol undoubtedly accounts partly for this concentration; but it is significant that some western counties are much more sparsely represented. Outside the heavy concentration in London and Middlesex, Yorkshire furnished the largest number to the London group.

The place of origin carries significance beyond the servant group; for if large numbers of servants were coming from certain centers, it is almost certain that there were also large numbers from these same centers who paid their own passage. The largest number of servants recorded in the Bristol group, slightly more than half, booked for Virginia. One is therefore not surprised to come upon the following passage from James Southall's sketch of a Virginia family, in which he discusses the section in England that was the source of so many of Virginia's early settlers. He describes an area

> about thirty miles north of Bristol in the west of England, running due north and south for a distance of about ten miles and with an average breadth of three miles, where a . . . ridge of the Malvern Hills divides the county of Hereford from the county of Worcester and on the southeast of these, on the south bank of the upper Severn, with yet ampler di-

mensions stretches the county of Gloucester, all three counties touching each other at a common point near the city of Gloucester.

It was in this district, the author says,

> and from Somersetshire, and the neighboring counties of Wales . . . from Warwick on the north, Devon in the southwest, Herts and the Isle of Wight in the south, and across the Bristol Channel from the coast of Ireland, that in Virginia, the counties of Henrico, James City, Charles City, Isle of Wight, Gloucester, Surrey, and Prince George were largely settled.

Except for including Ireland and the Isle of Wight, he has described almost exactly the area chiefly represented by the Bristol record. Along with East Anglia, and Lincolnshire and Yorkshire in the north, the West Country was the homeland of thousands of the early settlers. From the beginning there was in the West a strong tradition for the American adventure. The New World would not seem so far away to West Country boys, many of whose fathers and brothers earned their living as mariners and seamen on ships that plied between Plymouth, Bristol, and lesser ports to the New World. They were not, said a contemporary, of "the In-land sort," who were "wedded to their native soils like a Snaile to his shell, or . . . a mouse to his chest." Their grandfathers would have sailed or known people who sailed with Drake and Raleigh — and grandfathers are all alike. It was natural that Hugh Peter, telling the House of Lords in 1665 about his departure to New England, should say that he "by birth in Cornwall was not altogether ignorant of that place." It is then to the West Country that we must turn. For here lay the farm lands and villages from which almost eighty-five percent of the Bristol emigrants came.

Three centuries have inevitably changed the West Country. The most conspicuous difference is the growth of modern urban centers; yet there has been less change than in some parts of England, and one can drive through miles of rural Gloucestershire, Wiltshire, and Somerset, where the country must look much the same as it did three centuries and a half ago when many of its humbler people were preparing to leave. There are evidences now of more intensive agriculture, but the contours of hills and green sloping meadows remain the same. It is a good land to look upon. So also they must have thought who were departing from it. For it is a great mistake to assume that emigration, for whatever purpose, meant that people left home and familiar surroundings with no regrets. Even the most rabid of the New England Puritan clergy, full of spleen and invective, frequently expressed devotion to old England and the "mistaken ones" who stayed behind. These folk who left the West Country were not very articulate; they could not have said what they felt as did a later West Country man:

> 'Tis time, I think, by Wenlock town
> The golden broom should blow.

But chance words and phrases that appear in prosaic colonial records betray the same nostalgia. It was probably sheer homesickness that overcame the boy from a Gloucestershire village who went to Bristol with a friend intent on shipping to Virginia — he let the other boy go on without him, the record says, and "came back home."

The houses they lived in, especially the homes of the lesser folk, were made of whatever natural building materials the locality afforded. Some of the small stone houses that can be seen today in Cotswold villages were there then, some newly built, some already old — all evidence of the prosperity that Cotswold wool had brought to the locality. Beyond the Cotswolds to the west in the Severn Valley, a redder sandstone furnished excellent building material, but it was hard to quarry and in general was reserved for churches and the houses of great men. Farmers and tradesmen built their houses mostly of a combination of wood and some kind of plaster spread often over a wattle framework. "Cob," as it was called, used largely in Devon farmhouses, was a mixture of mud, straw, gravel, and chalk. These houses were small, varying from the two to three rooms of the less well-to-do to as many as eight or nine in the houses of wealthy yeomen, small clothiers, and tradespeople of some substance. The homes of the laborers have not survived; they were probably little more than hovels and, except for some very newly built, were almost certainly without much light. John Aubrey, himself a West Country man, wrote of Wiltshire in 1671 and remarked that within his remembrance the use of glass had been restricted: "Copyholders and ordinary poor people had none." The inventories attached to wills supply details of the interiors of these crude homes. Trestled furniture was still being used, although sometimes "joined" tables are mentioned. Pewter dishes were by now a commonplace in the cupboards of the middling people, but wooden trenches were still in everyday use. Occasionally there were a few prized silver teaspoons. Their standards of both comfort and cleanliness would, of course, be scorned by people of like position in modern society.

It is understandable that promoters found these middling people of the West Country satisfactory settlers and made special efforts to induce them to go to the colonies. It was not merely their skills that were wanted. They had other qualities born of the kind of lives they had lived that would stand them in good stead. They were not, it is true, accustomed to the peculiar type of pioneer hardship that prevailed in America, but their lives in England had known little comfort or ease. The craftsmen were accustomed to working from five in the morning until seven or eight at night. Farmers labored outside from daylight until dark and carried on indoor tasks by fire and candlelight. A man could not be idle and hold his own in the demanding world in which they lived. Idlers there were, of course, but lower and middle class families did not have the means to care for loafers.

Men of the West Country like those elsewhere were forced to adapt themselves to the competitive and acquisitive society common to their age. Those with a greater margin of wealth could weather the crises better. Because of their fairly simple standard of living and the fact that they were practically self-supporting, the farmers were less affected by the high prices of outside products than almost any other group. Despite market fluctuations, they could usually sell their sheep and grain at a very good profit.

Wealthy yeomen of the West Country not only had glass and chimneys in their houses, but were now installing wainscoting in their "halls" and "parlours." The members of this class were aggressive, and if they held their land in a good tenure — that is, if it were freehold or of that particular kind of copyhold which carried similar security — they were most probably affluent. But circumstances which brought success to many meant failure for others. Land hunger was rife among all classes. Wealthy clothiers, drapers, and merchants who had done well and wished to set themselves up in land were avidly watching the market, ready to pay almost any price for what was offered. Even prosperous yeomen often could not get the land they desired for their younger sons; and indeed those who did not hold their own land in a good tenure ran the risk of losing it.

The West Country was good farming country, especially for sheep raising. Somerset in particular also had excellent land for tillage, and its farmers were noted for their skill. Yet even if the title to his land were clear, a West Country farmer could fare badly compared with farmers in some sections of England. For the West was a conservative part of the country. Change came slowly there, and only a beginning had been made with inclosures. More than a century later George Turner, writing of farming conditions in the vale of Gloucestershire, could still say: "I know one acre which is divided into eight lands, and spread over a large common field, so that a man must travel two or three miles to visit it all. . . . But this is not the worst. . . ." And he continued to recite the woes that West Country farmers were still enduring.

A great deal of the land was still copyhold, and large landholders kept the village economy almost on a feudal basis. The farmers from Tetbury, Chipping Sodbury, and other Gloucestershire villages were still performing services that had long since been discarded in many parts of England. The tendency, moreover, to retain long leases (ninety-nine years was the most common), once an advantage to the leaseholders, was now catching up with western farmers. Many leases which had been made out in Elizabeth's reign were now "falling in," leaving the tenant to face increased fines and rents or the likelihood of seeing his land go to someone else. It is not surprising if farmers facing these and similar conditions lent a sympathetic ear to the tales of ship captains and their agents, colonial promoters, and returned travellers — tales of a country where land was to be had for the asking, or nearly so, where leases did not "fall in," nor rents come due, where, in short, a man was his own landlord. That these promises were often highly exaggerated, that there was not land in many places, at any rate, suitable land, to be had for the asking did not alter the landlord dream. It is a commonplace to say that land was the greatest inducement the New World had to offer; but it is difficult to overestimate its psychological and social importance to people in whose minds land had always been identified with security, success, and the good things of life. "Now we can get few English servants," said a member of the Barbados Assembly in 1665, "having no lands to give them at the end of their time which formerly was their main allurement." Tradesmen as well as yeomen and husbandmen looked forward to becoming landholders. Richard Norton was a Bristol millwright and John Hatten a watchmaker, but they, no less than John Rose, a Wiltshire husbandman, and Morgan Jones, son of a Monmouthshire yeoman, carried with them indentures that called for fifty acres of land in Virginia or Maryland. This was in 1655. In later years the Carolinas and Pennsylvania would make even more attractive land offers.

With the bulk of the family land going to the eldest son, it had been the traditional pattern for farmers in every section of England to apprentice one or more of their other sons to trade. This was especially true in the West Country, where the cloth trade had for generations been a source of employment. Hard times among the East Anglian clothworkers made it easier for Winthrop and the other Puritan leaders to gain recruits for New England. The exodus of West Country clothworkers to America in the second half of the century is less well known but merits equal attention. The plight of the West Country was made considerably worse by economic disruption during and after the Civil Wars. No part of the nation was unaffected by this conflict, but the West was especially hard hit. As a key city Bristol early became a major objective and was successively under the control of both armies. The neighboring countryside suffered accordingly. "This England," said one, "is merely the ghost of that England which it was lately." Ships rotted in Bristol harbor; Gloucestershire woolen mills were plundered; clothworkers in Somerset were left without employment for months.

Nor did matters improve when the wars were over. Returned soldiers found themselves without work. Slack periods in the cloth business came in close succession. Prices fluctuated. Problems growing out of the plight of war widows, disabled soldiers, and an increasing number of poor rose to plague local officials and cast a pall of gloom over village communities. "I wish I could hear what condition you live in," an Essex tradesman had written a few years earlier to his Virginia kinsman, "for I fear if these times hold long amongst us we must be all faine come to Virginia." If the emigrant records can be taken as a key, many West Country men and women were now thinking the same thing. The annual exodus of servants shipping from Bristol rose from slightly less than 300 in 1655 to almost 800 in 1659, and hundreds more emigrants were going with their families and paying their own fare.

Discontent in the West Country cloth towns was not new. The trade had suffered somewhat earlier in the century, but it was not until after the Civil Wars that the complaints so increased in volume and bitterness. Modern scholars are inclined to think that the depression in the cloth trade traditionally assigned to the late Commonwealth and early Restoration years was not as damaging to the industry as was earlier thought. They tend to see the complaints from clothiers as disgruntlement over a shift to new men and new methods rather than a decline in the industry itself. But they all agree on the bad effects of the situation for the workers. The local records at Taunton and Trowbridge and Gloucester are filled with the hardships of the clothworkers: those who "toiled in their cottages from Castle Colne and Malmsbury on the edge of the Cotswold country" and in the industrial towns on the Avon, "to Westbury, Edington and the other villages under the plain." And it was from Castle Colne, Malmsbury, Westbury, and other villages under the plain that John Niblett, the clothmaker, Thomas Allen, the worsted comber, Edward Webb, the feltmaker, and John Davis, the tailor, with dozens of their friends and neighbors, made their way to Bristol during the late fifties and early sixties, to sign the indentures which assured their free passage to America. Other tradesmen and farmers in the nearby countryside were likewise affected, for hard times cannot come to a basic industry in a rural area without affecting auxiliary trades and the whole working population.

Tradesmen, like farmers, were worried not merely by present uncertainties but by the lack of future opportunity. It had once been the expectation of journeymen that they would advance their status three or four years after apprenticeship. Many were beginning now to find that they would have to be wage earners all their lives. Skilled workers of certain kinds much needed in the colonies could sometimes get special favors written into their agreements. John Walker and Samuel Minor, both carpenters, had made such arrangements. Walker's term was only three years, with a wage of forty pounds per annum while he was still in service. Minor, probably younger, was bound for five years, to receive twenty pounds the first three years and twenty-five the last two. Most of the servants, however, were either not that forehanded or their skills were not such as would be so much needed in America. Land and high wages were counted on to make up for that.

Despite the fact that industry and the land had each its peculiar character and concerns, their interaction in the general economy was very marked. What each could offer or failed to offer to the individual was of paramount importance. Together they provided the economic framework within which West Country farmers and tradesmen shaped the course of their lives. The laborers, whether agricultural or urban, were perhaps most immediately affected by the current fluctuations common to both Cromwellian and Restoration years. They eked out a meager living on their daily wage if there was work for them. If the cloth works were "still" or harvests were thin, they became a public charge; the local records bear eloquent testimony to the efforts of harassed parish officials to look after their poor. For such among them as were ambitious there was little or no opportunity. Emigration offered it and, as we know, there were some who took advantage of the offer. But most of them were not ambitious. Their niche in the social and economic scale was not threatened as was often that of small landed men or craftsmen.

It would, however, be a great error to assume that these West Country people thought only of economic matters. It should also be remembered that numerous though the emigrants were from any region, far more people stayed at home than left. To think otherwise would be to distort the view of the background of American immigration. There had long been a good deal of mobility among England's working population, particularly among young single men who moved around in search of work when times were bad in their own communities. In some cases families whose sons emigrated to America were already accustomed to having them away from home. The life of country communities would not be markedly changed because here and there a young person or a few families left. Those at home would carry on with the normal pursuits of daily life as dictated by their rank and position in the community and by individual and group interests.

Aside from the demands of daily occupations, perhaps the central focus of their activities was religion. Their scale of values was in large part determined by it, and it profoundly affected the shape and substance of their mental and social outlook. To the middling people of the West Country, as to many of their kind elsewhere, religion meant non-conformity. It was not, of course, all of one brand — that is the essence of non-conformity. "How many ways do you make it to heaven in this place?" a royalist chaplain had asked in 1647 as he deplored the "rabble of heresies" around Bristol. The years under Cromwell had not eased their troubles as much as many had hoped for. There was probably not much actual religious persecution, although it was not wholly absent; Quakers were cruelly treated at Bristol in 1654–56 and hundreds of them went to America in the following years. A comparison of the Bristol list with Besse's "Sufferers" shows an identity of almost five hundred names. Granting the error which may originate in the prolific repetition among West Country names, these figures cannot be entirely without significance. And not only Quakers were troubled. The West was indeed as the royalist chaplain had found, a hotbed of activity of the various sects. The rise in the Bristol emigration for 1659 has already been indicated. It is significant that the largest annual exodus came in 1662, when the first Restoration statutes against dissenters went into effect. Between eight and nine hundred servants went to America in that year from this one port. If the non-comformists of the West Country had not fared too well in the Commonwealth, they certainly did not expect the return of the Stuarts to help matters. Nor did it.

George Herbert, earlier tracing the cycle through which he thought religion ran her course, startled some of his friends by saying:

> Religion stands on tiptoe in our land
> Readie to pass to the American strand.

Nor had he been unaware of the social and economic implications:

> Then shall Religion to America flee;
> . . . .
> My God, Thou dost prepare for them a way,
> By carrying first their gold from them away,
> For gold and grace did never yet agree
> Religion alwaies sides with povertie.

Josiah Child was only the best known of various writers in the second half of the century who pointed out the "great swarms of new inhabitants" whom the New World received because of the restrictions placed on dissenters in England.

Nowhere were non-conformity and the ferment which it bred more deeply rooted than in the clothmaking centers. Richard Baxter, a Puritan clergyman of yeoman origins, pointed out this relationship as he looked back upon the part played by the various classes in the Civil Wars. Writing in 1683, he said,

> On the side of Parliament were the smaller part (as some thought) of the gentry in most of the countries and the greatest part of the Tradesmen and Freeholders, and the Middle sort of men; especially in those corporations and countries [counties] which depend on Cloathing and such Manufactures.

The preoccupation of the middling classes with non-conformity has often been noted. It was, says Alan Simpson, "weavers at their looms, tradesmen in their shops, and yeoman farmers in their homes" among whom Puritanism chiefly took root. Certainly non-conformity, clothmaking, and emigration were active influences in East Anglia in the first half of the century. It was also a combination that was active in the West Country in the second half. Restrictions on non-conformity and the impoverishment of the clothmaking industry gave the New World a double appeal. By no means, of course, were all of these Somerset farmers and Wiltshire and Gloucestershire clothworkers deeply religious people. Far from it. But most of them had been brought up in non-conformist groups which had, to a great extent, shaped the pattern of their lives. As Oscar Handlin has said about the effect of the church on later comers to America, it was not so much that they "rationally accepted doctrines" as that their beliefs were "closely wrapped in the day-to-day events of their existence." And as was true of most people in seventeenth-century England, whatever their religious persuasion they accorded it intense loyalty and were ready to defend it with all of the energy — to say nothing of the invective — at their disposal. Religious controversy was in the very air they breathed; and it inevitably colored personal and neighborhood activities which often had nothing to do with religion.

With certain Puritan clergymen, religious conviction may well have been the primary motive for emigration. It may have motivated some other people, but this would not, I think, have been true of most. Among the farmers and tradesmen who left their native villages, religion was a kind of cement which gave unity and security to those who were thinking of moving to a new life in strange surroundings. Families would be readier to permit their young people to make the voyage if they went with neighbors of the same religious persuasion as their own. Threats and discrimination, moreover, were no balm to people already disgruntled; hence one more factor was added to the existing restiveness, one that provided the emotional and psychological stimulus sometimes needed to translate economic wants and needs into action.

The New World was the beneficiary of this state of mind. For many it seemed to provide the best answer to their needs and hopes. "They say there's bread and work for all, and the sun shines always there." The gospel of this line from an emigrant song of a later period was at the heart of the movement from its beginning. For West Country men and women Bristol was the nearest port from which ships went almost weekly during the summer months. For others it was London or one of the lesser ports. Laborers went if they could be persuaded. Convicts and, on several occasions, political prisoners were forced to go. But over the course of the years, the majority of "the others" who found shipping in the trading vessels that regularly plied the western waters were England's middling people — the most valuable cargo that any captain carried on his westbound voyage.

The Beginnings of Slavery

For over three centuries, the international slave trade transported millions of Africans to America, denuding one continent of precious human resources to enable whites to exploit another. Finding the Indians in Central and South America ill-suited to enslavement, the Spaniards turned for labor to the "Dark Continent," a source on which it was especially dependent, because relatively few people migrated from Spain to the colonies. The English sent abroad many of their own people and, therefore, relied less on blacks. Yet, even in British North America on the eve of the Revolution, slaves formed some 20 percent of the population. The "peculiar institution" had put down deep roots in the American Plantation colonies as the following selection by Thad W. Tate, Jr., makes clear.

The precise origins of slavery in America are clouded in uncertainty. Of this, however, we can be sure: the Spanish example, the drive for profits from large-scale plantation agriculture and white racism resulted in the debasement of the black man.

The first Africans arrived in Virginia about a decade after the first settlement, yet the legal status of Negroes remained unclear for almost a half century. Since slavery was a status that had long disappeared in Britain and was unrecognized in English law, the colonists had no familiar precedents with which to fix the black man's position. Some, in fact, were treated as indentured servants — those Englishmen who bound themselves to work for several years to pay for the cost of passage to America. Yet unlike indentured servants, from the outset, blacks could not count on being free after a term of service. Until the end of the seventeenth century, the number of blacks in the colonies was few, and they could be adequately managed by informal means. But as their numbers grew, problems of discipline, ownership, and descent became more vexing. As Negroes came to play an indispensable role in the emerging plantation economies of the southern colonies, their white masters felt the need to codify the black man's position into law. The results were the black codes which permanently and clearly fixed the Negro's future as a bondsman until the Civil War.

Facilitating the emergence of slavery in the British colonies were English attitudes toward black people. Commonly regarded as inferior creatures, not far removed from the beasts of the jungle, blacks — like Indians — were the victims of a dehumanization process that enabled whites to live with those qualms of conscience that few could entirely subdue. Yet as much as Europeans wished to believe that Africans were subhuman, they were never wholly convinced. Not even a slave trader such as Captain Thomas Phillips, commander of the ship *Hannibal,* 1693–1694, could escape doubts. "Nor can I imagine," the captain confessed, "why they should be despis'd for their color, being what they cannot help, and the effect of the climate it has pleas'd God to appoint them. I can't think there is an intrinsic value to one colour more than another, nor that white is better than black, only we think so because we are so. . . ."

FOR FURTHER READING:

Davis, David B. *The Problem of Slavery in Western Culture.* Ithaca, N.Y.: Cornell University Press, 1969.*
Jordan, Winthrop D. *White Over Black.* Baltimore: Penguin Books, 1969.*
Stampp, Kenneth. *The Peculiar Institution.* New York: Random House, Vintage Books, 1956.*

Asterisk denotes paperback edition.

From *The Negro in Eighteenth-Century Williamsburg*   THAD W. TATE, JR.

The Eighteenth Century: The Growth of Slavery

The 16,390 Negroes residing in Virginia in 1700 had grown to 26,559 by 1720, to 30,000 by 1730, or almost double the 1700 figure. In the next decade — the 1730's — the Negro population doubled once again, reaching an estimated 60,000. It was not long until annual importations of Negroes had climbed to a peak of three or four thousand a year, while the number of Virginia-born Negroes increased correspondingly.

By mid-century the estimates of population varied widely, but Governor Dinwiddie's 1756 figures were perhaps as reliable as any. Estimating from the count of tithables, he arrived at a total population in Virginia of 293,472, of which 173,316 were white and 120,156 Negro. By the 1760's the proportion of white to Negro was not quite half and half, a ratio which remained more or less constant to the end of the eighteenth century. As was to be expected, the highest density of Negroes occurred in the Tidewater, but slaves were also numerous in the Piedmont. Only in the Valley and in the mountain areas was the Negro population really small.

This rapid increase did not depend alone on the willingness of the colonial planters to employ Negro labor. It also demanded the evolution of an efficient, large-scale slave trade. Through much of the seventeenth century sporadic Dutch trading activity was responsible for most of the importations of Negroes. The Virginia Assembly attempted to encourage this trade in 1659 by exempting Dutch merchants from paying ten shillings per hogshead duty on tobacco received for Negroes, permitting them to pay instead the two shillings English duty.

English mercantile interests did not become actively involved in the African slave trade until the Restoration. In 1662 The Company of Royal Adventurers Trading to Africa received a monopoly of the slave trade. This company, however, survived for only ten difficult years and never recorded a contract for supplying Virginia with Negroes. In 1672 a new company, the Royal African Company, received a charter which passed along to it the monopoly of the slave trade to the English colonies. There has been a tendency to assume too easily that the company was able to take full advantage of its favored position. In reality, the Royal African Company found it difficult to protect itself against interlopers from both England and the colonies. Not even the support of the Crown, which consistently instructed royal governors to give all possible encouragement to the company, could help. The Royal African

---

Source: Thad W. Tate, Jr., *The Negro in Eighteenth-Century Williamsburg* (Williamsburg, Va.: Colonial Williamsburg, 1965), pp. 23–42, 101–113, 164–170, 176–181, 200–208.

Company contracted on several occasions in the 1670's for shipments of Negroes to Virginia and made some deliveries. But, even though Governor Culpeper's statement that the company had never sold slaves in the colony was obviously an exaggeration, the Royal African Company was unsuccessful in dominating the Virginia market.

Some of the challengers of the company monopoly seemed to have established good local connections in Virginia through men like the first William Byrd and William Fitzhugh. In the 1680's Byrd was interested in a number of transactions that involved bringing in small shipments of Negroes from the West Indies. About the same time Fitzhugh was in correspondence with a New England merchant about the details of trading tobacco for slaves.

Ultimately, in 1698, the Royal African Company lost its monopoly, being forced to give way to an arrangement which permitted "separate traders" to carry slaves by paying certain duties to the company. Other merchants could now openly compete, sending their vessels, among other places, to the landings and ports which dotted the Virginia rivers. The figures for 1699–1708, which show that the separate traders carried 5,692 Negroes to Virginia and the Royal African Company 679, are a clear indication of the weak position of the Company in the trade. After these years shipments of slaves by the Company became increasingly intermittent, though there were still a few to Virginia in the 1720's. Then, after 1730, it no longer shipped Negroes from the African coast. The flow of slaves continued, however, with Bristol and Liverpool merchants dominating the trade. A sprinkling of New England vessels also brought slave cargoes from Africa, and a number of Virginia ships were employed to bring small groups of Negroes from the West Indies into the colony.

As the century progressed, new Negroes were sold farther and farther up the rivers, until settlements on the Fall Line like Rocky Ridge, across the James from Richmond, became the most important slave markets in the colony. There was also a domestic trade in Virginia-born Negroes, prized for their greater skill and adjustment to white civilization and therefore commanding higher prices.

As much as they had come to value slave labor, Virginians viewed these large-scale importations of Negroes with misgivings. No one has yet managed a completely satisfactory explanation of why the colonists began to wish they could put some limit on the number of slaves to be introduced into the colony. An older generation of Virginia historians claimed to find evidence of moral and humanitarian objections to the trade in human beings. Some of them have even charged that slaves were forced on the Southern colonies by the pressure of greedy British and New England mercantile groups. Any close reading of the evidence quickly suggests how little support there is for this point of view, whether it be the prevailing attitudes of most of the planters toward the Negro or in the fact that no cargo of healthy slaves ever lacked for purchasers. It is clear that much less idealistic reasons were responsible for the planters' objections.

For one thing, social control of the Negro played a large part in the increasing uneasiness of the whites. Fear of slave insurrection became a daily fact of life in Virginia, and ultimately the slave owners came to feel that there must be a limit beyond which the proportion of Negroes in the population could not safely go. An economic factor was also involved. Often the explanation has been that owners of Negroes already in Virginia had a speculative interest in keeping additional African Negroes out in order to assure a steady increase in the value of their own human property. What seems more convincing, however, is the fact that many planters opposed the further drain of money and increase in colonial indebtedness that the purchase of African slaves necessarily imposed. Prosperity in the slave trade was directly related to economic conditions of the tobacco market with the result that it suffered some of the same consequences of overextended credit. The more perceptive colonists were fully aware of the connection.

The principal stratagem which the leaders of the colony evolved for discouraging too rapid an increase in the number of slaves was an import duty on African slaves that could be disguised as a revenue measure. The long series of laws which enacted these duties began as early as 1699, and, for the first few years, were honestly intended to raise funds rather than discourage trade. The initial act, for example, levied a charge of twenty shillings for each Negro imported specifically for the construction of the new Capitol at Williamsburg. With one renewal this duty continued in force until late 1703. After a three month interval in early 1704 during which no duty was in effect, the impost was revived in April, 1704. From then until 1718 some form of duty was in force without an important break. The tendency to make the duties prohibitory in character also began to appear, for during these years the amount climbed as high as £5 per Negro.

From 1718 to 1723 the Assembly made no attempt to continue the duty. Then, in 1723 an attempt to restore it at the rate of 40 shillings touched off the first organized opposition from English traders. The flood of petitions and representations by these men carried enough political weight to persuade the King to disallow the 1723 law and all subsequent attempts of the Assembly to pass a duty over the next nine years.

By a change of tactics that made a 5% *ad valorem* duty payable by the prospective buyer rather than by the importer the General Assembly broke the deadlock in 1732. Thereafter and until the outbreak of the Revolution an *ad valorem* duty on slaves was in effect in Virginia, except for six months during 1751. The 5% rate of 1732 was gradually increased, until it stood at 20% during part of the French and Indian War. The whole effort to discourage the foreign slave trade led ultimately to the unsuccessful petition of the Assembly in 1772 for a complete end to further importations and to the successful prohibition of the trade by the new state government in 1778. But these events are more logically a part of the American Revolution in Virginia. Down to the outbreak of that struggle African slavers and West Indian traders continued to land their human cargoes in the colony with but little discouragement.

The role which the African Negroes and their American-born descendants assumed in plantation society possesses a certain familiarity. The fact that most histories of slavery leap so quickly to the nineteenth century, where the details of plantation life survive so much more abundantly, does place difficulties in the way of a full picture of the eighteenth. However, the general outlines of the work of the Negro slaves, of their daily existence, and of their immovable position at the bottom of a stratified colonial society seem clear enough.

The largest proportion of Negroes — men, women, and children — were field hands, assigned to growing tobacco and the other marketable crops the colony produced. This was the real purpose for which slavery had evolved, and it represented the institution in its most impersonal, burdensome, and typical form. The account of the field slave's lot by J. F. D. Smyth, an English traveler in Virginia just before the Revolution, is admittedly an unflattering one and no more to be accepted uncritically than any other single observation; but it is probably accurate enough in its description of the working day:

> . . . He [the slave] is called up in the morning at day break, and is seldom allowed time enough to swallow three mouthfuls of homminy, or hoecake, but is driven out immediately to the field to hard labour, at which he continues, without intermission, until noon. . . . About noon is the time he eats his dinner, and he is seldom allowed an hour for that purpose. . . .
> They [*i.e.*, the slaves] then return to severe labour, which continues in the field until dusk in the evening, when they repair to the tobaccohouses, where each has his task in stripping alotted him, that employs him for some hours.

A smaller, but still significant number, of slaves fared somewhat better as household workers and personal servants of the master's family. Almost invariably accounts of slaves who enjoyed especially lenient treatment or some bond of affection from their masters refer to Negroes from the household staff. Even so, there has been an easy tendency to view this group of slaves in a romantic light, and there is much we really do not know about their life.

A third segment of the slave labor force was composed of skilled and semi-skilled craftsmen. In time Negroes performed substantially all of the work on plantations in certain trades, especially carpentry and cooperage. Frequently, they were also proficient millers, tanners, shoemakers, wheelwrights, spinners, and weavers. Not only did these slave artisans perform tasks necessary for individual plantations; they were also instrumental in the commercial development of the Southern colonies, especially in tanning, in the rudimentary iron industry which was developing, and in the preparation of lumber and staves for export.

There are not many extant lists of slaves which provide a specific breakdown of the division of labor on the plantation from which they came. There is one, however, for Green Spring Plantation in 1770, when the estate of its deceased owner, Philip Ludwell, was being settled. At that time Ludwell's son-in-law, William Lee, described the slaves at Green Spring as including 59 "crop Negroes," a figure which was "exclusive of boys"; 12 house servants; 4 carpenters; 1 wheelwright; 2 shoemakers; and 3 gardeners and hostlers.

It is easy to overestimate the number of slaves owned by an individual planter and even easier to miscalculate the number used to operate a single plantation or quarter. The eighty-odd Negroes at Green Spring were the largest single group from a combined total of 164 on all the lands belonging to Philip Ludwell's estate. This total was more than enough to mark Ludwell as one of the more substantial members of the planter aristocracy, as his membership on the Governor's Council also testified.

If we were to judge Ludwell by the pattern of slave ownership revealed in the tax records of the 1780's, he would belong very nearly at the middle of the hundred leading families of the colony. These tax records, which have been most effectively analyzed by Professor Jackson T. Main, furnish the only comprehensive records on how widely slave ownership was distributed in Virginia before the nineteenth century. While the position of the leading families had begun to decline somewhat by the 1780's, the change was as yet so slight that the statistics are generally reliable for the entire later colonial period.

What becomes immediately clear from these tax records is the error of regarding even most of the wealthiest planters as having owned "hundreds" of Negroes. One man, Charles Carter, owned 785. He was followed in turn by William Allen with 700, Robert Beverley of Essex County with 592, Robert Carter of Nomini Hall with 445, and David Ross, the Richmond merchant-planter, with 400. Aside from these top five there were only eighteen other men in the entire colony who owned more than 200 slaves. The average for the hundred leading families was about 180 slaves, eighty on the home plantation and about a hundred elsewhere. A number of families who fell within this top group owned far less than a hundred Negroes.

If there were relatively few large-scale slaveholders in Virginia, the vast majority of families in the average Tidewater or Piedmont county nonetheless owned at least a small number of Negroes. In a sampling of eight of these counties the records indicated that three-fourths of the heads of families held slaves. Forty per cent of them, however, owned fewer than five Negroes. In the light of these statistics a true picture of slavery in colonial Virginia must take into account the humbler man who owned no more than two or three slaves as well as the more substantial planter.

Until the rationale of the American Revolution had begun to work its logic on the minds of Virginians, any doubt which the average colonist ever had about the wisdom of slavery stemmed either from the unpleasant prospect that the slaves would one day rise up and butcher the master class or else from suspicion that, as a business proposition, slavery simply did not pay its way. The threat of insurrection was in part dealt with through the tightening of the black codes, as well as by the attempt to discourage new importations of Negroes; but it was less easy to deal so directly with the economics of slavery.

The relative advantages and disadvantages of slave labor was, however, a subject often on the mind of the planter. Philip Fithian's account of a conversation with the wife of Robert Carter adequately sums up the reaction in theory of many planters to a situation with which they were unable to deal in fact:

> After Supper I had a long conversation with Mrs Carter concerning Negroes in Virginia, & find that She esteems their value at no higher rate than I do. We both concluded, (& I am pretty certain that the conclusion is just) that if in Mr Carters, or in any Gentleman Estate, all the Negroes should be sold, & the Money put to Interest in safe hands, & let the Lands which these Negroes now work lie wholly uncultivated, the bare Interest of the Price of the Negroes would be a much greater yearly income than what is now received from their working the Lands, making no allowance at all for the trouble & Risk of the Masters as to the Crops, & Negroes. — How much greater then must be the value of an Estate here if these poor enslaved Africans were all in their native desired Country, & in their Room industrious Tenants, who being born in freedom, by a laudable care, would not onlyly inrich their Landlords, but would raise a hardy Offspring to be the Strength & honour of the Colony.

One reason the planters questioned the profit in slave labor was the high cost of investment in slaves. In more pessimistic moments they also criticized their Negroes as wasteful and unproductive workers, either from lack of skill or deliberate resistance to forced labor.

To a large degree, the planters were inclined to rationalize other deficiencies in the agricultural methods of the colony at the expense of their Negroes. If there was one way in which slavery succeeded, it was as an economic system. Any problems of debt or credit arising from large investment in slaves was in reality a by-product of the uncertainties of tobacco cultivation. The supposed inefficiency and ineptitude of slave labor was more likely to be the fault of the wasteful methods of farming common to almost everyone who tilled the Virginia soil. Moreover, the cheapness of a slave's maintenance easily outweighed high purchase price, lack of training or skill, and even the prospect of his unproductive old age.

Whatever doubts the Virginia planter may have felt about the wisdom of enslaving an alien people, it must have seemed in the mid-eighteenth century that slavery was certainly here to stay. The rapid growth of the Negro population, the size of the slaveowners' investment, the usefulness of the labor, and outright fear combined to make the replacement of slavery unthinkable.

The Social Life of the Negro in Williamsburg

An oppressed community nearly always has a furtive quality about its life that conceals what its members really think and do and feel among themselves. This is simply a matter of self-preservation, of protecting whatever degree of independence its members still possess. Negro neighborhoods in the South have as often as not retained to the present day vestiges of such a barrier against white intrusions. As slaves the Negroes had even more need of this defense, and there are occasional evidences of the resourcefulness of the slave inhabitants of eighteenth-century Williamsburg in this regard.

No better example exists of the way in which the Negroes who lived here were both an integral part of the busy life of the capital and yet a society that could not be completely comprehended by their masters than the ability of the local Negro community to hide runaways. It is perfectly clear that the Negroes who had lived here any length of time were well known to most of the white residents in the way of all small towns. Advertisers in the *Gazette* often felt it unnecessary to tell more about a Williamsburg slave than the executors of Josiah Royle's estate did about a mulatto girl, Jenny, of whom they stated, "As she is well known in the Neighbourhood of this City, a more particular Description is unnecessary. . . ."

Yet Jenny and other Negroes just as well known were runaways who were thought to have remained in hiding in or around Williamsburg. In some cases a master only suspected that his slave had remained here secretly. But there were other instances where slaves had been seen in Williamsburg since their "elopement" and still could not be recaptured. Many of these fugitives had relatives or acquaintances in town whom the owners realized were probably hiding the fugitives. William Carter, for instance, stated of his mulatto girl, Venus, who had run away in December of 1766, "I imagine she is either harboured by other slaves in kitchens and quarters in and about town, or else gone for *Nansemond* county, from whence she was purchased a few years ago."

There was also difficulty with slaves who had once lived in Williamsburg and returned as runaways. Edward Cary, Jr. owned an 18-year old female slave raised in York County and leased to Philip Moody in Williamsburg in 1774. The next year Cary hired her out to John Thruston in King and Queen County; but Kate — this was the girl's name — had acquired attachments in Williamsburg that led her to flee Thruston's plantation. As Cary announced, "She has got a husband in *Williamsburg*, and probably may pass for a free person, as she is well acquainted in that city, and I have repeatedly heard of her being there." It hardly seems possible that this slave girl could have been a fugitive almost two years, have been recognized frequently in Williamsburg during that time, and yet not have been recaptured and returned to either Cary or Thruston. Above all, she could hardly have succeeded, unless the slave community had ways and means of shielding its members that the slaveowner could not readily penetrate.

Kate's experiences illustrate another feature of the life of the Negro under slavery. She had run away to Williamsburg in the first place because she had a husband here, an important point for a number of reasons. The customs and practices of eighteenth-century slavery did not usually permit the marriage of slaves, even baptised ones, in any legal or religious sense. Yet for every slave who took advantage of, or was unable to resist, the open invitation to promiscuity inherent in such a situation, there were many others who tried under the most difficult conditions to pursue a normal family life. The slaveowners gave a certain recognition to these "marriages," although they often did not hesitate to destroy a slave marriage by selling one mate.

There are even accounts of a sort of marriage ceremony known as "jumping the broomstick," in which the Negro couple stepped across a broomstick together as a symbol of the fact that they considered each other husband and wife. One slave has left a personal recollection of her mother's broomstick marriage. As the mother recounted it to her daughter, the young couple simply decided on a Sunday that they would like to be married. Thereupon they went up to the kitchen and asked to see their master by sending word through the cook. After determining they were old enough — both the boy and the girl were 16 in this instance — the owner readily assented and sent them off to one of the Negro women, Aunt Lucy, who was probably either the midwife or the oldest woman; and she performed the broomstick ceremony. Since it was Sunday and all the Negroes were around their quarters, the old woman called them together immediately. They formed a circle around the couple, while Aunt Lucy recited a few verses from the Bible and laid a broomstick on the floor. The couple locked arms, jumped over the stick, and were then husband and wife in the eyes of the other slaves in the quarter.

The slaveowners understandably preferred to have their Negroes marry on the home plantation to lessen the chance of runaways and to insure that children born to the couple would belong to him. Permission to marry on a neighboring plantation was sometimes granted, though it usually restricted the couple to a single visit a week.

It is only possible to speculate about the problem slave marriages might create in a town such as Williamsburg, where a large number of slaves belonging to many different owners lived in close contact. The number of unions of slaves belonging to different owners undoubtedly increased, and the master's consent was probably much less vital than on an isolated plantation. He was also likely to be able to do far less about destroying a marriage made against his will. These slave marriages may well have been the occasion of a lot of trouble in Williamsburg. Certainly this is the source to which a large number of fugitive slaves can be traced. Edmund Cary's Kate, whose flight from King and Queen to Williamsburg has already provided so much by way of illustration, had lived in Williamsburg only a year and yet found a slave to whom she considered herself wed. Gaby, a male slave belonging to James Burwell at King's Creek, was listed twice in three years as a runaway. Both times he had fled into Williamsburg where his wife worked. Slaves brought into Williamsburg from some distance and thereby separated from a wife frequently ran off, too — in this case not into hiding around town but back to their original home.

The frustrations that slaveowners experienced in trying to recover slaves in hiding around town seems all the more surprising in the view of the living arrangements for slaves. While our exact knowledge about where slaves lived in Williamsburg is sketchy, we can be reasonably certain they lived on the master's property, perhaps close to the main house where surveillance should have been relatively easy.

The conventional arrangement on the large plantations with one or two rows of crude slave cabins, possibly at some little distance from the plantation house, was more extensive than even the larger town households required. There were Williamsburg properties on which undoubtedly an outbuilding or two was used specifically for slave quarters. When a house that had belonged to Peter Randolph was offered for sale, the description pointed out that it included five major outbuildings — two stables, a coach house, a kitchen, and a servant's house of the same dimension as the kitchen. One of the advertisements on runaways refers to "kitchens and quarters in and about town," as if there might have been a fairly large number of slave quarters scattered through Williamsburg. In other cases the living space for slaves seems not to have been a separate building but only the second-floor rooms over the kitchens. Eliza Baker remembered slaves living over the kitchen at the Garrett House in the nineteenth century. Household servants sometimes had no quarters of their own but simply spread pallets in the hall, on the staircase, or somewhere else in the house after the family had retired.

Whatever the arrangement of living quarters for the slaves, they never were provided with much furniture. At best there can hardly have been more than a bed or a cot and maybe a few discarded pieces from the main house. In the specific instance of Williamsburg not a single inventory has appeared that suggests anything definite about the furnishings of slave quarters. The inventory of the William Prentis estate did include a room-by-room listing of furnishings that also included outbuildings. It contains one or two entries of possible value. Described as being "In out House, Yard, &C" were a number of tools, some scrap metal, and a few chairs and chests. These last few pieces of furniture could have been used by the slaves, although no beds at all were included. Also, several items were "*At old Nann*[y's?]," one of Prentis's slaves being called old Nanny. This included only a frying pan, a pot, a grindstone, and a few tools, however, and no furniture at all.

The Negro slave had little time to spend as he wished — usually Saturday nights and Sundays plus additional time at one or two major holidays like Christmas and Whitsunday. Descriptions of plantation life substantially agree about the way in which the slaves spent their spare time. On Saturday nights they usually gathered in the slave quarters for dancing, which was as much their favorite recreation as it was that of most other Virginians. Philip Fithian has described how by five o'clock on Saturday at Nomini Hall "every Face (especially the Negroes) looks festive & cheerful — " Sundays the Negroes might tend their garden plots or spend as much time as possible sleeping and resting.

The slaves in Williamsburg probably enjoyed a social life that cannot have been much different, especially in amount of free time. Despite laws forbidding it, the Negroes here seemed able to procure and consume alcohol in some quantity. The Negro girl described as "fond of Liquor, and apt to sing indecent and Sailors Songs when so" is a good case in point. So is the series of charges and countercharges involving the merchants Daniel Fisher, John Holt, and John Greenhow. Fisher was charged by the other two with selling liquor to Negroes without the written permission of their masters. When the case came into court, Fisher turned on his accusers and claimed that Holt had "without the least scruple whatever" served two Negroes whom Fisher himself had turned away. The aggrieved Fisher also claimed that John

Greenow was "infamously remarkable for trafficking with Negroes in wine, or any other commodity, Sunday not excepted." These accusations involve so much personal bickering and name-calling that acceptance of them at face value is impossible; but their general tenor suggests that a certain amount of dealing with slaves in liquor went on in Williamsburg. Many of the masters may, for one thing, have been lenient at times about issuing permission for their slaves to have intoxicants. William Byrd recounted the well-known instance in which Governor Spotswood could not get his servants to remain sober for a large holiday entertainment at the Palace until they were promised the privilege of getting drunk the next day.

Most of the aspects of life discussed above would have been the private concern of a free person. The slave, of course, had no such right. Where he lived, whom he married, and sometimes even what he did for amusement were no more his to decide than the work he would do or the master he would serve. Yet by a combination of evasion and defiance the slaves were often able to achieve some degree of independence in their social life. Town life, if anything, seemed to increase this degree of freedom and to create a slave community with its own thoughts and pleasures and with the means of protecting its fugitives.

The Law and the Negro

The evolution of the Negro's legal status from ordinary indentured servant to servant for life to slave was followed by the development of a separate legal code, distinct trial procedures, and harsher punishments for Negroes accused of criminal acts. Inevitably the slave's lack of personal freedom would have necessitated some revision in the English legal system that had been transported to Virginia. But it was unrelenting fear of the Negro as a potential insurrectionist and constant determination to police his conduct rigidly that instigated most of the early laws affecting Negro slaves.

Only in the last two decades of the seventeenth century did anything more than the faintest beginning of a separate criminal law for Negroes begin to appear. An act of 1680 for preventing Negro insurrections was the first real "black code" in Virginia, providing specific punishments for the three crimes of leaving the master's property without permission; lifting a hand against a "Christian," that is, a white man; and for hiding or resisting capture after running away. Conviction on the last charge required the death penalty. A 1691 statute that was of the greatest importance as the first legal restriction on manumission of slaves in Virginia also provided a systematic plan for raising a force of men to recapture "outlying slaves," or runaways who were in hiding. Then in 1692 the legislature provided the first trial procedures, in particular the denial of jury trial, which applied specifically to Negro slaves.

There were three more or less comprehensive pieces of legislation in the eighteenth century covering the trial, punishment, and regulation of slaves. The first passed in 1705 to be replaced in 1723 by one which was in turn superseded by the act of 1748. These were the basic codes for the later colonial period, and most of the other legislation affecting Negro crimes, with the exception of laws dealing with runaways, was not much more than a minor modification of these two measures.

As has already been suggested, the first law aimed at a crime by Negroes other than running away was the 1680 statute designed to prevent insurrections by punishing slaves who kept their master's property without permission or resisted a white man in any way. On the supposition that this act went unnoticed the Assembly required two years later that it be read twice a year in every church. The more comprehensive statute of 1723 sought new safeguards against an armed rising by withdrawing the privilege of benefit of clergy from Negroes convicted of plotting or attempting such rebellion and by forbidding all assemblies of slaves that were not licensed by the masters and held for public worship. It also denied all Negroes free or slave the right to possess weapons, except that free Negroes who were householders or militiamen might keep a single gun and Negroes residing on the frontier might be licensed by the justice of the peace to carry arms. All of these restrictions continued in force under the law of 1748.

Most crimes other than running away or rising in rebellion that a Negro might commit were actions defined in laws that applied equally to all persons in the colony. It is revealing, however, that two felonies, hog stealing and the administration of poisonous medicines, were the occasion of special provisions dealing exclusively with slaves. Hog stealing reached the point that on the third conviction it became a capital offense without benefit of clergy. Such were the risks involved in the temptations of the delicate flavor of roast pig.

The restriction of poisonous medicines obviously arose out of the belief of the whites that a great many Negroes continued to practice the witchcraft and tribal medicine they had brought from Africa both in honest, if primitive, attempts to cure ailing slaves but also in malicious attempts to destroy an enemy. One section of the 1748 code provided capital punishment for Negroes who prepared and administered medicine of any sort, unless their owner had consented. Benefit of clergy was allowable only where the slave could prove there had been no evil intent. In the wave of Negro crimes which David Mays described in Caroline County from 1761–1764 there were no less than three trials under this law in a three months period during 1762 with convictions in two of them.

Beginning with the legislation of 1692 a separate court procedure developed for the trial of Negroes differing markedly in its rapid movement to trial and lack of constitutional guarantees from that accorded the free man. In capital cases the core of this process was (1) the immediate imprisonment of the slave, (2) issuance by the governor of a commission of oyer and terminer to persons in the county involved to arraign and indict the offender and to take for evidence the confession of the accused or the oaths of two witnesses, or one in some cases, and (3) "without the sollemnitie of jury" to pass such judgment as the law allowed. Throughout the colonial era there was but one modification in this method of trial. In 1765 the governor was permitted to issue general commissions of oyer and terminer to four or more justices of the peace in each county, including one of the quorum, thereby eliminating the necessity of a special commission for each trial.

Initially the procedure for trying slaves did not provide for testimony by other Negroes. In 1723, however, it became permissible in capital cases involving Negroes to take such testimony from Negroes, Indians, or mulattoes "as shall seem convincing," wording which clearly implied that they were not to be accepted as sworn witnesses nor to be questioned at all, except when absolutely necessary. However, this provision for the use of slave testimony in 1723 may have been an opening wedge for employing Negro witnesses far more widely than the law intended. For a new law of 1732 stated that no Negro, mulatto, or Indian should be admitted in court, be sworn as a witness, or give evidence in a case — practices which the law complained had been allowed, even in the General Court — except in the trial of a slave for a capital offense. One subsequent modification occurred in 1748 when free Christian Negroes, Indians, and mulattoes were allowed to appear in any case involving another Negro, Indian, or mulatto. In brief, however, all these technicalities come down to the fact that the slaves normally could testify only in a capital case involving another Negro. . . .

Just as the very nature of slave status had demanded trial procedures that to some extent abridged the traditional English and colonial guarantees of individual right, it just as logically required a system of punishment that was exclusively corporal. The courts might fine a master whose neglect contributed in some way to a criminal act of one of his Negroes, but the slave could not normally make satisfaction in this way. For minor offenses or when the slave was able to avail himself of benefit of clergy, whipping became the prescribed penalty — 10 lashes for coming on a plantation without permission, 39 lashes for attending an unlawful meeting, or 39 for possessing weapons illegally, to cite a few examples.

More serious crimes which did not warrant capital punishment, even in the harsh criminal codes of the day, required what may have been a more unpleasant fate than death itself. That penalty was mutilation or dismemberment. A slave giving false evidence would, for instance, receive his 39 lashes and then have his ears nailed to the pillory for half an hour, after which they would be cut off. Under the law of 1748 his ears would have been nailed to the pillory and then cut off one at a time rather than simultaneously. Dismemberment was a favorite punishment for the slave who continually ran away, went abroad at night, or lay in hiding. Both the 1723 and 1748 acts specify its use for these offenses. Since the dismemberment usually took the form of cutting off a foot, it was a practical, if cruel, way of curbing the sort of ungovernable Negro who really constituted the greatest threat of all against slavery as a police institution. That dismemberment sometimes reached proportions which struck even slaveowners as barbarous is, however, evidenced by a 1769 statute which in the future forbade the castration of a slave for continually lying out and reserved that punishment solely for Negroes guilty of the attempted rape of a white woman.

Finally there were the whole series of crimes for which conviction carried the death penalty, the felonies for which white persons would also have been executed plus offenses such as rebellion or the administering of medicines that applied only to slaves. According to the customary practice of colonial Virginia slaves were ordinarily hanged, but a slave named Eve who was convicted in Orange County of poisoning her master was drawn upon a hurdle to the place of execution and there burned at the stake. Then there are also instances in which the head of a slave who had been hanged was cut off and put on public exhibition.

One economic problem arose with capital punishment of a slave. The owner was apt to view the execution as costing him the loss of a valuable piece of property, no matter how serious the slave's crime had been. In the 1705 statute affecting trial procedure for capital offenses, the justices were impowered to put a reasonable valuation upon any slave they condemned. When this valuation had been certified to the Assembly, the owner would be reimbursed from public funds. This method of compensation remained in force throughout the colonial period with the result that few sessions of the Assembly fail to record favorable action on the request of some owner to be paid for an executed slave.

The punishment which the courts meted out to slaves for crimes against public order in no way interfered with the disciplining of slaves by their owners and overseers. In fact, the law protected to extreme limits the master's privilege of punishing his slaves. One of the earliest pieces of legislation affecting slavery was the 1669 statute exempting a master from indictment for felony if a slave were killed while under punishment. The law reasoned that there could be no felony without malicious intent and that no one could be presumed to destroy his own property deliberately and maliciously. The Assembly made some dent in this line of reasoning in 1723, by providing that the master might be indicted if there were at least one lawful witness to testify that the killing of the slave had been a willful act. But with this one unlikely exception owners remained exempt from prosecution for the death of a slave under correction, even though new royal governors were often instructed to work for laws to punish masters who deliberately killed or maimed a slave.

The dissection of a long list of laws is a tedious business at best; and once their contents have been outlined, there is not much more to be said. One significant development in the eighteenth century, however, was the collection of most of the criminal law affecting Negroes into the two comprehensive statutes of 1723 and 1748. They provided the colony with a "black code" nearly as well-defined and systematic as those of a later day.

This much can be said for the justice administered under these laws — it was often harsh, but it was uniform and not arbitrary. And it was rapid, for the slave did not often languish in jail awaiting trial. To that extent the slaves of colonial Virginia could have fared worse, as indeed they did in parts of the New World.

The net effect of these statutes, however, was to make the law for the Negro slave almost exclusively a police instrument for maintaining the stability of society and largely to demolish that more attractive side of law, the safeguarding of the individual from unnecessary invasions of his person. Perhaps only the uncomfortable fact that the slave was not fully a person in the eyes of the law saved this one-sidedness from seriously damaging, for free men even, the traditional guarantees to the individual that Virginia had inherited from English law.

* * *

There has already been occasion, in connection with the movement for high import duties on slaves, to comment on the lurking fear of insurrection which haunted every slaveowner. As the number of slaves mounted steadily toward half the population of the colony — and, of course, more than half in areas where the slaves were really concentrated — it became possible to conceive of the destruction of society itself, if a Negro uprising were really to take hold. Newspapers all over the colonies were quick to publish every available detail of a real or rumored attempt of slaves to rebel; and much of the restrictive legislation against Negroes in the colony was admittedly aimed at this unwelcome possibility.

To what extent was the alarm of the whites exaggerated? One count of uprisings or threats of uprisings during the entire course of slavery in Virginia lists 72 of which only 9 occurred before 1776. The truth is difficult to measure; for instead of specific, brief episodes more often there were periods of general unrest lasting several years at a time. Judged on this basis, about a fourth of the years from 1700 to 1775 were marred by an abnormal degree of this uneasiness. The fact remains, however, that no white person was killed in an organized slave insurrection in Virginia before the Nat Turner rising of 1831.

The first recorded attempt at a slave uprising in Virginia occurred in the Northern Neck in 1687. As so often happened, one of the men involved confessed and the attempt was checked. The slave who had been leader was not executed but was whipped around Jamestown from the prison to the gallows and back, forced to wear an iron collar for the rest of his life, and forbidden ever to leave his master's plantation.

A more serious plot, which centered in Surry and Isle of Wight Counties but also involved James City, was uncovered in March, 1709. Once again it was a slave who betrayed the plan to the whites — a Negro named Will, the property of Robert Ruffin of Surry. It fell to the Governor's Council to direct an investigation of the whole matter and issue instructions for the trial and punishment of the Negroes involved. The way in which they proceeded provides a good picture of the operation of all levels of government in the colony in the face of what, to these men, presented a serious crisis. First of all, the Council apparently issued warrants for the arrest of all suspects, similar to one issued for four Negroes in Bruton Parish, Angola Peter, Bumbara Peter, Mingo, and Robin. Then the county justices of Surry and Isle of Wight were ordered to examine all suspected slaves, releasing those only slightly involved with appropriate punishment and holding the leaders in the county jail, until the record of their examination could be examined by the President of the Council, Edmund Jenings. James City Negroes were not considered to be so deeply involved. Here, with a single exception, the slaves, who had been rounded up and held under guard, were to be tried at the next county court, punished, and released. There is an account of the close cross examination of several of these slaves in a letter from Philip Ludwell to Jenings. The questioning by Ludwell and three others had cleared Commissary Blair's slaves and a number of others of complicity, but it had also turned up the evidence against John Brodnax's Jamy, the one James City slave ordered held in prison.

About a month later the Council ordered the principal culprits, those still held in jail, to be tried before the General Court, where three of them were presumably convicted and hanged. One of the "chief Actors," Peter, belonging to Samuel Thompson of Surry, had escaped, and a reward of £10 alive or £5 dead was offered for his recapture.

The episode had a happier ending for Robert Ruffin's Will. After he had given away the insurrection, it became necessary to move him to the Northern Neck because some of the other Negroes threatened his life. Then at its meeting in the fall of 1710 the Assembly voted him his freedom as a reward for his service to the colony, the occasion being marred only by the complaint of his former master, Ruffin, that the £40 voted by the Assembly was less than he had been offered for the Negro by a prospective buyer.

Another plan for an uprising was headed off in 1722, prompting Governor Drysdale to include in his first message to the Assembly a request for improving the militia and for passing stricter laws as a protection against Negroes. The slave code was, in fact, strengthened that year.

The years of 1729 and 1730 seem to have brought a relatively longer period of unrest among slaves which may have continued through most of the decade of the 30's. The first incident occurred in June of 1729 on a new plantation near the head of the James River. There a group of about fifteen Negroes seized arms, provisions, and tools and made off for the mountains. The search party found them already settled in a secluded area, where they had even begun to clear ground for crops. A brief exchange of gunfire brought about the surrender of the slaves, however, and their small colony was destroyed.

There was more trouble the next year, touched off by a rumor that former Governor Spotswood, just back from England, had brought an order from the Crown to free all Christian slaves. This was more a matter of general unrest than a concerted plot. The governor, at the time Gooch, reported that by "keeping the Militia to their Duty, by Imprisonment and severe whipping of the most Suspected, this Disturbance was very soon Quashed, and until about six weeks afterwards we were easy. . . ." Then there was more trouble. About two hundred slaves in Norfolk and Princess Anne counties gathered on a Sunday at church time and elected officers to lead an intended rebellion. In this instance four of the Negroes involved were executed. A certain amount of continuing uneasiness is reflected in Gooch's address to the Assembly in 1736, in which he recommended strengthening the militia as a means of policing the slaves; in his proclamation of October 29, 1736, on the same subject; and in the 1738 revision of the law requesting the militia to include a system of four-men patrols to police slave quarters and suspected gathering places of Negroes in every county.

Another unsettled period occurred in and near Williamsburg during the 1770's. The number of runaways advertised seemed noticeably large, and accounts of trouble with slaves in York, James City, and Hanover counties circulated in newspapers as far away as New York. This was in part responsible for the establishment of a night watch in Williamsburg in 1772 to consist of four people to patrol the streets, cry the hours, and "use their best Endeavours to preserve Peace and good Order, by apprehending and bringing to Justice all disorderly People, Slaves, as well as others." About the same time there was a strict patrol in Yorktown, and Negroes found on the street were picked up and held overnight.

For suppression of an incipient revolt the colony relied largely on the county militia and, after 1738, the system of Patrols, reinforced by such local activity as the Williamsburg night watch. From what we know about the colonial militia, it is not likely that these men were over-diligent, until there was an indication of trouble. Still, the colony proved able to act swiftly in an emergency. Real emergencies, however, were relatively infrequent; for well-laid plots by slaves were much rarer in eighteenth-century Virginia than what could be more correctly described as periods of unusual restiveness.

The Plantation South

The United States was formed out of highly distinctive regions, so much so, that not until almost a century after the republic was born, did the nation establish, through civil war, its supremacy over its sections. The roots of sectionalism go back into America's colonial period. The New England, middle, and southern colonies each had enough common characteristics to distinguish them from one another. On the other hand, a heightened sense of sectional identity awaited the struggle for independence that propelled Americans into a national political arena where they competed and became more self-conscious of their differences.

Two institutions defined the American South before the Civil War, and both emerged in the colonial period: slavery and the plantation system. Slave labor made plantation agriculture possible. Most colonists were farmers, who relied principally on the labor of large families. Consequently, the amount of land they could cultivate was limited, since agricultural technology was still primitive. Plantations, however, employed capital and labor to produce commercial crops, such as tobacco and rice, on a large scale. Aubrey C. Land shows in the following essay that though there were relatively few plantations — that is, large-scale enterprises — there were many "planters."

The explanation of this paradox is that most southern farmers considered themselves planters even though they operated small family farms, occasionally with a slave or two. Yet almost all aspired to a life of ease and elegance on a large, impressive estate, with a great mansion and thousands of acres, tilled by hundreds of slaves. Few achieved this dream. Land was easy to acquire, but not many accumulated the necessary capital to buy slaves. Some tried by plowing back profits from tobacco or rice into acquiring more slaves. With these they could cultivate more land, raise larger crops, and buy still more slaves. Eventually, they could lift themselves into the ranks of the leading planters. But there were other, even more important, routes to the top. According to Professor Land, enterprising southerners also engaged in trade and manufacturing, practiced law, and speculated in land. Profits from these activities provided capital for the developing plantations. Still another important source came from wealthy English merchants who advanced credit to Americans while helping market southern exports overseas. Those most skillful and aggressive in taking advantage of these opportunities formed the plantation elite, proud of their elegant, gracious life and contemptuous of the commercial spirit that they ascribed to the money-grubbing, boorish Yankee sharpers.

FOR FURTHER READING:

MORTON, LOUIS. *Robert Carter of Nomini Hall: A Virginia Tobacco Planter of the Eighteenth Century.* Charlottesville, Va.: University Press of Virginia, 1964.*
PHILLIPS, ULRICH B. *Life and Labor in the Old South.* Boston: Little, Brown & Company, 1929.*
WOODMAN, HAROLD D. *Slavery and the Southern Economy: Sources and Readings.* New York: Harcourt, Brace & World, 1966.*

Asterisk denotes a paperback edition.

Economic Base and Social Structure: The Northern Chesapeake in the Eighteenth Century AUBREY C. LAND

The *Maryland Gazette* for 18 October 1749 carried an obituary of more than common interest:

> On the Eleventh Instant Died, at his Seat on Wye River in Queen Anne's County, Richard Bennett, Esq. in the Eighty-third Year of his Age, generally lamented by all that knew him. As his great fortune enabled him to do much good, so (happily for many) his Inclination was equal to his Ability, to relieve the indigent and distressed, which he did very liberally, without regarding of what Party, Religion or Country, they were. As he was the greatest Trader in this Province, so great Numbers fell in his Debt, and a more merciful Creditor could not be, having never deprived the Widows or Orphans of his Debtors of a Support; and when what the Debtors left, was not sufficient for that purpose, frequently supply'd the deficiency. His long Experience and great Knowledge in Business, as well as his known Candor and generosity, occasion'd many to apply to him for Advice and Assistance, and none were ever disappointed of what was in his Power, and several by his means, extricated out of great Difficulties. . . .

A later issue adds some particulars:

> On Wednesday last was solemnized the Funeral of Richard Bennett, Esq. of Wye River, in a very handsome and decent Manner, by the Direction of his sole executor, the Hon. Col. Edward Lloyd. Mr. Bennett, by his Will, has forgiven above one hundred and fifty of his poor Debtors, and has made Provision for the Maintainance of many of his Overseers, and other poor Dependents, and settled a Sum of Money to be paid annually to the Poor of a Parish in Virginia: and done many other Acts of Charity and Munificence. He was supposed to be the Richest Man on the Continent. . . .

Bennett's obvious virtues as a Christian gentleman need no underscoring, but two comments of the eulogist should be noted; his great wealth and his calling as a "trader." Perhaps the enthusiastic editor went beyond the exact truth in estimating Bennett's fortune, though probably not much. The field certainly included a few other candidates for the richest man. A neighbor across the Bay, Charles Carroll, counted his total worth at something like a hundred thousand pounds sterling, including £ 30,000 loaned at 6 per cent interest. Robert Carter, south of the Potomac in Virginia, could reckon himself worth nearly as much. The second William Byrd had left an impressive heritage which his son of the same name had already begun to dissipate. Even by the standards of London these were wealthy men.

All three alternate possibilities for the title of richest man are better known than Bennett, because they have had biographers, or because they played important political roles, or both. They belong to what has been variously called the aristocracy, the ruling oligarchy, or the squirearchy. The pejorative connotations of all three terms incline me toward a label suggested by a profound student of early American social and cultural history, "the southern agrarian leaders." We can understand them in a sense as leaders of an agrarian area. But when we inquire about the eco-

---

Source: Aubrey C. Land, "Economic Base and Social Structure: The Northern Chesapeake in the Eighteenth Century," *Journal of Economic History*, vol. 25 (1965), pp. 639–654.

nomic milieu in which they flourished or seek the mechanisms by which they acquired their dominant positions, we are faced with some difficulties.

The traditional historiography has leaned heavily on literary evidence, and when it does not ignore these questions often gives impressions that are positively misleading. As sources, personal letters, travel accounts, and memoirs have the great merit of being relatively easy to put into context and ideal to paraphrase. A few dozen up to a few thousand items of this kind can be quilted into interesting and convincing patterns. The procedure has the limitations of the sources. Even the most acute observer focuses on objects of high visibility. The high tor eclipses the molehill in the landscape until the king falls to his death because of the "little gentleman in black velvet."

In the eighteenth-century Chesapeake, the "great planters" were the element of high visibility. They held slaves, owned vast estates, and built magnificent houses that have survived as showpieces. Visitors came under the spell of these gracious livers and left charming accounts of their balls, their tables, and their luxury. Planters themselves contributed to the effect. They wrote letters and a few left diaries that have survived along with their great houses. Viewed through these sources they cut large figures and play the star roles in the arrangements that the people of the Chesapeake made for themselves in that period. These personages are accurately enough drawn, but they are a detail, though an important one, in the total production. Unfortunately the supporting cast and stage hands that made the production possible receive next to no attention, sometimes not even the courtesy of a billing. Just as *Hamlet* cannot be successfully staged without Hamlet, there can hardly be a play with Hamlet alone.

Not much literary evidence for the minor figures has come down; but another kind does exist and, even though bristling with difficulties and overawing in bulk, it can be compelled to yield some data for a fuller view. This body of material has been brought together in two despositories, the Maryland Hall of Records and the Virginia State Archives, and properly canvassed will fill in some gaps in our knowledge of Chesapeake affairs. It consists of inventories and accounts of the estates in personalty of all free men at the time of their death. The argument in this paper applies only to Maryland, for which a statistical analysis has been completed. The Virginia counties that have been analyzed give me the clear impression that differences between the areas north and south of the Potomac are not very great in respect of the basic contention here. Both were a part of a single economic region which political boundaries could not split asunder and were treated as a unit in contemporary British commercial records.

To obtain from the voluminous Maryland records a sample that faithfully reflects conditions in the northern Chesapeake, some of the usual economies are not possible. Geographical sampling by selected counties is ruled out. The process of carving new counties out of large older counties went on continuously from 1690 to the Revolution. Consequently the county of one decade is not necessarily the same unit in a later decade. Accordingly, all counties of the province are included. Over the entire eighty-year period 1690-1770 for which the records are reasonably complete the alternate decades from 1690-1699 to 1750-1759 have been tabulated. If it can be assumed that these sizable samples reflect with reasonable accuracy the spectrum of planters' estates, then we have some basis for understanding an otherwise shadowy aspect of the Chesapeake economy.

The profile of estates in the decade January 1, 1690, to December 31, 1699, shows an unexpected imbalance. Three quarters of these estates (74.6 per cent, to be precise) are of the magnitude £ 100 sterling or less. In the next bracket, £ 100 to £ 200, the percentage drops to 12.1, and in succeeding hundred-pound brackets to 5.5 per cent, 2.7 per cent, 1.4 per cent, 1.3 per cent, 0.6 per cent, and 0.3 per cent. After a break in the distribution, a meager 1.5 per cent at the top are valued at £ 1,000 sterling or greater.

Beyond the obvious fact that the less affluent far outnumber the better off, this analysis tells us little. The estates, small or great, are all those of planters — a handful of physicians, mariners, and clergymen specifically excepted. "Planter," then, simply describes an occupation without indicating economic status of the individual. To get at what this distribution means in terms of worldly goods, standard of living, and possibly social status, it is necessary to look at particulars in the inventories themselves. Here impressions become vivid.

The planters at the bottom of the scale, those with estates of £ 100 or less, have at best a "country living": a saddle horse or two, half a dozen or fewer cows, a few swine to furnish fresh or salt meat for the table according to the season, a modest assortment of household utensils — sometimes nothing more than a cooking pot or skillet, a few tools and agricultural implements. Many essentials of a household — for instance, plates and cups — are missing in fully half the inventories, an omission indicating that makeshifts such as wooden bowls and gourds took the place of these articles. The appraisers of estates overlooked no article, not even a cracked cup without a handle or a single glass bottle. In brief the standard of living might be described as rude sufficiency. The self-styled poet laureate of Maryland, Eben Cooke, calls planters at this level "cockerouses."

The inventories also speak to the productivity of these small planters. In those inventories made during the autumn and winter after the tobacco had been cut the appraisers carefully estimated the size of the deceased's crop. Crop entries range from twelve hundred pounds, a trifle over two hogsheads, up to three thousand pounds, or about six hogsheads. This represented the producer's cash crop, almost his entire annual income, excepting possibly the occasional sale of a heifer, a pig, or a few bushels of corn to a neighbor or local trader. Reckoning the price of tobacco at ten shillings a hundred, these small producers could count their disposable incomes at a figure between £ 6 and £ 15 a year.

Even taking into account the small planter's self-sufficiency in fresh vegetables from the kitchen garden, cereals from whatever field crops he grew besides tobacco, and meat from his own farm animals, an income of this size imposed iron limitations on him. Between investment and consumption he had no choice. Such necessities as thread, needles, powder and shot, coarse fabrics for clothing or featherbeds, and an occasional tool or a household utensil strained his credit at the country store until his crop was sold. For the small planter, provincial quitrents, church tithes, and taxes represented a real burden. He cast his ballot for a representative who could resist the blandishments of governors and hold public expenses to the barest minimum. In good part the pressures from men of his kind kept investment in the public sector to lowest dimensions, whether the object was a county courthouse, a lighthouse, or a governor's mansion. As a private person he could not invest from savings because he had none. With tobacco crops barely sufficient to cover his debt to the country merchant, a disastrous year could prostrate him. A lawsuit, the death of cattle in a winter freeze, or a fire in house or barn forced him to contract debts which had often not been paid at the time of his death and which ate up his entire personal estate, leaving his heirs without a penny. Not infrequently his administrator actually overpaid his estate in order to save trifling family heirlooms more precious than their valuation in the inventory. Investment in a slave or indentured servant to increase his productivity, though not completely out of the question, was very difficult.

The small planter clearly was not the beneficiary of the planting society of the Chesapeake. He bred his increase and added to the growing population that filled up vacant land from the shoreline to the mountains before the Revolution. In the language of the courts he qualified as a planter. Considering the circumstances of his life, it would stretch the usual meaning of the term to call him a yeoman, particularly if he fell in the lower half of his group.

In the brackets above £ 100, different characteristics of the estates immediately strike the eye. Sumptuary standards of planters above this line were obviously higher. Kitchens had ampler stocks of utensils; and for dining, earthenware and china replaced the gourds and wooden makeshifts that apparently were the rule on tables of families in the lowest economic bracket. Ticking stuffed with flock gave way to bedsteads and bedding. Even more striking is the prevalence of bond labor, both indentured servants and slaves, in this higher stratum. The transition comes abruptly. In estates below £ 100, servants or slaves rarely appear and then only in those within a few pounds of the line. In the estates at £ 100 to £ 200, the inventories of eight out of ten estates list bond labor — a higher percentage, actually, than in any of the succeeding £ 100 brackets up to £ 500.

In fact, these estates falling between £ 100 and £ 500 form a relatively homogeneous group. Altogether they comprise 21.7 per cent of all estates. Though existence for the planter is less frugal, his worldly goods show few signs of real luxury. Not a single estate was debt free, though fewer than a tenth had debts amounting to more than half the value of the inventory. The number of slaves in single estates does not run high: from one to five in 90 per cent of the estates that had them at all. Yet even this small number represented between half and two thirds of the appraised valuation. Reflecting the additional hands for husbandry, tobacco crops ran higher roughly in proportion to the number of slaves or indentured servants. Crops ranged from twelve hundred pounds (planters with no bond labor) up to nearly twenty thousand pounds, or from a little over two up to forty hogsheads. Again using ten shillings per hundred for transforming tobacco values to sterling, we can put the incomes from tobacco production alone between £ 6 and £ 100 a year. Other sources of income for families with bond labor should not be ruled out. Doubtless off-season occupations such as riving staves or shingles, sawing plank, and making cereal crops occupied some productive time. Unfortunately only occasional data on this type of product appear, enough to call for acknowledgment but insufficient for measurement.

Nevertheless, with annual incomes of these dimensions from their tobacco crops, planters in this group had alternatives not open to the lowest income group. As respectable citizens with community obligations to act as overseers of roads, appraisers of estates and similar duties, they might choose to lay by something to see their sons and daughters decently started in turn as planters or wives of planters. Or they might within the limitations of their estates live the good life, balancing consumption against income. Social pressure must have urged them in this direction, to a round of activities that included local politics and such country entertainments as dances, horseracing, and cockfights, occasionally punctuated with drinking brawls complete with eye-gougings and other practices not usually associated with the genteel life of the planter. Whatever the choice it is difficult to see how the planter in these circumstances could add appreciably to his estate in a short period of years, or even in a lifetime.

Still further up the scale, the estates appraised at sums above £ 500 form an even smaller percentage of the total. The five £ 100 brackets between £ 500 and £ 1,000 include altogether 2.2 per cent of all estates. At first glance this small group appears to be a plusher version of the preceding: somewhat more slaves, larger tobacco crops, more personal goods including some luxury items. These are planters of substance, much closer to the stereotype, as the character and contents of their inventories show. And in their activities they moved on a higher plane. One had represented his county for a term in the General Assembly and another had served on the county court as a justice of the peace. In the matter of indebtedness, however, some interesting differences appear. Just over half the inventories list debts owed to the estate among the major assets. In a few cases the portion of total assets in the form of debts owed the estate runs to half or more.

What I think we see here is an emerging business or entrepreneurial element, a small group of planters with sources of income other than planting alone. All were planters in the sense that they, or their bond labor, produced tobacco crops. But the appreciable number in the creditor category have other concerns. The nature of these concerns appear more clearly in the most affluent element, whose members can be studied individually as cases.

This element includes all persons with estates inventoried at more than £ 1,000 sterling. In the decade 1690–1699, they represent 1.6 per cent of the total. They were the "great planters" of the day.

The smallest estate in personalty, that of Nicholas Gassaway of Anne Arundel County, was inventoried at £ 1,017 14s. 11½d. sterling; the largest, that of Henry Coursey of Talbot County, at £ 1,667 17s. 1¼d. Perhaps estates of this size would have cut a mean figure beside those of the sugar planters of the West Indies. In the northern Chesapeake of the closing years of the seventeenth century, they loom high.

The composition of these largest estates varies a bit from what we might expect of the great planter's holdings. Slaves comprise less than a quarter of the assets and, in several, less than a fifth. It should be remembered that this decade lies in the transition period when slaves were displacing indentured servants as field labor. Even so, the numbers seem unimpressive — often no greater than slave holdings in estates a third as large. By contrast, the number and the amount of assets in the form of debts owed the estate are striking. Altogether they comprised between a quarter and a half of the assets in individual estates. In one of the largest estates, debts owed the deceased came to 78 per cent of the total assets.

The inventories themselves give some clues as to how these large planters had become creditors. Occasionally an industrious appraiser included information on how the debtor had incurred his obligation: for a pipe of wine, for a parcel of steers, for corn, for rent of a certain property, for goods. In short, the great planter had also become a "trader." Frequently a portion of the inventory is simply labeled "in the store" and the contents of that room or building listed under this heading. Then the origin of the debts becomes clear. Sometimes they ran well over a hundred major items and were carefully listed under captions "sperate debts" and "desperate debts."

Putting this cross section or sample against the general outlines of the Chesapeake economy, I suggest the hypothesis that the men of first fortune belonged functionally to a class whose success stemmed from entrepreneurial activities as much as, or even more than, from their direct operations as producers of tobacco. The Chesapeake closely resembles pioneer economies of other times and places. It was a region with a relatively low ratio of population to resources and an equally low ratio of capital to resources. External commerce was characterized by heavy staple exports and high capital imports. Internally this flow created a current of high capital investment, full employment, profit inflation, and rising property values. The tobacco staple did not lend itself to bonanza agriculture, as did sugar in the West India islands where fortunes could be made in a decade. Consequently the Chesapeake planters did not go "back home" to dazzle the populace with their wealth. Their returns derived in the first instance from tobacco production, which afforded a competence, and secondly from enterprise, which gave greater rewards. As entrepreneurs, they gave the Chesapeake economy both organization and direction. They took the risks, made the decisions, and reaped the rewards or paid the penalties. And they worked unremittingly at these tasks, which could not be performed in their absence by the small planter or by overseers.

It is not easy to analyze the activities of this economic elite into neat categories. They were at once planters, political leaders, and businessmen. The first two roles tend to obscure the last. Their role in politics is a textbook commonplace. As planters they lived in the great tradition, some even ostentatiously. On this point testimony is abundant and unambiguous. Had they depended solely on the produce of their tobacco fields, they doubtless would have lived up to or beyond current income. And some did. But in fact many among them increased their fortunes substantially and a few spectacularly, while still maintaining their reputations as good livers. During the early years of the eighteenth century, when the tobacco trade was far from booming, some of the first families of the Chesapeake established themselves as permanent fixtures. Several had come to the first rank, or very near it, both in politics and wealth by 1700: the Taskers, the Catholic Carrolls, the Lloyds, and the Trumans. Others, less well known but eventually architects of equal or greater fortunes, were rising in the scale within another decade: the Bordleys, the Chews, the Garretts, the Dulanys, the Bennetts, and the Protestant Carrolls. The secret of their success was business enterprise, though almost to a man they lived as planters separated from the kind of urban community in which their more conspicuously entrepreneurial counterparts to the north had their residences and places of business. An examination of the chief forms of enterprise discloses the mechanisms by which they came to the top of the heap.

One of the most profitable enterprises and one most commonly associated with the great planters of the Chesapeake, land speculation, appears early in the eighteenth century in both Virginia and Maryland. The Virginia Rent Roll of 1704, admitted as imperfect but the best that could be done at the time, shows half a dozen holdings that suggest speculative intent. After these tentative beginnings, speculators moved quite aggressively during the administration of Spotswood and his successors, when huge grants in the vacant back country became commonplace events for privileged insiders, with the governors themselves sharing the spoils of His Majesty's bounty. In the more carefully regulated land system of Maryland, agents of the Lords Baltimore made a few large grants to favored persons like Charles Carroll the Settler in the first two decades of the century. During these same decades other wary speculators took up occasional large grants. The Maryland system compelled speculators to be cautious, because it exacted some money for the patents and made evasion of quitrents nearly impossible. But by the 1730's, eager speculators had glimpsed a vision of the possible returns and kept the land office busy issuing warrants for unpatented areas. For a relatively modest outlay a small number of Marylanders obtained assets with which they experimented for years before discovering the last trick in turning them to account.

Speculators capitalized their assets in two chief ways, both enormously profitable. First, as landlords of the wild lands, they leased to tenants who paid rents and at the same time improved their leaseholds by clearing, planting orchards, and erecting houses, barns, and fences. Almost exclusively long-term leases, either for years (commonly twenty-one) or for lives, these instruments specified the improvements to be made. Tenants who could not save from current income thus under compulsion contributed their bit to capital formation to the ultimate benefit of the landlord. Literary sources give the impression that tenancy was not very widespread, but the records tell another story. Something over a third of the planters in the lowest £ 100 bracket in Maryland leased their land. Secondly, the large landholder sold off plantation-size parcels as settlement enveloped his holdings and brought values to the desired level. Not content to leave this movement to chance, many speculators hastened the process by encouraging immigration and by directing the movement of settlers toward their own properties. Jonathan Hagar in Maryland and William Byrd in Virginia are two among many who attempted to enhance the value of their properties in this way. It is difficult to determine profits even for single speculators except for short periods. Experience must have varied widely, and undoubtedly some speculators failed. But some of the successful ones made incredible gains in a relatively short span of years.

Even more ubiquitous than the planter-speculator was the planter-merchant. The inventories and accounts contain much evidence on the organization of commerce in the tobacco counties of the Chesapeake. Hardly a parish lacked one or more country stores, often no more than a tiny hut or part of a building on the grounds of a planter who could supply, usually on credit, the basic needs of neighboring small producers — drygoods, hoes and other small implements, salt, sugar, spices, tea, and almost always liquor. Inventories show some small stores with a mere handful of those articles in constant demand. Others had elaborate stocks of women's hats, mirrors, mourning gloves, ribbons, patent medicines, and luxury goods. The names of several great families are associated with country stores, particularly in the earlier generations of the line. Frequently, storekeeping duties fell to a trusted servant or to a younger member of the family as a part of his training. Occasionally, an apprentice from one of the county families came to learn the mysteries of trade by measuring out fabrics or liquors and keeping the accounts.

As with land speculation, determining profits of merchants is next to impossible. Consumers complained bitterly of high markups, and a few storekeepers boasted of them. Even so, the country merchant's profits were not limited to sale of goods alone. He stood to gain on another transaction. He took his payment in tobacco, the crops of the two- to six-hogshead producers. The small planter participated directly in the consignment system of the early eighteenth century only to a limited extent. His petty wants and his small crop hardly justified the London merchant's time and trouble in maintaining him as a separate account. His nexus to the overseas market was the provincial merchant, who took tobacco at prices that allowed at least a small profit to himself on every hogshead.

Closely allied to merchandising, moneylending presents almost as great problems of analysis. The Chesapeake economy operated on an elaborate network of credit arrangements. Jefferson's famous remark that Virginia planters were a species of property attached to certain great British merchant houses may have been true of some planters, as it was of Jefferson himself. But the observation has created a mischievous view of credit relations between England and the tobacco colonies and does not describe the debt pattern within the area at all accurately. A full account awaits the onslaught of an industrious graduate student armed with electronic tapes and computers. Meanwhile the accounts can tell us something. Country merchants had to be prepared to extend credit beyond that for goods purchased by their customers. They paid for some of their customers at least the church tithes, the tax levies, and the freedom dues of indentured servants who had served their terms. These petty book debts could be collected with interest in any county court. Loans to artisans — the shoemakers, tanners, and blacksmiths who multiplied in number toward mid century — were of a different order. For working capital, the artisan in need of £ 5 to £ 20 and upward turned to men of means, the "traders." Far from abating, the demand for capital increased as the century wore on.

Investment opportunities were never lacking for planters with ready money or with credit in England. As lenders, they squarely faced the conflict of the law and the profits. By law they could take interest at 6 per cent for money loans and 8 per cent for tobacco loans. One wonders why the Carrolls chose to loan their £ 30,000 sterling at 6 per cent, even on impeccable securities. Could the answer be in part that returns at this rate equaled those from further investment in planting? At any rate they did choose to lend, following the example of Bennett and a dozen or so others.

Far more profitable as an investment opportunity, manufacturing exercised an enduring fascination on imaginative men of the Chesapeake. During Virginia Company days, before the first settlement of Maryland, glass and iron had figured among the projects launched under Company stimulus. Although these had come to ruin in the massacre of 1622, Virginians never gave up hope of producing iron. Their success was limited; but in the upper reaches of the Bay a combination of easily worked ore, limitless forests for charcoal, oyster shell, and water transportation from the furnace site invited exploitation. British syndicates moved first to establish the Principio Works and later the Nottingham and Lancashire works. These remained in British hands until the Revolutionary confiscations. Last of the big four, the Baltimore Iron Works (1733) became the largest producer and the biggest money-maker. Five Maryland investors subscribed the initial capital of £ 3,500 sterling. The Baltimore enterprise was a triumph for native capital, though technicians and technology were both imported from Britain. After the first three years of operation the partners received handsome dividends but always plowed a substantial part of the profits back into the enterprise. By the early 1760's the share of each partner was valued at £ 6,000 sterling. The five partners were among the first fortunes in Maryland.

Beyond iron making, other forms of enterprise (mostly small-scale manufacturing or processing) attracted investment capital. In nearly all areas of the Chesapeake some shipbuilding, cooperage, and milling establishments provided essential local services or commodities. None of these required either the capital outlay or the organization of an ironworks. Consequently, as enterprises they were attractive to investors with modest capital but large ambitions. In the area of Baltimore, flour milling developed major proportions after mid century, as the upper counties of Maryland found grain more profitable than tobacco as a field crop.

An astonishing percentage of the personal fortunes of the northern Chesapeake had their roots in law practice. While not entrepreneurial in a technical sense, the rewards went to the enterprising. During the seventeenth century lawyers were neither numerous nor always in good odor. Private persons attended to their own legal business in the courts. By 1700, the fashion had changed as the courts insisted on greater formality in pleading and as the cumbersome machinery of the common law compelled the uninstructed to turn to the professional. Pleading "by his attorney" swiftly replaced appearances *in propria persona.* Still the legal profession remained trammeled. Laws strictly regulated fees attorneys could take and kept these at levels low enough that the ablest members of the Maryland bar went on strike in the 1720's. What lawyers lacked in size of fees they made up in number of cases. An attorney might, and frequently did, bring thirty or forty cases to trial in a three- or four-day session of a county court. Had these been litigation over land, an impression widely held by students who use the *Virginia Reports* and the *Maryland Reports,* attorneys might have spent their entire time in title searches, examining witnesses, and preparing their cases. The court proceedings at large, however, show fifty cases of debt collection for every case over land; and sometimes the ratio runs as high as a hundred to one. One traveler to the Chesapeake, remarking on the "litigious spirit," wryly concluded that this spectacle of everybody suing everybody else was a kind of sport peculiar to the area. In fact, the numbers of suits grew out of the very arrangements — a tissue of book debts, bills of exchange, and promissory notes — that kept the mechanism operating.

In this milieu the lawyer had an enviable position. From his practice he derived a steady income freed from direct dependence on returns from the annual tobacco fleet. In a phrase, he had ready money the year 'round. Furthermore, he had an intimate knowledge of the resources and dependability of the planters in the county — and, indeed, throughout the province if he also practiced at the bar of the superior courts. Consequently he could take advantage of opportunities on the spot, whether they were bargains in land, sales of goods or produce, or tenants seeking leases. He could besides avoid the costs of litigation that inevitably arose as he involved himself in land speculation, lending, or merchandising, as many did. As a rule the lawyers did well, and the most enterprising moved into the highest brackets of wealth. Perhaps the most spectacular example, Thomas Bordley, a younger son of a Yorkshire schoolmaster, came from an impecunious immigrant apprentice in a Maryland law office to distinction in the law, in politics, and in Maryland society within the span of a short lifetime. After his premature death in 1726 his executors brought to probate the largest estate in the history of the province to that time.

Quite commonly, lawyers added a minor dimension to their income from office holding. A fair percentage of Maryland offices were sinecures that could be executed by deputies for a fraction of the fees. Most carried modest stipends, but a few eagerly-sought prizes paid handsomely. Baltimore's provincial secretary received £ 1,000 per annum.

This is not the place to argue the returns from planting, pure and simple. Many planters did well without other sources of income. But impressive fortunes went to those who, in addition, put their talents to work in some of the ways described above. A few engaged in all. The list is finite, for we are referring here to a small percentage of planters, those with estates above £ 1,000: in the decade 1690-1699 to 1.6 per cent, in 1710-1719 to 2.2 per cent, in 1730-1739 to 3.6 per cent, and in 1750-1759 to 3.9 per cent. When tabulated and examined for group characteristics, they resemble functionally a type that could easily come under that comprehensive eighteenth-century term, merchant. They look very unlike the planter of the moonlight-and-magnolias variety. It is a commentary on the prosperity of the northern Chesapeake that, as this favored category increased in percentage and in absolute numbers, so did the magnitude of its members' individual fortunes. The sample taken just before the turn of the century shows top fortunes between £ 1,000 and £ 2,000, with none above. The sample decade 1730-1739 includes an appreciable number over £ 2,000. The two largest were those of Samuel Chew (£ 9,937) and Amos Garrett (£ 11,508), both merchants. Even these did not match the fortunes left by Dr. Charles Carroll and Daniel Dulany the Elder in the decade 1750-1759, nor that of Benjamin Tasker in the next.

The poor were not excluded, individually or as a group, from the general prosperity of the Chesapeake. Four individuals — Thomas Macnemara, Thomas Bordley, Daniel Dulany, and Dr. Charles Carroll — moved up the scale from nothing to the top bracket of wealth, two of them from indentured servitude. These were extraordinary men, but their careers indicate the avenues open to their combination of talents for the law, land speculation, moneylending, merchandising, and manufacturing in which they engaged. Of course all were planters as well.

But for the mass, advance was by comparison glacial. The composition of the base on which such performances took place changed more slowly. In the fourth decade of the eighteenth century the percentage of planters in the lowest economic group, those with estates of £ 100 or less, had fallen to 54.7 per cent, in marked contrast to the 74.6 per cent of the decade 1690-1699. Between the same two sample decades the percentage in the next higher category of estates (£ 100 to £ 500) had increased to 35.7 per cent from 21.7 per cent. If this means that the poor were getting richer, it also means for the great majority that they were doing so by short and slow steps. Together, these two lowest categories still made up 90.4 per cent of the planting families in 1730-1739, as compared with 96.3 per cent in the last decade of the seventeenth century. Nonetheless, the shift toward a higher standard of living within this huge mass of lesser planters is quite as important a commentary on the economic well-being of the Chesapeake as is the growth in numbers and magnitude of the great fortunes.

It is never easy to know just how much to claim for statistical evidence. Perhaps there is enough here to raise doubts about the descriptive accuracy of reports from Chesapeake planters themselves. These sound like a protracted wail of hard times, rising occasionally in crescendo to prophesies of impending ruin. Yet even during the early and least prosperous decades, the northern Chesapeake experienced some growth. During the second quarter of the century and on into the following decades the samples made for this study indicate a quickened rate. The results worked no magic change in the way of life or economic station for the small planter, the mass of Maryland. These were always the overwhelming percentage of the producers. As a social group they come in for little notice. Their lives lack the glitter and incident that has made the great planter the focus of all eyes. By the standards of the affluent society theirs was a drab, rather humdrum, existence bound to the annual rhythm of the field crop. The highest rewards were for those who could transcend the routine of producing tobacco and develop the gainful activities that kept the economy functioning.

Colonial Roots of Popular Government

In the middle of the eighteenth century, a Scottish physician Andrew Hamilton visited the American colonies and severely criticized their political institutions. In Pennsylvania "their government is a kind of anarchy," he observed, in New Jersey "the House of Assembly . . . was chiefly composed of mechanics and ignorant wretches, obstinate in the last degree," while in Rhode Island, royal officials were afraid to "exercise their office for fear of the fury and unruliness of the people." Though Hamilton exaggerated, he correctly recognized that government in America was more turbulent than government in England. The colonists were laying the foundations for popular rule which matured from these colonial origins. This occurred more by accident rather than design. The first settlers expected that in America, as in England, political power would be the privilege of the great families and aristocrats. They also assumed that the mass of people would have little voice since property qualifications in England excluded most from the suffrage. Finally, all expected that the Crown, from which each colony derived its authority, would be the locus of ultimate power.

None of these assumptions proved true. The Crown was far away and often preoccupied with more important matters than governing the colonies. And the king's representatives in America, from the royal governors down to the lowliest customs officials, more often than not proved unfaithful and ineffective standard-bearers of British authority. In theory, the Crown and Parliament were supreme, but in practice, the Americans carved out large areas of self-government.

In every colony, as the following essay by Milton Klein demonstrates for New York, ambitious families emerged to provide local leadership. Wealthy landholders, who served as justices of peace, ruled their counties through courthouse rings. Rich merchants whose wealth gave them importance and influence at home and in London proved formidable antagonists to stubborn royal officials who dared enforce the Navigation Laws. Governors learned that the best way to stay in office and enjoy the financial rewards that sent them to the provinces in the first place, was to make their peace with the local power brokers.

The result was that the lines of authority in America were terribly confused. Not only was English authority easily flouted and silently subverted, but among the colonists themselves, chronic competition between rival American factions — the "ins" versus the "outs" — complicated the picture. Those on top at any one time, were never secure because the absence of a hereditary aristocracy, the abundance of resources, especially land, and the numerous other opportunities a new society offers the ambitious resulted in a social structure which was constantly in flux, especially at the top. The traditional deference of the common people to their social "betters," in whose hands power customarily resided, was slowly but effectively being eroded by social instability in America. First of all, a much larger percentage of adult males could vote in the colonies than could vote in Britain. Moreover, it became harder than ever to know to whom to defer in the colonies when so many competed for leadership. Surely it was unnecessary to defer to Crown officials, for they were often at the mercy of the colonial elite. Yet even powerful native ruling groups fell from power as others more ruthless, skillful or shrewd pushed them aside. The decline of deference was a psychological revolution necessary before popular rule — government based on the consent of, and participation by, the governed — could become practical. American colonists neither practiced nor believed in democracy, but colonial politics was clearly heading in that direction.

FOR FURTHER READING:

BAILYN, BERNARD. "Politics and Social Structure in Virginia." In *Seventeenth-Century America*, edited by James M. Smith. Chapel Hill: University of North Carolina Press, 1959.
KAMMEN, MICHAEL, ed. *Politics and Society in Colonial America: Democracy or Defense.* New York: Holt, Rinehart & Winston, 1967.*
SYDNOR, CHARLES. *American Revolutionaries in the Making.* Original title: *Gentlemen Freeholders.* New York: The Macmillan Company, Free Press, 1965.*

Asterisk denotes paperback edition.

Democracy and Politics in Colonial New York MILTON M. KLEIN

The classic description of the political structure of colonial New York was provided by Carl Becker a half-century ago. In his doctoral dissertation and in two articles in the *American Historical Review,* Becker set forth the thesis that throughout most of the colonial period provincial politics were controlled by a few rich and powerful families whose wealth was based on land and commerce. This small coterie, linked among themselves by marriage, exercised a type of leadership that was "essentially medieval in nature — that is, informal and personal"; and political parties were consequently little more than "factions based on personal influence." Party allegiance was thus determined more by personal ties than by differences of political or economic principle, and "personal loyalty, rather than faith in a proposition was the key to political integrity."

Becker did single out one fundamental source of disagreement between political factions, the continuing dispute between governor and assembly, but he qualified this. While those supporting the executive at any particular moment might be designated the "court" or "British" party and those opposing him the "popular" or "anti-British" party, men moved into or out of the governor's "interest" not out of conviction or principle but rather as he was able to grant them special favors. When political leaders desired to enlarge their followings, Becker insisted, they did not appeal for popular support by party programs but rather engineered "prudential intermarriages" with other families of the aristocracy. The alliances thus created constituted the real sources of political strength.

The political stage could be monopolized by the aristocracy, according to Becker, because the bulk of the colony's population constituted a passive and inarticulate audience, or, at best, a well-trained and obedient claque. The suffrage was ex-

Source: Milton M. Klein, "Democracy and Politics in Colonial New York," *New York History,* vol. 40 (1959), pp. 221–246.

tremely limited, and the undemocratic landholding system of the colony placed most of the population in economic dependence upon a few great proprietors, who insured the political fidelity of their tenants by the coercive surveillance that open voting made possible. Nominations were managed by the aristocracy, tenants were herded to the polls to register their approval of hand-picked candidates, and if revolt should threaten, the leaders could meet it by deferring the election or holding it at odd times and inaccessible places.

The democratization of the political machinery, Becker maintained, took place in the last half of the eighteenth century, and particularly after 1765; and the evidences of the change were the rise of popular nominating devices like the mass meeting, the use of the press to rally popular support, and the disappearance of the "purely personal element" as the cement of political association. A newly articulate electorate took advantage of the democratized machinery to demand a larger share in the political process, and as the Revolution approached, the conflict between mother country and colony was fought alongside the local struggle between the old aristocracy and the new democracy.

Becker's analysis parallels that drawn for most of the other colonies, and his conclusion that the Revolution in New York had a dual character has been generalized into the oft-repeated and felicitous aphorism that the war was fought over the issue of "who should rule at home" as well as over the issue of "home rule."

Both the analysis and the conclusion are still attractive, but recent reappraisals of the political structure of colonial Massachusetts suggest the desirability of a fresh examination of the New York scene. No attempt can be made in a short paper to subject Becker's conclusions to exhaustive reexamination, but three questions arising from his analysis will be reconsidered here: 1. Were New York's political parties largely medieval-type personal factions? 2. Was the electoral machinery controlled by the aristocracy through the landlord-tenant relationship? and 3. Was the franchise severely restricted?

As Becker saw it, the political divisions of the first half of the eighteenth century were personal in character, and the so-called parties that developed during this period were no better than "factions based on personal influence." As evidence, Becker offered the well-known contest between the Livingston and De Lancey families, which appears to run like an unbroken thread through the colony's political history. Becker did not suggest the origin or the basis of the contest, but he saw these two families emerging, after fifty years of feuding among the various factions, as "the leaders in the struggle which was, though political in some degree, after all very largely personal in its nature . . . and that the struggle was personal rather than political is indicated by the fact that the parties were known by the names of their respective leaders."

The rivalry between the Livingstons and the De Lanceys was indeed long and bitter, but their disagreement was neither private nor personal in its origination, and the political parties that formed around them were rooted in substantial differences of a political and economic character. The contest began during the administration of Governor William Burnet (1720–1728), and it was inspired not by simple attachment or opposition to the governor's interest but rather by large differences between two rival economic groups over Indian policy and the fur trade.

Robert Livingston, the founder of that family's American fortunes and the first

Lord of the Livingston Manor, was also the colony's Secretary for Indian Affairs. A fur trader in addition, he conceived an ambitious and far-sighted program of imperial-Indian relations designed to promote the interests of the Empire and of his own trade at the same time.

The heart of the Livingston program was a discontinuance of the traffic in furs that had developed between some traders in Albany and certain Montreal fur dealers. The latter got their skins from the Indians and from the French trappers (*coureurs de bois*) who lived among the western tribes. They then exchanged the pelts on a wholesale basis with the Albanians, who paid in English "stroud" and wares, which the natives preferred to the inferior French manufactures. In conducting this trade, both the Canadians and the Albanians ignored the interests of their home governments. French policy made the export of beaver from New France a legal monopoly and required all skins to be shipped to France; English policy demanded that the western Indians be diverted from their French allegiance, a policy that could hardly succeed as long as the natives depended upon Montreal for their supply of cloth, guns, and hardware.

Livingston was disturbed at the continuing business relationship between Albany and Montreal for economic as well as political reasons. As a "direct" or "retail" trader who sent his agents into the Indian country to secure skins directly from the native source, Livingston came into competition with those Albanians who conducted their trade "wholesale" through the Montreal merchants. He became convinced that unless the Indians could be induced to redirect the flow of furs to the English, France would ultimately dominate not only the fur trade but the Indians and the Continent as well. To prevent this, he suggested that a chain of fortified posts be built in the Indian country to impress the natives with British power and to serve as centers of the fur trade, that young New Yorkers be trained as scouts and "bushlopers" to compete with the *coureurs de bois*, and that Protestant missionaries be sent among the natives to counteract the work of the Jesuits. To make the program effective, a ban on trade between Albany and Montreal must be imposed.

Around Livingston rallied the other retail traders, the imperialists, and the land speculators with holdings in the Mohawk Valley. The success of the Livingston scheme would pacify the natives, encourage settlement in the back country, and boost land values. Men like Robert Livingston, Jr., Lewis Morris, and Cadwallader Colden joined to promote the new policy. They organized a "Livingston-Morris Party," secured the support of Governor Burnet, and launched the program with a law prohibiting trade with Canada and the establishment of a trading post and fort at Oswego, on Lake Ontario.

An opposition party was quickly organized by the wholesale traders and their allies, and its leadership was provided by Stephen De Lancey, Peter Schuyler, and Adolph Philipse. Schuyler was the spokesman of the Albanians who monopolized the traffic with Montreal; De Lancey and Philipse represented the New York merchants who supplied the traders with their English wares. The Livingston program threatened their interests in two ways. The prohibitory legislation would undermine the source of their prosperity, and the money for the new trading posts would be secured by fresh import levies that would fall most heavily on merchants like De Lancey who were so deeply involved in the Canada trade.

The immediate victory of the Livingstons was shortly nullified as the De Lanceys managed to win control of the assembly, to oust Livingston as speaker in favor of Adolph Philipse, and to secure a royal disallowance of the law barring trade with

Canada; but the significance of the contest, in terms of the Becker thesis, is the politico-economic character of the party division and the superficial part that personal relationships played in the contest. Family ties, indeed, served less to clarify the lines of political divergence than to obscure them. Thus, Stephen De Lancey and Peter Schuyler, leaders of the anti-Livingston forces, were both related to Robert Livingston by marriage, the one as nephew, the other as brother-in-law; the De Lancey's son, Peter, married the daughter of Cadwallader Colden, a leader of the Livingston faction!

Kinship was equally inconspicuous in dictating the political loyalty of the second generation of the Livingston family. Philip Livingston inherited his father's wealth, but not his political principles. Himself a Canada trader, he was unenthusiastic about the Livingston-Burnet trade program. While he remained nominally allied with his father's former supporters, thus gaining a seat on the Governor's Council under Burnet, he also maintained good relations with the De Lanceys, not quite certain which of the Indian policies would become permanent. This happy faculty of keeping a discreet foot in both camps served Livingston especially well during the hectic days of the Zenger Trial. Personal relationship should have placed him in the camp of the Zengerite "popular" party, since its leaders were his father's old friends, Lewis Morris, James Alexander, Cadwallader Colden, and William Smith, Sr.; but as a member of the Executive Council, he found himself, perforce, one of the De Lancey "court" party. Publicly, Livingston professed his attachment to the De Lanceys, unwilling to jeopardize his place on the council; privately, he lent his aid to the Zengerites in their efforts to thwart Governor William Cosby. But Livingston's defection from the De Lanceys was not the result of his personal affection for or his family ties with the Alexander-Morris group. Cosby's high-handed tactics in challenging existing land titles simply threatened Livingston's own fortune.

Superficially, the dispute between Cosby and his critics revolved about the governor's attempt to collect the salary paid to Rip Van Dam, who had served as acting governor during the interval between Cosby's appointment and his arrival in New York. To collect, and to keep the case away from a jury, Cosby established a Court of Exchequer in which the proceedings could be conducted. Livingston, along with the Zengerite leaders, feared that the new juryless court might also be used to achieve Cosby's personal ambition to carve out a landed estate for himself. When Cosby began to resurrect old land titles and to demand quit rents long in arrears, Livingston took alarm. Some of his own land acquisitions from the Indians were so tainted that they could hardly stand the light of scrupulous examination. Land titles, he conceded, were "not drawn in right form" and "flaws may be found in Severall of them." To James Alexander, the mouthpiece of the Zengerites, he wrote that "If Mr. Van Dam had suffered himself to be devoured, certainly another Morcell would have followed, [and] no Person could have expected to escape." In extending his secret support to the Zenger leadership, Livingston confessed frankly that "we Change Sides as Serves our Interest best."

For the next two decades, the Livingstons pursued the same calculating political course, now allying with the De Lanceys, now opposing them, and at times preserving a cautious neutrality. When Governor George Clinton (1743–1753) turned upon Philip Livingston and attacked him for defrauding the Indians and trading with the enemy during King George's War, the family renewed their alliance with the De Lanceys. With the death of Philip Livingston, the second manor lord, in 1749, the personal ties between the Livingstons and the Alexander-Morris group became even stronger, but the family remained in the De Lancey fold while the old Zengerites moved into the circle of "the court." Not until 1754 did the descendants of Robert Livingston and his earliest political allies rejoin forces, and again it was "interest" not friendship that determined the Livingston choice. The De Lancey-controlled assembly refused to assist the family in its dispute with Massachusetts over the manor's boundary and was slow in soliciting Parliament to defer the new Iron Act long enough to allow the manor's iron works to be expanded. In deserting the De Lanceys once again, the Livingstons demonstrated how well they had learned the hard lesson that in politics there was "no such thing as friendship, abstracted from political Views."

In the light of the above evidence, it is difficult to accept Becker's assertion that "strictly speaking . . . there were no political parties" but rather "two centers of influence," or that family connections provided the solid underpinnings of the colony's political structure. Contemporary observers were well aware of the tenuous character of family loyalty as the cohesive element in political organization. James Alexander himself confessed with a wisdom born out of long experience that "Interest often connects people who are entire strangers and sometimes separates those who have the strongest natural ties." William Smith, Jr., conceded that the Livingston party "did not always proceed from motives approved of by that family." And Cadwallader Colden, a veteran of New York's political battles, summed up his own extensive acquaintance with the colony's history in the observation that although parties "at different times have taken their denominations from some distinguished Person or Family who have appeared at their head," their roots lay in the "different political and religious Principles of the Inhabitants."

The Revolution may well have hastened the transformation of New York's political parties from "personal factions" to modern-type associations on "a basis of principle," as Becker suggested, but the process had been initiated early in the eighteen century. The political rivalry between the Livingstons and the De Lanceys bears a closer resemblance to the later contests between Federalists and Democratic-Republicans than it does to the medieval feud between the Guelphs and the Ghibellines. And if Becker is right in insisting that the "essence of the aristocratic method" in politics is "that men are governed by personality rather than by principle," then colonial New York's early political parties were less aristocratic than democratic.

Next to the marriage relationship, the principal instrument of aristocratic political control, according to Becker, was "the economic relation of tenant to proprietor." New York's undemocratic system of landholding, perhaps the most undemocratic of all the colonies, appears at first glance to substantiate Becker's thesis. A few individuals engrossed vast estates, manorial and non-manorial; most small farmers held their lands as tenants rather than as owners; and the terms of many leases were irritating and onerous, involving personal services of a medieval nature and restrictions on the sale and use of the property. From these conditions, Becker drew the inference that tenant voters were politically dependent upon the will of their economic overlords. The inference was never specifically documented, Becker being content with the statement: "That tenant voters would be largely influenced by lords of manors is perhaps sufficiently obvious."

Economic power certainly endowed the great proprietors with a large share of political influence, but landlord control was neither automatic nor absolute, nor were lessees universally at the mercy of the owners because of stringent conditions of tenure. The leases on the Livingston Manor were generally considered among the most burdensome, but even here some tenants held their lands on generous terms. In 1737, for example, Philip Livingston granted land to some German families rent-free for the first nine years and supplied each of them with three horses, two cows, and provisions for a year besides. Three years later he offered leases "gratis" and others rent-free for the first ten years in order to attract "good people." On the James Duane estate, such liberal terms were not unusual.

Tenants on all the estates were usually permitted to begin farming without any down payment, rents were often nominal, and non-payment was not always followed by eviction. In 1757, William Smith, Jr., reported that on the Van Rensselaer and Livingston Manors, rents had "as yet been neither exacted nor paid" even though they amounted to only a tenth of the produce of the leaseholds. The total rent on a 160 acre farm was seldom more than twenty-five dollars, and some lands rented for as little as two or four pounds per 100 acre.

Tenant status did not render the small farmers politically impotent, nor did it preclude their political independence. On the Westchester County manors there was a considerable amount of self-government, the "inhabitants" of Philipsburgh, for example, meeting regularly to "mak[e] town laws" and to choose constables, collectors, assessors, poundmasters, clerks, and highway overseers. Even where political "bossism" prevailed, it was not impossible for the small farmers to revolt against the "organization" nominee and threaten to set up a candidate of their own. In 1748 such an incipient revolt occurred among the farmers of Canajoharie against the Albany County machine, and two years later a similar protest movement originated among the tenants of Henry Beekman, Jr., in Ulster and Dutchess counties. Beekman's machine was a well-disciplined one, but not even his political control was foolproof. In 1751 he expressed fears that unless his friends united around his nominee for the assembly seat, the place would go to "one w[hi]ch we will Like worse."

According to Becker, once the political "bosses" of the counties selected the candidates for provisional office, the tenant voters followed "their lead as a matter of course." But if the landlords were so sure of the votes of their tenantry, one wonders why they went to such considerable extents to buy votes. Not even the most powerful of the political machines or the greatest proprietor could guarantee success in an election campaign without a large war chest. By 1753, the business of "election jobbing" and political bribery was so widespread that it became the subject of public protest from one anguished citizen who was outraged that so many voters should be willing to barter away their prized and traditional franchise for no more than "Beer and Brandy," "a Pound of Beef," or "a Treat" and "a Frolick."

The practice was common in Beekman territory, Henry Beekman regularly providing his tenants with free beef, bacon, cider, and rum a day or two before the polls opened. In Albany, votes were bought at prices that ranged from a mere bottle of wine to as much as forty pounds! Perhaps the most revealing evidence to dispute Becker's contention that tenants merely registered the wishes of the great proprietors is the experience of Robert Livingston in 1761. Despite his economic power as lord of the manor, Livingston could not guarantee the political adherence of his tenants unless they were paid for their votes. "The Camps will not move to an Election without being payed for their time," he advised his friend, Abraham Yates, Jr., who was running for the assembly seat in Albany County. At forty shillings a man, however, Livingston had no doubts that "they may be had." He warned Yates quite plainly that unless sufficient funds could be raised, the election would be lost, "for money are the Senues of War, in this as well as in other affairs."

Just as Becker appears to have overestimated the extent of political control that stemmed from proprietorship, so did he exaggerate the role that open voting played in insuring landlord control. Becker's statement that "Every voter was watched, we may be sure, and his record was known," is another of those irritating generalizations based largely on assumption rather than proof. As a matter of fact, there is little evidence to suggest that tenants considered *viva voce* voting either oppressive or undemocratic, or that the great proprietors regarded it as essential to their political control.

There were many small farmer uprisings in the eighteenth century, culminating in the "Great Rebellion of 1766," but the complaints of the tenantry always centered around land titles, rents, security of tenure, and their personal obligations to the manor lords. The secret ballot was never one of the demands of the dissidents. How lightly the aristocracy considered the practice as an instrument of political control is revealed by the attempt, in 1769, to pass a secret ballot bill in the assembly. The bill was given its strongest endorsement in the house by the Livingston party, the traditional spokesmen of the landed interest, and was attacked by the De Lanceys on the grounds that it would enable "crafty and subtle" lawyers to *influence* the voters! The question was argued most heatedly in New York City where landlord control was not a significant issue; and among the most ardent supporters of the measure, in addition to the Livingstons, were the Sons of Liberty, a group that was entirely out of sympathy with the tenants during their "rebellion" a few years earlier.

When the written ballot was ultimately incorporated into the New York State Constitution of 1777, it was done at the suggestion not of a representative of the tenantry but of John Jay, whose conservatism is epitomized in his comment that "those who own the country ought to govern it." The innovation did not work any great change in tenant voting habits or in landlord control. Van Rennselaer tenants continued to elect the patroon or a member of his family to the state legislature, and for twenty-one years they chose a Van Rensselaer to represent them in Congress.

If *viva voce* voting was an essential ingredient of the undemocratic political structure of New York, then there is patent incongruity in the failure of both the aristocracy and tenantry to recognize it as such. Undoubtedly the landed aristocrats exercised great influence in the colony's politics, but their influence is better ascribed to voter illiteracy and indifference than to open balloting or the landlord-tenant relationship. It is not without significance that when in 1788 a tenant in Albany County recalled publicly that he had often in the past given his "assent" to the will of his landlord "in supporting his political importance," he added: "I was ignorant of my own rights."

Becker's contention that suffrage restrictions left over half the adult white male population without any political privileges is difficult to corroborate because of the few census returns and the even fewer election statistics available for the colonial period. The figure is open to considerable question, however, based upon Becker's own reckoning. The unfranchised, he claimed, included the smaller freeholders, the leasehold tenants, and the "mechanics," and this resulted in an electorate so narrow that in 1790 it comprised only twelve per cent of the total population. The latter figure is, in the first place, deceptive, since the "total" population included women, children, and Negroes. A recent calculation of the electorate in New York City in

1790 discloses that virtually 100 per cent of the *adult white males* qualified under the suffrage requirement of the state constitution of 1777. Moreover, Becker was absolutely wrong in excluding the mechanics of New York City and Albany on the ground that they were neither freeholders nor freemen, and in casually dismissing the number of freemen in these cities as "insignificant."

The freemen of Albany and New York City were those merchants and handicraftsmen who had been admitted to the freedom of the town by the municipal corporation. The practice was a European one, intended originally to reserve the benefits of town industry to its inhabitants, but in New York freemanship quickly lost its original character. Wholesale traders were early exempt from its limitations, the city never enforced the monopoly, and by the eighteenth century an increasing number of tradespeople were carrying on business in open violation of the law. New Yorkers continued to seek the privilege, however, for the political rather than the economic benefits it bestowed: freemen along with freeholders could vote in municipal and provincial elections and hold municipal office.

In New York City, freemanship was conferred liberally, and the number of freemen who participated in the city's elections was scarcely "insignificant." Indeed, freemen played a decisive role at the polls. The privilege was not restricted to skilled laborers, the term "handicraftsman" being interpreted so loosely that among those admitted under this category were carmen, porters, painters, fishermen, boatmen, gardeners, yeomen, and mariners, along with others classified simply as "laborers." The cost of purchasing the freedom of the town might well have served to bar mass admissions. In Albany it ranged from thirty-six shillings to three pounds twelve shillings for merchants, and from eighteen to thirty-six shillings for handicraftsmen. In New York City, rates fluctuated similarly, merchants paying from twenty shillings to five pounds and handicraftsmen from six shillings to one pound four shillings, with three pounds and twenty shillings being the respective averages. However, skilled laborers did not find the sum excessive during a period when they earned an average of more than seven shillings a day, and natives of the city and those completing an apprenticeship in the city were even less concerned with the cost, since they could secure their freedom by simply paying the clerical fee of about two shillings. Finally, in New York City, those citizens "that are poor and not able to purchase their Freedoms" were admitted "gratis," by a decree of the Common Council in 1703.

These liberal regulations permitted an increasing number of mechanics and laborers to secure the freedom of the city. By the middle of the eighteenth century, they comprised two-thirds of all the admissions; in 1765, they made up almost half the new freemen. Still another index of the increasing accessibility of freemanship is the rising number of persons admitted as "Registrants" rather than "Purchasers," the former being those who because of their birth or apprenticeship in New York merely had to have their names recorded on the rolls and pay the nominal clerical fees. From 1735 to 1740, three times as many new freemen were registered as purchased their freedom, and in 1765 twice as many were admitted by registration as by purchase.

Albany's regulations paralleled those of New York City, freemanship here too proving more important as a political than as an economic institution. The town fathers were less interested in barring non-freemen from the economic life of the city than in encouraging them to purchase their freedom. Here also the privilege was extended liberally, natives of the city paying only a few shillings to be registered and others being admitted free. In 1702, for example, the right was conferred by action of the Common Council on the entire military company stationed at the fort! About the only persons disfranchised in Albany as a result were bound servants and foreigners not naturalized.

Freemanship played a vital role in the political life of the two largest cities of the colony of New York. In New York City itself, admissions to freemanship serve as a kind of barometer of political activity, rising in periods of political excitement and falling during the calms between political storms. Freemen were not "an insignificant portion of the electorate," as Becker believed, nor was the institution of freemanship a handmaiden of the aristocracy's system of political control. In the elections of 1768 and 1769 in New York City, no less than two-thirds of the voting electorate were freemen. Freemanship was not an obstacle to popular participation in politics but rather a democratic device which opened the polls to all classes of citizens and gave virtually all the adult white males the opportunity of exercising the franchise.

Outside of Albany and New York City, the franchise was probably more restricted, but perhaps not nearly as much as Becker indicated. The large number of tenant farmers who made up the bulk of the rural population were not necessarily barred from voting by the colony's suffrage restrictions. In 1699 the legislature limited the right to vote in provincial elections (apart from the freemen of New York City and Albany) to freeholders over twenty-one years of age who possessed lands or tenements to the value of forty pounds, free of all encumbrances; but two years later it defined as "freeholder" any person who held land for his own life or that of his wife's, mortgages notwithstanding. The modification amounted to a liberalization since it qualified all those tenants whose leases ran for a term of lives or for at least twenty-one years.

The number of persons thus enfranchised is difficult to determine in the absence of sufficient tax rolls. However, all the tenants on the Livingston and Van Rensselaer Manors undoubtedly qualified as freeholders, leases on the former being for at least one life and those on the latter being freehold estates. The status of the tenants on the Van Cortlandt and Philipse Manors is less clear, but whatever the terms of their leases, the tenants of the Westchester County manors were regarded as politically powerful. In any case contemporaries were unable to draw clear distinctions in tenant status, Lieutenant Governor Cadwallader Colden reporting to the Board of Trade in 1765 that all the farmers in the province were regarded as holding their lands in "fee simple." This would presumably have made all of them eligible to vote providing their lands were of sufficient value.

Just how many estates were valued at forty pounds or more is not known, but contemporaries like the historian, William Smith, Jr., complained that the great proprietors had a tendency to rate their lands "exorbitantly high." On the manors, where the assessors were selected locally, it would not be difficult for the manor lords to secure courtesy valuations of forty pounds for as many of their leaseholds as they desired. Certainly tenants played an important and at times a decisive role in elections in Albany, Westchester, and Dutchess Counties, but in the absence of fuller statistical data, their precise numerical significance is unknown. A few figures are available, but they are disappointingly inconclusive. In Westchester County in 1763, for example, less than 25 per cent of the adult white male population was able to meet the *sixty-pound* freehold qualification for service on juries. In Albany

County in 1720, however, about 44 per cent of the adult white males were listed as freeholders in a census of that year, and in New York City at least 48 per cent were freeholders in 1768.

If disfranchisement under the existing suffrage requirements was a source of tenant discontent, it was singularly missing, along with *viva voce* voting, among the grievances loudly voiced by rural leaseholders during the agrarian disturbances of the 1750's and 1760's.

One other basis of disfranchisement is worth noting. Catholics and Jews were both barred from the polls by actions of the assembly in 1701 and 1737, respectively, but the effect of these restrictions was minimal. The number of Catholics in the colony was insignificant, and the law seems not to have been applied to Jews with any regularity. In the city of New York, where virtually all of the Jews of the province resided, the poll lists of 1761, 1768, and 1769 carry such Jewish names as Moses Benjamin Franks, Baruch Hays, Judah Hays, Solomon Hays, Benjamin Laziere, Hayman Levy, Isaac Moses, Aaron Myer, and Isaac Myer.

Somewhat more information exists for those who *did* vote than for those who *could* vote. In New York City, voting returns for four years disclose the following degrees of participation:

	Adult White Males	Number of Votes	Per Cent of Adult White Males
1735	1465	812	55.4
1761	2581	1447	56.1
1768	3589	1924	53.6
1769	3733	1515	40.6

In Westchester County, figures are available for the famous poll of 1733 on the green of St. Paul's Church, Eastchester, in which Lewis Morris, recently deposed from the chief justiceship by Governor Cosby because of his role in the Van Dam affair, ran for the assembly seat. In that election, which became a *cause célèbre* in the Zenger Trial, participation was smaller than in the New York City polls already noted:

Adult White Males	Number of Votes	Per Cent of Adult White Males
1276	420	32.9

If participation in elections during the colonial period was only as extensive as it was in 1788, when about half of those eligible in New York City voted, then the electorate of the colony was still an extremely broadly based one, amounting to virtually all the adult white males in New York City (and probably in Albany), and to about 65 per cent in the rural counties. The latter figure, moreover, may well be an underestimate in view of the fact that transportation difficulties, political indifference, and illiteracy kept rural participation in elections below the level of New York City's. The *qualified* electorate in the rural areas may quite possibly, then, have been as large as that of New York City and Albany.

While there is no intention of suggesting that the reappraisal offered in this paper is conclusive, there appears to be enough evidence to warrant redrawing the conventional picture of colonial New York's politics. Surely Becker's relegation of early political parties to quasi-feudal factions of a personal nature requires reconsideration in view of the continuing economic self-interest, rather than the ties of blood and marriage, which explains the political tergiversations of great families like the Livingstons and De Lanceys. Their political somersaults placed them alternately within or outside the circle of "the court," but this was purely incidental. The De Lanceys could shift from the gubernatorial to the popular side without disturbing the essential bases of their party organization, and the Livingstons could similarly pose as champions of prerogative or flaming representatives of the people depending upon their own political or economic principles. That such political gyrations disturbed family ties or personal relationships was also quite incidental. Coldens married De Lanceys and Livingstons married Alexanders without reconciling existing political enmities between the respective families.

One of the Livingstons diagnosed the fundamental bases of the colony's political alignments with acute perception when he noted of the Morrises that they "set their witts to work to gain a party" only when their personal interests were "touched." Kinship took but second place to "interest."

There appears considerable exaggeration, too, in Becker's impression of early parties as highly informal in character and undisciplined in organization. Party machinery seems to have been well developed long before 1765, with party "bosses," campaign chests, vote-getting devices, and patronage rewards all in existence. Appeals for popular support on the grounds of "principle" and through the medium of the press were common in the late 1740's and early 1750's. "Paper war" accompanied almost every election. That of 1750 in Westchester County produced a particularly heavy barrage of pamphlets and broadsides. Two years later, the election campaign in New York City was so violent that the printer of one of the local newspapers, the *Gazette,* made public apology for the many vituperative essays that appeared in its columns. During 1754–1755, the controversy over the founding of King's College generated so much literary heat in the *New York Mercury* that its printer was frequently compelled to publish supplements to carry the non-controversial news and regular advertisements.

The frequency with which political leaders resorted to the press and the regularity with which they lured voters to the polls with financial blandishments suggest a far greater degree of political independence among the small farmer electorate than Becker assumed. The economic bond between landlord and tenant was never so strong that shrewd party leaders could afford to take the latter's allegiance for granted. Even so firmly entrenched a political leader as Henry Beekman was careful to solicit the wishes of his constituents and to introduce legislation in the assembly that would prove "Beneficiall for the county." Other party leaders were equally aware of the strength of the independent voter. When the triumvirate of young lawyers, William Livingston, William Smith, Jr., and John Morin Scott, undertook to thwart the Anglican scheme to establish King's College on terms favorable to the Church of England, their political strategy was to arouse the country voters to deluge the assembly with petitions against the plan and thus to maintain such "an unremitting pressure from their constituents" as to keep "irresolute" assemblymen "warm in their attachment to the anti-Episcopal cause." And while they sought support from the wealthy landlords who controlled political machines in the rural counties, their major appeal was addressed to the small farmers themselves, with local lawyers, public officials, and Presbyterian clergymen acting as their agents and campaign managers.

The electorate was not only more articulate and more active than Becker believed, but it was also more extensive. Even the incomplete figures offered in this paper indicate a franchise that was surprisingly broadly based, particularly in New York City and Albany where about one-third of the adult white male population of the colony resided, and an electorate that took advantage of its suffrage in at least as great a measure as did the qualified voters under the new state constitution after the Revolution.

The Revolution in New York was not "the open door through which the common freeholder and the unfranchised mechanic and artisan pushed their way into the political arena," to use Becker's language, simply because the door had never really been closed throughout most of the colonial period. The local aristocracy did occupy a commanding position in the colony's politics, and they continued to do so after independence; but the explanation for their political leadership must be sought in factors other than the strength of family ties, their economic power as landlords, or an excessively restricted franchise.

Religion in the New World

"But it does me no injury for my neighbor to say there are twenty gods, or no God. It neither picks my pocket nor breaks my leg," wrote Thomas Jefferson in the 1780s. Few of those who settled America would have agreed with the Sage of Monticello. Most early European settlers, especially the middle classes and the peasantry, which supplied the bulk of the immigrants, believed that man's relations with God were the central experience of life. Yet by Jefferson's time, and increasingly so since, most Americans have been more preoccupied with life in this world than in the next. The emergence of a secular outlook facilitated the ultimate triumph of religious tolerance and the separation of church and state, since people who are indifferent toward religion are less likely to insist on conformity from dissenters and persecute them for heterodoxy, than those who are preoccupied with salvation and certain that their faith is the only true road to Heaven.

Tolerance and separation of church and state — two foundations of the American religious tradition — did not simply await the corrosive effects of secularism on religious belief, as Perry Miller explains in the following essay. Most colonists brought across the ocean the common assumption of the time that no well-ordered society could exist without an established church to which all people belonged, which all supported financially, and which all accepted as the "true" faith. The Protestant Reformation, however, had divided Christendom into dozens of competing denominations, each claiming to be the only authentic interpretation of Christianity. It also triggered a century of religious wars and persecutions that sent defeated minorities in search of refuge to America. Puritans came to Massachusetts, Catholics to Maryland, Quakers and German Lutherans to Pennsylvania. But the persecuted, with some exceptions, did not seek freedom for all men. Their formula was freedom for themselves, but not for others who were "heretics." Diversity, however, played havoc with efforts to create in the colonies state churches that tolerated no dissent. In some, as in Virginia and Massachusetts, dissenters became so numerous and influential that eventually the established churches grudgingly made concessions and later, during the Revolutionary era, lost their privileged positions. Elsewhere, such as in Pennsylvania, there was never a state church because the Quaker founders believed, as a matter of principle rather than of Jeffersonian expediency, that faith was a private and holy affair between man and God and that state involvement would only corrupt the church and oppress those seeking God.

FOR FURTHER READING:

GREENE, EVARTS B. *Religion and the State: The Making & Testing of an American Tradition.* Ithaca, N.Y.: Cornell University Press, 1959.*
MEAD, SIDNEY E. *The Lively Experiment.* New York: Harper & Row, Publishers, 1963.*
SWEET, WILLIAM W. *Religion in Colonial America.* New York: Cooper Square Publishers, 1942.*

Asterisk denotes paperback edition.

The Contribution of the Protestant Churches to Religious Liberty in Colonial America   PERRY MILLER

While endeavouring to formulate these remarks I have come to suspect that there may possibly lurk in the title of my paper a misleading implication. The word "contribution" would seem to connote on the part of the Protestant churches a deliberate and concerted effort toward the triumph of religious liberty. Those of us who prize ecclesiastical freedom would like to feel that our colonial ancestors of their own free will and choice undertook the march to liberty. Liberal-minded historians in particular are prone to sing the praises of this individual or that church for furthering this advance; they are inclined to gloss over or to apologize for the men and the institutions that hindered it.

Such an attitude, though inspired by the most admirable of motives, has been, I am convinced, an encumbrance to the student of history. There is no way to deny — and as far as I can see, no use in denying — that Protestants coming to this country in the seventeenth century were almost unanimous in their conviction that toleration was a dangerous and heathen notion. They came fresh from Europe of the Reformation, where experience had demonstrated that if two divergent churches were permitted to exist within striking distance of each other, it would only be a question of time before throats were cut. And Protestants were far from deploring this belligerency. If you believe, as men believed in that era, that you are altogether on the Lord's side, and that your enemies are and must be entirely on the devil's, you can see no virtue in the idea of tolerating them. Statesmen knew that a policy of toleration would not work; theologians were grimly determined that it never should work. As the Reverend Nathaniel Ward of Ipswich in Massachusetts Bay emphatically declared:

> He that is willing to tolerate any Religion, or descrepant way of Religion besides his own, unless it be in matters merely indifferent, either doubts of his own, or is not sincere in it. He that is willing to tolerate any unsound Opinion, that his own may also be tolerated, though never so sound, will for a need hang God's Bible at the Devil's girdle.

When a Protestant church came into a colony at the beginning of settlement, with no other churches on the ground, with a clear field before it, that church deliberately set up an exclusive régime, it conscientiously strove to establish one official church in absolute uniformity, it frankly employed the civil power to compel all inhabitants to conform and contribute. Both Virginia and Massachusetts furnish examples of this disposition. The Anglicans in the one colony and the Puritans in the other, entertaining utterly different conceptions of polity and theology, were at one in their philosophy of uniformity. Among the early enactments of the House of Burgesses was a statute demanding that there "be a uniformity in our Church as near as may be to the Cannons in England, both in substance and in circumstance, and that all persons yield obedience under pain of censure." Puritan ministers and the Puritan settlement at Nansemond were driven out, and in 1671 that picturesque and outspoken governor, Sir William Berkeley, reported with glowing pride that no free

---

Source: Perry Miller, "The Contribution of the Protestant Churches to Religious Liberty in Colonial America," *Church History*, vol. 4 (1935), pp. 57-66.

schools disgraced the landscape in Virginia: "I hope we shall not have [them] these hundred years: for learning has brought disobedience and heresy and sects into the world." This, quite clearly, is nipping religious liberty in the bud.

The Puritans were equally clear and decisive. Many writers have already called attention to the fact that though the Puritans came to New England to escape persecution, they did not come to bestow upon those who disagreed with them any such immunity within the confines of their colonies. John Cotton patiently explained their position to Roger Williams thus: anybody in possession of his senses must recognize what is true and what is false when a learned Congregational minister demonstrates truth and falsehood to him. If a man, after such instruction, then maintains certain errors, he deserves punishment, not for being in error, but for persisting in it. In his heart of hearts, his own better judgment must acknowledge as much, even if he won't admit it. Accordingly, the laws of Massachusetts and the explicit pronouncements of her apologists pile up incontrovertible evidence that the leaders of the Bay Colony were intentionally and consistently intolerant; the banishment of Williams and Anne Hutchinson, the fining of Dr. Child, the whipping of Obadiah Holmes, and the dangling bodies of four Quakers hanged on Boston Common attest the fidelity with which the Puritans scouted the idea of toleration.

Speaking still as a historian, I must confess my gratitude to such men as Berkeley and Cotton. We know, at any rate, where we stand with them. With many figures of this stripe for our authorities, we can confidently assert that the Protestant *intention* in America was not towards religious toleration, let alone liberty. Yet it is also true that the colonies of Virginia and Massachusetts were the exceptions; they were the only colonies in which a program of intolerance had any real success, the only colonies in which a religious uniformity was achieved, and even in them for a relatively short time. The colonial period witnessed a fairly steady growth of practical religious freedom. From time to time some men in one or another of the churches might foresee the end and even approve. But by and large, I can find very little evidence that the Protestant churches ever really entertained the conception of complete liberty as their ultimate goal, or that they often moved in that direction unless forced to do so by the pressure of events or by the necessities of the social environment. As I say, there are exceptions, notably of course Williams and Penn, but the contribution of the majority of the Protestant churches must in the final analysis be described as inadvertent.

My time is limited, and it would manifestly be impossible to relate the whole narrative here. I wish therefore only to indicate, however briefly, what seems to my mind to be three important factors determining the development of religious liberty in America. To enumerate them roundly, they seem to me to have been, first the practical situation of the sects in the colonies, second the influence and interference of England, and third the shift in issues and concerns produced by the introduction or development of both the rationalistic and evangelical temper in the eighteenth century.

Most of the colonies were not as fortunate as Virginia or Massachusetts; they did not begin with unsettled expanses, or they could not people them with men of only one persuasion. The proprietors of the Carolinas, for instance, intended some day to establish the Church of England in their domains, but from the beginning had to reckon with a hopeless variety of creeds, Puritans from England and from New England, Huguenots, Dutch Calvinists, Scotch Calvinists, Quakers and several sorts of Baptists. The uniformity for which the noble proprietors hoped was impossible, unless they were prepared to expel nine-tenths of their settlers. So religious principle gave way to economic interest; practical toleration became the rule. The official clique still contemplated a full establishment of the Anglican church and in 1704 felt themselves strong enough in South Carolina to enact legislation excluding dissenters from the assembly and establishing an ecclesiastical court. A revolution was averted only when these acts were annulled by Parliament and toleration was restored.

The story in New York is much the same. The Dutch had been fairly tolerant and hospitable, following the national policy at home. When the English took over the colony, the number of sects already flourishing precluded any effective establishment. As Governor Dongan complained in 1687:

> Here bee not many of the Church of England; few Roman Catholics; abundance of Quaker preachers, men and women especially; Singing Quakers; Ranting Quakers; Sabbatarians; Anti-Sabbatarians; some Anabaptists; some Independents; some Jews; in short, of all sorts of opinions there are some, and the most part of none at all. The most prevailing opinion is that of the Dutch Calvinists. . . . As for the King's natural born subjects that live on Long Island, and other parts of the Government, I find it a hard task to make them pay their Ministers.

The governors did what they could, but the best they could wring from a predominantly Dutch Calvinistic assembly was the peculiar Ministry Act of 1693, which established in four counties six Protestant churches, not necessarily Anglican. Very few denominations were clearly advocating religious liberty on principle in New York; they were all opposing an established church, and the result was that religious liberty in large measure they all had. Circumstances placed insuperable obstacles in the way of intolerance. Where a multiplicity of creeds checkmate each other, they find themselves to their surprise maintaining religious liberty.

Indeed, the reasons that made uniformity difficult or ineffective in the Carolinas or in New York ultimately made it impossible in Virginia and Massachusetts. The established order in Virginia was never a very efficient organization; as early as 1629 the Burgesses were endeavouring to stop the clergy from "drinking or ryott" or "playing at dice." Meantime the dissenters began trickling in, Quakers and Baptists, and then the Scotch-Irish with their militant Presbyterianism streamed down the Shenandoah. Many of these were valuable settlers, particularly on the frontier, and the government had to give them allowance, either by express enactment or by tacit agreement. In Massachusetts also Quakers and Baptists forced an opening, and Anglicans came to stay in the train of the royal governors. By the 1730's the province had to allow some dissenters from the established Congregational order to pay their rates to churches of their own persuasion.

Thus in the colonies a generous amount of liberty or at least of toleration had come to prevail by the time of the Revolution. But this situation was hardly the result of conscious and deliberate theory; it was the result of circumstances. Diversity of belief compelled it. Rhode Island is, of course, an exception to this statement, thanks to the teachings of Roger Williams. Inspiring a figure as Williams may be, he nevertheless devised theories that were not palatable to the majority of Protestant churches in his day. Williams may speak for the essentially individualistic tendency inherent in all Protestantism; in the perspective of time we may see that his was the only solution for the ecclesiastical problem in a Protestant world, but Protestants in the colonies did not want to think so. If we desire to state accurately the "contribution" of the Protestant churches in all colonies beside Rhode Island and Pennsylvania to the development of religious liberty, we are forced to say that they made it inevitable by their dogged persistence in maintaining their own beliefs and practices. They persisted so resolutely that the governments had either to exterminate them or to tolerate them. In this connection it is worth noting that once a sect was tolerated it was generally ready to thrust itself into intolerance if it could get the upper hand. The Anglicans in Maryland, for example, given toleration by the Catholic proprietor in 1649, spent every effort to secure a Protestant establishment and the disfranchisement of their benefactors. Once the Church of England was established in Maryland, we have the old story again; the dissenting sects that had opposed the proprietor's church at once banded together, with the Catholics this time, to antagonize the royal governor's. By 1776 the established church in Maryland had become a shadow. The New Side Presbyterians and the Baptists in eighteenth century Virginia brought down upon their own heads the official persecution to which they were subjected by their own scurrility in assaulting the deplorable established church. "They treat all other modes of worship with the utmost scorn and contempt," complained the broad-minded Governor Gooch in 1745. The Protestant churches in America finally accepted the idea of religious liberty because they had become habituated to it. Most of them had not moved toward it with intelligent foresight; they had been forced to accustom themselves to it, because experience demonstrated the futility of exclusive domination by any one church, because settlers were too valuable to be antagonized over-much by acts of conformity, and because there were simply so many Protestant organizations that no power on earth could whip them into a system of uniformity.

A second source of liberal developments in colonial America is to be found in the example of English opinion and English law. The many sects that sprang up like mushrooms in the frenzied years of the Civil Wars had banded together with the English Independents against the Presbyterians to demand toleration. The dissenters were finally given toleration by the Parliament and the Established Church in the act of 1689. Though this act by no means created religious liberty, it marked the demise in England of that philosophy of absolute uniformity and enforced conformity which had characterized all Protestant churches during the Reformation.

It is with this development of opinion in England that we are to connect the experiment of William Penn. The Quakers were one of the enthusiastic groups that came into being during the wars. They began their existence when the idea of toleration had already been embraced by the Independents. Although in the first flush of their zeal the Quakers had flung themselves against all other churches in a spirit that betrayed little comprehension of toleration, they soon aligned themselves with the Independents. Their peculiar theology made it possible for them to admit, much more easily than other creeds could do, that men might be holy and good even if they belonged to other organizations. In that spirit Penn founded his colony, on an explicit theory of liberty for all churches, though his conceptions were still not as broad as those of Williams and he would not enfranchise Jews or give harbor to atheists. His plan was a little too broad for the home government, so that in 1705 the colony yielded to compulsion from Queen Anne and required the test-oath to be taken by office-holders, thus excluding Catholics from official positions.

Yet if the English government was instrumental in curtailing religious liberty in Pennsylvania, the act of 1689 fashioned a weapon by which minority groups in other colonies could pry loose the laws of conformity. The dissenters of South Carolina successfully appealed to the Whigs in Parliament to block the exorbitant acts of 1704. Francis Makemie, by demanding a license to preach in Virginia under the terms of the act of 1699, compelled the Burgesses to incorporate them into Virginia law. Samuel Davies appealed to the act again in 1753 to procure liberty for itinerant ministers. The Royal charter of Massachusetts, drawn up in 1691, guaranteed that "there shall be liberty of conscience allowed, in the worship of God, to all Christians (except Papists)." When Connecticut in 1708 grudgingly gave toleration to dissenters from the Congregational system, it specifically cited "the act of William and Mary." Thus once more, liberty was forced upon the colonies from without. The Quakers were intentionally libertarian; the other churches used English principles and laws for self-protection. In the end they furthered the growth of religious liberty, but not with malice aforethought; they achieved that end in the course of securing relief and opportunities for themselves.

The eighteenth century saw a steady extension of toleration in the colonies until with the Revolution established churches collapsed, in Massachusetts and Connecticut somewhat belatedly. But again an examination of the activity and statements of the churches before the Revolution does not offer much evidence that they took the lead. In the shift of the general intellectual climate, and the pressure of one or two political factors, religious liberty came to seem attractive. A complete account of this transformation would entail a chapter in intellectual history that has yet to be written; lacking that chapter we can here only enumerate a few of the factors. Before the Revolution the dissenting churches were thrown into co-operation and alliance against the threat of an Anglican bishop; this served to lessen the hostility of one toward another. Furthermore, in this century the question of church-polity ceased to be a serious issue; the young Jonathan Edwards would as soon serve in a Presbyterian as in a Congregational parish. Probably the most irritating of controversies was thus minimized. Then also, the differences between the sects began to seem of minor significance in the face of the towering danger of scientific rationalism and deism, which threatened all traditional creeds alike. Against the spread of "infidelity" all the churches drew closer together. Finally the movement for religious liberty was carried to a speedy triumph in the Revolutionary decades because the leadership was taken by a rational aristocracy, shot through with deistical beliefs, willing to see any number of religions have their freedom because they believed in none of them. As Nathaniel Ward had said, nothing is easier than to tolerate when you do not seriously believe that differences matter. So the Adamses, Masons, Franklins, and Jeffersons could advocate dis-establishment and religious liberty in a spirit which is, from an orthodox Christian point of view, simply cynical. As James Madison cheerfully put it: "In a free government, the security for civil rights must be the same as that for religious rights; it consists in the one case in a multiplicity of interests and in the other in the multiplicity of sects." At the same time the transformation of religious issues wrought by the Great Awakening and the introduction of revivalistic evangelicalism had created a situation in which the new Protestant groups were able to see clearly that a policy of religious liberty offered them definite advantages. Evangelical Baptists and New Side Presbyterians, and eventually the Methodists, came to perceive that they were opposing conceptions of institutionalized civic religion inherited from the previous century; they had to demolish established churches along with intricate theological structures in order to have the track cleared for their own program of spiritual regeneration and impassioned zeal. I do not think it has ever been sufficiently emphasized, or that it can be too much stressed, that there is a subtle and close connection between the shift of vital religious interest from elaborate intellectual systems of theology to the simplified emotional fervor of the new revivalism and the turning of Protestant Americans from a concern with ecclesiastical exclusiveness to the demand for liberty to all churches. It is not only that two or three more militant minorities now existed to contend for privileges against vested institutions, but that the whole bent and temper of this evangelicalism required that organization, external regulation and formal discipline become subordinated to the reawakening of the spirit and the revivifying of morality. It is in Massachusetts where the ruling classes most stoutly resisted what they considered the crude mysticism of the camp meetings that the retention of an established church was the most protracted. Such apparent champions of religious liberty as the Baptists Backus and Manning, or the Presbyterian Davies, have about them an apparent liberalism which is inspiring to behold, which yet can easily be made too much of. The truth of the matter was that they understood the situation, they realized that old institutions had to be replaced by less systematized forms if the sort of religious incitement they prized was to have full opportunity. James Manning — symbolizing the vast difference of evangelical Protestantism in the eighteenth century from Puritanism of the seventeenth, as we have seen that Puritanism incarnated in Nathaniel Ward — said to the Massachusetts delegates to the Continental Congress in October, 1774, "Establishments may be enabled to confer worldly distinctions and secular importance. They may make hypocrites, but cannot create Christians." So for the time being such leaders often made common cause with the rational aristocracy to attack established order and medieval theology. Yet all the time they were perfectly aware that their cause would not be lost, but in reality furthered, if various denominations were allowed to practise it in various ways. In terms of an ideal of ethics rather than of evangelical emotion, the same ultimately became true of the Unitarians. As Professor Hall has remarked, "It was easier for Harvard College to take up Unitarianism than it would have been to introduce at that date sports on Sunday."

It therefore seems to me that it is possible to speak too glibly of the "contributions" of Protestant groups to religious liberty; we can be easily betrayed by our own approbation for the idea into prizing and unduly exalting such instances of advance as we can find in our forebears. It has often seemed to me that the worshippers of Roger Williams have done more harm than good not only to the Puritans of the Bay but to their hero himself by their extravagant laudation of his ideas without at the same time maintaining sufficient historical perspective upon the general intellectual background from which he so dramatically emerged. Exceptionally liberal men in Protestant ranks undoubtedly exist, and they deserve all honor and veneration; but by and large Protestants did not contribute to religious liberty, they stumbled into it, they were compelled into it, they accepted it at last because they had to, or because they saw its strategic value. In their original intention, Protestants were intolerant; because of the sheer impossibility of unifying colonies made up of a hodge-podge diversity, because of the example of toleration set and enforced by England, and because of a complete shift in the intellectual situation in the eighteenth century, whereby religious liberty became a perfect solution for new issues — for these reasons, the Protestant churches did not so much achieve religious liberty as have liberty thrust upon them.

Class and Status in the New World

"In America," reported a South Carolina newspaper toward the end of the colonial period, "every Tradesman is a Merchant, every Merchant is a Gentleman, and every Gentleman one of the Noblesse. . . . We are a Country of Gentry. . . . We have no such Thing as a common People among us. . . ." In reality there was no shortage of "common people" in the American colonies as the following analysis by James Henretta of Boston's changing social structure makes clear. Nonetheless, the American social order differed in significant ways from the European.

In the absence of a hereditary, landed aristocracy, America's elite was perforce self-made, at least at the beginning. Forming the colonial ruling class were merchants, planters, and professionals who acquired substantial wealth; and wealth, rather than birth or blood, was the principal basis of social differentiation. As Henretta notes, this elite differed from its European counterpart in another respect: it did not form a closed caste. For one thing, its eminence was not based on inherited privilege. For another, there was a good deal more access to the leading circles than was the case in Britain. In a new society with seemingly limitless resources and social opportunities, the ambitious had a far better chance of moving up the social ladder. As a result, those on top constantly received infusions of new blood from enterprising newcomers. Moreover, those on top could not sit back and rest on their past achievements. Both trade and planting required constant attention. Those who neglected them for other business, as did Jefferson and Washington, saw their fortunes decline.

Incomplete at top, the social structure was also incomplete at the bottom. Unlike in Europe, in America the masses of country folk were neither landless peasants, nor city proletarians. Most were freehold farmers, or artisans and mechanics, who could vote and participate in government. As a result, the American social order was more open, and social distinctions not quite so clear-cut. Titles, such as mister or madame, which located a person's position in the more precisely graded social structure of England, lost much of their meaning in the colonies. Petty traders insisted on calling themselves merchants, and newly "arrived" merchants considered themselves gentlemen. And no one could stop them or their wives from wearing finery that in the Old World was the mark of a superior social class.

Though American society was more open and fluid than European, James Henretta discovered that it became less so as a city such as Boston matured. In the eighteenth century, a few families accumulated large fortunes and came to engross a disproportionate share of the town's wealth. At the same time, the percentage of the propertyless increased, though they were still substantially in the minority just before the Revolution, and even they could hold town office. A somewhat similar process occurred in the older rural regions. Here, when the best lands were taken up and a farmer's sons preferred to stay and settle on marginal lands rather than migrate to greener pastures far away from relatives, friends, and familiar sights, a landless group began to appear. Yet, to acute European observers the abundance of free land was the most distinctive characteristic of America. It transformed European peasants, they claimed, "from nothing to start into being; from a servant to the rank of a master; from being the slave of some despotic prince to become a freeman, invested with lands to which every municipal blessing is annexed."

FOR FURTHER READING:

BRIDENBAUGH, CARL. *Myths and Realities: Societies of the Colonial South.* New York: Atheneum Publishers, 1963.*

MAIN, JACKSON T. *Social Structure of Revolutionary America.* Princeton: Princeton University Press, 1965.*

TOLLES, FREDERICK B. *Meeting House and Counting House.* New York: W. W. Norton & Company, 1963.*

Asterisk denotes paperback edition.

Economic Development and Social Structure in Colonial Boston

JAMES A. HENRETTA

A distinctly urban social structure developed in Boston in the 150 years between the settlement of the town and the American Revolution. The expansion of trade and industry after 1650 unleashed powerful economic forces which first distorted, then destroyed, the social homogeneity and cohesiveness of the early village community. All aspects of town life were affected by Boston's involvement in the dynamic, competitive world of Atlantic commerce. The disruptive pressure of rapid economic growth, sustained for over a century, made the social appearance of the town more diverse, more complex, more modern — increasingly different from that of the rest of New England. The magnitude of the change in Boston's social composition and structure may be deduced from an analysis and comparison of the tax lists for 1687 and 1771. Containing a wealth of information on property ownership in the community, these lists make it possible to block out, in quantitative terms, variations in the size and influence of economic groups and to trace the change in the distribution of the resources of the community among them.

The transformation of Boston from a land-based society to a maritime center was neither sudden nor uniform. In the last decade of the seventeenth century, a large part of the land of its broad peninsula was still cultivated by small farmers. Only a small fraction was laid out in regular streets and even less was densely settled. The north end alone showed considerable change from the middle of the century when almost every house had a large lot and garden. Here, the later-comers — the mariners, craftsmen, and traders who had raised the population to six thousand by 1690 — were crowded together along the waterfront. Here, too, in the series of docks and shipyards which jutted out from the shore line, were tangible manifestations of the commercial activity which had made the small town the largest owner of shipping

---

Source: James A. Henretta, "Economic Development and Social Structure in Colonial Boston," *William and Mary Quarterly,* 3d ser., vol. 22 (1965), pp. 75–92.

and the principal port of the English colonies. Over 40 per cent of the carrying capacity of all colonial-owned shipping was in Boston hands.

Dependence on mercantile endeavor rather than agricultural enterprise had by 1690 greatly affected the extent of property ownership. Boston no longer had the universal ownership of real estate characteristic of rural Massachusetts to the end of the colonial period. The tax list for 1687 contained the names of 188 polls, 14 per cent of the adult male population, who were neither owners of taxable property of any kind nor "dependents" in a household assessed for the property tax. Holding no real estate, owning no merchandise or investments which would yield an income, these men constituted the "propertyless" segment of the community and were liable only for the head tax which fell equally upon all men above the age of sixteen. Many in this group were young men, laborers and seamen, attracted by the commercial prosperity of the town and hoping to save enough from their wages to buy or rent a shop, to invest in the tools of an artisan, or to find a start in trade. John Erving, a poor Scotch sailor whose grandson in 1771 was one of the richest men in Boston, was only one propertyless man who rose quickly to a position of wealth and influence.

But many of these 188 men did not acquire either taxable property or an established place in the social order of Boston. Only sixty-four, or 35 per cent, were inhabitants of the town eight years later. By way of contrast, 45 per cent of the polls assessed from two to seven pounds on the tax list, 65 per cent of those with property valued from eight to twenty pounds, and 73 per cent of those with estates in excess of twenty pounds were present in 1695. There was a direct relation between permanence of residence and economic condition. Even in an expanding and diversifying economic environment, the best opportunities for advancement rested with those who could draw upon long-standing connections, upon the credit facilities of friends and neighbors, and upon political influence. It was precisely these personal contacts which were denied to the propertyless.

A second, distinct element in the social order consisted of the dependents of property owners. Though propertyless themselves, these dependents — grown sons living at home, apprentices, and indentured servants — were linked more closely to the town as members of a tax-paying household unit than were the 188 "unattached" men without taxable estates. Two hundred and twelve men, nearly one sixth of the adult male population of Boston, were classified as dependents in 1687. The pervasiveness of the dependency relationship attested not only to the cohesiveness of the family unit but also to the continuing vitality of the apprenticeship and indenture system at the close of the seventeenth century.

Yet even the dependency relationship, traditionally an effective means of alleviating unemployment and preventing the appearance of unattached propertyless laborers, were subjected to severe pressure by the expansion of the economy. An urgent demand for labor, itself the cause of short indentures, prompted servants to strike out on their own as soon as possible. They became the laborers or semiskilled craftsmen of the town, while the sons of the family eventually assumed control of their father's business and a share of the economic resources of the community.

The propertied section of the population in 1687 was composed of 1,036 individuals who were taxed on their real estate or their income from trade. The less-skilled craftsmen, 521 men engaged in the rougher trades of a waterfront society, formed the bottom stratum of the taxable population in this pre-industrial age. These carpenters, shipwrights, blacksmiths, shopkeepers owned only 12 per cent of the taxable wealth of the town. Few of these artisans and laborers had investments in shipping or in merchandise. A small store or house, or a small farm in the south end of Boston, accounted for their assessment of two to seven pounds on the tax list. (Tables 1 and 3.)

Between these craftsmen and shopkeepers and the traders and merchants who constituted the economic elite of the town was a middle group of 275 property owners with taxable assets valued from eight to twenty pounds. Affluent artisans employing two or three workers, ambitious shopkeepers with investments in commerce, and entrepreneurial-minded sea masters with various maritime interests, bulked large in this center portion of the economic order. Of the 275, 180 owned real estate assessed at seven pounds or less and were boosted into the third quarter of the distribution of wealth by their holdings of merchandise and shares in shipping. (Table 3.) The remaining ninety-five possessed real estate rated at eight pounds or more and, in addition, held various investments in trade. Making up about 25 per cent of the propertied population, this middle group controlled 22 per cent of the taxable wealth in Boston in 1687. Half as numerous as the lowest group of property owners, these men possessed almost double the amount of taxable assets. (Table 1.)

Merchants with large investments in English and West Indian trade and individuals engaged in the ancillary industries of shipbuilding and distilling made up the top quarter of the taxable population in 1687. With taxable estates ranging from twenty to 170 pounds, this commercial group controlled 66 per cent of the town's wealth. But economic development had been too rapid, too uneven and incomplete, to allow the emergence of a well-defined merchant class endowed with a common outlook and clearly distinguished from the rest of the society. Only eighty-five of these men, one third of the wealthiest group in the community, owned dwellings valued at as much as twenty pounds. The majority held landed property valued at ten pounds, only a few pounds greater than that of the middle group of property holders. The merchants had not shared equally in the accumulated fund of capital and experience which had accrued after fifty years of maritime activity. Profits had flowed to those whose daring initiative and initial resources had begun the exploitation of the lucrative colonial market. By 1687, the upper 15 per cent of the property owners held 52 per cent of the taxable assets of the town, while the fifty individuals who composed the highest 5 per cent of the taxable population accounted for more than 25 per cent of the wealth. (Table 1.)

By the end of the seventeenth century widespread involvement in commerce had effected a shift in the locus of social and political respectability in Boston and distinguished it from the surrounding communities. Five of the nine selectmen chosen by the town in 1687 were sea captains. This was more than deference to those accustomed to command. With total estates of £83, £29, £33, £33, and £24, Captains Elisha Hutchinson, John Fairweather, Theophilus Frary, Timothy Prout, and Daniel Turell were among the wealthiest 20 per cent of the population. Still, achievement in trade was not the only index of respectability. Henry Eames, George Cable, Isaac Goose, and Elnathan Lyon, the men appointed by the town to inspect the condition of the streets and roads, had the greater part of their wealth, £105 of £130, invested in land and livestock. And the presence of Deacon Henry Allen among the selectmen provided a tangible indication of the continuing influence of the church.

These legacies of an isolated religious society and a stable agricultural economy

TABLE 1 Distribution of Assessed Taxable Wealth in Boston in 1687*

Total Value of Taxable Wealth	Number of Taxpayers in Each Wealth Bracket	Total Wealth in Each Wealth Bracket	Cumulative Total of Wealth	Cumulative Total of Taxpayers	Cumulative Percentage of Taxpayers	Cumulative Percentage of Wealth
£ 1	0	£ 0	£ 0	0	0.0%	0.0%
2	152	304	304	152	14.6	1.8
3	51	153	457	203	19.5	2.7
4	169	676	1,133	372	35.9	6.8
5	33	165	1,298	405	39.0	7.8
6	97	582	1,880	502	48.5	11.3
7	19	133	2,013	521	50.2	12.1
8	43	344	2,357	564	54.4	14.2
9	22	198	2,555	586	56.6	15.4
10	45	450	3,005	631	60.9	18.1
11	17	187	3,192	648	62.5	19.2
12	30	360	3,552	678	65.4	21.4
13	13	169	3,721	691	66.6	22.4
14	12	168	3,889	703	67.9	23.4
15	22	330	4,219	725	69.9	25.4
16	21	336	4,555	746	72.0	27.5
17	1	17	4,572	747	72.0	27.6
18	18	324	4,896	765	73.8	29.5
19	1	19	4,915	766	73.9	29.6
20	30	600	5,515	796	76.8	33.2
21–25	41	972	6,487	837	80.7	39.0
26–30	48	1,367	7,854	885	85.4	47.3
31–35	29	971	8,825	914	88.2	53.1
36–40	21	819	9,644	935	90.2	58.1
41–45	19	828	10,472	954	92.1	63.1
46–50	16	781	11,253	970	93.6	67.8
51–60	16	897	12,150	986	95.1	73.2
61–70	19	1,245	13,395	1,005	97.0	80.7
71–80	7	509	13,904	1,012	97.8	83.8
81–90	3	253	14,157	1,015	97.9	85.3
91–100	7	670	14,827	1,022	98.6	89.3
100–	14	1,764	16,591	1,036	100.0	100.0

* Money values are those of 1687. Many of the assessments fall at regular five pound intervals and must be considered as an estimate of the economic position of the individual. No attempt was made to compensate for systematic overvaluation or undervaluation inasmuch as the analysis measures relative wealth. The utility of a relative presentation of wealth (or income) is that it can be compared to another relative distribution without regard to absolute monetary values. See Mary Jean Bowman, "A Graphical Analysis of Personal Income Distribution in the United States," *American Economic Review*, XXXV (1944–45), 607–628, and Horst Mendershausen, *Changes in Income Distribution during the Great Depression* (New York, 1946).

disappeared in the wake of the rapid growth which continued unabated until the middle of the eighteenth century. In the fifty years after 1690, the population of the town increased from 6,000 to 16,000. The farms of the south end vanished and the central business district became crowded. In the populous north end, buildings which had once housed seven people suddenly began to hold nine or ten. Accompanying this physical expansion of Boston was a diversification of economic endeavor. By 1742, the town led all the colonial cities in the production of export furniture and shoes, although master craftsmen continued to carry on most industry on a small scale geared to local needs. Prosperity and expansion continued to be rooted, not in the productive capacity or geographic position of the town, but in the ability of the Boston merchants to compete successfully in the highly competitive mercantile world.

After 1750, the economic health of the Massachusetts seaport was jeopardized as New York and Philadelphia merchants, exploiting the rich productive lands at their backs and capitalizing upon their prime geographic position in the West Indian and southern coasting trade, diverted a significant portion of European trade from the New England traders. Without increasing returns from the lucrative "carrying" trade, Boston merchants could no longer subsidize the work of the shopkeepers, craftsmen, and laborers who supplied and maintained the commercial fleet. By 1760, the population of Boston had dropped to 15,000 persons, a level it did not exceed until after the Revolution.

The essential continuity of maritime enterprise in Boston from the late seventeenth to the mid-eighteenth century concealed the emergence of a new type of social system. After a certain point increases in the scale and extent of commercial endeavor produced a new, and more fluid, social order. The development of the economic system subjected the family, the basic social unit, to severe pressures. The fundamental link between one generation and another, the ability of the father to train his offspring for their life's work, was endangered by a process of change which rendered obsolete many of the skills and assumptions of the older, land-oriented generation and opened the prospect of success in new fields and new places. The well-known departure of Benjamin Franklin from his indenture to his brother was but one bright piece in the shifting mosaic of colonial life.

The traditional family unit had lost much of its cohesiveness by the third quarter of the eighteenth century. The Boston tax lists for 1771 indicate that dependents of property owners accounted for only 10 per cent of the adult male population as opposed to 16 per cent eighty-five years earlier. Increasingly children left their homes at an early age to seek their own way in the world.

A second factor in the trend away from dependency status was the decline in the availability of indentured servants during the eighteenth century. Fewer than 250 of 2,380 persons entering Boston from 1764 to 1768 were classified as indentured servants. These were scarcely enough to replace those whose indentures expired. More and more, the labor force had to be recruited from the ranks of "unattached" workers who bartered their services for wages in a market economy.

This laboring force consisted of the nondependent, propertyless workers of the community, now twice as numerous relative to the rest of the population as they had been a century before. In 1687, 14 per cent of the total number of adult males were without taxable property; by the eve of the Revolution, the propertyless accounted for 29 per cent. The social consequences of this increase were manifold. For every wage earner who competed in the economy as an autonomous entity at the end of the seventeenth century, there were four in 1771; for every man who slept in the back of a shop, in a tavern, or in a rented room in 1687, there were four in the later period. The population of Boston had doubled, but the number of propertyless men had increased fourfold.

The adult males without property, however, did not form a single unified class, a monolithic body of landless proletarians. Rather, the bottom of society consisted of a congeries of social and occupational groups with a highly transient maritime element at one end of the spectrum and a more stable and respected artisan segment at

TABLE 2 Distribution of Assessed Taxable Wealth in Boston in 1771*

Total Value of Taxable Wealth	Number of Taxpayers in Each Wealth Bracket	Total Wealth in Each Wealth Bracket	Cumulative Total of Wealth	Cumulative Total of Taxpayers	Cumulative Percentage of Taxpayers	Cumulative Percentage of Wealth
£ 3–30	78	£1,562	£1,562	78	5.0%	0.3%
31–40	86	2,996	4,558	164	10.6	0.9
41–50	112	5,378	9,936	276	17.9	2.2
51–60	74	4,398	14,334	350	22.6	3.5
61–70	33	3,122	17,456	383	24.7	3.8
71–80	165	12,864	30,320	548	35.4	6.5
81–90	24	2,048	32,368	572	36.9	7.0
91–100	142	13,684	46,052	714	46.1	10.0
101–110	14	494	46,546	728	47.1	10.1
111–120	149	17,844	64,390	877	56.7	13.9
121–130	20	2,570	66,960	897	58.0	14.5
131–140	26	4,600	71,560	923	59.7	15.5
141–150	20	2,698	74,258	943	60.9	16.1
151–160	88	14,048	88,306	1,031	66.6	19.1
161–170	11	1,846	90,152	1,042	67.4	19.6
171–180	18	3,128	93,280	1,060	68.6	20.3
181–190	10	1,888	95,168	1,070	69.2	20.7
191–200	47	9,368	104,536	1,117	72.2	22.7
201–300	126	31,097	135,633	1,243	80.4	29.4
301–400	60	21,799	157,432	1,303	84.2	34.1
401–500	58	24,947	182,379	1,361	88.0	39.6
501–600	14	7,841	190,220	1,375	88.9	41.3
601–700	24	15,531	205,751	1,399	90.4	44.6
701–800	26	19,518	225,269	1,425	92.2	48.9
801–900	20	17,020	242,289	1,445	93.4	52.6
901–1,000	16	15,328	257,617	1,461	95.4	55.9
1,001–1,500	41	48,364	305,963	1,502	97.1	66.4
1,501–5,000	37	85,326	391,289	1,539	99.5	84.9
5,001–	7	69,204	460,493	1,546	100.0	100.0

* The extant tax list is not complete. In ward 3, there are two pages and 69 polls missing; in ward 7, one page and 24 polls; in ward 12, an unknown number of pages and 225 polls. Only the total number of polls (224) is known for ward 11. The missing entries amount to 558, or 19.3 per cent of the total number of polls on the tax list. Internal evidence (the totals for all wards are known) suggests the absent material is completely random. Nevertheless, it should be remembered that this table represents an 80 per cent sample.

The value of shipping investments and of "servants for life" was not included in the computation of the table as it was impossible to determine the assessor's valuation. For the law regulating the assessment, see *The Arts and Resolves, Public and Private, of the Province of the Massachusetts Bay . . . IV* (Boston, 1881), 985–987. Money values are those of 1771.

the other. Although they held no taxable property, hard-working and reputable craftsmen who had established a permanent residence in Boston participated in the town meeting and were elected to unpaid minor offices. In March 1771, for instance, John Dyer was selected by the people of the town as "Fence Viewer" for the following year. Yet according to the tax and valuation lists compiled less than six months later, Dyer was without taxable property. At the same town meeting, four carpenters, Joseph Ballard, Joseph Edmunds, Benjamin Page, and Joseph Butler, none of whom was listed as an owner of taxable property on the valuation lists, were chosen as "Measurers of Boards." That propertyless men should be selected for public office indicates that the concept of a "stake in society," which provided the theoretical underpinning for membership in the community of colonial Boston, was interpreted in the widest possible sense. Yet it was this very conception of the social order which was becoming anachronistic under the pressure of economic development. For how could the growing number of propertyless men be integrated into a social order based in the first instance on the principle that only those having a tangible interest in the town or a definite family link to the society would be truly interested in the welfare of the community?

Changes no less significant had taken place within the ranks of the propertied groups. By the third quarter of the eighteenth century, lines of economic division and marks of social status were crystalizing as Boston approached economic maturity. Present to some degree in all aspects of town life, these distinctions were very apparent in dwelling arrangements. In 1687, 85 per cent of Boston real estate holdings had been assessed within a narrow range of two to ten pounds; by the seventh decade of the eighteenth century, the same spectrum ran from twelve to two hundred pounds. (Table 3.) Gradations in housing were finer in 1771 and had social connotations which were hardly conceivable in the more primitive and more egalitarian society of the seventeenth century. This sense of distinctiveness was reinforced by geographic distribution. Affluent members of the community who had not transferred their residence to Roxbury, Cambridge, or Milton built in the spacious environs of the south and west ends. A strict segregation of the social groups was lacking; yet the milieu of the previous century, the interaction of merchant, trader, artisan, and laborer in a waterfront community, had all but disappeared.

The increasing differences between the social and economic groups within the New England seaport stemmed in part from the fact that craftsmen, laborers, and small shopkeepers had failed to maintain their relative position in the economic order. In the eighty-five years from 1687 to 1771, the share of the taxable wealth of the community controlled by the lower half of the propertied population declined from 12 to 10 per cent. (Table 2.) If these men lived better at the end of the century than at the beginning, it was not because the economic development of Boston had effected a redistribution of wealth in favor of the laboring classes but because the long period of commercial prosperity had raised the purchasing power of every social group.

The decline in the economic distinctiveness of the middle group of property holders, the third quarter of the taxable population in the distribution of wealth, is even more significant. In 1771, these well-to-do artisans, shopkeepers, and traders (rising land values had eliminated the farmers and economic maturity the versatile merchant-sea captain) owned only 12½ per cent of the taxable wealth, a very substantial decrease from the 21 per cent held in 1687. These men lived considerably better than their counterparts in the seventeenth century; many owned homes and possessed furnishings rarely matched by the most elegant dwellings of the earlier period. But in relation to the other parts of the social order, their economic position had deteriorated drastically. This smaller middle group had been assessed for taxable estates twice as large as the bottom 50 per cent in 1687; by 1771 the assets of the two groups were equal.

On the other hand, the wealthiest 25 per cent of the taxable population by 1771 controlled 78 per cent of the assessed wealth of Boston. This represented a gain of 12 per cent from the end of the seventeenth century. An equally important shift had taken place within this elite portion of the population. In 1687, the richest 15 per cent of the taxpayers held 52 per cent of the taxable property, while the top 5 per cent owned 26.8 per cent. Eighty-five years later, the percentages were 65.9 and 44.1. (Tables 1 and 2 and Chart A.)

CHART A
Lorenz Curves Showing the Distribution of Wealth in Boston in 1687 and 1771 (Drawn from Data in Tables 1 and 2)

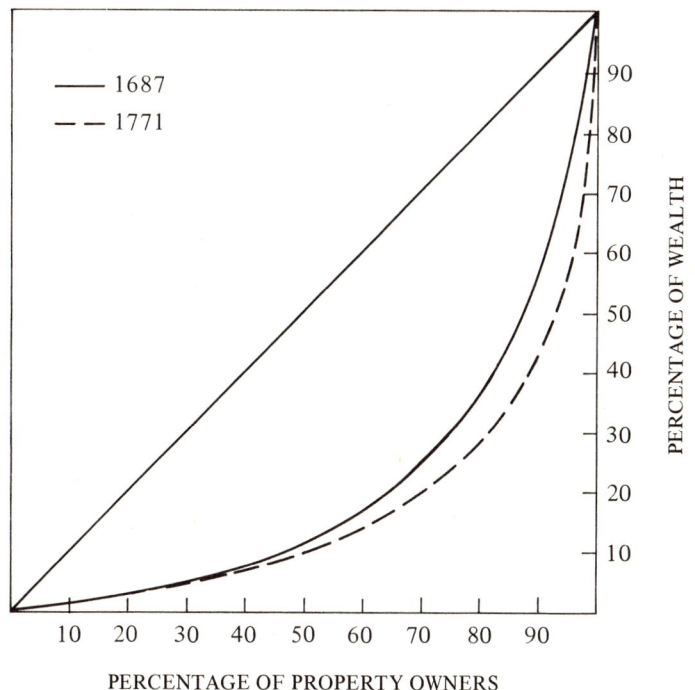

Certain long-term economic developments accounted for the disappearance of a distinct middle group of property owners and the accumulation of wealth among a limited portion of the population. The scarcity of capital in a relatively underdeveloped economic system, one in which barter transactions were often necessary because of the lack of currency, required that the savings of all members of the society be tapped in the interest of economic expansion. The prospect of rapid commercial success and the high return on capital invested in mercantile activity attracted the small investor. During the first decade of the eighteenth century, nearly one of every three adult males in Boston was involved directly in trade, owning at least part of a vessel. In 1698 alone, 261 people held shares in a seagoing vessel. Trade had become "not so much a way of life as a way of making money; not a social condition but an economic activity." This widespread ownership of mercantile wealth resulted in the creation of a distinct economic "middle class" by the last decades of the seventeenth century.

A reflection of a discrete stage of economic growth, the involvement of disparate occupational and social groups in commerce was fleeting and transitory. It lasted only as long as the economy of the New England seaport remained underdeveloped, without large amounts of available capital. The increase in the wealth and resources of the town during the first half of the eighteenth century prompted a growing spe-

TABLE 3 Real Estate Ownership in Boston in 1687 and 1771*

1687 Assessed Total Value of Real Estate	Number of Owners	Cumulative Total of Owners	1771 Assessed Annual Worth of Real Estate	Number of Owners	Cumulative Total of Owners
£ 1	0	0	£ 1	0	0
2	168	168	2	1	1
3	75	243	3	9	10
4	203	446	4	49	59
5	85	531	5	22	81
6	167	698	6	79	160
7	3	701	7	0	160
8	54	755	8	115	275
9	2	757	9	3	278
10	107	864	10	91	369
11	0	864	11	4	373
12	24	888	12	43	416
13	0	888	13	163	579
14	3	891	14	10	589
15	25	916	15	3	592
16	8	924	16	148	740
17	0	924	17	6	746
18	7	930	18	7	753
19	1	931	19	5	758
20	46	932	20	236	994
21–30	25	1,003	21–25	41	1,035
31–40	11	1,014	26–30	163	1,198
41–50	2	1,016	31–35	93	1,291
			36–40	92	1,383
			41–45	5	1,388
			46–50	42	1,430
			51–60	32	1,462
			61–70	10	1,472
			71–80	9	1,481
			81–90	3	1,484
			91–100	3	1,487

* The assessed annual worth of real estate in the 1771 valuation must be multiplied by six to give the total property value.

cialization of economic function; it was no longer necessary to rely on the investments of the less affluent members of the community for an expansion of commerce. This change was slow, almost imperceptible; but by 1771 the result was obvious. In that year, less than 5 per cent of the taxable population of Boston held shares in shipping of ten tons or more, even though the tonnage owned by the town was almost double that of 1698. Few men had investments of less than fifty tons; the average owner held 112 tons. By way of contrast, the average holding at the end of the seventeenth century had been about twenty-five tons. Moreover, on the eve of the Revolution ownership of shipping was concentrated among the wealthiest men of the community. Ninety per cent of the tonnage of Boston in 1771 was in the hands of those whose other assets placed them in the top quarter of the population. With the increase in the wealth of the town had come a great increase in the number of propertyless men and a bifurcation of the property owners into (1) a large amorphous body of shopkeepers, artisans, and laborers with holdings primarily in real estate and (2) a smaller, somewhat more closely defined segment of the population with extensive commercial investments as well as elegant residences and personal possessions.

A similar trend was evident in other phases of town life. In the transitional decades of the late seventeenth and early eighteenth century, the fluidity inherent in the primitive commercial system had produced a certain vagueness in the connotations of social and economic status. Over 10 per cent of the adult males in Boston designated themselves as "merchants" on the shipping registers of the period from 1698 to 1714, indicating not only the decline in the distinctiveness of a title traditionally limited to a carefully defined part of the community but also the feeling that any man could easily ascend the mercantile ladder. Economic opportunity was so evident, so promising, that the social demarcations of the more stable maritime communities of England seemed incongruous. By the sixth decade of the eighteenth century, however, rank and order were supplanting the earlier chaos as successful families tightened their control of trade. The founding in 1763 of a "Merchants Club" with 146 members was a dramatic indication that occupations and titles were regaining some of their traditional distinctiveness and meaning.

An economic profile of the 146 men who composed this self-constituted elite is revealing. Of those whose names appeared on the tax and valuation lists of 1771, only five had estates which placed them in the bottom three quarters of the distribution of wealth. Twenty-one were assessed for taxable property in excess of £1,500 and were thus in the top 1 per cent of the economic scale. The taxable assets of the rest averaged £650, an amount which put them among the wealthiest 15 per cent of the population.

That 146 men, 6½ per cent of the adult male population, were considered eligible for membership in a formal society of merchants indicates, however, that mercantile activity was not dominated by a narrow oligarchy. The range of wealth among the members of the top quarter of the propertied population was so great and the difference of social background so large as to preclude the creation of a monolithic class or guild with shared interests and beliefs.

Yet the influence of this segment of society was pervasive. By the third quarter of the eighteenth century, an integrated economic and political hierarchy based on mercantile wealth had emerged in Boston to replace the lack of social stratification of the early part of the century and the archaic distinctions of power and prestige of the religious community of the seventeenth century. All of the important offices of the town government, those with functions vital to the existence and prosperity of the town, were lodged firmly in the hands of a broad elite, entry into which was conditioned by commercial achievement and family background. The representatives to the General Court and the selectmen were the leaders of the town in economic endeavor as well as in political acumen. John Hancock's taxable wealth totaled £18,000; James Otis was assessed at £2,040, while Colonel Joseph Jackson had property valued at £1,288. Other levels of the administrative system were reserved for those whose business skills or reputation provided the necessary qualifications. Samuel Abbot, John Barrett, Benjamin Dolbeare, John Gore, William Phillips, William White, and William Whitewell, Overseers of the Poor in 1771, had taxable estates of £815, £5,520, £850, £1,747, £5,771, £1,953, and £1,502 respectively. All were among the wealthiest 7 per cent of the property owners; and Barrett and Phillips were two of the most respected merchants of the town. John Scollay, a distiller with an estate of £320, and Captain Benjamin Waldo, a shipmaster assessed at £500, who were among those chosen as "Firewards" in 1771, might in an earlier period have been dominant in town affairs; by the seventh decade of the century, in a mature economic environment, the merchant prince had replaced the man of action at the apex of the social order.

Gradations continued to the bottom of the scale. Different social and occupational levels of the population were tapped as the dignity and responsibility of the position demanded. It was not by accident that the estates of the town assessors, Jonathan Brown, Moses Deshon, and John Kneeland, were £208, £200, and £342. Or that those of the "Cullers of Staves," Henry Lucas, Thomas Knox, and Caleb Hayden, totaled £120, £144, and £156. The assumption of a graded social, economic, and political scale neatly calibrated so as to indicate the relation of each individual to the whole was the basic principle upon which the functioning of town-meeting "democracy" depended. William Crafts, with a taxable estate of £80, was elected "Fence Viewer." Half this amount qualified William Barrett to be "Measurer of Coal Baskets," while Henry Allen and John Bulfinch, "Measurers of Boards," were assessed at £80 and £48. The design was nearly perfect, the correlation between town office and social and economic position almost exact.

As in 1687, the distribution of political power and influence in Boston conformed to the standards and gradations of a wider, more inclusive hierarchy of status, one which purported to include the entire social order within the bounds of its authority. But the lines of force which had emerged on the eve of the American Revolution radiated from different economic and social groups than those of eighty-five years before, and now failed to encompass a significant portion of the population. The weakening of the "extended" family unit and the appearance of a large body of autonomous wage earners, "proletarians" in condition if not in consciousness, had introduced elements of mobility and diversity into the bottom part of society. Equally significant had been the growing inequality of the distribution of wealth among the propertied segment of the community, notably the greater exclusiveness and predominance of a mercantile "elite." Society had become more stratified and unequal. Influential groups, increasingly different from the small property owners who constituted the center portion of the community, had arisen at either end of the spectrum. Creations of the century-long development of a maritime economy in an urban setting, these "merchant princes" and "proletarians" stood out as the salient characteristics of a new social order.

PART 2
The Birth of the Republic 1763–1815

Roots of the American Revolution

From the Revolutionary generation to the present, Americans have never ceased trying to explain why the American colonies, after more than 150 years as loyal outposts of Great Britain, suddenly revolted and established an independent republic. Americans at that time had a simple explanation: wicked English politicians sought to deprive them of their liberty, and the colonists manfully and successfully resisted. Later generations, skeptical of such simple black-and-white interpretations, discovered that the British taxes and regulations which triggered American resistance in the 1760s resulted from sincere, if not always wise, efforts to deal with difficult, indeed intractable, problems of imperial government that grew out of England's victory in the Seven Years' War (1754-1761). The need for a revenue and for tighter central control, as perceived by London, clashed with well-entrenched traditions of decentralized rule, from which Americans profited and which they were reluctant to give up. Still other historians have maintained that conflicting economic interests tore the Empire apart as British merchants and officials attempted to enrich themselves at the expense of the colonists. The following selection by Bernard Bailyn is an important recent major contribution to Revolutionary historiography. Bailyn argues that whatever the actual motives of British policy-makers, the Americans became convinced of a plot against their freedom.

The conspiratorial mentality — an irrational pattern of explanation that attributes dire events to hidden, malign forces — has appeared many times since in American history: in Andrew Jackson's War against the Bank of the United States, in the Populist crusade against Wall Street, and more recently in Senator Joe McCarthy's demagogic attack on supposed Communist subversion in high places. It made its first full-blown debut in America during the turbulent decade preceding the Revolution. It flourished then and later because people, living in times of rapid change, are often bewildered and do not understand why their lives are being disrupted. Americans, for instance, did not perceive the Stamp Act and other British measures as reforms in imperial governance. The new policies clearly departed from past ones and seemed to fly in the face of the long-accepted theory that the best way to advance the interests of the mother country was to permit the colonists ample freedom. Unable or unwilling to understand the real reasons for having to pay new taxes or submit to new trade regulations, Americans could only imagine themselves the victims of a wicked plot against their freedom.

Colonial political developments and English political thought further predisposed Americans to this view. The colonists did enjoy more freedom than any other people in the Western world; they regarded America, moreover, as a refuge to which victims of tyranny had fled. Their own experience as well as their study of history and politics taught them that, because man is inherently self-seeking, willing to enslave others for his own benefit, those who are free always live in danger from others. The chief danger came from the state, since the men who controlled it possessed a monopoly of force. The best defense against the abuse of authority was a properly balanced constitution that placed limits on rulers. Americans thought they lived under such a constitution until the 1760s. Then, Professor Bailyn argues, when they thought legislatures, courts, and churches to be under attack from England, they became convinced of a plot to subvert the British constitution and to destroy their liberty.

FOR FURTHER READING:

BAILYN, BERNARD. *Ideological Origins of the American Revolution.* Cambridge, Mass.: Harvard University Press, 1967.*

BILLIAS, GEORGE A., ed. *American Revolution: How Revolutionary Was It.* Magnolia, Mass.: Peter Smith, 1965.*

MORGAN, EDMUND G. *Stamp Act Crisis.* Chapel Hill: University of North Carolina Press, 1963.*

Asterisk denotes paperback edition.

From *The Ideological Origins of the American Revolution*   BERNARD BAILYN

. . . The colonists believed they saw emerging from the welter of events during the decade after the Stamp Act a pattern whose meaning was unmistakable. They saw in the measures taken by the British government and in the actions of officials in the colonies something for which their peculiar inheritance of thought had prepared them only too well, something they had long conceived to be a possibility in view of the known tendencies of history and of the present state of affairs in England. They saw about them, with increasing clarity, not merely mistaken, or even evil, policies violating the principles upon which freedom rested, but what appeared to be evidence of nothing less than a deliberate assault launched surreptitiously by plotters against liberty both in England and in America. The danger to America, it was believed, was in fact only the small, immediately visible part of the greater whole whose ultimate manifestation would be the destruction of the English constitution, with all the rights and privileges embedded in it.

This belief transformed the meaning of the colonists' struggle, and it added an inner accelerator to the movement of opposition. For, once assumed, it could not be easily dispelled: denial only confirmed it, since what conspirators profess is not what they believe; the ostensible is not the real; and the real is deliberately malign.

It was this — the overwhelming evidence, as they saw it, that they were faced with conspirators against liberty determined at all costs to gain ends which their words dissembled — that was signaled to the colonists after 1763, and it was this above all else that in the end propelled them into Revolution.

Suspicion that the ever-present, latent danger of an active conspiracy of power against liberty was becoming manifest within the British Empire, assuming specific form and developing in coordinated phases, rose in the consciousness of a large segment of the American population before any of the famous political events of the

---

Source: Bernard Bailyn, *The Idealogical Origins of the American Revolution* (Cambridge, Mass.: Harvard University Press, 1967), pp. 94–97, 98–101, 101–106, 107–110, 112–115, 117–120, 124–125, 129–130, 135–136, 138–143.

struggle with England took place. No adherent of a nonconformist church or sect in the eighteenth century was free from suspicion that the Church of England, an arm of the English state, was working to bring all subjects of the crown into the community of the Church; and since toleration was official and nonconformist influence in English politics formidable, it was doing so by stealth, disguising its efforts, turning to improper uses devices that had been created for benign purposes. In particular, the Society for the Propagation of the Gospel in Foreign Parts, an arm of the Church created in 1701 to aid in bringing the Gospel to the pagan Indians, was said by 1763 to have "long had a formal design to root out Presbyterianism, etc., and to establishing both episcopacy and bishops."

This suspicion, which had smoldered in the breasts of New Englanders and nonconformists throughout the colonies for half a century or more, had burst into flame repeatedly, but never so violently as in 1763, in the Mayhew-Apthorp controversy which climaxed years of growing anxiety that plans were being made secretly to establish an American episcopate. To Mayhew, as to Presbyterian and Congregational leaders throughout the colonies, there could be little doubt that the threat was real. Many of the facts were known, facts concerning maneuvers in London and in America. Anglican leaders in New York and New Jersey had met almost publicly to petition England for an American episcopate, and there could be little doubt also of the role of the Society for the Propagation of the Gospel in this undercover operation. For if the ostensible goal of the Society was the gospelizing of the pagan Indians and Negroes, its true goal was manifestly revealed when it established missions in places like Cambridge, Massachusetts, which had not had a resident Indian since the seventeenth century and was well equipped with "orthodox" preachers. Such missions, Mayhew wrote, have "all the appearance of entering wedges . . . carrying on the crusade, or spiritual siege of our churches, with the hope that they will one day submit to an episcopal sovereign." Bishops, he wrote unblinkingly in reply to the Archbishop of Canterbury, have commonly been instruments in arbitrary reigns of "establishing a tyranny over the bodies and souls of men," and their establishment in America would mark the end of liberty in Massachusetts and elsewhere. By 1765, when the final exchanges in this pamphlet war were published, it was commonly understood in New England and elsewhere that "the stamping and episcopizing [of] our colonies were . . . *only different branches of the same plan of power.*"

Fear of an ecclesiastical conspiracy against American liberties, latent among nonconformists through all of colonial history, thus erupted into public controversy at the very same time that the first impact of new British policies in civil affairs was being felt. And though it was, in an obvious sense, a limited fear (for large parts of the population identified themselves with the Anglican Church and were not easily convinced that liberty was being threatened by a plot of Churchmen) it nevertheless had a profound indirect effect everywhere, for it drew into public discussion — evoked in specific form — the general conviction of eighteenth-century Englishmen that the conjoining of "temporal and spiritual tyranny" was, in John Adams' words, an event totally "calamitous to human liberty" yet an event that in the mere nature of things perpetually threatened. . . . Fear of the imposition of an Anglican episcopate thus brought into focus a cluster of ideas, attitudes, and responses alive with century-old Popish-Stuart-Jacobite associations that would enter directly into the Revolutionary controversy in such writings as John Adams' *Dissertation on the Canon and Feudal Law* (1765) and Samuel Adams' "A Puritan" pieces published in the *Boston Gazette* in 1768. And more than that, it stimulated among highly articulate leaders of public opinion, who would soon be called upon to interpret the tendency of civil affairs, a general sense that they lived in a conspiratorial world in which what the highest officials professed was not what they in fact intended, and that their words masked a malevolent design.

Reinforcement for this belief came quickly. Even for those who had in no way been concerned with the threat of an episcopal establishment, the passage of the Stamp Act was not merely an impolitic and unjust law that threatened the priceless right of the individual to retain possession of his property until he or his chosen representative voluntarily gave it up to another; it was to many, also, a danger signal indicating that a more general threat existed. For though it could be argued, and in a sense proved by the swift repeal of the act, that nothing more was involved than ignorance or confusion on the part of people in power who really knew better and who, once warned by the reaction of the colonists, would not repeat the mistake — though this could be, and by many was, concluded, there nevertheless appeared to be good reason to suspect that more was involved. For from whom had the false information and evil advice come that had so misled the English government? From officials in the colonies, said John Adams, said Oxenbridge Thacher, James Otis, and Stephen Hopkins — from officials bent on overthrowing the constituted forms of government in order to satisfy their own lust for power, and not likely to relent in their passion. Some of these local plotters were easily identified. To John Adams, Josiah Quincy, and others the key figure in Massachusetts from the beginning to the end was Thomas Hutchinson who by "serpentine wiles" was befuddling and victimizing the weak, the avaricious, and the incautious in order to increase his notorious engrossment of public office. In Rhode Island it was, to James Otis, that "little, dirty, drinking, drabbing, contaminated knot of thieves, beggars, and transports . . . made up of Turks, Jews, and other infidels, with a few renegado Christians and Catholics" — the Newport junto, led by Martin Howard, Jr., which had already been accused by Stephen Hopkins and others in Providence of "conspiring against the liberties of the colony."

But even if local leaders associated with power elements in England had not been so suspect, there were grounds for seeing more behind the Stamp Act than its ostensible purpose. The official aim of the act was, of course, to bring in revenue to the English treasury. But the sums involved were in fact quite small, and "some persons . . . may be inclined to acquiesce under it." But that would be to fall directly into the trap, for the smaller the taxes, John Dickinson wrote in the most influential pamphlet published in America before 1776, the more dangerous they were, since they would the more easily be found acceptable by the incautious, with the result that a precedent would be established for making still greater inroads on liberty and property.

> Nothing is wanted at home but a PRECEDENT, the force of which shall be established by the tacit submission of the colonies . . . If the Parliament succeeds in this attempt, other statutes will impose other duties . . . and thus the Parliament will levy upon us such sums of money as they choose to take, *without any other* LIMITATION *than their* PLEASURE.

. . . To John Adams it seemed "very manifest" that the ultimate design behind the Stamp Act was an effort to forge the fatal link between ecclesiastical and civil despotism, the first by stripping the colonists "in a great measure of the means of knowledge, by loading the press, the colleges, and even an almanac and a newspaper with restraints and duties," the second, by recreating the inequalities and dependencies of feudalism "by taking from the poorer sort of people all their little subsistence, and conferring it on a set of stamp officers, distributors, and their deputies." This last point was the most obvious: "as the influence of money and places generally procures to the minister a majority in Parliament," Arthur Lee wrote, so an income from unchecked taxation would lead to a total corruption of free government in America, with the result that the colonies would "experience the fate of the *Roman* people in the deplorable times of their slavery."

But by then, in 1768, more explicit evidence of a wide-ranging plot was accumulating rapidly. Not only had the Townshend Duties, another revenue act, been passed by Parliament despite all the violence of the colonists' reaction to the Stamp Act, but it was a measure that enhanced the influence of the customs administration, which for other reasons had already come under suspicion. There had been, it was realized by the late 1760's, a sudden expansion in the number of "posts in the [colonial] 'government' . . . worth the attention of persons of influence in Great Britain" — posts, Franklin explained, like the governorships, filled by persons who were

> generally strangers to the provinces they are sent to govern, have no estate, natural connection, or relation there to give them an affection for the country . . . they come only to make money as fast as they can; are sometimes men of vicious characters and broken fortunes, sent by a minister merely to get them out of the way.

By the late 1760's, in the perspective of recent events, one could see that the invasion of customs officers "born with long claws like eagles," had begun as far back as the last years of the Seven Years' War and was now being reinforced by the new tax measures. The wartime Orders in Council demanding stricter enforcement of the Navigation Laws; the Sugar Act of 1764, which had multiplied the customs personnel; and the American Board of Customs Commissioners created in 1767 with "power," Americans said, "to constitute as many under officers as they please" — all of these developments could be seen to have provided for an "almost incredible number of inferior officers," most of whom the colonists believed to be "wretches . . . of such infamous characters that the merchants cannot possibly think their interest safe under their care." More important by far, however, was their influence on government.

For there was an obvious political and constitutional danger in having such "a set of *idle drones*," such "lazy, proud, worthless *pensioners* and *placemen*," in one's midst. It was nothing less than "a general maxim," James Wilson wrote,

> that the crown will take advantage of every opportunity of extending its prerogative in opposition to the privileges of the people, [and] that it is the interest of those who have *pensions* or *offices at will* from the crown to concur in all its measures.

These "baneful harpies" were instruments of power, of prerogative. They would upset the balance of the constitution by extending "*ministerial influence* as much beyond its former bounds as the late war did the British dominions." Parasitic officeholders, thoroughly corrupted by their obligations to those who had appointed them, would strive to "*distinguish themselves* by their sordid zeal in defending and promoting measures which *they know beyond all question* to be *destructive* to the *just rights* and *true interests* of their country." Seeking to "*serve the ambitious purposes of great men* at home," these "*base-spirited wretches*" would urge — were already urging — as they logically had to, the specious attractions of "SUBMISSIVE behavior." They were arguing

> with a plausible affection of *wisdom* and *concern* how *prudent* it is to please the *powerful* — how *dangerous* to provoke them — and then comes in the perpetual incantation that freezes up every generous purpose of the soul in cold, inactive expectation — "that if there is any request to be made, compliance will obtain a favorable attention."

In the end, this extension of executive patronage, based on a limitless support of government through colonial taxation, would make the whole of government "merely a ministerial engine"; by throwing off the balance of its parts, it would destroy the protective machinery of the constitution.

But even this did not exhaust the evidence that a design against liberty was unfolding. During the same years the independence of the judiciary, so crucial a part of the constitution, was suddenly seen to be under heavy attack, and by the mid-1760's to have succumbed in many places.

This too was not a new problem. The status of the colonial judiciary had been a controversial question throughout the century. The Parliamentary statute of 1701 which guaranteed judges in England life tenure in their posts had been denied to the colonies, in part because properly trained lawyers were scarce in the colonies, especially in the early years, and appointments for life would prevent the replacement of ill-qualified judges by their betters, when they appeared; and in part because, judicial salaries being provided for by temporary legislative appropriations, the removal of all executive control from the judiciary, it was feared, would result in the hopeless subordination of the courts to popular influences. The status of the judiciary in the eighteenth century was therefore left open to political maneuvering in which, more often than not, the home government managed to carry its point and to make the tenure of judges as temporary as their salaries. Then suddenly, in the early 1760's, the whole issue exploded. In 1759 the Pennsylvania Assembly declared that the judges of that province would thereafter hold their offices by the same permanence of tenure that had been guaranteed English judges after the Glorious Revolution. But the law was disallowed forthwith by the crown. Opposition newspapers boiled with resentment; angry speeches were made in the Assembly; and a pamphlet appeared explaining in the fullest detail the bearing of judicial independence on constitutional freedom.

In New York the issue was even more inflamed and had wider repercussions. There, the judges of the Supreme Court, by a political maneuver of 1750, had managed to secure their appointments for life. But this tenure was interrupted by the death of George II in 1760 which required the reissuance of all crown commissions. An unpopular and politically weak lieutenant governor, determined to prevent his enemies from controlling the courts, refused to recommission the judges on life tenure. The result was a ferocious battle in which the opposition asserted New York's "*undoubted right* of having the judges of our courts on a constitutional basis," and demanded the "liberties and privileges" of Englishmen in this connection as in all others. But they were defeated, though not by the governor. In December 1761 orders were sent out from the King in Council to all the colonies, permanently forbidding the issuance of judges' commissions anywhere on any tenure but that of "the pleasure of the crown. . . ."

"More and more," as the people contemplated the significance of crown salaries for a judiciary that served "at pleasure," was it clear that "the designs of administration [were] totally to subvert the constitution." Any judge, the House in Massachusetts ultimately stated, who accepted such salaries would thereby declare "that he has not a due sense of the importance of an impartial administration of justice, that he is an enemy to the constitution, and has it in his heart to promote the establishment of an arbitrary government in the province. . . ."

The more one looked the more one found evidences of deliberate malevolence. In Massachusetts, Thomas Hutchinson's elaborate patronage machine, long in existence but fully organized only after the arrival of Governor Francis Bernard in 1760, appeared to suspicious tribunes like Oxenbridge Thacher and John Adams to constitute a serious threat to liberty. The Hutchinsons and the Olivers and their ambitious allies, it was said (and the view was widely circulated through the colonies), had managed, by accumulating a massive plurality of offices, to engross the power of all branches of the Massachusetts government thereby building a "foundation sufficient on which to erect a tyranny."

> Bernard had all the executive, and a negative of the legislative; Hutchinson and Oliver, by their popular arts and secret intrigues, had elevated to the [Council] such a collection of crown officers and their own relations as to have too much influence there; and they had three of a family on the superior bench . . . This junto, therefore, had the legislative and executive in their control, and more natural influence over the judicial than is ever to be trusted to any set of men in the world.

With encouragement, no doubt, from England, they were stretching their power beyond all proper bounds, becoming "conspirators against the public liberty. . . ."

Meanwhile an event even more sinister in its implications had taken place in the colonies themselves. On October 1, 1768, two regiments of regular infantry, with artillery, disembarked in Boston. For many months the harassed Governor Bernard had sought some legal means or excuse for summoning military help in his vain efforts to maintain if not an effective administration then at least order in the face of Stamp Act riots, circular letters, tumultuous town meetings, and assaults on customs officials. But the arrival of troops in Boston increased rather than decreased his troubles. For to a populace steeped in the literature of eighteenth-century English politics the presence of troops in a peaceful town had such portentous meaning that resistance instantly stiffened. It was not so much the physical threat of the troops that affected the attitudes of the Bostonians; it was the bearing their arrival had on the likely tendency of events. Viewed in the perspective of Trenchard's famous tracts on standing armies and of the vast derivative literature on the subject that flowed from the English debates of the 1690's, these were not simply soldiers assembled for police duties; they were precisely what history had proved over and over again to be prime movers of the process by which unwary nations lose "that precious jewel *liberty*." The mere rumor of possible troop arrivals had evoked the age-old apprehensions. "The raising or keeping a standing army within the kingdom in time of peace, unless it be with the consent of Parliament, is against the law," the alarmed Boston Town Meeting had resolved. It is, they said,

> the indefeasible right of [British] subjects to be *consulted* and to give their *free consent in person* or by representatives of their own free election to the raising and keeping a standing army among them; and the inhabitants of this town, being free subjects, have the same right derived from nature and confirmed by the British constitution as well as the said royal charter; and therefore the raising or keeping a standing army without their consent in person or by representatives of their own free election would be an infringement of their natural, constitutional, and charter rights; and the employing such army

for the enforcing of laws made without the consent of the people, in person or by their representatives, would be a grievance.

But the troops arrived, four regiments in all: in bold, stark actuality a standing army — just such a standing army as had snuffed out freedom in Denmark, classically, and elsewhere throughout the world. True, British regulars had been introduced into the colonies on a permanent basis at the end of the Seven Years' War; that in itself had been disquieting. But it had then been argued that troops were needed to police the newly acquired territories, and that they were not in any case to be regularly garrisoned in peaceful, populous towns. No such defense could be made of the troops sent to Boston in 1768. No simple, ingenuous explanation would suffice. The true motive was only too apparent for those with eyes to see. One of the classic stages in the process of destroying free constitutions of government had been reached.

To those most sensitive to the ideological currents of the day, the danger could scarcely have been greater. "To have a standing army!" Andrew Eliot wrote from Boston to Thomas Hollis in September, 1768, "Good God! What can be worse to a people who have tasted the sweets of liberty! Things are come to an unhappy crisis; there will never be that harmony between Great Britain and her colonies that there hath been; all confidence is at an end; and the moment there is any blood shed all affection will cease." He was convinced, he wrote, that if the English government "had not had their hands full at home they would have crushed the colonies." As it was, England's most recent actions tended only "to hasten that independency which at present the warmest among us deprecate." "I fear for the nation," he concluded, and his fears were shared not only by all liberty-minded Bostonians but also, through the stimulation of the "Journal of the Times," a day-by-day account of Boston "under military rule" that was, in effect, syndicated throughout the colonies, it was shared by politically and ideologically sensitive Americans everywhere. Time did not ease these anxieties; it merely complicated them. Fear and hatred became edged with contempt. "Our people begin to despise a military force," Eliot observed a year after the troops had first appeared; they coolly woo away the soldiers and drag offending officers before the courts — which, he grimly added, continue to function "notwithstanding all their efforts." But "things cannot long remain in the state they are now in; they are hastening to a crisis. What will be the event, God knows. . . ."

Unconstitutional taxing, the invasion of placemen, the weakening of the judiciary, plural officeholding, Wilkes, standing armies — these were major evidences of a deliberate assault of power upon liberty. Lesser testimonies were also accumulating at the same time: small episodes in themselves, they took on a large significance in the context in which they were received. Writs of assistance in support of customs officials were working their expected evil: "our houses, and even our bedchambers, are exposed to be ransacked, our boxes, trunks, and chests broke open, ravaged and plundered by wretches whom no prudent man would venture to employ even as menial servants." Legally convened legislatures had been "adjourned . . . to a place highly inconvenient to the members and greatly disadvantageous to the interest of the province"; they had been prorogued and dissolved at executive whim. Even the boundaries of colonies had been tampered with, whereby *rights of soil* had been eliminated at a stroke. When in 1772 the Boston Town Meeting met to draw up a full catalogue of the "infringements and violations" of the rights of the colonists, and of this province in particular, as men, as Christians, and as subjects," it approved a list of twelve items, which took seventeen pamphlet pages to describe.

But then, for a two-year period, there was a détente of sorts created by the repeal of the Townshend Duties, the withdrawal of troops from Boston, and the failure of other provocative measures to be taken. It ended abruptly, however, in the fall and winter of 1773, when, with a rush, the tendencies earlier noted were brought to fulfillment. In the space of a few weeks, all the dark, twisted roots of malevolence were finally revealed, plainly, for all to see.

The turning point was the passage of the Tea Act and the resulting Tea Party in Boston in December 1773. Faced with this defiant resistance to intimidation, the powers at work in England, it was believed, gave up all pretense of legality — "threw off the mask," John Adams said in a phrase that for a century had been used to describe just such climactic disclosures — and moved swiftly to complete their design. In a period of two months in the spring of 1774 Parliament took its revenge in a series of coercive actions no liberty-loving people could tolerate: the Boston Port Act, intended, it was believed, to snuff out the economic life of the Massachusetts metropolis; the Administration of Justice Act, aimed at crippling judicial processes once and for all by permitting trials to be held in England for offenses committed in Massachusetts; the Massachusetts Government Act, which stripped from the people of Massachusetts the protection of the British constitution by giving over all the "democratic" elements of the province's government — even popularly elected juries and town meetings — into the hands of the executive power; the Quebec Act, which, while not devised as a part of the coercive program, fitted it nicely, in the eyes of the colonists, by extending the boundaries of a "papist" province, and one governed wholly by prerogative, south into territory claimed by Virginia, Connecticut, and Massachusetts; finally, the Quartering Act, to take effect in all colonies, which permitted the seizure for the use of troops of all buildings, public and private, deserted and occupied.

Once these coercive acts were passed there could be little doubt that "the system of slavery fabricated against America . . . is the offspring of mature deliberation."

To the leaders of the Revolutionary movement there was, beyond question, "a settled, fixed plan for *enslaving* the colonies, or bringing them under arbitrary government, and indeed the nation too." By 1774 the idea "that the British government — the *King, Lords,* and *Commons* — have laid a regular plan to enslave America, and that they are now deliberately putting it in execution" had been asserted, Samuel Seabury wrote wearily but accurately, "over, and over, and over again." The less inhibited of the colonial orators were quick to point out that "the MONSTER of a standing ARMY" had sprung directly from "a PLAN . . . *systematically* laid, and pursued by the British *ministry,* near twelve years, for enslaving America"; the Boston Massacre, it was claimed, had been "planned by Hillsborough and a knot of treacherous knaves in Boston." Careful analysts like Jefferson agreed on the major point; in one of the most closely reasoned of the pamphlets of 1774 the Virginian stated unambiguously that though "single acts of tyranny may be ascribed to the accidental opinion of a day . . . a series of oppressions, begun at a distinguished period and pursued unalterably through every change of ministers, too plainly prove a deliberate and systematical plan of reducing us to slavery." So too the fastidious and scholarly John Dickinson, though in 1774 he still clung to the hope that inadvertence, at least on the part of the King, was involved, believed that "a plan had been deliberately framed and pertinaciously adhered to, unchanged even by frequent changes of ministers, unchecked by any intervening gleam of humanity, to sacrifice to a passion for arbitrary dominion the universal property, liberty, safety, honor, happiness, and prosperity of us unoffending yet devoted Americans." So too Washington, collaborating with George Mason in writing the Fairfax Resolves of 1774, agreed that the trouble had arisen from a "regular, systematic plan" of oppression, the English government "endeavoring by every piece of art and despotism to fix the shackles of slavery upon us"; he was convinced "beyond the smallest doubt," he wrote privately, "that these measures are the result of deliberation . . . I am as fully convinced as I am of my own existence that there has been a regular, systematic plan formed to enforce them. . . ."

The most common explanation, however — an explanation that rose from the deepest sources of British political culture, that was a part of the very structure of British political thought — located "the spring and cause of all the distresses and complaints of the people in England or in America" in "a kind of fourth power that the constitution knows nothing of, or has not provided against." This "overruling arbitrary power, which absolutely controls the King, Lords, and Commons," was composed, it was said, of the "ministers and favorites" of the King, who, in defiance of God and man alike, "extend their usurped authority infinitely too far," and, throwing off the balance of the constitution, make their "despotic will" the authority of the nation.

> For their power and interest is so great that they can and do procure whatever laws they please, having (by power, interest, and the application of the people's money to *placemen* and *pensioners*) the whole legislative authority at their command. So that it is plain (not to say a word of a particular reigning arbitrary *Stuarchal* power among them) that the rights of the people are ruined and destroyed by ministerial *tyrannical* authority, and thereby . . . become a kind of slaves to the ministers of state.

This "junto of courtiers and state-jobbers," these "court-locusts," whispering in the royal ear, "instill in the King's mind a divine right of authority to command his subjects" at the same time as they advance their "detestable scheme" by misinforming and misleading the people. . . .

Perhaps the most explicit and detailed explanation of the assault upon America by a conspiratorial ministry, encapsulating a century of opposition thought, came from the pen of a country parson in Connecticut writing "to enlighten the people of a country town not under the best advantages for information from the newspapers and other pieces wrote upon the controversy." Seeking to rouse the villagers "to a sense of the danger to which their liberties are now involved," the Rev. Ebenezer Baldwin of Danbury explained that during the last war "the state of the colonies was much more attended to than it had been in times past," and "a very exalted idea of the riches of this country" had been conveyed back to England by the returning officers and soldiers. This exciting information fitted the plans of the ministry neatly, for

> notwithstanding the excellency of the British constitution, if the ministry can secure a majority in Parliament who will come into all their measures [and] will vote as they bid them, they may rule as absolutely as they do in *France* or *Spain,* yea as in *Turkey* or *India.* And this seems to be the present plan: to secure a majority of Parliament, and thus enslave the nation with their own consent. The more places or pensions the ministry have in their gift the more easily they can *bribe* a majority of Parliament by bestowing

those places on them or their friends. This makes them erect so many new and unnecessary offices in America, even so as to swallow up the whole of the revenue . . . by bestowing these places — places of considerable profit and no labor — upon the children or friends or dependents of the members of Parliament, the ministry can secure them in their interest. This doubtless is the great thing the ministry are driving at, to establish arbitrary government with the consent of Parliament. And to keep the people of England still, the first exertions of this power are upon the colonies.

Thus the balance of the constitution had been thrown off by a gluttonous ministry usurping the prerogatives of the crown and systematically corrupting the independence of the Commons. Corruption was at the heart of it — the political corruption built on the general dissoluteness of the populace, so familiar in the history of tyranny and so shocking to observers of mid-eighteenth-century England. The evil, public and private, that had appalled Dickinson in 1754 had ripened, it seemed clear, in the subsequent decade. . . .

. . . "Liberty," John Adams wrote, "can no more exist without virtue and independence than the body can live and move without a soul," and what liberty can be expected to flow from England where "luxury, effeminacy, and venality are arrived at such a shocking pitch" and where "both electors and elected are become one mass of corruption"? It was not hard to see where England stood: it was, Adams declared, precisely at the point "where the Roman republic was when Jugurtha left it, and pronounced it 'a venal city, ripe for destruction, if it can only find a purchaser.'" The analogy to the decline and fall of Rome and its empire was intriguing and informative; others carried it further and became more specific. Like Rome in its decline, England, "from being the nursery of heroes, became the residence of musicians, pimps, panders, and catamites." The swift decline of her empire, which, it was observed, had reached its peak only between 1758 and the Stamp Act, resulted from the same poison that had proved so fatal to free states in classical antiquity: the corruption, effeminacy, and languor that came from "the riches and luxuries of the East" and led to a calamitous "decay of virtue" and the collapse of the constitution. Even Franklin, his old caution and careful optimism gone, agreed, writing in 1775 to his one-time political ally Joseph Galloway, that he would himself, reluctantly, have to oppose Galloway's plan for reconciliation.

. . . when I consider the extreme corruption prevalent among all orders of men in this old rotten state, and the glorious public virtue so predominant in our rising country, I cannot but apprehend more mischief than benefit from a closer union. I fear they will drag us after them in all the plundering wars which their desperate circumstances, injustice, and rapacity may prompt them to undertake; and their wide-wasting prodigality and profusion is a gulf that will swallow up every aid we may distress ourselves to afford them. Here numberless and needless places, enormous salaries, pensions, perquisites, bribes, groundless quarrels, foolish expeditions, false accounts or no accounts, contracts and jobs, devour all revenue and produce continual necessity in the midst of natural plenty. I apprehend, therefore, that to unite us intimately will only be to corrupt and poison us also. . . .

The fact that the ministerial conspiracy against liberty had risen from corruption was of the utmost importance to the colonists. It gave a radical new meaning to their claims: it transformed them from constitutional arguments to expressions of a world regenerative creed. For they had long known — it had been known everywhere in the English-speaking world in the eighteenth century — that England was one of the last refuges of the ancient gothic constitution that had once flourished everywhere in the civilized world. And now, in the outpourings of colonial protest, it was again repeated, but with new point and urgency, that by far "the greatest part of the human race" already lies in "total subjection to their rulers." Throughout the whole continent of Asia people are reduced "to such a degree of abusement and degradation"

> that the very idea of liberty is unknown among them. In *Africa,* scarce any human beings are to be found but barbarians, tyrants, and slaves: all equally remote from the true dignity of human nature and from a well-regulated state of society. Nor is *Europe* free from the curse. Most of her nations are forced to drink deep of the bitter cup. And in those in which freedom seem to have been established, the vital flame is going out. Two kingdoms, those of *Sweden* and *Poland,* have been betrayed and enslaved in the course of one year. The free towns of *Germany* can remain free no longer than their potent neighbors shall please to let them. *Holland* has got the forms if she has lost the spirit of a free country. *Switzerland* alone is in the full and safe possession of her freedom.

And if now, in this deepening gloom, the light of liberty went out in Britain too — in Britain, where next to "self-preservation, political liberty is the main aim and end of her constitution" — if, as events clearly portended and as "senators and historians are repeatedly predicting . . . continued corruption and standing armies will prove mortal distempers in her constitution" — what then? What refuge will liberty find?

"To our own country," it was answered, "must we look for the biggest part of that liberty and freedom that yet remains, or is to be expected, among mankind . . . For while the greatest part of the nations of the earth are held together under the yoke of universal slavery, the North American provinces yet remain *the country of free men:* the *asylum,* and the last, to which such may yet flee from the common deluge." More than that: "our native country . . . bids the fairest of any to promote *the perfection and happiness of mankind.*" No one, of course, can predict "the state of mankind in future ages." But insofar as one can judge the ultimate "designs of providence by the number and power of the causes that are already at work, we shall be led to think that the perfection and happiness of mankind is to be carried further in America than it has ever yet been in any place." Consider the growth the colonies had enjoyed in so short a time — growth in all ways, but especially in population: a great natural increase it had been, supplemented by multitudes from Europe, "tired out with the miseries they are doomed to at home," migrating to America "as the only country in which they can find food, raiment, and rest." Consider also the physical vigor of the people. But above all consider the moral health of the people and of the body politic.

> The fatal arts of luxury and corruption are but comparatively beginning among us . . . Nor is corruption yet established as the common principle in public affairs. Our representatives are not chosen by bribing, corrupting, or buying the votes of the electors. Nor does it take one half of the revenue of a province to manage her house of commons . . . We have been free also from the burden and danger of standing armies . . . Our defense has been our *militia* . . . the general operation of things among ourselves indicate strong tendencies towards a state of greater perfection and happiness than mankind has yet seen.

No one, therefore, can conceive of the cause of America as "the cause of a mob, of a party, or a faction." The cause of America "is the cause of *self-defense,* of *public faith,* and of the *liberties of mankind* . . . 'In our destruction, liberty itself expires, and human nature will despair of evermore regaining its first and original dignity.'"

This theme, elaborately orchestrated by the colonial writers, marked the fulfillment of the ancient idea, deeply embedded in the colonists' awareness, that America had from the start been destined to play a special role in history. The controversy with England, from its beginning in the early 1760's, had lent support to that belief, so long nourished by so many different sources: the covenant theories of the Puritans, certain strands of Enlightenment thought, the arguments of the English radicals, the condition of life in the colonies, even the conquest of Canada. It had been the Stamp Act that had led John Adams to see in the original settlement of the colonies "the opening of a grand scene and design in providence for the illumination of the ignorant and the emancipation of the slavish part of mankind all over the earth." And Jonathan Mayhew, celebrating the conclusion of the same episode, had envisioned future streams of refugees escaping from a Europe sunk in "luxury, debauchery, venality, intestine quarrels, or other vices." It was even possible, Mayhew had added, "who knows?" that "our liberties being thus established . . . on some future occasion . . . we or our posterity may even have the great felicity and honor to . . . keep Britain herself from ruin."

Now, in 1774, that "future occasion" was believed to be at hand. After the passage of the Coercive Acts it could be said that "all the spirit of patriotism or of liberty now left in England" was no more than "the last snuff of an expiring lamp," while "the same sacred flame . . . which once showed forth such wonders in Greece and in Rome . . . burns brightly and strongly in America." Who ought then to suppress as "whimsical and enthusiastical" the belief that the colonies were to become "the foundation of a great and mighty empire, the largest the world ever saw to be founded on such principles of liberty and freedom, both civil and religious . . . [and] which shall be the principal seat of that glorious kingdom which Christ shall erect upon earth in the latter days" ? America "ere long will build an empire upon the ruins of Great Britain; will adopt its constitution purged of its impurities, and from an experience of its defects will guard against those evils which have wasted its vigor and brought it to an untimely end." The hand of God was "in America now giving a new epocha to the history of the world."

In the invigorating atmosphere of such thoughts, the final conclusion of the colonists' logic could be drawn not with regret but with joy. For while everyone knew that when tyranny is abroad "submission is a crime"; while they readily acknowledged that "no obedience is due to arbitrary, unconstitutional edicts calculated to enslave a free people"; and while they knew that the invasion of the liberties of the people "constitutes a state of war with the people" who may properly use "all the power which God has given them" to protect themselves — nevertheless they hesitated to come to a final separation even after Lexington and Bunker Hill. They hesitated, moving slowly and reluctantly, protesting "before God and the world that the utmost of [our] wish is that things may return to their old channel." They hesitated because their *sentiments of duty and affection* were sincere; they hesitated because their respect for constituted authority was great; and they hesitated too because their future as an independent people was a matter of doubt, full of the fear of the unknown.

What would an independent American nation be? A republic, necessarily — and properly, considering the character and circumstances of the people. But history clearly taught that republics were delicate polities, quickly degenerating into anarchy and tyranny; it was impossible, some said, to "recollect a single instance of a nation who supported this form of government for any length of time or with any degree of greatness." Others felt that independence might "split and divide the empire into a number of petty, insignificant states" that would easily fall subject to the will of "some foreign tyrant, or the more intolerable despotism of a few American demagogues"; the colonies might end by being "parceled out, Poland-like."

But if what the faint-hearted called "the ill-shapen, diminutive brat, INDEPENDENCY" contained within it all that remained of freedom; if it gave promise of growing great and strong and becoming the protector and propagator of liberty everywhere; if it were indeed true that "the cause of America is in a great measure the cause of all mankind"; if " 'Tis not the concern of a day, a year, or an age; posterity are virtually involved in the contest, and will be more or less affected even to the end of time by our proceedings now" — if all of this were true, ways would be found by men inspired by such prospects to solve the problems of a new society and government. And so let every lover of mankind, every hater of tyranny,

> stand forth! Every spot of the old world is overrun with oppression. Freedom hath been hunted round the globe. Asia and Africa have long expelled her. Europe regards her like a stranger, and England hath given her warning to depart. O! receive the fugitive, and prepare in time an asylum for mankind.

The Nature of the American Revolution

Periodically, newspaper reporters, without identifying the document, ask Americans if they would be willing to sign the Declaration of Independence. Typically most Americans refuse, some describing it as "Commie junk," others certain that "Somebody ought to tell the FBI about this sort of rubbish." A nation, conceived in revolution, thus seems fearful of acknowledging its revolutionary history, perhaps because revolution, in our own time, has become identified with turbulent worldwide conditions that many believe threaten American society. Yet America was a revolutionary nation, and its example once inspired the downtrodden elsewhere to fight for their liberty.

In the following essay, Thomas C. Barrow seeks to discover how revolutionary the American Revolution was, and to determine how it compares with other great revolutions in modern history, such as the French and Russian. Barrow argues that, at least at the outset, the American Revolution was a struggle against foreign rule, rather than an internal upheaval, as it occurred in France and Russia where the oppressed masses toppled their rulers in the hope of creating a more just social order. Such social revolutions stem from deep-seated and long-standing conflicts over the very nature of the social system. The American quarrel with Great Britain, however, was of a much more limited nature. It was essentially a demand for home rule. Moreover, the origins of the Revolution profoundly influenced the direction the new nation took. Though the American Revolution did bring about important changes in the social order, they were relatively modest compared to the transformations occurring in France after 1789, or Russia after 1917, or China after 1948.

The principal problem Americans faced after 1776 was not redistributing wealth or privilege, but coping successfully with the demands of nation-building. These included devising constitutions and governments that citizens would respect and obey, integrating diverse elements into a nation strong enough to defend itself against other nations, and promoting the general welfare even when it conflicted with parochial interests.

Yet the absence from the American Revolution of a reign of terror or of bloody purges of the ruling classes should not obscure its genuinely revolutionary character. In 1776, kings and aristocrats ruled almost everywhere. Few, except the Americans, believed that republican government, resting on a measure of popular control, was practical. Conventional wisdom held that men were too turbulent to be governed except by kings and noblemen, that liberty and order were incompatible, and that people must sacrifice freedom for the sake of stability. The Americans understood how perilous their experiment in republicanism was, but they were confident that they could discover how to reconcile liberty with order. Sustaining them during the early years, when the country was an untested beleaguered nation, was the faith, expressed by James Madison that "the citizens of the United States are responsible for the greatest trust ever confided to a political authority." That trust was to demonstrate to a skeptical world the practicality of a government based on the consent of the governed, a notion truly revolutionary in most of the world until recently.

FOR FURTHER READING:

GIPSON, LAWRENCE H. *The Coming of The Revolution.* New York: Harper & Row, Publishers, 1954.*

GREENE, JACK P., ed. *The Reinterpretation of the American Revolution.* New York: Harper & Row, Publishers, 1969.*

PALMER, R. R. *Age of Democratic Revolution: The Challenge.* Princeton: Princeton University Press, 1969.*

Asterisk denotes paperback edition.

The American Revolution as a Colonial War for Independence THOMAS C. BARROW

The current historiographical controversies over the American Revolution owe much to Carl Becker. From Becker's day to the present, historians have debated the question of the existence or non-existence of an "internal revolution" in American society. Some historians, following Becker's lead, search for traces of internal social or political turmoil. Others, disagreeing with Becker, stress the continuity of institutions and traditions during the Revolution. At issue is the basic question of just "how revolutionary was the American Revolution," and in the failure of historians to agree on an answer to that question lies the source of controversy. And so the great debate continues.

Unfortunately, there is no adequate definition of a "revolution." The dictionary description of a revolution as a "total or radical change" certainly provides no effective guideline. Since history is the study of change in human society, locating a revolution according to that formula becomes a matter of appraising just how much change is involved in a given event, which inevitably comes down to a question of where one wants to place the emphasis. In any case, precise definitions are somewhat beside the point. When the word *revolution* is used today in connection with a political system, its meaning, if not its precise definition, is abundantly clear. The image called to mind is inescapably that of the French and Russian revolutions, which have provided us with our classic formulas for revolutionary re-structurings of society. A revolution in these terms represents the replacement of an archaic, repressive regime or regimes with something new, something more open, more flexible, more adaptable. In effect, in the interests of "progress," within the political system stability is replaced by instability until some new synthesis is achieved. Only then is stability restored, at which point the revolutionary drama is closed.

For generations now American historians have struggled to fit their "revolution" into this classic mold. The difficulties they have encountered in doing so are reflected in the present historiographical impasse. It is a problem that might have been avoided had we remembered that the American people were, until 1776, colonials. By its very nature, a colonial society must be, in certain vital ways, unstable. Unable to exercise complete political control, subject to continual external interven-

---

Source: Thomas C. Barrow, "The American Revolution as a Colonial War for Independence," *William and Mary Quarterly*, 3d ser., vol. 25 (1968), pp. 452–464.

tion and negative interference, a colonial society cannot achieve effective "maturity" — that is, cannot create and control a political system that will be suited to the requirements of the interests indigenous to that society. A colonial society is an "incomplete" society, and consequently an inherently unstable society. This was as true of American society prior to 1776 as it is today of the colonial societies left in our world. And, consequently, if instability is the given fact in American society at the beginning of the imperial crisis, it is hard to see how the classic pattern of "stability replaced by instability" can be imposed upon it. The answer, of course, is that it cannot, that in fact colonial wars for independence or "liberation" are generically different from revolutions of the French or Russian variety. And, after all, the American Revolution was just that — a colonial war of liberation. Given the widespread existence of such wars in today's world, it is odd that for so long a time we have overlooked the full implications of this fact.

Colonial wars for independence have an inner logic of their own. The first problem is to achieve self-determination. Once that is accomplished, it then becomes a matter of organization, about which, naturally, there always will be fundamental disagreement. What course this disagreement will take, and how bitter it will be, will be determined by the nature of the particular society. In former colonies which have emerged into nationhood in this century, the determining factor has largely been the heterogeneous nature of their societies; with little internal unity or coherence, these new nations generally have fallen back at first on authoritarian centralism. When this has proved incapable of solving the complex problems confronting the society, it has been replaced usually by some kind of collective leadership, often based on the only effective national organization in existence, the military. It is at this point that many of the emergent nations of today find themselves.

Americans were more fortunate in their escape from colonialism. Thanks to the nature of the First British Empire, with its emphasis on commercial growth rather than on imperial efficiency, its loose organization, and the high degree of self-government allowed to the colonists, Americans had developed effective political units which commanded the allegiance of most inhabitants and served as adequate vehicles for the transition from colonial status to nationhood. Given a common English inheritance and a common struggle against British "tyranny," these states made the transition with a minimum of disagreement and dissension. In effect, by 1760 self-government in America, while still incomplete, had gone far. A tightening of English imperial authority after the last war with France brought about a reaction within the colonies toward complete self-determination, which was achieved finally through military success.

Yet, whatever the difference of the American experience from other colonial wars of liberation, certain elements were of necessity shared in common. Within any colonial society there exists an establishment, a group of men whose interests and situation tie them to the existing structure and whose orientation is towards the preservation of the colonial status. When the issue of independence or self-determination begins to be debated, these men are caught in powerful crosscurrents. As natives to the society, they identify to some degree with its problems. At the same time, as beneficiaries of their privileged position within the existing colonial structure, they are not enthusiastic for change. Such men fall back on arguments of moderation, particularly stressing the economic benefits of association with the dominant country and also emphasizing the immaturity of their own society. The gains associated with independence are outweighed for them by the prospects of social and political disorganization. So these men cast their lot with their colonial rulers. Such a man was Thomas Hutchinson. So, too, were many of his Tory associates.

And men like Hutchinson found much to disturb them within American society. Actually, not only was American colonial society subjected to the instability normally inherent in colonial status but there were certain peculiar circumstances which complicated matters further. The melting-pot aspects of American society, the diversity of ethnic, religious, and cultural backgrounds to be found within it, created problems of communication. And, of equal importance, American colonial society was, after all, an artificial creation. Unlike most other historic colonial episodes, the American case was not a matter of an indigenous native society being expropriated and exploited by outsiders. In such instances, the pre-existing patterns of such native societies provide a degree of internal continuity and stability. But the English colonies in North America had at their disposal no such pre-existence. They were created specifically and artificially to perform certain functions in relation to the mother country. Most particularly, from the very beginning their economy was geared to production for distant markets over which they had no control and little influence.

At the same time, while there were sizable non-English elements within the colonial population which created special problems, nevertheless the majority of the colonists were of the same national origin as their "rulers." It was not an instance of a conquered native population forced to bow fatalistically before the superior skills and power of an alien culture. Rather, it was a case in large part of Englishmen being governed and exploited by Englishmen. The result was a high degree of friction between governed and governors — an insistence by the colonists on their rights as Englishmen — that gave a special flavor and complexity to colonial politics.

Thoughtful colonials were well aware of and influenced by these problems. Thomas Hutchinson and John Adams — Tory and Whig — disagreed not so much on the question of the eventual independence of the American colonies as on the question of timing. Hutchinson's toryism sprang in part from his conviction that American society was too immature, too unstable, to stand alone. External force and authority, it seemed to him, would be required for many years to maintain internal order and stability in America. Realistically, he understood that eventually independence was probable: "It is not likely that the American Colonies will remain part of the Dominions of Great Britain another Century." But, Hutchinson added, until then, "as we cannot otherwise subsist I am consulting the best interest of my country when I propose measures for maintaining this subjection [to England]." What particularly disturbed Hutchinson about the changes in English policy after 1760 was that they tended to increase the instability and disorder inherent within American society: "Sieur Montesquieu is right in supposing men good or bad according to the Climate where they live. In less than two centuries Englishmen by change of country are become more barbarous and fierce than the Savages who inhabited the country before they extirpated them, the Indians themselves."

John Adams viewed American development in a different way. Contrasting the New World with the Old, he found the former far superior. The settlement of America had produced men who "knew that government was a plain, simple, intelligible thing, founded in nature and reason, and quite comprehensible by common sense. They detested all the base services and servile dependencies of the feudal system . . . and they thought all such slavish subordinations were equally inconsistent with the constitution of human nature and that religious liberty with which Jesus had made them free." The problem was that this purity of mind and behavior was always threatened by contact with the corruption of the Old World. Specifically, subordination of Americans to a distant Parliament which knew little of their needs and desires was not only frustrating but dangerous to the American experiment: "A legislature that has so often discovered a want of information concerning us and our country; a legislature interested to lay burdens upon us; a legislature, two branches of which, I mean the lords and commons, neither love nor fear us! Every American of fortune and common sense, must look upon his property to be sunk downright one half of its value, the moment such an absolute subjection to parliament is established." Independence was a logical capstone to such reasoning, although it took Adams some time to take that final step.

The differences between Hutchinson and Adams suggest that the divisions in American society between conservatives and radicals on the question of separation from Great Britain were related in part to a disagreement over the means to achieve coherence or stability within American society. For one side, continued tutelage under English authority was a necessity until such a time as maturity was achieved. For the other, it seemed that the major roadblock to maturity, to internal harmony and unity, was that self-same English authority. In effect, it was a disagreement on means, not ends. And disagreements similar to that between Hutchinson and Adams can be found within any society — whether in the eighteenth or twentieth century — which is in the process of tearing itself loose from its colonial ties.

It is possible, too, to suggest certain similarities between American intellectual development in these years and the experience of other colonial peoples. From his study of politics in eighteenth-century America, and particularly from his analysis of the pamphlet literature of the Revolutionary years, Bernard Bailyn has concluded that the "configuration of ideas and attitudes" which comprised the "Revolutionary ideology could be found intact — completely formed — as far back as the 1730's" and that these ideas had their origin in the "transmission from England to America of the literature of political opposition that furnished the substance of the ideology of the Revolution." Colonial societies are both fascinated and yet antagonized by the culture of the dominant exploiting nation. They tend to borrow much from their rulers. The English background of a majority of the American colonists in their case made such borrowing a natural and easy process, particularly for those who, for one reason or another, identified themselves with British rule.

However, in colonial societies even many of those who are anxious to assert, or preserve, their native interests or culture cannot resist that fascination exerted by the dominant "mother country." These "patriots" borrow, too, but they are likely to borrow from the dissenting tradition within the dominant culture, from the literature of "opposition," to utilize in their own defense the language and literature of those elements within the ruling society which are critical, or subversive, of the governing traditions. In this way the prestige of the "superior" society can be used against that society itself. On the evidence of Bailyn's research, it seems that the Americans followed just such a line of development, fitting the "opposition" tradition into the framework of their own evolving institutions and traditions — a process which was facilitated by the natural connections between the American religious dissenting traditions and the "opposition" traditions of eighteenth-century English society.

Again, once the movement for independence enters its final phase within a colonial society and becomes an open contest of strength, other divisions tend to become obscured. The most determined supporters of the colonial rule are silenced or forced to rely increasingly on the military strength of their rulers to maintain their position. On the other side, the advocates of independence submerge momentarily whatever differences they may have and present a common front. It is a time of common effort, of mutual support within the forces interested in achieving self-determination. At the same time the "patriot" groups develop special organizations capable of coercing those elements within society, often a majority of the population, which are inclined towards neutrality or moderation. Such were the Sons of Liberty in the American Revolution, and the evidence suggests that they performed their work effectively. Partly because of their efforts, and more generally because of the peculiar character of American colonial society and the nature of the imperial conflict, American society weathered the crisis with relative stability and harmony. As John Adams put it, "The zeal and ardor of the people during the revolutionary war, supplying the place of government, commanded a degree of order, sufficient at least for the temporary preservation of society."

With independence come altered circumstances for a former colonial society. Victorious patriots, confronted with the task of creating a permanent political structure, gradually begin to disagree among themselves as to how it can best be done. Since the only effective central direction came previously from the colonial rulers, the problem in each newly independent society is to fit the surviving local units into some coherent national structure. Here the forces of localism and centralism come into conflict. Those men or interests firmly entrenched in their positions at the local level see in increased centralism a threat to their existence and power. On the other hand, those men or interests of a more cosmopolitan nature, geared to extra-local activities and contacts, can see the benefits that would accrue to them through the introduction of the smoother flow of communications and transactions that effective centralization would bring. The disagreement pits the particularism of the entrenched local interests and individuals against the nationalism of the cosmopolitan interests and individuals. In most contemporary emergent societies these latter groups are by far the weaker. Fortunately, in America the cosmopolitan groups were stronger and more effective, partly again because of the unusual origin and nature of American colonial society. From the beginning the English colonies had been geared to production for European markets; it was the reason for their existence. The result was the development of an economy which had geographical variations but a common external orientation. Merchants and large-scale producers of items for export dominated this society. In the period after independence was achieved, these men provided a firm base for the construction of an effective national political system. Their success came with the substitution of the Constitution of 1787 for the Articles of Confederation.

Historians following the Becker-Beard approach put a different interpretation on the period following the achievement of de facto independence. For them, it was the moment of the triumph of radical democratic elements within American society. The wording of the Declaration of Independence, the constitutions of the new state governments, and particularly the drawing up of the Articles of Confederation represent for these historians the influence of a form of "radicalism." Yet, as Elisha Douglass has noted, in the formation of the governments for the new states, rather puzzlingly the one political reorganization that was subjected to the most democratic method of discussion and adoption — that of Massachusetts — turned out to be not only the most conservative of all the state constitutions but more conservative, in fact, than the previous system. Somehow in Massachusetts, at least, an excess of democracy seems to have led to an enthronement of conservatism. And, indeed, the new constitutions or systems adopted in all the states were remarkable generally for their adherence to known and familiar forms and institutions.

Obviously, given the disruption of the traditional ties to England, the interruption of the natural economic dependence on English markets, the division of American society into opposing Whig and Tory camps, and the presence on American soil of enemy troops (which occupied at different moments the most important commercial centers), some confusion and dissension was inevitable within American society. What is remarkable is how little upheaval and disagreement there actually was. Had American society been ripe for a social upheaval, had it been comprised of oppressing and oppressed classes, no better opportunity could have been offered. The conservative nature of the American response suggests that something other than a radical re-structuring of society was what was debated or desired.

Again, some historians have interpreted the decentralized political system created under the Articles of Confederation as a "triumph" of radical democracy. However, if instability, associated with colonial status and with the peculiar character of American colonial society, was a recurrent problem, and if inability to achieve positive control of their own political system was a major irritant, then the decentralization of the Articles was a logical development. In effect, if home rule was the issue and the cure, it was only natural that each local unit should seek as much autonomy within the national framework as possible. Seemingly, decentralization was the best method to bring coherence and stability, or maturity, to American society. Each local unit could look to its own needs, could arrange for the effective solution of its own special problems, could work to create that internal balance and harmony of conflicting interests that are the earmark of stability and maturity.

The problem with the Articles was not an excess of democracy. What brought about an effective opposition to them was their failure to achieve their purpose. The history of the states under the Articles, at least in the eyes of many contemporaries, suggested that decentralization, rather than being a source of stability, was a source of confusion and turmoil. James Madison explained the nature of the mistake in his Tenth Federalist. In spite of independence, under the system created by the Articles, wrote Madison, "complaints are everywhere heard from our most considerate and virtuous citizens . . . that our governments are too unstable." The problem, for Madison, was to control faction within society, and the most dangerous type of faction is that which includes a majority. Unfortunately, the "smaller the society, the fewer probably will be the distinct parties and interests composing it; the fewer the distinct parties and interests, the more frequently will a majority be found of the same party; and the smaller the number of individuals composing a majority, and the smaller the compass within which they are placed, the more easily will they concert and execute their plans of oppression." The solution is to enlarge the sphere, because if "you take in a greater variety of parties and interests," then "you make it less probable that a majority of the whole will have a common motive to invade the rights of other citizens . . . The influence of factious leaders may kindle a flame within their particular States, but will be unable to spread a general conflagration through the other States."

Nor was the opposition to the Constitution less concerned than Madison about order and stability within society. Again, disagreement was fundamentally over means, not ends. The anti-Federalists clung to the former ideas of local autonomy. They were, in fact, not more democratic than their opponents but more conservative. They were afraid of change: "If it were not for the stability and attachment which time and habit gives to forms of government, it would be in the power of the enlightened and aspiring few, if they should combine, at any time to destroy the best establishments, and even make the people the instruments of their own subjugation." The trouble was that the system created under the Articles was not yet sanctified by time: "The late revolution having effaced in a great measure all former habits, and the present institutions are so recent, that there exists not that great reluctance to innovation, so remarkable in old communities . . . it is the genius of the common law to resist innovation." George Clinton agreed with Madison on the dangers of faction: "The people, when wearied with their distresses, will in the moment of frenzy, be guilty of the most imprudent and desperate measures. . . . I know the people are too apt to vibrate from one extreme to another. The effects of this disposition are what I wish to guard against." It was on the solution to the problem, not on the nature of the problem, that Clinton differed from Madison. For Clinton, the powerful central government created by the Constitution might too easily become a vehicle for popular tyranny. It was this same sentiment which led eventually to the adoption of the first ten amendments, the Bill of Rights, with their reservations of basic rights and powers to local units and individuals.

It would not do to carry the comparison between the American Revolution and other colonial wars of liberation, particularly those of the twentieth century, too far. But there is enough evidence to suggest certain basic similarities between the American experience and that of other emergent colonial peoples — enough evidence, at least, to suggest that the efforts of historians to impose on the American Revolution the classic pattern of the French and Russian revolutions have led to a distorted view of our national beginnings. A French Revolution is the product of unbearable tensions within a society. The purpose of such a revolution is to destroy society as it exists, or at least to destroy its most objectional aspects, and to replace the old with something new. In contrast, a colonial "revolution" or war of liberation has as its purpose the achievement of self-determination, the "completion" or fulfillment of an existing society, rather than its destruction. A French Revolution is first of all destructive; a colonial revolution, first of all constructive. In either case the process may not be completed. In the instance of the French Revolution, the re-constructed society may contain more of the old than the original revolutionaries desired. And in the case of the colonial revolution, the process of winning independence and the difficulties of organizing an effective national political structure may open the gates to change, may create a radicalism that carries the original society far from its former course; the result may be more destruction than was originally envisaged. Yet, the goals of these two revolutions are fundamentally different, and their different goals determine a different process of fulfillment. The unfolding of the revolutionary drama, the "stages" of revolution, will be quite different, if not opposite.

For John Adams, the American Revolution was an epochal event, a moment of wonder for the world to behold and consider. At times his rhetoric carried him beyond the confines of his innate caution, and he sounded like a typical revolutionary: "The progress of society will be accelerated by centuries by this revolution . . . Light spreads from the dayspring in the west, and may it shine more and more until the perfect day." But, as Edward Handler has noted, "The truth is that if Adams was a revolutionary, he was so in a sense very different than that produced by the other great modern revolutions." Adams did indeed feel that his revolution had a meaning for the world but it was not related to the violent re-structurings of society. Rather its message, for Adams, was that free men can decide voluntarily to limit their freedom in the interests of mutual association, that rational men can devise a system that can at once create order and preserve liberty. The American success was in contrast to the traditional authoritarian systems of the Old World: "Can authority be more amiable or respectable, when it descends from accidents or institutions established in remote antiquity, than when it springs fresh from the hearts and judgments of an honest and enlightened people?"

Most wars of liberation are not so orderly as that of the American Revolution. Most, at least in this century, have led to increasing radicalism and division within the liberated society. National unity has not been easily achieved. That the American emergence from colonialism had a different ending is significant. A firm basis for unity obviously existed within American society, which, naturally, suggests that the reverse, too, was true — that such tensions and divisions as did exist within American society were relatively minor and harmless. It is no wonder that historians determined to find an internal social or political revolution of the French variety within the American Revolution have encountered such difficulties. Nor is it a wonder that the Revolution has become so beclouded with historiographical debates and arguments. The problem has been in our approach. We have been studying, it would seem, the wrong revolution.

Nation-Building, American Style

The Revolutionary Era (1763-1789) was the most creative period in American political history. Drawing on a century and a half of colonial political experience, forced by the crisis of the 1760s to think long and hard about the nature of government, and confronted with the vexing task of reconciling liberty with authority, Americans worked out, after much painful trial and error, new rules for political life — procedures and arrangements they have employed ever since.

Once they renounced British authority, the Americans had to construct new governments of their own devising, both on the state and national level. They wrote and rewrote more than a dozen state constitutions in that many years and composed two for the nation — the Articles of Confederation and the federal Constitution of 1787. By the time the Founding Fathers met at Philadelphia to draft the federal Constitution, constitutional thought had clarified and matured.

From the beginning of the controversy with England, two of the central issues in the debate with Parliament involved the meaning and nature of a constitution — in this case the British constitution — and the most appropriate constitutional forms for guaranteeing individual liberty, yet at the same time providing the state with means to maintain public order. A government with excessive power could become tyrannical; one that was too weak could become the victim of anarchy. In either case, men would lose their freedom.

Convinced that the new taxes imposed by Parliament in the 1760s threatened their own local assemblies, which until then were the only bodies that had levied taxes in America, the colonists sought to find a rationale for limiting parliamentary authority. From the claim that the British constitution guaranteed all Englishmen "no taxation without representation," they went on to insist that the British constitution restricted Parliament's power over the colonists. The British replied that the constitution was whatever Parliament said it was; new laws automatically became part of the constitution. Legally and historically the British were correct. Unconsciously the Americans were creatively groping toward a new conception of a constitution as a higher law which prescribed fundamental rules of the political game in order to protect people from arbitrary authority. Legislatures that derived their authority from the constitution, they argued, must therefore act within the limits prescribed by the fundamental law. Thus Americans made this conception explicit by adding a Bill of Rights to their new revolutionary constitution to protect individual liberty from arbitrary government.

As the Americans reconceived the nature of constitutions, they also faced the procedural problem of how to write and institute them. At first, the provisional revolutionary legislatures, set up after independence was declared, drafted constitutions. But many questioned the appropriateness of this procedure, for, if a legislature could make a constitution, it could change it and would, therefore, not be bound by it. The solution was to convene conventions to draft constitutions which then were to be ratified either by the voters or, as in the case of the federal Constitution, by specially chosen ratifying conventions. In the following essay, Robert R. Palmer argues that one of the principal achievements of the Americans in the Age of Democratic Revolution (1760–1800) was to devise new constitutional procedures, such as the Constitutional Convention, and new principles, such as the idea that constitutions were fundamental laws, that formed the underlying framework of popular government.

FOR FURTHER READING:

DOUGLAS, ELISHA P. *Rebels and Democrats: The Struggle for Equal Political Rights and Majority Rule during the American Revolution.* Chicago: Quadrangle Books, 1965.*

TAYLOR, ROBERT, ed. *Massachusetts, Colony to Commonwealth: Documents on the Formation of Its Constitution.* Chapel Hill: University of North Carolina Press, 1961.*

WOOD, GORDON S. *Creation of the American Republic.* Chapel Hill: University of North Carolina Press, 1969.*

Asterisk denotes paperback edition.

The American Revolution: The People as Constituent Power ROBERT R. PALMER

If it be asked what the American Revolution distinctively contributed to the world's stock of ideas, the answer might go somewhat along these lines. It did not contribute primarily a social doctrine — for although a certain skepticism toward social rank was an old American attitude, and possibly even a gift to mankind, it long antedated the Revolution, which did not so much cut down, as prevent the growth of, an aristocracy of European type. It did not especially contribute economic ideas — for the Revolution had nothing to teach on the production or distribution of goods, and the most advanced parties objected to private wealth only when it became too closely associated with government. They aimed at a separation of economic and political spheres, by which men of wealth, while free to get rich, should not have a disproportionate influence on government, and, on the other hand, government and public emoluments should not be used as a means of livelihood for an otherwise impecunious and unproductive upper class.

The American Revolution was a political movement, concerned with liberty, and with power. Most of the ideas involved were by no means distinctively American. There was nothing peculiarly American in the concepts, purely as concepts, of natural liberty and equality. They were admitted by conservatives, and were taught in the theological faculty at the Sorbonne. Nor could Americans claim any exclusive understanding of the ideas of government by contract or consent, or the sovereignty of the people, or political representation, or the desirability of independence from foreign rule, or natural rights, or the difference between natural law and positive law, or between certain fundamental laws and ordinary legislation, or the separation of powers, or the federal union of separate states. All these ideas were perfectly fa-

Source: Robert R. Palmer, *The Age of the Democratic Revolution: A Political History of Europe and America 1760–1800* (Princeton: Princeton University Press, 1964), vol. 1, *The Challenge*, chap. 8, "The American Revolution: The People as Constituent Power," pp. 213–235.

miliar in Europe, and that is why the American Revolution was of such interest to Europeans.

The Distinctiveness of American Political Ideas

The most distinctive work of the Revolution was in finding a method, and furnishing a model, for putting these ideas into practical effect. It was in the implementation of similar ideas that Americans were more successful than Europeans. "In the last fifty years," wrote General Bonaparte to Citizen Talleyrand in 1797, "there is only one thing that I can see that we have really defined, and that is the sovereignty of the people. But we have had no more success in determining what is constitutional, than in allocating the different powers of government." And he said more peremptorily, on becoming Emperor in 1804, that the time had come "to constitute the Nation." He added: "I am the constituent power."

The problem throughout much of America and Europe, for half a century, was to "constitute" new government, and in a measure new societies. The problem was to find a constituent power. Napoleon offered himself to Europe in this guise. The Americans solved the problem by the device of the constitutional convention, which, revolutionary in origin, soon became institutionalized in the public law of the United States.

The constitutional convention in theory embodied the sovereignty of the people. The people chose it for a specific purpose, not to govern, but to set up institutions of government. The convention, acting as the sovereign people, proceeded to draft a constitution and a declaration of rights. Certain "natural" or "inalienable" rights of the citizen were thus laid down at the same time as the powers of government. It was the constitution that created the powers of government, defined their scope, gave them legality, and balanced them one against another. The constitution was written and comprised in a single document. The constitution and accompanying declaration, drafted by the convention, must, in the developed theory, be ratified by the people. The convention thereupon disbanded and disappeared, lest its members have a vested interest in the offices they created. The constituent power went into abeyance, leaving the work of government to the authorities now constituted. The people, having exercised sovereignty, now came under government. Having made law, they came under law. They put themselves voluntarily under restraint. At the same time, they put restraint upon government. All government was limited government; all public authority must keep within the bounds of the constitution and of the declared rights. There were two levels of law, a higher law or constitution that only the people could make or amend, through constitutional conventions or bodies similarly empowered; and a statutory law, to be made and unmade, within the assigned limits, by legislators to whom the constitution gave this function.

Such was the theory, and it was a distinctively American one. European thinkers, in all their discussion of a political or social contract, of government by consent and of sovereignty of the people, had not clearly imagined the people as actually contriving a constitution and creating the organs of government. They lacked the idea of the people as a constituent power. Even in the French Revolution the idea developed slowly; members of the French National Assembly, long after the Tennis Court oath, continued to feel that the constitution which they were writing, to be valid, had to be accepted by the King as a kind of equal with whom the nation had to negotiate. Nor, indeed, would the King tolerate any other view. On the other hand, we have seen how at Geneva in 1767 the democrats advanced an extreme version of citizen sovereignty, holding that the people created the constitution and the public offices by an act of will; but they failed to get beyond a simple direct democracy; they had no idea of two levels of law, or of limited government, or of a delegated and representative legislative authority, or of a sovereign people which, after acting as a god from the machine in a constituent convention, retired to the more modest status of an electorate, and let its theoretical sovereignty become inactive.

The difficulty with the theory was that the conditions under which it could work were seldom present. No people really starts *de novo;* some political institutions always already exist; there is never a *tabula rasa*, or state of nature, or Chart Blanche as Galloway posited for conservative purposes. Also, it is difficult for a convention engaged in writing a constitution not to be embroiled in daily politics and problems of government. And it is hard to live voluntarily under restraint. In complex societies, or in times of crisis, either government or people or some part of the people may feel obliged to go beyond the limits that a constitution has laid down.

In reality, the idea of the people as a constituent power, with its corollaries, developed unclearly, gradually, and sporadically during the American Revolution. It was adumbrated in the Declaration of Independence: the people may "institute new government." Jefferson, among the leaders, perhaps conceived the idea most clearly. It is of especial interest, however, to see how the "people" themselves, that is, certain lesser and unknown or poorer or unsatisfied persons, contributed to these distinctive American ideas by their opposition to the Revolutionary elite.

There were naturally many Americans who felt that no change was needed except expulsion of the British. With the disappearance of the British governors, and collapse of the old governor's councils, the kind of men who had been active in the colonial assemblies, and who now sat as provincial congresses or other *de facto* revolutionary bodies, were easily inclined to think that they should keep the management of affairs in their own hands. Some parallel can be seen with what happened in Europe. There was a revolution, or protest, of constituted bodies against authorities set above them, and a more popular form of revolution, or protest, which aimed at changing the character or membership of these constituted bodies themselves. As at Geneva the General Council rebelled against the patriciate, without wishing to admit new citizens to the General Council; as in Britain the Whigs asserted the powers of Parliament against the King, without wishing to change the composition of Parliament; as in Belgium, in 1789, the Estates party declared independence from the Emperor, while maintaining the preexisting estates; as in France, also in 1789, the nobility insisted that the King govern through the Estates-General, but objected to the transformation of the three estates into a new kind of national body; as in the Dutch provinces in 1795 the Estates-General, after expelling the Prince of Orange, tried to remain itself unchanged, and resisted the election of a "convention"; so, in America in 1776, the assemblies that drove out the officers of the King, and governed their respective states under revolutionary conditions, sought to keep control of affairs in their own hands, and to avoid reconstitution at the hands of the "people."

Ten states gave themselves new constitutions in 1776 and 1777. In nine of these states, however, it was the ordinary assembly, that is, the revolutionary government of the day, that drafted and proclaimed the constitution. In the tenth, Pennsylvania, a constituent convention met, but it soon had to take on the burden of daily government in addition. In Connecticut and Rhode Island the colonial charters remained in force, and the authorities constituted in colonial times (when governors and councils had already been elected) remained unchanged in principle for half a century. In Massachusetts the colonial charter remained in effect until 1780.

Thus in no state, when independence was declared, did a true constituent convention meet, and, as it were, calmly and rationally devise government out of a state of nature. There was already, however, some recognition of the principle that constitutions cannot be made merely by governments, that a more fundamental power is needed to produce a constitution than to pass ordinary laws or carry on ordinary executive duties. Thus, in New Hampshire, New York, Delaware, Maryland, North Carolina, and Georgia, the assemblies drew up constitutions only after soliciting authority for that purpose from the voters. In Maryland and North Carolina there was a measure of popular ratification.

Constitution-making in North Carolina, Pennsylvania, and Massachusetts

The popular pressures that helped to form American political doctrine are best illustrated from North Carolina, Pennsylvania, and Massachusetts.

In North Carolina class lines had been sharply drawn by the Regulator movement and its suppression. The people of the back-country even inclined to be loyalist, not eager for an independence that might only throw them into the hands of the county gentry. In the turbulent election of October 1776 the voters knew that the assembly which they elected would draft a state constitution. There was no demand for a convention to act exclusively and temporarily as a constituent power. But several counties drew up instructions for the deputies, in which the emerging doctrine was set forth clearly.

Orange and Mecklenburg counties used identical language. This is a sign, as in the case of identical phrasing in the French *cahiers* of 1789, where the matter has been carefully studied, that some person of influence and education, and not some poor farmer ruminating in his cabin, had probably written out a draft. Still, the public meetings of both counties found it to their taste. "Political power," they said, "is of two kinds, one principal and superior, the other derived and inferior. . . . The principal supreme power is possessed only by the people at large. . . . The derived and inferior power by the servants which they employ. . . . The rules by which the inferior power is exercised are to be constituted by the principal supreme power. . . ." In other words, government was not a form of guardianship. Office was to be no longer a perquisite of the gentry, or "an aristocracy of power in the hands of the rich," to use their own language, but a form of employment by the people, whom they did not hesitate to call "the poor." Mecklenburg favored a unicameral legislature, Orange a bicameral one, but both called for a separation of powers. It was not that any organ of government should enjoy independence from the electorate (the essence of balance-of-power theory in the European, British, and loyalist view), but rather that the various functions of government should be defined and distributed among different men, to prevent what had happened in colonial times. The fact that before 1776 the council had possessed executive, legislative, and judicial functions, and that members of the assembly had served as justices of the peace, or had their relatives appointed judges and sheriffs, was the basis on which North Carolina had been dominated by small groups of gentry. It was popular objection to this situation, probably more than a reading of European books, that made the separation of powers a principal American doctrine.

The North Carolina constitution, as written and adopted, enlarged the electorate by granting all taxpayers the right to vote for members of the lower house. It equalized the representation by giving more deputies to the western counties. It required a freehold of 100 acres for members of the lower house, and of 300 acres for those of the upper house, who were to be elected only by voters possessing 50 acres. The governor, elected by the two houses, had to have a freehold worth £1,000. The constitution was a compromise between populace and landed gentry. It lasted until the Civil War.

The situation in Pennsylvania was complex. The Quaker colony, idealized by European intellectuals as the haven of innocent equality and idyllic peace, had long been plagued by some of the most acrimonious politics in America. Quaker bigwigs had long clashed with the non-Quaker lesser orders of Philadelphia and the West. In the spring of 1776 Pennsylvania was the only colony in which the assembly was still legal under the old law. It still showed a desire for reconciliation with England, and, with it, maintenance of the old social and political system. This persistence of conservatism in high places made a great many people all the more radical. A year of open war with Britain had aroused the determination for independence, and in May 1776 a mass meeting of 4,000 people in Philadelphia demanded the calling of a constitutional convention. Various local committees got to work, and a convention was elected by irregular methods. Where the three eastern counties had formerly been heavily over-represented, the situation was now not equalized, but reversed. The West, with the same population as the three eastern counties, had 64 delegates in the convention to only 24 for the East. "The Convention in Pennsylvania was a political expedient, and not, as in Massachusetts, the cornerstone of constitutional government." Its real function was to promote the Revolution, and assure independence from England, by circumventing the assembly and all other opposition. Like the more famous French Convention elected in 1792, it rested on a kind of popular mandate which did not reflect an actual majority of the population; like it, it became the government of the country during war and revolution; like it, it behaved dictatorially. The constitutions drafted in Pennsylvania in 1776, and in France in 1793, were, in their formal provisions, by far the most democratic of any produced in the eighteenth century. The Pennsylvania constitution of 1776, unlike the French constitution of the Year I, was never submitted even to the formalities of popular ratification. But the two constitutions became a symbol of what democrats meant by democracy.

The Pennsylvania constitution vested legislative power in a single house. For the executive it avoided the name and office of governor, entrusting executive power to a council and "president," a word which then meant no more than chairman. All male taxpayers twenty-one years of age had the vote, and were eligible for any office. To sit in the assembly, however, it was necessary publicly to acknowledge the divine inspiration of the Old and New Testaments. Voters elected the legislators, the executive councillors, sheriffs, coroners, tax-assessors, and justices of the peace. Voting was by ballot. The president was chosen by the legislature and the executive council; he had no veto or appointive powers, and what powers he did have he could exercise only in agreement with his council. All officers were elected for one year, except that councillors served for three. Rotation of office was provided for; legislators, councillors, president, and sheriffs could be reelected only a certain number of times. Doors of the legislative assembly must always be open to the public. There was a kind of referendum, in that no bill passed by the assembly, short of emergency, became law until submitted for public consideration and enacted in the assembly of the following year, if there was no public objection. Officeholders received pay, but if revenues of any office became too large the assembly could reduce them. All officers and judges could be impeached by the assembly. Judges of the Supreme Court could be removed by the assembly for "misbehavior." There was an elected council of censors, or board of review, which every seven years ascertained whether the constitution had been preserved inviolate, and called a convention if amendment seemed necessary.

The Pennsylvania constitution represented the doctrine of a single party, namely the democrats, people of the kind who had formerly had little to do with government, and whose main principle was that government should never become a separate or vested interest within the state. This was indeed an understandable principle, at a time when government, in all countries in varying degree, had in fact become the entrenched interest of a largely hereditary governing class. The Pennsylvania constitution substituted almost a direct democracy, in which no one in government could carry any responsibility or pursue any sustained program of his own. Many people in Pennsylvania objected to it from the beginning. It must be remembered that the democratic constitution did not signify that Pennsylvania was really more democratic than some of the other states; it signified, rather, that Pennsylvania was more divided, and that conservatism was stronger, certain upper-class and politically experienced elements, which elsewhere took a leading part in the Revolution, being in Pennsylvania tainted with Anglophilism. Whether the constitution of 1776 was workable or not, these people soon put an end to it. It lasted only until 1790.

The most interesting case is that of Massachusetts. Here the great political thinker was John Adams, who became the main author of the Massachusetts constitution of 1780, which in turn had an influence on the Constitution of the United States. In his own time Adams was denounced as an Anglomaniac and a Monocrat. In our own time some sympathizers with the eighteenth-century democrats have considered him very conservative, while on the other hand theorists of the "new conservatism" would persuade us that John Adams was in truth the American Edmund Burke. I confess that I see very little in any of these allegations.

Adams in January 1776 published some *Thoughts on Government*, for the guidance of those in the various colonies who were soon to declare independence and begin to govern themselves. This was in some ways a conservative tract. Adams thought it best, during the war, for the new states simply to keep the forms of government that they had. He obviously approved the arrangement under the Massachusetts charter of 1691, by which the popular assembly elected an upper house or council. In other ways he was not very conservative. He declared, like Jefferson, that the aim of government is welfare or happiness, that republican institutions must rest on "virtue," and that the people should support a universal system of public schools. He wanted one-year terms for governors and officials (the alternative would be "slavery"), and he favored rotation of office. He quite agreed that someday the state governors and councillors might be popularly elected, as they were in Connecticut already. He gave six reasons for having a bicameral legislature, but in none of these six reasons did he show any fear of the people, or belief that, with a unicameral legislature, the people would plunder property or degenerate into anarchy. He was afraid of the one-house legislature itself. He never committed the folly of identifying the deputies with the deputizers. He was afraid that a single house would be arbitrary or capricious, or make itself perpetual, or "make laws for their own interest, and adjudge all controversies in their own favor." He himself cited the cases of Holland and the Long Parliament. The fear of a self-perpetuating political body, gathering privileges to itself, was certainly better grounded in common observation than vague alarms about anarchy or pillage.

The *Thoughts* of 1776 were conservative in another way, if conservatism be the word. Adams had not yet conceived the idea of a constitutional convention. He lacked the notion of the people as constituent power. He had in mind that existing assemblies would draft the new constitutions, when and if any were drafted. Adams was familiar with all the high-level political theory of England and Europe. But the idea of the people as the constituent power arose locally, from the grass roots.

The revolutionary leadership in Massachusetts, including both Adamses, was quite satisfied to be rid of the British, and otherwise to keep the Bay State as it had always been. They therefore "resumed" the charter of 1691. They simply undid the Massachusetts Government Act of 1774. Some of the commonalty of Boston, and farmers of Concord and the western towns, envisaged further changes. It is hard to say what they wanted, except that they wanted a new constitution. Experts in Massachusetts history contradict each other flatly; some say that debtors, poor men, and Baptists were dissatisfied; others that all kinds of diverse people naturally owed money anyway, that practically no one was too poor to vote, and that Baptists were an infinitesimal splinter group in a solidly Congregationalist population. It may be that the trouble was basically psychological; that many people of fairly low station, even though they had long had the right to vote, had never until the Revolution participated in politics, were aroused by the Revolution, the war, and excitement of soldiering, and, feeling that affairs had always been managed by people socially above them, wanted now to act politically on their own.

Demands were heard for a new constitution. It was said that the charter of 1691 was of no force, since the royal power that had issued it was no longer valid. It was said that no one could be governed without his consent, and that no living person had really consented to this charter. Some Berkshire towns even hinted that they did not belong to Massachusetts at all until they shared in constituting the new commonwealth. They talked of "setting themselves apart," or being welcomed by a neighboring state. Echoes of the social contract floated through the western air. "The law to bind all must be assented to by all," declared the farmers of Sutton. "The Great Secret of Government is governing all by all," said those of Spencer. It began to seem that a constitution was necessary not only to secure liberty but to establish authority, not only to protect the individual but to found the state.

The house of representatives proposed that it and the council, that is, the two houses of legislation sitting together, should be authorized by the people to draw up a constitution. All adult males were to vote on the granting of this authorization, not merely those possessing the customary property qualification. In a sense, this was to recognize Rousseau's principle that there must be "unanimity at least once": that everyone must consent to the law under which he was to live, even if later, when constitutional arrangements were made, a qualification was required for ordinary voting. The council objected to a plan whereby it would lose its identity by merging with the house. A little dispute occurred, not unlike that in France in 1789 between "vote by head" and "vote by order." The plan nevertheless went through. The two houses, sitting as one, and authorized by the people, produced a constitution in

1778. It was submitted for popular ratification. The voters repudiated it. Apparently both democrats and conservatives were dissatisfied. This is precisely what happened in Holland in 1797, when the first constitution of the Dutch revolution was rejected by a coalition of opposite-minded voters.

A special election was therefore held, in which all towns chose delegates to a state convention, "for the sole purpose of forming a new Constitution." John Adams, delegate from Braintree, was put on the drafting committee. He wrote a draft, which the convention modified only in detail. The resulting document reflected many influences. It is worth while to suggest a few.

There is a modern fashion for believing that Rousseau had little influence in America, particularly on such sensible characters as John Adams. I do not think that he had very much. Adams, however, had read the *Social Contract* as early as 1765, and ultimately had four copies of it in his library. I suspect that, like others, he found much of it unintelligible or fantastic, and some of it a brilliant expression of his own beliefs. He himself said of the Massachusetts constitution: "It is Locke, Sidney, Rousseau, and de Mably reduced to practice."

Adams wrote in the preamble: "The body politic is formed by a voluntary association of individuals. It is a social compact, by which the whole people covenants with each citizen, and each citizen with the whole people, that all shall be governed by certain laws for the common good." The thought here, and the use of the word "covenant," go back to the Mayflower compact. But whence comes the "social" in *social* compact? And whence comes the word "citizen"? There were no "citizens" under the British constitution, except in the sense of freemen of the few towns known as cities. In the English language the word "citizen" in its modern sense is an Americanism, dating from the American Revolution. It is entirely possible that Jean-Jacques Rousseau had deposited these terms in Adams' mind. The whole passage suggests Chapter vi, Book 1, of the *Social Contract*. The convention adopted this part of Adams' preamble without change.

In the enacting clause of the preamble Adams wrote: "We, therefore, the delegates of the people of Massachusetts . . . agree upon the following . . . Constitution of the Commonwealth of Massachusetts." The convention made a significant emendation: "We, therefore, the people of Massachusetts . . . agree upon, ordain and establish. . . ." The formula, *We the people ordain and establish*, expressing the developed theory of the people as constituent power, was used for the first time in the Massachusetts constitution of 1780, whence it passed into the preamble of the United States constitution of 1787 and the new Pennsylvania constitution of 1790, after which it became common in the constitutions of the new states, and in new constitutions of the old states. Adams did not invent the formula. He was content with the matter-of-fact or purely empirical statement that the "delegates" had "agreed." It was the popularly elected convention that rose to more abstract heights. Providing in advance for popular ratification, it imputed the creation of government to the people.

Adams wrote, as the first article of the Declaration of Rights: "All men are born equally free and independent, and have certain natural, essential and unalienable rights," which included defense of their lives, liberties, and property, and the seeking of "safety and happiness." The Virginia Declaration of Rights, drafted by George Mason in June 1776, was almost identical, and Adams certainly had it in mind. The Massachusetts convention made only one change in this sentence. It declared: "All men are born free and equal." The convention, obviously, was thinking of the Declaration of Independence, that is, Jefferson's more incisive rewording of Mason's Virginia declaration.

The convention had been elected by a true universal male suffrage, but it adopted, following Adams' draft, a restriction on the franchise. To vote, under the constitution, it was necessary to own real estate worth £3 a year, or real and personal property of a value of £60. The charter of 1691 had specified only £2 and £40 respectively. The state constitution was thus in this respect more conservative than the charter. How much more conservative? Here we run into the difference between experts already mentioned. A whole school of thought, pointing to a 50 per cent increase in the voting qualification, has seen a reaction of property-owners against dangers from below. Closer examination of the values of money reveals that the £3 and £60 of 1780 represent an increase of only one-eighth over the figures of 1691. Even if half the people of Boston were unfranchised, all Boston then had only a twentieth of the population of the state. In the rural areas, where farm ownership was usual, it was mainly grown sons living for a few years with their parents who lacked the vote. There seems to have been only sporadic objection to the suffrage provision.

Adams put into the constitution, and the convention retained it, that ghost of King, Lords, and Commons that now assumed the form of governor, senate, and house of representatives. Partisans of the British system, in England or America, would surely find this ghost highly attenuated. The point about King and Lords, in the British system, was precisely that they were not elected by anyone, that they were immune to popular pressure, or any pressure, through their enjoyment of life tenure and hereditary personal rights to political position. Governor and senators in Massachusetts, like representatives, both in Adams' draft and in the final document, were all elected, all by the same electorate, and all for one-year terms. To Adams (as, for example, to Delolme), it was of the utmost importance to prevent the executive from becoming the mere creature of the legislature. He even wished the governor to have an absolute veto, which the convention changed to a veto that could be overridden by a two-thirds majority of both houses. Adams continued to prefer a final veto. Jeffersonians and their numerous progeny found this highly undemocratic. In all states south of New York, at the end of the Revolution, governors were elected by the legislative houses, and none had any veto. Adams justified the veto as a means "to preserve the independence of the executive and judicial departments." And since governors could no longer be appointed by the crown, an obvious way to prevent their dependence on legislatures was to have them issue, like legislators, from the new sovereign, the people. It was legislative oligarchy that Adams thought the most imminent danger. As he wrote to Jefferson in 1787: "You are afraid of the one — I, of the few."

As for the phantom "lords," or senators, though they were directly elected by the ordinary voters for one-year terms, they were in a way supposed to represent property rather than numbers. They were apportioned among the counties of Massachusetts not according to population but according to taxes paid, that is, according to assessed value of taxable wealth. Suffolk County, which included Boston, thus received 6 senators out of 40, where on a purely numerical basis it would have received only four. The Maine districts, Cape Cod, and the western counties were numerically somewhat underrepresented. The three central and western counties received 11 senators, where a representation in proportion to numbers would have given them 12 or 13. Inequalities in wealth in Massachusetts, as between individuals or as between city and country, were not yet great enough to make a senate apportioned according to "property" (which included the small man's property as well as the rich man's) very different from a senate apportioned according to numbers.

The Massachusetts constitution prescribed certain qualifications for eligibility. The governor was required to have a freehold worth at least £1,000, senators a freehold of £300 or £600 total estate, representatives a freehold of £100 or £200 total estate. (British law at this time required £300 or £600 *annual income* from land to qualify for the House of Commons.) These Massachusetts requirements resembled those in North Carolina, where the governor had to have a £1,000 freehold, and members of the upper and lower houses freeholds of 300 or 100 acres respectively. In the absence of comparative statistics on land values and distribution of land ownership in the two states, it is impossible to compare the real impact of these legal qualifications for office. In Massachusetts, however, whatever may have been true in North Carolina, the average 100-acre one-family farm was worth well over £300, and there were a great many such farms, so that the ordinary successful farmer could qualify for either house of the legislature, and a few well-to-do ones in almost every village might if they chose have aspired to the office of governor. The requirements in Massachusetts, as set forth by John Adams, were, if anything, Jeffersonian or agrarian in their tendency, since they favored the farm population, and made it even harder for middle-class townspeople, who might own no land, to occupy public office. The aim was clearly to limit office to the substantial segment of the population, but the substantial segment was broadly defined. Still, there were people who by this definition were not "substantial," and some of them objected to these provisions, though not many would in any case have ventured to run for office or been elected if they did, in the Massachusetts of 1780.

It was Article III of the Declaration of Rights, both in Adams' draft and in the finished constitution, that caused most debate in the convention and most disagreement among the voters during ratification. This article, declaring religion to be the foundation of morality and of the state, authorized the legislature to "enjoin" people to go to church, and required the use of public funds to maintain the churches, while allowing any "subject" to have his own contribution paid to the denomination of his choice. While it received a large majority of the popular vote, 8,885 to 6,225, it was the one article which most clearly failed to obtain a two-thirds majority, and the one which may have never been legally ratified, though declared so by the convention. Those voting against it expressed a desire to separate church and state. These, in turn, included perhaps a few Baptists who favored such separation on religious principle, a great many Protestants who feared that the article might legalize Roman Catholicism, and an unknown number of people, one suspects, who were no longer very regular in attending any church at all.

The Massachusetts constitution of 1780 was adopted by a two-thirds majority in a popular referendum from which no free adult male was excluded. The vote was light, for opinion on the matter seems not to have been excited. It was six years since the rebellion against King George, and four years since the British army had left Massachusetts; doubtless many people wished to be bothered no longer. The action of the people as constituent power is, after all, a legal concept, or even a necessary legal fiction where the sovereignty of any concrete person or government is denied. It does not signify that everyone is actually engrossed in the fabrication of constitutions. On the other hand, it does not seem necessary to believe that the convention, when it declared the constitution ratified, put something over on an innocent or apathetic or reluctant people. The people of Massachusetts had rejected the constitution proposed in 1778. They could have rejected the one proposed in 1780. It was adopted, not because it was thought perfect or final by everyone, but because it offered a frame of government, or basis of agreement, within which people could still lawfully disagree. It has lasted, with many amendments, until the present day.

A Word on the Constitution of the United States

The idea that sovereignty lay with the people, and not with states or their governments, made possible in America a new kind of federal structure unknown in Europe. The Dutch and Swiss federations were unions of component parts, close permanent alliances between disparate corporate members. For them no other structure was possible, because there was as yet no Dutch or Swiss people except in a cultural sense. It was in the Dutch revolution of 1795 and the Swiss revolution of 1798 that these two bundles of provinces or cantons were first proclaimed as political nations. In America it was easier to make the transition from a league of states, set up during the Revolution, to a more integral union set up in the United States constitution of 1787. The new idea was that, instead of the central government drawing its powers from the states, both central and state governments should draw their powers from the same source; the question was the limit between these two sets of derived powers. The citizen, contrariwise, was simultaneously a citizen both of the United States and of his own state. He was the sovereign, not they. He chose to live under two constitutions, two sets of laws, two sets of courts and officials; theoretically, he had created them all, reserving to himself, under each set, certain liberties specified in declarations of rights.

It has been widely believed, since the publication in 1913 of Charles A. Beard's *Economic Interpretation of the Constitution,* that the federal constitution of 1787 marked a reaction against democratic impulses of the Revolution, and was a device by which men of property, particularly those holding securities of the state or continental governments, sought to protect themselves and their financial holdings against the dangers of popular rule. The Philadelphia convention has been represented as an almost clandestine body, which exceeded its powers, and which managed (as has also been said of the Massachusetts convention of 1780) to impose a conservative constitution on a confused or apathetic people. Recently the flimsiness of the evidence for this famous thesis has been shown by Professor Robert Brown. The thesis takes its place in the history of historical writing, as a product of that Progressive and post-Progressive era in which the common man could be viewed as the dupe or plaything of private interests.

It seems likely enough that there was a conservative reaction after the American Revolution, and even a movement among the upper class (minus the old loyalists) not wholly unlike the "aristocratic resurgence" which I shall soon describe in the Europe of the 1780's. The difference is that these neo-aristocrats of America were less obstinate and less caste-conscious than in Europe. They did not agree with each other, and they knew they could not rule alone. The men at Philadelphia in 1787 were too accomplished as politicians to be motivated by anything so impractical as ideology or mere self-interest. They hoped, while solving concrete problems, to arouse as little opposition as possible. They lacked also the European sense of the permanency of class status. Thinking of an upper class as something that individuals might move into or out of, they allowed for social mobility both upward and downward. The wealthy Virginian, George Mason, at the Philadelphia convention, on urging that the upper class should take care to give adequate representation to the lower, offered it as one of his reasons that, however affluent they might be now, "the course of a few years not only might, but certainly would, distribute their posterity through the lowest classes of society." No one seems to have disputed this prognostication. Such acceptance of future downward mobility for one's own grandchildren, if by no means universal in America, was far more common than in Europe. Without such downward mobility there could not long remain much room for newcomers at the top, or much assurance of a fluid society. With it, there could not be a permanent aristocracy in the European sense.

It was the state legislatures that chose the delegates to the Philadelphia convention, in answer to a widely expressed demand for strengthening the federal government under the Articles of Confederation. The Philadelphia convention proceeded, not to amend the Articles, but to ignore and discard them. It repudiated the union which the thirteen states had made. Beard in 1913 found it satisfying to call this operation a revolution, a revolution from above to be sure, which he compared to a *coup d'état* of Napoleon. His critic, Professor Brown, in 1956, found it satisfying and important to deny any revolutionary action in what happened.

What did really happen? The men at Philadelphia did circumvent the state governments, and in a sense they betrayed those who sent them. They did so by adopting the revolutionary principle of the American Revolution, which had already become less purely revolutionary and more institutionalized as an accepted routine, as shown in the Massachusetts convention of 1780, which had been followed by a New Hampshire convention, and new constitution for New Hampshire in 1784. The Philadelphia convention went beyond the existing constituted bodies, that is, the state governments and the Congress under the Articles, by appealing for support directly to the people, who in each state elected, for this purpose only, conventions to discuss, ratify, or refuse to ratify the document proposed by the convention at Philadelphia. The authors of the proposed federal constitution needed a principle of authority; they conceived that "the people were the fountain of all power," and that if popularly chosen conventions ratified their work "all disputes and doubts concerning [its] legitimacy" would be removed. In each state, in voting for ratifying conventions, the voters voted according to the franchise as given by their state constitutions. No use was made of the more truly revolutionary idea, still alive in Massachusetts in 1780, that on the acceptance of a government *every* man should have a vote. In some states the authorized voters were a great majority; in none were they a small minority. The actual vote for the ratifying conventions was light, despite protracted public discussion, because most people lost interest, or never had any, in abstract debates concerning governmental structure at the distant federal level. Eleven states ratified within a few months, and the constitution went into effect for the people of those eleven states. The remaining two states came in within three years. The whole procedure was revolutionary in a sense, but revolution had already become domesticated in America. The idea of the people as the constituent power, acting through special conventions, was so generally accepted and understood that a mere mention of the word "convention," in the final article of the proposed constitution, was thought sufficient explanation of the process of popular endorsement.

Nevertheless, men of popular principles, those who would soon be called democrats, and who preferred the arrangements of the Pennsylvania constitution, with its single-house legislature to which the executive was subordinated, found much in the new federal constitution not to their liking, at least at first sight. The new instrument reproduced the main features of the Massachusetts constitution of 1780: the strong president, the senate, the house of representatives, the partial executive veto, the independent judiciary, the separation and balance of powers. In fact, the longer tenure of offices — four years for the president, six for senators, two for representatives, in place of the annual terms for corresponding functionaries in Massachusetts — shows a reaction away from revolutionary democracy and toward the giving of more adequate authority to those entrusted with public power. The president was not popularly elected, like the governor in Massachusetts; but neither was he designated by the legislative assembly, like the president in Pennsylvania and governors in the Southern states. He was elected by an electoral college, with each state free to determine how its own share of these electors should be chosen. Although as early as 1788 almost half the states provided for popular election of presidential electors, it was not until 1828 that this became the general and permanent rule. In the federal constitution the unique feature, and key to the main compromise, was the senate. Not only did large and small states have the same number of senators, but it was the state legislatures that chose them. Since it was the state legislatures that conservative or hard-money men mainly feared in the 1780's, this provision can hardly have been introduced in the hope of assuring economic conservatism. It was introduced to mollify the states as states. In the senate the new union was a league of preexisting corporate entities. In the house of representatives it rested more directly on the people. Anyone who had the right to vote in his state could vote for a member of the lower house of Congress. In one respect the federal constitution, by its silence, was more democratic in a modern sense than any of the state constitutions. No pecuniary or religious qualification was specified for any office.

The new constitution was a compromise, but that it produced a less popular federal government, less close to the people, than that of the Articles of Confederation, seems actually contrary to the facts. It created a national arena for political controversy. There were now, for the first time, national elections in which voters could dispute over national issues. One result was the rise, on a national scale, of the Jeffersonian democratic movement in the 1790's.

Ambivalence of the American Revolution

In conclusion, the American Revolution was really a revolution, in that certain Americans subverted their legitimate government, ousted the contrary-minded and confiscated their property, and set the example of a revolutionary program, through mechanisms by which the people was deemed to act as the constituent power. This much being said, it must be admitted that the Americans, when they constituted their new states, tended to reconstitute much of what they already had. They were as fortunate and satisfied a people as any the world has known. They thus offered both the best and the worst example, the most successful and the least pertinent precedent, for less fortunate or more dissatisfied peoples who in other parts of the world might hope to realize the same principles.

Pennsylvania and Georgia gave themselves one-chamber legislatures, but both had had one-chamber legislatures before the Revolution. All states set up weak governors; they had been undermining the authority of royal governors for generations. South Carolina remained a planter oligarchy before and after independence, but even in South Carolina fifty-acre freeholders had a vote. New York set up one of the most conservative of the state constitutions, but this was the first constitution under which Jews received equality of civil rights — not a very revolutionary departure, since Jews had been prospering in New York since 1654. The Anglican Church was disestablished, but it had had few roots in the colonies anyway. In New England the sects obtained a little more recognition, but Congregationalism remained favored by law. The American revolutionaries made no change in the laws of indentured servitude. They deplored, but avoided, the matter of Negro slavery. Quitrents were generally abolished, but they had been nominal anyway, and a kind of manorial system remained long after the Revolution in New York. Laws favoring primogeniture and entail were done away with, but apparently they had been little used by landowners in any case. No general or statistical estimate is yet possible on the disposition of loyalist property. Some of the confiscated estates went to strengthen a new propertied class, some passed through the hands of speculators, and some either immediately or eventually came into the possession of small owners. There was enough change of ownership to create a material interest in the Revolution, but obviously no such upheaval in property relations as in France after 1789.

Even the apparently simple question of how many people received the right to vote because of the Revolution cannot be satisfactorily answered. There was some extension of democracy in this sense, but the more we examine colonial voting practices the smaller the change appears. The Virginia constitution of 1776 simply gave the vote to those "at present" qualified. By one estimate the number of persons voting in Virginia actually declined from 1741 to 1843, and those casting a vote in the 1780's were about a quarter of the free male population over twenty-one years of age. The advance of political democracy, at the time of the Revolution, was most evident in the range of officers for whom voters could vote. In the South the voters generally voted only for members of the state legislatures; in Pennsylvania and New England they voted also for local officials, and in New England for governors as well.

In 1796, at the time of the revolution in Europe, and when the movement of Jeffersonian democracy was gathering strength in America, seven of the sixteen states then in the union had no property qualification for voters in the choice of the lower legislative house, and half of them provided for popular election of governors, only the seabord South, and New Jersey, persisting in legislative designation of the executive. The best European historians underestimate the extent of political democracy in America at this time. They stress the restrictions on voting rights in America, as in the French constitution of 1791. They do so because they have read the best American historians on the subject and have in particular followed the school of Charles Beard and others. The truth seems to be that America was a good deal more democratic than Europe in the 1790's. It had been so, within limits, long before the revolutionary era began.

Nor in broad political philosophy did the American Revolution require a violent break with customary ideas. For Englishmen it was impossible to maintain, in the eighteenth century or after, that the British constitution placed any limits on the powers of Parliament. Not so for Americans; they constantly appealed, to block the authority of Parliament or other agencies of the British government, to their rights as Englishmen under the British constitution. The idea of limited government, the habit of thinking in terms of two levels of law, of an ordinary law checked by a higher constitutional law, thus came out of the realities of colonial experience. The colonial Americans believed also, like Blackstone for that matter, that the rights of Englishmen were somehow the rights of all mankind. When the highest English authorities disagreed on what Americans claimed as English rights, and when the Americans ceased to be English by abjuring their King, they were obliged to find another and less ethnocentric or merely historical principle of justification. They now called their rights the rights of man. Apart from abstract assertions of natural liberty and equality, which were not so much new and alarming as conceptual statements as in the use to which they were applied, the rights claimed by Americans were the old rights of Englishmen — trial by jury, *habeas corpus,* freedom of the press, freedom of religion, freedom of elections, no taxation without representation. The content of rights was broadened, but the content changed less than the form, for the form now became universal. Rights were demanded for human beings as such. It was not necessary to be English, or even American, to have an ethical claim to them. The form also became more concrete, less speculative and metaphysical, more positive and merely legal. Natural rights were numbered, listed, written down, and embodied in or annexed to constitutions, in the foundations of the state itself.

So the American Revolution remains ambivalent. If it was conservative, it was also revolutionary, and vice versa. It was conservative because colonial Americans had long been radical by general standards of Western Civilization. It was, or appeared, conservative because the deepest conservatives, those most attached to King and empire, conveniently left the scene. It was conservative because the colonies had never known oppression, excepting always for slavery — because, as human institutions go, America had always been free. It was revolutionary because the colonists took the risks of rebellion, because they could not avoid a conflict among themselves, and because they checkmated those Americans who, as the country developed, most admired the aristocratic society of England and Europe. Henceforth the United States, in Louis Hartz's phrase, would be the land of the frustrated aristocrat, not of the frustrated democrat; for to be an aristocrat it is not enough to think of oneself as such, it is necessary to be thought so by others; and never again would deference for social rank be a characteristic American attitude. Elites, for better or for worse, would henceforth be on the defensive against popular values. Moreover the Americans in the 1770's, not content merely to throw off an outside authority, insisted on transmuting the theory of their political institutions. Their revolution was revolutionary because it showed how certain abstract doctrines, such as the rights of man and the sovereignty of the people, could be "reduced to practice," as Adams put it, by assemblages of fairly levelheaded gentlemen exercising constituent power in the name of the people. And, quite apart from its more distant repercussions, it was certainly revolutionary in its impact on the contemporary world across the Atlantic.

The Founding Fathers: Democrats or Aristocrats?

The revolutionary generation learned that it was far easier to declare American independence in 1776 than to set up a viable republic. For almost fifteen years, Americans searched for a workable political structure that would give them a central government, powerful enough to promote those general interests and perform functions beyond the capacity of the states, without creating a monster which undermined local authority and ignored local concerns. Their experience with Britain taught Americans to fear centralized government, and so the first attempt at nation-building — the Articles of Confederation — left sovereign power in the hands of the states, while at the same time thrusting formidable responsibilities for foreign affairs, the conduct of war and public finance, on Congress. The Confederation proved inadequate and various schemes to strengthen it foundered.

Convened to repair the Articles, the convention which assembled in Philadelphia in May 1787 designed instead a wholly new framework for the Union. For generations, the intent of the Founding Fathers has been a source of controversy in the courts, in the political arena, and among historians.

Throughout most of the nineteenth century, Americans venerated the Founding Fathers as supreme statesmen, as men touched with semi-divine wisdom and blessed with impartial benevolence, who constructed the most perfect instrument of democratic self-government in the history of man. This view received a rude jolt more than fifty years ago from Charles A. Beard and other historians who argued that the founders were human beings, not demigods, and that like most humans, they followed the dictates of class interest. The Constitution, Beard argued, established a strong central government, attuned to the interests of wealthy merchants and public security holders, a government in which they would have a dominant voice. Such a government would protect them from tyrannical popular majorities in the states, which were endangering property interests. Beard discovered that the members of the Convention owned substantial amounts of public securities. These were bound to increase in value because the new federal government had the power to fund the national debt, a power which the Confederation had lacked.

This thesis, long accepted by sophisticated students of the American past, no longer seems adequate. Critics of Beard point out that neither the class origins nor the property-holdings of those who opposed the federal Constitution distinguished them from those who backed it. This fact raised serious doubts that the Constitution was the product of rival economic interests as Beard defined them. In the following essays, Douglass G. Adair further argues that the Founding Fathers were neither the democrats enslaved by nineteenth-century constitution worship nor the aristocrats unmasked by Beard. They were skeptical of relying entirely on popular majorities to govern wisely but they had no more faith in the wisdom or benevolence of the wealthy few. Rich and poor alike, majorities and minorities, were subject to all the passions that led men to injure one another in the pursuit of self-interest. The task was to devise a government that restrained man's baser nature and released his nobler impulses. As students of history and close readers of political theory, the founders had no illusions that Americans could easily escape the sad fate of earlier republics which had invariably succumbed to tyranny or oligarchy. But they believed that a properly balanced government, such as they attempted to contrive in Philadelphia, offered Americans a new hope.

FOR FURTHER READING:

BEARD, CHARLES A. *Economic Interpretation of the Constitution of the United States.* New York: The Macmillan Company, Free Press, 1969.*
GOODMAN, PAUL, ed. *The American Constitution.* New York: John Wiley & Sons, 1970.*
MCDONALD, FORREST. *We the People, The Economic Origins of the Constitution.* Chicago: University of Chicago Press, 1958.*

Asterisk denotes paperback edition.

"Experience Must Be Our Only Guide": History, Democratic Theory, and the United States Constitution

DOUGLASS G. ADAIR

"The history of Greece," John Adams wrote in 1786, "should be to our countrymen what is called in many families on the Continent, a *boudoir,* an octagonal apartment in a house, with a full-length mirror on every side, and another in the ceiling. The use of it is, when any of the young ladies, or young gentlemen if you will, are at any time a little out of humour, they may retire to a place where, in whatever direction they turn their eyes, they see their own faces and figures multiplied without end. By thus beholding their own beautiful persons, and seeing, at the same time, the deformity brought upon them by their anger, they may recover their tempers and their charms together."

Adams' injunction that his countrymen should study the history of ancient Greece in order to amend their political behavior suggests two points for our consideration. First, John Adams assumed without question that history did offer lessons and precepts which statesmen could use in solving immediate problems. Secondly, Adams urged the study of the classical Greek republics as the particular history especially relevant, most full of useful lessons and precepts for Americans in 1787.

Adams, as is well known, practiced what he preached. Working at high speed between October 1786 and January 1787, in time stolen from his duties as United States Minister to Great Britain, he composed his *Defence of the Constitutions of the United States* — a 300-page book exhibiting for his countrymen the lessons of history. And though he included material from all periods of western civilization, a large part of his data was collected from the classical republics of antiquity.

Source: Douglass G. Adair, "'Experience Must Be Our Only Guide': History, Democratic Theory, and the United States Constitution," in *The Reinterpretation of Early American History,* ed. Ray A. Billington (San Marino, Cal.: Huntington Library, 1966), pp. 129–144.

Nor did his American audience who read Adams' work in the weeks immediately prior to the meeting of the Philadelphia Convention deny his assumptions or purposes in urging them to study the lessons of Greek history. Benjamin Rush, for example, reporting to the Reverend Richard Price in England on the attitude of the Pennsylvania delegation to the Convention, gave Adams' study the highest praise. "Mr. Adams' book," he wrote, "has diffused such excellent principles among us that there is little doubt of our adopting a vigorous and compounded federal legislature. Our illustrious Minister in this gift to his country has done us more service than if he had obtained alliances for us with all the nations of Europe."

Do Adams and Rush in their view on the utility of history for the constitutional reforms of 1787 represent the typical attitude of the members of the Convention? Did the fifty-five men gathered to create a more perfect union consciously turn to past history for lessons and precepts that were generalized into theories about the correct organization of the new government? Did lessons from the antique past, applied to their present situation, concretely affect their actions at Philadelphia? The evidence is overwhelming that they did, although the weight of modern commentary on the Constitution either ignores the Fathers' conscious and deliberate use of history and theory or denies that it played any important part in their deliberations.

Max Farrand, for example, after years of study of the debates in the Convention concluded that the members were anything but historically oriented. Almost all had served (Farrand noted) in the Continental Congress and had tried to govern under the impotent Articles of Confederation. There is little of importance in the Constitution (Farrand felt) that did not arise from the effort to correct specific defects of the Confederation.

Robert L. Schuyler, an able and careful student of the Constitution, goes even further in denying the Convention's dependence upon history. "The Fathers were practical men. They lived at a time when a decent respect for the proprieties of political discussion required at least occasional reference to Locke and Montesquieu . . . but . . . such excursions into political philosophy as were made are to be regarded rather as purple patches than as integral parts of the proceedings. The scholarly Madison had gone extensively into the subject of Greek federalism . . . but it was his experience in public life and his wide knowledge of the conditions of his day, not his classical lucubrations that bore fruit at Philadelphia. . . . The debate . . . did not proceed along theoretical lines. John Dickinson expressed the prevailing point of view when he said in the Convention: 'Experience must be our only guide. Reason may mislead us.'"

Dickinson's statement on August 13th: "Experience must be our only guide" does indeed express the mood of the delegates; no word was used more often; time after time "experience" was appealed to as the clinching argument for a controverted opinion. But "experience" as used in the Convention, more often than not, referred to the precepts of history. This is Dickinson's sense of the word when he warned the Convention that "reason" might mislead. "It was not reason," Dickinson continued, "that discovered the singular and admirable mechanism of the English Constitution . . . [or the] mode of trial by jury. Accidents probably produced these discoveries, and experience has given a sanction to them." And then Dickinson, turning to James Wilson and Madison who had argued that vesting the power to initiate revenue bills exclusively in the lower house of the Legislature had proved "pregnant with altercation in every [American] State where the [revolutionary] Constitution had established it," denied that the short "experience" of the American

States carried as weighty a sanction as the long historic "experience" of the English House of Commons. "Shall we oppose to this long [English] experience," Dickinson asked, "the short experience of 11 years which we had ourselves, on this subject." Dickinson's words actually point to the fact that theories grounded in historical research are indeed integral parts of the debate on the Constitution.

For Dickinson is not alone in using "experience" in this dual fashion to refer both to political wisdom gained by participation in events, and wisdom gained by studying past events. Franklin and Madison, Butler and Mason, Wilson and Hamilton all appeal to historical "experience" in exactly the same way. "Experience shows" or "history proves" are expressions that are used interchangeably throughout the Convention by members from all sections of the United States. Pure reason not verified by history might be a false guide; the mass of mankind might indeed be the slave of passion and unreason, but the fifty-five men who gathered at Philadelphia in 1787 labored in the faith of the enlightenment that experience-as-history provided "the least fallible guide of human opinions," that historical experience is "the oracle of truth, and where its responses are unequivocal they ought to be conclusive and sacred."

Schuyler's insistence that the Fathers were "practical men" who abhorred theory, associates him with a standard theme of American anti-intellectualism that honors unsystematic "practicality" and distrusts systematic theoretical thought. His argument, undoubtedly too, reflects nineteenth-century theories of "progress-evolution" that assume the quantititative lapse in time between 400 B.C. and A.D. 1787 *a priori* makes the earlier period irrelevant for understanding a modern and different age. And, of course, what came to be called "sound history" after 1880 when the discipline came to roost in academic groves, is quite different itself from the "history" that eighteenth-century statesmen found most significant and useful. Modern historians have tended to insist that the unique and the particular is the essence of "real history"; in contrast the eighteenth-century historian was most concerned and put the highest value on what was universal and constant through time.

Eighteenth-century historians believed "that there is a great uniformity among the actions of men, in all nations and ages, and that human nature remains still the same, in its principles and operations. The same motives always produce the same actions; the same events follow from the same causes. Ambition, avarice, self-love, vanity, friendship, generosity, public spirit; these passions, mixed in various degrees, and distributed through society, have been from the beginning of the world, and still are the source of all the actions and enterprizes, which have ever been observed among mankind. Would you know the sentiments, inclinations, and course of life of the Greeks and Romans? Study well the temper and actions of the French and English." Thus David Hume, distinguished eighteenth-century historian and philosopher.

The method of eighteenth-century history for those who would gain political wisdom from it followed from this primary assumption — it was historical-comparative synthesis. Again Hume speaks: "Mankind are so much the same, in all times and places, that history informs us of nothing new or strange, in this particular. *Its chief use is only to discover the constant and universal principles of human nature,* by showing men in all varieties of circumstances and situations, and furnishing us with materials, from which we may form our observations and become acquainted with the regular springs of human action and behavior. These records . . . are so many collections of experiments, by which the politician or moral philosopher fixes the principles of his science, in the same manner as the physician or natural philosopher becomes acquainted with the nature of plants, minerals, and other external objects, by the experiments which he forms concerning them."

John Adams would echo Hume's argument and use the identical metaphor in the preface to his *Defence*. "The systems of legislators are experiments made on human life, and manners, society and government. Zoroaster, Confucius, Mithras, Odin, Thor, Mohamet, Lycurgus, Solon, Romulus and a thousand others may be compared to philosophers making experiments on the elements." Adams was too discreet to list his own name with the Great Legislators of the past, but in his own mind, we know from his *Diary* and letters to his wife, he identified himself with Moses, Lycurgus, and Solon as the Lawgiver of his state, Massachusetts, whose republican constitution, based on his study of history, he had written almost single-handed in October 1779. Now eight years later his *Defence* both justified the form of government he had prepared for his own state and "fixed the principles" — to use Hume's words — of the science of government that ought to be followed in modeling a more perfect union of the states. Adams' book, in complete accord with eighteenth-century canons, was a comparative-historical survey of constitutions reaching back to Minos, Lycurgus, and Solon.

History proved, Adams felt sure, "that there can be no free government without a democratical branch in the constitution." But he was equally sure that "Democracy, simple democracy, never had a patron among men of letters." Rousseau, indeed, had argued, as Adams pointed out, that "a society of Gods would govern themselves democratically," but this is really an ironic admission by "the eloquent philosopher of Geneva that it is not practicable to govern *Men* in this way." For very short periods of time pure democracy had existed in antiquity, but "from the frightful pictures of a democratical city, drawn by the masterly pencils of ancient philosophers and historians, it may be conjectured that such governments existed in Greece and Italy . . . [only] for short spaces of time." Such is the nature of pure democracy, or simple democracy, that this form of government carries in its very constitution, infirmities and vices that doom it to speedy disaster. Adams agreed completely with Jonathan Swift's pronouncement that if the populace of a country actually attempted to rule and establish a government by the people they would soon become their "own dupe, a mere underworker and a purchaser in trust for some single tyrant whose state and power they advance to their own ruin, with as blind an instinct as those worms that die with weaving magnificent habits for beings of a superior order to their own." It was not surprising then to Adams that when he surveyed contemporary Europe he found no functioning democracy. Indeed, governments that had even the slightest "democratical mixture" in their constitutions "are annihilated all over Europe, except on a barren rock, a paltry fen, an inaccessible mountain, or an impenetrable forest." The one great exception outside of the American states where a democratic element was part of the constitution was Britain, the great monarchical or regal republic. And as Adams contemplated the English Constitution, he felt it to be "the most stupendous fabric of human invention. . . . Not the formation of languages, not the whole art of navigation and shipbuilding does more honor to the human understanding than this system of government."

The problem for Americans in 1787 was to recognize the principles exemplified in Britain, Adams thought, and to frame governments to give the people "a legal, constitutional" *share* in the process of government — it should operate through representation; there should be a balance in the legislature of lower house and upper house; and there should be a total separation of the executive from the legislative power, and of the judicial from both. Above all, if the popular principles of government were to be preserved in America it was necessary to maintain an independent and powerful executive: "If there is one certain truth to be collected from the history of all ages, it is this; that the people's rights and liberties, and the democratical mixture in a constitution, can never be preserved without a strong executive, or, in other words, without separating the executive from the legislative power. If the executive power . . . is left in the hands either of an aristocratical or democratical assembly, it will corrupt the legislature as necessarily as rust corrupts iron, or as arsenic poisons the human body; and when the legislature is corrupted, the people are undone."

And then John Adams took on the role of scientific prophet. If Americans learned the lessons that history taught, their properly limited democratic constitutions would last for ages. Only long in the future when "the present states become . . . rich, powerful, and luxurious, as well as numerous, [will] their . . . good sense . . . dictate to them what to do; they may [then] make transitions to a nearer resemblance of the British constitution," and presumably make their first magistrates and their senators hereditary.

But note the ambiguity which underlies Adams' historical thinking. Science, whether political or natural, traditionally has implied determinism — scientific prediction is possible only because what was, is, and ever shall be. Reason thus might be free to discover the fixed pattern of social phenomena, but the phenomena themselves follow a pre-destined course of development. The seventeenth-century reason of Isaac Newton discovered the laws of the solar system, but no man could change those laws or the pattern of the planets' orbits; Karl Marx might in the nineteenth century discover the scientific laws of economic institutions, but no man could reform them or change the pattern in which the feudal economy inevitably degenerated into bourgeois economy, which in its turn worked inexorably toward its predetermined and proletarian end.

In the same fashion Adams' scientific reading of history commited him and his contemporaries in varying degrees of rigidity to a species of *political determinism.* History showed, so they believed, that there were only three basic types of government: monarchy, aristocracy, and democracy, or government of the one, the few, or the many. Moreover history showed, so they believed, that each of these three types when once established had particular and terrible defects — "mortal diseases," Madison was to call these defects — that made each pure type quickly degenerate: Every monarchy tended to degenerate into a tyranny. Every aristocracy, or government of the few, by its very nature, was predestined to evolve into a corrupt and unjust oligarchy. And the democratic form, as past experience proved, inevitably worked toward anarchy, class-conflict, and social disorder of such virulence that it normally ended in dictatorship.

On this deterministic-theory of a uniform and constant human nature, inevitably operating inside a fixed-pattern of limited political forms, producing a predictable series of evil political results, John Adams based his invitation to Americans to study the classical republics. This assumption of determinism explains the constant and reiterated appeal to Greek and Roman "experience," both during the Philadelphia Convention and in the State ratifying conventions. At the beginning of the Revolution Adams had invited his rebellious compatriots to study English history, for from 1765 to 1776 the immediate and pressing questions of practical politics related to the vices and corruption of the English monarchy. But after 1776 at which time Americans committed their political destinies to thirteen democratic frames of government loosely joined in a Confederation, English monarchical history became temporarily less relevant to American problems. The American States of 1776 in gambling on democratic republics stood alone in the political world. Nowhere in contemporary Europe or Asia could Americans turn for reassuring precedents showing functioning republican government. So, increasingly from 1776 to 1787, as Americans learned in practice the difficulties of making republican systems work, the leaders among the Revolutionary generation turned for counsel to classical history. They were *obliged* to study Greece and Rome if they would gain "experimental" wisdom on the dangers and potentialities of the republican form. Only in classical history could they observe the long-range predictable tendencies of those very "vices" of their democratic Confederacy that they were now enduring day by day.

It was these frightening lessons from classical history added to their own present difficulties under the Confederation that produced the total dimension of the crisis of 1787. Standing, as it were, in John Adams' hall of magic mirrors where past and present merged in a succession of terrifying images, the Founding Fathers could not conceal from themselves that Republicanism in America might already be doomed. Was it indeed possible to maintain stable republican government in any of the thirteen American States? And even if some of the States units could maintain republicanism, could union be maintained in a republican confederation?

The answer of history to both of these questions seemed to be an emphatic "no." As Alexander Hamilton reminded the Convention June 18th and later reminded the country speaking as Publius, "It is impossible to read the history of the petty Republics of Greece and Italy without feeling sensations of horror and disgust at the distractions with which they were continually agitated, and at the rapid succession of revolutions, by which they were kept in a state of perpetual vibration between the extremes of tyranny and anarchy. If they exhibit occasional calms, these only serby as short-lived contrasts to the furious storms that are to succeed. If now and then intervals of felicity open themselves to view, we behold them with a mixture of regret, arising from the reflection, that the pleasing scenes before us are soon to be overwhelmed by the tempestuous waves of sedition and party rage."

Hamilton along with Madison, Adams, Jefferson, and every educated eighteenth-century statesman thus knew from history that the mortal disease of democratical republics was and always would be the class struggle that had eventually destroyed every republican state in history. And *now* with the "desperate debtor" Daniel Shays, an American Cataline — an American Alcibiades — proving only ten years after independence, the class struggle was raising monitory death's-heads among the barely united republican States of America. If potential class war was implicit in every republic, so too did war characterize the interstate relations of adjacent republics. The only union that proved adequate to unite Athens and Sparta, Thebes and Corinth in one functioning peaceful whole was the monarchical power of Philip of Macedon; Rome, after conquering her neighbor city states, it is true, had maintained republican liberty for a relatively long period, in spite of internal conflict of plebes and patricians, but when the Empire increased in extent, when her geographical boundaries were enlarged, Roman liberty died and an Emperor displaced the Senate as the center of Roman authority. In 1787 the authority of scholars, philosophers, and statesmen was all but unanimous in arguing (from the experience of history) that no republic ever could be established in a territory as extended as the United States — that even if established for a moment, class war must eventually destroy every democratic republic.

These were the two lessons that Hamilton insisted in his great speech of June 18 the Constitutional Convention must remember. These were the lessons that were stressed in John Adams' morbid anatomy of fifty historic republican constitutions. This was the theme of Madison's arguments (which the Convention accepted) for junking entirely the feeble Articles of the Confederation in favor of a government that would, it was hoped, neutralize interstate conflict and class war. It was because these lessons were accepted by so many educated men in America that the commercial crisis of 1784–5 had become a political crisis by 1786, and a moral crisis by 1787.

Had the Revolution been a mistake from the beginning? Had the blood and treasure of Americans spent in seven years of war against England ironically produced republican systems in which rich and poor New Englanders must engage in bloody class war among themselves? Had independence merely guaranteed a structure in which Virginians and Pennsylvanians would cut each others' throats until one conquered the other or some foreign crown conquered both?

From our perspective, 179 years later, this may appear an hysterical and distorted analysis of the situation of the United States in 1787, but we, of course, are the beneficiaries of the Fathers' practical solution to this problem that *their* reading of history forced upon them. Americans today have the historic experience of living peacefully in the republic stabilized by their Constitution. History has reassured us concerning what only the wisest among them dared to hope in 1787: that the republican form could indeed be adapted to a continental territory. Priestley, a sympathetic friend of the American Revolution was speaking the exact truth in 1791 when he said: "It was taken for granted that the moment America had thrown off the yoke of Great Britain, the different states would go to war among themselves."

When Hamilton presented his analysis of the vices of republicanism to his acceptant audience in Philadelphia, he also offered the traditional remedy which statesmen and philosophers from antiquity on had proposed as the *only* cure for the evils of the three types of pure government. This remedy was to "mix" or "compound" elements of monarchy, aristocracy, and democracy into one balanced structure. There was, Hamilton reasoned, little danger of class war in a state which had a king vested with more power than the political organs of government representing either the rich or the poor. The "size of the country" and the "amazing turbulence" of American democracy made him despair of republicanism in the United States, without an elective monarch who once in office could not be voted out by majority rule. The people, i.e., the multitudinous poor, would directly elect the lower house of the legislature; a Senate to represent the rich would be elected for life; and to guard against the poison of democracy in the separate States, they would be transformed into administrative districts with their governors appointed by the elected King.

We mistake the significance of Hamilton's proposal of an elective monarch as a solution of the crisis of 1787 if we think of his plan as either *original* or *unrepresentative* of the thought of important segments of American opinion in 1787. The strength of Hamilton's logical position lay in the fact that his proposal was the traditional, the standard, indeed, as history showed the *only* solution for the specific dangers of interclass and interstate conflict that were destroying the imperfect Union. As early as 1776 Carter Braxton had offered almost this identical plan as the ideal constitution for Virginia. In May, 1782, reasoning parallel to Hamilton's had emboldened Colonel Lewis Nicola to invite Washington to use the Army to set himself up as a King. And after Shays' rebellion voices grew louder, particularly in the New England and the Middle States, proposing two cures for the ills of America. One cure was to divide the unwieldy Confederation into two or three small units; the other was the creation of an American throne. We have Washington's word for it that the most alarming feature of this revival of monarchical sentiment was its appearance among staunch "republican character" — men who like Hamilton had favored independence in 1776 but who had become disillusioned about ever achieving order and security in a republic. Add to this group of new converts the large bloc of old Tories who had never forsaken their allegiance to monarchy, and it is easy to see why Washington, Madison and other leaders were seriously alarmed that Union would break up and that kings would reappear in the Balkanized segments.

Furthermore, at the very time the Philadelphia Convention was rejecting Hamilton's mixed-monarchy as a present solution for the vices of American democracy, leading members of the Convention most tenacious of republicanism accepted the fact that an American monarchy was inevitable at some future date. As Mr. Williamson of North Carolina remarked, on July 24, "it was pretty certain . . . that we should at some time or other have a king; but he wished no precaution to be omitted that might postpone the event as long as possible." There is a curious statistical study of Madison's which points to his certainty also, along with the precise prophecy that the end of republicanism in the United States would come approximately 142 years after 1787 — about the decade of the 1930's. John Adams' *Defence* contains the same sort of prophecy. "In future ages," Adams remarked, "if the present States become great nations, rich, powerful, and luxurious, as well as numerous," the "feelings and good snese" of Americans "will dictate to them" reform of their governments "to a nearer resemblance of the British Constitution," complete with a hereditary king and a hereditary Senate. Gouverneur Morris is reported to have argued during the Covention "we must have a Monarch sooner or later . . . and the sooner we take him while we are able to make a Bargain with him, the better." Nor did the actual functioning of the Constitution during its first decade of existence lighten Morris' pessimism; in 1804 he was arguing that the crisis would come sooner rather than later. Even Franklin, the least doctrinaire of the Fathers — perhaps with Jefferson the most hopeful among the whole Revolutionary generation regarding the potentialities of American democracy — accepted the long-range pessimism of the Hamiltonian analysis. Sadly the aged philosopher noted, June 2, "There is a natural inclination in mankind to kingly government. . . . I am apprehensive, therefore — perhaps too apprehensive — that the government of these States may in future times end in monarchy. But this catastrophe, I think may be long delayed. . . ."

The "precious advantage" that the United States had in 1787 that offered hope for a "republican remedy for the diseases most incident to republican government" — the circumstance which would delay the necessity of accepting Hamilton's favored form of mixed monarchy — lay in the predominance of small free-hold farmers among the American population. Since the time of Aristotle, it had been recognized that yeoman farmers — a middle class between the greedy rich and the envious poor — provided the most stable foundation upon which to erect a popular government. This factor, commented on by Madison, Pinckney, Adams and others, helps explain why the Convention did not feel it necessary to sacrifice either majority rule or popular responsibility in their new Constitution.

Of equal importance was the factor of expedience. Less doctrinaire than Alexander Hamilton, the leaders of the Convention realized that a theoretical best — and member after member went on record praising the British Constitution as *the best* ever created by man — a theoretical best might be the enemy of a possible good. As Pierce Butler insisted, in a different context, "The people will not bear such innovations. . . . Supposing such an establishment to be useful, we must not venture on it. We must follow the example of Solon who gave the Athenians not the best government he could devise, but the best they would receive."

Consequently the Constitution that emerged from the Convention's debates was, as Madison described it a "novelty in the political world" — a "fabric" of government which had "no model on the face of the globe." It was an attempt to approximate in a structure of balanced republican government the advantages of stability that such mixed governments as Great Britain's had derived from hereditary monarchy and a hereditary House of Lords.

It was an "experiment" as members of the Convention frankly admitted, but one about which most of the Fathers could be hopeful because it adapted to the concrete circumstances of the United States of 1787, the experience of mankind through all ages as revealed by history. Driven by the collapse of the Confederation, the depression of 1785–86, and Shays' Rebellion to take stock of their political situation six years after Yorktown had won for Americans the opportunity for self-government, the Fathers had turned to history, especially classical history, to help them analyze their current difficulties. Their reading of history, equally with their immediate experience, defined for them both the short-range and the long-range potentialities for evil inherent in a uniform human nature operating in a republican government. But their reading of history also suggested a specific type of government that would remedy the evils they already knew and those worse evils they expected to come. Utilizing this knowledge, building on the solid core of agreement which historical wisdom had helped supply, they created, by mutual concession and compromise, a governmental structure as nearly like mixed government as it was possible to approach while maintaining the republican principle of majority rule. And this they offered the American people *hoping* it would be ratified, *hoping* that after ratification their "experiment" with all its compromises of theory and interest would provide a more perfect union.

If there is substance in the argument offered in the foregoing paragraphs, it should throw some light, at least, on the intellectual confusion exhibited during the last half-century by many learned commentators in discussing the nature of our Constitution. This confused and confusing debate has focused in part on the question: "did the Fathers write a 'democratic' Constitution?" The answers given have been almost as "mixed" as the theory to which the Framers subscribed.

Part of the bother lies in the lack of precision with which the word *democracy* was used then, and the even more unprecise way that we use it now. The more a word is used the less exact its meaning becomes, and in our day *democratic/democracy* has been extended to describe art, foreign policy, literature, etc., etc. Thus, from being a somewhat technical word of political discourse, in 1787, it has become a perfect sponge of squashy vagueness. Luckily, the context of formal theory that mixed government did imply in 1787 does allow us to recognize certain rather concrete and specific features usually associated, then, with the democratic form of government. In the first place, the very concept of "mixture" implies a relativism that modern doctrinaire democrats often forget: a political system, in 1787, was thought of as more-or-less democratic, as possessing few or many democratic features. Only in the pure form was democracy an either/or type of polity. In the second place, the simple democratic form was almost always thought of as appropriate only for a tiny territorial area — Madison in *Federalist 10*, for instance, would only equate the word with the direct democracy of the classical city-state. Thirdly, the functional advantages and disadvantages of the pure democratic form of government were almost universally agreed upon. A government *by* the people (so it was thought) always possessed *fidelity* to the common good; it was impossible for a people not to *desire* and to *intend* to promote the general welfare. However, the vices of democracy were that the people, collectively, were not *wise* about the correct measures to serve this great end and that the people could be easily duped by demagogues, who, flattering their good hearts and muddled heads, would worm their way to unlimited power. It was this well-meaning stupidity, the capacity for thoughtless injustice, the fickle instability of the popular will, that led the classical theorists, whom the Fathers were familiar with, to designate "pure democracy" as a form doomed to a short existence that tended to eventuate, with a pendulum swing, in the opposite extreme of tyranny and dictatorship.

In dark contrast to this *fidelity* of the democratic many was the vice afflicting both monarchy and aristocracy: an inveterate and incorrigible tendency to use the apparatus of government to serve the special selfish interests of the one or the few. However, the aristocratic form offered, so it was believed, the best possibility of *wisdom*, in planning public measures, while monarchy promised the necessary *energy, secrecy,* and *dispatch* for executing policy.

It is in this ideological context that one can deduce some of the intentions of the authors of our Constitution. It is clear, I think, that the office and power of the President was consciously designed to provide the *energy, secrecy,* and *dispatch* traditionally associated with the monarchical form. Thus Patrick Henry, considering the proposed Chief Executive and recognizing that the President was not unlike an elective king, could cry with reason that the Constitution "squints toward monarchy." But it was equally possible for Richard Henry Lee, focusing on the Senate, to complain that the document had a "strong tendency to aristocracy." This was said by Lee six months before Madison, in *Federalists 62–63*, explicitly defended the Senate as providing the *wisdom* and the *stability* — "aristocratic virtues" — needed to check the fickle lack of wisdom that Madison predicted would characterize the people's branch of the new government, the Lower House. Nor were there other critics lacking who, recognizing that the Constitution ultimately rested on popular consent, who, seeing that despite the ingenious apparatus designed to temper the popular will by introducing into the compound modified monarchical/aristocratic ingredients, could argue that the new Constitution was too democratic to operate effectively as a national government in a country as large and with a population as heterogeneous as the Americans'. One such was William Grayson, who doubted the need of *any* national government, but who felt, if one was to be established, it ought to provide a President and a Senate elected for life terms, these to be balanced by a House of Representatives elected triennially.

It is, thus, significant that if modern scholars are confused and disagreed about the nature of the Constitution today, so, too, in 1787–1788, contemporary observers were also confused and also disagreed as to whether it was monarchical, aristocratic, or democratic in its essence.

My own opinion is that the Constitution of 1787 is probably best described in a term John Adams used in 1806. Writing to Benjamin Rush, September 19, 1806, Adams, disapproving strongly of Jefferson's style as President, bemoaned the fact that Jefferson and his gang had now made the national government "to all intents and purposes, in virtue, spirit, and effect a democracy." — Alas! "I once thought," said Adams, "our Constitution was *quasi* or mixed government" — but alas!

"Quasi," or better still "quasi-mixed" — for, given the American people's antipathy to monarchy after 1776, and given the non-aristocratic nature (in a European sense) of the American upper class of 1787, the Constitution at best, or worst, could only be "*quasi*-mixed," since there were not "ingredients" available in the United States to compose a genuine mixture in the classic sense. So what the Fathers fashioned was a "quasi-mixed" Constitution that, given the "genius" of the American people, had a strong and inevitable tendency that "squinted" from the very beginning towards the national democracy that would finally develop in the nineteenth century.

The First American Party System, 1790–1820

The modern political party, an institution vital to the conduct of democratic government in the modern world, was born in the United States in the decade following adoption of the federal Constitution in 1789. In the following essay, William N. Chambers explains why.

Before parties emerged in America, political organization revolved around small groups of powerful families in towns and counties. Though the suffrage was broadly distributed, voter turnout was low, reflecting the belief of most citizens that politics was the business of the "better sort." Moreover, the colonists or their ancestors had migrated from Europe where the majority was disfranchised, and government was the preserve of landed aristocrats and wealthy mercantile and financial groups. People, therefore, had little experience with political participation. Even in America, political passivity had prevailed except when the colonists had from time to time become aroused by threats to their interests or had desired to advance their welfare through political action. On the whole, however, elections went uncontested, and citizens did not conceive of politics as a way of furthering a program or a policy.

The first American party system changed all that. Growing out of controversies at the nation's Capital over the course to be followed by the government initiated in 1789, parties represented a new method of organizing political life. They were coalitions which cut across state and local boundaries and brought men together to nominate candidates and win office. The creation of a national political arena after 1789 in a large, diverse nation, necessitated some means of managing Congress and electing Presidents. The cement that held coalitions of diverse elements together — northerners and southerners, Deists and Baptists, merchants and farmers — were common interests and attitudes that shaped a party's ideology and program. Parties were thus instruments by which people sought power to make government sensitive to their needs.

At first, American politicians from President Washington on down condemned the emerging parties, even when they themselves were engaged in the process of party-building. The Founding Fathers had specifically sought to contain organized political conflict because they believed that the rivalry of factions posed the chief danger to liberty. But the parties that emerged in the 1790s were nothing like the factions the founders had in mind — small groups of men, willing to sacrifice the general good for private advantage, adept at manipulation, and flourishing where the indifference of the many gave a free run to the scheming of a few. The first parties were broad-based coalitions that had to serve many interests to gain power. They operated in the open, for the most part, and felt compelled to justify their policies as serving the general welfare. Finally, parties aroused the electorate as never before. Presented periodically with a choice between rival programs and personalities, Americans went to the polls in unprecedented numbers in the 1790s, to vote for newly-formed party organizations that employed propaganda, money, and party workers to win votes. In 1800, when the Republicans under Thomas Jefferson captured the Presidency from the Federalists, led by President John Adams, it was a triumph for party government which had provided a peaceful and orderly means of settling differences and transferring power.

FOR FURTHER READING:

BEARD, CHARLES A. *Economic Origins of Jeffersonian Democracy.* New York: The Macmillan Company, Free Press, 1965.*

CHAMBERS, WILLIAM N. *Political Parties in the New Nation: The American Experience.* New York: Oxford University Press, 1963.*

GOODMAN, PAUL, ed. *The Federalists vs. the Jeffersonian Republicans.* New York: Holt, Rinehart & Winston, 1967.*

Asterisk denotes paperback edition.

Parties and Nation-Building in America

WILLIAM N. CHAMBERS

Political parties emerge out of certain sets of conditions, confront certain problems or loads in the political system, and perform interrelated functions which may include functions contributing to political integration. What the conditions are determines in part the shapes party structures will take, the functions they will perform, and how they will perform them. Yet the way in which political elites and party leaders handle political loads also determines the result in part and the impact parties may have on political development in general. In short there is a reciprocal relationship between political development and loads on the one hand and the effects of party action on the other. This relationship carries profound consequences for the political system, particularly in the era of national formation or nation-building.

Once political parties emerge, they may take on stable structures and establish stable patterns of interaction which constitute party systems. It is probably more useful for analysis to think in terms of developing party systems rather than simply of parties. For the United States it is certainly true that the relationship between parties and national integration can be understood only in terms of the party system and the net balance of integrative and malintegrative consequences of that system as a whole. Approached in this way, early American experience provides a useful laboratory. The United States constituted the first modern "new nation" in the sense that the American people were the first to throw off colonial rule, establish an independent polity, and achieve a fresh national identity. It was also the United States that brought into being the first modern political parties and party system with the emergence of the Federalist and Republican formations within two decades of the assertion of independence. In short, American development presents a case study of nation-building and party-building of great potential use in general and compara-

---

Source: William N. Chambers, "Parties and Nation-Building in America," in *Politics, Parties and Political Development,* eds. Joseph LaPalombara and Myron Weiner (Princeton: Princeton University Press, 1966), pp. 79–106.

tive political analysis. The address to these phenomena here will be to discuss the context and conditions out of which early American parties arose, the shape parties took and the functions they performed, the character of the party system, and the net impact that system had on national integration. The effect of parties on integration was a kind of end-product of the totality of functions the parties performed and of their relationships with one another.

The discussion will focus on the Federalists and Republicans in the 1790's, the crucial party-building decade. Neither of these formations survived beyond the period around 1820, and the first American party system was followed by a second system in the Jacksonian era in the 1830's. Yet the parties of the 1790's marked the way for later Democrats, Whigs, and second Republicans and for the party systems they evolved. These parties and systems showed important similarities to their predecessors as well as some differences.

Basic Conditions in Party Development

Political parties in America did not spring from growing resistance to colonial rule from 1763 to 1776 in a manner that is familiar in many new nations in Asia and Africa today. In the revolutionary struggle sharp divisions did develop between Patriots and Loyalists. The Patriots established committees of correspondence in the thirteen colonies or states, formed the Continental Congress as a coordinating agency for the revolutionary effort and as a quasi-government thereafter, and undertook other means of agitation, cooperation, and action. Yet the Patriots did not become a party in the full sense and did not persist as a distinct political formation past the period of the struggle for independence. Cleavage between so-called Federalists and anti-Federalists appeared in the controversy over the ratification of the new Constitution in 1788–1789. Yet once again these alignments did not take on party form, and the actual contest over ratification was waged among a pluralistic congeries of leaders and groups that varied significantly from place to place in the thirteen state arenas involved. In the internal politics of the several states, moreover, the contest for power was waged by a variety of factional formations rather than by parties. Only relatively advanced Pennsylvania developed something like a party system.

Thus the first American parties, or national parties, emerged out of new conflicts only in the 1790's. In terms of economic groups, what distinguished Federalists from Republicans were cleavages between mercantile, investing, and manufacturing interests and certain segments of agriculture on the one side and most planting and agrarian interests on the other. Differences also arose out of disagreements over the degree to which power should be consolidated in the new national government; over proposed policies to promote economic growth and capitalist development through government action; and over the extent to which foreign policy should be oriented toward traditionalist-monarchist England or revolutionary-republican France. Lastly, conflict grew out of contentions between leading personalities such as the Federalists Alexander Hamilton and John Adams on the one hand and the Republicans James Madison and Thomas Jefferson on the other, contentions that were sometimes as petty as they were colorful; and out of cleavages among a variety of other group, sectional, religious, local, and personal interests and persuasions. The whole story does not require retelling in its historical detail. The Federalists and

Republicans also developed out of a set of basic conditions, which are more to the point here.

As a general theory or hypothesis, the most basic conditions associated with the development of political parties in the modern sense may be summarized under four major headings:

1. The emergence or prospect of a significant national or common political arena, within which influence or power may be sought with reference to the decision-making centers and the offices of a common political system.

2. The development of differentiation or complexity within the political system in terms of divergences in group structures and conflicts of interest and opinion and in terms of governmental structures and functions.

3. The emergence of social structures and of ideologies or utopias which permit or encourage some form of popular or mass politics and a substantial electorate.

4. A sense of felt need to develop political structures to establish relationships between leaders and popular followings if leaders are to win and hold power and governmental functions are to be performed.

This statement of conditions can readily be related to the American instance by mediating the general theory through statements of particular sets of conditions which, taken together, constitute an immediate-conditional or relative-historical explanation for the emergence of the first American parties. The recital of American conditions will be summarized as a set of middle-range generalizations about American political development.

1. A national political arena was opened with the ratification of the new Constitution and the establishment of the national government in 1789.

Even in the colonial years a considerable degree of intercolonial communication and what might be called continental consciousness, or proto-national identity, had begun to emerge on the American scene. This development at once helped to sustain and received new impetus from the Revolutionary War effort and the Continental Congress of 1775–1789. The limited powers of this Congress, however, together with the fact that it could not exercise direct power over citizens but was only a quasi-government which depended on the states, and the fact that the Congress consisted of delegates appointed by state legislatures rather than of representatives chosen by the voters, kept it from providing a truly national political arena. The new general government with its single indirectly elected executive and its representative two-house Congress did become the center of a rapidly developing national arena. It was in and around this government that groups, leaders, and parties struggled and the great issues of the day were fought out.

2. The indigenous pluralism within the American nation produced a high degree of differentiation among groups, social strata, and states or sections and a complex interplay of interests, loyalties, sentiments, and opinions; and most of these forces quickly found expression in politics and turned increasingly to the national scene.

The cross-currents which the pluralism of early American life threw up were complex indeed. There were small-freehold farmers and great planters owning thousands of slaves; merchants, shippers and shipbuilders, importers and exporters, investors, and struggling manufacturers; artisans or "mechanics"; varied ethnic stocks and different religious faiths; would-be "aristocrats" and nascent "democrats," and sanguine "Gallomen" and sober "Anglomen"; states competing with one another; and a host of subgroupings, such as near-subsistence farmers or farmers who looked to the market. There extended across the new nation a congeries of interests that had to be given expression and accommodated if the system was to sustain itself and perform its functions; and parties developed in considerable part as a response to such felt needs. Certain interstate comparisons are also revealing in connection with this condition for party formation. Indices are difficult to assign, but Pennsylvania exhibited a particularly high degree of differentiation in the interplay of interests, which helps to explain the fact that Pennsylvania alone developed a state party system in the 1780's and also moved rapidly toward shaping local units of the national parties in the 1790's. A significant degree of complexity might also be attributed to New York, for example, where the pace of national party development was second only to that of Pennsylvania; but in New York old patterns of domination by great families and clique politics, characteristics which were much less in evidence in Pennsylvania, impeded party development. It may be suggested as a hypothesis that the higher the degree of differentiation of group and other relationships is in a political system, the greater is the probability for the development of political parties, though this probability may be reduced by the presence of other impending conditions. Such differentiation certainly existed in American national politics by the 1790's, as various group interests took on nation-wide form and sought national expression.

Substantial differentiation also characterized the national government. It was not only formally separated into executive, legislative, and judicial branches with distinct prescribed powers but the two houses of Congress had different electoral foundations and constituencies and somewhat different functions. The Constitution also provided among the various organs of government an intricate set of checks or reciprocal relationships that in effect constituted a further differentiation of functions. Again, parties arose in part in response to the problems leaders faced in trying to operate this complex governmental machinery effectively.

3. Social structures and basic perspectives in the American experience provided a strong impetus for popular involvement in politics, demands for representation and mechanisms of consent, and the emergence of a substantial electorate.

In comparison with contemporary European societies American society was remarkably open, atomistic, affluent, and fluid. It was not bound to feudal traditions, graded structures of estates or classes, or old corporate configurations. Most men owned a piece of farm land or other property as a foundation for individual independence; a vast continent and its wealth of resources offered unprecedented opportunities; distances between rich and poor were not so great as they were in Old World societies; social distinctions and deference patterns were not so sharp or rigid, and there was no genuine aristocracy or fixed hierarchy; and social mobility was a frequent fact as well as a hope. Distinctions there were, particularly between great planters and lesser farmers and Negro slaves in the South; and where social gradations were particularly sharp and persistent, patterns of deference held on longer than they did elsewhere. Yet distinctions were generally on the wane, partly as a result of economic opportunity and partly because of the democratization that had accompanied the Revolution and swept many states in the 1780's. This development was furthered by the impact of the social outlook, *ethos,* or mood that Hartz has aptly called the American "liberal tradition." This fundamental perspective, with John Locke as its ideologue, was to develop steadily in American conditions from a utopia to an increasingly common general ideology and foundation for emerging consensus; and in drafting the Declaration of Independence, which became the basic statement of the American creed, Jefferson drew on Lockian ideas as "the common sense of the subject." The liberal tradition placed heavy stress on such important if sometimes conflicting values as free individualism, opportunity, individual achievement, equalitarianism, and liberal democracy. It is not surprising that movement toward democratic participation, representation, and consent was rapid, and it is also not surprising that these forces brought the emergence of an extensive electorate in state after state. In terms of interstate comparisons all of these forces and particularly the stress on equalitarianism and a mass base for politics were especially pronounced in Pennsylvania, where party action developed most rapidly. On the other hand equalitarianism and the extension of suffrage took hold more slowly in the Southern states, where full-scale party structures and action came comparatively late, although even there the impact of remaining tax or property qualifications on suffrage has been exaggerated by older historians.

It may be suggested as a further general hypothesis that the greater the degree to which equalitarian political ideologies and extended suffrage obtain, the greater is the probability that political parties will develop in the absence of other, impeding factors. Recent research findings for the American case indicate that after the Revolution the great majority of white adult males in an era of widely held agricultural property could vote. Not all of them did, but the democratic impulse and keen party competition brought voting participation in the period 1799–1802 and after to the substantial proportion of 39 per cent or more of white adult males in important elections, a level that was not to be exceeded until new party rivalry appeared in the Jacksonian era. Moreover access to other avenues to the political arena was comparatively open. Freedom of political belief, expression, and action was also generally accepted, despite important uncertainties and exceptions in the early years.

4. Within the context of these conditions, a sense of felt need gradually arose for efficient means to represent and combine interests, amass power, conduct elections, and manage government.

Innumerable obstacles stood in the way of party development, and no one set out to construct parties with a blueprint in mind. Men thought in terms of devices to meet immediate needs, or bickered about immediate interests; many important political figures including George Washington spoke out against the idea of parties. The process of party-building was one of groping expediences as well as brilliant innovations, and it was some time before leaders came to think consciously in party-building terms. Yet in the space of a few years after the ratification of the Constitution in 1789 stable structures were evolved, and the Federalist and Republican formations emerged as parties.

This analysis is hardly unique in its basic terms. It is consistent with suggestions contained in the classical work of Ostrogorski, with the emphasis Weber puts on the relationship between popular or mass politics and "parties of politicians," and with many of the ideas offered by Duverger. Yet the summary here is based primarily on investigation of the American instance. Circumstances will certainly reveal variations from context to context in the significance of any one condition in the development of political parties even though the general pattern of relevant conditions may remain constant. Indeed it may be argued that generic conditions as they affect the development of parties can be firmly established only in terms of comparative historical processes carefully analyzed through a theoretically oriented historiography or time-oriented science of political development. As V. O. Key puts it: ". . . a conception of the party system must take into account its dimension of time. It may be useful to think of the party system as an historical process rather than as patterned and static institutional behavior. . . . if the party process is viewed through time, additional aspects of the working of party [systems] may be identified." This, presumably, is the task of developmental political science or analytical history.

A possible factor in party development as it has operated in many new nations today should be noted. This is the effect of external influences on the peoples of developing areas who are seeking to achieve the modernization that most Western societies have already accomplished. The adaptation of foreign ideas or models as part of the European legacy, including general models for political parties, has played a significant part in political development in Asia and Africa today, although of course local conditions continue to have profound effects. Such mimetic elements were virtually absent in the early American experience. The terms "Whig" and "Tory" had been in use in England for a century or more, but they denoted broad persuasions and shifting alliances of factions or personal clique-"connexions," in the old spelling and the old style, rather than parties as such; suffrage remained extremely narrow; and these early English political formations did not develop continuing and pervasive structures to provide stable links between leaders at the parliamentary center and substantial popular followings in the nation as a whole. It was not until the rise of the Liberal and Conservative formations after the limited first Reform Act of 1832 that England may be said to have arrived at genuine political parties. Nor were modern party models available in the 1790's in other European countries. In short the Federalist and Republican formations in the United States had to find their own way toward party structure and party action.

Political Development, Party Structures, and Party Functions

The argument that American parties in the 1790's were the first modern parties is more than a mere historiographical contention. It involves conceptions of what a political party is and does and of how American parties were related to the whole question of political development, and a conceptual distinction between party politics and faction politics. Political development may be understood as a movement toward a political system which is capable of handling the loads it confronts, characterized by significant differentiation of structures and specificity of functions, increasingly centralized and able to maintain itself. It may not be as easy to measure political development as it would be to measure economic development, for example, yet one might argue that a highly developed political system is characterized by some measure of rationalized political efficiency, defined as a substantial degree of coherence in policy output and a capacity for innovation in the face of new problems. Parties and party systems may have an important impact on the course of such development.

In the American case the emergence of parties marked a significant elaboration of structures and a movement toward relative political efficiency. Before the advent of parties politics was a pluralistic, kaleidoscopic flux of personal cliques like those that gathered around the great magnate families in New York, caucuses of the sort that came and went in many New England towns, select and often half-invisible juntos in the capitals or courthouse villages in the Southern states, or other more or less popular but usually evanescent factions. All of these political formations in their pluralistic variety may be brought under the general heading of faction politics. With few exceptions such old-style "connexions" or multiple factions were characterized by lack of continuity from election to election, by tenuous or shifting relationships between leaders in government on the one hand and the electorate on the other, by comparatively narrow ranges of support from interest groupings, and thus by a confusing degree of raw, unaggregated pluralism in politics. One result was that it was difficult for the voters to hold any one group of men responsible for the direction of public policy. Another was that policy-making was generally erratic or incoherent except where it was under the control of a dominant "connexion," clique, or junto.

The advent of the Federalists and Republicans as comprehensive parties, on the other hand, brought a new dualistic order into politics. The parties emerged as durable, differentiated, visible, rationalized formations which developed stable operating structures. Continuing relationships were evolved between leaders and cadre at the center of government and between lesser leaders and cadre in the states, counties, and towns; and in turn between this structure and broad popular followings in the electorate. It is appropriate in the American instance to consider the structure of leaders and cadre as "the party," or party proper, and its supporters or adherents in the public as its following. At the beginning American parties accomplished little toward organization strictly construed as a regularized differentiation of internal functions and corresponding division of labor. Indeed the Federalists never achieved significant organization, although the Republicans by the late 1790's and early 1800's devised party caucuses, conventions, and committees in several states which foreshadowed the full development of organization proper in the Jacksonian era. Yet both party structures in the 1790's did reach out to amass stable popular followings of considerable range and density that carried them well beyond the fluid and limited support pre-party factions had enjoyed. Lastly, both parties developed distinctive sets of in-group perspectives with emotional overtones, or ideologies, that helped to bind party structures together and popular followings to the parties. In short the first American parties can be described as developing historical patterns of stable structures linked to broad popular followings, with distinguishing ideologies, and as structures that were able and ready to perform crucial political functions. It is in terms of this general idea of what a party is that the Federalists and Republicans may be thought of as the first modern parties.

In the functions they came to perform the first American parties exerted an important influence on the course of political development in general. In the process of nation-building any people is likely to face a number of interrelated problems which impose significant loads on the political system. Among the most salient of these we may list the following:

1. Establishing and maintaining a national authority, or the operating political system itself.
2. Expressing and aggregating interests as essential functions and, if possible, containing conflict within a spectrum which will prevent immobilism or disruption.
3. Meeting the "crisis of participation" and meeting related problems of coordinating political action in a politics of popular participation.
4. Recruiting and training at all levels new leaders who are capable of managing the problems or loads at hand.

5. Effecting a "pay-off," in Lipset's terms, or meeting the "crisis of distribution" in order to maintain the political system by convincing at least substantial segments of the population that it is an instrument through which they may accomplish their objectives.

6. Arriving at a position with reference to possible opposition to governing elites within the polity.

Each problem noted here certainly does not carry the same weight in every emerging nation, but the loads are sufficiently universal in political development to give an analysis of their impact a general relevance. How political parties affected the way each was met in the American instance can be recounted briefly.

First, although parties did not establish the national constitutional authority in the United States, they did much to assure its effective operation. Despite controversy over the balance of federal and state powers in the new political system, both Federalists and Republicans worked within it. Both parties also discountenanced periodic eruptions of violence for political purposes; thus, for example, party spokesmen did not take up the violence of the Whisky Insurrection of 1794 or the Fries Rebellion of 1799 as a weapon of opposition but condemned it instead. As time passed, parties and party leaders also came to manage the structures of the central government, establish informal connections between its separated agencies, and staff its offices. In short, the parties filled gaps in the constitutional structure of national authority in a constitutional manner and thus performed a crucial constitutional function.

Second, parties dealt effectively with one of the major problems of the new American polity in expressing and aggregating conflicting interests. Given the manifold pluralism and sectional divisions on the American scene, and given a continuation of the politics of raw group pressures and of factions, conflicts of interest might have brought immobilism in the political system along with severe strains or social disruption. Both the Federalists and the Republicans amassed followings which included national coalitions or combinations of interests and opinions, however, held together by working formulas of agreement or compromises, and the Federalists enjoyed at the outset a far wider range of group support than early historians were willing to attribute to them. Conflict continued in party channels, but within viable limits.

Third, early American parties helped to meet the load of popular participation and related problems. Many Federalists were far from happy at the prospect of having to curry votes in order to hold power, but they adjusted at least in part to the imperatives an increasingly open, liberal society imposed. Their Republican opponents meanwhile actively encouraged popular involvement in politics and made the emerging general ideology of liberal democracy a particular ideology for their party, thereby winning an increasingly large following that helped to make them a dominant party after 1800. Indeed the Federalists tended to remain a "party of notables," in Weber's phrase, maintained a condescending tone, and were inclined to view elections as referenda on the policies they had already forged in government. On the other hand the Republicans, partly a "party of notables" but also and increasingly a "party of politicians," revealed a responsiveness to sentiments and opinions among their followers and in the electorate which made them what may be called a "popular party," a party highly sensitive to such currents. Yet both parties turned to general propaganda to inform voters and influence public opinion, most significantly through partisan media at the capital like the *Gazette of the United States* (Federalist) and the *National Gazette* (Republican) and satellite newspapers in the states, although the Republican *Gazette* was soon replaced by the Philadelphia *Aurora* as a national party organ. Moreover both parties gradually evolved procedures to coordinate action in the nomination of candidates and the conduct of election campaigns, and to appeal to and bring out the vote.

Fourth, the parties brought up leaders or enlisted new cadres who helped to manage political business throughout the political system. The roster of major leaders includes such brilliant figures as Hamilton, Adams, Jefferson, and Madison at the party "point," in the capital; editor-politicians like John Fenno, Philip Freneau, Benjamin Franklin Bache, or Noah Webster; such Congressional leaders as Fisher Ames, Theodore Sedgwick, James Monroe, or Albert Gallatin; and scores of prominent local leaders like John Jay in New York or Alexander Dallas in Pennsylvania. Yet the parties, particularly the Republicans, also developed national behind-the-scenes cadre figures like John Beckley, who served the Republicans as a kind of informal national chairman, and untold legions of lesser cadre in the supportive echelons of the party phalanx, in the states, counties, and towns. Most early American party managers were young, and many were intellectuals to a greater or lesser degree. The average age of nine representative Federalist leaders in 1792, when incipient parties were beginning to take recognizable form, was 44, and the average age of thirteen representative Republican leaders was 36. Nearly all had attended college at a time when higher education was not common, and most had significant intellectual talents as writers or in other areas. One of the most remarkable devices for bringing forward political leadership came with the growth of indigenous Democratic or Republican societies as formal political associations in several states and cities. These societies had a short life and never became mass-membership units in the Republican party as such; but they provided a useful training ground for new political elites.

Fifth, parties also provided mechanisms to assure that the new political system produced a pay-off. They not only quickly developed to the point where they could provide representation for important interests, but as each party partly emerged out of controversy over important national issues each maintained different positions on these issues. On economic policy, for example, Hamilton and the Federalists advocated government measures to encourage hothouse capitalist development even at the expense of economic inequality within the society, while Jefferson and most Republicans were content to speak for a predominantly agricultural economy as the foundation of an equalitarian simple-republican order even at the cost of a slow pace of national economic growth. In the positions they took on these and other issues the two parties in effect provided the electorate with a choice. In the coherence and innovation they brought into government they also helped to shape reasonably consistent courses for public policy. A comparison of Congressional behavior before and after the development of national parties makes clear the transition from confusion to some measure of order and coherence in policy decisions. No group perhaps got all it wanted, but all important groups had some means to express their demands; and serious dysfunction was avoided.

Sixth, American parties arrived at the acceptance of opposition. To be sure, not only Hamilton but also many other Federalist leaders were suspicious or impatient of opposition, and the Alien and Sedition Acts of 1798, which Adams as well as extreme Federalists supported, were aimed at Republican critics. Yet no general program of repression was undertaken, and when the Republicans won the presidency and both houses of Congress in 1800 the Federalists yielded power in 1801 without recourse to force. Despite overheated rhetoric in the campaign and later Congressional maneuvers to make Aaron Burr president instead of Jefferson, it was the first instance of such a peaceful transition in modern politics. Meanwhile the Republicans in opposition had followed a wholly peaceful course, had carefully avoided overtones of disruptive separatism in the Kentucky and Virginia Resolutions of Jefferson and Madison that censured the Alien and Sedition Acts, and had come rather more readily than the Federalists to the acceptance of opposition after they won power. American parties achieved a *modus vivendi* of adjustment to opposition and peaceful rivalry instead of repression or violence.

In short, parties helped to meet many of the loads the new nation faced and did so in an ideological spirit of open, innovative, and pragmatic accommodation. Parties moreover contributed to political development as a whole by providing mechanisms for the rationalization of politics through the party structures and by helping to introduce a measure of political efficiency which faction politics could scarcely have achieved. Within the general scheme advanced by Almond and Coleman for the analysis of non-Western or under-developed as well as Western or developed societies, the first American parties may be said to have undertaken important aspects of the crucial functions of socialization, recruitment, interest articulation, interest aggregation, communication, and rule-making. The intricate machinery of the Constitution could scarcely have functioned as it did without the role parties and the party system played.

It is possible to offer a conceptual generalization based on the American experience. The American parties of the 1790's took the form of cadre structures rather than mass-membership parties, in Duverger's terms; and they did not perform as comprehensive a range of internal functions as many parties in new nations in Asia and Africa have undertaken today, or at least not so intensively point by point. Other differences in specific structure and function could be pointed out from party system to party system. Yet it may also be argued that the American experience lays bare useful generic aspects of the process of party development. If this is the case, all modern parties may be thought of, in a conceptual hypothesis, as historical instances of social formations directed toward the acquisition of governmental power whose definitive characteristics are stable structures, stable relationships linking leaders and popular followings, performance or an offer to perform a wide range of crucial functions in the political system, and the generation of in-group perspectives or ideologies. The specific shape of parties will vary with conditions, loads, and responses, but all modern parties seem likely to exhibit at an irreducible minimum the four general characteristics suggested by the American case.

Party Systems and Party Roles

The ultimate impact parties have depends on the party system. Whether there is one party or more than one makes a difference; the kinds of relationships that exist between parties where more than one appears also count; and so does the kind of leadership that develops within the parties. Thus one-party systems will have their own consequences; the impact of plural party systems may differ in societies characterized by widely-shared agreement as compared with societies riven by the centrifugal forces of bipolarized pluralism, and a party system marked by intransigence is likely to produce quite different results from one in which pragmatic adaptation is the mode. Few if any of these matters can be taken as wholly foreordained, at least in the early stages of political development.

Continuing competition between the Federalists and Republicans in the 1790's produced the first modern two-party system. The American experience suggests that the defining characteristic of stable competitive two-party systems is continuing interaction between the parties in which each must take the other into account in its conduct, particularly as it touches on their relations with the electorate in their bids for power and their relations to the centers of government authority. The character of this interaction may be put in terms of four interrelated criteria:

1. The existence of continuing conflict between parties, at once based on and implying the development of policy positions and ideologies which appear as "we-they" perspectives. Differences between parties in policy and ideology may be relatively broad or relatively narrow.

2. The provision of stable links or connections between elements in the public or electorate on the one hand and government on the other as the parties contend with one another.

3. The conduct of party conflict short of social disruption, with at least some degree of acceptance of the idea of a loyal opposition. If party conflict passes beyond the bounds of the spectrum suggested here, it is difficult to conceive of the parties as operating within a stable system, because the seeds of the breakdown of the system or its transition to a different kind of system would always be present. In a stable competitive party system there must at a minimum be some kind of agreement to disagree without recourse to repression or disruption.

4. The existence of a reasonable chance for "out" parties to win governmental power and become "in" parties, and therefore the possibility of the alternation of parties in power. Where one party holds an unassailably dominant position even though opposition exists, we can scarcely speak of a genuinely competitive system.

In the United States the first parties established a pattern of dual party competition. This pattern gave way in the 1800's to a period of Republican ascendency in which the Federalists grew less and less able to provide a significant national challenge to the governing party of Jefferson, Madison, and Monroe; and this pattern of one-party dominance in turn gave way to a new period of faction politics as the Republicans themselves suffered disintegration. In the Jacksonian era, however, new parties revived the pattern of dual party competition, and it has persisted in America despite periodic third-party challenges in the national arena and variations in state arenas. In its broad form the model of a stable competitive party system derived from the early-American experience and suggested here may serve as a basic model of such systems in general, within which variations in particular characteristics may be taken into account.

Political parties may also be thought of as tending toward democratic or plebiscitarian poles in their behavior and roles in the party system. The issue hinges on the different ways parties respond to the load of participation in the course of political development. On the one hand the attitude of political elites may be that mass involvement in politics is something to be contended with through manipulation or control. This may be accomplished through parties as directing and mobilizing but not responsive structures; by molding interests and opinions rather than by giving them open expression; and by elections as formal referenda rather than effective choices. On the other hand elites may adjust to or stimulate patterns of effective participation in the power structure, assume attitudes of responsiveness to a variety of freely expressed interests and opinions in the party system, and view elections as open choices on broad policy options, which in turn should have an effect on public policy. Given their inclination to look upon elections as referenda on policies they had already forged, the Federalists tended toward a plebiscitarian outlook — or a restricted plebiscitarian outlook if one includes their additional inclination to view with misgivings the emergence of a sizable electorate — while the Republicans moved toward an increasingly democratic response. Yet the bent of social structure, Lockian ideology, and the polity tended to push the party system as a whole along a democratic course. The fact that parties developed in a competitive system in which each party had to appeal to a substantial electorate if it was to gain power also provided an internal dynamic in the party system itself which moved it still further in a democratic direction. The existence of open and continuing Federalist and Republican rivalry at virtually all levels of government meant that the party system provided a choice for the public or electorate. This opportunity for choice became the fulcrum of democratic consent and control in the American experience.

Variations in structure between the Federalists and Republicans are also relevant to the question of democratic and plebiscitarian patterns. The Federalists persisted in their notabilistic structure; they were internally created, in Duverger's phrase, originating as they did in and building out from a powerful nucleus at the center of government; and they never developed great sensitivity to popular demands. Because the Republicans were relatively free from such notabilistic characteristics, they developed more and more as a "popular party." Although they too built out from the center of government, they were also in an important part externally created, out of indigenous elements in the states and localities, in a manner Duverger finds unusual for cadre parties; and they were inclined to see elections as expressions of the popular will even to the point of investing them with a Lockian mystique. In the relationships the Republican party evolved with its popular following important patterns of two-way communication emerged, and what was said at either end of lines of communication was likely to be heard and considered at the other, at the top as well as at the bottom. In part such relationships emerged out of the fact that the Republicans grew up in opposition and were faced with the necessity of mobilizing support to counter the advantages in power the Federalists enjoyed as a government party. The result, however, was a further impetus toward democratization of the American party system.

Lastly, the democratic bent in the development of American parties found expression in the manner in which the parties performed political functions. Their style was more specific than diffuse, more instrumental than affective, and their appeal more general than particular, although personal ties continued as an important undercurrent in party life; and American parties developed in a direction that stressed mass appeals and popular mobilization in elections. Moreover the fact that the parties had a comprehensive governmental structure to work through meant that they enjoyed significant opportunities to carry popular choices in policy into effect once they had won office. Indeed the Federalists and Republicans probably achieved a higher degree of efficiency on this count than later American parties have done when internal factionalism has worked against coherent translation of national electoral choices into governmental decisions.

For the democratic and plebiscitarian alternatives the crucial point is the role party systems as a whole play. They may provide channels for open recruitment, effective participation, and effective representation, or they may not; if they do, they may exhibit a substantial measure of intraparty democracy. They may provide meaningful, relatively orderly, continuing options on policy as well as leaders among which the public or electorate can choose, or they may not; if they do, they offer choices as the operative meaning of interparty democracy. It may be argued as a general hypothesis that competive dual-party systems carry a stronger probability not only of democratic consent but of democratic control than do pluralistic multiparty systems, in the sense of the translation of broad popular choices into public policy; whereas multiparty systems or dual systems with a high incidence of intraparty factionalism are less efficient in promoting democratic control because the clarity of either-or alternatives is lacking and parties or factions must enter into *ad hoc* coalitions to govern. Yet these features and problems on consent and control are not involved at all in any effective sense in plebiscitarian systems, where domination replaces meaningful consent and manipulation replaces free choice.

Parties and National Integration

In an important sense nearly every aspect of the discussion of American nation-building and party-building here is related to the question of integration. It remains, however, to isolate and analyze the elements involved from the point of view of this particular aspect of political development.

Most broadly, national integration may be taken as a process of incorporating various parts of a society into a functioning whole. Where a relatively high degree of integration obtains, a political system can perform essential functions with a substantial measure of acceptance, order, and efficiency. Integration also tends to proceed by phases, meeting various problems, so to speak, as it moves from lower to higher stages. Among these we may note the growth of obedience and loyalties to the nation which transcend loyalties to its parts; the reduction of barriers between various parts of the whole, the opening of communication, and ultimately the toleration of differences within unity; the emergence of faith in the political system; and the emergence of shared values and perspectives, or consensus. Where norms or promises of democracy exist, integration appears to require general access to effective participation in the processes of the political system. Successful integration in a society of any complexity also appears to require some rationalization of political processes so that the variety of elements in the nation may be related effectively to a single government. These aspects of political development will be taken here not as integration itself, or as "participation integration" and "process integration"; but as requisites for national integration, construed as the process of incorporation of parts into a whole. This notion of integration in general has been put suggestively by Deutsch in a summary of possible stages: "Open or latent resistance to political amalgamation into a common national state; minimal integration to the point of passive compliance with the orders of such an amalgamated government; deeper political integration to the point of active support for such a common state but with continuing ethnic or cultural group cohesion and diversity; and, finally, the coincidence of political amalgamation and integration with the assimilation of all groups to a common language and culture. . . ."

National integration may be found in different dimensions at different junctures in time. Much also depends on the sequence and clustering of issues. If a developing polity faces all at once the loads of establishing legitimacy and achieving some measure of integration and also the problems of participation and distribution and of rationalizing political processes, serious strains are likely to occur. In the American case the timing of issues was fortunate. It was no easy task to amalgamate thirteen previously separate, often squabbling states into a single nation. Yet the emergence of communication among the colonies and various sections even before the Revolution, the development of a continental consciousness, the Revolutionary experience and American tribulations after 1783 as a lonely republic in a generally hostile world, the existence of a substantial measure of cultural as well as linguistic identity, the rise of economic interdependence, and the increasing sway of the liberal tradition all helped toward the development of national identity in a way that few new nations in Asia or Africa today have enjoyed. The federal character of the new national political system under the Constitution, with its explicit recognition of diversity within unity, marked another important step. Finally the charismatic legitimacy George Washington brought to the new government, and his refusal to allow his personal appeal to be converted into a foundation for perennial power, also did much to smooth a transition from personal foundations for legitimacy to rational foundations in a legal-constitutional order. It was only after most of these phases in the process of integration had been passed through or were underway that other loads came to the fore in the nation as a whole. There was already a significant development toward integration before national political parties appeared.

Many aspects of party action did more to hinder this development than to advance it. The Federalists and Republicans not only expressed but even exacerbated cleavage in their representation of conflicts of interest in the society and in their maneuvering for office and power; in the way in which they helped to pit men against one another "like two cocks," as Jefferson put it in describing his relations with Hamilton in the cabinet; and by contributing to a general heating-up of the political atmosphere. Indeed conflict is inherent in competive party systems as they have been described here because such systems provide open channels for the clash of interests, sentiments, and opinions which already exist in the population and introduce new elements of antagonism on their own in their continuing rivalry for power. The we-they perspectives of parties, the stress on the virtues of "our" leaders and policies and symbols and the evil of "theirs," are all likely to stir strident outcries among rival partisans. Moreover early American party cadres were not always above sharp dealing and even occasional fraud in elections in the scramble for power; there was at least one occasion in the 1790's when invective between partisans in the American Congress came to blows; the suspicion and partisan motives which spawned the Alien and Sedition Acts carried over into the partisan strains of the election of 1800; and party conflict exacerbated personal dislikes, leading Burr and Hamilton to a duel in which the latter was killed. It was such aspects of political rivalry that Washington condemned when he spoke out against "the spirit of party" as a spirit sure to "distract the public councils." There is no discounting the malintegrative impact of such aspects of party rivalry in the American case.

Yet it is important to note two additional elements in this connection, which may be expressed as general hypotheses. First, it may be that parties of the general American type, by channeling the conflicts which already exist within the society and subjecting them to mediating structures, reduce on the whole the amount of conflict that would otherwise occur even though they generate distinctively partisan cleavages on their own. Second, it may be that such parties by expressing conflict openly in a patterned manner within the rules of the political system promote integration by facilitating rhetorical modes of expression as channels of social and psychological catharsis, thereby drawing off potential strains in the political system as a whole. In any case the American polity weathered the storms of its formative period and has weathered all such storms but one that blew up over the most continually divisive issue in American life, the place of the Negro in the national community — and in that one the loosing of the national and integrative ties of the party system in 1860 was the prelude to civil war in 1861. Although parties in the 1790's scarcely ushered in a millennium of harmony, conflict was kept within peaceful bounds.

In this connection the place of ideology requires some specification. Federalists and Republicans were divided ideologically on many questions of domestic policy. Issues of world politics such as the Jay Treaty with England in 1795 touched off frenzies of logomachy in which each party hinted that the other verged on treason, and Washington thought that the Jay Treaty controversy agitated the public to a point that equaled the excitements of the revolutionary era itself. Extreme or "High" Federalists in the late 1790's could scarcely stomach the thought of the Republicans gaining power, and a few of them in the early 1800's even toyed with abortive schemes for the secession of New England from the union as an answer to Republican ascendency. Yet by and large ideology among party leaders took the form of giving vent to emotional release in rhetoric; and as a controlling element in behavior it did not reach the point of ultimate intransigence. Extremist Federalists remained a minority in the party as a whole, and John Adams as a party leader as well as President insisted on following a moderate course in foreign policy; Jefferson's conduct in office has been described as a triumph of practical adaptation over ideological inflexibility — "what is practicable," he himself commented, "must often controul what is pure theory." On the whole ideological divisions between Federalists and Republicans were sharper than they have usually been between major American parties, but not sharp enough to produce disruptive consequences in the polity.

In their competion, meanwhile, early American parties made significant contributions to some of the crucial requisites for national integration. They helped to fulfill the democratic promises of the American liberal tradition by providing effective channels for popular participation. They assisted in meeting the problem of distribution by their transmission to government of the demands of important groups across the nation and in the states and localities. They contributed to solving the problem of orderly management in a complex polity by their conduct of nominations and elections and by helping to manage the agencies of the national government. In short, parties helped to realize a measure of political efficiency which could never have been achieved through faction politics.

As integration was involved in the problem of establishing constitutional legitimacy and the evolution of a viable national consensus, parties also performed directly integrative tasks in their relation with the public in several ways:

1. By supporting the new constitutional order in its hour of uncertainty and testing, even in the face of disagreements over specific interpretation of the Constitution itself.

2. By strengthening and maintaining communication and a sense of shared stakes among different groups in the several states. Thus, for example, both Massachusetts men and Virginians could join across state lines in being either Federalists or Re-

publicans, though there were more of the former in Massachusetts and more of the latter in Virginia. Without national parties malintegration among the several states might have persisted far longer than it did.

3. By undertaking recruitment and socialization, or bringing up and training new elites to man posts in the political system and providing popular education in politics on an informal basis.

In these ways parties helped to promote a sense of political community and efficacy and thereby further strengthened the new government. If they did not perform a range of directly integrative functions comparable to those that parties have undertaken in many new nations today, this was in part because the American problem of integration was less demanding by the time parties appeared.

In the final analysis, however, the effect of parties on national integration depends on the role of the party system as a whole. The fruitful issue for analysis appears to be not a general either-or question of whether parties integrate or don't integrate. The question is: Under what conditions do party systems of what kinds promote a net balance of integration or of nonintegration, and in what ways? It is the contention here that the first American party system, despite the malintegrative results of certain aspects of party action, produced a net balance of integrative results. This was the case in large part because of certain salient features of the system itself and their consequences.

First, there is the fact that the Federalists and the Republicans took on the form of stable, broad-gauge parties as contrasted with shifting, narrow factions. Thus the parties and their followings operated as broadly inclusive combinations of interest groups. In the long-term interaction of the parties in competition for support these combinations could be held together only by political brokerage and compromise in the party structures and in their relations with their followings. The net result was that the party system turned group conflict from unlimited pluralistic into manageable dualistic channels before it reached the decision-making centers of government. As compared with the tensions of deadlock that might have ensued if indigenous pluralism had continued unchecked, party dualism reduced malintegrative strains.

Second, because the parties developed as formations given more to the practical pursuit of power and office than to ideological intransigence, they tended to conduct conflict within a moderate range. They did so in part as a result of the moderate bent of American politics generally and in part out of the exigencies of their interaction in the party system itself. Yielding too much to the views of extremist groups or leaders threatened the loss of important blocs of votes that were essential to political success. The result was a tendency to push the party system toward moderation or centralism and to limit the ambit of extremist elements. All of these forces combined to produce a net balance of integrative results, particularly as compared with the degree of malintegration that would have followed from constant extremes in party policy or action. In this context the party system also arrived at the acceptance and legitimization of a coordinated political opposition.

Third, by providing instruments for electoral consent and democratic choice the party system helped to drain off dissatisfaction before it reached the point of serious dissaffection. It opened avenues of expression for those who were at the moment out of power as well as in, gave hope to the "outs" that they might become "ins" as a result of electoral choices, provided concrete mechanisms through which the far-flung national electorate could hold someone responsible for the conduct of government, and offered working tools for a peaceful change of elites if the electorate wished it. It is hard to imagine how major national elections could have been managed in a satisfactory manner without the machinery of operating democratic choice the party system made available. By 1800, for example, widespread dissatisfaction with Federalist leaders and policies had built up within many important groups in the population, however much parties intensified it. If the party system had not existed to help effect a transfer of power to the Republicans in a way the dispersed mechanisms of faction politics could scarcely have done, dissatisfaction might have grown to seriously disruptive proportions or turned to violence, as earlier antagonisms toward ruling elites and their policies had done in the Regulator movement in North Carolina, in Shays' Rebellion in Massachusetts, or in the Whisky Insurrection and the Fries Uprising. On balance again, the party system may be said to have reduced potential disaffection and disruption, with a net gain for integrative over malintegrative consequences.

Lastly, parties in the party system operated within the rules of the developing polity as a whole, with the obvious integrative results which this fact entailed.

This analysis of the American experience suggests as a general hypothesis that a democratic two-party system can produce a net balance of integrative impacts on political development if the parties embrace a wide range of interests and opinions in their followings held together by pragmatic adjustment, if they keep conflict within moderate bounds, and if they are ready to operate within a larger basic agreement or an accepted set of fundamental rules. The hypothesis contains a substantial set of "ifs," however; and they raise a final important question.

Leadership, Purposes, and Political Styles

The net impact of early American parties on national integration was what it was to an important degree because of key features which the party system came to exhibit as a whole — notably the features just outlined here, and its pragmatic development in general. It remains to explore why, or how, the American party system took on these particular characteristics; why, or how, it came to operate within the rules.

A large part of the explanation lies in the comparatively narrow range of conflict American conditions produced and in the rise of the American liberal tradition toward national consensus. The distribution of interests and opinions tended to fall into a curve of dualistic centrality, with most interests and opinions encompassed in two central peaks of concentration which tapered off into much lower measures of extremes, as it were, rather than into a bimodal curve of disruptive extremes or a centrifugal scattering of disruptive drives. Such matters of social fact, prevailing ideology, a relatively limited spectrum of social conflict, and the distribution of interests may be taken as a necessary condition in any explanation of how the American party system came to perform as it did. Yet the explanation as a whole goes beyond such matters and brings us again to the responses of American party leaders to the conditions and loads they faced.

Particularly in a period of national formation, what leaders do and how they do it may have a crucial impact. In the American case the bulk of party leaders were guided by purposes and convictions which included a deep concern for the future of the new nation or the success of its "republican experiment," as well as by concerns for more immediate or particular political goals. Moreover they had before them the example and counsel of Washington, who served far more as a moderator than he did as a mobilizer or dramatizer, as many later prophet-leaders of nationalism have. In the long run American party leaders avoided pushing issues and ideologies to the breaking-point of violence or disruption, as they might have done, and upheld the Constitution and the rules of the polity; and when the test of 1800 came the Federalists as a whole accepted the result rather than resort to force to prevent it. In short, no major party leader was ready to chance the destruction of the new nation in order to gain partisan or factional advantage. The role of leadership in this connection is underscored by the fact that the story might have been quite different if men like the intransigent ultra-High Federalists of Connecticut, for example, had dominated in national party leadership.

Lastly, American party leaders developed unusual skills in intergroup adjustment and combination, in compromise, in aggregating as well as mobilizing interests, and in the practical rationalization of political methods and processes; and through such skills they helped to establish patterns of adjustment as well as of conflict in the party system. These crucial matters of purpose, commitment, and skill became the foundations of the basically pragmatic style the preponderance of American party leaders achieved. It is in important part the lack of such commitments, skills, and styles that has prevented many new nations in Asia or Africa today from establishing a viable measure of national integration and efficiency, and many nations in Latin America from managing peaceful transfers of power by democratic procedures. If there are lessons for developing nations today that may be learned from the early American experience in political development, they lie in large part here — in the area of leadership and in the manner in which leaders conduct politics in general and party politics in particular.

Considered as a whole, the response of American party leaders to the problems of nation-building and party-building was more than a reflex action to social conditions and emerging ideology. It was also a creative element operating in reciprocal interaction with these elements, an active and positive factor itself. It was forwarded by human purposes, modes of behavior, and shared hopes, notably the hope of building a strong nation and making the republican innovation work in a hostile world. Rivals though they were and spokesmen of strongly different points of view, Hamilton the Federalist and Jefferson the Republican were outstanding examples of this creative personal element, one by virtually inventing a program to point the nation toward economic growth, the other by embodying the spirit of American nationhood and liberal democracy. If the total historical process in its groping, its occasional pettiness, and its conflict as well as its creative aspects was by no means all smooth and orderly, it did bring the United States from uncertainty to stable nationhood, from faction politics to working party politics, and to a political system that was cohesive, internally legitimate, and autonomous, in Deutsch's terms. The measure of integration early America achieved was in part a byproduct of underlying forces. It was also in part the result of active responses to conditions and loads by political leaders.

The Enigma of Thomas Jefferson

The revolutionary generation produced a galaxy of great Americans each of whom reflected different aspects of American character. None has proved more fascinating, or so full of paradoxes as Thomas Jefferson. If any single individual can lay claim to being the Father of American Democracy, Jefferson is the strongest candidate. Few of his contemporaries expressed deeper faith in popular government or did more to demonstrate the possibility of enlightened leadership in a democratic society. In the following essay, Richard Hofstadter shrewdly picks his way through conflicting historical interpretations of the Sage of Monticello as well as through the apparent contradictions within Jefferson himself.

Jefferson believed that all men were created equal, yet he owned dozens of slaves; he idealized the yeoman farmer as God's chosen class on whose simple honesty and virtue the success of the American experiment rested, yet he and his closest associates were great planters, masters of broad estates and numerous bondsmen, living in stately mansions surrounded by luxury and elegance. He insisted that virtue could only flourish in the countryside and that vice found its natural habitat in cities, yet as minister of finance in the 1780s, as secretary of state in the 1790s and, afterwards, as leader of the Republican party he fought fiercely to defend America's maritime claims to sail the seas freely, claims on which the prosperity of the cities rested. Devoted to his native Virginia whose yeomen served as his model of the good citizen, he was the commonwealth's severest critic. A state in which most citizens were illiterate and political power was monopolized by the slaveholding planter elite hardly conformed to Jefferson's conception of a republican order. Though he sought to reform his native state early in his career, he met with only limited success in the face of the conservative opposition from his own class. Ultimately he found far greater success as an apostle of reform in Paris, New York, Boston, and Washington.

Professor Hofstadter suggests that the Jeffersonian contradictions grew out of the counterpoint in the Virginian's life between the ideal and the practical. An agrarian republic, he thought, was the ideal society, but he was too much the realist to imagine that men would forego the opportunities commerce and manufacturing offered. He had faith in the ability of the people to govern themselves, but he knew that they were not infallible and that wise, benevolent, and selfless leaders, such as he presented himself to be, were indispensable. An irrepressible optimist, he believed that slavery — the greatest blot on the republic — was declining because it had become economically unprofitable, at the very time when the sudden and rapid emergence of the Cotton Kingdom was riveting it on the South more firmly than ever. Yet none saw more clearly than Jefferson that slavery someday would plunge the Union into a holocaust. Realist and idealist, cunning politician and aloof intellectual, provincial Virginian and cosmopolitan, Jefferson's life and career were full of paradox. More perhaps than any other American, his life reveals the ambivalences and contradictions of America itself.

FOR FURTHER READING:

CHINARD, GILBERT. *Thomas Jefferson: The Apostle of Americanism.* Ann Arbor: University of Michigan Press, 1957.*
NOCK, ALBERT J. *Jefferson.* New York: Hill & Wang, American Century Series, 1960.*
PETERSON, MERRIL. *The Jeffersonian Image in the American Mind.* New York: Oxford University Press, 1960.*

Asterisk denotes paperback edition.

Thomas Jefferson: The Aristocrat as Democrat RICHARD HOFSTADTER

The sheep are happier of themselves, than under the care of the wolves. THOMAS JEFFERSON

The mythology that has grown up around Thomas Jefferson is as massive and imposing as any in American history. Although the bitterly prejudiced views of Federalist historians have never had wide acceptance, the stereotype perpetuated by such adherents of the Jeffersonian tradition as Claude Bowers and the late V. L. Parrington has been extremely popular. Jefferson has been pictured as a militant, crusading democrat, a Physiocrat who repudiated acquisitive capitalistic economics, a revolutionist who tore up the social fabric of Virginia in 1776, and the sponsor of a "Revolution of 1800" which destroyed Federalism root and branch. Although there is fact enough to give the color of truth to those notions, they have been torn down by shrewd Jefferson scholars like Charles A. Beard, Gilbert Chinard, and Albert J. Nock, and it is certainly not lack of good criticism that accounts for the dominant Jefferson legend. The issues of his time have been overdramatized, and Jefferson has been overdramatized with them.

It would have been strange if Jefferson had become one of those bitter rebels who live by tearing up established orders and forcing social struggles to the issue. He was born into an eminent place in the Virginia aristocracy. Peter Jefferson, his father, was a self-made man, but through his mother, Jane Randolph, who came from the distinguished Virginia family, he had an assured social position. Peter Jefferson died in 1757, leaving his son, then fourteen, over 2,700 acres and a large number of bondsmen. During most of his mature life Thomas Jefferson owned about 10,000 acres and from one to two hundred Negroes. The leisure that made possible his great writings on human liberty was supported by the labors of three generations of slaves.

Jefferson was a benevolent slavemaster, and his feeling for the common people was doubtless affected by an ingrained habit of solicitude for the helpless dependents who supported him. He prided himself on not being overprotective, once writing Dupont that the difference between their affections for the people was that Dupont loved them as infants who must be nursed, while he loved them as adults who could govern themselves. But no aristocrat, reared in a society rent by such a

---

Source: Richard Hofstadter, *The American Political Tradition, and the Men Who Made It* (New York: Alfred A. Knopf, 1948), chap. 2, "Thomas Jefferson: The Aristocrat as Democrat," pp. 18–43.

gulf between rich and poor, learned and unlearned, could be quite the democrat Jefferson imagined himself. As Charles M. Wiltse puts it, "He remains always aloof from the masses, and if he claims equality for all men, it is not because he feels that men are equal, but because he reasons that they must be so." An element of gentle condescension is unmistakable in his democracy; its spirit is caught in one of his letters to Lafayette:

> It will be a great comfort to you to know from your own inspection, the condition of all the provinces of your own country, and it will be interesting to them at some future day, to be known to you. This is, perhaps, the only moment of your life in which you can acquire that knowledge. And to do it most effectually, you must be absolutely incognito, you must ferret the people out of their hovels as I have done, look into their kettles, eat their bread, loll on their beds under pretence of resting yourself, but in fact, to find if they are soft. You will feel a sublime pleasure in the course of this investigation, and a sublimer one hereafter, when you shall be able to apply your knowledge to the softening of their beds, or the throwing of a morsel of meat into their kettle of vegetables.

Jefferson was educated at the College of William and Mary at Williamsburg, where in spite of his youth he was immediately accepted by the most brilliant and enlightened society. After graduation he fell into the expected pattern of the Virginia gentry, among whom political leadership was practically a social obligation. At twenty-four he was admitted to the bar, at twenty-six elected to a seat in the House of Burgesses, which he held for six years. At twenty-nine, a successful but unenthusiastic consulting lawyer, he married a young widow and settled at Monticello. His marriage brought large landholdings to add to his patrimony, but also a debt of four thousand pounds. Like many other Virginia planters, he developed from his own relations with British creditors a bilious view of the province's economic subordination to England and fell in with the anti-British group among the Burgesses. The ringing phrases he had learned from English republican philosophers began to take on more vivid meaning for him. In 1774 he wrote a bold tract applying the natural-rights doctrine to the colonial controversy, which won immediate attention throughout the colonies and gave him the reputation for literary craftsmanship that later made him the draftsman of the Declaration of Independence.

The Revolution found Jefferson in the prime of life and at the full flush of his reforming enthusiasm; during its first few years he did some of the most creative work of his life. Under his leadership the Virginia reformers abolished primogeniture and entail and laid the base for freedom of thought and religion by disestablishing the Anglican Church and forbidding legal or political disabilities for religious dissent. They also attempted, with paltry results, to found a good common-school system. Jefferson wrote the bills destroying primogeniture and entail, and on behalf of the bill for religious freedom drafted one of the most brilliant and trenchant pleas for free thought in the history of literature.

The accomplishments of this reform movement were considerable, but they have been subject to fantastic exaggeration by historians and biographers who look upon Jefferson and his colleagues as revolutionists putting through a sweeping program of social reform, destroying the Virginia aristocracy, and laying the foundations for democratic government. Even Jefferson, who was usually modest and accurate about his achievements, claimed too much when he said that these reforms "laid the axe" to the root of the Old Dominion's aristocracy. If the changes were actually so important, one would expect bitter resistance. The truth is that, with the exception of the bill for religious freedom (which, Jefferson testified, gave rise to "the severest contests in which I have ever been engaged"), the old institutions fell almost without a push. Jefferson wrote to Franklin that "this important transformation" was accomplished with the most remarkable ease; only "a half-dozen aristocratic gentlemen, agonizing under the loss of pre-eminence," had opposed it, and they "have been thought fitter objects of pity than of punishment."

The explanation of this "revolution by consent" is simple: there was no revolution. Primogeniture in the full meaning of the word did not really exist in Virginia. It was never mandatory upon the landowner. It applied only when he died without leaving a will disposing of his land. It was not regularly practiced by the landed families of the Old Dominion, for Virginians usually did leave wills dividing their land among their sons, and sometimes even among their daughters. Entail was actually a nuisance to the aristocracy because it interfered with the sale of estates they often found inconvenient to hold. During the years before 1776 petition after petition came into the Virginia legislature from leading families asking that their lands be exempted from entail.

Much has been made by rapt biographers of Jefferson's interest in abolishing slavery at this time. As a member of a committee to revise the legal code, he did draft a law for gradual emancipation, but never presumed to introduce it. "It was found," he explained, "that the public mind would not bear the proposition. . . . Yet the day is not distant when it must bear and adopt it, or worse will follow." Trying to force through any law, however desirable, which "the public mind would not bear" would have been thoroughly uncharacteristic of Jefferson's pragmatic political temperament.[1]

After a most unhappy experience as war Governor of Virginia, Jefferson, at thirty-eight, was eager for permanent retirement from politics, but the death of his wife drove him away from Monticello and back into furiously active service for the Congress. From 1785 to 1789 he was American Minister to France, where his experience may have been crucial in determining the direction of his political thinking. While his friends at home were watching the failure of the Articles of Confederation, looking anxiously upon the political advances of the dirt farmers, and turning rightward in their politics, he was touring Europe, taking the measure of feudal and monarchical institutions, observing the bitter exploitation of the workers of England and the peasantry of France, and confirming his republicanism. Appalled at the extremes of wealth and misery in European countries, he found kings, nobles, and priests "an abandoned confederacy against the happiness of the mass of the people," saw in the royalty of Europe only "fools" and "idiots," and described the treatment of the English laboring classes in the bitterest language. Europe fortified his conviction that America, with its republican government, broad distribution of landed property, agrarian economy, and oceanic isolation, was the chosen spot of the earth. Although he found much to admire in the European common people, they too brought him back to the political superiority of America. A lifelong prejudice is summed up in a few words from one of his letters to Lafayette: "The yeomanry of the United States are not the *canaille* of Paris."

In France during the early days of the French Revolution, Jefferson was naturally consulted by the moderate leaders of its first phase. Once he committed the indiscretion of allowing Lafayette and a few friends to meet at his house. He promptly apologized to the French Foreign Minister, Montmorin; but Montmorin, who evidently understood Jefferson well, answered that he hoped Jefferson "would habitually assist at such conferences, being sure I would be useful in moderating the warmer spirits and promoting a wholesome and practicable reformation only." When the King showed the first signs of a conciliatory state of mind, appearing in public with the popular cockade on his head, Jefferson concluded that the time had come for a compromise with the crown. But the draft of terms which he gave to his revolutionary friends was rejected — because it was too moderate.

What of the notion that Jefferson was an impractical visionary, that he was, as Charles Carroll of Carrollton called him, "a theoretical and fanciful man"? There is a sense in which this was true, but it has little to do with his public activity or his cast of mind. He *was* fatally generous, borrowed funds to give to beggars, entertained with a lavishness far beyond the capacities of his purse, and in his last years gave his declining fortunes the *coup de grâce* by signing the note of a floundering neighbor.

But did his mind run naturally to high abstractions? Did he spend his spare moments on them? On the contrary, when he found time to write at length, he turned his energies to such matter-of-fact projects as the encyclopedic *Notes on Virginia*, a parliamentary manual for the use of the Senate, a study of Indian languages, and his autobiography. He never attempted to write a systematic book of political theory — which was well, because he had no system and lacked the doctrinaire's compulsion to be consistent. Although he found time and energy for everything from epistemology to the mechanical arts, it was the latter that interested him most. He had an almost compulsive love of counting, observing, measuring. ("Not a sprig of grass shoots uninteresting to me," he once wrote to his daughter.) His standard of values was eminently practical. ("The greatest service which can be rendered any country is to add a useful plant to its culture.") He was the architect of his own home, ran his farm on a fairly self-sufficient basis, and made elaborate efficiency studies of his slaves' work. He invented a hempbeater, worked out the formula for a moldboard plow of least resistance, for which the French Institute of Agriculture of the Department of Seine-et-Oise gave him a prize, devised a leather buggy top, a swivel chair, and a dumbwaiter. He kept elaborate journals about the farms, gardens, social conditions, and natural phenomena he saw on his travels. Albert Jay Nock concludes that he "examined every useful tree and plant in western Europe and studied its cultivation." For long periods he kept daily thermometric and barometric readings. He was constantly studying new plows, steam engines, metronomes, thermometers, elevators, and the like, as well as the processing of butters and cheeses. He wrote a long essay for Congress on standards of weights and measures in the United States, and an excellent critique of the census returns, with detailed suggestions for collecting more minute information. On his travels he procured the plans of twelve large European cities, which he was able to lend L'Enfant to help him lay out the scheme of Washington. He conceived the American decimal system of coinage, demonstrating on this score his superiority to the financier Robert Morris. Such are the contributions to practical arts of this "theoretical and fanciful man."

What of the Jefferson who said that the tree of liberty must be watered periodically with the blood of tyrants, who thought that a rebellion every twenty years was an excellent thing, and who urged throughout his life that constitutions should be completely remade every twenty-five or thirty years? What of the Jefferson who was considered dangerous by so many conservative contemporaries, who was everywhere understood to be a strongheaded doctrinaire?

Jefferson was a complex person who must be measured in whole, not in part, in action as well as thought. There were deep ambiguities in his thinking, which made any effort at consistency impossible. Although Federalist historians have cited these ambiguities as evidence of a moral taint, a constitutional shiftiness of mind, they may in fact be traced to a continuously ambivalent personal and political history. He valued much more highly the achievements of his father, whom he intensely admired, than the high social status of his mother, whose influence he never acknowledged; but from the beginning he was aware of both the assurance of the aristocracy and the real merits and talents of men who came from unknown families. In his autobiography he remarked dryly of the Randolph genealogy: "They trace their pedigree far back in England and Scotland, to which let everyone ascribe the faith and merit he chooses." When he came to maturity, Jefferson was a slaveowner and yet a revolutionist, who could say that man's rights were "unalienable" at the very moment when he owned several dozen souls. All his life he circulated among men of wealth, learning, and distinction, and as befitted one who disliked acrimony he learned to accommodate himself to them — but he also absorbed the most liberal and questionable opinions of his age and associated on congenial terms with men like Thomas Paine and Joel Barlow. In American politics he became a leader of yeomen farmers — but also of great planters. He was the head of a popular faction that stood against the commercial interests — but it was also a propertied faction with acquisitive aspirations of its own. Well read in the best philosophical literature of his century, he accepted broad cosmopolitan ideas, but he was also an ardent American patriot. He was a pacifist in personal temperament and philosophy, a nationalist by training, and yet a Virginian with strong parochial loyalties. He wanted with all his heart to hold to the values of agrarian society, and yet he believed in progress. Add to all this the fact that he lived an unusually long life, saw many changes, and tried to adapt his views to changing circumstances.

Jefferson had warm impulses. His cosmopolitan mind refracted the most advanced and liberating ideas of his time. He believed in those ideas, and rephrased and reiterated them in language that has become classic; but he was not in the habit of breaking lances trying to fulfill them. The generous and emancipating thoughts for which his name is so justly praised are to be found almost entirely in his *private* correspondence; after he wrote the Declaration of Independence and the Virginia Statute for Religious Freedom he avoided expressing his more unacceptable ideas in public. He understood that in the workday world of public activity his most lofty ideals were chiefly valuable to indicate the direction in which society should be guided. He never really expected them to be realized in his time and preferred to place his hopes in progress, in the promise that mankind would consummate his ideals in some magnificent future. ("Your taste is judicious," John Adams once taunted him, "in liking better the dreams of the future than the history of the past.")

Jefferson's practical activity was usually aimed at some kind of minimum program that could be achieved without keen conflict or great expenditure of energy. He hated vigorous controversy, shrank from asserting his principles when they would excite the anger of colleagues or neighbors. He tried to avoid a wide circulation of his *Notes on Virginia* because he did not want Virginians to read his bitter remarks on slavery and a few tart observations on the province's Constitution. Jefferson did not lack courage — his futile embargo policy, carried out under bitter protest from every part of the country, proves that — but rather that hardihood of spirit which makes a political fight bearable. Although he had strong political prejudices and sometimes violent animosities, he did not enjoy power and could not bear publicity. He was acutely sensitive to criticism, admitting to Francis Hopkinson in 1789: "I find the pain of a little censure, even when it is unfounded, is more acute than the pleasure of much praise." Abnormally shy and troubled by a slight speech defect, he found it impossible to read his messages in person to Congress as Washington and Adams had done. He had not the temperament of an agitator, hardly even of a leader in the qualities that leadership requires under modern democracy. Not once did he deliver an exciting speech. His private life was one of enormous variety and interest, and there were many times when he would have been happy to desert public service to enjoy his farm, his family, and his books.

Jefferson's Federalist opponents feared, above all, power lodged in the majority. Jefferson feared power lodged anywhere else. In his First Inaugural Address he asked concerning the common observation "that man cannot be trusted with the government of himself": "Can he, then, be trusted with the government of others?" He would have agreed with Madison that power is "of an encroaching nature," and he was sure that power corrupts those who possess it. "If once the people become inattentive to the public affairs," he wrote Edward Carrington from Paris, "you and I and Congress and Assemblies, Judges and Governors, shall all become wolves. It seems to be the law of our general nature, in spite of individual exceptions."

Admitting that a majority will often decide public questions wrongly, Jefferson argued that "the duperies of the people are less injurious" than the self-interested policies of kings, priests, and aristocrats. He refused to be alarmed by popular uprisings like the Shays Rebellion. In the safety of his private correspondence he felt free to say that "honest republican governments" should be "so mild in their punishment of rebellions as not to discourage them too much." "A little rebellion now and then is a good thing, and as necessary in the political world as storms in the physical." The people are not always well informed, but it is better that they have misconceptions that make them restless than that they be lethargic — for lethargy in the people means death for republics.

Again and again Jefferson urged that the people be educated and informed through a broad common-school system and a free press. Although he had small faith in the power of republics to resist corruption and decay, he hoped that mass education would stem this degenerative process.[2] Education not only would give stability and wisdom to the politics of a commonwealth, but would widen opportunities, bring out the natural talents that could be found in abundance among the common people. Throughout Jefferson's life there runs this humane concern for "the pursuit of happiness," for the development of the individual without regard to limitations of class.

By and large, however, when Jefferson spoke warmly of the merits and abilities of "the people" he meant "the farmers." He did not see a town until he was almost eighteen, and he believed deeply that rural living and rural people are the wellspring of civic virtue and individual vitality, that farmers are the best social base of a democratic republic. "Those who labor in the earth are the chosen people of God, if ever he had a chosen people," he proclaimed in his *Notes on Virginia.* "Corruption of morals in the mass of cultivators is a phenomenon of which no age nor nation has furnished an example."[3]

> . . . generally speaking, the proportion which the aggregate of the other classes of citizens bears in any State to that of its husbandmen, is the proportion of its unsound to its healthy parts, and is a good enough barometer whereby to measure its degree of corruption. While we have lands to labor then, let us never wish to see our citizens occupied at a work bench or twirling a distaff. . . . Let our workshops remain in Europe.

The American economy, then, should be preserved in its agricultural state. Manufacturers, cities, urban classes, should be held at a minimum. So Jefferson believed, at any rate, until the responsibilities of the White House and the conduct of foreign policy caused him to modify his views. He once went so far as to say that he hoped the United States would remain, with respect to Europe, on the same economic footing as China. Commerce he would encourage — it supplied the needs of agriculture — but this was the extent of his early concessions to the urban classes.

Thus far Jefferson, with his faith in the farmers, his distrust of the urban classes, and his belief in the long-range value of rebellions and social disturbances, seems at the opposite pole from the Constitution-makers — and so he might have been if his political theory had been elaborated into a coherent system. But he had more in common with the conservative thinkers of his age than is usually recognized. His differences with the political theory of the Constitution-makers were differences of emphasis, not of structure. He shared their primary fears. He did not think that political constitutions could safely rely on man's virtue. In a letter to Mann Page in 1795 he declared that he could not accept the idea of the Rochefoucaulds and Montaignes that "fourteen out of fifteen men are rogues." "*But I have always found that rogues would be uppermost*, and I do not know that the proportion is too strong for the higher orders and for those who, rising above the swinish multitude, always contrive to nestle themselves into the places of power and profit." It was the upper, not the lower orders of society that he thought especially unregenerate — but it was Jefferson, too, who could use words like "canaille" and "swinish multitude." [4]

Jefferson, of course, accepted the principle of balanced government and the idea that the people must be checked. "It is not by the consolidation, or concentration of powers, but by their distribution that good government is effected," he wrote in his autobiography. He designed a constitution for Virginia in 1776 which employed the principle of checks and balances and required property qualifications of voters.[5] Of the two houses of the legislature, only the lower was to be elected by the people: the senate was to be chosen by the house, as was the governor, so that two of the three parts of the lawmaking body were at one remove from the citizens. Five years later, criticizing the Constitution that had been adopted by Virginia instead of his own, he complained primarily of its lack of checks: the Senate and the House of Delegates were too much alike because both were chosen by the voters in the same way. "The purpose of establishing different houses of legislation is to introduce the influence of different interests or different principles." He continued:

> All the powers of government, legislative, executive, and judiciary, result to the legislative body. The concentrating these in the same hands is precisely the definition of despotic government. It will be no alleviation that these powers will be exercised by a plurality of hands and not by a single one. One hundred and seventy-three despots would surely be as oppressive as one. . . . As little will it avail us that they are chosen by ourselves. An *elective despotism* was not the government we fought for, but one which should not only be founded on free principles, but in which the powers of government should be so divided and balanced among several bodies of magistracy, as that no one

could transcend their legal limits without being effectually checked and restrained by the others.

This would have been accounted sound doctrine at the Philadelphia Convention of 1787. A government that does not divide and balance powers in a system of checks is precisely what Jefferson means by despotic; the fact that the governing body is chosen by the people does not qualify his complaint; such a government, without checks, is merely "an elective despotism." Jefferson, then, refused to accept simple majority rule, adopting instead the idea that "different interests or different principles" should be represented in government.

All this sounds close to the theories of Madison and Adams. In fact, Jefferson did not differ with them strongly enough to challenge their conservative writings of the constitutional period. In 1788 he wrote to Madison praising the *Federalist* as "the best commentary on the principles of government which ever was written." Two years later, advising his nephew Thomas Mann Randolph on a course of reading, Jefferson praised Locke's work as being "perfect as far as it goes," and then added: "Descending from theory to practice, there is no better book than the Federalist." In 1787 he told John Adams that he had read his *Defence* "with infinite satisfaction and improvement. It will do great good in America. Its learning and its good sense will, I hope, make it an institute for our politicians, old as well as young." [6]

When the text of the federal Constitution of 1787 reached him in France, Jefferson confessed to Adams that he was staggered at what had been attempted, but soon recovered his composure. He informed Madison that he saw many good features in it, but objected strongly to two things: the absence of a bill of rights (later included in the first ten amendments), and the eligibility of the president for more than one term. In the end he gave it a substantial endorsement: "It is a good canvas, on which some strokes only want retouching." His regard for it grew with the years.

As much as Madison or Morris, Jefferson disliked the idea of city mobs — "the panders of vice and the instruments by which the liberties of a country are generally overturned" — but he believed that they would not emerge in the calculable future because America's lands would be open to make substantial farmers of the ragged and discontented. In his First Inaugural he said that the land would last the American people "to the hundredth and thousandth generation"! The United States would be a nation of farmers, tilling their own soil, independent, informed, unexcitable, and incorruptible. Such a national destiny, he must have felt, would be secured by the Louisiana Purchase.

The future, then, would be founded on a propertied class in a propertied nation. Jefferson leaned strongly to the idea that a propertied interest in society is necessary to a stable political mentality. In 1800 he wrote a friend that he had always favored universal manhood suffrage; but this was one of those theoretical notions to which he was not firmly wedded. "Still I find some very honest men," he added, "who, thinking the possession of some property necessary to give due independence of mind, are for restraining the elective franchise to property." His 1776 draft of a constitution for Virginia had required that voters own either a freehold estate of twenty-five acres in the country or one fourth of an acre in town, or pay taxes within two years of the time of voting. Never did Jefferson try to introduce universal manhood suffrage anywhere.[7]

The outstanding characteristic of Jefferson's democracy as its close organic relation to the agrarian order of his time. It seems hardly enough to say that he thought that a nation of farmers, educated, informed, and blessed with free institutions, was the best suited to a democratic republic, without adding that he did not think any *other* kind of society a good risk to maintain republican government. In a nation of large cities, well-developed manufactures and commerce, and a numerous working class, popular republicanism would be an impossibility — or at best an improbability.

Certainly the balance of Jefferson's good society is a tenuous thing: the working class is corrupt; merchants are corrupt; speculators are corrupt; cities are "pestilential"; only farmers are dependably good. Sunder human nature from its proper or "natural" nourishment in the cultivation of the soil and the ownership of real property, and he profoundly distrusts it. Sunder democracy from the farm and how much more firmly does he believe in it than John Adams? Yet this is just what the relentless advance of modern industrial capitalism has done: it has sundered four fifths of society from the soil, has separated the masses from their property, and has built life increasingly on what Jefferson would have called an artificial basis — in short, has gradually emptied the practical content out of Jefferson's agrarian version of democracy. This process had its earliest beginnings during Jefferson's lifetime, and, as we shall see, he yielded a good part of his agrarian prejudices (like the pragmatic, undoctrinaire soul that he was) without sacrificing his democratic preferences. But although he clung to his humane vision of democracy, he left it without the new economic rationale that it required.

In after years Jefferson declared that the struggle between his party and the Federalists was one between those who cherished the people and those who distrusted them. But he had been associated with a number of men like Elbridge Gerry, Pierce Butler, Charles Pinckney, and Edmund Randolph who did not cherish the people in the least, and the differences in abstract principle were hardly intense enough to account for the fierceness of the conflict or for the peculiar lines along which it was drawn. Although democratically minded Americans did stand with Jefferson, the line of division was essentially between two kinds of property, not two kinds of philosophy.

The Federalists during Hamilton's service as Secretary of the Treasury had given the government a foundation of unashamed devotion to the mercantile and investing classes. Through his method of funding the national debt, through his national bank, and through all the subsidiary policies of the government, Hamilton subsidized those who invested in manufactures, commerce, and public securities, throwing as much of the tax burden as possible on planters and farmers. The landed interests, however, were in a majority, and it was only a matter of time before they could marshal themselves in a strong party of their own. Jefferson's party was formed to defend specific propertied interests rather than the abstract premises of democracy, and its policies were conceived and executed in the sober, moderate spirit that Jefferson's generation expected of propertied citizens when they entered the political arena.

When Jefferson was elected in 1800, the more naïve Federalists, frightened to the marrow by their own propaganda, imagined that the end of the world had come. Fisher Ames anticipated that he would soon scent "the loathsome steam of human victims offered in sacrifice." Among those who knew the President-elect, however, there was no such hysteria — especially not among insiders who had private knowledge of the circumstances under which he had been chosen.

The election of 1800 was unique in American history. Because no distinction had yet been made in the Constitution between ballots cast for presidential and vice-presidential candidates, Jefferson and his running mate, Aaron Burr, won the same number of votes in the electoral college. The tied contest was thrown into the House of Representatives, where it fell to Federalist Congressmen to choose between two Republicans. To some this seemed merely a choice of executioners; others, looking upon Jefferson as their supreme enemy, gravitated naturally toward Burr. Not so Alexander Hamilton, who had long been Burr's political rival in New York. In a remarkable letter to a Federalist Representative, Hamilton gave a shrewd estimate of Jefferson's character. He admitted that his old foe's views were "tinctured with fanaticism; that he is too much in earnest with his democracy." But it is not true, he continued, in an appraisal that is as penetrating in substance as it is unfair in phrasing,

> that Jefferson is zealot enough to do anything in pursuance of his principles which will contravene his popularity or his interest. He is as likely as any man I know to temporize — to calculate what will be likely to promote his own reputation and advantage; and the probable result of such a temper is the preservation of systems, though originally opposed, which, being once established, could not be overturned without danger to the person who did it. To my mind a true estimate of Mr. Jefferson's character warrants the expectation of a temporizing rather than a violent system. . . . Add to this that there is no fair reason to suppose him capable of being corrupted, which is a security that he will not go beyond certain limits.

Not entirely satisfied with Hamilton's advice, Federalist leaders sought for assurance from Jefferson. The Virginian refused to commit himself in response to direct approach, but a friend who sounded him out informally was able to convey to the Federalists the comforting knowledge that Jefferson's intentions were moderate. That Jefferson abandoned any of his original plans, and in that sense bargained away any principles to win the office, is extremely unlikely; but when he entered the White House it was after satisfying the Federalists that he and they had come to some kind of understanding.

A little thought on the difficult position in which Jefferson now found himself should convince anyone that for a man of his moderate temperament there was small choice in fundamental policy. The Hamiltonian system, now in operation for twelve years, had become part of the American economy. The nation was faring well. To unscramble Hamilton's system of funding, banks, and revenues would precipitate a bitter struggle, widen the breach between the classes, and drive moderates out of the Republican ranks; it might bring a depression, perhaps even rend the Union. And when the strife was over, there would always be the need of coming to terms with the classes that carried on commerce and banking and manufactures. Further, even if the landed interests were charged with the burden of Hamilton's debts, there was always the probability that they were better off when the system was working smoothly than they would be after a ruinously successful assault upon it. Jefferson, in short, found himself in a position much like that of modern social-democratic statesmen who, upon attaining power, find themselves the managers of a going concern that they fear to disrupt. Just as they have been incapable of liquidating capitalism, so Jefferson found himself unable to keep it from growing and extending its sway over the agrarian masses. Instead he wisely confined himself to trimming carefully at the edges of the Hamiltonian system.

Jefferson's First Inaugural Address was a conciliatory document contrived to bind up the wounds of the bitter period from 1798 to 1800 and to attract moderate Federalists to his support. "We are all Republicans — we are all federalists," he declared. Soon the President was writing to Dupont de Nemours in words that show how well Hamilton had taken his measure:

> When this government was first established, it was possible to have kept it going on true principles, but the contracted, English, half-lettered ideas of Hamilton destroyed that hope in the bud. We can pay off his debts in 15 years: but we can never get rid of his financial system. It mortifies me to be strengthening principles which I deem radically vicious, but this vice is entailed on us by the first error. In other parts of our government I hope we shall be able by degrees to introduce sound principles and make them habitual. What is practicable must often control what is pure theory.

Jefferson kept his promises to friends and enemies alike. So successfully did he whittle away at the Federalist machinery by reducing expenditures that he was able to abolish the hated excise duties that had stirred up the Whisky Rebellion and still make great inroads on the public debt. He tried hard to tame the federal judiciary — the last arm of the national government still under Federalist control — but to little effect. Through the Louisiana Purchase he widened the area for agrarian expansion. In 1811, two years after his terms were over, his party also allowed the First Bank of the United States to die upon the expiration of its charter.

But no attack was made upon other vital parts of the Hamiltonian system. No attempt was made to curb such abuses as speculation in public lands; nor did the well-organized Republican machines try hard to democratize the mechanics of government in the states or the nation. Limitations on the suffrage, for example, were left untouched. Professor Beard observes that the Republican states were "no more enamored of an equalitarian political democracy" than the Federalist states. Had Jefferson suggested a broad revision of the suffrage, many of his state leaders who had no use for theoretical democracy would have looked at him askance; if he had been the crusading democrat of Jeffersonian legend he could not have been so successful a machine leader.

Since his policies did not deviate too widely from those of the Federalists, Jefferson hoped to win over the moderates from their ranks and planned to use the patronage in doing so. "If we can hit on the true line of conduct which may conciliate the honest part of those who were called federalists," he wrote to Horatio Gates soon after taking office, "and do justice to those who have so long been excluded from [the patronage], I shall hope to be able to obliterate, or rather to unite the names of federalists and republicans."

In politics, then, the strategy was conciliation; in economics it was compromise. Soon the Republican machines began flirting with the financial interests they had sworn to oppose. Republican state legislatures issued charters liberally to local banks, which, in turn, tended to cleave to the Republican Party in politics. Jefferson gave his benediction to this process of mutual accommodation. When the Bank of Baltimore applied to the administration for assistance, he wrote to Secretary of the Treasury Albert Gallatin:

> It is certainly for the public good to keep all the banks competitors for our favors by a judicious distribution of them and thus to engage the individuals who belong to them in support of the reformed order of things or at least in an acquiescence under it.

And:

> ... I am decidedly in favor of making all the banks Republican by sharing deposits among them in proportion to the disposition they show. ... It is material to the safety of Republicanism to detach the mercantile interest from its enemies and incorporate them into the body of its friends. A merchant is naturally a Republican, and can be otherwise only from a vitiated state of things.

John Adams, in the quiet of his retirement at Quincy, might have been amused to see a new elite, closely linked to the fiscal interests, emerging in the heart of the Republican Party, but the militant agrarian John Taylor was deeply discouraged. In 1811 he wrote:

> ... those who clearly discerned the injustice and impolicy of enriching and strengthening the federalists by bank or debt stock, at the publick expense, will seldom refuse to receive a similar sinecure. In short, a power in the individuals who compose legislatures, to fish up wealth from the people, by nets of their own weaving ... will corrupt legislative, executive and judicial publick servants, by whatever systems constituted.

The inability of the Republicans to follow a pure policy of democratic agrarianism was matched by their inability to fashion a positive theory of agrarian economics. The predominant strain in their economic thinking was laissez-faire, their primary goal essentially negative — to destroy the link between the federal government and the investing classes. Acute and observant, their economic writing was at its best in criticism, but it offered no guide to a specific agrarian program. They had no plan; indeed, they made a principle of planlessness.

Jefferson has been described as a physiocrat by many writers — among them V. L. Parrington — but there is little more substance to this notion than there is to the preposterous idea that he was influenced chiefly by French thought. He was naturally content to remain an eclectic in economics. "No one axiom," he wrote to J. B. Say in 1815, "can be laid down as wise and expedient for all times and circumstances." Their defense of free trade was responsible for whatever appeal the physiocrats had for Jefferson; but after he read *The Wealth of Nations* he became a convert to the doctrines of Adam Smith.[8]

Like other theorists of the "natural law" era, Jefferson was quite ready to believe that the "natural" operations of the system of self-seeking private enterprise were intrinsically beneficent and should not normally be disturbed by government. In his First Inaugural he called for "a wise and frugal government, which shall restrain men from injuring one another, *which shall leave them otherwise free to regulate their own pursuits of industry and improvement,* and shall not take from the mouth of labor the bread it has earned."[9] In a letter to Joseph Milligan, April 6, 1816, in which he discussed the proper limits of taxation, he concluded that the state ought not be aggressive in redistributing property:[10]

> To take from one, because it is thought his own industry and that of his fathers has acquired too much, in order to spare to others, who, or whose fathers have not exercised equal industry and skill, is to violate arbitrarily the first principle of association, "the *guarantee* to everyone a free exercise of his industry and the fruits acquired by it."

John Taylor, perhaps the cleverest of the agrarian writers, likewise believed that "it is both wise and just to leave the distribution of property to industry and talents."

This conception of state policy was not anti-capitalist but anti-mercantilist. Jefferson and his followers had seen the unhappy effects of British governmental interference in American economic affairs, and they regarded Hamilton's system of state economic activity ("the contracted, English, half-lettered ideas of Hamilton") as merely a continuation at home of English economic ideas. Hamilton had set the government to helping the capitalists at the expense of the agrarians. The Jeffersonian response was not to call for a government that would help the agrarians at the expense of the capitalists, but simply for one that would let things alone. Where modern liberals have looked to government interference as a means of helping the poor, Jefferson, in common with other eighteenth-century liberals, thought of it chiefly as an unfair means of helping the rich through interest-bearing debts, taxation, tariffs, banks, privileges, and bounties. He concluded that the only necessary remedy under republican government would be to deprive the rich of these devices and restore freedom and equality through "natural" economic forces. Because he did not usually think of economic relationships as having an inherent taint of exploitation in them, he saw no necessity to call upon the state to counteract them. It was not the task of government to alter the economic order: the rich were not entitled to it and the poor would not find it necessary.

Jefferson rejected from his political philosophy the idea that one man has any intrinsic superiority over another; but he implicitly and perhaps unwittingly took it back again when he accepted competitive laissez-faire economics with its assumption that, so long as men were equal in law, and government played no favorites, wealth would be distributed in accordance with "industry and skill." Such a philosophy seemed natural enough to American farmers and planters who were in their own rights entrepreneurs, businessmen, exporters, and often, in a small way, speculators with a weather eye on land values — men accustomed to stand on their own feet.

In due time, of course, Jeffersonian laissez-faire became the political economy of the most conservative thinkers in the country. Fifty years after Jefferson's death men like William Graham Sumner were writing sentences exactly like Jefferson's and John Taylor's to defend enterprising industrial capitalists and railroad barons from government regulation and reform. And one hundred years after the Jeffersonians first challenged John Adams at the polls, William Jennings Bryan, leading the last stand of agrarianism as an independent political power, was still striving to give his cause the color of respectability by showing that, after all, the farmer too was a businessman!

The practical conduct of foreign relations forced the Jeffersonians into a position no less frustrating than the maintenance of Hamilton's domestic system. In the East they found themselves almost as dependent on foreign commerce as were the sea traders of New England; their cheapest manufactured goods were bought abroad, and abroad their surplus was sold. In the West, where they looked about hungrily for new lands, fear of the Indians and of the closure of their trade outlet at New Orleans intensified their expansionist appetites. Expansion of their export market on the land and defense of it on the sea finally started them on a headlong retreat from Jeffersonian principles.

Jefferson himself was both a fierce patriot and a sincere pacifist. During the Napoleonic Wars, when England and France began to prey upon American commerce, he tried to retaliate by a pacifistic policy of economic coercion. In December 1807 Congress passed his drastic Embargo Act, which simply confined American ships to port. His aim was to bring both sides to terms by withholding food and other supplies. This was the one doctrinaire and impractical measure of his career, and it proved a miserable failure. The Embargo not only failed to force Britain and France to respect American rights on the high seas, but also brought economic paralysis to the trading cities of the Northeast and the farms and plantations of the West and South. Jefferson finally admitted that the fifteen months of its operation cost more than a war. At the close of his second term the Embargo was replaced by a Nonintercourse Act, which opened trade with the rest of Europe but continued the costly ban on England and France.

Although Jefferson's successor, James Madison, continued to be harried by the maritime controversy, it was expansionism — what John Randolph called "agrarian cupidity" — rather than free trade that in the end brought the War of 1812. Southern planters wanted the Floridas and Northern farmers wanted Canada. Jefferson, always an ardent expansionist, approved of both aims and accepted the popular clichés with which expansion was justified. ("The possession of Canada," he wrote Adams in the summer of 1812, "secures our women and children forever from the tomahawk and scalping knife, by removing those who excite them.") As Julius W. Pratt has shown, enthusiasm for war with England raged along the broad arc of the frontier; resistance to war was hottest in the old Federalist and mercantile sections.

But if the United States was to withdraw from Europe economically, as under Jefferson, or to lose its best market through war, as under Madison, it had to find a way of employing its energies and supplying its people with manufactured goods. Accordingly, capital, cut off from its normal investment outlet in overseas commerce, began to turn to manufacturing. The period of the Embargo and the War of 1812 proved to be the seedtime of American industrialism; Henry Adams remarked on the ironic fact that "American manufactures owed more to Jefferson than to northern statesmen who merely encouraged them after they were established."

Jefferson, of course, realized the immediate implications of his desire to pursue an independent economic course and as early as 1805 became a convert to the development of manufactures. "The spirit of manufacture has taken deep root among us," he wrote Dupont in 1809, "and its foundations are laid in too great expense to be abandoned." "Our enemy," he wailed to William Short in 1814, "has indeed the consolation of Satan on removing our first parents from Paradise: from a peaceable and agricultural nation he makes us a military and manufacturing one." To another he wrote: "We must now place the manufacturer by the side of the agriculturist." If the United States was to be peaceful, it must be self-sufficient, must end its dependence on foreign goods and overseas trade. The Napoleonic Wars destroyed the Jeffersonian dream of an agrarian commonwealth. Since Jeffersonian democracy, as embodied in measures of public policy, was entirely dependent upon the agrarian order, these wars also erased the practical distinction between Republicans and Federalists.

Manufactures, if they were to be maintained, needed tariffs, especially when British capitalists, hoping to crush their new competitors at once, began dumping goods in the American market at the close of the war. In 1816 the Republicans passed a much higher tariff than Hamilton's. They, not the Federalists, began the American protective system.

And war must be financed. Hard hit by the economic drain of military operations and the financial sabotage of the Northeast, the Republicans were confronted with a bitter dilemma: either they must go begging to the fiscal interests for support, or they must charter a new national bank to fill the vacuum they had created by letting Hamilton's bank expire. They chose the second course — and soon Republican newspapers were reprinting Alexander Hamilton's arguments in favor of the constitutionality of the First Bank of the United States! In vain did Jefferson rage in his letters against the banking system. A second bank, similar in structure to Hamilton's, was chartered by the Republicans in 1816. By the end of that year Jefferson's party had taken over the whole complex of Federalist policies — manufactures, bank, tariffs, army, navy, and all — and this under the administration of Jefferson's friend, neighbor, and political heir, James Madison. As Josiah Quincy complained, the Republicans had "out-Federalized Federalism." By 1820 they had driven the rival party completely off the field, but only at the cost of taking over its program. Federalism, Jefferson wrote to Albert Gallatin in 1823, "has changed its name and hidden itself among us . . . as strong as it has ever been since 1800." Nathaniel Macon, one of the last of the intransigent agrarians, lamented: "The opinions of Jefferson and those who were with him are forgot."

And Jefferson himself? He lived through his last years without bitterness or anger, certainly without a sense of defeat. His country, in spite of one short-lived depression, was growing and flourishing, and as he looked down upon it from his mountaintop he predicted hopefully that the process of civilization would continue to sweep across the continent from east to west "like a cloud of light." He busied himself answering his voluminous correspondence, interpreting for inquirers the history of his times, trading opinions with scientists and inventors, trying to steady his failing fortunes, and laying the foundations of the University of Virginia, which gave him special pride. He renewed his old friendship with John Adams, and once again argued with him the case of democracy. At the age of seventy-eight he wrote to the old man at Quincy: "I shall not die without a hope that light and liberty are on steady advance." When Adams asked if he would choose to live his life over again, he replied in the affirmative, at least for the greater part of it. "From twenty-five to sixty, I would say yes; and I might go further back, but not come lower down." "I enjoy good health," he went on, "I am happy in what is around me, yet I assure you I am ripe for leaving all, this year, this day, this hour. Nothing proves more than this that the Being who presides over the world is essentially benevolent."

Here speaks the antithesis of the tragic temperament. Through all Jefferson's work there runs like a fresh underground stream the deep conviction that all will turn out well, that life will somehow assert itself. Wherever he was, he managed to find it good, and in these last years he never felt the need of moving more than a few miles from Monticello. Life had always come more than halfway to meet him, just as visitors now came from everywhere in the Western World to find him out on his mountain. For him no defeat could ever be more than a temporary interruption in the smooth flow of things toward their beneficent end. It was not, after all, a system of economics or politics that he was leaving, not even a political party, but an imperishable faith expressed in imperishable rhetoric. It did not matter that his agrarianism was in retreat, that his particularism was falling into the hands of proslavery apologists whom he would have detested, that his individualism would become the doctrine of plutocrats and robber barons. His sense of values would survive. Men like Hamilton could argue that manufactures ought to be promoted because they would enable the nation to use the labor of women and children, "many of them at a tender age," but Jefferson was outraged at such a view of humanity. Hamilton schemed to get the children into factories; Jefferson planned school systems. While Hamilton valued institutions and abstractions, Jefferson valued people and found no wealth more important than life. If he had gone astray as to means, he had at least kept his eyes on his original end — the pursuit of happiness.

One of the last survivors among the founders, Jefferson lived to see himself become an object of veneration, and as his life ebbed out he might easily have observed with the dying Roman Emperor: "I feel myself becoming a god." But he had no desire that he and his contemporaries should become oracles to future generations. "The earth," he was fond of saying, "belongs to the living." The world changes, and truths cannot be embalmed.

NOTES

1. Jefferson was characteristically circumspect about attacking slavery in his own state, but more aggressive in intercolonial affairs when he could expect Northern backing. Thus he included a bitter attack upon the slave trade in the Declaration of Independence — which was struck out — and tried to get slavery banned from the Northwest Territory in his Ordinance of 1784.
2. In his Bill for the More General Diffusion of Knowledge (1779) he declared that "experience hath shewn, that even under the best forms [of government] those entrusted with power have, in time, and by slow operations perverted it into tyranny. . . ."
3. In 1787 he wrote: "I think our governments will remain virtuous for many centuries; as long as they remain chiefly agricultural; and this will be as long as there shall be vacant lands in any part of America. When they get piled upon one another in large cities, as in Europe, they will become corrupt as in Europe."

    After he had observed the machinations of the Federalists, his faith in the husbandman's monopoly on civic virtue became even more rigid than before, and a shrill note rang through his letters: "Farmers, whose interests are entirely agricultural . . . are the true representatives of the great American interest, and are alone to be relied on for expressing the proper American sentiments."

    In his belief that one economic class, the freeholding farmers, had more political virtue than the other orders, Jefferson made a significant breach in the abstract conception that human nature is everywhere the same, but he does not seem to have developed the implications of this insight.
4. Not long after the first edition of this volume was published, Mr. Charles Carroll Ransom, Jr., was kind enough to call to my attention that the phrase "swinish multitude" was in very common use among the Federalists in 1795, in connection with the controversy over Jay's treaty. Mr. Ransom suggests — I believe correctly — that Jefferson's own use of the phrase was ironic rather than literal. My original construction of his meaning seems therefore to have been incorrect. R.H.
5. And yet in his *Notes on Virginia* he voiced his displeasure with the limited suffrage of the state: "The majority of the men in the State who pay and fight for its support, are unrepresented in the legislature, the roll of freeholders entitled to vote not including generally the half of those on the roll of the militia, or of the taxgatherers."
6. Later he also endorsed heartily John Taylor's *An Inquiry into the Principles and Policy of the Government of the United States* (1814), which was in large part a headlong assault on Adams's theories. This of course was after the Federalist-Republican antagonism had ripened.
7. It is important to add, however, that in 1776 Jefferson proposed that Virginia grant fifty acres of land to every white of full age who had less than that amount. This would have made suffrage practically universal. It also illustrates his belief in broadening economic opportunities where free land made the policy possible, as well as the vital linkage in his mind between landed property and democracy. He was, at this time, more democratic in his conception of the economic *base* of government than in his conception of the *structure* of government.
8. Ultimately he came to prefer J. B. Say's adaptations of Smith as more lucid and readable, and showed much admiration for the work of Destutt de Tracy.
9. In his Second Inaugural, when he listed the things government should do, he asserted that it should maintain "that state of property, equal or unequal, which results to every man from his own industry or that of his fathers."
10. He added that if an individual's wealth becomes so overgrown that it seems a danger to the State, the best corrective would not be discriminatory taxation but a law compelling equal inheritance in equal degree by all the heirs.

The Perils of a Young Republic

When the Americans declared their independence from England they presumed that they had also escaped further involvement in national rivalries and periodic warfare that afflicted Europe. The 3000 miles of ocean that separated the New World from the Old World seemed to guarantee the United States the blessings of peace and national security without the need to maintain a large and expensive army or navy. Yet, within a decade after Britain and America made peace in 1783, the young American republic found itself embroiled in conflicts between the new revolutionary French Republic and the coalition of monarchies, including Great Britain, determined to contain the spread of revolutionary fever.

Enjoying valuable trading ties with the belligerents, Americans insisted on continuing to do business with all nations. But the British, who controlled the seas, objected because the French relied on American supplies carried in American vessels. In the 1790s, accordingly, Britain seized American shipping and brought the two countries to the brink of war, averted only by the Jay Treaty (1794). The French, regarding the treaty as a pro-British move, attacked American shipping, precipitating an undeclared naval war, also ended by negotiations.

Unless it were willing to renounce trade with other nations, apparently there was no way the United States could escape involvement or remain perfectly neutral. To surrender freedom of the seas, however, was to confess that the United States could not defend its rights as a sovereign nation. Yet to insist on trading risked war for which the country was unprepared and which no one wanted.

In the 1790s, the United States managed to escape this cruel dilemma twice, first in the confrontation with Britain and then with France. But when war broke out once again in Europe after 1803 the United States was not so lucky. This time France and Britain fought to the finish, each blockading the other, and in the process trampling on American commerce. President Jefferson tried an experiment in peaceful coercion — the Embargo (1807–1808) — but it failed to force the European powers to respect American rights. In 1812, the United States declared war against Great Britain.

In the following essay, Norman K. Risjord critically examines changing interpretations of the cause of the War of 1812. He concludes that no explanation is sufficient that neglects the overriding importance the dominant Republican party placed on vindicating American honor. Yet, why were Republicans so preoccupied with national honor? Perhaps the answer lies in the fact that the United States was a young and untested nation, that its republican form of government was a novel experiment that few Europeans thought would last very long. Republics, in the past, had always succumbed either to internal decay or to external aggression. If the United States could not defend its sovereignty, could it survive for very long? And if the United States perished, the last best hope of mankind to liberate itself from tyranny would vanish with it. "We have been long enough at peace," a leading Republican intoned. "We are losing our spirit, our character, and our independence. We are degenerating into a mere nation of traders and are forgetting the honor of our ancestors and the interest of posterity. We must be roused by some great event that may stir up the ancient patriotism of the people." When the war came, it deeply divided the American people, but when it ended — though the peace treaty settled none of the disputed issues — Americans felt more confident of the viability of the young republic that had fought to a standoff the world's most powerful nation.

FOR FURTHER READING:

BROWN, ROBERT H. *The Republic in Peril: Eighteen-Twelve.* New York: Columbia University Press, 1964.
PERKINS, BRADFORD, ed. *The Causes of the War of 1812: National Honor or National Interest.* New York: Holt, Rinehart & Winston, 1961.*
SMELSER, MARSHALL. *The Democratic Republic.* New York: Harper & Row, Publishers, New American Nation Series, 1968.*

Asterisk denotes paperback edition.

1812: Conservatives, War Hawks, and the Nation's Honor NORMAN K. RISJORD

The modern tendency to seek materialistic motives and economic factors in all human relations has greatly obscured one of the basic causes of the War of 1812. A generation of historians, brought up on the disillusionment that followed the failure of the attempt to "make the world safe for democracy" in 1919, has persistently searched for the hidden economic factors behind all wars. Yet a cursory glance at the statistics of American commerce in the first decade of the nineteenth century will show that the War of 1812 was the most uneconomic war the United States has ever fought. A casual search through the letters and speeches of contemporaries reveals that those who fought the war were primarily concerned with the honor and integrity of the nation.

Students of the period are familiar with the standard explanation for the war: the election of 1810, by providing 63 new faces in a House of 142, represented a popular disillusionment with the Jeffersonian system and supplied the new Twelfth Congress with a number of young war hawks, such as Henry Clay, John C. Calhoun, and Felix Grundy, who were determined to assert America's position in the world. Since the loudest demand for strong measures, as well as some of the ablest of the war hawks, came from the West, historians have been channeled into a search for reasons why the West should have demanded a war for "free trade and sailors' rights"; the historiography of the period has been almost exclusively concerned with "Western war aims." The desire for land, Canadian or Indian, fear of a British-backed Indian conspiracy, concern over the declining prices of agricultural products and the restriction of markets abroad — all at one time or another have been represented as basic causes of the war.

The weakness in this interpretation is that it virtually ignores the vote on the dec-

Source: Norman K. Risjord, "1812: Conservatives, War Hawks, and the Nation's Honor," *William and Mary Quarterly,* vol. 18 (1961), pp. 196-210.

laration of war in June 1812. The West may have been influenced by economic as well as patriotic motives, but the West, after all, had only ten votes in the House of Representatives. The South Atlantic states from Maryland to Georgia cast thirty-nine, or nearly half, of the seventy-nine votes for war in 1812. Any explanation of the war must place primary emphasis on the Southern Congressmen, and neither feature of the standard interpretation — the concept of a "revolution" in popular sentiment in 1810 and the emphasis on economic factors — satisfactorily explains their votes for war.

Most of these Southern Congressmen were "old Republicans," conservatives whose political Bible was the Republican platform of 1800 and who had sat in Congress for years. In the South there is no evidence of a sudden popular demand in the election of 1810 for a more energetic government and a more vigorous foreign policy. Maryland, which voted six to three for war in June 1812, had four new members in the Twelfth Congress, one a Federalist. The three new Republicans either won the election without opposition or they replaced men who had supported military preparations and a stronger foreign policy in the Eleventh Congress.

Virginia, which held her elections for the Twelfth Congress in the spring of 1811, returned a virtually identical delegation of seventeen Republicans and five Federalists. The two Quids, John Randolph and Edwin Gray, were re-elected, as were most of the conservative Republicans of the Eleventh Congress. The Shenandoah Valley remained as solidly Federalist as it had been in 1800, and the tramontane region, the one part of the state that might have been concerned with Indians and Western lands, elected Thomas Wilson, its first Federalist since 1793.

Virginia's election as a whole produced five new Republican members; none apparently was elected on the issue of peace or war. John Wayles Eppes, the only strong leader Virginia had sent to the Eleventh Congress, moved to John Randolph's district in the Southside and was defeated by Randolph in the election. The contest was close even though Eppes never formally declared himself a candidate, but the objections to Randolph centered on his vigorous opposition to the Madison administration. No one maintained that the election of Eppes would ensure stronger measures toward Great Britain. Eppes's seat in his former district was taken by James Pleasants, a war Republican who in the postwar period was to revert to the old Jeffersonian strict constructionist doctrines. In Thomas Jefferson's own district, which included Albemarle County, David S. Garland was replaced by Hugh Nelson, a close friend of James Monroe and member of the "minority" that had supported Monroe against James Madison's election in 1808 because it felt that Madison was too nationalistic. Nelson entered the Twelfth Congress with a decided preference for peace at any price. In the Fredericksburg area the administration regular, Walter Jones, declined to run again, and in the election Major John P. Hungerford defeated John Taliaferro by six votes. Hungerford was a former Quid and had sat on the Monroe electoral committee in 1808. Taliaferro contested the election, received the support of the war hawks in the House, and was awarded the seat. In the Fauquier-Culpeper district John Love, who had generally supported preparedness measures in the Eleventh Congress, declined re-election and was replaced by another war Republican, Dr. Aylet Hawes.

Nearly half the Virginia Congressmen were elected without opposition, and even where there was a contest the election seldom turned on the issue of foreign policy. Typical of Virginia conservatives re-elected in 1811 was John Clopton, who had represented the Richmond district since 1801. If a letter to his constituents published in the *Virginia Argus* is a fair summary of his campaign platform, Clopton was running in support of the nonintercourse law and against the Bank of the United States, giving no indication of any departure from the Jeffersonian system. Clopton had two opponents, one of whom withdrew before the election, while the other made public statements agreeing with Clopton on every issue.

The election of 1810 in North Carolina similarly produced no great change in her representation. Of her twelve Congressmen eight were re-elected, two of them Federalists and one, Richard Stanford, a Randolph Quid. Two of the four newcomers had served in Congress during the Jefferson administration (William Blackledge from 1803 to 1808 and Thomas Blount from 1804 to 1808). The only new faces in the North Carolina group, Israel Pickens and William R. King, were war hawks, but neither defeated an incumbent.

The political "revolution" in South Carolina in the election of 1810, which produced a unanimous vote for war in June 1812, was more apparent than real. The election of the three great war hawk leaders, John C. Calhoun, William Lowndes, and Langdon Cheves, was more an addition of talent than of numbers to the war party in Congress. In the campaign Calhoun had openly advocated war, but he was elected without opposition since the incumbent — his cousin Joseph Calhoun, a war hawk in the Eleventh Congress — declined re-election and supported him. William Lowndes succeeded to the seat of John Taylor, one of the administration's floor leaders in the Eleventh Congress who had been elected to the Senate. Cheves was elected in 1810 to fill a vacant seat in the Eleventh Congress and was re-elected to the Twelfth.

The other prominent war hawk, David Rogerson Williams, took the seat of his brother-in-law Robert Witherspoon, who declined re-election and threw his support to Williams. Williams, moreover, as a member of the Ninth Congress, had followed John Randolph in rebellion against the Jefferson administration in 1806 and thus fits more into the pattern of the converted conservative. Indeed, as late as May 1812 a Federalist member of the House observed that Williams was still trying to make up his mind between peace and war. The only real contest in South Carolina was the defeat of Lemuel J. Alston by Elias Earle, but no current issue was involved for the two men had taken turns defeating each other for years.

The election in South Carolina illustrates the real significance of the election of 1810. Without any fundamental change in public opinion, and partly by coincidence, South Carolina produced some of the outstanding leaders of the Twelfth Congress. But the change, as in the Western elections that produced Henry Clay and Felix Grundy, was primarily in ability rather than in numbers. Indeed, speaking strictly in terms of numbers, the actual war hawks elected in 1810 were outvoted by Federalists and antiwar Republicans in the Twelfth Congress. The young war hawks from the South and West were certainly able men, and largely by force of character alone they led an unwilling and apathetic country to war.

Yet was leadership alone enough? Several prominent war hawks — Clay, Richard M. Johnson, Ezekiel Bacon, Cheves, and Peter B. Porter — were members of the Eleventh Congress, but despite their ability they had been unable to lead that body in any consistent direction. At least as significant as the sudden appearance of a few talented war hawks in the Twelfth Congress was the gradual conversion of the average Republican from Jeffersonian pacifism to a vigorous defense of America's neutral rights. It was these men, most of them Southerners who had been in Congress for years, who provided the necessary votes for war, just as they had provided the main support for the embargo and nonintercourse laws. Their conversion seems to have stemmed primarily from a disillusionment with the old system of commercial retaliation and a growing realization that the only alternative to war was submission and national disgrace. Every expedient to avoid war honorably had been tried without success. Submission to the orders in council presaged a return to colonial status; war seemed the only alternative. The war, at least as far as the South was concerned, was brought on by men who had had a "bellyful" of England, not by men who were interested in Western lands, or Indians, or prices in the lower Mississippi Valley.

The major weakness in the various economic interpretations is their failure to explain the demand for war in the Middle Atlantic states and in the South. The "expansionist" school of historians, with internal variations, generally maintains that the war was the result of the Western desire for land, in Canada as well as in Indian-dominated Indiana, and that the conquest of Canada was demanded both for its own sake and because the British were backing the Tecumseh confederacy. The difficulty is that the areas most concerned with these problems — Indiana, Illinois, and Michigan — were territories with no vote in Congress. Even Ohio, which presumably had a direct interest in the Wabash lands, was by no means unanimously in favor of war. Its one representative, Jeremiah Morrow, voted for war in 1812 just as he had voted for the embargo in 1807, but Ohio's two senators, Thomas Worthington and Alexander Campbell, opposed war in 1812 because the nation was unprepared and they feared an Indian attack on the defenseless frontier. Both preferred to retain the old system of commercial retaliation. Some have suggested that Ohio's senators were out of touch with public sentiment, but a recent biographer of Worthington feels that a plebiscite held in the spring of 1812 would probably have shown a majority of the people of Ohio against war. Kentucky and Tennessee, it is true, showed considerable interest in the Indian lands and in Canada, but even so their votes in Congress were hardly enough to carry the country to war.

Julius W. Pratt, leading proponent of the "expansionist" thesis, circumvented this difficulty by conjecturing a "frontier crescent" of war hawks extending from New Hampshire (John A. Harper) to Kentucky (Clay and Johnson) and Tennessee (Felix Grundy) and ending in South Carolina (Calhoun, Lowndes, and Cheves) and Georgia (George M. Troup). Yet this seems an arbitrary conjunction of dissimilar areas. Why should New Hampshire or Vermont have been interested enough in the Wabash lands to go to war? And how explain a Southern interest in the Wabash or in Canada? Pratt plugged this hole by surmising a bargain between Southern and Western war hawks in which Florida would be brought into the Union to balance the conquest of Canada. The only evidence he cites, however, is one editorial in a Tennessee newspaper.

It is true that Southern war hawks talked much about the conquest of Canada, but they seem to have regarded it as primarily a method of conducting the war rather than as an ultimate objective. Secretary of State Monroe, for instance, felt that Canada might be invaded, "not as an object of the war but as a means to bring it to a satisfactory conclusion." On the other hand there is evidence that some Southerners actually feared the annexation of Canada. John Randolph certainly considered the possibility that Canada might be acquired the best of reasons for not going to war, and a fellow Virginian elected in 1810 wrote home in December 1811: "The New Yorkers and Vermonters are very well inclined to have upper Canada united with them, by way of increasing their influence in the Union." As to the other half of the bargain there is little evidence that outside of the border area the South was much interested in Florida, and recent scholars have tended to minimize the importance of Florida in the Southern demand for war.

Somewhat more plausible is the economic interpretation of the war in terms of declining farm prices and the restriction of markets abroad. This point of view was first put forth in the early 1930's by George Rogers Taylor, who suggested that the declining price of agricultural products, particularly in the lower Mississippi Valley, may have been a factor in the Western demand for war. The gist of this argument is summed up in a letter of a Louisiana planter of July 25, 1811: "Upon the subject of cotton we are not such fools, but we know that . . . the British are giving us what they please for it. . . . But we happen to know that we should get a much greater price for it, for we have some idea of the extent of the Continent, and the demand there for it; . . . and, therefore, upon the score of lucre, as well as national honor, we are ready." More recently, this argument has been adopted to explain the West-South alliance. Both sections were concerned with the declining prices of the great staple exports, cotton, tobacco, and hemp, and were inclined to blame the British orders in council for restricting their markets. The South and West, in this view, went to war primarily to defend the right to export their products without interference from Britain.

That prices for these great staples declined gradually throughout the first decade of the century cannot be denied, but to what extent the British blockades were responsible is more difficult to determine. The direct trade in agricultural products was not generally affected by the orders in council; not till the winter of 1811–12 did the British interfere with cotton shipments, though their action at that time helped to justify war — at least in the mind of the North Carolina planter Nathaniel Macon. It is interesting, however, that despite the British orders the market for cotton was rapidly increasing both in quantity exported and in geographical area. The declining price was a long-term phenomenon only temporarily interrupted by the postwar prosperity, rather than a result of British restrictions. Statistics on the export of tobacco similarly give no real indication that the British orders in council were responsible for the constriction in markets or the drop in prices.

It is true, however, that the opinion that British restrictions were responsible for lower prices, even if unjustified, seems to have been widely held in the South. Margaret Kinard Latimer has recently brought to light evidence that this was a major factor in the demand for war at least in South Carolina. "Whether or not fighting a war with England," she concludes, "was the logical step to take as a remedy to the commercial and thus agricultural distress is not the question — the South Carolinians of 1812 were convinced that a war would help." Yet this leaves unanswered the question of why South Carolinians preferred to ignore the probability that war would further disrupt their commerce, while others, notably the New Englanders, were so painfully aware of it. Is it possible that those South Carolina politicians who stressed the cotton depression as a cause for war were merely supplying additional reasons that might influence the wavering?

It must also be remembered that the decline in prices was not universal. Prices for beef, corn, and flour, the main exports of the Middle Atlantic states, actually increased over the decade, while the price of pork declined only slightly. In 1810–11 total exports in these products nearly doubled as American farms fed the Duke of Wellington's army in Spain. Pennsylvania, which voted sixteen to two for war with England, can hardly have been following the dictates of economic interest.

The South and the Middle Atlantic states, whose Congressmen furnished the major support for war, had little to gain economically from the conflict. Their direct trade in agricultural products was scarcely affected by the orders in council, and England had long been the major foreign market for both sections. Indeed, it might even be argued that these sections stood to lose as much by war as did New England. When, therefore, Nathaniel Macon spoke of going to war "to obtain the privilege of carrying the produce of our lands to a market" — an oft-quoted passage — he undoubtedly had in mind the "privilege" as much as the trade. Southerners went to war primarily to defend their rights, not their purses.

This is not to deny that economic factors were present. The final synthesis of the causes of the war will have to take into account various material factors — the fear of an Indian conspiracy in the West, for instance, and the concern over declining prices in the South — but it will also have to recognize that none of these economic theses furnishes a satisfactory explanation for the general demand for war. The only unifying factor, present in all sections of the country, was the growing feeling of patriotism, the realization that something must be done to vindicate the national honor. In recent years historians have tended more and more to stress this factor, particularly in its influence on the West, where a feeling of national pride was an obvious concomitant of the youth and exuberance of that section. Even Julius W. Pratt admitted that the war fever in the West "was doubtless due to various causes — perhaps most of all to sheer exasperation at the long continued dilatory fashion of handling the nation's foreign affairs." This factor was probably even more important in the Middle Atlantic states and in the South where fewer material interests were at stake.

The system of commercial retaliation itself had not been defended on economic grounds. The first nonintercourse resolution had been introduced in the spring of 1806 by a Pennsylvanian, Andrew Gregg, as an instrument for gaining by peaceful means some recognition of America's neutral rights. The embargo and the later nonintercourse laws were intended to furnish the President with a lever of negotiation, to maintain the national dignity short of war. It was the growing disillusionment with this system, the growing feeling that war was the only means for maintaining the nation's integrity that eventually brought on the conflict. This mental conversion is aptly illustrated by the following letter of John Clopton of Virginia:

> Let us consider what our government has done — how long it has borne with the repeated injuries which have been touched on in this letter — how often negotiations have been resorted to for the purpose of avoiding war; and the aggressions, instead of having been in any measure relaxed have been pursued with aggravating violence without a single ray of expectation that there exists any sort of disposition in the B[ritish] Cabinet to relax, but the strongest disposition to persist in their career.
>
> . . . The outrages in impressing American seamen exceed all manner of description. Indeed the whole system of aggression now is such that the real question between G. Britain and the U. States has ceased to be a question merely relating to certain rights of commerce about which speculative politicians might differ in opinion — it is now clearly, positively, and directly *a question of independence*, that is to say, whether the U. States are really an independent nation.

Not all Republicans came to a similar conclusion at the same time. The process was a gradual one, beginning with the *Chesapeake* affair and the failure of the embargo to secure a recognition of American rights. The prominent Virginia Republican, Wilson Cary Nicholas, was one of the first to conclude that war was inevitable.

Shortly after the Randolph schism in 1806, Nicholas had entered Congress at the behest of Jefferson, who needed an able floor leader in the House. The failure of the embargo convinced him that the whole policy of commercial retaliation was unsound, for it could not be enforced effectively enough to coerce the belligerents and it resulted only in the ruin of American agriculture. Since the Madison administration was unwilling to abandon the policy, Nicholas, rather than go into opposition, resigned his seat in the autumn of 1809. "We have tried negotiation until it is disgraceful to think of renewing it," he wrote Jefferson. "Commercial restrictions have been so managed as to operate only to our own injury. War then or submission only remain. In deciding between them I cannot hesitate a moment." George Washington Campbell of Tennessee reached a similar conclusion shortly after the *Chesapeake* affair, and he became one of the leading advocates for military preparations in the Tenth and Eleventh Congresses.

The gradual realization of the need for a more militant foreign policy was also reflected in the prominent Republican newspapers. Thomas Ritchie of the Richmond *Enquirer* considered the embargo the only honorable alternative to war, and when it was repealed Ritchie and the *Enquirer* began openly advocating war with England. William Duane, editor of the Philadelphia *Aurora,* generally supported the system of commercial retaliation, but the repudiation of David Erskine's agreement and the mission of Francis "Copenhagen" Jackson in the fall of 1809 convinced him that Britain did not intend to negotiate the question of neutral rights. By December 1809 he was advocating military preparations, the arming of American merchant ships, and, if those measures failed to intimidate Britain, "defensive war."

The old Jeffersonian, Nathaniel Macon, struggled long and valiantly with his conscience in an effort to reconcile Republican dogma with the obvious need for a vigorous defense of American rights. Throughout the Eleventh Congress he had been one of the administration leaders in the House, yet his basic conservatism was frequently evident. In the spring of 1810 he co-operated with John Randolph's efforts to reduce the size of the army and navy, even advocating that they be abolished altogether. As chairman of the foreign relations committee, Macon reported the nonintercourse bill of April 1810, known as Macon's Bill Number Two, but he personally opposed it because he felt it too provocative. Not until the beginning of the Twelfth Congress did he reach the conclusion that war was the only alternative. War was justified, he told the House in December 1811, because of the recent British seizures of ships carrying American agricultural products. This new aggression, he felt, showed that the British, instead of becoming more lenient, were actually tightening their system, and that further negotiation was useless. Macon thereafter co-operated with the war hawks but with some reluctance and with an occasional lapse. He voted against every effort to increase the size of the navy, and he consistently opposed all efforts during the session to raise the taxes to finance the war.

A number of Republicans, though they co-operated with the preparedness measures of the war hawks, could not make up their minds on the basic issue of peace or war until the last minute. As late as May 1812 a Massachusetts Federalist reported, perhaps somewhat wishfully, that a majority of the Virginia delegation was still against war. Besides the Federalists and the Quids, Randolph and Gray, he listed Taliaferro, Nelson, William A. Burwell, John Smith, and Matthew Clay as opposed to war. Representative of this group was Hugh Nelson. Nelson had been elected in 1811, but entered the Twelfth Congress with a lingering sympathy for the old Republican "minority" whose leader was John Randolph of Roanoke and whose prophet was John Taylor of Caroline. "I am a messmate of J[ohn] R[andolph]," he wrote to a friend in Charlottesville shortly after his arrival in Washington. "The more I see him the more I like him. He is as honest as the sun, with all his foibles, and as much traduced I believe as any man has ever been. . . . Do not be surprised if before the session closes I am classified with him as a minority man." Nelson's maiden speech in the House came on the resolution to increase the size of the regular army. It was a rehash of all the old Republican antiwar arguments — war would centralize the government, strengthen the executive, burden the people with taxes, armies, and navies, undermine our "republican simplicity," and subvert the Constitution. "I care not for the prices of cotton and tobacco as compared with the Constitution," he averred. Moreover he felt it unlikely that the United States could ever gain recognition of her neutral rights, particularly since the only program the war hawks suggested was a territorial war begun by an invasion of Canada. Canada could not be conquered, but even if it could, would this enforce our rights? "Certainly not. The way to enforce these rights was by way of a great maritime force, which the nation were incompetent to raise and support." Nelson nevertheless felt the country should prepare for any eventuality because unless Britain relented there was no alternative to war. "I shall vote for the increase of the regular force," he concluded, "to go hand in hand with my friends, even in a war, if necessary and just." The most important of these friends was Nelson's neighbor from Charlottesville, Secretary of State Monroe, who by the spring of 1812 was a vigorous advocate of strong measures. In June, John Randolph wrote to John Taylor of Caroline that Monroe was "most furiously warlike & carries the real strength of the Southern representation with him."

Even more important than the personal influence of Monroe was the stimulus provided by President Madison. Most of the conservatives considered themselves loyal Republicans and were accustomed to following Presidential leadership in dealing with Britain and France. The policy of commercial retaliation had been largely an administration measure, and when the Twelfth Congress assembled in November 1811 Congress naturally looked to the Executive for guidance. Madison not only encouraged the war fever but he co-operated with the war hawks to a degree that has only recently begun to be fully recognized. His Annual Message to Congress in November 1811 outlined a program of military and naval preparations that was adopted virtually intact by the war hawks. His release of the correspondence of Captain John Henry in March 1812 and his request in April for a thirty-day embargo as a prelude to war have been interpreted by his most recent biographer, Irving Brant, as attempts to stimulate the war sentiment in Congress.

The war hawks took full advantage of these moves by the President in their efforts to hold the conservatives in line. In the later stages of the session, when a number of Republicans began to get cold feet, the war hawks informed them that it was too late to back out. When in April the bill initiating a temporary embargo was reported for debate, Henry Clay warned the House that if it stopped now after all the war measures it had passed, it would cover itself "with shame and indelible disgrace." That this argument was effective is indicated by John Smilie, who followed Clay on the floor. Smilie, whose western-Pennsylvania Republicanism dated back to the fight over the Constitution in 1787, admitted that from the beginning of the session he had only reluctantly voted for the various proposals of the war hawks. He actually preferred continuing commercial retaliation to a war and an army of

25,000. But he realized it was too late to back down now; the nation's honor was at stake: "If we now recede we shall be a reproach to all nations."

Added to this internal stimulus was the pressure of continuing British intransigence. On May 22 dispatches arrived in Washington from British Foreign Secretary Lord Castlereagh that contained nothing but a restatement of the British position. President Madison himself concluded that this was the last formal notice intended by the British government and sent his war message to Congress on June 1. It is not difficult to conceive that many a reluctant Republican came to the same decision.

It was thus with mixed motives that a majority of Republicans followed the war hawks to war. It is nevertheless clear that a primary factor in the mind of each was the conclusion that the only alternative to war was submission to the British commercial system. The balance of power in the House was held by men who had been in Congress for years, who had tried every expedient short of war to secure a recognition of American rights, and who at last had become surfeited with British commercial regulations. The war hawks, it is true, provided with their skill and energy the necessary impetus to war, but they could not have done so had not a majority of the Republican Party, particularly in the South, become gradually converted to the idea that war was the only alternative to national humiliation and disgrace. In this sense the war hawks acted as the intangible catalyst for a reaction whose basic elements were already present.

The State of the Union: 1800

By 1815, the United States had successfully passed through the initial stages of national development. It had avoided internal disruption and had successfully defended its interests against other nations. The revolutionary generation, preoccupied with founding a republic on a lasting basis, was passing from the scene. Taking its place after 1815 was a new generation that looked westward and became preoccupied with developing the vast resources of the American continent, now doubled in size as a result of Jefferson's Louisiana Purchase.

In the following selections from his monumental eight-volume history of the United States during the administrations of Jefferson and Madison, Henry Adams (1838–1918), probably the greatest historian America has produced, surveys the state of the union in 1800. Adams plays upon the contrast between the extraordinary creativity of the revolutionary generation in the field of politics and government and the backwardness of the country's material and intellectual life. The American Revolution altered the structure of government and the locus of authority, but it left the economic and social structures largely intact. In vivid strokes of the pen, Adams reminds us how rude a society America was in 1800 — its roads and technology primitive, its intellectual and cultural life thin, its resources enormous but largely unexploited. And he tries to explain why a people, so adventurous politically, was so backward in other respects. Americans, Adams argues, were a conservative people preoccupied with individual enterprise, so much so that they refused to support internal improvements or scientific learning until they glimpsed that these held the keys to far greater wealth. That discovery, made by more and more Americans in the decades after 1815, unleashed new energies that spread settlement to the Pacific in one generation, and touched off a transportation revolution which, in turn, stimulated the growth of manufacturing. At the time Adams wrote, the United States was becoming the world's leading industrial nation. How and why Americans threw off the conservatism that Adams believed held back economic progress for so long, becomes clearer as one studies the history of the American people in the nineteenth century as explored in the next group of selections.

FOR FURTHER READING:

DANGERFIELD, GEORGE. *The Awakening of American Nationalism.* New York: Harper & Row, Publishers, Torchbooks, 1965.*

SMELSER, MARSHALL. *The Democratic Republic, 1801–1815.* New York: Harper & Row, Publishers, Torchbooks, 1968.*

YOUNG, JAMES S. *The Washington Community.* New York: Columbia University Press, 1966.*

Asterisk denotes paperback edition.

From *History of the United States During the Administrations of Jefferson and Madison* HENRY ADAMS

According to the census of 1800, the United States of America contained 5,308,483 persons. In the same year the British Islands contained upwards of fifteen millions; the French Republic, more than twenty-seven millions. Nearly one fifth of the American people were negro slaves; the true political population consisted of four and a half million free whites, or less than one million able-bodied males, on whose shoulders fell the burden of a continent. Even after two centuries of struggle the land was still untamed; forest covered every portion, except here and there a strip of cultivated soil; the minerals lay undisturbed in their rocky beds, and more than two thirds of the people clung to the seaboard within fifty miles of tide-water, where alone the wants of civilized life could be supplied. The centre of population rested within eighteen miles of Baltimore, north and east of Washington. Except in political arrangement, the interior was little more civilized than in 1750, and was not much easier to penetrate than when La Salle and Hennepin found their way to the Mississippi more than a century before.

A great exception broke this rule. Two wagonroads crossed the Alleghany Mountains in Pennsylvania — one leading from Philadelphia to Pittsburg; one from the Potomac to the Monongahela; while a third passed through Virginia southwestward to the Holston River and Knoxville in Tennessee, with a branch through the Cumberland Gap into Kentucky. By these roads and by trails less passable from North and South Carolina, or by water-ways from the lakes, between four and five hundred thousand persons had invaded the country beyond the Alleghanies. At Pittsburg and on the Monongahela existed a society, already old, numbering seventy or eighty thousand persons, while on the Ohio River the settlements had grown to an importance which threatened to force a difficult problem on the union of the older States. One hundred and eighty thousand whites, with forty thousand negro slaves, made Kentucky the largest community west of the mountains; and about ninety thousand whites and fourteen thousand slaves were scattered over Tennessee. In the territory north of the Ohio less progress had been made. A New England colony existed at Marietta; some fifteen thousand people were gathered at Cincinnati; half-way between the two, a small town had grown up at Chillicothe, and other villages or straggling cabins were to be found elsewhere; but the whole Ohio territory contained only forty-five thousand inhabitants. The entire population, both free and slave, west of the mountains, reached not yet half a million; but already they were partly disposed to think themselves, and the old thirteen States were not altogether unwilling to consider them, the germ of an independent empire, which was to find its outlet, not through the Alleghanies to the seaboard, but by the Mississippi River to the Gulf.

Nowhere did eastern settlements touch the western. At least one hundred miles of mountainous country held the two regions everywhere apart. The shore of Lake Erie, where alone contact seemed easy, was still unsettled. The Indians had been

---

Source: Henry Adams, *History of the United States During the Administrations of Jefferson and Madison* (New York: Charles Scribner's Sons, 1891–1896), vol. 1, pp. 1–5, 16–19, 20–23, 27–33, 39–40, 43, 60–63, 65–67, 72–74.

pushed back to the Cuyahoga River, and a few cabins were built on the site of Cleveland; but in 1800, as in 1700, this intermediate region was only a portage where emigrants and merchandise were transferred from Lake Erie to the Muskingum and Ohio valleys. Even western New York remained a wilderness: Buffalo was not laid out; Indian titles were not extinguished; Rochester did not exist; and the county of Onondaga numbered a population of less than eight thousand. In 1799 Utica contained fifty houses, mostly small and temporary. Albany was still a Dutch city, with some five thousand inhabitants; and the tide of immigration flowed slowly through it into the valley of the Mohawk, while another stream from Pennsylvania, following the Susquehanna, spread toward the Genesee country.

The people of the old thirteen States, along the Atlantic seaboard, thus sent westward a wedge-shaped mass of nearly half a million persons, penetrating by the Tennessee, Cumberland, and Ohio rivers toward the western limit of the Union. The Indians offered sharp resistance to this invasion, exacting life for life, and yielding only as their warriors perished. By the close of the century the wedge of white settlements, with its apex at Nashville and its flanks covered by the Ohio and Tennessee rivers, nearly split the Indian country in halves. The northern half — consisting of the later States of Wisconsin, Michigan, Illinois, Indiana, and one third of Ohio — contained Wyandottes and Shawanese, Miamis, Kickapoos, and other tribes, able to send some five thousand warriors to hunt or fight. In the southern half, powerful confederacies of Creeks, Cherokees, Chickasaws, and Choctaws lived and hunted where the States of Mississippi, Alabama, and the western parts of Georgia, Tennessee, and Kentucky were to extend; and so weak was the State of Georgia, which claimed the southwestern territory for its own, that a well-concerted movement of Indians might without much difficulty have swept back its white population of one hundred thousand toward the ocean or across the Savannah River. The Indian power had been broken in halves, but each half was still terrible to the colonists on the edges of their vast domain, and was used as a political weapon by the Governments whose territory bounded the Union on the north and south. The governors-general of Canada intrigued with the northwestern Indians, that they might hold in check any aggression from Washington; while the Spanish governors of West Florida and Louisiana maintained equally close relations with the Indian confederacies of the Georgia territory.

With the exception that half a million people had crossed the Alleghanies and were struggling with difficulties all their own, in an isolation like that of Jutes or Angles in the fifth century, America, so far as concerned physical problems, had changed little in fifty years. The old landmarks remained nearly where they stood before. The same bad roads and difficult rivers, connecting the same small towns, stretched into the same forests in 1800 as when the armies of Braddock and Amherst pierced the western and northern wilderness, except that these roads extended a few miles farther from the seacoast. Nature was rather man's master than his servant, and the five million Americans struggling with the untamed continent seemed hardly more competent to their task than the beavers and buffalo which had for countless generations made bridges and roads of their own. . . .

If the physical task which lay before the American people had advanced but a short way toward completion, little more change could be seen in the economical conditions of American life. The man who in the year 1800 ventured to hope for a new era in the coming century, could lay his hand on no statistics that silenced doubt. The machinery of production showed no radical difference from that familiar to ages long past. The Saxon farmer of the eighth century enjoyed most of the comforts known to Saxon farmers of the eighteenth. The eorls and ceorls of Offa and Ecgbert could not read or write, and did not receive a weekly newspaper with such information as newspapers in that age could supply; yet neither their houses, their clothing, their food and drink, their agricultural tools and methods, their stock, nor their habits were so greatly altered or improved by time that they would have found much difficulty in accommodating their lives to that of their descendants in the eighteenth century. In this respect America was backward. Fifty or a hundred miles inland more than half the houses were log-cabins, which might or might not enjoy the luxury of a glass window. Throughout the South and West houses showed little attempt at luxury; but even in New England the ordinary farmhouse was hardly so well built, so spacious, or so warm as that of a well-to-do contemporary of Charlemagne. The cloth which the farmer's family wore was still homespun. The hats were manufactured by the village hatter; the clothes were cut and made at home; the shirts, socks, and nearly every other article of dress were also homemade. Hence came a marked air of rusticity which distinguished country from town — awkward shapes of hat, coat, and trousers, which gave to the Yankee caricature those typical traits that soon disappeared almost as completely as coats of mail and steel headpieces. The plough was rude and clumsy; the sickle as old as Tubal Cain, and even the cradle not in general use; the flail was unchanged since the Aryan exodus; in Virginia, grain was still commonly trodden out by horses. Enterprising gentlemen-farmers introduced threshing-machines and invented scientific ploughs; but these were novelties. Stock was as a rule not only unimproved, but ill cared for. The swine ran loose; the cattle were left to feed on what pasture they could find, and even in New England were not housed until the severest frosts, on the excuse that exposure hardened them. Near half a century afterward a competent judge asserted that the general treatment of cows in New England was fair matter of presentment by a grand jury. Except among the best farmers, drainage, manures, and rotation of crops were uncommon. The ordinary cultivator planted his corn as his father had planted it, sowing as much rye to the acre, using the same number of oxen to plough, and getting in his crops on the same day. He was even known to remove his barn on account of the manure accumulated round it, although the New England soil was never so rich as to warrant neglect to enrich it. The money for which he sold his wheat and chickens was of the Old World; he reckoned in shillings or pistareens, and rarely handled an American coin more valuable than a large copper cent.

At a time when the wealth and science of London and Paris could not supply an article so necessary as a common sulphur-match, the backwardness of remote country districts could hardly be exaggerated. Yet remote districts were not the only sufferers. Of the whole United States New England claimed to be the most civilized province, yet New England was a region in which life had yet gained few charms of sense and few advantages over its rivals. Wilson, the ornithologist, a Pennsylvania Scotchman, a confirmed grumbler, but a shrewd judge, and the most thorough of American travellers, said in 1808: "My journey through almost the whole of New England has rather lowered the Yankees in my esteem. Except a few neat academies, I found their schoolhouses equally ruinous and deserted with ours; fields covered with stones; stone fences; scrubby oaks and pine-trees; wretched orchards; scarcely one grain-field in twenty miles; the taverns along the road dirty, and filled with loungers brawling about lawsuits and politics; the people snappish and extortioners, lazy, and two hundred years behind the Pennsylvanians in agricultural improvements." The description was exaggerated, for Wilson forgot to speak of the districts where fields were not covered with stones, and where wheat could be grown to advantage. . . .

A better measure of the difficulties with which New England struggled was given by the progress of Boston, which was supposed to have contained about eighteen thousand inhabitants as early as 1730, and twenty thousand in 1770. For several years after the Revolution it numbered less than twenty thousand, but in 1800 the census showed twenty-five thousand inhabitants. In appearance, Boston resembled an English market-town, of a kind even then old-fashioned. The footways or sidewalks were paved, like the crooked and narrow streets, with round cobblestones, and were divided from the carriage way only by posts and a gutter. The streets were almost unlighted at night, a few oil-lamps rendering the darkness more visible and the rough pavement rougher. Police hardly existed. The system of taxation was defective. The town was managed by selectmen, the elected instruments of town-meetings whose jealousy of granting power was even greater than their objection to spending money, and whose hostility to city government was not to be overcome.

Although on all sides increase of ease and comfort was evident, and roads, canals, and new buildings, public and private, were already in course of construction on a scale before unknown, yet in spite of more than a century and a half of incessant industry, intelligent labor, and pinching economy Boston and New England were still poor. A few merchants enjoyed incomes derived from foreign trade, which allowed them to imitate in a quiet way the style of the English mercantile class; but the clergy and the lawyers, who stood at the head of society, lived with much economy. Many a country clergyman, eminent for piety and even for hospitality, brought up a family and laid aside some savings on a salary of five hundred dollars a year. President Dwight, who knew well the class to which he belonged, eulogizing the life of Abijah Weld, pastor of Attleborough, declared that on a salary of two hundred and twenty dollars a year Mr. Weld brought up eleven children, besides keeping a hospitable house and maintaining charity to the poor.

On the Exchange a few merchants had done most of the business of Boston since the peace of 1783, but a mail thrice a week to New York, and an occasional arrival from Europe or the departure of a ship to China, left ample leisure for correspondence and even for gossip. The habits of the commercial class had not been greatly affected by recent prosperity. Within ten or fifteen years before 1800 three Banks had been created to supply the commercial needs of Boston. One of these was a branch Bank of the United States, which employed there whatever part of its capital it could profitably use; the two others were local Banks, with capital of $1,600,000, toward which the State subscribed $400,000. Altogether the banking capital of Boston might amount to two millions and a half. A number of small Banks, representing in all about two and a half millions more, were scattered through the smaller New England towns. The extraordinary prosperity caused by the French wars opened to Boston a new career. Wealth and population were doubling; the exports and imports of New England were surprisingly large, and the shipping was greater than that of New York and Pennsylvania combined; but Boston had already learned, and was to learn again, how fleeting were the riches that depended on foreign commerce, and conservative habits were not easily changed by a few years of accidental gain.

Of manufactures New England had many, but none on a large scale. The people could feed or clothe themselves only by household industry; their whaleoil, salt fish, lumber, and rum were mostly sent abroad; but they freighted coasters with turners' articles, home-made linens and cloths, cheese, butter, shoes, nails, and what were called Yankee Notions of all sorts, which were sent to Norfolk and the Southern ports, and often peddled from the deck, as goods of every sort were peddled on the flat-boats of the Ohio. Two or three small mills spun cotton with doubtful success; but England supplied ordinary manufactures more cheaply and better than Massachusetts could hope to do. A tri-weekly mail and a few coasting sloops provided for the business of New England with domestic ports. One packet sloop plied regularly to New York.

The State of New York was little in advance of Massachusetts and Maine. In 1800 for the first time New York gained the lead in population by the difference between 589,000 and 573,000. The valuation of New York for the direct tax in 1799 was $100,000,000; that of Massachusetts was $84,000,000. New York was still a frontier State, and although the city was European in its age and habits, travellers needed to go few miles from the Hudson in order to find a wilderness like that of Ohio and Tennessee. . . .

As a rule American capital was absorbed in shipping or agriculture, whence it could not be suddenly withdrawn. No stock-exchange existed, and no broker exclusively engaged in stock-jobbing, for there were few stocks. The national debt, of about eighty millions, was held abroad, or as a permanent investment at home. States and municipalities had not learned to borrow. Except for a few banks and insurance offices, turnpikes, bridges, canals, and land-companies, neither bonds nor stocks were known. The city of New York was so small as to make extravagance difficult; the Battery was a fashionable walk, Broadway a country drive, and Wall Street an uptown residence. Great accumulations of wealth had hardly begun. The Patroon was still the richest man in the State. John Jacob Astor was a fur-merchant living where the Astor House afterward stood, and had not yet begun those purchases of real estate which secured his fortune. Cornelius Vanderbilt was a boy six years old, playing about his father's ferryboat at Staten Island. New York city itself was what it had been for a hundred years past — a local market. . . .

Of all parts of the Union, Pennsylvania seemed to have made most use of her national advantages; but her progress was not more rapid than the natural increase of population and wealth demanded, while to deal with the needs of America, man's resources and his power over Nature must be increased in a ratio far more rapid than that which governed his numbers. Nevertheless, Pennsylvania was the most encouraging spectacle in the field of vision. Baltimore, which had suddenly sprung to a population and commerce greater than those of Boston, also offered strong hope of future improvement; but farther South the people showed fewer signs of change.

The city of Washington, rising in a solitude on the banks of the Potomac, was a symbol of American nationality in the Southern States. The contrast between the immensity of the task and the paucity of means seemed to challenge suspicion that the nation itself was a magnificent scheme like the federal city, which could show only a few log-cabins and negro quarters where the plan provided for the traffic of London and the elegance of Versailles. When in the summer of 1800 the government was transferred to what was regarded by most persons as a fever-stricken morass, the half-finished White House stood in a naked field overlooking the Potomac, with two awkward Department buildings near it, a single row of brick houses and a few isolated dwellings within sight, and nothing more; until across a swamp, a mile and a half away, the shapeless, unfinished Capitol was seen, two wings without a body, ambitious enough in design to make more grotesque the nature of its surroundings. The conception proved that the United States understood the vastness of their task, and were willing to stake something on their faith in it. Never did hermit or saint condemn himself to solitude more consciously than Congress and the Executive in removing the government from Philadelphia to Washington: the discontented men clustered together in eight or ten boarding-houses as near as possible to the Capitol, and there lived, like a convent of monks, with no other amusement or occupation than that of going from their lodgings to the Chambers and back again. Even private wealth could do little to improve their situation, for there was nothing which wealth could buy; there were in Washington no shops or markets, skilled labor, commerce, or people. Public efforts and lavish use of public money could alone make the place tolerable; but Congress doled out funds for this national and personal object with so sparing a hand, that their Capitol threatened to crumble in pieces and crush Senate and House under the ruins, long before the building was complete.

A government capable of sketching a magnificent plan, and willing to give only a half-hearted pledge for its fulfilment; a people eager to advertise a vast undertaking beyond their present powers, which when completed would become an object of jealousy and fear — this was the impression made upon the traveller who visited Washington in 1800, and mused among the unraised columns of the Capitol upon the destiny of the United States. As he travelled farther south his doubts were strengthened, for across the Potomac he could detect no sign of a new spirit. Manufactures had no existence. Alexandria owned a bank with half a million of capital, but no other was to be found between Washington and Charleston, except the branch Bank of the United States at Norfolk, nor any industry to which loans and discounts could safely be made. Virginia, the most populous and powerful of all the States, had a white population of 514,000, nearly equal to that of Pennsylvania and New York, besides about 350,000 slaves. Her energies had pierced the mountains and settled the western territory before the slow-moving Northern people had torn themselves from the safer and more comfortable life by the seaboard; but the Virginia ideal was patriarchal, and an American continent on the Virginia type might reproduce the virtues of Cato, and perhaps the eloquence of Cicero, but was little likely to produce anything more practical in the way of modern progress. The Shenandoah Valley rivalled Pennsylvania and Connecticut in richness and skill of husbandry; but even agriculture, the favorite industry in Virginia, had suffered from the competition of Kentucky and Tennessee, and from the emigration which had drawn away fully one hundred thousand people. The land was no longer very productive. Even Jefferson, the most active-minded and sanguine of all Virginians — the inventor of the first scientific plough, the importer of the first threshing-machine known in Virginia, the experimenter with a new drilling-machine, the owner of one hundred and fifty slaves and ten thousand acres of land, whose negroes were trained to carpentry, cabinet-making, house-building, weaving, tailoring, shoe-making — claimed to get from his land no more than six or eight bushels of wheat to an acre, and had been forced to abandon the more profitable cultivation of tobacco. Except in a few favored districts like the Shenandoah Valley, land in Virginia did not average eight bushels of wheat to an acre. The cultivation of tobacco had been almost the sole object of land-owners, and even where the lands were not exhausted, a bad system of agriculture and the force of habit prevented improvement.

The great planters lavished money in vain on experiments to improve their crops and their stock. They devoted themselves to the task with energy and knowledge; but they needed a diversity of interests and local markets, and except at Baltimore these were far from making their appearance. Neither the products, the markets, the relative amount of capital, nor the machinery of production had perceptibly changed. "The Virginians are not generally rich," said the Duc de Liancourt, "especially in net revenue. Thus one often finds a well-served table, covered with silver, in a room where for ten years half the window panes have been missing, and where they will be missed for ten years more. There are few houses in a passable state of repair, and of all parts of the establishment those best cared for are the stables." Wealth reckoned in slaves or land was plenty; but the best Virginians, from President Washington downward, were most outspoken in their warnings against the Virginia system both of slavery and agriculture. . . .

If any portion of the United States might hope for a sudden and magnificent bloom, South Carolina seemed entitled to expect it. Rarely had such a situation, combined with such resources, failed to produce some wonderful result. Yet as Washington warned Sinclair, these advantages were counterbalanced by serious evils. The climate in summer was too relaxing. The sun was too hot. The sea-coast was unhealthy, and at certain seasons even deadly to the whites. Finally, if history was a guide, no permanent success could be prophesied for a society like that of the low country in South Carolina, where some thirty thousand whites were surrounded by a dense mass of nearly one hundred thousand negro slaves. Even Georgia, then only partially settled, contained sixty thousand slaves and but one hundred thousand whites. The cotton States might still argue that if slavery, malaria, or summer heat barred civilization, all the civilization that was ever known must have been blighted in its infancy; but although the future of South Carolina might be brilliant, like that of other oligarchies in which only a few thousand freemen took part, such a development seemed to diverge far from the path likely to be followed by Northern society, and bade fair to increase and complicate the social and economical difficulties with which Americans had to deal.

A probable valuation of the whole United States in 1800 was eighteen hundred million dollars, equal to $328 for each human being, including slaves; or $418 to each free white. This property was distributed with an approach to equality, except in a few of the Southern States. In New York and Philadelphia a private fortune of one hundred thousand dollars was considered handsome, and three hundred thousand was great wealth. Inequalities were frequent; but they were chiefly those of a landed aristocracy. Equality was so far the rule that every white family of five persons might be supposed to own land, stock, or utensils, a house and furniture, worth about two thousand dollars; and as the only considerable industry was agriculture, their scale of life was easy to calculate — taxes amounting to little or nothing, and wages averaging about a dollar a day.

Not only were these slender resources, but they were also of a kind not easily converted to the ready uses required for rapid development. Among the numerous difficulties with which the Union was to struggle, and which were to form the interest of American history, the disproportion between the physical obstacles and the material means for overcoming them was one of the most striking.

The growth of character, social and national — the formation of men's minds — more interesting then any territorial or industrial growth, defied the tests of censuses and surveys. No people could be expected, least of all when in infancy, to understand the intricacies of its own character, and rarely has a foreigner been gifted with insight to explain what natives did not comprehend. Only with diffidence could the best-informed Americans venture, in 1800, to generalize on the subject of their own national habits of life and thought. . . .

. . . The path their development might take was one of the many problems with which their future was perplexed. Such few habits as might prove to be fixed, offered little clew to the habits that might be adopted in the process of growth, and speculation was useless where change alone could be considered certain.

If any prediction could be risked, an observer might have been warranted in suspecting that the popular character was likely to be conservative, for as yet this trait was most marked, at least in the older societies of New England, Pennsylvania, and Virginia. Great as were the material obstacles in the path of the United States, the greatest obstacle of all was in the human mind. Down to the close of the eighteenth century no change had occurred in the world which warranted practical men in assuming that great changes were to come. Afterward, as time passed, and as science developed man's capacity to control Nature's forces, old-fashioned conservatism vanished from society, reappearing occasionally, like the stripes on a mule, only to prove its former existence; but during the eighteenth century the progress of America, except in political paths, had been less rapid than ardent reformers wished, and the reaction which followed the French Revolution made it seem even slower than it was. In 1723 Benjamin Franklin landed at Philadelphia, and with his loaf of bread under his arm walked along Market Street toward an immortality such as no American had then conceived. He died in 1790, after witnessing great political revolutions; but the intellectual revolution was hardly as rapid as he must, in his youth, have hoped.

In 1732 Franklin induced some fifty persons to found a subscription library, and his example and energy set a fashion which was generally followed. In 1800 the library he founded was still in existence; numerous small subscription libraries on the same model, containing fifty or a hundred volumes, were scattered in country towns; but all the public libraries in the United States — collegiate, scientific, or popular, endowed or unendowed — could hardly show fifty thousand volumes, including duplicates, fully one third being still theological.

Half a century had passed since Franklin's active mind drew the lightning from heaven, and decided the nature of electricity. No one in America had yet carried further his experiments in the field which he had made American. This inactivity was commonly explained as a result of the long Revolutionary War; yet the war had not prevented population and wealth from increasing, until Philadelphia in 1800 was far in advance of the Philadelphia which had seen Franklin's kite flying among the clouds. . . .

Noah Webster, who before beginning his famous dictionary edited the "New York Commercial Advertiser," and wrote on all subjects with characteristic confidence, complained of the ignorance of his countrymen. He claimed for the New Englanders an acquaintance with theology, law, politics, and light English literature; "but as to classical learning, history (civil and ecclesiastical), mathematics, astronomy, chemistry, botany, and natural history, excepting here and there a rare instance of a man who is eminent in some one of these branches, we may be said to have no learning at all, or a mere smattering." Although defending his countrymen from the criticisms of Dr. Priestley, he admitted that "our learning is superficial in a shameful degree . . . our colleges are disgracefully destitute of books and philosophical apparatus . . . and I am ashamed to own that scarcely a branch of science can be fully investigated in America for want of books, especially original works. This defect of our libraries I have experienced myself in searching for materials for the History of Epidemic Diseases. . . . As to libraries, we have no such things. There are not more than three or four tolerable libraries in America, and these are extremely imperfect. Great numbers of the most valuable authors have not found their way across the Atlantic."

This complaint was made in the year 1800, and was the more significant because it showed that Webster, a man equally at home in Philadelphia, New York, and Boston, thought his country's deficiencies greater than could be excused or explained by its circumstances. George Ticknor felt at least equal difficulty in explaining the reason why, as late as 1814, even good schoolbooks were rare in Boston, and a copy of Euripides in the original could not be bought at any book-seller's shop in New England. For some reason, the American mind, except in politics, seemed to these students of literature in a condition of unnatural sluggishness; and such complaints were not confined to literature or science. If Americans agreed in any opinion, they were united in wishing for roads; but even on that point whole communities showed an indifference, or hositility, that annoyed their contemporaries. . . .

. . . So strong was the popular prejudice against paying for the privilege of travelling on a highway that in certain States, like Rhode Island and Georgia, turnpikes were long unknown, while in Virginia and North Carolina the roads were little better than where the prejudice was universal.

In this instance the economy of a simple and somewhat rude society accounted in part for indifference; in other cases, popular prejudice took a form less easily understood. So general was the hostility to Banks as to offer a serious obstacle to enterprise. The popularity of President Washington and the usefulness of his administration were impaired by his support of a national bank and a funding system. Jefferson's hostility to all the machinery of capital was shared by a great majority of the Southern people and a large minority in the North. For seven years the New York legislature refused to charter the first banking company in the State; and when in 1791 the charter was obtained, and the Bank fell into Federalist hands, Aaron Burr succeeded in obtaining banking privileges for the Manhattan Company only by concealing them under the pretence of furnishing a supply of fresh water to the city of New York.

This conservative habit of mind was more harmful in America than in other communities, because Americans needed more than older societies the activity which could alone partly compensate for the relative feebleness of their means compared with the magnitude of their task. Some instances of sluggishness, common to Europe and America, were hardly credible. For more than ten years in England the steam-engines of Watt had been working, in common and successful use, causing a revolution in industry that threatened to drain the world for England's advantage;

yet Europe during a generation left England undisturbed to enjoy the monopoly of steam. France and Germany were England's rivals in commerce and manufactures, and required steam for self-defence; while the United States were commercial allies of England, and needed steam neither for mines nor manufactures, but their need was still extreme. Every American knew that if steam could be successfully applied to navigation, it must produce an immediate increase of wealth, besides an ultimate settlement of the most serious material and political difficulties of the Union. Had both the national and State Governments devoted millions of money to this object, and had the citizens wasted, if necessary, every dollar in their slowly filling pockets to attain it, they would have done no more than the occasion warranted, even had they failed; but failure was not to be feared, for they had with their own eyes seen the experiment tried, and they did not dispute its success. For America this question had been settled as early as 1789, when John Fitch — a mechanic, without education or wealth, but with the energy of genius — invented engine and paddles of his own, with so much success that during a whole summer Philadelphians watched his ferry-boat plying daily against the river current. No one denied that his boat was rapidly, steadily, and regularly moved against wind and tide, with as much certainty and convenience as could be expected in a first experiment; yet Fitch's company failed. He could raise no more money; the public refused to use his boat or to help him build a better; they did not want it, would not believe in it, and broke his heart by their contempt. Fitch struggled against failure, and invented another boat moved by a screw. The Eastern public still proving indifferent, he wandered to Kentucky, to try his fortune on the Western waters. Disappointed there, as in Philadelphia and New York, he made a deliberate attempt to end his life by drink; but the process proving too slow, he saved twelve opium pills from the physician's prescription, and was found one morning dead.

Fitch's death took place in an obscure Kentucky inn, three years before Jefferson, the philosopher president, entered the White House. Had Fitch been the only inventor thus neglected, his peculiarities and the defects of his steamboat might account for his failure; but he did not stand alone. . . .

Possibly Fulton and Fitch, like other inventors, may have exaggerated the public apathy and contempt; but whatever was the precise force of the innovating spirit, conservatism possessed the world by right. Experience forced on men's minds the conviction that what had ever been must ever be. At the close of the eighteenth century nothing had occurred which warranted the belief that even the material difficulties of America could be removed. Radicals as extreme as Thomas Jefferson and Albert Gallatin were contented with avowing no higher aim than that America should reproduce the simpler forms of European republican society without European vices; and even this their opponents thought visionary. The United States had thus far made a single great step in advance of the Old World — they had agreed to try the experiment of embracing half a continent in one republican system; but so little were they disposed to feel confidence in their success, that Jefferson himself did not look on this American idea as vital; he would not stake the future on so new an invention. "Whether we remain in one confederacy," he wrote in 1804, "or form into Atlantic and Mississippi confederations, I believe not very important to the happiness of either part." Even over his liberal mind history cast a spell so strong, that he thought the solitary American experiment of political confederation "not very important" beyond the Alleghenies.

The task of overcoming popular inertia in a democratic society was new, and seemed to offer peculiar difficulties. Without a scientific class to lead the way, and without a wealthy class to provide the means of experiment, the people of the United States were still required, by the nature of their problems, to become a speculating and scientific nation. They could do little without changing their old habit of mind, and without learning to love novelty for novelty's sake. Hitherto their timidity in using money had been proportioned to the scantiness of their means. Henceforward they were under every inducement to risk great stakes and frequent losses in order to win occasionally a thousand fold. In the colonial state they had naturally accepted old processes as the best, and European experience as final authority. As an independent people, with half a continent to civilize, they could not afford to waste time in following European examples, but must devise new processes of their own. A world which assumed that what had been must be, could not be scientific; yet in order to make the Americans a successful people, they must be roused to feel the necessity of scientific training. Until they were satisfied that knowledge was money, they would not insist upon high education; nor until they saw with their own eyes stones turned into gold, and vapor into cattle and corn, would they learn the meaning of science.

PART 3

*The Middle Years
1815–1877*

The Urban Wage Earner in the Early Republic

The period between independence and about 1830 was one of considerable progress in the economic institutions of the United States. During the confederation period, the basic outlines of federal land policy were drawn. New trade routes were opened up, following the end of British trade restrictions. Businessmen increasingly adopted the corporate form for private business enterprise. The first true commercial banks were established in major port cities. Following 1787, the new Constitution established a government equipped to protect American economic interests abroad and to encourage economic integration at home. During the administration of Washington, the Hamiltonian program reestablished public credit and created a national bank to stimulate commerce and industry. These and other institutional changes set the stage for rapid economic progress in later years, but the period itself was probably one of slow advance in income and welfare of the average American. Evidently, war, the heavy costs of opening up the West, the slow improvement in technology — all conspired to confine improvement per person in the output of the farms and workshops of the nation to modest dimensions.

In 1830, most Americans were still rural farm folk. Of the four million men, women, and children in the labor force in 1830, almost 3 million were still on farms, with many others employed in other extractive industries. The urban wage-earning class was still relatively small, though growing in size. They were not factory workers, as David Montgomery notes, but craftsmen, seamen, apprentices, and common laborers. They lived in a transitional period in the economy: between the era when many jobs were performed by self-employed craftsmen and the era when many of these working folk would be gathered into large factories.

They were not, it is clear, affluent people, yet they were far better off than their European counterparts, and they found it possible to move up the social ladder. Despite the relatively slow pace of economic growth in this period, it would seem that the lot of the working man was generally better than it had been in eighteenth-century Boston, as described earlier by James Henretta.

FOR FURTHER READING:

HUGINS, WALTER. *Jacksonian Democracy and the Working Class: A Study of the New York Workingmen's Movement.* Stanford, Cal.: Stanford University Press, 1967.*
TAYLOR, GEORGE R. *The Transportation Revolution.* New York: Harper & Row, Publishers, 1968.*
WARE, NORMAN. *The Industrial Worker 1840–1860.* Chicago: Quadrangle Books, 1964.*

Asterisk denotes paperback edition.

The Working Classes of the Pre-Industrial American City, 1780–1830

DAVID MONTGOMERY

In the years since Raymond W. Goldsmith submitted to Congress his statistical findings on the rise of per capita income in the United States many economic historians have come to date the beginnings of sustained industrial growth at some time during the 1830s. This chronology has provided historians of the working class with a significant bench-mark to guide their own research and analysis. Among other things it raises questions concerning the sources, size, and character of the labor supply which was at hand before the acceleration of economic growth and the ideological baggage (attitudes, customs, institutions) which the available workers carried with them when they entered the industrial era. The objective of this article is to suggest some parameters for both sets of questions derived from an examination of the working classes in the young nation's four northern cities: Boston, New York, Philadelphia, and Baltimore.

During the five decades before 1830 these cities were essentially depots for transoceanic shipping, and their labor force was largely tied to maritime commerce. Surrounding each of them was "a vast scene of household manufacturing" where, wrote Alexander Hamilton, country folk produced clothing, shoes, and other necessities, "in many instances, to an extent not only sufficient for the supply of the families in which they are made, but for sale, and even, in some cases, for exportation." Such a countryside Albert Gallatin found twenty years later in New Hampshire, where the average farmer's house had at least one spinning wheel, and every second house boasted a loom on which from 100 to 600 yards of saleable cloth were woven annually (at a time when journeymen weavers in their homes averaged only 829 yards per year and factory looms, 1,111 yards). Most manufacturing, in other words, was carried on outside of the major cities. By 1820 some 12 percent of the nation's labor force was engaged in manufacturing and construction, and 28 percent in all non-agricultural occupations, but at that time the residents of these cities and their contiguous suburbs totalled only 356,452, or 3.7 percent of the American people.

The merchant elite of these communities, furthermore, was concerned not so much with hiring labor as with vending the produce of labor, both agricultural and mechanical. Mathew Carey went so far as to accuse the merchants of hostility toward manufacturing interests, of striving "to impress upon the public mind, that the national prosperity depended almost altogether on commerce; that the protection of manufactures by duties on imports was impolitic and unjust." Understandably the broadsides of Carey, Gallatin, Tench Coxe, and other promoters of manufacturing bore the aspect of appeals to the dominant agricultural and commercial interests of the land to pay some heed to the needs of industry and to believe that the growth of domestic manufactures could take place without depriving farmers and merchants of either manpower or customers.

But Carey's conception of the merchant as industry's relentless foe slighted the

---

Source: David Montgomery, "The Working Classes of the Pre-Industrial American City, 1780–1830," *Labor History*, vol. 9 (1968), pp. 3–22.

encouragement offered manufacturing by the commercial city itself. The concentration of population in seaports required by a growing flow of commerce prevented urban residents from producing their own necessities in the fashion of farm families. It generated a social division of labor within the city itself and hence a need for sedentary artisans. The accumulation of merchant fortunes, furthermore, created a demand for luxury goods and thus for expert craftsmen: for silversmiths, goldbeaters, clockmakers, wig and peruke makers, printers of books and journals, tailors, and cordwainers familiar with European fashions and capable of reproducing them. By the end of the eighteenth century, moreover, seaboard merchants had opened a substantial oceanic trade in shoes, clothing, barrels, and ironwares with the regions of slave plantations. This trade encouraged the development of both the putting-out system and the early efforts toward factory organization of production.

Although most manufacturing was carried on outside the great urban centers, the seaport itself, therefore, generated a demand for labor in production as well as trade. In the eighteenth century most manufacture had been performed in the workshops of mechanics who, with the aid of family, apprentices, and occasional journeymen, made the wares they vended themselves. The printer, for example, was usually a bookseller and a journalist as well, in the manner of Mathew Carey, who in the 1790s composed his own editorials in type and then hawked the paper about Philadelphia. Only after 1810 did urban newspapers gravitate into the hands of publishers who were not printers but, in the language of the journeymen, "speculators on the labor of printers" who installed "hireling editors" to write the columns printers now set in type.

The colonial conception of a journeyman as tomorrow's master mechanic was neither dead nor fully obsolete by 1820, for vertical mobility was still remarkable. Among the early members of the Franklin Typographical Association of New York, a trade society of journeymen founded in 1799, were David Bruce, the future owner of the city's largest printing shop and a pioneer typefounder; Thurlow Weed, a future boss of state politics; Samuel Woodworth, the poet of "Old Oaken Bucket" fame; and Peter Force, America's most eminent historical archivist. Two of the master shoemakers who testified against the cordwainers union in Philadelphia's 1805 conspiracy trial were former journeymen and union members, as were two of the employers at the similar Pittsburgh trial ten years later. But by the first two decades of the nineteenth century the emergence of distinct societies of journeymen and of masters among printers, tailors, shoemakers, carpenters, stone cutters, and other trades in every seaport indicated a new awareness of distinct class interests. The seventeen benevolent societies of Philadelphia carpenters, ship masters, stone cutters, and other trades listed by James Mease in 1811 were clearly organizations of master mechanics. Their initiation fees ranging from $10 up and their annual dues of four or five dollars contrast remarkably with the one dollar initiation and the 25 cents monthly dues (waived after ten years' membership) charged by that city's printers union. Societies of journeymen that sought to combine benevolent functions with the enforcement of union wage scales ultimately found it necessary to either expel members who had risen to the rank of employers, or to succumb to the urgings of "alimoners" in their midst and abandon the effort to regulate trade conditions. Thus the printers' organizations in Philadelphia and Boston during the 1820s converted themselves into friendly societies open to employers and workmen alike, while the New York society, bent on controlling wages and aware that "the interests of the journeymen are separate and in some respects opposite to those of the employers," resolved in 1817 "that when any member of this society shall become an employing printer he shall be considered without the limits of this society."

The myth of harmonious personal relationships among masters, journeymen, and apprentices in a setting of domestic paternalism may be quite anachronistic when applied to post-Revolutionary decades. Ian Quimby's study of apprentice contracts in eighteenth century Philadelphia revealed a persistent erosion of filial duties and loyalties by the emerging ethos of commercialism. The mutual moral obligations of apprentices and masters in such matters as work expected of the boy, and the education and clothing due him were converted over the course of the century into money values and specified in ever-increasing detail in the contracts. The experience of cabinetmakers, furthermore, suggests that journeymen seldom remained long enough with any master to develop a sense of personal attachment. The journeymen of Samuel Ashton's Philadelphia cabinet shop between 1795 and 1803 averaged scarcely six months in his employ. So rapid was the turnover of craftsmen that, though Ashton rarely needed more than five workmen at a time, forty-nine different men worked for him during those eight years. Under such circumstances class antagonisms based on chronic disputes over wages could be quite consistent with a high level of upward social mobility.

By the 1820s, therefore, the urban working classes comprised recognizable and self-conscious elements of urban society. The "classes . . . who are wholly dependent upon wages," wrote Reverend Joseph Tuckerman, "are very numerous" and, he continued:

> would, indeed, be numerous, if we looked for them among only those who have no trade, and who are generally distinguished alone, as labouring men. This large division includes shop, market, and other porters; carmen; those who are employed in lading, and unlading vessels; wood-sawyers; hod carriers; house servants; those employed by mechanics in a single branch of their business; and multitudes, who are men and women of any work, occasionally required in families, as washing, scouring, etc.; or on the wharves, or in the streets of the city. Besides these, the number is great of those, who are journeymen, and many of whom will never be anything but journeymen, in the various mechanic arts; and considerable numbers are also employed in the different departments of large manufactories, who possess no capital; and who know, and will continue to know, little or nothing in any other department of these establishments, except that in which they are themselves employed. All these, in the strictest sense, and in the common acceptation of the term, are dependent on the wages which they obtain for their services.

Tuckerman's definition of the wage earning classes suggests that journeymen, mechanics, casual laborers, and factory operatives must be analyzed separately. Even though many mechanics would "never be anything but journeymen," they enjoyed the highest incomes and status of any wage earners and were psychologically the most firmly wedded to the social values and practices of the traditional artisan. Apprenticeship was the historic route of access to "the art and mysteries" of any trade, and the journeymen of this period strove to bar any other avenue of entry. The Philadelphia Typographical Society, which sought with occasional success to reserve all printing positions in town for its own members, excluded from membership anyone "who shall not have served an apprenticeship satisfactory to the board of directors" of the union, and subsequently tried to keep from the presses anyone who had "broken into the trade" after he was twenty-one years old. Both the income and the honor associated with the printer's art were thus to be reserved to those who elected to ply it when they first attained the age of productive manhood at fifteen or sixteen years old. Altogether Philadelphia's complete records of apprentices bound between October 1771 and October 1773 revealed 1,075 youths apprenticed to sixty-eight trades (including many girls indentured to learn "housewifery"). Ten percent of them were to learn the cordwainer's art, and the trades of tailor, mariner, carpenter, and cooper followed shoemaking in order of preference.

Sons of mechanics apprenticed to trades were supplemented by those of farmers who, for example, constituted the bulk of Massachusetts' supply of shoemakers, and in Baltimore by young slaves. The emancipation of northern slaves meant the eclipse of Negro apprenticeship in most urban trades elsewhere. Because the training of slave craftsmen had rarely been complete, freed Negro artisans, who faced intense animosity from white craftsmen and had lost the protection of their masters, rarely survived in positions where they could train apprentices of their own race, and even fewer whites would engage black youth for training. The influx of white farm boys to urban trades, on the other hand, was inhibited by that "desire of being an independent proprietor of land" which Alexander Hamilton believed would always keep small the numbers of those "who would be diverted from it towards manufacturers." Youths who did elect urban trades, furthermore, often fled their apprenticeships after only a year or two of service and, to the great distress of established journeymen, easily found employment as half-trained workmen at substandard wages. The supply of labor was thus rapidly increased at the expense of its quality. The founding of mechanics' institutes (vocational schools) in every major northern city in the 1820s bears witness to the breakdown of traditional apprenticeship training.

The fact remains that residents of rural areas in the Northeast were being lured toward the city, just as others were migrating westward, and frequently such migrants had been craftsmen, rather than (or as well as) farmers. In every decade between 1790 and 1840, the population of all four cities under review grew at a rate substantially above the 33 percent to 36 percent growth for the nation as a whole, with two exceptions: both Philadelphia and New York grew at less than the national rate between 1810 and 1820, and Baltimore's increase after 1820 was chronically below the national pace. This urbanization of native Americans was supplemented by the arrival of European immigrants, but the extent of the trans-oceanic contribution to the growth of these seaports is difficult to measure. Although newcomers to America totalled 400,000 between 1790 and 1830, with 1801–1807, 1816 and 1828–1830 being the years of greatest influx, the bulk of them came not to the American seaport but through it. It was the demand for farm laborers in the hinterland which produced, for example, the large scale trafficking in redemptioners Frances Wright witnessed in the Philadelphia of 1818.

Among the immigrants who tarried in the city, however, were many skilled mechanics. British emigrants and British trade union practices (complete to the oaths sworn over union scales and the trappings of secrecy necessitated in the old country by the Combination Acts but retained here as a matter of custom) showed up in every conspiracy trial of union journeymen. When the prosecutor charged Philadelphia cordwainers in 1805 with "crimes" committed by union members a decade earlier, the defense replied with only slight exaggeration that none of the journeymen on trial had been in America when those acts were committed. Stocking weavers in Germantown and Kensington outside of Philadelphia had almost all learned their trade in Leicester or Nottingham or the Rhineland. Linen weavers had poured out of northern Ireland in the early 1770s and again at the close of the American Revolution, many of them coming to the new republic. In 1784 alone 11,000 passengers embarked from Dublin, most of them emigrants of this type.

An extreme case of immigrants' providing an industry with its skilled labor was offered by the thousand or so carpet weavers in the country in the early 1830s, at least nine-tenths of whom were Scots, largely from Kilmarnock and Ayr. So well did these mechanics know each other that when sixty-three of them struck the Thompsonville Carpet Manufacturing Company in Connecticut, they quickly assembled, compiled from memory a list of the eleven other principal carpet manufactories in the nation, wrote personal letters to friends in each of them explaining the dispute, notified the Blue Bonnet Tavern in New York City, which served as the country's hiring hall for carpet weavers, to divert men from the struck plant, and dispatched an appeal to the *Old Countryman* in that city to warn off any Scots not reached by the other methods.

Such incidents suggest the hypothesis that America was then a land of opportunity for handicraftsmen whose skills were being undermined by the industrial revolution in England but still in high demand in the more backward American economy. True, the number of handloom weavers and stockingers working in England continued to grow rapidly down to 1820 and perhaps beyond, despite the unmistakeable deterioration of income and status in those trades. Many older craftsmen, Arthur Redford found, moved to manufacturing cities in England, there continuing to ply their obsolete trades while depending increasingly on the earnings of their factory-employed children. The Scottish carpet weavers brought to trial in Connecticut for their strike, however, were remarkably young men, twenty-two years of age or less. The presumption is that the craftsman-immigrant tended to be neither the daring innovator nor the veteran artisan who could not quit his obsolescent trade, but the mobile youth who spurned Briton's factory for the possibility of plying the (to him) preferable family trade in a new location.

This hypothesis is consistent with Hamilton's belief that "the disparity" between the "dearness of labor" in America and that in England was "much less in regard to artificers and manufacturers, than in regard to country labourers," a belief recently concurred in by H. J. Habakkuk and Stuart Bruchey. During the first two decades of the nineteenth century skilled tradesmen in England engaged in "hounourable work" (a high quality work not yet subjected to a division of labor and deterioration of apprenticeship standards) looked upon 30s. weekly ($7.50) as an expected income, while some earned £3 and over. Such a 30s. standard fell below the $8.25 of an American shoemaker or the $9 a more seasonal carpenter might ordinarily have expected when working at union standards by precisely the differential of 12 percent-20 percent in America's favor which J. Leander Bishop found for glass workers. True, American workmen paid considerably fewer taxes than their English counterparts, and as D. B. Warden observed of Philadelphia, "Smiths, shoemakers, weavers, and tailors have generally one or two acres of land, which afford pasture for a cow, fuel, and esculent plants." But such bucolic benefits were by no means unknown to English weavers, croppers, and shoemakers, most of whom still worked in their cottages in rural villages.

Far more extreme was the contrast between the American municipal or canal laborer's expectation of some $4.50 a week (often paid partly in board) and the earnings of the English casual laborer, which then ranged from perhaps 11s. weekly in cotton factories to 1s. a day for wheelbarrow men in Birmingham. Taking 10s. (i.e.,

$2.50) as good weekly pay for such laborers in the second decade of the century, the unskilled American enjoyed a premium of 80 percent over his British counterpart. That the wage differential was less rather than greater for the artisan than for casual labor is thus evident even without investigation of the real values of money wages in the two countries. Yet British craftsmen did migrate, spurred by the deteriorating conditions in their trades at home and lured, as one emigrant manual declared, by the openings in American trades left by "the strong emulation of the *cute* native Yankee to elevate himself above the common labour class."

Whether graduates of American or British apprenticeships, urban tradesmen were both geographically mobile enough and sufficiently well informed about the state of the labor market elsewhere to maintain rather uniform wage standards throughout the northeastern cities. When Philadelphia shoemakers demanded a schedule of prices based on $4 a pair for back strap boots in October 1805, they were aware that the New York union had established precisely that scale in March. Similarly, when Pittsburgh shoemakers unionized at the end of that decade, they quickly drove up their prices from 75 cents below the Philadelphia wage to parity with it — but when they sought a scale higher than Philadelphia's, they were roundly defeated by their masters. Both the New York and Washington societies of printers undertook — by correspondence with their counterparts in Philadelphia, Baltimore, Boston, and Albany — to establish uniform scales, and all these societies exchanged "rat lists" with each other, so that typographers who violated union rules and standards could not find refuge in other communities. At times employers cooperated with these efforts of the journeymen, as did master printers in New York in 1815, or, more dramatically, the master weavers of Baltimore, who in 1829 did everything in their power to ostracize a fellow employer for slashing his journeymen's wages below the city norm.

Although the mechanic was ranked by Tuckerman within the wage-earning classes, there is little evidence that prior to the 1830s he either identified himself with "the poor" or felt in any way alienated from the existing social order. Despite the absence from common American parlance of the rigid British distinction between "honourable" and "dishonourable" work, only the scale of the New York shoemakers out of all the union price lists which have been preserved from that period (mainly those of printers, shoemakers, tailors, and weavers) included a specified wage for coarse work, partially completed work, or the work of helpers. While the Pittsburgh shoemakers union did explicitly deem coarse work "out of society" and posed no objections to non-members performing such tasks, there is no such clear evidence from any of the seaport cities. It is remarkable, however, that the prosecutor in the New York shoemakers' trial, while conceding that many journeymen were not members, insisted that "all the best workmen were of the society." Similarly Philadelphia shoemakers considered themselves fully unionized between 1798 and 1804, when their society had 100 to 150 members, while the city directory for 1798 listed 292 shoemakers and cordwainers. A plausible inference is that cheap shoes for slaves and for auction sale, which did not appear in the union's scale of prices, were deliberately relegated to inferior workmen whom the society made no effort to recruit.

The mechanics proudly preserved an ideological heritage blended of Ben Franklin's maxims and Tom Paine's "rights of man." The best local legal talent defended their societies in the several conspiracy trials to which they were subjected, as witness Philadelphia's shoemakers enlisting Caesar Rodney, whom President Jefferson was soon to appoint Attorney General of the United States. When seventeen years earlier that city's mechanics had paraded with their masters in joyous celebration of the ratification of the federal constitution, they had borne such emblems as "the weavers' flag, a rampant lion in a green field, holding a shuttle in his dexter paw — motto — '*may the government* protect us,'" the boat builders' flag (atop the thirty-three foot schooner *Federal Union* drawn down Market Street for the occasion) bearing "an axe and an adze crossing each other — motto, 'by these we live,'" or the bricklayers' flag, with "the federal city rising out of a forest, workmen building it, and the sun illuminating it," motto, "*both buildings and rulers are the works of our hands.*'" At the close of the procession, bakers distributed bread to the poor, victuallers slew their "two stately oxen" and gave away the meat, and millers provided the needy with flour. The best the printers could do was to read the destitute a poem, but clearly the citizen craftsmen were dispensers, not recipients, of charity.

Very different was the outlook of the impoverished residents of the Rittenhouse Square vicinity, who petitioned the Philadelphia city council in 1830 to halt the dumping in the square of offal swept from neighboring streets, "which being in heaps, occasions numerous ponds of stagnant and putrescent water in the immediate spots, which in summer send forth pestilential vapours wafted by every breeze to the dwellings of your petitioners, whose only comfort, health, is thus destroyed." These poor argued that "being of the working class, their whole time is indispensably employed in various labour to maintain their families," so that sickness is "a scourge the most severe." Here was a group whose annual incomes ranged far closer to $200 than to $400 or $425 expected by craftsmen, a group who Reverend Tuckerman feared" have lived, and to a great extent are living, as a *caste* — cut off from those in more favoured circumstances; and doomed to find their pleasures, and sympathy in their suffering, alone among themselves."

The seaport poor were by no means a new phenomenon at the end of the 1820s. James Henretta has clearly traced their emergence in eighteenth-century Boston as a function of the growth of overseas commerce. He discovered from the Boston tax rolls of 1687 that only 14 percent of the adult male population of the city, that is, 188 men, were neither "dependent" nor owners of property. In contrast to them stood the 17 percent of the adult males who as servants, apprentices, or participants in family home enterprise were classified as dependent. The propertied classes numbered 1,036 (69 percent of the adult males) and included 521 poor craftsmen, 275 artisans of the "middling sort" with two or three journeymen apiece, and the wealthier tradesmen, professionals, and merchants. By 1771 only 10 percent of the adult males were dependent in the traditional sense, while 29 percent were neither dependent nor propertied. These were wage earners in the full meaning of the term, and while the city's population had doubled between the two counts, their number had increased fourfold. They ranged in occupation from seamen and longshoremen at one end of the scale to journeymen at the other, but, while the latter ranked close to the small property-holding mechanic, the division of wealth between the upper and lower halves of property owners was far sharper than had been the case in the seventeenth century.

Most day laborers participated directly in transportation and commerce. It was the demand for seamen, longshoremen, carters, and domestic servants which absorbed unskilled wage earners already in the eighteenth century. By the early nineteenth century, construction work, wood cutting, and road building employed many, while thousands of Philadelphia's poor, Mathew Carey found, "travel hundreds of miles in quest of employment on canals at 62½, 75 and 87½ cents per day, paying a dollar and a half or two dollars per week for their board, leaving families behind, depending on them for support." By 1830 Carey estimated "labourers, hodmen, seamstresses, families of workmen on canals and rail-roads" at 40 percent of the working classes and 25 percent of the total population of Philadelphia.

Many laborers reached the city from the farm by way of the sea. The merchant fleet of Massachusetts, wrote Samuel Eliot Morison, "was manned by successive waves of adventure-seeking boys, and officered by such of them as determined to make the sea their calling." The great majority on the crew lists professed "to be native-born Yankees, and probably were." Seamen would register with federal revenue agents after 1796 and receive, for a fee of 25 cents, papers certifying their United States citizenship. Between that year and 1812, 106,757 seamen collected their papers, and of them only 1,530, or 1.4 percent were naturalized citizens. The registrations reported for the years after 1808 were certainly still incomplete, for district revenue collectors were very tardy in submitting their reports to Washington. The fact that registration was heaviest in years such as 1797 and 1805, when the danger of British impressment was most severe, indicates that enrollment was never very thorough. These figures, nevertheless, can suggest the large number of native Americans who took to the sea.

So high were the rates of promotion, death, and desertion that the man who spent more than twelve years before the mast was rare indeed. No other occupation offered an unskilled farmboy so great an opportunity to rise quickly in wealth and standing — or to topple from yardarm into the cold Atlantic. Few seamen dwelt long in any port, but while ashore they augmented the local casual labor supply significantly. Illustrative of their role was young Charles Erskine, whose mother moved to Boston in the early 1820s after his father (a currier) had deserted her. Playing about the docks, Erskine heard the tales of sailors and through them was lured to sea. Between voyages he and his mates earned their keep ashore by whatever employment was available wherever they happened to be. He once helped construct an aqueduct in Washington and at another time worked in a Philadelphia hook and eye factory.

In marked contrast to the artisan's tendency to ply for life the trade he had learned in his adolescence, the laborer was the epitome of versatility. To move from the sea to canal digging to hod carrying to factory work was well within the realm of possibility. Many of the half-trained journeymen and "botches" who bedevilled mechanics' efforts to retain high quality and wage standards were of this sort. New England's first factory to use cotton spinning machinery, founded in Beverly, Massachusetts, in 1787, wasted precious quantities of material in training its workmen, then was driven close to ruin when it had to raise wages to prevent its partly-taught employees from deserting to rival firms. Mercifully, perhaps, the factory burned down in 1808. A happier experience with such labor was reported by a cotton mill near Providence, which employed fifty-three workers in the factory and 125 on putting-out by 1810. The owners, reported Albert Gallatin, at first suffered "in being put to much expense by English workmen, who pretended to much more knowledge in the business than they really possessed." But the phony Samuel Slaters were discharged, "and Americans, as apprentices, &c. are getting the art very fast," though the company did not anticipate dividends "for a considerable time."

The fact that machine operatives could be trained made the "factory controversy" of this period focus not on the fate of the workers, as was to be the case in the 1830s and 1840s, but on the potential impact of manufacturing upon the nation's supply of farm labor. Wages of farm hands, Henry Carey reported, were higher in the vicinity of the cities than in more rustic settings. Whether this differential in money wages was a sign of competition from urban employments or simply an indication that the market economy was more mature near the cities (that a smaller portion of the farm laborer's income was paid in kind and more in cash than was the case to the West) is not clear. Whichever it meant, advocates of governmental aid to manufactures from Coxe through Carey felt obliged to echo Hamilton's famous assurance that manufacturing would not attract able-bodied men away from the land, that it would rather "afford occasional and extra employment to industrious individuals and families," through which farmers could profit by the home produce of their wives and daughters, and provide steady employment for "persons who would otherwise be idle, and in many cases a burthen on the community," and render women and children "more useful, and the latter more early useful . . . than they should otherwise be."

At this period, therefore, it was impossible to speak of the factory labor force without directing attention to women, children, and charitable institutions. This was the case long before the mills of Lowell arose. Philadelphia's first large-scale use of spinning jennies was undertaken by the United Company of Philadelphia for Promoting American Manufactures, founded by patriotic subscriptions in 1775. By the late 1780s it employed 400 women, most of them recruited from the city's poor rolls. Despite the pride with which the Society displayed a jenny of eighty spindles in the Federal Procession of 1788, and boasted that the woman operating it was "a native of and instructed in this city," the company's building was destroyed by an arsonist only two years later. Newly-inaugurated President Washington found a similar labor force when he visited a Boston sail duck factory. Here pairs of little girls spun and wove flax from eight in the morning until six at night, but their demeanor favorably impressed the President, who described them as "daughters of decayed families" and "girls of character — none others are admitted."

Two decades later the Secretary of the Treasury reported that eighty-seven cotton mills then in operation or about to commence operations in the United States needed a labor force of about 500 men and 3,500 women and children. Such a work force was for Gallatin proof positive that manufacturing need not lure men from the farm. Tench Coxe agreed:

> Female aid in manufactures, which prevents the diversion of men and boys from agriculture, has greatly increased. Children are employed, as well as the infirm and the crippled. The assylums of the poor and unfortunate, and the penitentiaries of indiscretion and immorality are improved and aided by the employment and profits of manufactures.

The markets of seamstresses were especially crowded with unmarried and widowed women, not to speak of those whose husbands were "travelling" — in the informal divorce procedure of the day. When such women bid on sewing work, they competed with both married women trying to supplement their own families' meager incomes and recipients of work relief. While female operatives in Philadelphia factories earned two or three dollars a week in the 1820s, seamstresses rarely surpassed $1.25, and the city's home relief system helped keep those earnings low. In slack seasons so many women applied to the Provident Society and other charities for work to tide them over that the scale offered by almshouses became, during the 1820s, the standard price offered by private firms. Thus the U.S. War Department offered seamstresses 12½ cents a shirt, the very wage given by the Provident Society. In reply to a plea that such a price reduced the seamstresses "to the degradation of pauperism," the Secretary of War termed the subject "of such delicacy, and so intimately connected with the manufacturing interests, and the general prices of this kind of labour in the city of Philadelphia" that he dared not change his Department's practice.

While the seamstress stood with one foot in the poor house, this was not the case with the weaver, for in the urban areas most cloth was still put out to families with handlooms. The city and county of Philadelphia in 1809 produced 65,326 yards of cloth in its six factories on both hand and power looms, but its home production amounted to 233,232 yards. Furthermore, the spinning mills, while they continued to be staffed primarily by women and children, tended to free themselves by the second decade of the century from dependence on public charities. The reason is that unmarried women, widows, and orphaned families gravitated toward them by free choice.

Especially was this the case in New England, where the textile mill became a means of emancipation for the "maiden aunts" who lived with so many of the region's families. In Massachusetts the 1810 male population under the age of sixteen outnumbered females of the same age in the ratio of 104 to 100. Between the ages of sixteen and forty-five, however, the proportions were reversed. During the marrying season (ages sixteen through twenty-five) there were 103 women for every 100 men, but in the post twenty-six age of the spinster, women outnumbered men by a ratio of 107 to 100. And Massachusetts had 3,335 more women of that age than it had men. Theirs was the choice, at best, of boarding with parents, or a married sister, or entering a mill. Since the loss of males was a result of the westward movement, it would seem that, as far as New England's early textile industry is concerned, the famous "safety-valve" worked in reverse. The migration of men to the West created a surplus of female labor in the East.

Neither New York State nor Pennsylvania exhibited such an imbalance of the sexes, for both were receiving substantial immigration, and considerable westward movement still occurred within their boundaries. But within the cities of New York and Philadelphia free white women between the ages of sixteen and twenty-five sharply outnumbered the men of the same age. The New York ratio in 1820, for example, was 119 women to 100 men in that age bracket, while in Philadelphia women of this marriageable age outnumbered men 122 to 100. Similarly, the Boston ratio was 127 to 100, and that of Baltimore 108 to 100. Although the terrible toll of childbirth, among other hazards, more than corrected the balance of the sexes in all four cities after the age of twenty-six, each of the seaports was naturally provided with a sizeable force of women for whom there was no prospect of marriage and for whom entry into the labor market was a necessity.

Each of these groups of city workers of the pre-industrial epoch (journeymen mechanics, male laborers, and women) merits careful historical study. Little new work has been done in this area since David J. Saposs contributed his chapters to John R. Commons' *History of Labour in the United States* in 1917, and because of this deficiency the labor historian's view of this period has fallen seriously out of phase with that of the economic historian. For example, Saposs' contention that "the wages of the unskilled were going up while those of the skilled were kept down by the merchant-capitalist" in the century's first two decades finds no support in the wage data of this article or in recent economic studies.

The problem assumes considerable significance in the light of George Rogers Taylor's hypothesis that per capita income in America declined rather steadily between 1807 and the early 1830s. The impact of such a trend could logically have been different for mechanics, for factory operatives, for casual laborers, and for women sewing in their rented rooms. Only specific studies of particular groups of workers can yield conclusive data on the standard of living. Jackson Turner Main and James Henretta have shown that enough evidence exists in tax rolls, judicial records, and the press of the eighteenth century to enable the historian to reconstruct patterns of property and income distribution quite clearly. Their work challenges other historians to trace the evolution of these patterns in early nineteenth-century city life and to reduce their reliance on impressionistic evidence.

Still greater is the need for research into the cultural and intellectual life of the working classes of this period. We need to know what the urban poor expected of life, how they reacted to the commercial ethos of their cities, and how they conceived their relationship to the governing merchant elites. Were they, as some historians have recently portrayed the poor of Naples or London, simultaneously devoted to the traditional social order, aware of their power as a mob, confident the city would care for them in times of want, and, profoundly hostile toward the emerging impersonal and amoral market economy? Was it such a mentality which made some 200 assembled New York sailors, idled by the embargo, respond obediently when Mayor Marinus Willet commanded them to disperse, with assurances that the embargo was "the *Captain's Orders*," and that the city would "do everything possible for your relief"? Such questions cannot yet be answered because a fixation on the clash of "agrarian" and "industrial" values has distracted us from exploring pre-industrial urban values and customs.

Similarly American historians have yet to probe the culture of the American mechanic as, say, E. P. Thompson did for his British counterpart. Our concern has been either with the journeyman's economic circumstances (where there is still much to be learned) or with whether he voted for Andrew Jackson (and may we be spared that debate for a while). Because the mechanics were frequently organized and far more articulate than the urban poor, research into the mind of the journeyman should prove relatively easy. The ideas suggested in this article need careful testing, to begin with, and beyond them lie several major issues for research. How open was economic mobility for the journeymen, and what changes did the post-Revolutionary generation experience in this regard? Why did this class provide most of the country's early nineteenth-century adherents to deism, and just how widespread and significant was infidelity among them? What new circumstances made craftsmen in every major city between 1827 and 1837 expand the horizons of their concern beyond the limits of their own trades, create city Trades' Unions as new institutions to fuse the efforts of the several crafts, undertake unprecedented united action with the unskilled laborers, giving rise to something worthy of the name labor movement?

These problems suggest that we have rushed ahead to evaluate labor's response to industrialism without first ascertaining labor's pre-industrial behavior and attitudes. In exploring the shock of change after the Civil War our attention has been directed half a century too late, and our concern with the fate of agrarian values has led us to ignore the impact of the spreading factory system on the cultural heritage of urban America's lower orders.

The Frontier and American Society

One of the most impressive attempts to explain the special qualities of America and Americans was the frontier thesis of Frederick Jackson Turner. Long before Turner, observers of the United States had assigned a distinctive place to the West in the molding of American thought and institutions. But the brilliant analysis by Turner of that role in his 1893 paper "On the Significance of the Frontier in American History" raised the observations of commentators to the level of a powerful theory and profoundly influenced the way both historians and laymen thought about the American past.

Turner's thesis was that "the existence of an area of free land, its continuous recession, and the advance of American settlement westward, explain American development." This central fact explained American politics, for democracy, in its various manifestations, came from the frontier. It explained American affluence and social stability, for the West was a land of economic opportunity and a "safety valve" for the deprived and the unsuccessful. It explained American individualism, for in the new western communities each man had only himself to rely on for safety and survival. All these traits of character and mind and these institutional distinctions were what made America exceptional and what, Turner might well have said, made America better.

Turner's seminal essay, and its elaboration in a dozen or so articles and a number of books, swept away the earlier emphasis by historians on the continuities between America and the European, particularly the Anglo-Saxon, heritage. Even during his lifetime, Turner was not unchallenged, but at least half of the historians of the country, for the first thirty years of this century, might be labeled "Turner's disciples." During these years the history of the West and the frontier flourished, and analyses of American politics emphasizing East–West conflict became standard elements in textbooks. In the 1930s, Turner went into eclipse. The scholars' disenchantment with capitalism and individualism during the depression made them skeptical of Turner's belief in American uniqueness. They subjected his insights to close scrutiny and often found them seriously wanting. Democracy did not seem to flow from the West; universal manhood suffrage came earlier in the East. The safety valve did not operate; farm-making costs were too high for the unemployed labor of the cities to take advantage of unoccupied land. Individualism was not particularly western; the West often demanded cooperation and conformity for survival.

One of Turner's most persistent and intelligent followers is Ray Allen Billington of the Huntington Library in San Marino, California. Billington is by no means an uncritical disciple. He finds much in Turner's concept of frontier individualism that is exaggerated and simplistic. On the other hand, he sees more merit in the picture of the West as egalitarian and mobile, a region where men did not defer to rank and wealth, and where both were within grasp of the able and the lucky. In the end, he concludes, America has still not entirely lost some of the exceptional qualities it inherited from its frontier past.

FOR FURTHER READING:

BILLINGTON, RAY ALLEN. *America's Frontier Heritage.* New York: Holt, Rinehart & Winston, 1967.*
SMITH, HENRY NASH. *Virgin Land: The American West as Symbol and Myth.* New York: Random House, Vintage Books, 1957.*
TURNER, FREDERICK JACKSON. *On the Significance of the Frontier in American History.* New York: Frederick Ungar Publishing Co., 1963.*

Asterisk denotes paperback edition.

Frontier Democracy: Social Aspects

RAY ALLEN BILLINGTON

To understand the uniqueness of *American* democracy we must consider not only the form of government and the extent of popular participation, but the way in which the people of the United States view government and society as a whole. Do they regard the state as the master or servant of its citizens? Do they consider their fellow men as equals, or as inferiors and superiors? In seeking answers to these questions, our concern is not with what *is,* but with what is *thought* to be. If the image of the social order common among Americans differs from that usual among Europeans, and if the differences can be explained by the pioneering experience, we can conclude that the frontier has altered the national character as well as institutions.

In this quest, two concepts are especially important: that of "individualism" and that of "equality." Visitors from abroad feel that the people of the United States have endowed these words with distinctive meanings. In no other nation is the equality of all men so loudly proclaimed; in no other country is the right of individual self-assertion (within certain areas) so stoutly defended. Travelers have also noted the relationship between the two concepts. Because all men are judged to be equal, all are assured the same freedom of individual expression. "They are apt to imagine," wrote Alexis de Tocqueville in the early nineteenth century, "that their whole destiny is in their own hands." Tocqueville believed that this attitude was dangerous, threatening as it did the atomization of society.

His fears were groundless, for even as he wrote conformity was displacing individualism as a national cult, save in one important aspect. To Ralph Waldo Emerson and Henry David Thoreau society may have been the sum of atomized individuals, but to the generations that followed the emergence of an industrial-urban complex that made social interdependence essential to survival was one of the stark realities of life. In this integrated society, the fact of individualism, if not the *theory* of individualism, was gradually altered. In theory individualism meant the right of every person to make his own decisions and choices without regard to their effect on the

---

Source: Ray Allen Billington, *America's Frontier Heritage* (New York: Holt, Rinehart & Winston, 1966), chap. 7, "Frontier Democracy: Social Aspects," pp. 139–157.

social group. In practice, this was acceptable only in the sphere of economic activity. In that realm, a sink-or-swim philosophy gained acceptance and still prevails. If a man makes a wrong decision, and a business fails or a job is lost, no one is to blame but the person himself. If his decision is correct and he does well, we believe that he should be rewarded by advancement to positions of ever higher prestige. The direction in which he moves is his responsibility alone; the successful person enjoys a sense of his own greatness quite unrelated to those around him. Individualism in the economic world seems fair to Americans as long as equal and plentiful opportunity exists for all, and who can doubt its existence in a land of abundance? Social-security systems, unemployment benefits, Medicare, and a host of other security measures today challenge the fact of economic individualism, but the theory is still vigorously defended.

Individualism in its distinctly American usage does not apply to the noneconomic world. It grants no license for freedom of personal expression; no respectable citizen would dream of exhibiting a unique personality in the clothes that he wears, the manners he adopts, or the behavior that he exhibits in public. The Frenchman instinctively distrusts the outsider and shuns cooperation; the American instinctively follows the herd. "Americans," observed Peter Ustinov, "are always attempting to run away from conformity, but unfortunately they always start running in the same direction." Twentieth-century travelers have pointed out the monotonous uniformity of the streets, the towns, the cities, of the United States. "Not a single American," wrote one, "can distinguish Main Street in one town from Main Street in one of hundreds of others." Let a Hollywood actress or a spotlighted pop singer adopt a new hair style and women rush to their hairdressers to imitate her. Let a public figure appear in a novel hat, or trousers, or haircut, and men fall into line. Even political behavior is regimented, as Americans dutifully cast their ballots for Democratic or Republican candidates rather than for the dozens of parties that range across the political spectrum in Europe. And woe unto the American who defends a belief that is currently unpopular, either of the extreme left or the extreme right.

The oft-defended individualism of the United States is no guarantee of the individual's freedom of expression, but is manifested in two ways, each related to the other. One is a relative lack of respect for the law; the typical American is more inclined to flaunt regulations, or to whittle a few illegal dollars from his income tax, than his British cousins. The other is a resentment of governmental meddling in private affairs. Some Americans preached individual freedom when the Eighteenth Amendment told them what not to drink, and the bootleggers' paradise of the 1920s was the result. Some raised an umbrella of "rugged American individualism" over their heads when the regulatory measures of Progressivism or the New Deal threatened to interfere with their free use of property. Some, living in the Southern states, hoisted the banner of states' rights when federal agencies told them to integrate their schools, but what they really defended was the right of every individual to like or dislike persons of his own choice, whatever the effect on society. All were proclaiming their defiance of the government, and demanding that it cease telling them how to live or manage their affairs. The American is willing to conform if he personally decides to conform, as he does in adopting the style of his clothes or the brand of popular music that he will enjoy. But the American is not willing to allow his elected representatives to decide that conformity is for him. This is the essential difference between the individualism of the United States and that of Europe.

As long as we dwell in the realm of theory, nothing could be easier than to link this distinctly American faith with the frontier experience. The modern American believes that each person shall be allowed to rise or fall in the workaday world as his own grit and ability decrees; he also clings to the belief that the government should not interfere. Such a system could operate only in a land of equal opportunity, where the dispossessed could begin life anew without too much difficulty, where new jobs were being created to absorb an expanding population, and where resources were so abundant that all could share in their wealth without governmental intervention in the role of umpire. Only in frontier America did this combination of beatitudes exist. Hence American individualism is the product of the frontiering experience. So men reasoned in the nineteenth century, and so many believe today.

This myth has been fastened on the public mind by the plausibility of logic. Nothing is more obvious than that the pioneer would resent social controls, or that he would be able to escape dependence on society. He had, after all, fled his fellows to battle the wilderness alone. In his new home the solitude in which he lived, the vastness of the world about him, and the assurance that he acquired as he combatted nature, contributed to a spirit of self-reliance that was universal among pioneers. This was accentuated by the richness of the land, and the equally shared opportunity to exploit those riches. Where all were potential millionaires, property assumed a new importance, even to the propertyless. Men on the frontier, Americans of the nineteenth century believed, were so confident of affluence that they needed no help from society and wanted no meddling by society. "Here," wrote a visitor to the Colorado mines, "a man looks upon the wealth of others as held in trust for himself, and will suffer no diminution of its sanctity." This attitude fostered rugged American individualism in its truly American sense.

Just as persuasive was the frequent testimony of travelers and Westerners that the West actually was a land of unbridled liberty where men behaved according to the dictates of their consciences, and devil take their neighbors. "Liberty here," wrote an Englishman from the Kentucky backwoods, "means to do each as he pleases, to care for nothing and nobody." This was natural in the borderlands, where men were free to shape the course of their lives without nearby neighbors inflicting their wills or watchful officials meddling in their affairs. There every man was king, and kings could rule themselves. When passengers on a keelboat tried to stop a frontiersman from singing on the Sabbath they were heatedly informed that they were in a "land of liberty" and had no right to interfere. A recruit among the fur trappers of the Rocky Mountain country was told by an old-timer that he had only to mind his own affairs to get along. "If you see a man's mule running off," the newcomer was advised, "don't stop it — let it go to the devil; it isn't yourn. If his possibles sack falls off, don't tell him of it; He'll find it out." A pioneer who told a visitor that he was moving from Arkansas to Texas because he "had heern there was no sich thing as a government there, and not one varmint of a lawyer in the *hull* place" only personified what the United States believed to be the spirit of the whole frontier.

This nineteenth-century image of the West perpetuated the belief that the pioneer was opposed to all governmental regulation of economic activity. If steamboats had accidents that killed hundreds of persons yearly, nothing should be done, for steamboats were the lifeblood of the Mississippi Valley, and a few lives were a cheap price to pay for the economic activity that they fostered. If speculators absorbed the best lands, or miners appropriated mineral wealth, or lumbermen stripped away the forests, or "Sooners" illegally usurped the prime acreage in land openings, the social losses were insignificant compared to the benefits that accrued when the free-enterprise spirit was unleashed amidst the West's resources. These were the tales spread across the nation by the frontiersmen and their visitors, until they became a part of the nation's folklore. The frontier was a land of individualism, and American individualism was its natural offspring. This was a myth accepted throughout the nineteenth century and beyond.

Actually, the legend of frontier individualism rested on what people thought should be true, rather than what was true. The West was in truth an area where cooperation was just as essential as in the more thickly settled East. The danger of Indian attack, the joint efforts needed to clear the forests or break the prairie sod, the community of labor required for the variety of enterprises necessary in establishing a settlement, all decreed that new communities be occupied by groups, and never by solitary individuals. "In a young country," noted a visiting Englishman, "they must assist each other, if they wish to be assisted themselves — and there always will be a mutual dependence." Alexis de Tocqueville expressed nothing less than the truth when he observed that "In no country in the world has the principle of association been more successfully used, or applied to a greater multitude of objects, than in America."

This "principle of association" was more essential on the frontier than in the East. Cooperative enterprise is instinctive among all groups, even of the most primitive tribesmen, for habits of mutual dependence developed by family life during infancy are extended as people realize that the benefits of joint activity compensate for the work involved. Cooperation is normal within every in-group, but accentuates when the in-group is in conflict with an out-group and group solidarity is strengthened. This was the situation in frontier communities, where conflicts with Indians, with raw nature, and with dominating Easterners heightened the spirit of interdependence. In the West social cohesiveness, standardized behavior, and restrictive limitations on individual freedom were more acceptable than in the East.

So closely knit were pioneer groups that privacy of person or mind was virtually unattainable. Where neighbors were relatively few and newcomers a treasured rarity, every stranger was of rapt interest and a heaven sent opportunity to relieve the tedium of existence. "You are in a house of glass," complained one annoyed traveler as he endured the probing of the frontiersmen; another added that "privacy, either in eating, sleeping, conversation, or government, seems quite unknown, and unknowable." So prevailing was the community spirit that no one dared express individuality; people lived and dressed and thought exactly alike. "Whoever ventures to differ essentially from the mass," recorded a newcomer to the Michigan frontier, "is sure to become the object of unkind feeling, even without supposing any bitter personal animosity." And Charles Dickens, vitriolic as usual in his impressions of the Mississippi Valley pioneers, complained of "such a deadly, leaden people; such systematic plodding weary insupportable heaviness." These may have been exaggerations, but they were accurate in the over-all estimate of the spirit of cohesiveness existing in pioneer communities. Amidst the anonymity of a city, a person might dare to be different; amidst the intimacy of the frontier, he did not.

Much of this spirit was rooted in the stark realities of backwoods life, for cooperation was as essential to survival as a "Kentucky" rifle or a Colt revolver. Men went west in groups to minimize the Indian danger and the hardships of travel. When the journey was long and difficult, they organized a walking republic, complete with administrative and judicial officials to whom they delegated needed authority. As soon as they reached their destination they provided for the common defense by building a blockhouse or forming a militia company. These log or adobe forts became the centers of neighborhood life, especially in time of danger when the whole community "forted up" and shared guard duty until the threat passed. "Their common security," a pioneer told a traveler, "locked them in amity." Years after the times of danger a frontiersman remembered the pleasure they had provided because "we were so kind and friendly to one another." Commonly shared perils were a cohesive force among the homesteaders of the Great Plains no less than among earlier pioneers, for there grass fires, grasshopper invasions, and cattle wars banded the people together to combat mutual enemies. Any who refused to share were banished as traitors to society; there was no place for the uncooperative eccentric in a land where joint effort was the key to survival.

Cooperation was just as essential in times of peace as in times of war. Needed goods were imported by mutually owned caravans. Neighbors assisted in the "cabin raisings" and "barn raisings" that provided every newcomer with a home, and in the "logrollings" that helped him clear his fields. They joined in "corn huskings" and "quilting bees" and "fulling parties" where newly woven cloth was prepared for the housewife's needle. Scarce an activity in a frontier community that did not lend itself to neighborhood enterprise; records of pioneer settlements bristle with accounts of spinning parties, goose pickings, apple parings, rag cuttings, carpet tackings, wool pickings, and a dozen more. "A life in the woods," observed a visitor from Britain, "teaches many lessons, and this among the rest, that you must both give assistance to your neighbor, and receive it in return, without either grudging or pouting." Little wonder that students of the frontier refer to the "principle of mutuality" when speaking of life in the West.

The community benefited no less than individuals from mutual enterprise, because the necessity of common labor for society's good was cheerfully accepted as a part of pioneer life. Was a new church required, or a new school to be built, all hands turned out with axes and adzes to buckle to the task. "The neighbors divided themselves into choppers, hewers, carpenters, and masons," recalled an Indiana settler. "Those who found it impossible to report for duty might pay an equivalent in nails, boards, or other materials." When a road was to be constructed, or a bridge thrown across a stream, all were expected to help, since on the frontier division of labor was little known. Communities organized "Claim Clubs" to guard land from or for speculators, and in the Great Plains country recruited members to drive cattle from planted fields. Pioneer farmers, wherever they lived, were not so wedded to individualism that they would scorn help when help was needed.

Even these crown princes of individualism, the ranchers and miners, depended far more on joint effort than on self-prowess. Cattlemen on the Great Plains lost no time in forming associations that not only supervised the semiannual roundups, but that seriously restricted private enterprise by regulating pasturage on the open range. Community activity also quickened in time of emergency, furnishing men and horses to hunt down herds scattered by fire or drought. Cowboys as well as ranchers recognized the value of group activity; in 1883 some 325 in Texas organized to demand a $20 monthly raise, which they won after striking five ranches at roundup time. So did miners. The lone prospector is a figure from fiction rather than reality, for no single man could live long in the rugged mountain country of the early West. Most prospecting was done in groups of five to twenty men, usually well-mounted and provisioned, and led by a miner sufficiently versed in geology that no time was wasted on unlikely spots. Mining was never an individual enterprise, but was conducted by partners or teams who divided the labor and shared the profits. The rugged individualist, defending his claim with a six-shooter, had no place in the real Far West. "The Americans," wrote a Scottish visitor to the California gold fields, "have a very great advantage, for . . . they are certainly of all people in the world the most prompt to organize and combine to carry out a common object."

On all frontiers community effort found particular expression in law enforcement. Renegades from society posed a problem in new settlements, attracted as they were by the hope of quick wealth and the absence of machinery to administer justice, but when they became sufficiently numerous to threaten life and property, the sober citizens banded together to meet the situation head on. Known variously as Regulators or the Regulation in the forested regions, as Anti-Horse-Thief Associations on the Great Plains, and as Vigilantes in the Far West, they served as law officers, courts, and executioners, rounding up the worst offenders, subjecting them to a summary trial, and either hanging them to the nearest tree or banishing them from the community. So effective were they that in one California mining district 500 miles long, occupied by a hundred thousand turbulent men who had riches to tempt the outlaw but neither government nor locks as protection, "there was," noted a visitor in 1850, "as much security of life and property as in any part of the Union." This security was won at a grim price; vigilantes sometimes degenerated into lynching mobs that took the life of many an innocent man. Yet the readiness of frontiersmen to cooperate for protection, and their instinctive skill in organizing, underlines the myth of frontier individualism.

This was made even more obvious by the willingness of pioneers to accept governmental regulations that might have aroused protests in eastern cities. Blue laws were commonplace in many areas, restricting private behavior in a manner reminiscent of seventeenth-century Boston. Ohio in 1816 levied heavy fines for swearing by God, Christ, or the Holy Ghost; shooting bullets across a stream; and running horses in towns. Still heavier penalties awaited anyone guilty of arranging a puppet show, wire dancing, or tumbling. Illinois decreed a fine of $25 for any person selling cards, dice, or billiard balls. Towns studded their statute books with laws forbidding the playing of ninepins, serenading, or making a noise with "drums, fifes, horns, pans, kettles or with anything whatsoever." Frontiersmen accepted infringements on individual freedom needed to protect the community against gambling, time-wasting entertainment, or sleep-disturbing noise, just as had the Puritans.

Less well known was the willingness of the pioneers to adopt laws governing economic behavior, at least in the infant urban communities of the Midwest. Citizens were required to sweep the streets before their doors, and to conform to certain standards in advertising their products. Trade was regulated more exactingly than in the East, because firm measures were necessary in near-monopoly situations to protect the uncertain food supply, prevent speculative pricing in times of shortage, and force licensed merchants to compete honestly with each other. Chicago confined the sale of meats and vegetables to certain times and places where they could be inspected to protect the public health. Other pioneer cities fixed the price of bread, regulated fees of hackmen and carters, and regularly checked the accuracy of weights and measures. Not even private property was too sanctified to escape controls designed for the public good.

Regulation by state and national agencies was equally acceptable to the pioneer — when he judged the laws to be in his own interest. Texas in 1883 set up machinery to control railroad rates and force roads to haul cars of their competitors, although such a measure invaded property rights that had been held sacred. Texan cattlemen welcomed laws governing the conduct of drovers on the "long drives" to the Kansas railroads, even though their own liberties were threatened. A few years later the embattled farmers of the Great Plains raised the banner of Populism to demand governmental regulation of the railroads, a "socialistic" parcel post service, and the curbing of monopolies. To the frontier-oriented Westerner, the government could be a valuable ally as readily as a dangerous enemy, and should be viewed in either light as the immediate situation dictated.

On the basis of this analysis of Western opinion, we can now seek answers to two questions: Was frontier individualism a myth, and if not, how did it differ from traditional individualism? One conclusion is obvious: in the social realm the pioneer was a complete traditionalist, leaning on the community no less than his city cousins. Cooperation with his neighbors was commonplace for defense, the accomplishment of essential pioneering tasks, law enforcement, and a host of other necessities. In the economic realm the frontiersman's attitudes were less sharply defined. Consistency was not one of his sins, he favored regulation that seemed beneficial to his interests, and opposed regulation that threatened immediate or potential profits. His views were, in other words, comparable to those of Eastern business leaders who demanded from the government protective tariffs, railroad land grants, and federal subsidies, while mouthing the virtues of "rugged individualism."

Yet in one sense, the frontiersman moved somewhat beyond his counterparts in the East. He was, to a unique degree, living in a land where everyone was a real or potential capitalist. Nowhere could a stake in society be more easily obtained, and nowhere was the belief that this was possible more strongly entrenched. Moreover the frontier was developed largely by capital imported from the seaboard or from Europe. The fur trade, mining, and cattle raising prospered only because a flow of money from the East and abroad made prosperity possible. "The real peculiarity of our present Pacific civilization," wrote the editor of the *Overland Monthly* in 1883, "is that it is, perhaps, the most completely realized embodiment of the purely commercial civilization on the face of the earth." Dependent as they were on this flow of capital, and certain as they were that the humblest tenant farmers would someday enjoy wealth, Westerners were even more acutely conscious of the value of private property than Easterners, and more grimly determined to defend their right to use property as they wished. They would favor regulatory measures needed to attract capital or assure a healthy return on investments, but they would oppose laws that threatened profits even more vigorously than Easterners.

The frontiersmen, then, were opportunists rather than consistent theorists, but to an even greater degree than the capitalists of the seaboard. They had to be. Gambling against an unpredictable nature, they were willing to follow any path that promised success. If their ends could be achieved by individualistic effort, they preached individualism. If, more commonly, cooperative labor was necessary, or the use of governmental controls, they showed no reluctance in approving these devices. Their purpose was to make a profit, not prove a political theory, and their views swung with the circumstances. Yet the widespread property holdings in the West, and the belief that every man would achieve affluence, inclined the Westerner to insist on his right to profits somewhat more stridently than others. His voice spoke for individualism louder than that of his fellows, even though he was equally willing to find haven in cooperation when danger threatened or need decreed.

The rural Westerner's inclination toward individualism was strengthened by the fact that except in periods of danger or disaster he was somewhat less integrated into society than a city dweller, especially after the frontier on which he lived had passed its pioneer stage. The Easterner, living in a land where the economy was based on division of labor, was only a cog in a machine that must keep on operating if he were to survive. The Westerner, even though he leaned on his neighbors for defense and cabin raisings and husking parties, was relatively more self-sufficient. He harbored the belief that his self-sufficiency would increase, knowing that his own abilities would assure him a prosperous future as he exploited the natural resources about him. He might need government help to regulate rates of railroads that carried his grain to market or prices of manufacturers who sold him his implements, but he wanted no government interference with his freedom as he followed the road to riches.

To this extent, the frontiersman was an individualist, and his brand of individualism was remarkably like that which has persisted in the United States as a whole. The American follows the herd in his social habits, and he is eager to accept government aid that promises benefits to his business. But he is loudest in protest when regulatory measures threaten his profits or his economic freedom. Individualism, in the uniquely American sense, does seem to duplicate the individualism of the pioneer.

Basically, frontier individualism stemmed from the belief that all men were equal (excluding Negroes, Indians, Orientals, and other minority groups), and that all should have a chance to prove their personal capabilities without restraint from society. This seemed fair in a land of plenty, where superabundant opportunity allowed each to rise or fall to his proper level as long as governments did not meddle. Faith in the equality of men was the great common creed of the West. Only an understanding of the depth of this belief can reveal the true nature of social democracy on successive frontiers.

To European visitors, this was the most unique feature of Western life and thought: the attitude that set that region apart from Europe or the East. "There is nothing in America," wrote one, "that strikes a foreigner so much as the real republican equality existing in the Western States, which border on the wilderness." The whole attitude of the people was different; calmly confident of their own future, they looked on all men as their peers and acted accordingly. One Westerner who defined the frontier as a region where a poor man could enter a rich man's house without feeling uneasy or unequal was not far astray. Menial subservience was just as unpopular there as haughty superiority. Dame Shirley, writing from the California gold fields, felt the "I'm as good as you are" spirit all about her, and believed that only an American frontiersman could

> Enter a palace with his old felt hat on —
> To address the King with the title of Mister,
> And ask the price of the throne he sat on.

Everywhere men of all ranks exuded that easy air of confidence that went with complete self-assurance, meeting travelers on terms of equality that charmed those democratically inclined and shocked those of opposite prejudice. "The wealthy man assumes nothing to himself on account of his wealth," marveled one, "and the poor man feels no debasement on account of his poverty, and every man stands on his own individual merits." The spirit of Western democracy was captured by a cowboy addressing a disagreeable scion of British nobility: "You may be a son of a lord back in England, but that ain't what you are out here."

In the give and take of daily life, Western egalitarianism was expressed in the general refusal to recognize the class lines that were forming in every community. Some of the self-proclaimed "better sort" might hold themselves aloof and put on aristocratic airs, but they were atypical of the great mass of the people. The majority, in evaluating those about them, applied value judgments that differed from those in communities where tradition played a stronger role. Men were weighed on their present and future contributions to society, with total disregard for their background. Each played a role in the developing social order, and as long as he played it well he was respected. "To be useful is here the ruling principle," wrote a Swedish visitor to the West; "it is immaterial what one does so long as he is respected and does his work efficiently." Drones and aristocratic idlers were not bearing their fair share and were outcasts; men of menial rank were contributing to the community welfare and were respected. "There is in the West," noted an unusually acute observer during the 1830s, "a real equality, not merely an equality to talk about, an equality on paper; everybody that has on a decent coat is a gentleman."

Contemporaries speculated often on the reasons for frontier social democracy. Most agreed that the burgeoning Western economy was basically responsible, offering as it did a chance for the lowliest to acquire prestige through accumulated wealth. All had an equal chance to improve themselves, and so all should be treated as equals; conversely, the servant who believed that he would someday be a millionaire saw no reason to be servile to his temporary betters. This was common sense, since every new community boasted dozens of living examples of rags-to-riches success: the tenant farmer who was now a county judge, the mechanic newly elected to the legislature, the farmer grown rich by the sale of lands. As a British traveler saw, "the means of subsistence being so easy in the country, and their dependence on each other consequently so trifling, that spirit of servility to those about them so prevalent in European manners, is wholly unknown to them." Why be servile when the man above today might be the man below tomorrow? Why cling to traditional views of rank when the heir apparent to a British earldom could be seen mowing hay, assisted by two sons of a viscount, while nearby the brother of an earl was feeding grain into a threshing machine? Clearly standards on the frontier were different, and equality more nearly a fact of life.

The common level of wealth encouraged this spirit, for while differences did exist, the gulf between rich and poor was relatively less in frontier regions than in older societies. Poverty was rare in pioneer communities that had graduated from the backwoods stage; one governor complained that the number of dependent paupers in his state was "scarcely sufficient to give exercise to the virtue of charity in individuals." Wealth might and did exist on rural frontiers, but its presence was less obvious than in the East, for money would buy little but land and land was available to all. Ostentatious spending existed but was uncommon, partly because luxuries and leisure were largely unavailable, partly because it would breed hostility in neighbors who resented display. "Their wealth," it was observed, "does very little in the way of purchasing even the outward signs of respect; and as to *adulation*, it is not to be purchased with love or money." This leveling process underlined the sense of equality that was so typical of the frontier.

It was further emphasized by the fact that on the newer frontiers rich and poor lived, dressed, and acted much more alike than in the East. Most owned their own houses, though some might be of logs and some of bricks. Most dressed in homespun clothes and shunned the powdered wigs and knee breeches that were the badge of the gentry in the early nineteenth century; travelers frequently complained that it was impossible to distinguish the well-born from the lowly by the garments they wore. Most bore themselves proudly, scorning the humble mien that marked the lower classes in Europe. "The clumsy gait and bent body of our peasant is hardly ever seen here," wrote an Englishman from Kentucky in 1819; "every one walks erect and easy." When people looked and acted alike, as they did along the frontiers, treating them alike came naturally.

No less important in fanning the spirit of egalitarianism was the newness of the West, and the lack of traditional aristocratic standards there. No entrenched gentry governed social intercourse, setting the practices of those below them and closing their ranks against newcomers. Those who rose in station did not have to surmount the barrier of learning new customs as do those achieving higher status today, for conventions, deferences, and distinctions were rare among the "tree-destroying sovereigns" of the West. A man's ancestry and prior history were less important than the contribution that he could make to a new society badly in need of manpower. One Westerner who remarked: "It's what's above ground, not what's under, that we think on," and another who added: "Not 'What has he done in the East?' but 'What does he intend to do in Kansas and for Kansas?'" summed up the reasons for much of the social democracy that thrived along the frontiers.

This combination of causal forces — economic equality, commonly shared living standards, and the absence of traditional aristocratic values — enshrined belief in equality as the common faith of Western society. Class distinctions did exist, of course; innate differences in talent, ambition, and skill divided the various strata at an early stage in the evolution of every Western community. But relatively, these distinctions played a lesser role in the West than in the East. Instead belief in equality compelled frontiersmen to uplift the lowly and degrade the superior as they sought a common democratic level.

Elevation of the lowly was most commonly expressed by refusal to use terms designating class distinctions. Every man on the frontier, whatever his status in life, was a "gentleman," and every woman a "lady." Travelers from older societies were frequently amused to find the ragged wagoner or the ill-kempt seller of old bones addressed in this fashion; one who asked a tavern keeper in an infant settlement in New York to find his coachman was delighted when that worthy called out: "Where is the gentleman that brought this man here?" "Ladies" were as carelessly designated; one traveling in the West might hear, as did Mrs. Trollope, references to "the lady over the way that takes in washing," or "that there lady, out by the Gulley, what is making dip-candles." If titles could serve as social escalators, no one on the frontiers need stay long in menial ranks.

The leveling spirit of Western democracy sought not only to elevate the lowly but also to dethrone the elite. Any attempt at "putting on airs," was certain to be met with rude reminders of the equality of all men. New settlers were warned by guidebooks to mingle freely and familiarly with neighbors, and above all to pretend no superiority, if they wished to be accepted. They were told that nothing ruined a man's chances on the frontier so fatally as a suspicion of pride, which, once established, would ruin his reputation. "The cry of 'Mad Dog,'" wrote a Michigan pioneer, "is not more surely destructive. Travelers were also instructed to dress in simple fashion, and to avoid display in their clothes or their speech; those garbed as mechanics risked insults far less than those dressed as gentlemen. Those who failed to heed these warnings might be greeted with such remarks as: "Hold on, tha'r, stranger! When ye go through this yer town, go slow, so folks kin take you in," or in dry tones: "Mister, how much do you ask for it?" "For what, sir?" "Well, for the town; you look as though you owned it." One English newcomer who asked to be addressed as "Esquire" found that within a few days not only his host but the hired hands were calling him "Charlie"; another had the brass buttons unceremoniously ripped from his coat by a frontiersman who objected to such display. Texas rangers gambled or gave away the fancy uniforms issued to them, and stole the gold-braided suits of officers so that these aristocratic evidences of rank would not be seen. "Superiority," observed an English visitor, "is yielded to men of acknowledged talent alone."

Outward signs of social snobbery might arouse resentment in the West, but so did any conduct that seemed to suggest superiority. Families with sizable incomes found themselves better accepted if they lived and dressed as simply as their poorest neighbors; politicians soon realized that for success they must insist on being addressed as "Mister" or "Governor," and not as "Excellency." Even such a born-to-the-purple native aristocrat as Theodore Roosevelt took pains to understate his wealth and ancestry when on his Dakota ranch. When Colonel Thomas Dabney appeared at a frontier cabin raising in the Southwest with twenty slaves to do his work he was ostracized by the community; when a traveler had the good sense to dispose of expensive luggage, he was at last accepted on friendly terms. Natives and visitors alike learned that in the West refusal to drink with a stranger was interpreted as a sign of social superiority; unless they could convince their would-be hosts that they had "sworn off," even redeye whisky was preferable to the trouble that followed if word spread that they were "too good" for the community.

So strong was the spirit of equality along the frontiers that any deviation was met with resentment that was sometimes carried to ludicrous ends. Frontier housewives found themselves in disfavor if they kept their homes neater or cleaner than those of their neighbors; one who had waited three years for her first caller was told: "I woulda come before but I heard you had Brussels carpet on the floor." Another who offered to lend teaspoons for a party was rudely informed that no such luxuries were wanted, for the guests would not be used to them. Even those with a few choice possessions apologized; carpets were excused as "*one* way to hide the dirt," a mahogany table as "dreadful plaguy to scour," and kitchen conveniences as "lumberin' up the house for nothin'." When an Englishman remonstrated about the lack of ceremony in Western life he was told: "Yes, that may be quite necessary in England, in order to overawe a parcel of ignorant creatures, who have no share in making the laws; but with us a man's a man, whether he have a silk gown on him or not." The spirit of Western social democracy could have found no more eloquent expression than that.

In practice this spirit found its most outspoken expression in the attitude of hired workers. A "servant" in the traditional sense was impossible to find in the West because any form of servility was demeaning and hence intolerable; some of the most wealthy hosts and hostesses interrupted their dinner parties to wait on table or busy themselves in the kitchen. When servants could be drafted from the ranks of newly arrived immigrants or the families of less well-to-do pioneers they refused to accept that designation, but insisted on being called "helps," or "hired hands," or "ladies." The term "waiter" was equally unpopular, and was likely to call forth a spirited rejoinder from the person so addressed. Still more insulting was the word "master." A misguided traveler asking "Is your master at home?" would probably be told "I have no master"; one in the Wyoming cattle country was heatedly informed that "the son of Baliel ain't been born yet." So deep was the resentment against any implication of servility that young men and women preferred to labor at poor pay under bad conditions rather than accept a post as servant.

Those who did so guarded their respectability by abolishing all traditional symbols of servitude. Livery was never used; bells to summon servants in Western inns were unknown because the "helpers" refused to respond. All insisted on being treated as equals, dining with the family, meeting guests, and joining in all social functions under threat of immediate departure. One who had been told she must eat in the kitchen turned up her lip, announced "I guess that's cause you don't think I'm good enough to eat with you," and flounced from the house. Nor was this rebellious spirit peculiar to household help. The oft-heard remark: "If a man is good enough to work for me, he is good enough to eat with me" was literally applied. A family who had hired several carpenters to build a barn made the mistake of an early breakfast without them one day; the next day they left. A honeymooning couple were abandoned by their hired driver when they tried to eat alone just once. In public houses or conveyances the story was the same; travel accounts abound with tales of stewards who joined the card game after serving drinks, of waitresses who leaned over chairs to join in the conversation or borrow a guest's fan, of messengers who seated themselves and demanded a drink while serving their messages, of waiters in inns who joined their patrons when their tasks were done. In the West men felt equal, and acted the part.

Menial tasks were as resented by servants as were menial titles. Travelers were often forced to clean their own boots in frontier inns, or to rub down their own horses while "helpers" looked on disdainfully. One who asked to be awakened in the morning was answered "call yourself and be damned." On another occasion a titled Englishman in the Wyoming wilds was told to take a swim instead of a bath when he asked his hired helper to fill a tub; when he refused the angry helper shot the tub full of holes, shouting: "You ain't quite the top-shelfer you think you is, you ain't even got a shower-bath for cooling your swelled head, but I'll make you a present of one, boss!" Nor did servants alone resent the suggestion of servility. A pioneer Michigan housewife who tired of seeing a guest attack the roast with his own knife and offered to carve was rudely informed: "I'll help myself, I thankye. I never want no waitin' on."

Travelers who were shocked by these evidences of social democracy in the West were equally appalled by the democratic spirit which prevailed in frontier inns. There no "First Class" or "Second Class" accommodations separated patrons; tradesmen, slave dealers, farmers, congressmen, generals, fur trappers, and roustabouts ate side by side at the long tables, and all were treated the same. Sleeping accommodations were allotted on a first-come-first-serve basis, with governors and herdsmen, senators and farmers, rich and poor, clean and unclean, all crowded three or four to a bed. "It has been my lot," recorded an experienced traveler, "to sleep with a diversity of personages; I do believe from the driver of the stage coach, to men of considerable name." Complaints against these arrangements were summarily rejected by pioneer landlords; one visitor from overseas who objected to using a dirt-encrusted washbowl with a dozen other guests was told that "one rain bathes the just and the unjust, why not one wash-bowl"; another's protest that the sheets were dirty was answered with: "since *Gentlemen* are all alike, people do not see why they should not sleep in the same sheets." The frontier inn was, as one traveler put it, "a most almighty beautiful democratic amalgam."

The social democracy and frontier-type individualism that characterized America's growing period have not persisted unchanged into the twentieth century. Individualism has retreated before the advance of social cohesiveness essential in an urban-industrial society. The nation's folk hero may still be the rugged individualist, but the lone wolves of the past have found that they cannot fight the pack and that in cut-throat competition all throats are cut. At least since the 1890s the economic community had grudgingly accepted the regulation that the pioneer resisted save when it was to his advantage, and today cooperation and reliance on government are almost as commonplace in the United States as in the older countries of Europe. Yet American individualism differs from that of France or England in its continued insistence on a degree of economic freedom that has long since vanished in those countries, and in a glorification of the individual's ability to care for himself despite daily proof that joint effort alone will succeed in a society increasingly enmeshed.

Just as vestiges of frontier individualism remain to distinguish the social attitudes of modern America from those of modern Europe, so do remnants of pioneer democracy. The United States is no longer a country free of class distinctions and so wedded to egalitarianism that manifestations of wealth arouse public resentment. But its social democracy does differ from that of older nations, marked by its relative lack of class awareness, and by the brash assurance of the humble that they are as worthy of respect as the elite. The house painter who addresses a client by his first name, the elevator operator who enters into casual conversation with his passengers, the garage mechanic who condescendingly compares his expensive car with your aging model, could exist only in the United States. Their counterparts are unknown in England or on the Continent partly because America's frontiering experience bred into the people attitudes toward democracy that have persisted down to the present.

The Second Party System

Politics in America has been a game, a spectacle, a religion, a way of doing homage to heroes, and a way of expressing disapproval of one's neighbors. It has also been a dead-serious way of distributing wealth and power. American politics began as an extension of English politics, often in response to English political events. As the colonies matured, men had divided over local issues, but they had also organized around differing responses to the English ministry and to its representatives, the colonial governors.

Factions, rather than parties, continued to characterize the first years of independence. These were groupings often owing allegiance, not to a program or set of principles, but to a leader and his "interest." Factions were usually temporary, rising and declining as one powerful or charismatic political or social leader appeared or died. Often they lasted only for a single electoral campaign.

A full national party system with permanent machinery, an official program, and continuity from year to year emerged during the 1790s in response to a flock of new issues: local versus national authority, the financial measures of Alexander Hamilton, and the ideological issues generated by the French Revolution. Those supporting the use of national power to effect social and economic change, who endorsed the Bank of the United States and the Hamiltonian funding program, and who favored England over France, became Federalists. Their opponents followed the leadership of Jefferson and came, eventually, to be called Republicans or Democratic-Republicans.

While national issues dominated this "first party system," Americans divided politically over ethnic and religious antagonisms, over local conflicts of economic interest, and over what we today would call differing "life styles." On the local level, these were often more important than larger national questions in determining which of the two major parties men joined.

Between 1800 and 1815, the first party system faltered and collapsed. It had never been fully accepted as legitimate by Americans who had vainly hoped that the new nation would be free of party squabbling. When the early issues that divided Federalists from Republicans began to recede, the two bodies started to erode. The weaker of the two, the Federalist, disappeared first, leaving the field to its opponent. This Republican triumph was temporary, for the Republicans, in turn, began to lose support. The next few years represented an unusual hiatus in the American party system. Factions, centering around personalities rather than clear-cut issues, once again became the norm, though men continued to call themselves by the old Jeffersonian labels.

Beginning in 1824, a new political structure materialized. This "second party system" is the subject of Richard McCormick's essay that follows. McCormick is not interested in the parties of the period 1824–1860 for their individual characteristics. His concern is the party structure as it functioned in this period. Using some of the approaches and concepts of political scientists, he examines the origins, development, and operations of the parties during the era of Whig-Democratic strife, and distinguishes them from their Federalist-Republican antecedents. His intention is to suggest in what ways the two differed and what the new system meant for the political life of the country.

FOR FURTHER READING:

BENSON, LEE. *The Concept of Jacksonian Democracy: New York as a Test Case.* New York: Atheneum Publishers, 1964.*

MCCORMICK, RICHARD P. *The Second American Party System: Party Formation in the Jacksonian Era.* Chapel Hill: University of North Carolina Press, 1966.*

SCHLESINGER, ARTHUR M., JR. *The Age of Jackson.* Boston: Little, Brown & Company, 1945.*

Asterisk denotes paperback edition.

Political Development and the Second Party System   RICHARD P. McCORMICK

Historians engaged in the study of political parties in the United States have commonly focused their attention on individual parties as distinctive entities or on the contests between parties. Studies of particular parties abound, both at the state level and in larger contexts, and much of our political history is written in terms of the clashing rivalry of Jeffersonian Republicans and Federalists, Whigs and Democrats, or Democrats and Republicans. This approach has tended to emphasize the differences between parties, especially in terms of their ideologies and their constituencies. Worthy, rewarding, and time-honored as this usual type of inquiry may be, there is an alternative — or complementary — approach that can be expected to yield important insights into American political development. We can view the parties in existence at any given time as comprising a party system; and with the party system, rather than individual parties, as the phenomenon under scrutiny, we can proceed to new categories of questions and hypotheses.

In studying individual political parties, for example, we may properly direct our attention to certain activities in which parties engage, such as nominating candidates, conducting campaigns, aggregating interests, formulating ideological positions, and managing governmental power. We may also be concerned with the structure, or pattern of organized relationships between leaders and identifiers, of a particular party. If on the other hand the party system is the object of our concern, we may endeavor to formulate understandings of how and under what circumstances party systems emerge, define the character of the party system in terms of various proposed typologies, and evaluate the contribution of the party system — as an element in the larger political system — to the handling of certain "problems" or the meeting of specified "crises." To the degree that we are able to develop suitable and meaningful concepts of broad applicability, we can engage in the comparative

---

Source: Richard P. McCormick, "Political Development and the Second Party System," in *The American Party Systems: Stages of Political Development,* eds. William Nisbet Chambers and Walter Dean Burnham (New York: Oxford University Press, 1967), pp. 90–116.

analysis of successive party systems within our own nation over a period of time as well as of party systems in different nations. By engaging in such comparative studies, we may hope to formulate and test hypotheses regarding the role of party systems in our culture.[1]

Proceeding within this frame of reference, we can say that in the period between the establishment of a new government under the federal Constitution in 1789 and the disruption of the Union in 1860, two party systems rose and declined and a third was in the process of being formed as the nation confronted the crisis of disunion. The first party system, properly recognized as the first modern party system in any nation, was formed in the 1790's, deteriorated after 1815, and in a loose sense came to an end in 1824. The second party system had its origins in the presidential contest of 1824, acquired its full dimensions by 1840, and began to disintegrate in the early 1850's. By 1856, with the sudden rise of the Republican party to national prominence, there were signs that a third party system was emerging, although the disunited condition of the opposition parties down through 1860 and the cataclysmic effects of the Civil War and the subsequent era of Reconstruction left the eventual outlines of this party system in doubt until the 1870's.[2]

These three party systems shared many attributes. They were all, for example, two-party systems. But they differed in the circumstances surrounding their origins — and in the cases of the first and second party systems in the circumstances associated with their disintegration — as well as in such important respects as the character of their sectional alignments, the comprehensiveness of their appeal to potential participants, and their apparent capacity for resolving conflicts. They are, however, comparable, and when sufficient descriptive studies become available, it should be fruitful to engage in a comparative analysis of all three. Then it may be possible to identify similarities and differences and advance hypotheses to explain them.

This brief introduction will suffice to establish the general conceptual framework within which my particular subject — the second American party system — is presented. My main concern will be to offer a descriptive account of the formation of this party system and its growth to maturity in the 1840's.[3] In order to place the subject in proper perspective, I shall deal briefly with some aspects of party development before 1824 and after 1840 and suggest some comparisons among the party systems under consideration.

By way of background, it is relevant to offer some very general observations on the conduct of politics before the emergence of the first party system. Unlike most nations of the world, the United States had considerable experience in operating representative institutions long before the advent of parties. Passing over the colonial period, which, as current research has demonstrated, was marked by a lively brand of politics inspired by an ideology that came to assume an increasingly democratic thrust, it should be recognized that even after 1776 republican governments functioned without political parties. In all of the states leaders were recruited, substantial proportions of the adult males were involved in the electoral process, stability was maintained, the legitimacy of governmental authority was recognized, and important conflicts were resolved. In this era of popular or semipopular non-party politics, independence was secured, grievous postwar problems were met, a new Constitution was adopted, and the federal government was established. Many of the obvious pre-conditions for the rise of parties existed in many of the states —

elected legislatures, broad suffrage provisions, open competition for offices, a society of differentiated interests sharing common goals — but there was no semblance of a national party system, and, with two or three interesting but questionable exceptions, no party formation at the state level. Politics remained essentially local in scope and factional in character, and was therefore readily managed through informal structures.

Any general approach to the comparative study of American party systems must surely include some analysis of this pre-party era, for only through such an analysis can we test adequately any hypotheses that may be advanced to explain the emergence of parties shortly after 1789. Similarly, by comparing how certain functions conventionally ascribed to parties were actually performed in the pre-party period and after the advent of parties, we may be able to obtain valid understanding of what parties have contributed to our political system. Or, to put the matter differently, what obvious deficiencies existed in the political system before the 1790's that were rectified by the formation of parties? These questions can only be raised at this point; not until we have available well-conceived studies of colonial and state politics before 1789 can they be answered with any assurance.

National parties did not form during the Confederation period, but within a few years after the establishment of the new federal government, and surely by 1795, there were clear signs that party formation was well under way at all levels of government.[4] The origins of these parties can be detected first in cleavages that developed within the highest level of the national administration. Next, comparable factions formed within Congress. The emergence of these congressional factions encouraged the formation of parties at the state level. Finally, successive contests for the presidency in 1796 and 1800 provided an additional stimulant and served to focus and reinforce party feelings.

In endeavoring to account for the creation of parties at this particular time, we are obliged to ask what new conditions arose in the 1790's that seemingly created an environment more favorable to the formation of national parties than had maintained a decade earlier. It is my view that the critical new factor was the creation of a national political arena as the result of the adoption of the federal Constitution. Politics assumed an entirely new dimension — a national dimension — and the informal techniques of political management that had sufficed previously were replaced by party techniques. In particular, the constitutional arrangements for electing a President encouraged co-operation among political leaders throughout the nation in behalf of particular candidates. In quite a different way, the election of members of the House of Representatives by popular vote served to relate state and national politics. As parties were delineated on this national basis, the same alignments became operative in contests for state and even local offices.

Overly simple as this formulation may appear, it is not without its complications. It would seem that down to 1796, at least, we are confronted with a fairly clear case of parties whose origins were of the "interior" type, or "internally created" parties, to employ Maurice Duverger's typology.[5] That is, parties were formed first within the Congress and then were extended to the electorate. The complication arises because almost at once — in 1796 — quite a different influence entered the scene; namely, the contest for the presidency. The rivalry between John Adams and Thomas Jefferson in 1796 and again in 1800 served not only to dramatize and polarize the emerging partisan cleavage: it also enlarged party strife beyond the bounds of congressional districts, bringing it to embrace entire states and, by extension, the whole nation. Without pausing to develop this admittedly crucial point, I would contend that it was the contest for the presidency that was to exert the determining influence on the structure of the American party system.

The first party system, launched with such enterprise and vigor in the 1790's, soon entered upon what might be termed a stage of arrested development. It did not become established in the newer states that entered the Union after 1796; it soon languished in the Southern states; and in some other areas it succumbed to factional discord. By 1824 the remnants of the first party system possessed some vitality in only five states — Maine, Massachusetts, New Jersey, Delaware, and Maryland — although there were numerous isolated instances elsewhere of Federalists still offering challenges to their Republican adversaries.[6] Vestiges of old party organizations survived in some cases and party identities lingered on, but elections were rarely contested within the framework of the party system.

The first party system, then, can be seen in terms of failure as well as success. It failed to achieve truly national dimensions and, quite obviously, it failed to survive; and it also came perilously close to recording an even more serious failing. As the party system matured it became increasingly unbalanced. That is, the Republicans achieved such a lopsided superiority on a national basis that their Federalist opponents could scarcely hope to compete. What rendered this situation especially ominous was that the Federalist strength was sectionally concentrated, chiefly in New England, and that strength could now scarcely be effective in national politics. In consequence, the Federalists experienced a keen sense of political frustration, amounting to a sense of loss of their political efficacy. Much of New England's disaffection during the War of 1812 can be related to this factor, and the Hartford Convention, with its demands for revision of the constitutional "rules of the game," and even its implied threat of a division of the Union, brought the tensions to a crisis. What the ultimate result might have been had Andrew Jackson's victory at New Orleans in 1815 not transformed popular reactions to the war and to the record of the national administration must remain problematical. It can at least be suggested that the first party system as of 1814 was failing lamentably in achieving national integration and was even bringing the very legitimacy of the government into question. In other terms, the first party system was a failure because the parties became excessively unbalanced and took on a sectional alignment to the point where one sectionally oriented party, feeling that it could not compete, would no longer play the game according to the recognized rules.

In sequel, the first party system in its latter years — after 1815 — can be held responsible for a peculiar example of a "crisis of participation." Having failed to secure a revision of the rules, and having lost any prospect of electoral success, the Federalists in many states simply withdrew entirely from the arena of politics. In New Hampshire, for example, where the Federalists ceased to contest for state offices after 1817, voter participation declined from a high of slightly more than 80 per cent of those eligible in the gubnernatorial election of 1814 to a low of 44 per cent by 1822. In Connecticut, for similar reasons, voter participation dropped from 45 per cent in 1819 to 22 per cent by 1822; in Vermont there was a comparable decline from 66 per cent in 1818 to 25 per cent by 1821; and in Rhode Island there was an abrupt falloff from nearly 50 per cent in 1818 to 15 per cent in 1819.[7] In other states, as party competition languished, voter participation generally sank to a low level.

Why did the first party system disintegrate? If we could answer this question with complete authority we should no doubt possess an important key to understanding the nature of the system. Without attempting to offer a comprehensive explanation for the breakdown of the parties, we could propose the simple proposition that the failure of the Federalists to extend, or even maintain, the bases of support they held in 1800 brought about a condition of extreme party imbalance. At this point the Federalists confronted the alternatives of rebelling against the system or withdrawing from it. After experiencing failure with the first alternative, they adopted the second in most states. No longer confronted by a formidable opposition, the Republicans in most areas succumbed to internal factionalism.

Approaching the problem from even a narrower perspective, we could advance the hypothesis that the first party system disintegrated because the chief purpose for which it had been formed had lost its urgency. That is, the fact that the contest for the presidency subsided after 1800 deprived the party system of the main source of its vitality and even the reason for its existence. The fortuitous availability of the members of the "Virginia Dynasty," the succession of Jefferson, Madison, and Monroe, and the failure of the Federalists as politicians to grasp the full significance of the importance of the presidential contest, together with certain impediments that inhered in the existing constitutional and social environment, all combined to reduce and ultimately eliminate the contest for the presidency as the stimulus to party action. This hypothesis — that the contest for the presidency provided the first party system with its crucial function — would obviously require extensive testing. Here it can only be noted that in the absence of a contest for the presidency there was little tendency for parties to form within individual states for the purpose of competing for state and local offices. Moreover, there is no evidence to suggest that cleavages within the Congress, even after 1815, could provide the basis for the rehabilitation or reconstruction of the party system. Finally, the revival of the contest for the presidency after 1824 had the immediate effect of stimulating the formation of a new party system.

As the national party system disintegrated, especially after 1815, it is noteworthy that there was not much of a tendency toward the formation of state-oriented parties, that is, parties organized solely for the purpose of contesting offices at the state level. The obvious exceptions to this generalization were New York, with its Bucktail and Clintonian parties; Georgia, with its peculiar Troup-Clark alignments; and Kentucky, where Old Court and New Court parties carried on a brief struggle.[8] It is also significant, I believe, that divisions did not form within Congress to provide the basis for a new party alignment even when such crises as those attendant upon the economic depression of 1819 or the furor over the admission of Missouri to statehood agitated public feelings.

It would seem to be quite clear that the stimulus for the formation of the second party system was supplied by the revival of the contest for the presidency in 1824. With the expiration of Monroe's second term there was no notable Virginian to take his place; the weak and discredited Republican congressional caucus was unable to produce a disciplined solution to the problem of succession; and soon there were four candidates — all self-styled Republicans — contending for the presidency. Except in New England, where John Quincy Adams had virtually no opposition, the contest was extremely confused and did not at once produce new party alignments. Because it was so chaotic, and also because in many states one or another of the candidates enjoyed overwhelming support from local political leaders, voter participation was remarkably low.

The most important consequence of 1824, in terms of party formation, was that it projected Andrew Jackson to the fore as the rival to Adams. Looking ahead to 1828, rival political leaders from state to state began to calculate their courses of action with respect to what was termed the "presidential question." Obviously, many considerations entered into their appraisals, but the fact that loomed largest, no doubt, was the highly sectional nature of the appeal of the two candidates.

This sectional bias was clearly revealed in the election of 1828. Adams swept New England, securing majorities of three-to-one or better in four of the six states. Jackson was equally impressive in the South, and won commanding majorities in most of the newer states of the West. Having no sectional candidate of their own in the race, the Middle States provided the major battleground of the election, and — except in Pennsylvania — the vote was extremely close. The party alignments that formed in the Middle States by 1828 tended to be durable, as Table 1 shows,[9] al-

TABLE 1 Differential between Percentages of Total Vote Obtained by Major Presidential Candidates, 1828–44

State	1828	1832	1836	1840	1844
Maine	20	10	20	1	13
New Hampshire	7	13	50	11	19
Vermont	50	10	20	29	18
Massachusetts	66	30	9	16	12
Rhode Island	50	14	6	23	20
Connecticut	50	20	1	11	5
New York	2	4	9	4	1
New Jersey	4	1	1	4	1
Pennsylvania	33	16	4	1	2
Delaware	—	2	6	10	3
Maryland	2	1	7	8	5
Virginia	38	50	13	1	6
North Carolina	47	70	6	15	5
Georgia	94	100	4	12	4
Kentucky	1	9	6	29	8
Tennessee	90	90	16	11	1
Louisiana	6	38	3	19	3
Alabama	80	100	11	9	18
Mississippi	60	77	2	7	13
Ohio	3	3	4	9	2
Indiana	13	34	12	12	2
Illinois	34	37	10	2	12
Missouri	41	32	21	14	17
Arkansas	—	—	28	13	26
Michigan	—	—	9	4	6
Average differential	36	36	11	11	9

though in both New York and Pennsylvania the anti-Jackson forces lacked cohesion and were distracted by Antimasonry. With these important exceptions, we could say that a new two-party system had emerged in the Middle States by 1828 and that it had been given definition by the presidential contest. In New England, because of the overwhelming loyalty to the sectional favorite, the opposition Jacksonian parties were able to make little headway until after Adams had been defeated. But by 1829 the political balance had altered considerably, and the Jacksonians rapidly moved into a competitive position in most states. In the South and West — except for the very special case of Kentucky — the election of 1828 stimulated the temporary formation of parties. Once the election was over, however, the alignments did not persist and politics continued to be conducted in what was essentially an unstructured fashion.

Despite the large issues that presumably were involved, the election of 1832 had remarkably little effect on party formation. In the South and West there were feeble efforts to organize support for Henry Clay, but in most states he fared even less well than had Adams in 1828. In the Middle States, the close balance that had become evident in 1828 persisted. The most striking shift occurred in New England, where in every state the Jacksonians made tremendous gains and captured Maine and New Hampshire. Perhaps this remarkable upheaval can be attributed to the popularity of Jackson's policies regarding the bank, tariff, and internal improvements. Yet I am inclined to believe that the explanation is to be found quite simply in the fact that Clay lacked the strong sectional appeal that Adams had possessed.

How well developed, then, was the new party system by the end of 1832? In broad terms, it was well established in New England and the Middle States, despite the complications of Antimasonry. In every state the Jacksonians had acquired recognized leaders, constructed an elaborate party apparatus, and enlisted in their ranks multitudes of voters who identified with the Jackson party. The opposition, plagued by the lack of a persistent standard bearer, nevertheless managed to maintain a competitive position, whether under the Adams, National Republican, or Antimasonic label. The South, except for Kentucky, could best be described as politically monolithic. Where nearly all political leaders and candidates were nominally, at least, of the Jacksonian persuasion, there could scarcely be a functioning two-party system. In certain of the newer states of the West what can only be described as a dual party system existed. There were temporary party formations in 1828 and 1832 for the purpose of contesting the presidential election, but in state and congressional elections the contests were either conducted on a non-party basis or, in some instances, on the basis of alignments quite different from those that obtained in the presidential elections. It is common, in describing American politics in this era, to assert that by 1828 or by 1832 a functioning party system existed; but it would be my contention that in many states the crucial stage of party formation had not yet been reached.

Slight as was the effect of the election of 1832 on party formation, it did reveal an undercurrent that was soon to assume the proportions of a tidal wave. Although Jackson retained, and even increased, his huge majorities throughout the South, there were strong manifestations of dissatisfaction with his running mate and heir-apparent, Martin Van Buren of New York. In Virginia, North Carolina, Georgia, and Alabama, factions that professed loyalty to Jackson also launched organized efforts to oppose Van Buren's candidacy for the vice-presidency, and there were similar signs of restiveness in other Southern states as well. Some of these early anti-Van Burenites were admirers of John C. Calhoun, and others were appalled at the prospect of having to support a Northerner for the presidency. Still others, no doubt, were calculating how they might exploit anti-Van Buren sentiment to advance their political fortunes within their particular states.

What can best be characterized as a political explosion rocked the South from

Virginia to Mississippi in 1834 and 1835. With Jackson nearing the end of his tenure, the political consensus that seemingly had prevailed was abruptly replaced by a sharp cleavage in almost every state. Those who remained loyal to the Jackson party found themselves confronted with a virulent opposition that shared a common antagonism to Martin Van Buren. While some of those "antis" continued to profess their undying loyalty to Old Hickory and his policies, others declaimed against executive usurpation, the removal of bank deposits, and the tariff, or sounded the changes on states' rights. The new sides were drawn in the state and congressional elections of 1834 and 1835, and by 1836 the Southern opposition parties — often bearing the name Whig — had found their standard bearer in Hugh Lawson White of Tennessee.

In the Western states, too, the approach of the election of 1836 spurred the slow process of party formation. More-or-less well-organized Van Buren-Democratic parties faced bitter struggles with opposition parties pledged variously to a local hero — William Henry Harrison of Indiana — or to mixed White-Harrison tickets. In part because of the unprecedented personal campaign waged by Harrison, the election aroused considerable interest. The alignments that emerged in this election persisted, even though state elections in Illinois, Indiana, and Missouri continued for a few years to bear only a vague resemblance to party contests.

The least studied of all our presidential elections, the election of 1836, was of crucial importance in determining the ultimate outlines of the second party system. In marked contrast to the situation that had existed in 1832, there were now two parties contesting elections in every state, and — no less significantly — in the large majority of the states the parties were competitive. Although Van Buren eked out a victory in the 1836 election, the party that he headed had very different dimensions from the one that had twice swept Jackson into office. In the South, where Jackson had encountered little more than token opposition, Van Buren polled slightly less than 50 per cent of the popular vote. Jackson had won 100 per cent of the votes in Georgia and 95 per cent of the votes in Tennessee in 1832; Van Buren lost both of these states in 1836. In the West, too, Van Buren's strength was far less than that of Jackson. Only in New England did Van Buren enhance the strength of the Democratic party. In the evenly balanced Middle States there was no large shift.

In brief, the effect of Van Buren's candidacy was to end the monolithic character of Southern politics and delineate and strengthen alignments in the West, thereby giving a truly national dimension to the second party system. While in 1832 the victorious candidate had secured a two-to-one margin in eleven states, only one state remained in that category in 1836: New Hampshire, which Van Buren carried by a three-to-one margin. Fittingly enough, the state in which Van Buren found his weakest support was Vermont. Here, indeed, is a conundrum for political analysts.

The anti-Buren or Whig parties that had formed in the several states between 1834 and 1836, together with those in New England and the Middle States that had originated earlier, had yet to develop national cohesion and leadership. Such an achievement would be essential if they were to contest successfully for the presidency. Meeting at Harrisburg in December 1839, in one of the most astutely contrived conventions ever held, they performed the difficult feat by agreeing to unite on the best available hero, Old Tippecanoe Harrison, and by sedulously avoiding any semblance of a party platform. Thus effectively mobilized, the Whigs proceeded to put on a spectacular campaign that was to fix a new style in American political drama.[10] The exciting contest, waged furiously now in every state, stimulated an unprecedented outpouring of voters and sent Van Buren down to a crushing defeat in the electoral college, although the popular vote was far less lopsided.

The campaign of 1840 brought the second American party system at last to fruition. In every region of the country, and indeed in every state, politics was conducted within the framework of a two-party system, and in all but a handful of states the parties were so closely balanced as to be competitive.[11] In broad terms, it was the contest for the presidency that shaped this party system and defined its essential purpose. The same party system, however, was to be utilized as the framework within which competition for office at all other levels of government would be conducted. The two parties were similar in structure, employed similar campaign techniques, and performed similar functions. Although in specific features the parties remained somewhat differentiated from state to state, there had in fact occurred a nationalization of institutional forms and political styles. There was also a nationalization of political identities. Voters everywhere would respond to candidates and issues as Whigs or Democrats.

With this brief and even partial synopsis of party development in mind, it becomes possible to attempt some analyses of what it all signifies. We can approach this question by attempting some broad comparisons between the first and second party systems. But before engaging in this exercise, we might well pause to consider how politics was conducted in the absence of parties, for only with some understanding of this phase of our political history can we measure and evaluate the effects of parties.

Even after the appearance of the first party system, many states continued to conduct politics on a non-party basis. An example is Tennessee, which did so for roughly forty years.[12] With no vestige of political parties, the Tennessee brand of politics featured hard-fought contests for seats in the legislature and in Congress that not uncommonly brought over 70 per cent of the electorate to the polls. In the process, the state produced a host of outstanding political figures, including not only Andrew Jackson but James K. Polk, Hugh Lawson White, John Bell, and Felix Grundy as well. Reference could readily be made to a dozen other states where as late as the 1820's, or even 1830's, political parties were nonexistent. Leaving aside the intriguing question of why parties were not formed, at least for the purpose of conducting state politics, it would no doubt be illuminating if we could answer the question of what functions usually ascribed to political parties were not being performed in some manner in Tennessee and other non-party states. Probably none of us would insist that representative government was inconceivable without political parties, but we may readily err in attributing to parties a larger and more comprehensive role in the American political process than they in fact deserve. Unfortunately, we know even less about pre-party politics in the United States than we do about party politics, with the result that as yet we are not well prepared to make reliable comparisons between the two systems.

We are on slightly firmer ground when we endeavor to compare the first and the second party systems, although admittedly our knowledge of both is inadequate and the conceptual framework within which we structure our comparisons is incomplete. For the purposes of this essay, the comparative analysis must necessarily be kept within brief limits and deal only with large and readily visible attributes.

The first and second American party systems did not have precisely the same origins. It would seem that cleavages within Congress preceded and even forecast the formation of parties in the 1790's. In theoretical terms, it would be extremely important to be able to affirm that the first party system represented an "internally created" or "interior" type of party formation. Unfortunately, we cannot be sure how far this interior process of party formation might have proceeded, for superimposed on the impulse supplied by the congressional parties was the mobilization for the presidential contests in 1796 and 1800. It is my view that these contests for the presidency supplied a greater stimulus to party formation than did the congressional groupings. Nevertheless, the early existence of congressional alignments in the 1790's has no counterpart in the 1820's. Moreover, the parties of the 1790's possessed at the outset an issue-orientation that can hardly be discerned in 1824 or 1828. Finally, the first party system had a relatively rapid emergence, whereas the second was formed in stages over a period of roughly sixteen years.

Both party systems, the second more clearly than the first, were oriented toward contesting presidential elections. This orientation presents a striking contrast to the situation in other Western political systems, where parties have been oriented toward securing as large a representation as possible in the national legislature (although it must be noted that in most cases it has been the legislature that names the functioning executive in such systems). It is this peculiarity, among others, that makes it so difficult to conceptualize American party systems in terms that would be relevant to other nations. In organizational terms, the congressional district has presented awkward problems for our parties, quite unlike the parliamentary constituencies in Europe. Why should the executive rather than the legislative branch have been the focal point for the party system, especially in the first half of the nineteenth century? No doubt an extended answer to this question could tell us much about the special character of American parties.

There were pronounced differences in the organizational structures of parties in the first and second party systems. The caucus reflected in part the prominent role taken by legislators — national and state — in guiding early party development, and it was extensively employed as a management device under the first party system.[13] In most states, as well as at the national level, party members within the legislature, often joined by non-legislators, performed extensive nominating functions and — usually through such agencies as central committees — directed party affairs generally. In many states, conspicuously in New England and Virginia, the caucus and its agencies operated a highly centralized party apparatus, although in time local party units increasingly employed delegate conventions to nominate candidates for lesser offices. Two states, New Jersey and Delaware, were exceptional in that they instituted the state convention. Because of the great variations in constitutional structures from state to state, the precise forms of party organization and even the functions performed by the caucus differed widely; but in its most highly developed form — notably in Massachusetts — the caucus structure was highly integrated and extremely efficient. At the national level, party management was relatively weak. The Republican congressional caucus was a promising institution, which under slightly altered circumstances might have exerted a lasting influence on the structure of American parties, but for reasons that must be passed over it failed to develop and maintain its authority and grew increasingly ineffective, especially after 1816. The Federalists, with their small and geographically unrepresentative delegation in

Congress, could scarcely use the caucus as an authoritative national agency, and they had little success in developing the convention as an alternative.

Under the second party system, the caucus was almost completely replaced by the convention as the characteristic device for party management. The changeover, which has not yet been studied thoroughly, had great theoretical significance. In addition to reflecting demands for popular participation in party affairs the convention also represented a highly practical solution to problems facing party leaders at a time when party identities in legislative bodies were extremely confused, or when incipient parties had too few legislative representatives to organize a respectable caucus. Much might be made of the fact that the Antimasonic party, the first clear example of what Maurice Duverger calls an "externally created" or "exterior" type of party in the United States, was especially zealous in developing the convention technique and, as we know, held the first national party convention. Whether the extralegislative origins of the Jackson and Adams parties in most — but not all — states would justify our describing them as "exterior" parties could lead to considerable debate. What would seem to be indisputable is that the shift from caucus to convention implied a loss in the political authority of legislative bodies. While they were suffering this loss, they were also experiencing general curtailment of their elective functions, as evidenced by the trend toward the popular choice of electors, governors, and other state officials. Again, one would like to be able to understand fully why this downgrading of the legislative branch occurred and what implications it had for our system of politics.

The widespread adoption of the convention system in the 1830's, with its hierarchy of delegate conventions and party committees extending from the smallest electoral unit up to the national conventions, made for an exceedingly elaborate and complex organizational structure. Because candidates had to be nominated at so very many different levels of government, elections were held so frequently, and the party system embraced the entire range of offices, the organizations that had evolved in most states by the 1840's were marvels of ingenuity and intricacy and required enormous manpower to staff them. In contrast to the diversity of organizational forms under the first party system, there was now a high degree of uniformity throughout the nation and in both major parties.

It is possible that the shift from the caucus to the convention may have tended greatly to emphasize the purely electoral functions of the party apparatus. The members of a caucus, in their dual capacity as legislators and party managers, may have been more concerned with matters of program and policy than were the members of conventions. It would also appear that in its most centralized form, the caucus structure imposed a much higher degree of discipline than was to prevail under the convention system. Despite their elaborate organization, the new parties of the second party system were actually decentralized structures. The party apparatus at each level of government, or within each type of constituency, possessed considerable autonomy. Party mechanisms were better designed for achieving agreement on nominations than for formulating policies. Perhaps the very complexity and magnitude of the formal organizational structure contributed to the rise of the professional party manager and the informal leader, or boss.

In discussing any formal party structures, whether of the caucus or convention type, the problem inevitably arises as to whether the formal structure reflected the actual locus of power or influence. Superficially, the delegate convention system of the 1830's and 1840's resulted in the "democratization" of parties, but we have yet to determine the degree to which conventions were genuine decision-making bodies. Perhaps they were, but they must also be viewed as having what might be termed a cosmetic function; that is, they gave a democratic appearance to what might in fact have been decisions determined by a party oligarchy. Indeed, Ostrogorski used the term "democratic formalism" to describe the convention structure.

The two party systems could also be compared with respect to participation. The installation of the convention party structure unquestionably multiplied opportunities for party followers to assume roles as activists. This development was especially prominent in those states where previously there had been little or no formal party organization, but its effects could be noted everywhere. Moreover, intense interparty competition stimulated unprecedented levels of voter participation, not uncommonly rising to 80 per cent of the electorate, whereas prior to 1824 in a very large number of states it was exceptional for half of the eligible voters to participate regularly in elections.[14] Both in the comprehensiveness of their structures and in the universality of their appeal, then, the new parties could truly be characterized as mass parties.

One may properly speculate as to whether the measurable increase in voter participation had a direct influence on party programs and governmental actions. To put the question differently, when vast numbers of men who had formerly lacked the franchise or who had been apathetic entered the electoral arena, were there discernible shifts in party attitudes or public policy? Did the parties and the governments become more "democratic"? This would be an extremely difficult question to answer, but I have the impression that the "new" voters tended to divide between the two parties in much the same proportion as the "old" voters.[15] We might conclude that both parties accommodated the new voters by modifying their appeals and their programs. An alternative conclusion could be that because the new voters did not enter predominantly into one party and make it the instrument for achieving their political goals, they had no great effect on the parties. Any sure evaluation of the effects of enlarged participation must depend on further studies, but at least we might agree that the mass participation that we associate with the second party system did affect the style of politics.

The extended form of participation in politics in the era of the second party system can scarcely be comprehended in purely political terms — that is, only in terms of rivalry between opposing power elites or interest groups for dominance in the state and for control over public policy. It would be difficult to account for all the phenomena of the system within these limited concepts, and the varieties of experiences that parties in this era afforded to the electorate went beyond the political sphere.[16] Those tens of thousands of men and women who attended the mammoth Whig festival at Nashville in 1840; those untold millions who carried torches, donned uniforms, chanted slogans, or cheered themselves hoarse at innumerable parades and rallies; those puffed-up canvassers of wards, servers of rum, and distributors of largesse; and all those simple folk who whipped themselves into a fury of excitement and anxiety as each election day approached, were thrilling to a grand dramatic experience, even a cathartic experience. There was no spectacle, no contest, in America that could match an election campaign, and all could identify with and participate in it.

Innumerable foreign observers saw clearly this amazing dimension of American politics. As Michael Chevalier perceived it, the political campaign and all its attendant pageantry and exaltation meant to Americans what religious festivals had meant to the peoples of Catholic Europe. Witnessing a post-election celebration of New York City Democrats, he was struck by the resemblance.

> The procession was nearly a mile long; the democrats marched in good order to the glare of torches; the banners were more numerous than I had ever seen them in any religious festival; all were in transparency, on account of the darkness. On some were inscribed the names of the democratic societies or sections . . . others bore imprecations against the Bank of the United States; *Nick Biddle* and *Old Nick* here figured largely and formed the pendant of our *libera nos a malo*. Then came portraits of General Jackson afoot and on horseback . . . Those of Washington and Jefferson, surrounded with democratic mottoes, were mingled in all tastes and of all colors. Among these figured an eagle, not a painting, but a real live eagle, tied by the legs, surrounded by a wreath of leaves, and hoisted upon a pole, after the manner of the Roman standards. The imperial bird was carried by a stout sailor, more pleased than ever was a sergeant permitted to hold one of the strings of the canopy, in a Catholic ceremony. From further than the eye could reach, came marching on the democrats. I was struck with the resemblance of their air to the train that escorts the *viaticum* in Mexico or Puebla. . . . The democratic procession, also, like the Catholic procession, had its halting places; it stopped before the house of the Jackson men to fill the air with cheers, and halted at the doors of the leaders of the Opposition, to give three, six, or nine groans.
> . . . If these scenes were to find a painter, they would be admired at a distance, not less than the triumphs and sacrificial pomps, which the ancients have left us delineated in marble and brass; for they are not mere grotesques after the manner of Rembrandt, they belong to history, they partake of the grand; they are the episodes of a wondrous epic which will bequeath a lasting memory to posterity, that of the coming of democracy.[17]

Finally, the first and second party systems exhibited pronounced differences in their extent and their alignment. The parties of the 1790's had never really been extended to more than fifteen states, and in several of those they scarcely became rooted. The second party system comprehended every state, although there might well be some reservations about South Carolina. The first party system was, from one point of view, very badly aligned. Early in its history the New England states were heavily inclined toward the Federalist party, while in the South the Republicans possessed a lopsided supremacy. Although New England in time achieved a brief balance of parties, the South became virtually a one-party region. The second party system was extraordinary in that the two parties were fairly evenly balanced in every region.[18] Between 1836 and 1852, as in no other period in our history, each of the parties was truly national in its extent.

It would be possible and even profitable to explain why the two party systems differed in so many attributes, but such a disquisition would probably have to be very lengthy if it were to be at all persuasive. Within the limited compass of this essay it is appropriate to attempt no more than a brief reference to the most salient factors.

Of foremost importance in affecting the structures of parties as well as the specific tasks that elements within the party organization had to perform were certain fundamental changes in the constitutional and legal environment.[19] To put the matter simply, the rules under which the political game was to be played changed greatly between 1800 and 1840. The most obvious development was a trend from diversity to uniformity in governmental structures and electoral procedures from state to state. The magnitude and significance of this quiet revolution in the electoral environment has generally been ignored, except for a curious preoccupation with modifications in suffrage qualifications.[20] We have yet to assess adequately the relevance to our party system of the movements toward the popular, at-large election of presidential electors, the choice of congressmen by districts, the popular election of governors, and the multiplication in numbers of locally elected officials. In a related realm, the adoption of printed ballots, the creation of small voting districts, and the consolidation of elections on a single day had enormous consequences for political parties.

One general effect of this quiet revolution was to complicate the tasks of the parties. In a situation where, for example, members of a legislature were elected from the county as a unit and where the legislature in turn appointed the governor, presidential electors, and county officials, parties would have very limited tasks, as contrasted with a situation where members of each house of the legislature were chosen from different constituencies, and presidential electors, the governor, and county officials were popularly elected. Compelled to elaborate an intricate organization capable of making nominations and conducting campaigns within a bewildering variety of constituencies, and obliged at the same time to appeal for the broadest possible base of support, the new parties confronted a staggering challenge, especially when they might be called upon to engage in electoral combat two or three times within a single year. It is no wonder that they were reduced to little more than electoral machines.

If one change in the electoral environment loomed larger than all the rest it was the shift to the popular, at-large election of presidential electors. This development gave a popular dimension to the contest for the presidency, reduced the political authority of the state legislatures, called forth elaborate and intensive campaign efforts, facilitated the building of national parties, reduced the effectiveness of third parties, and made the presidential election the focal point of the party system — to suggest but a few consequences. How and through what influences this transformation of the process of choosing electors was brought about has yet to be studied, but a complete understanding of its implications might well be crucial to any conceptualization of the American party system.

The political environment was profoundly influenced not only by these constitutional and legal developments, but also by fairly obvious technological, economic, and social changes. Revolutionary improvements in means of transportation and communication made it feasible, for example, for parties to hold state and even national conventions and conduct nationwide campaigns. Rising economic expectations associated with the transformation and expansion of the economy gave new energy to democratic dogmas and spurred mass participation in politics. The entrance of new states into the union broadened the spatial dimensions of the party system, and the growth of urban areas and the sharp rise in immigration created new challenges. Above all, the increasingly egalitarian flavor of American society, now given voice in an incontestable rhetoric, compelled both parties to project the same democratic image.

These briefly enumerated changes in the constitutional and cultural environment may account for certain fairly obvious differences in organization and style between the first and second party systems. But they do not fully explain what was most distinctive about the latter, namely, its lack of sectional bias. As the second party system reached maturity in the 1840's, it scarcely reflected the fact that the basic cleavage within the nation, transcending all others, was that which may be vaguely defined as North-South sectionalism. The first party system had mirrored this tension to the degree that after 1800 the Federalists were very largely a Northern party. The third party system as it finally became aligned in the 1870's also contained a decided sectional bias, with its solidly Democratic South and its Northern-oriented Republican party. In attempting to explain how the second party system produced not sectional parties but parties that were remarkably well balanced throughout the nation, we are confronted with a paradox. In the successive contests for the presidency between 1824 and 1836 strong sectional loyalties shaped the responses of political leaders and voters in each region to the opposing candidates. But by 1836 the end result of the series of realignments was a sectionally balanced party system. In brief, the explanation for the paradoxical character of the second party system is to be found in the peculiar circumstances associated with the contests for the presidency.

To recapitulate, the second party system did not emerge suddenly; it developed in a series of stages, and at each stage it was shaped by the sectional identifications of the candidates. With Andrew Jackson and John Quincy Adams as the candidates in 1828, a highly sectionalized vote resulted; New England went almost as overwhelmingly for Adams as the South did for Jackson; only the Middle States were evenly divided. When Henry Clay was substituted for Adams, New England was no longer held together by its loyalty to a sectional favorite, and parties throughout the North came into balance. When Martin Van Buren was substituted for Jackson — and opposed by White and Harrison — the South and much of the new West ceased to be politically monolithic, as anti-Van Buren parties quickly mobilized. These sectional responses to the presidential candidates were crucial at the time of party formation. Once the parties had been formed and identities had been acquired by the voters, alignments tended to remain relatively firm. Thus highly sectional responses in a series of presidential elections resulted in the formation of non-sectional parties.

Merely to emphasize their distinctiveness, I have chosen to call these national parties "artificial" because their ultimate alignments bore no direct relationship to the realities of sectional antagonism. At maturity, each party sought to aggregate interests that were national in scope; and within each party almost equally powerful Northern and Southern wings contested for supremacy. Intra-party tensions were greater than the tensions between the two parties. The federalized character of our constitutional structure and the inability of any national party agency to exercise firm discipline made it all but impossible to restrain the intra-party tensions. Responsible leaders of both parties understood that such parties could be destroyed by issues that were sectional in character. The parties could indulge themselves in furious controversies over the "Monster Bank," but they might be rent asunder by such issues as expansionism or the status of slavery in the territories.

The second American party system was truly a wondrous creation. Emerging over a period of sixteen years from the circumstances associated with the successive contests for the presidency, it elaborated a complex organizational structure within which there could be orderly competition for offices of all levels of government. It also provided maximal opportunities for mass participation and produced a political style that took on the aspects of a democratic religion. It could perform a wide range of electoral functions, and it could resolve conflicts that were not highly charged with sectional antagonisms. But, like the first party system, it, too, met with failure.

Apparently it was still in a healthy condition down to about 1850. Then, under the strain of the sectional issues confronting the nation, it began to crumble. The first sign was the collapse of the Whig party in the lower South, and by 1856 the already altered Democratic party was confronted by the newly marshalled Republican party and, in some areas, by the short-lived American, or "Know-Nothing," party as well. At last, in 1860, the Democrats succumbed to a fateful division and the Civil War followed. Although in the North a viable new party system operated, it was not until the 1870's, with the nation reunited and the South released from the abnormal years of Reconstruction, that the third party system assumed national dimensions.

Why did the second party system fail? One answer could be that it was inadequate to cope with conflicts that arrayed section against section. The first party system had come perilously close to foundering on this rock in 1814; but the second party system, for the reason that its parties were truly national in scope and lacked a pronounced sectional bias, was presumably better designed to manage divisive pluralism. Here we face a dilemma. If in a democratic two-party system the parties became so aligned as to reflect crucial ideological, class, social, or sectional cleavages, and they therefore present the electorate with drastic alternatives, the strain on the political system as a whole, and particularly at the level of government, may be disruptive. If, on the other hand, each party is expected to mediate conflicting interests by aggregating the broad spectrum of those interests, the strain on the political system at the level of the parties may be disruptive. I have no solution to propose to this dilemma, other than to suggest that a party system that is *too* comprehensive — as was the second party system — may be potentially as explosive as a party system that is polarized around drastic alternatives — as was the third party system in its formative years.[21] Perhaps this is to say that threatening problems or the strains of crises must be shared between the party system and the government.

In conclusion, some crude assessments of the contributions of the party systems to American political development down to 1860 might be attempted. Such an appraisal must be extremely tentative because the concept of political development, as formulated by LaPalombara and Weiner or others, is awkwardly elusive.[22] And even if one accepts the notion that such problems as national integration, political participation, distribution, legitimacy, and management of conflict are relevant to political development, it is all but impossible to measure the specific contributions of party systems to the solution of those problems. Consequently, what follows must be regarded as impressionistic and even subjective.

We must begin with the understanding that the United States in the 1790's did not confront crises of the same kind and magnitude as those facing the newly emergent nations of today. An extensive experience with the operation of representative institutions that dated back to early in the seventeenth century gave the new nation a politically skilled leadership corps, a broad and alert electorate, and an informed respect for constitutional order. In addition to possessing a common language, a cultural heritage that stemmed largely from British origins, and a relatively homogeneous Protestant religious background, the former colonies had strengthened their sense of national identity through their struggle for independence and had reaffirmed their unity by adopting the federal Constitution. The legitimacy of the new government was not challenged by a party of disaffection, nor was it threatened with subversion by a hereditary elite, an entrenched bureaucracy, or a powerful military establishment. The economy seemed to be capable of gratifying the expectations of the citizens. In relative terms, a high degree of literacy existed; and a flourishing, free press sustained political communication. Not least of all, if we accept the persuasive formulation of Louis Hartz concerning the flowering of a liberal tradition in America, there was consensual agreement on basic national values.[23]

The new American republic was designed as a federal republic, however, in recognition of the sovereign authority held by the several states, and the powers assigned to the national government were explicitly limited. This intricate, carefully adjusted political system was decidedly experimental, and by its very nature it placed restraints on national integration and even permitted the possibility of contests over legitimacy between state and national authorities. Given the complex of factors that conditioned the formation of the national union, we can appreciate the virtues of these arrangements, but they were to occasion very special problems for American party systems. These problems were to become especially formidable as the nation expanded in size and — most ominously — as sectional interests diverged and took precedence over other cleavages.

In gross terms I would take the view that the first and second American party systems were not confronted with serious crises of participation, nor with major crises of distribution. Neither were they required to meet challenges to the legitimacy of the constitutional regime, unless we choose to regard the menace of secession as a threat to legitimacy rather than to national integration. The two areas in which the party systems might be expected to contribute to political development were in advancing national integration and in managing conflicts.

We know, of course, that internal conflicts were not successfully managed in the 1850's and that the nation disintegrated in 1860-61, after having somewhat fortuitously averted a similar crisis in 1814. Now two possible courses of argument are open to us. We might adduce evidence to sustain the position that the first two party systems, despite their defects, held the nation together and resolved a number of conflicts over a period of sixty years, only to fail when confronted by irreconcilable cleavages. Or we might defend the position that the party systems, perhaps because of the difficulties inherent in the federal system, were ill-adapted to resolving conflicts that were sectional in character and that in 1814 and again in 1860 they were malintegrative in their effects.

Whichever position seems to us most plausible, one conclusion is inescapable: the early American party systems are no less notable for their failures than for their successes. We may properly hail the ingenuity of the political architects who constructed the first modern party system in history, but we must record that that party system fell victim to a kind of entropy after 1815. We can marvel at the comprehensiveness and popularity of the second party system, and at the incredible technical proficiency of its professional corps of managers, but that system collapsed within a generation. And as the third party system began to form, the nation divided. Whatever the contributions of the party systems to American political development, they were not after all adequate to avert the disaster of civil war.

NOTES

1. My own interest in the comparative study of party systems has been influenced in various ways by Gabriel A. Almond and James S. Coleman (eds.), *The Politics of the Developing Areas* (Princeton, 1960); Maurice Duverger, *Political Parties: Their Organization and Activity in the Modern State* (New York, 1954); Seymour Martin Lipset, *The First New Nation* (New York, 1963); Sigmund Neumann (ed.), *Modern Political Parties* (Chicago, 1956); and Joseph LaPalombara and Myron Weiner (eds.), *Political Parties and Political Development* (Princeton, 1966). For an admirable and full bibliography, see the last work, pp. 439–64. William N. Chambers has broken new ground with his brilliant conceptualizations of American party systems in *Political Parties in a New Nation: The American Experience, 1776–1809* (New York, 1963); and in "Party Development and Party Action: The American Origins," *History and Theory, III* (1963), 111–17. I have found many of his formulations suggestive.
2. Two useful but outdated standard histories of American parties are Wilfred E. Binkley, *American Political Parties: Their Natural History* (New York, 1962); and Edgar E. Robinson, *The Evolution of American Political Parties* (New York, 1924).
3. Much of the material in this essay is drawn from my study, *The Second American Party System: Party Formation in the Jacksonian Era* (Chapel Hill, 1966).
4. In addition to Chambers's *Political Parties in a New Nation*, which provides the best summary account of early party formation, two outstanding works are Joseph Charles, *The Origins of the American Party System* (Williamsburg, Va., 1956); and Noble E. Cunningham, Jr., *The Jeffersonian Republicans: The Formation of Party Organizations, 1789–1801* (Chapel Hill, 1957); see also Manning J. Dauer, *The Adams Federalists* (Baltimore, 1953). I share many of the understandings that Paul Goodman has set forth in his essay on "The First American Party System," in this volume. In particular, I agree with his insistence that the creation of a national political arena and its particular character was the crucial factor in the array of preconditions for the formation of national parties.
5. Duverger, *Political Parties,* xxiii–xxxvii.
6. Contrary to some understandings, the Federalist party did not experience an abrupt demise in 1815. Indeed, it was still amazingly vigorous as late as 1826 in Delaware — see John A. Munroe, *Federalist Delaware, 1775–1815* (New Brunswick, N.J., 1954). Two of the best studies on the Federalists are David Hackett Fischer, *The Revolution of American Conservatism: The Federalist Party in the Era of Jeffersonian Democracy* (New York, 1965); and Shaw Livermore, *The Twilight of Federalism* (Princeton, 1962).
7. For the sources of these, and other voting data cited, see my *Second American Party System,* 373–9.
8. Although I recognize that some may contend that the formations in New York, Georgia, and Kentucky were not parties, I believe that they are entitled to this designation. The point to be emphasized, however, is that these formations were exceptional and that in the absence of the stimulus of the contest for the presidency, parties did not form around state issues or group cleavages within states.
9. See Table 1 for an index of the balance — or imbalance — of parties in each state for the presidential elections from 1828 through 1844. It will be observed that the average differential between the total vote obtained by the presidential candidates in 1828 was 36 points, which would mean an average percentage of 68 for the victor and 32 for the defeated candidate.
10. The story of this memorable campaign is ably detailed in Robert G. Gunderson, *The Log Cabin Campaign* (Lexington, Ky., 1957).
11. See Table 1. In twenty of the states in 1840 the margin between the two parties was 15 points or less and the average differential was only 11 points. Note the contrast between 1832 and 1840.
12. Tennessee might be called a "one-party" state in the sense that nearly all public figures, as well as voters, identified themselves as Jeffersonian Republicans, or — after 1824 — as Jacksonians. But there was no formal party structure, and vigorously contested elections were conducted without relevance to parties.
13. For interesting material on the caucus-style party organization under the first party system, see Cunningham, *Jeffersonian Republicans,* 162–6; Cunningham, *The Jeffersonian Republicans in Power: Party Operations 1801–1809* (Chapel Hill, 1963), 111–12, 127, 133, 137, 142, 145–6; and Fischer, *Revolution of American Conservatism,* 60–90 passim.
14. See my "New Perspectives on Jacksonian Politics," *American Historical Review, LXV* (1960), 288–301, for illustrative data on the increase in voter participation. In those states where the parties were competitive after 1800, it was not uncommon for 70 per cent or more of the adult white males to vote, and on occasion higher levels were reached. But in states where the parties were unbalanced, or where elections were not contested on a party basis, participation would usually be under 50 per cent. There are, however, curious exceptions to these generalizations. Alabama recorded the suspiciously high figure of 97 per cent in a gubernatorial election in 1819, and Tennessee reached 80 per cent in the gubernatorial election of 1817. These, and other data that could be cited, suggest that high participation could be achieved in the absence of parties, and even in the absence of the stimulus of a presidential contest.
15. See my "Suffrage Classes and Party Alignments: A Study in Voter Behavior," *Mississippi Valley Historical Review, XLVI* (1959), 397–410.

16. M. Ostrogorski, among other foreign observers, has some extremely perceptive comments on the "ritual character" of American parties in *Democracy and the Party System in the United States* (New York, 1910), 408–12.
17. Michael Chevalier, *Society, Manners and Politics in the United States* (Boston, 1839), 318–19.
18. See Table 1.
19. Constitutions and electoral laws, as demonstrated by the studies of Duverger and others, strongly conditioned the nature of party systems. This is not to maintain that all attributes of parties are explainable in these terms, and in seeking to account for cleavages between parties, political styles, or the characteristics of political elites, for example, relevant social factors must be considered. But I would agree with Lipset that "electoral laws determine the nature of the party system as much as any other structural variable." See Lipset, *The First New Nation*, 293.
20. There have been scarcely any comparative studies of constitutional change at the state level, although this field offers rich opportunities for scholars. For a pioneering study, which still stands alone, see Fletcher M. Green, *Constitutional Development in the South Atlantic States, 1776–1860* (Chapel Hill, 1930).
21. For an interesting discussion of the conditions under which a two-party system may be less able to resolve conflict than a multi-party system, see Lipset, *The First New Nation*, 308–12.
22. The discussion that follows draws upon some of the concepts advanced by LaPalombara and Weiner in *Political Parties and Political Development*, 399–435. Similar concepts have been perceptively applied to an analysis of American party development by William N. Chambers in an extremely important essay in the same volume, "Parties and Nation Building in America," 79–106. For a contrasting view, which minimizes the effects of parties as independent variables, see Morton Grodzins's essay, "Political Parties and the Crisis of Succession in the United States: The Case of 1800," in the same volume, 303–27. I would suggest that the election of 1824 is an even better illustration of Grodzins's point.
23. Louis Hartz, *The Liberal Tradition in America* (New York, 1955).

Women in Ante-Bellum America

American men have always been confused about women, and in the process have often made women confused about themselves. On the one hand women were thought of as vessels of sin, tempting men from the path of purity and continence. On the other hand, they were represented as temples of virtue and the repositories and protectors of all that was holy in the family. They were treated as if they were delicate and fragile, but they were also burdened with nursing, comforting, teaching, and drudging for their families. Men cherished them, but they also mistreated them, and underneath, often despised them.

Without a doubt, the net effect of all this was not happy for women. Much as slavery frustrated the creative potential of blacks, the prevailing attitudes and mores of ante-bellum America severely limited the self-realization of women. The female mind was considered frail, as was the female body, and the education thought proper for a girl excluded the sciences, the learned professions, and the practical world of affairs. Until Oberlin College admitted women in 1833, higher education was closed to them. The first women who attempted to prepare for the medical profession faced enormous difficulties in forcing their way into medical colleges. Women interested in politics or public issues were ridiculed and abused and held to be "unsexed." When the Grimké sisters, Lucretia Mott, Abbey Kelly, and other strong-willed, idealistic women, sought to lecture for the abolitionists, they caused such a furor that otherwise brave antislavery men endeavored to stop them.

More important to most women of the period were the legal disabilities under which they suffered. The common law made women virtually their husbands' or fathers' chattels. Their property and earnings belonged to their men, and they could be physically abused by their men without the law's intervention. The children of a married woman were her husband's, and in a divorce action, even though he might be the guilty party, the father could claim them along with whatever property his wife possessed. In the realm of civil rights, she was virtually nonexistent, forbidden either to vote or hold office.

And yet it might be suggested that her situation was not all bad. If she was restricted, she was also protected. Most women, in those days, were probably happy to be spared the rough-and-tumble of a man's world. If she happened to be middle class and urban, she could count on servants to ease her household burdens, leaving her free to devote herself to self-adornment, the polite arts, and the pleasures of social intercourse. At least for the prosperous then, the "Cult of True Womanhood," as Barbara Welter shows in the following essay, had its advantages. From our perspective it is hard to say whether they offset the drawbacks.

FOR FURTHER READING:

FLEXNER, ELEANOR. *Century of Struggle*. New York: Atheneum Publishers, 1968.*
O'NEILL, WILLIAM. *Everyone Was Brave: The Rise and Fall of Feminism in America*. Chicago: Quadrangle Books, 1969.*

SINCLAIR, ANDREW. *The Emancipation of the American Woman.* New York: Harper & Row, Publishers, Colophon Books, 1966.*

Asterisk denotes paperback edition.

The Cult of True Womanhood 1820–1860 BARBARA WELTER

The nineteenth-century American man was a busy builder of bridges and railroads, at work long hours in a materialistic society. The religious values of his forebears were neglected in practice if not in intent, and he occasionally felt some guilt that he had turned this new land, this temple of the chosen people, into one vast countinghouse. But he could salve his conscience by reflecting that he had left behind a hostage, not only to fortune, but to all the values which he held so dear and treated so lightly. Woman, in the cult of True Womanhood [1] presented by the women's magazines, gift annuals and religious literature of the nineteenth century, was the hostage in the home.[2] In a society where values changed frequently, where fortunes rose and fell with frightening rapidity, where social and economic mobility provided instability as well as hope, one thing at least remained the same — a true woman was a true woman, wherever she was found. If anyone, male or female, dared to tamper with the complex of virtues which made up True Womanhood, he was damned immediately as an enemy of God, of civilization and of the Republic. It was a fearful obligation, a solemn responsibility, which the nineteenth century American woman had — to uphold the pillars of the temple with her frail white hand.

The attributes of True Womanhood, by which a woman judged herself and was judged by her husband, her neighbors and society could be divided into four cardinal virtues — piety, purity, submissiveness and domesticity. Put them all together and they spelled mother, daughter, sister, wife — woman. Without them, no matter whether there was fame, achievement or wealth, all was ashes. With them she was promised happiness and power.

Religion or piety was the core of woman's virtue, the source of her strength. Young men looking for a mate were cautioned to search first for piety, for if that were there, all else would follow.[3] Religion belonged to woman by divine right, a gift of God and nature. This "peculiar susceptibility" to religion was given her for a reason: "the vestal flame of piety, lighted up by Heaven in the breast of woman" would throw its beams into the naughty world of men.[4] So far would its candle power reach that the "Universe might be Enlightened, Improved, and Harmonized by WOMAN!!"[5] She would be another, better Eve, working in cooperation with the Redeemer, bringing the world back "from its revolt and sin."[6] The world would be reclaimed for God through her suffering, for "God increased the cares and sorrows of woman, that she might be sooner constrained to accept the terms of salvation."[7] A popular poem by Mrs. Frances Osgood, "The Triumph of the Spiritual Over the Sensual" expressed just this sentiment, woman's purifying passionless love bringing an erring man back to Christ.[8]

Source: Barbara Welter, "The Cult of True Womanhood, 1820–1860," *American Quarterly*, vol. 18 (1966), pp. 151–174.

Dr. Charles Meigs, explaining to a graduating class of medical students why women were naturally religious, said that "hers is a pious mind. Her confiding nature leads her more readily than men to accept the proffered grace of the Gospel." [9] Caleb Atwater, Esq., writing in *The Ladies' Repository*, saw the hand of the Lord in female piety: "Religion is exactly what a woman needs, for it gives her that dignity that best suits her dependence." [10] And Mrs. John Sandford, who had no very high opinion of her sex, agreed thoroughly: "Religion is just what woman needs. Without it she is ever restless or unhappy. . . ." [11] Mrs. Sandford and the others did not speak only of that restlessness of the human heart, which St. Augustine notes, that can only find its peace in God. They spoke rather of religion as a kind of tranquilizer for the many undefined longings which swept even the most pious young girl, and about which it was better to pray than to think.

One reason religion was valued was that it did not take a woman away from her "proper sphere," her home. Unlike participation in other societies or movements, church work would not make her less domestic or submissive, less a True Woman. In religious vineyards, said the *Young Ladies' Literary and Missionary Report*, "you may labor without the apprehension of detracting from the charms of feminine delicacy." Mrs. S. L. Dagg, writing from her chapter of the Society in Tuscaloosa, Alabama, was equally reassuring: "As no sensible woman will suffer her intellectual pursuits to clash with her domestic duties" she should concentrate on religious work "which promotes these very duties." [12]

The women's seminaries aimed at aiding women to be religious, as well as accomplished. Mt. Holyoke's catalogue promised to make female education "a handmaid to the Gospel and an efficient auxiliary in the great task of renovating the world." [13] The Young Ladies' Seminary at Bordentown, New Jersey, declared its most important function to be "the forming of a sound and virtuous character." [14] In Keene, New Hampshire, the Seminary tried to instill a "consistent and useful character" in its students, to enable them in this life to be "a good friend, wife and mother" but more important, to qualify them for "the enjoyment of Celestial Happiness in the life to come." [15] And Joseph M' D. Mathews, Principal of Oakland Female Seminary in Hillsborough, Ohio, believed that "female education should be preeminently religious." [16]

If religion was so vital to a woman, irreligion was almost too awful to contemplate. Women were warned not to let their literary or intellectual pursuits take them away from God. Sarah Josepha Hale spoke darkly of those who, like Margaret Fuller, threw away the "One True Book" for others, open to error. Mrs. Hale used the unfortunate Miss Fuller as fateful proof that "the greater the intellectual force, the greater and more fatal the errors into which women fall who wander from the Rock of Salvation, Christ the Saviour. . . ." [17]

One gentleman, writing on "Female Irreligion" reminded his readers that "Man may make himself a brute, and does so very often, but can woman brutify herself to his level — the lowest level of human nature — without exerting "special wonder?" Fanny Wright, because she was godless "was no woman, mother though she be." A few years ago, he recalls, such women would have been whipped. In any case, "woman never looks lovelier than in her reverence for religion" and, conversely, "female irreligion is the most revolting feature in human character." [18]

Purity was as essential as piety to a young woman, its absence as unnatural and unfeminine. Without it she was, in fact, no woman at all, but a member of some lower order. A "fallen woman" was a "fallen angel," unworthy of the celestial company of her sex. To contemplate the loss of purity brought tears; to be guilty of such a crime, in the women's magazines at least brought madness or death. Even the language of the flowers had bitter words for it: a dried white rose symbolized "Death Preferable to Loss of Innocence." [19] The marriage night was the single great event of a woman's life, when she bestowed her greatest treasure upon her husband, and from that time on was completely dependent upon him, an empty vessel,[20] without legal or emotional existence of her own.[21]

Therefore all True Women were urged, in the strongest possible terms, to maintain their virtue, although men, being by nature more sensual than they, would try to assault it. Thomas Branagan admitted in *The Excellency of the Female Character Vindicated* that his sex would sin and sin again, they could not help it, but woman, stronger and purer, must not give in and let man "take liberties incompatible with her delicacy." "If you do," Branagan addressed his gentle reader, "you will be left in silent sadness to bewail your credulity, imbecility, duplicity, and premature prostitution." [22]

Mrs. Eliza Farrar, in *The Young Lady's Friend*, gave practical logistics to avoid trouble: "Sit not with another in a place that is too narrow; read not out of the same book; let not your eagerness to see anything induce you to place your head close to another person's." [23]

If such good advice was ignored the consequences were terrible and inexorable. In *Girlhood and Womanhood: Or Sketches of My Schoolmates*, by Mrs. A. J. Graves (a kind of mid-nineteenth-century *The Group*), the bad ends of a boarding school class of girls are scrupulously recorded. The worst end of all is reserved for "Amelia Dorrington: The Lost One." Amelia died in the almshouse "the wretched victim of depravity and intemperance" and all because her mother had let her be "high-spirited not prudent." These girlish high spirits had been misinterpreted by a young man, with disastrous results. Amelia's "thoughtless levity" was "followed by a total loss of virtuous principle" and Mrs. Graves editorializes that "the coldest reserve is more admirable in a woman a man wishes to make his wife, than the least approach to undue familiarity." [24]

A popular and often-reprinted story by Fanny Forester told the sad tale of "Lucy Dutton." Lucy "with the seal of innocence upon her heart, and a rose-leaf on her cheek" came out of her vine-covered cottage and ran into a city slicker. "And Lucy was beautiful and trusting, and thoughtless: and he was gay, selfish and profligate. Needs the story to be told? . . . Nay, censor, Lucy was a child — consider how young, how very untaught — oh! her innocence was no match for the sophistry of a gay, city youth! Spring came and shame was stamped upon the cottage at the foot of the hill." The baby died; Lucy went mad at the funeral and finally died herself. "Poor, poor Lucy Dutton! The grave is a blessed couch and pillow to the wretched. Rest thee there, poor Lucy!" [25] The frequency with which derangement follows loss of virtue suggests the exquisite sensibility of woman, and the possibility that, in the women's magazines at least, her intellect was geared to her hymen, not her brain.

If, however, a woman managed to withstand man's assaults on her virtue, she demonstrated her superiority and her power over him. Eliza Farnham, trying to prove this female superiority, concluded smugly that "the purity of women is the everlasting barrier against which the tides of man's sensual nature surge." [26]

A story in *The Lady's Amaranth* illustrates this dominance. It is set, improbably, in Sicily, where two lovers, Bianca and Tebaldo, have been separated because her family insisted she marry a rich old man. By some strange circumstance the two are in a shipwreck and cast on a desert island, the only survivors. Even here, however, the rigid standards of True Womanhood prevail. Tebaldo unfortunately forgets himself slightly, so that Bianca must warn him: "We may not indeed gratify our fondness by caresses, but it is still something to bestow our kindest language, and looks and prayers, and all lawful and honest attentions on each other." Something, perhaps, but not enough, and Bianca must further remonstrate: "It is true that another man is my husband, but you are my guardian angel." When even that does not work she says in a voice of sweet reason, passive and proper to the end, that she wishes he wouldn't but "still, if you insist, I will become what you wish; but I beseech you to consider, ere that decision, that debasement which I must suffer in your esteem." This appeal to his own double standards holds the beast in him at bay. They are rescued, discover that the old husband is dead, and after "mourning a decent season" Bianca finally gives in, legally.[27]

Men could be counted on to be grateful when women thus saved them from themselves. William Alcott, guiding young men in their relations with the opposite sex, told them that "Nothing is better calculated to preserve a young man from contamination of low pleasures and pursuits than frequent intercourse with the more refined and virtuous of the other sex." And he added, one assumes in equal innocence, that youths should "observe and learn to admire, that purity and ignorance of evil which is the characteristic of well-educated young ladies, and which, when we are near them, raises us above those sordid and sensual considerations which hold such sway over men in their intercourse with each other." [28]

The Rev. Jonathan F. Stearns was also impressed by female chastity in the face of male passion, and warned woman never to compromise the source of her power: "Let her lay aside delicacy, and her influence over our sex is gone." [29]

Women themselves accepted, with pride but suitable modesty, this priceless virtue. *The Ladies' Wreath*, in "Woman the Creature of God and the Manufacturerer of Society" saw purity as her greatest gift and chief means of discharging her duty to save the world: "Purity is the highest beauty — the true pole-star which is to guide humanity aright in its long, varied, and perilous voyage." [30]

Sometimes, however, a woman did not see the dangers to her treasure. In that case, they must be pointed out to her, usually by a male. In the nineteenth century any form of social change was tantamount to an attack on woman's virtue, if only it was correctly understood. For example, dress reform seemed innocuous enough and the bloomers worn by the lady of that name and her followers were certainly modest attire. Such was the reasoning only of the ignorant. In another issue of *The Ladies' Wreath* a young lady is represented in dialogue with her "Professor." The girl expresses admiration for the bloomer costume — it gives freedom of motion, is healthful and attractive. The "Professor" sets her straight. Trousers, he explains, are "only one of the many manifestations of that wild spirit of socialism and agrarian radicalism which is at present so rife in our land." The young lady recants immediately: "If this dress has any connexion with Fourierism or Socialism, or fanaticism in any shape whatever, I have no disposition to wear it at all . . . no true woman would so far compromise her delicacy as to espouse, however unwittingly, such a cause." [31]

America could boast that her daughters were particularly innocent. In a poem on "The American Girl" the author wrote proudly:

> Her eye of light is the diamond bright,
> Her innocence the pearl,

> And these are ever the bridal gems
> That are worn by the American girl.[32]

Lydia Maria Child, giving advice to mothers, aimed at preserving that spirit of innocence. She regretted that "want of confidence between mothers and daughters on delicate subjects" and suggested a woman tell her daughter a few facts when she reached the age of twelve to "set her mind at rest." Then Mrs. Child confidently hoped that a young lady's "instinctive modesty" would "prevent her from dwelling on the information until she was called upon to use it."[33] In the same vein, a book of advice to the newly-married was titled *Whisper to a Bride*.[34] As far as intimate information was concerned, there was no need to whisper, since the book contained none at all.

A masculine summary of this virtue was expressed in a poem "Female Charms":

> I would have her as pure as the snow on the mount —
>   As true as the smile that to infamy's given —
> As pure as the wave of the crystalline fount,
>   Yet as warm in the heart as the sunlight of heaven.
> With a mind cultivated, not boastingly wise,
>   I could gaze on such beauty, with exquisite bliss;
> With her heart on her lips and her soul in her eyes —
>   What more could I wish in dear woman than this.[35]

Man might, in fact, ask no more than this in woman, but she was beginning to ask more of herself, and in the asking was threatening the third powerful and necessary virtue, submission. Purity, considered as a moral imperative, set up a dilemma which was hard to resolve. Woman must preserve her virtue until marriage and marriage was necessary for her happiness. Yet marriage was, literally, an end to innocence. She was told not to question this dilemma, but simply to accept it.

Submission was perhaps the most feminine virtue expected of women. Men were supposed to be religious, although they rarely had time for it, and supposed to be pure, although it came awfully hard to them, but men were the movers, the doers, the actors. Women were the passive, submissive responders. The order of dialogue was, of course, fixed in Heaven. Man was "woman's superior by God's appointment, if not in intellectual dowry, at least by official decree." Therefore, as Charles Elliott argued in *The Ladies' Repository*, she should submit to him "for the sake of good order at least."[36] In *The Ladies Companion* a young wife was quoted approvingly as saying that she did not think woman should "feel and act for herself" because "When, next to God, her husband is not the tribunal to which her heart and intellect appeals — the golden bowl of affection is broken."[37] Women were warned that if they tampered with this quality they tampered with the order of the Universe.

The Young Lady's Book summarized the necessity of the passive virtues in its readers' lives: "It is, however, certain, that in whatever situation of life a woman is placed from her cradle to her grave, a spirit of obedience and submission, pliability of temper, and humility of mind, are required from her."[38]

Woman understood her position if she was the right kind of woman, a true woman. "She feels herself weak and timid. She needs a protector," declared George Burnap, in his lectures on *The Sphere and Duties of Woman*. "She is in a measure dependent. She asks for wisdom, constancy, firmness, perseverance, and she is willing to repay it all by the surrender of the full treasure of her affections. Woman despises in man every thing like herself except a tender heart. It is enough that she is effeminate and weak; she does not want another like herself."[39] Or put even more strongly by Mrs. Sandford: "A really sensible woman feels her dependence. She does what she can, but she is conscious of inferiority, and therefore grateful for support."[40]

Mrs. Sigourney, however, assured young ladies that although they were separate, they were equal. This difference of the sexes did not imply inferiority, for it was part of that same order of Nature established by Him "who bids the oak brave the fury of the tempest, and the alpine flower lean its cheek on the bosom of eternal snows."[41] Dr. Meigs had a different analogy to make the same point, contrasting the anatomy of the Apollo of the Belvedere (illustrating the male principle) with the Venus de Medici (illustrating the female principle). "Woman," said the physician, with a kind of clinical gallantry, "has a head almost too small for intellect but just big enough for love."[42]

This love itself was to be passive and responsive. "Love, in the heart of a woman," wrote Mrs. Farrar, "should partake largely of the nature of gratitude. She should love, because she is already loved by one deserving her regard."[43]

Woman was to work in silence, unseen, like Wordsworth's Lucy. Yet, "working like nature, in secret" her love goes forth to the world "to regulate its pulsation, and send forth from its heart, in pure and temperate flow, the life-giving current."[44] She was to work only for pure affection, without thought of money or ambition. A poem, "Woman and Fame," by Felicia Hemans, widely quoted in many of the gift books, concludes with a spirited renunciation of the gift of fame:

> Away! to me, a woman, bring
> Sweet flowers from affection's spring.[45]

"True feminine genius," said Grace Greenwood (Sara Jane Clarke) "is ever timid, doubtful, and clingingly dependent; a perpetual childhood." And she advised literary ladies in an essay on "The Intellectual Woman" — "Don't trample on the flowers while longing for the stars."[46] A wife who submerged her own talents to work for her husband was extolled as an example of a true woman. In *Women of Worth: A Book for Girls,* Mrs. Ann Flaxman, an artist of promise herself, was praised because she "devoted herself to sustain her husband's genius and aid him in his arduous career."[47]

Caroline Gilman's advice to the bride aimed at establishing this proper order from the beginning of a marriage: "Oh, young and lovely bride, watch well the first moments when your will conflicts with his to whom God and society have given the control. Reverence his *wishes* even when you do not his *opinions.*"[48]

Mrs. Gilman's perfect wife in *Recollections of a Southern Matron* realizes that "the three golden threads with which domestic happiness is woven" are "to repress a harsh answer, to confess a fault, and to stop (right or wrong) in the midst of self-defense, in gentle submission." Woman could do this, hard though it was, because in her heart she knew she was right and so could afford to be forgiving, even a trifle condescending. "Men are not unreasonable," averred Mrs. Gilman. "Their difficulties lie in not understanding the moral and physical nature of our sex. They often wound through ignorance, and are suprised at having offended." Wives were advised to do their best to reform men, but if they couldn't, to give up gracefully. "If any habit of his annoyed me, I spoke of it once or twice, calmly, then bore it quietly."[49]

A wife should occupy herself "only with domestic affairs — wait till your husband confides to you those of a high importance — and do not give your advice until he asks for it," advised the *Lady's Token.* At all times she should behave in a manner becoming a woman, who had "no arms other than gentleness." Thus "if he is abusive, never retort."[50] *A Young Lady's Guide to the Harmonious Development of a Christian Character* suggested that females should "become as little children" and "avoid a controversial spirit."[51] *The Mother's Assistant and Young Lady's Friend* listed "Always Conciliate" as its first commandment in "Rules for Conjugal and Domestic Happiness." Small wonder that these same rules ended with the succinct maxim: "Do not expect too much."[52]

As mother, as well as wife, woman was required to submit to fortune. In *Letters to Mothers* Mrs. Sigourney sighed: "To bear the evils and sorrows which may be appointed us, with a patient mind, should be the continual effort of our sex. . . . It seems, indeed, to be expected of us; since the passive and enduring virtues are more immediately within our province." Of these trials "the hardest was to bear the loss of children with submission" but the indomitable Mrs. Sigourney found strength to murmur to the bereaved mother: "The Lord loveth a cheerful giver."[53] *The Ladies' Parlor Companion* agreed thoroughly in "A Submissive Mother," in which a mother who had already buried two children and was nursing a dying baby saw her sole remaining child "probably scalded to death. Handing over the infant to die in the arms of a friend, she bowed in sweet submission to the double stroke." But the child "through the goodness of God survived, and the mother learned to say 'Thy will be done.' "[54]

Woman then, in all her roles, accepted submission as her lot. It was a lot she had not chosen or deserved. As *Godey's* said, "the lesson of submission is forced upon woman." Without comment or criticism the writer affirms that "To suffer and to be silent under suffering seems the great command she has to obey."[55] George Burnap referred to a woman's life as "a series of suppressed emotions."[56] She was, as Emerson said, "more vulnerable, more infirm, more mortal than man."[57] The death of a beautiful woman, cherished in fiction, represented woman as the innocent victim, suffering without sin, too pure and good for this world but too weak and passive to resist its evil forces.[58] The best refuge for such a delicate creature was the warmth and safety of her home.

The true woman's place was unquestionably by her own fireside — as daughter, sister, but most of all as wife and mother. Therefore domesticity was among the virtues most prized by the women's magazines. "As society is constituted," wrote Mrs. S. E. Farley, on the "Domestic and Social Claims on Woman," "the true dignity and beauty of the female character seem to consist in a right understanding and faithful and cheerful performance of social and family duties."[59] Sacred Scripture re-enforced social pressure: "St. Paul knew what was best for women when he advised them to be domestic," said Mrs. Sandford. "There is composure at home; there is something sedative in the duties which home involves. It affords security not only from the world, but from delusions and errors of every kind."[60]

From her home woman performed her great task of bringing men back to God. *The Young Ladies' Class Book* was sure that "the domestic fireside is the great guardian of society against the excesses of human passions."[61] *The Lady at Home* expressed its convictions in its very title and concluded that "even if we cannot reform the world in a moment, we can begin the work by reforming ourselves and our households — It is woman's mission. Let her not look away from her own little family circle for the means of producing moral and social reforms, but begin at home." [62]

Home was supposed to be a cheerful place, so that brothers, husbands and sons would not go elsewhere in search of a good time. Woman was expected to dispense comfort and cheer. In writing the biography of Margaret Mercer (every inch a true woman) her biographer (male) notes: "She never forgot that it is the peculiar province of woman to minister to the comfort, and promote the happiness, first, of those most nearly allied to her, and then of those, who by the Providence of God are placed in a state of dependence upon her." [63] Many other essays in the women's journals showed woman as comforter: "Woman, Man's Best Friend," "Woman, the Greatest Social Benefit," "Woman, A Being to Come Home To," "The Wife: Source of Comfort and the Spring of Joy." [64]

One of the most important functions of woman as comforter was her role as nurse. Her own health was probably, although regrettably, delicate.[65] Many homes had "little sufferers," those pale children who wasted away to saintly deaths. And there were enough other illnesses of youth and age, major and minor, to give the nineteenth-century American woman nursing experience. The sickroom called for the exercise of her higher qualities of patience, mercy and gentleness as well as for her housewifely arts. She could thus fulfill her dual feminine function — beauty and usefulness.

The cookbooks of the period offer formulas for gout cordials, ointment for sore nipples, hiccough and cough remedies, opening pills and refreshing drinks for fever, along with recipes for pound cake, jumbles, stewed calves head and currant wine.[66] *The Ladies' New Book of Cookery* believed that "food prepared by the kind hand of a wife, mother, sister, friend" tasted better and had a "restorative power which money cannot purchase." [67]

A chapter of *The Young Lady's Friend* was devoted to woman's privilege as "ministering spirit at the couch of the sick." Mrs. Farrar advised a soft voice, gentle and clean hands, and a cheerful smile. She also cautioned against an excess of female delicacy. That was all right for a young lady in the parlor, but not for bedside manners. Leeches, for example, were to be regarded as "a curious piece of mechanism . . . their ornamental stripes should recommend them even to the eye, and their valuable services to our feelings." And she went on calmly to discuss their use. Nor were women to shrink from medical terminology, since "If you cultivate right views of the wonderful structure of the body, you will be as willing to speak to a physician of the bowels as the brains of your patient." [68]

Nursing the sick, particularly sick males, not only made a woman feel useful and accomplished, but increased her influence. In a piece of heavy-handed humor in *Godey's* a man confessed that some women were only happy when their husbands were ailing that they might have the joy of nursing him to recovery "thus gratifying their medical vanity and their love of power by making him more dependent upon them." [69] In a similar vein a husband sometimes suspected his wife, "almost wishes me dead — for the pleasure of being utterly inconsolable." [70]

In the home women were not only the highest adornment of civilization, but they were supposed to keep busy at morally uplifting tasks. Fortunately most of housework, if looked at in true womanly fashion, could be regarded as uplifting. Mrs. Sigourney extolled its virtues: "The science of housekeeping affords exercise for the judgment and energy, ready recollection, and patient self-possession, that are the characteristics of a superior mind." [71] According to Mrs. Farrar, making beds was good exercise, the repetitiveness of routine tasks inculcated patience and perseverance, and proper management of the home was a surprisingly complex art: "There is more to be learned about pouring out tea and coffee, than most young ladies are willing to believe." [72] *Godey's* went so far as to suggest coyly, in "Learning vs. Housewifery" that the two were complementary, not opposed: chemistry could be utilized in cooking, geometry in dividing cloth, and phrenology in discovering talent in children.[73]

Women were to master every variety of needlework, for, as Mrs. Sigourney pointed out, "Needle-work, in all its forms of use, elegance, and ornament, has ever been the appropriate occupation of woman." [74] Embroidery improved taste; knitting promoted serenity and economy.[75] Other forms of artsy-craftsy activity for her leisure moments included painting on glass or velvet, Poonah work, tussy-mussy frames for her own needlepoint or water colors, stands for hyacinths, hair bracelets or baskets of feathers.[76]

She was expected to have a special affinity for flowers. To the editors of *The Lady's Token* "A Woman never appears more truly in her sphere, than when she divides her time between her domestic avocations and the culture of flowers." [77] She could write letters, an activity particularly feminine since it had to do with the outpourings of the heart,[78] or practice her drawingroom skills of singing and playing an instrument. She might even read.

Here she faced a bewildering array of advice. The female was dangerously addicted to novels, according to the literature of the period. She should avoid them, since they interfered with "serious piety." If she simply couldn't help herself and read them anyway, she should choose edifying ones from lists of morally acceptable authors. She should study history since it "showed the depravity of the human heart and the evil nature of sin." On the whole, "religious biography was best." [79]

The women's magazines themselves could be read without any loss of concern for the home. *Godey's* promised the husband that he would find his wife "no less assiduous for his reception, or less sincere in welcoming his return" as a result of reading their magazine.[80] *The Lily of the Valley* won its right to be admitted to the boudoir by confessing that it was "like its namesake humble and unostentatious, but it is yet pure, and, we trust, free from moral imperfections." [81]

No matter what later authorities claimed, the nineteenth century knew that girls *could* be ruined by a book. The seduction stories regard "exciting and dangerous books" as contributory causes of disaster. The man without honorable intentions always provides the innocent maiden with such books as a prelude to his assault on her virtue.[82] Books which attacked or seemed to attack woman's accepted place in society were regarded as equally dangerous. A reviewer of Harriet Martineau's *Society in America* wanted it kept out of the hands of American women. They were so susceptible to persuasion, with their "gentle yielding natures" that they might listen to "the bold ravings of the hard-featured of their own sex." The frightening result: "such reading will unsettle them for their true station and pursuits, and they will throw the world back again into confusion." [83]

The debate over women's education posed the question of whether a "finished" education detracted from the practice of housewifely arts. Again it proved to be a case of semantics, for a true woman's education was never "finished" until she was instructed in the gentle science of homemaking.[84] Helen Irving, writing on "Literary Women," made it very clear that if women invoked the muse, it was as a genie of the household lamp. "If the necessities of her position require these duties at her hands, she will perform them nonetheless cheerfully, that she knows herself capable of higher things." The literary woman must conform to the same standards as any other woman: "That her home shall be made a loving place of rest and joy and comfort for those who are dear to her, will be the first wish of every true woman's heart." [85] Mrs. Ann Stephens told women who wrote to make sure they did not sacrifice one domestic duty. "As for genius, make it a domestic plant. Let its roots strike deep in your house. . . ." [86]

The fear of "blue stockings" (the eighteenth-century male's term of derision for educated or literary women) need not persist for nineteenth-century American men. The magazines presented spurious dialogues in which bachelors were convinced of their fallacy in fearing educated wives. One such dialogue took place between a young man and his female cousin. Ernest deprecates learned ladies ("A *Woman* is far more lovable than a *philosopher*") but Alice refutes him with the beautiful example of their Aunt Barbara who "although she *has* perpetrated the heinous crime of writing some half dozen folios" is still a model of "the spirit of feminine gentleness." His memory prodded, Ernest concedes that, by George, there was a woman: "When I last had a cold she not only made me a bottle of cough syrup, but when I complained of nothing new to read, set to work and wrote some twenty stanzas on consumption." [87]

The magazines were filled with domestic tragedies in which spoiled young girls learned that when there was a hungry man to feed French and china painting were not helpful. According to these stories many a marriage is jeopardized because the wife has not learned to keep house. Harriet Beecher Stowe wrote a sprightly piece of personal experience for *Godey's,* ridiculing her own bad housekeeping as a bride. She used the same theme in a story "The Only Daughter," in which the pampered beauty learns the facts of domestic life from a rather difficult source, her mother-in-law. Mrs. Hamilton tells Caroline in the sweetest way possible to shape up in the kitchen, reserving her rebuke for her son: "You are her husband — her guide — her protector — now see what you can do," she admonishes him. "Give her credit for every effort: treat her faults with tenderness; encourage and praise whenever you can, and depend upon it, you will see another woman in her." He is properly masterful, she properly domestic and in a few months Caroline is making lumpless gravy and keeping up with the darning. Domestic tranquillity has been restored and the young wife moralizes: "Bring up a girl to feel that she has a responsible part to bear in promoting the happiness of the family, and you make a reflecting being of her at once, and remove that lightness and frivolity of character which makes her shrink from graver studies." [88] These stories end with the heroine drying her hands on her apron and vowing that *her* daughter will be properly educated, in piecrust as well as Poonah work.

The female seminaries were quick to defend themselves against any suspicion of interfering with the role which nature's God had assigned to women. They hoped to enlarge and deepen that role, but not to change its setting. At the Young Ladies' Seminary and Collegiate Institute in Monroe City, Michigan, the catalogue admitted few of its graduates would be likely "to fill the learned professions." Still, they were called to "other scenes of usefulness and honor." The average woman is to be "the presiding genius of love" in the home, where she is to "give a correct and elevated literary taste to her children, and to assume that influential station that she ought to possess as the companion of an educated man." [89]

At Miss Pierce's famous school in Litchfield, the students were taught that they had "attained the perfection of their characters when they could combine their elegant accomplishments with a turn for solid domestic virtues." [90] Mt. Holyoke paid pious tribute to domestic skills: "Let a young lady despise this branch of the duties of woman, and she despises the appointments of her existence." God, nature and the Bible "enjoin these duties on the sex, and she cannot violate them with impunity." Thus warned, the young lady would have to seek knowledge of these duties elsewhere, since it was not in the curriculum at Mt. Holyoke. "We would not take this privilege from the mother." [91]

One reason for knowing her way around a kitchen was that America was "a land of precarious fortunes," as Lydia Maria Child pointed out in her book *The Frugal Housewife: Dedicated to Those Who Are Not Ashamed of Economy*. Mrs. Child's chapter "How To Endure Poverty" prescribed a combination of piety and knowledge — the kind of knowledge found in a true woman's education, "a thorough religious *useful* education." [92] The woman who had servants today, might tomorrow, because of a depression or panic, be forced to do her own work. If that happened she knew how to act, for she was to be the same cheerful consoler of her husband in their cottage as in their mansion.

An essay by Washington Irving, much quoted in the gift annuals, discussed the value of a wife in case of business reverses: "I have observed that a married man falling into misfortune is more apt to achieve his situation in the world than a single one . . . it is beautifully ordained by Providence that woman, who is the ornament of man in his happier hours, should be his stay and solace when smitten with sudden calamity." [93]

A story titled simply but eloquently "The Wife" dealt with the quiet heroism of Ellen Graham during her husband's plunge from fortune to poverty. Ned Graham said of her: "Words are too poor to tell you what I owe to that noble woman. In our darkest seasons of adversity, she has been an angel of consolation — utterly forgetful of self and anxious only to comfort and sustain me." Of course she had a little help from "faithful Dinah who absolutely refused to leave her beloved mistress," but even so Ellen did no more than would be expected of any true woman.[94]

Most of this advice was directed to woman as wife. Marriage was the proper state for the exercise of the domestic virtues. "True Love and a Happy Home," an essay in *The Young Ladies' Oasis*, might have been carved on every girl's hope chest.[95] But although marriage was best, it was not absolutely necessary. The women's magazines tried to remove the stigma from being an "Old Maid." They advised no marriage at all rather than an unhappy one contracted out of selfish motives.[96] Their stories showed maiden ladies as unselfish ministers to the sick, teachers of the young, or moral preceptors with their pens, beloved of the entire village. Usually the life of single blessedness resulted from the premature death of a fiancé, or was chosen through fidelity to some high mission. For example, in "Two Sisters," Mary devotes herself to Ellen and her abandoned children, giving up her own chance for marriage. "Her devotion to her sister's happiness has met its reward in the consciousness of having fulfilled a sacred duty." [97] Very rarely, a "woman of genius" was absolved from the necessity of marriage, being so extraordinary that she did not need the security or status of being a wife.[98] Most often, however, if girls proved "difficult," marriage and a family were regarded as a cure.[99] The "sedative quality" of a home could be counted on to subdue even the most restless spirits.

George Burnap saw marriage as "that sphere for which woman was originally intended, and to which she is so exactly fitted to adorn and bless, as the wife, the mistress of a home, the solace, the aid, and the counsellor of that ONE, for whose sake alone the world is of any consequence to her." [100] Samuel Miller preached a sermon on women: "How interesting and important are the duties devolved on females as WIVES . . . the counsellor and friend of the husband; who makes it her daily study to lighten his cares, to soothe his sorrows, and to augment his joys; who, like a guardian angel, watches over his interests, warns him against dangers, comforts him under trials; and by her pious, assiduous, and attractive deportment, constantly endeavors to render him more virtuous, more useful, more honourable, and more happy." [101] A woman's whole interest should be focused on her husband, paying him "those numberless attentions to which the French give the title of *petits soins* and which the woman who loves knows so well how to pay . . . she should consider nothing as trivial which could win a smile of approbation from him." [102]

Marriage was seen not only in terms of service but as an increase in authority for women. Burnap concluded that marriage improves the female character "not only because it puts her under the best possible tuition, that of the affections, and affords scope to her active energies, but because it gives her higher aims, and a more dignified position." [103] *The Lady's Amaranth* saw it as a balance of power: "The man bears rule over his wife's person and conduct. She bears rule over his inclinations: he governs by law; she by persuasion. . . . The empire of the woman is an empire of softness . . . her commands are caresses, her menaces are tears." [104]

Woman should marry, but not for money. She should choose only the high road of true love and not truckle to the values of a materialistic society. A story "Marrying for Money" (subtlety was not the strong point of the ladies' magazines) depicts Gertrude, the heroine, rueing the day she made her crass choice: "It is a terrible thing to live without love. . . . A woman who dares marry for aught but the purest affection, calls down the just judgments of heaven upon her head." [105]

The corollary to marriage, with or without true love, was motherhood, which added another dimension to her usefulness and her prestige. It also anchored her even more firmly to the home. "My Friend," wrote Mrs. Sigourney, "If in becoming a mother, you have reached the climax of your happiness, you have also taken a higher place in the scale of being . . . you have gained an increase of power." [106] The Rev. J. N. Danforth pleaded in *The Ladies' Casket*, "Oh, mother, acquit thyself well in thy humble sphere, for thou mayest affect the world." [107] A true woman naturally loved her children; to suggest otherwise was monstrous.[108]

America depended upon her mothers to raise up a whole generation of Christian statesmen who could say "all that I am I owe to my angel mother." [109] The mothers must do the inculcating of virtue since the fathers, alas, were too busy chasing the dollar. Or as *The Ladies' Companion* put it more effusively, the father "weary with the heat and burden of life's summer day, or trampling with unwilling foot the decaying leaves of life's autumn, has forgotten the sympathies of life's joyous springtime. . . . The acquisition of wealth, the advancement of his children in worldly honor — these are his self-imposed tasks." It was his wife who formed "the infant mind as yet untainted by contact with evil . . . like wax beneath the plastic hand of the mother." [110]

The Ladies' Wreath offered a fifty-dollar prize to the woman who submitted the most convincing essay on "How May An American Woman Best Show Her Patriotism." The winner was Miss Elizabeth Wetherell who provided herself with a husband in her answer. The wife in the essay of course asked her husband's opinion. He tried a few jokes first — "Call her eldest son George Washington," "Don't speak

French, speak American" — but then got down to telling her in sober prize-winning truth what women could do for their country. Voting was no asset, since that would result only in "a vast increase of confusion and expense without in the smallest degree affecting the result." Besides, continued this oracle, "looking down at their child," if "we were to go a step further and let the children vote, their first act would be to vote their mothers at home." There is no comment on this devastating male logic and he continues: "Most women would follow the lead of their fathers and husbands," and the few who would "fly off on a tangent from the circle of home influence would cancel each other out."

The wife responds dutifully: "I see all that. I never understood so well before." Encouraged by her quick womanly perception, the master of the house resolves the question — an American woman best shows her patriotism by staying at home, where she brings her influence to bear "upon the right side for the country's weal." That woman will instinctively choose the side of right he has no doubt. Besides her "natural refinement and closeness to God" she has the "blessed advantage of a quiet life" while man is exposed to conflict and evil. She stays home with "her Bible and a well-balanced mind" and raises her sons to be good Americans. The judges rejoiced in this conclusion and paid the prize money cheerfully, remarking "they deemed it cheap at the price." [111]

If any woman asked for greater scope for her gifts the magazines were sharply critical. Such women were tampering with society, undermining civilization. Mary Wollstonecraft, Frances Wright and Harriet Martineau were condemned in the strongest possible language — they were read out of the sex. "They are only semi-women, mental hermaphrodites." The Rev. Harrington knew the women of America could not possibly approve of such perversions and went to some wives and mothers to ask if they did want a "wider sphere of interest" as these nonwomen claimed. The answer was reassuring. " 'NO!' they cried simultaneously, 'Let the men take care of politics, *we will take care of the children!*' " Again female discontent resulted only from a lack of understanding: women were not subservient, they were rather "chosen vessels." Looked at in this light the conclusion was inescapable: "Noble, sublime is the task of the American mother." [112] "Women's Rights" meant one thing to reformers, but quite another to the True Woman. She knew her rights,

> The right to love whom others scorn,
> The right to comfort and to mourn,
> The right to shed new joy on earth,
> The right to feel the soul's high worth . . .
> Such women's rights, and God will bless
> And crown their champions with success.[113]

The American woman had her choice — she could define her rights in the way of the women's magazines and insure them by the practice of the requisite virtues, or she could go outside the home, seeking other rewards than love. It was a decision on which, she was told, everything in her world depended. "Yours it is to determine," the Rev. Mr. Stearns solemnly warned from the pulpit, "whether the beautiful order of society . . . shall continue as it has been" or whether "society shall break up and become a chaos of disjointed and unsightly elements." [114] If she chose to listen to other voices than those of her proper mentors, sought other rooms than those of her home, she lost both her happiness and her power — "that almost magic power, which, in her proper sphere, she now wields over the destinies of the world." [115]

But even while the women's magazines and related literature encouraged this ideal of the perfect woman, forces were at work in the nineteenth century which impelled woman herself to change, to play a more creative role in society. The movements for social reform, westward migration, missionary activity, utopian communities, industrialism, the Civil War — all called forth responses from woman which differed from those she was trained to believe were hers by nature and divine decree. The very perfection of True Womanhood, moreover, carried within itself the seeds of its own destruction. For if woman was so very little less than the angels, she should surely take a more active part in running the world, especially since men were making such a hash of things.

Real women often felt they did not live up to the ideal of True Womanhood: some of them blamed themselves, some challenged the standard, some tried to keep the virtues and enlarge the scope of womanhood.[116] Somehow through this mixture of challenge and acceptance, of change and continuity, the True Woman evolved into the New Woman — a transformation as startling in its way as the abolition of slavery or the coming of the machine age. And yet the stereotype, the "mystique" if you will, of what woman was and ought to be persisted, bringing guilt and confusion in the midst of opportunity.[117]

The women's magazines and related literature had feared this very dislocation of values and blurring of roles. By careful manipulation and interpretation they sought to convince woman that she had the best of both worlds — power and virtue — and that a stable order of society depended upon her maintaining her traditional place in it. To that end she was identified with everything that was beautiful and holy.

"Who Can Find a Valiant Woman?" was asked frequently from the pulpit and the editorial pages. There was only one place to look for her — at home. Clearly and confidently these authorities proclaimed the True Woman of the nineteenth century to be the Valiant Woman of the Bible, in whom the heart of her husband rejoiced and whose price was above rubies.

NOTES

1. Authors who addressed themselves to the subject of women in the mid-nineteenth century used this phrase as frequently as writers on religion mentioned God. Neither group felt it necessary to define their favorite terms, they simply assumed — with some justification — that leaders would intuitively understand exactly what they meant. Frequently what people of one era take for granted is most striking and revealing to the student from another. In a sense this analysis of the ideal woman of the mid-nineteenth century is an examination of what writers of that period actually meant when they used so confidently the vague phrase True Womanhood.
2. The conclusions reached in this article are based on a survey of almost all of the women's magazines published for more than three years during the period 1820–60 and a sampling of those published for less than three years; all the gift books cited in Ralph Thompson, *American Literary Annuals and Gift Books, 1825–1865* (New York, 1936) deposited in the Library of Congress, the New York Public Library, the New York Historical Society, Columbia University Special Collections, Library of the City College of the University of New York, Pennsylvania Historical Society, Massachusetts Historical Society, Boston Public Library, Fruitlands Museum Library, the Smithsonian Institution and the Wisconsin Historical Society; hundreds of religious tracts and sermons in the American Unitarian Society and the Galatea Collection of the Boston Public Library: and the large collection of nineteenth century cookbooks in the New York Public Library and the Academy of Medicine of New York. Corroborative evidence not cited in this article was found in women's diaries, memoirs, autobiographies and personal papers, as well as in all the novels by women which sold over 75,000 copies during this period, as cited in Frank Luther Mott, *Golden Multitudes: The Story of Best Sellers in the United States* (New York, 1947) and H. R. Brown, *The Sentimental Novel in America, 1789–1860* (Durham, N. C., 1940). This latter information also indicated the effect of the cult of True Womanhood on those most directly concerned.

3. As in "The Bachelor's Dream," in *The Lady's Gift: Souvenir for All Seasons* (Nashua, N. H., 1849), p. 37.
4. *The Young Ladies' Class Book: A Selection of Lessons for Reading in Prose and Verse,* ed. Ebenezer Bailey, Principal of Young Ladies' High School, Boston (Boston, 1831). p. 168.
5. A Lady of Philadelphia, *The World Enlightened, Improved, and Harmonized by WOMAN!!!* A lecture, delivered in the City of New York, before the Young Ladies' Society for Mutual Improvement, on the following question proposed by the society, with the offer of $100 for the best lecture that should be read before them on the subject proposed: What is the power and influence of woman in moulding the manners, morals and habits of civil society? (Philadelphia, 1840), p. 1.
6. *The Young Lady's Book: A Manual of Elegant Recreations, Exercises, and Pursuits* (Boston, 1830), p. 29.
7. *Woman As She Was, Is, and Should be* (New York, 1849), p. 206.
8. "The Triumph of the Spiritual Over the Sensual: An Allegory," in *Ladies' Companion: A Monthly Magazine Embracing Every Department of Literature, Embellished With Original Engravings and Music, XVII* (New York) (1842), 67.
9. *Lecture on Some of the Distinctive Characteristics of the Female,* delivered before the class of the Jefferson Medical College, Jan. 1847 (Philadelphia, 1847), p. 13.
10. "Female Education," *Ladies' Repository and Gatherings of the West: A Monthly Periodical Devoted to Literature and Religion, I* (Cincinnati), 12.
11. *Woman, in Her Social and Domestic Character* (Boston, 1842), pp. 41–42.
12. *Second Annual Report of the Young Ladies' Literary and Missionary Association of the Philadelphia Collegiate Institution* (Philadelphia, 1840), pp. 20, 26.
13. *Mt. Holyoke Female Seminary: Female Education. Tendencies of the Principles Embraced, and the System Adopted in the Mt. Holyoke Female Seminary* (Boston, 1839), p. 3.
14. *Prospectus of the Young Ladies' Seminary at Bordentown, New Jersey* (Bordentown, 1836), p. 7.
15. *Catalogue of the Young Ladies' Seminary in Keene, New Hampshire* (n.p., 1832), p. 20.
16. "Report to the College of Teachers, Cincinnati, October, 1840" in *Ladies' Repository, I* (1841), 50.
17. *Woman's Record: or Sketches of All Distinguished Women from 'The Beginning' Till A.D. 1850* (New York, 1853), pp. 665, 669.
18. "Female Irreligion," *Ladies' Companion, XIII* (May–Oct. 1840), 111.
19. *The Lady's Book of Flowers and Poetry,* ed. Lucy Hooper (New York, 1842), has a "Floral Dictionary" giving the symbolic meaning of floral tributes.
20. See, for example, Nathaniel Hawthorne, *The Blithedale Romance* (Boston, 1852), p. 71, in which Zenobia says: "How can she be happy, after discovering that fate has assigned her but one single event, which she must contrive to make the substance of her whole life? A man has his choice of innumerable events."
21. Mary R. Beard, *Woman As Force in History* (New York, 1946) makes this point at some length. According to common law, a woman had no legal existence once she was married and therefore could not manage property, sue in court, etc. In the 1840s and 1850s laws were passed in several states to remedy this condition.
22. *Excellency of the Female Character Vindicated: Being an Investigation Relative to the Cause and Effects on the Encroachments of Men Upon the Rights of Women, and the Too Frequent Degradation and Consequent Misfortunes of The Fair Sex* (New York, 1807), pp. 277, 278.
23. By a Lady (Eliza Ware Rotch Farrar), *The Young Lady's Friend* (Boston, 1837), p. 293.
24. *Girlhood and Womanhood: or, Sketches of My Schoolmates* (Boston, 1844), p. 140.
25. Emily Chubbuck, *Alderbrook* (Boston, 1847), 2nd. ed., *II,* 121, 127.
26. *Woman and Her Era* (New York, 1864), p. 95.
27. "The Two Lovers of Sicily," *The Lady's Amaranth: A Journal of Tales, Essays, Excerpts — Historical and Biographical Sketches, Poetry and Literature in General* (Philadelphia), *II* (Jan. 1839), 17.
28. *The Young Man's Guide* (Boston, 1833), pp. 229, 231.
29. *Female Influence: and the True Christian Mode of Its Exercise; a Discourse Delivered in the First Presbyterian Church in Newburyport, July 30, 1837* (Newburyport, 1837), p. 18.
30. W. Tolles, "Woman The Creature of God and the Manufacturer of Society," *Ladies' Wreath* (New York), *III* (1852), 205.
31. Prof. William M. Heim, "The Bloomer Dress," *Ladies' Wreath, III* (1852), 247.
32. *The Young Lady's Offering: or Gems of Prose and Poetry* (Boston, 1853), p. 283. The American girl, whose innocence was often connected with ignorance, was the spiritual ancestress of the Henry James heroine. Daisy Miller, like Lucy Dutton, saw innocence lead to tragedy.
33. *The Mother's Book* (Boston, 1831), pp. 151, 152.
34. Mrs. L. M. Sigourney, *Whisper to a Bride* (Hartford, 1851), in which Mrs. Sigourney's approach is summed up in this quotation: "Home! Blessed bride, thou art about to enter this sanctuary, and to become a priestess at its altar!," p. 44.
35. S. R. R., "Female Charms," *Godey's Magazine and Lady's Book* (Philadelphia), *XXXIII* (1846), 52.
36. Charles Elliott, "Arguing With Females," *Ladies' Repository, I* (1841), 25.
37. *Ladies' Companion, VIII* (Jan. 1838), 147.
38. *The Young Lady's Book* (New York, 1830), American edition, p. 28. (This is a different book than the one of the same title and date of publication cited in note 6.)

39. *Sphere and Duties of Woman* (5th ed., Baltimore, 1854), p. 47.
40. *Woman,* p. 15.
41. *Letters to Young Ladies* (Hartford, 1835), p. 179.
42. *Lecture,* p. 17.
43. *The Young Lady's Friend,* p. 313.
44. Maria J. McIntosh, *Woman in America: Her Work and Her Reward* (New York, 1850), p. 25.
45. *Poems and a Memoir of the Life of Mrs. Felicia Hemans* (London, 1860), p. 16.
46. Letter "To an Unrecognized Poetess, June, 1846" (Sara Jane Clarke), *Greenwood Leaves* (2nd ed.; Boston, 1850), p. 311.
47. "The Sculptor's Assistant: Ann Flaxman," in *Women of Worth: A Book for Girls* (New York, 1860), p. 263.
48. Mrs. Clarissa Packard (Mrs. Caroline Howard Gilman), *Recollections of a Housekeeper* (New York, 1834), p. 122.
49. *Recollections of a Southern Matron* (New York, 1838), pp. 256, 257.
50. *The Lady's Token: or Gift of Friendship,* ed. Colesworth Pinckney (Nashua, N. H., 1848), p. 119.
51. Harvey Newcomb, *Young Lady's Guide to the Harmonious Development of Christian Character* (Boston, 1846), p. 10.
52. Rules for Conjugal and Domestic Happiness," *Mother's Assistant and Young Lady's Friend, III* (Boston), (April 1843), 115.
53. *Letters to Mothers* (Hartford, 1838), p. 199. In the diaries and letters of women who lived during this period the death of a child seemed consistently to be the hardest thing for them to bear and to occasion more anguish and rebellion, as well as eventual submission, than any other event in their lives.
54. "A Submissive Mother," *The Ladies' Parlor Companion: A Collection of Scattered Fragments and Literary Gems* (New York, 1852), p. 358.
55. "Woman," *Godey's Lady's Book, II* (Aug. 1831), 110.
56. *Sphere and Duties of Woman,* p. 172.
57. Ralph Waldo Emerson, "Woman," *Complete Writings of Ralph Waldo Emerson* (New York, 1875), p. 1180.
58. As in Donald Fraser, *The Mental Flower Garden* (New York, 1857). Perhaps the most famous exponent of this theory is Edgar Allan Poe who affirms in "The Philosophy of Composition" that "the death of a beautiful woman is unquestionably the most poetical topic in the world. . . ."
59. "Domestic and Social Claims on Woman," *Mother's Magazine, VI* (1846), 21.
60. *Woman,* p. 173.
61. *The Young Ladies' Class Book,* p. 166.
62. T. S. Arthur, *The Lady at Home: or, Leaves from the Every-Day Book of an American Woman* (Philadelphia, 1847), pp. 177, 178.
63. Caspar Morris, *Margaret Mercer* (Boston, 1840), quoted in *Woman's Record,* p. 425.
64. These particular titles come from: *The Young Ladies' Oasis: or Gems of Prose and Poetry,* ed. N. L. Ferguson (Lowell, 1851), pp. 14, 16; *The Genteel School Reader* (Philadelphia, 1849), p. 271; and *Magnolia, I* (1842), 4. A popular poem in book form, published in England, expressed very fully this concept of woman as comforter: Coventry Patmore, *The Angel in the Home* (Boston, 1856 and 1857). Patmore expressed his devotion to True Womanhood in such lines as:
    The gentle wife, who decks his board
    And makes his day to have no night,
    Whose wishes wait upon her Lord,
    Who finds her own in his delight. (p. 94)
65. The women's magazines carried on a crusade against tight lacing and regretted, rather than encouraged, the prevalent ill health of the American woman. See, for example, *An American Mother, Hints and Sketches* (New York, 1839), pp. 28 ff. for an essay on the need for a healthy mind in a healthy body in order to better be a good example for children.
66. The best single collection of nineteenth-century cookbooks is in the Academy of Medicine of New York Library, although some of the most interesting cures were in hand-written cookbooks found among the papers of women who lived during the period.
67. Sarah Josepha Hale, *The Ladies' New Book of Cookery: A Practical System for Private Families in Town and Country* (5th ed.; New York, 1852), p. 409. Similar evidence on the importance of nursing skills to every female is found in such books of advice as William A. Alcott, *The Young Housekeeper* (Boston, 1838), in which, along with a plea for apples and cold baths, Alcott says "Every female should be trained to the angelic art of managing properly the sick," p. 47.
68. *The Young Lady's Friend,* pp. 75–77, 79.
69. "A Tender Wife," *Godey's. II* (July 1831), 28.
70. "MY WIFE! A Whisper," *Godey's, II* (Oct. 1831), 231.
71. *Letters to Young Ladies,* p. 27. The greatest exponent of the mental and moral joys of housekeeping was the *Lady's Annual Register and Housewife's Memorandum Book* (Boston, 1838), which gave practical advice on ironing, hair curling, budgeting and marketing, and turning cuffs — all activities which contributed to the "beauty of usefulness" and "joy of accomplishment" which a woman desired (*I,* 23).

72. *The Young Lady's Friend,* p. 230.
73. "Learning vs. Housewifery," *Godey's,* X (Aug. 1839), 95.
74. *Letters to Young Ladies,* p. 25. W. Thayer, *Life at the Fireside* (Boston, 1857), has an idyllic picture of the woman of the house mending her children's garments, the grandmother knitting and the little girl taking her first stitches, all in the light of the domestic hearth.
75. "The Mirror's Advice," *Young Maiden's Mirror* (Boston, 1858), p. 263.
76. Mrs. L. Maria Child, *The Girl's Own Book* (New York, 1833).
77. P. 44.
78. T. S. Arthur, *Advice to Young Ladies* (Boston, 1850), p. 45.
79. R. C. Waterston, *Thoughts on Moral and Spiritual Culture* (Boston, 1842), p. 101. Newcomb's *Young Lady's Guide* also advised religious biography as the best reading for women (p. 111).
80. *Godey's, I* (1828), 1. (Repeated often in *Godey's* editorials.)
81. *The Lily of the Valley,* n. v. (1851), p. 2.
82. For example, "The Fatalist," *Godey's, IV* (Jan. 1834), 10, in which Somers Dudley has Catherine reading these dangerous books until life becomes "a bewildered dream. — O passion, what a shocking perverter of reason thou art!"
83. Review of *Society in America* (New York, 1837) in *American Quarterly Review* (Philadelphia), *XXII* (Sept. 1837), 38.
84. "A Finished Education," *Ladies' Museum* (Providence), *I* (1825), 42.
85. Helen Irving, "Literary Women," *Ladies' Wreath, III* (1850), 93.
86. "Women of Genius," *Ladies' Companion, XI* (1839), 89.
87. "Intellect vs. Affection in Woman," *Godey's, XVI* (1846), 86.
88. "The Only Daughter," *Godey's, X* (Mar. 1839), 122.
89. *The Annual Catalogue of the Officers and Pupils of the Young Ladies' Seminary and Collegiate Institute* (Monroe City, 1855), pp. 18, 19.
90. *Chronicles of a Pioneer School* from 1792 to 1833: Being the History of Miss Sarah Pierce and Her Litchfield School, Compiled by Emily Noyes Vanderpoel; ed. Elizabeth C. Barney Buel (Cambridge, 1903), p. 74.
91. *Mt. Holyoke Female Seminary,* p. 13.
92. *The American Frugal Housewife* (New York, 1838), p. 111.
93. "Female Influence," in *The Ladies' Pearl and Literary Gleaner: A Collection of Tales, Sketches, Essays, Anecdotes, and Historical Incidents* (Lowell), *I* (1841), 10.
94. Mrs. S. T. Martyn, "The Wife," *Ladies' Wreath, II* (1848–49), 171.
95. *The Young Ladies' Oasis,* p. 26.
96. "On Marriage," *Ladies' Repository, I* (1841), 133; "Old Maids," *Ladies' Literary Cabinet* (Newburyport), *II* (1822) (Microfilm), 141; "Matrimony," *Godey's, II* (Sept. 1831), 174; and "Married or Single," *Peterson's Magazine* (Philadelphia) *IX* (1859), 36, all express the belief that while marriage is desirable for a woman it is not essential. This attempt to reclaim the status of the unmarried woman is an example of the kind of mild crusade which the women's magazines sometimes carried on. Other examples were their strictures against an overly-genteel education and against the affectation and aggravation of ill health. In this sense the magazines were truly conservative, for they did not oppose all change but only that which did violence to some cherished tradition. The reforms they advocated would, if put into effect, make woman even more the perfect female, and enhance the ideal of True Womanhood.
97. *Girlhood and Womanhood,* p. 100. Mrs. Graves tells the stories in the book in the person of an "Old Maid" and her conclusions are that "single life has its happiness too" for the single woman "can enjoy all the pleasures of maternity without its pains and trials" (p. 140). In another one of her books, *Woman in America* (New York, 1843), Mrs. Graves speaks out even more strongly in favor of "single blessedness" rather than "a loveless or unhappy marriage" (p. 130).
98. A very unusual story is Lela Linwood, "A Chapter in the History of a Free Heart," *Ladies' Wreath, III* (1853), 349. The heroine, Grace Arland, is "sublime" and dwells "in perfect light while we others struggled yet with the shadows." She refuses marriage and her friends regret this but are told her heart "is rejoicing in its *freedom.*" The story ends with the plaintive refrain:

> But is it not a happy thing,
> All fetterless and free,
> Like any wild bird, on the wing,
> To carol merrily?

But even in this tale the unusual, almost unearthly rarity of Grace's genius is stressed; she is not offered as an example to more mortal beings.
99. Horace Greeley even went so far as to apply this remedy to the "dissatisfactions" of Margaret Fuller. In his autobiography, *Recollections of a Busy Life* (New York, 1868) he says that "noble and great as she was, a good husband and two or three bouncing babies would have emancipated her from a deal of cant and nonsense" (p. 178).
100. *Sphere and Duties of Woman,* p. 64.
101. *A Sermon: Preached March 13, 1808, for the Benefit of the Society Instituted in the City of New-York, For the Relief of Poor Widows with Small Children* (New York, 1808), pp. 13, 14.

102. *Lady's Magazine and Museum: A Family Journal* (London) *IV* (Jan. 1831), 6. This magazine is included partly because its editorials proclaimed it "of interest to the English speaking lady at home and abroad" and partly because it shows that the preoccupation with True Womanhood was by no means confined to the United States.
103. *Sphere and Duties of Woman*, p. 102.
104. "Matrimony," *Lady's Amaranth, II* (Dec. 1839), 271.
105. Elizabeth Doten, "Marrying for Money," *The Lily of the Valley*, n. v. (1857), p. 112.
106. *Letters to Mothers*, p. 9.
107. "Maternal Relation," *Ladies' Casket* (New York, 1850?), p. 85. The importance of the mother's role was emphasized abroad as well as in America. *Godey's* recommended the book by the French author Aimeé-Martin on the education of mothers to "be read five times," in the original if possible (*XIII*, Dec. 1842, 201). In this book the highest ideals of True Womanhood are upheld. For example: "Jeunes filles, jeunes épouses, tendres mères, c'est dans votre âme bien plus que dans les lois du législateur que reposent aujourd'hui l'avenir de l'Europe et les destinées du genre humain," L. Aimeé-Martin, *De l'Education des Mères de famille ou De la civilisation du genre humain par les femmes* (Bruxelles, 1857), *II*, 527.
108. *Maternal Association of the Amity Baptist Church:* Annual Report (New York, 1847), p. 2: "Suffer the little children to come unto me and forbid them not, is and must ever be a sacred commandment to the Christian woman."
109. For example, Daniel Webster, "The Influence of Woman," in *The Young Ladies' Reader* (Philadelphia, 1851), p. 310.
110. Mrs. Emma C. Embury, "Female Education," *Ladies' Companion, VIII* (Jan. 1838), 18. Mrs. Embury stressed the fact that the American woman was not the "mere plaything of passion" but was in strict training to be "the mother of statesmen."
111. "How May An American Woman Best Show Her Patriotism?" *Ladies' Wreath, III* (1851), 313. Elizabeth Wetherell was the pen name of Susan Warner, author of *The Wide Wide World* and *Queechy*.
112. Henry F. Harrington, "Female Education," *Ladies' Companion, IX* (1838), 293, and "Influence of Woman — Past and Present," *Ladies' Companion, XIII* (1840), 245.
113. Mrs. E. Little, "What Are the Rights of Women?" *Ladies' Wreath, II* (1848–49), 133.
114. *Female Influence*, p. 18.
115. *Ibid.*, p. 23.
116. Even the women reformers were prone to use domestic images, i.e. "sweep Uncle Sam's kitchen clean," and "tidy up our country's house."
117. The "Animus and Anima" of Jung amounts almost to a catalogue of the nineteenth-century masculine and female traits, and the female hysterics whom Freud saw had much of the same training as the nineteenth-century American woman. Betty Friedan, *The Feminine Mystique* (New York, 1963), challenges the whole concept of True Womanhood as it hampers the "fulfillment" of the twentieth-century woman.

The Black Slave

If America was exceptional, it was so not only in positive but also in negative ways. By 1860, the "land of the free" was also the home of four million black slaves, who constituted 13 percent of the whole population. Some of these bondsmen were African by birth; many more were descended from the wretched victims stolen from Africa by slavers in the colonial period. By the eve of the Civil War, blacks had been in North America for as long as Europeans, yet the overwhelming majority were chattel slaves, a "peculiar species of property," whose status would become more controversial with each passing year.

Slavery in the ante-bellum South was not a benign institution. Most masters sought to avoid using the lash and the branding iron to enforce their will, but everywhere in the South some slaves were punished brutally and peremptorily. More important, slavery denied its subjects' fundamental human needs by weakening the ties between husband and wife, children and parents. It also wasted tremendous human potential. A few slaves were able to develop and exercise their minds and their skills, but most were locked permanently into a life of mindless, backbreaking, common toil.

Yet human beings can adjust to many frustrating and coercive experiences. Most bondsmen learned to survive within the system by virtue of avoiding its penalties as much as they were able. Slaves shirked their duties, or did them in the easiest, and often the most inefficient, way possible. They expressed their resistance to the regime by feigning clumsiness or stupidity, by breaking tools and equipment, by mistreating farm stock. They often ran away. Sometimes they struck back physically at the master, though the penalty for such behavior was savage and summary punishment. A number of times during the slave era, bloody slave uprisings took place, upheavals that sent tremendous shocks through all of southern society.

Though slavery was founded on coercion, it would be a mistake to assume that the average bondsmen encountered nothing but beatings and brandings in his day-to-day existence. Work, rather than force, was the most common experience of the slave. They were employed in almost every conceivable occupation and in almost every conceivable setting in the Old South. Bondsmen were used as house servants in every capacity, from butler and cook to laundress, housemaid, and stable boy. A few worked at the skilled trades — carpentry, masonry, blacksmithing, and numerous others — both on the plantation and in the towns. They were common laborers on canals and railroads and were even employed as operatives in the South's cotton mills and iron works.

But above all they were agricultural laborers. The South was overwhelmingly agrarian. By 1860, the North, particularly the Northeast, was beginning to industrialize. The South had some industry too, but was well behind New England and the Middle Atlantic states in the size, number, and output of its factories and workshops. In colonial times, southern slaves had grown tobacco, rice, and indigo along the Chesapeake and the Carolina and Georgia coasts. Tobacco and rice continued to be cultivated in these older regions by slave labor, but by the 1790s these were no longer expanding crops, and it looked to many men as if slavery were doomed. The slave population continued to expand by natural increase, but it became more and more difficult to find profitable labor for it. Then came cotton and the rapid spread of slavery through the entire lower South. Thousands of slaves were drawn off to the burgeoning cotton kingdom to grow the white fiber. Men got rich, slave prices rose, and slavery once more became a viable and profitable labor system. By 1830, the South was a prosperous part of the American and the world economy, fiercely committed to the perpetuation of the plantation system and the labor regime that sustained it.

In the selection that follows, Kenneth M. Stampp, of the University of California at Berkeley, describes the work of the slave on the plantations and in the homes and workshops of the South. Stampp does not sentimentalize slavery. His book *The Peculiar Institution* is deeply colored by his repugnance for chattel slavery. Although he seeks to evaluate the institution objectively, he refuses to believe that, at heart, it was more than a way of squeezing profits from the lives and toil of black men.

FOR FURTHER READING:

ELKINS, STANLEY. *Slavery: A Problem in American Institutional and Intellectual Life.* Chicago: University of Chicago Press, 1968.*
JORDAN, WINTHROP. *White Over Black.* Baltimore: Penguin Books, Pelican, 1969.*
PHILLIPS, ULRICH B. *American Negro Slavery.* Magnolia, Mass.: Peter Smith, 1966.*

Asterisk denotes paperback edition.

From Day Clean to First Dark

KENNETH M. STAMPP

The day's toil began just before sunrise. A visitor on a Mississippi plantation was regularly awakened by a bell which was rung to call the slaves up. "I soon hear the tramp of the laborers passing along the avenue. . . . All is soon again still as midnight. . . . I believe that I am the only one in the house that the bell disturbs; yet I do not begrudge it a few minutes' loss of sleep it causes me, it sounds so pleasantly in the half dreamy morning."[1] On James H. Hammond's South Carolina plantation a horn was blown an hour before daylight. "All work-hands are [then] required to rise and prepare their cooking, etc. for the day. The second horn is blown just at good day-light, when it is the duty of the driver to visit every house and see that all have left for the field."[2] At dusk the slaves put away their tools and returned to their quarters.

The working day was shorter in winter than in summer, but chiefly because there was less daylight, not because there was much less to do. Seldom at any time of the year was the master at a loss to find essential work to keep his hands busy. Those

---

Source: Kenneth M. Stampp, *The Peculiar Institution: Slavery in the Ante-Bellum South* (New York: Alfred A. Knopf, 1956), chap. 2, "From Day Clean to First Dark," pp. 44–85.

who planned the routine carefully saved indoor tasks for rainy days. An Alabama planter told his father in Connecticut that cotton picking continued until January, "and after that [we] gathered our corn which ripened last August. We then went to work with the waggons ha[u]ling rails and repairing and rebuilding fences, say two weeks, we then knocked down cotton stalks and pulled up corn stalks and commenced plowing. There is no lying by, no leisure, no long sleeping season such as you have in New England."[3] The terse plantation records of the year-round routine of slaves whose principal work was growing cotton usually ran something like this:

January–February: Finished picking, ginning, and pressing cotton and hauling it in wagons to the point of shipment; killed hogs and cut and salted the meat; cut and hauled wood; cut and mauled fence rails; repaired buildings and tools; spread manure; cleaned and repaired ditches; cleared new ground by rolling and burning logs and grubbing stumps; knocked down corn and cotton stalks and burned trash; plowed and "bedded up" corn and cotton fields; planted vegetables.

March–April: Opened "drills," or light furrows, in the corn and cotton beds; sowed corn and cotton seeds in the drills and covered them by hand or with a harrow; replanted where necessary; cultivated the vegetable garden; plowed and hoed in the corn fields.

May–August: "Barred" cotton by scraping dirt away from it with plows; "chopped" cotton with hoes to kill weeds and grass and to thin it to a "stand"; "molded" cotton by "throwing dirt" to it with plows; cultivated corn and cotton until it was large enough to be "laid by"; made repairs; cleared new ground; "pulled fodder," i.e., stripped the blades from corn stalks; cleaned the gin house.

September–December: Picked, ginned, pressed, and shipped cotton; gathered peas; hauled corn and fodder; dug potatoes; shucked corn; cleaned and repaired ditches; repaired fences; cut and hauled wood; cleared new ground.[4]

Thus the operations of one growing cycle overlapped those of the next. There were, of course, variations from planter to planter and differences in the time of planting crops in the upper and lower parts of the cotton belt. Slaves who grew long-staple, or sea-island, cotton in the coastal areas of South Carolina and Georgia had to exercise greater care in picking, ginning, and packing this finer and more expensive variety. But these were differences only in detail. The routine work of cotton growers was essentially the same everywhere, and their basic tools were always the hoe and the plow.

Slaves who cultivated sugar, rice, tobacco, or hemp were involved in a similar year-round routine. They used the same basic tools and much of the time performed the same kinds of supplementary tasks. But each of the staples required special techniques in planting, cultivating, harvesting, and preparing for market.

Some slaves in Texas, Florida, Georgia, and other scattered places in the Deep South produced a little sugar, but those who worked on plantations lining the rivers and bayous of southern Louisiana produced ninety-five per cent of this crop. Most of them were attached to large estates whose owners had heavy investments in land, labor, and machinery. On sugar plantations in the late fall and winter the slaves prepared the land with plows and harrows; before the end of February they planted the seed cane in deep furrows. The shoots grew from eyes at the joints of the seed cane, or ratooned from the stubble of the previous crop. Then came months of cultivation with hoes and plows until the crop was laid by in July. Meanwhile, other slaves cut huge quantities of wood and hauled it to the sugar house, and coopers made sugar hogsheads and molasses barrels. Much heavy labor also went into ditching to provide drainage for these lands which sloped gently from the rivers toward the swamps.

The first cane cut in October was "matalayed" (laid on the ground and covered with a little dirt) to be used as the next year's seed cane. During the frantic weeks from then until December most of the slaves worked at cutting the cane and stripping the leaves from the stalks, loading it into carts, and hauling it to the sugar house. At the mill other slaves fed the cane through the rollers, tended the open kettles or vacuum pans, kept the fires burning, hauled wood, and packed the unrefined sugar into hogsheads. When the last juice was boiled, usually around Christmas, it was almost time to begin planting the next crop.[5]

Soon after the Revolution South Carolina planters abandoned the cultivation of one of their staples — indigo.[6] But to the end of the ante-bellum period rice continued to be the favorite crop of the great planters along the rivers of the South Carolina and Georgia Low Country. Slaves had turned the tidal swamps into fertile rice fields by constructing an intricate system of banks, "trunks" (sluices), and ditches which made possible periodic flooding and draining with the rising and falling tides. Throughout the year slaves on rice plantations devoted much of their time to cleaning the ditches, repairing the banks and trunks, and keeping the tide-flow irrigation system in efficient operation.

In winter the slaves raked the rice fields and burned the stubble. After the ground was broken and "trenched" into drills, the seeds were planted in March and early April. During the first flooding (the "sprout flow") other crops on higher ground were cultivated. When the rice fields were drained and dried they were hoed to loosen the ground and to kill grass and weeds. The next flooding (the "stretch flow") was followed by a long period of "dry growth" during which hoeing went on constantly. Then came the final flooding (the "harvest flow") which lasted until September when the rice was ready to be cut. The slaves cut the rice with sickles, tied it into sheaves, and stacked it to dry. After it had dried they carried the rice to the plantation mill to be threshed, "pounded" to remove the husks from the kernels, winnowed, screened, and packed in barrels.[7] The other crops grown on lands above the swamps were gathered in time to begin preparations for the next year's planting.

The Tobacco Kingdom stretched into the border states of Maryland, Kentucky, and Missouri, but in the ante-bellum period its heart was still the "Virginia District." This district embraced the piedmont south of Fredericksburg, including the northern tier of counties in North Carolina. Here the plantations were smaller than in the Lower South, because each hand could cultivate fewer acres and because the crop had to be handled with great care. The unique aspects of tobacco culture included the preparing of beds in which the tiny seeds were sown during the winter, the transplanting of the shoots in May, and the worming, topping, and suckering of the plants during the summer months. In the late summer the tobacco stalks were split, cut, and left in the fields to wilt. Then they were carried to the tobacco houses to be hung and cured during the fall and winter. The following year, when work had already begun on the next crop, the leaves were stripped from the stalks, sorted, tied into bundles, and "prized" into hogsheads.[8]

The Bluegrass counties of Kentucky and the Missouri River Valley were the chief hemp producing regions of the Old South. Slaves were almost always the working force on hemp farms, because free labor avoided the strenuous, disagreeable labor required to prepare a crop for market. After the ground was prepared, the seeds were sown broadcast in April and May and covered lightly with a harrow or shovel plow. Unlike the other staples, hemp required no cultivation during the growing season, and slaves were free to tend other crops. In late summer the hemp was cut, laid on the ground to dry, and then tied in sheaves and stacked. In November or December it was again spread out in the fields for "dew rotting" to loosen the fiber. A month or so later the hemp was stacked once more, and the lint was laboriously separated from the wood with a hand "brake." The fiber was taken to the hemp house where it was hackled or sold immediately to manufacturers.[9]

In 1850, the Superintendent of the Census estimated that 2,500,000 slaves of all ages were directly employed in agriculture. Of these, he guessed that 60,000 were engaged in the production of hemp, 125,000 in the production of rice, 150,000 in the production of sugar, 350,000 in the production of tobacco, and 1,815,000 in the production of cotton. Somewhat casually he observed that these slaves also produced "large quantities of breadstuffs."[10] This was scarcely adequate recognition of the amount of time they devoted to such crops, even on many of the plantations which gave chief attention to one of the five staples.

To be sure, some planters in the Lower South were so preoccupied with staple production that they grew almost nothing else — not even enough corn and pork to feed their slaves. This pattern was common in the Louisiana sugar district. One planter explained that when sugar sold for fifty dollars a hogshead, "it is cheaper to buy pork[,] for it is utterly impossible to raise hogs here without green pastures and plenty of corn[,] and all lands here fit for pasturage will make a hogshead [of] sugar pr acre — The great curse of this country is that we are all planters and no farmers."[11] An Alabama cotton planter was alarmed when pork failed to arrive from Tennessee: "All of our towns and most of our large Planters are dependent on Drovers for their meat." Even some of the cotton and tobacco planters in North Carolina bought food supplies for their slaves.[12] Such planters were convinced that it was most profitable to concentrate on the production of a single cash crop.

Most planters, however, did not share this point of view. Almost all of the hemp and tobacco growers of the Upper South planted many acres of food crops to supply their own needs — and frequently additional acres to produce surpluses for sale. A major feature of the agricultural revival in ante-bellum Virginia was an improved system of crop rotation with increased emphasis upon corn, wheat, and clover.[13] Many of the tobacco planters gave enough attention to these and other crops to approximate a system of diversified farming. Their field-hands often devoted less than half of their time to tobacco.

Few planters in the Deep South approached such levels of diversification, but most of them produced sizeable food crops for their families and slaves. In southern agricultural periodicals they constantly admonished each other to strive for self-sufficiency. They instructed their overseers to produce adequate supplies of corn, sweet potatoes, peas, and beans, and to give proper attention to the poultry, hogs, and cattle. A Mississippi planter warned his overseer "that failure to make a bountiful supply of corn and meat for the use of the plantation, will be considered as notice that his services will not be required for the succeeding year."[14] The average planter, however, was tempted to forgive a great deal if his overseer managed to make enough cotton. Interest in other crops tended to vary with fluctuations in cotton prices. Even so, most of the field-hands on cotton plantations were at least familiar with the routine of corn cultivation.

Though southern planters showed that slaves could grow other crops besides the five great staples, there was a widespread belief that it was impractical to devote plantations to them exclusively. But here and there in the Lower South a planter disproved this assumption. In Richmond County, Georgia, an owner of more than a hundred slaves successfully used his labor force to raise grain and meat for sale in Augusta.[15]

In the Upper South many large slaveholders grew neither tobacco nor hemp but engaged in diversified farming. In Talbot County, Maryland, Colonel Edward Lloyd worked his two hundred and seventy-five slaves on profitable farms which produced wheat, corn, hams, wool, and hides.[16] On Shirley Plantation on the James River, Hill Carter, like many of his Virginia neighbors, made wheat his major cash crop. An incomplete list of the products of a plantation in King and Queen County included wheat, corn, oats, rye, vegetables, Irish potatoes, sweet potatoes, wool, hogs, apples, and strawberries.[17]

In North Carolina, corn was the chief crop on a number of Roanoke River plantations. In Tyrrell County, Ebenezer Pettigrew annually shipped thousands of bushels of wheat and corn to Norfolk and Charleston.[18] Clearly, the slave-plantation system had greater flexibility and was less dependent upon the production of a few staples than some have thought.

There is a different tradition about the agricultural operations of farmers who owned less than ten slaves. Here a high degree of diversification is assumed — presumably the smaller farms were better adapted to this type of farming than to the cultivation of the staples. Thousands of slaveholders in this group did engage in what was almost subsistence farming with cash incomes well below five hundred dollars a year. Others, especially in the Upper South, marketed large surpluses of pork, corn, and wheat. The amount of commercialization in the operations of non-staple producing small slaveholders depended upon the quality of their lands, their proximity to markets and transportation, and their managerial skill.

But a large proportion of these slaveholding farmers depended upon one of the five southern staples for a cash crop. In Kentucky and Missouri many of them produced a few tons of hemp; there and in Virginia and North Carolina they often gave tobacco their chief attention. A few small slaveholders in the Deep South even planted rice and sugar — sometimes surprisingly large amounts — in spite of the handicaps they faced in trying to compete with the planters. In St. Mary Parish, Louisiana, for example, an owner of seven slaves in 1859 produced forty hogsheads of sugar. These small operators depended upon their neighbors' sugar making facilities or ran their own crude horse-driven mills.[19]

In cotton production those with modest slaveholdings faced no overwhelming competitive disadvantage. Some of the smaller cotton growers were as preoccupied with this staple as were their neighbors on the large plantations. Some even depended upon outside supplies of food. Many of them reported astonishing cotton-production records to the census takers, the number of bales per hand easily matching the records of the planters.[20]

Nevertheless, the majority of small slaveholders did engage in a more diversified type of agriculture than most of the large planters. Slavery could be, and was, adapted to diversified agriculture and to the labor needs of small farms. It did not necessarily depend upon large plantations or staple crops for its survival.

For the owner of a few slaves, labor management was a problem of direct personal relationships between individuals. For the owner of many, the problem was more difficult and required greater ingenuity. Both classes of masters desired a steady and efficient performance of the work assigned each day. They could not expect much cooperation from their slaves, who had little reason to care how much was produced. Masters measured the success of their methods by the extent to which their interest in a maximum of work of good quality prevailed over the slaves' predilection for a minimum of work of indifferent quality. Often neither side won a clear victory.

Slaveowners developed numerous variations of two basic methods of managing their laborers: the "gang system" and the "task system." Under the first of these systems, which was the one most commonly used, the field-hands were divided into gangs commanded by drivers who were to work them at a brisk pace. Competent masters gave some thought to the capacities of individual slaves and to the amount of labor that a gang could reasonably be expected to perform in one day. But the purpose of the gang system was to force every hand to continue his labor until all were discharged from the field in the evening.

Under the task system, each hand was given a specific daily work assignment. He could then set his own pace and quit when his task was completed. The driver's job was to inspect the work and to see that it was performed satisfactorily before the slave left the field. "The advantages of this system," according to a Georgia rice planter, "are encouragement to the laborers, by equalizing the work of each agreeable to strength, and the avoidance of watchful superintendence and incessant driving. As . . . the task of each [slave] is separate, imperfect work can readily be traced to the neglectful worker." [21]

The task system was best adapted to the rice plantation, with its fields divided into small segments by the network of drainage ditches. Outside the Low Country of South Carolina and Georgia planters occasionally used this system or at least experimented with it, but many of them found it to be unsatisfactory. For one thing, they could get no more work out of their stronger slaves than out of their weaker ones, since the tasks were usually standardized. The planters also found that the eagerness of slaves to finish their tasks as early as possible led to careless work. After using the task system for twenty years, an Alabama planter abandoned it because of evils "too numerous to mention." A South Carolina cotton planter, who also gave it up, noted with satisfaction that under the gang system his slaves did "much more" and were "not so apt to strain themselves." [22]

Actually, most planters used a combination of the two systems. Cotton planters often worked plow-hands in gangs but gave hoe-hands specific tasks of a certain number of cotton rows to hoe each day. Each hand was expected to pick as much cotton as he could, but he might be given a minimum quota that had to be met. Sugar, rice, and tobacco planters applied the task system to their coopers, and hemp growers used it with hands engaged in breaking or hackling hemp. Masters generally tasked their hands for digging ditches, cutting wood, or mauling rails.

Thus most slaves probably had some experience with both systems. From their point of view each system doubtless had its advantages and drawbacks. A strong hand might have preferred to be tasked if he was given an opportunity to finish early. But many slaves must have been appalled at the ease with which they could be held responsible for the quality of their work. The gang system had the disadvantages of severe regimentation and of hard driving which was especially onerous for the weaker hands. But there was less chance that a slave would be detected and held individually responsible for indifferent work. In the long run, however, the rigors of either system were determined by the demands of masters and overseers.

The number of acres a slaveholder expected each of his field-hands to cultivate depended in part upon how hard he wished to work them. It also depended upon the nature of the soil, the quality of the tools, and the general efficiency of the agricultural enterprise. Finally, it depended upon the crop. Cotton growers on flat prairies and river bottoms planted as many as ten acres per hand but rarely more than that. Those on hilly or rolling lands planted from three to eight acres per hand. Since a slave could ordinarily cultivate more cotton than he could pick, acreage was limited by the size of the available picking force. By the 1850's each hand was expected to work from nine to ten acres of sugar but seldom more than five acres of rice or three of tobacco, plus six or more of corn and other food crops.[23] The yield per acre and per hand varied with the fertility of the soil, the care in cultivation, the damage of insects, and the whims of the weather.

When calculating his yield per field-hand a slaveholder was not calculating his yield per slave, for he almost always owned fewer field-hands than slaves. Some of his slaves performed other types of work, and the very young and the very old could not be used in the fields. The master's diseased, convalescing, and partially disabled slaves, his "breeding women" and "sucklers," his children just beginning to work in the fields, and his slaves of advanced years were incapable of laboring as long and as hard as full-time hands.

Most masters had systems of rating such slaves as fractional hands. Children often began as "quarter hands" and advanced to "half hands," "three-quarter hands," and then "full hands." As mature slaves grew older they started down this scale. "Breeding women" and "sucklers" were rated as "half hands." Some planters organized these slaves into separate gangs, for example, into a "sucklers gang." Children sometimes received their training in a "trash gang," or "children's squad," which pulled weeds, cleaned the yard, hoed, wormed tobacco, or picked cotton. Seldom were many more than half of a master's slaves listed in his records as field-hands, and always some of the hands were classified as fractional. Olmsted described a typical situation on a Mississippi cotton plantation: "There were 135 slaves, big and little, of which 67 went to the field regularly — equal, the overseer thought, to 60 able-bodied hands." [24]

The master, not the parents, decided at what age slave children should be put to work in the fields. Until they were five or six years old children were "useless articles on a plantation." Then many received "their first lessons in the elementary part of their education" through serving as "water-toters" or going into the fields alongside their mothers.[25] Between the ages of ten and twelve the children became fractional hands, with a regular routine of field labor. By the time they were eighteen they had reached the age when they could be classified as "prime field-hands."

Mature slaves who did not work in the fields (unless they were totally disabled or extremely old) performed other kinds of valuable and productive labor. Old women cooked for the rest of the slaves, cared for small children, fed the poultry, mended and washed clothes, and nursed the sick. Old men gardened, minded stock, and cleaned the stable and the yard.

Old or partially disabled slaves might also be put to spinning and weaving in the loom houses of the more efficient planters. The printed instructions in a popular plantation record book advised overseers to adopt this policy: "Few instances of good management will better please an employer, than that of having all the winter clothing spun and woven on the place. By having a room devoted to that purpose . . . where those who may be complaining a little, or convalescent after sickness, may be employed in some light work, and where all of the women may be sent in wet weather, more than enough of both cotton and woolen yarn can be spun for the supply of the place."[26] One planter reported that he had his spinning jenny "going at a round rate[.] Old Charles [is] Spinning and Esther reeling the thread. . . . Charles will in this way be one of my most productive laborers and so will several of the women[.]"[27] Thus a master's productive slaves were by no means limited to those listed as field-hands.

The bondsmen who were valued most highly were those who had acquired special skills which usually exempted them from field work entirely. This select group of slave craftsmen included engineers, coopers, carpenters, blacksmiths, brickmakers, stone masons, mechanics, shoemakers, weavers, millers, and landscapers. The excellence of the work performed by some of them caused slaveowners to make invidious comparisons between them and the free artisans they sometimes employed. An Englishman recalled an interview with the overseer on a Louisiana sugar plantation: "It would have been amusing, had not the subject been so grave, to hear the overseer's praises of the intelligence and skill of these workmen, and his boast that they did all the work of skilled laborers on the estate, and then to listen to him, in a few minutes, expatiating on the utter helplessness and ignorance of the black race, their incapacity to do any good, or even to take care of themselves."[28]

Domestic servants were prized almost as much as craftsmen. The number and variety of domestics in a household depended upon the size of the establishment and the wealth of the master. They served as hostlers, coachmen, laundresses, seamstresses, cooks, footmen, butlers, housemaids, chambermaids, children's nurses, and personal servants. On a large plantation specialization was complete: "The cook never enters the house, and the nurse is never seen in the kitchen; the wash-woman is never put to ironing, nor the woman who has charge of the ironing-room ever put to washing. Each one rules supreme in her wash-house, her ironing-room, her kitchen, her nursery, her house-keeper's room; and thus . . . a complete system of domesticdom is established to the amazing comfort and luxury of all who enjoy its advantages."[29]

But the field-hands remained fundamental in the slave economy. Though their work was classified as unskilled labor, this of course was a relative term. Some visitors described the "rude" or "slovenly" manner in which slaves cultivated the crops, how "awkwardly, slowly, and undecidedly" they moved through the fields.[30] But other observers were impressed with the success of many masters in training field-hands to be efficient workers, impressed also by the skill these workers showed in certain crucial operations in the production of staple crops. Inexperienced hands had their troubles in sugar houses and rice fields, in breaking and hackling hemp, and in topping, suckering, sorting, and prizing tobacco. Even the neophyte cotton picker soon wondered whether this was unskilled labor, as one former slave testified: "While others used both hands, snatching the cotton and depositing it in the mouth of the sack, with a precision and dexterity that was incomprehensible to me, I had to seize the boll with one hand, and deliberately draw out the white, gushing blossom with the other." On his first day he managed to gather "not half the quantity required of the poorest picker."[31]

Field workers kept up a ceaseless struggle to make the lands fruitful, against the contrary efforts of the insects and the elements. The battle seemed at times to be of absorbing interest to some of the slaves, conscripts though they were. In a strange and uneasy kind of alliance, they and their masters combatted the foes that could have destroyed them both.

In 1860, probably a half million bondsmen lived in southern cities and towns, or were engaged in work not directly or indirectly connected with agriculture. Some farmers and planters found it profitable, either temporarily or permanently, to employ part of their hands in non-agricultural occupations. Along the rivers slaves cut wood to provide fuel for steamboats and for sale in neighboring towns. In swamplands filled with juniper, oak, and cypress trees they produced shingles, barrel and hogshead staves, pickets, posts, and rails. In North Carolina's Dismal Swamp slave gangs labored as lumberjacks.[32] In the eastern Carolina pine belt several thousand slaves worked in the turpentine industry. An owner of one hundred and fifty slaves in Brunswick County, North Carolina, raised just enough food to supply his force; he made his profits from the annual sale of thousands of barrels of turpentine. Many smaller operators also combined turpentine production with subsistence farming.[33]

Elsewhere in the South bondsmen worked in sawmills, gristmills, quarries, and fisheries. They mined gold in North Carolina, coal and salt in Virginia, iron in Kentucky and Tennessee, and lead in Missouri. On river boats they were used as deck hands and firemen. Slave stokers on a Mississippi River steamer bound for New Orleans, who sang as they fed wood to the boiler fires, intrigued a European traveler: "It was a fantastic and grand sight to see these energetic black athletes lit up by the wildly flashing flames . . . while they, amid their equally fantastic song, keeping time most exquisitely, hurled one piece of firewood after another into the yawning fiery gulf." [34]

Other slaves were employed in the construction and maintenance of internal improvements. They worked on the public roads several days each year in states which required owners to put them to such use. For many years slaves owned by the state of Louisiana built roads and cleared obstructions from the bayous. Slaves also worked for private internal improvements companies, such as the builders of the Brunswick and Altamaha Canal in Georgia and the Cape Fear and Deep River Navigation Company in North Carolina. In Mississippi a hundred were owned by a firm of bridge contractors, the Weldon brothers.[35]

Railroad companies employed bondsmen in both construction and maintenance work. As early as 1836 the Richmond, Fredericksburg, and Potomac Railroad Company advertised for "a large number" of slave laborers. In the same year the Alabama, Florida, and Georgia Railroad Company announced a need for five hundred "able-bodied negro men . . . to be employed in felling, cutting, and hewing timber, and in forming the excavations and embankments upon the route of said Rail Road." During the 1850's southern newspapers carried the constant pleas of railroad builders for slaves. Almost every railroad in the ante-bellum South was built at least in part by bondsmen; in Georgia they constructed more than a thousand miles of roadbed. In 1858, a Louisiana newspaper concluded: "Negro labor is fast taking the place of white labor in the construction of southern railroads." [36]

Bondsmen in southern cities and towns, in spite of the protests of free laborers, worked in virtually every skilled and unskilled occupation. They nearly monopolized the domestic services, for most free whites shunned them to avoid being degraded to the level of slaves. Many of the Southerners who owned just one or two slaves were urban dwellers who used them as cooks, housekeepers, and gardeners. The wealthier townspeople often had staffs of domestic servants as large as those of rural planters. Other domestics found employment in hotels and at watering places.

Town slaves worked in cotton presses, tanneries, shipyards, bakehouses, and laundries, as dock laborers and stevedores, and as clerks in stores. Masters who owned skilled artisans such as barbers, blacksmiths, cabinet makers, and shoemakers often provided them with shops to make their services available to all who might wish to employ them. Many white mechanics used slave assistants. In short, as a visitor to Natchez observed, town slaves included "mechanics, draymen, hostlers, labourers, hucksters, and washwomen, and the heterogeneous multitude of every other occupation, who fill the streets of a busy city — for slaves are trained to every kind of manual labour. The blacksmith, cabinet-maker, carpenter, builder, wheelwright — all have one or more slaves labouring at their trades. The negro is a third arm to every working man, who can possibly save money enough to purchase one. He is emphatically the 'right-hand man' of every man." [37] The quality of the work of slave artisans had won favorable comment as early as the eighteenth century. Among them were "many ingenious Mechanicks," wrote a colonial Georgian, "and as far as they have had opportunity of being instructed, have discovered as good abilities, as are usually found among people of our Colony." [38]

Some Southerners were enthusiastic crusaders for the development of factories which would employ slaves. They were convinced that bondsmen could be trained in all the necessary skills and would provide a cheaper and more manageable form of labor than free whites. "When the channels of agriculture are choked," predicted an industrial promoter, "the manufacturing of our own productions will open new channels of profitable employment for our slaves." Others thought that slavery was one of the South's "natural advantages" in its effort to build industries to free it from "the incessant and vexatious attacks of the North." [39] They believed that industrialization and slavery could proceed hand in hand.

Southern factory owners gave evidence that this was more than idle speculation. Every slave state had industrial establishments which made some use of slave labor. In Kentucky, the "ropewalks" which manufactured cordage and the hemp factories which produced cotton bagging and "Kentucky jeans" employed slaves extensively.[40] Almost all of the thirteen thousand workers in the tobacco factories of the Virginia District were bondsmen. The majority of them were employed in the three leading tobacco manufacturing cities — Richmond, Petersburg, and Lynchburg. These slave workers were not only a vital part of this industry but also a curiously paradoxical element in the society of the tobacco towns.[41]

From its earliest beginnings the southern iron industry depended upon skilled and unskilled slaves. Negro iron workers were employed in Bath County, Kentucky, and along the Cumberland River in Tennessee. In the Cumberland country the majority of laborers at the iron furnaces were slaves. Montgomery Bell, owner of the Cumberland Iron Works, engaged his own three hundred slaves and many others in every task connected with the operation of forge and furnace.[42] In the Great Valley of Virginia, where the southern industry was centered during the early nineteenth century, slaves constituted the chief labor supply.

Until the 1840's, the famed Tredegar Iron Company in Richmond used free labor almost exclusively. But in 1842, Joseph R. Anderson, then commercial agent of the company, proposed to employ slaves as a means of cutting labor costs. The board of directors approved of his plan, and within two years Anderson was satisfied with "the practicability of the scheme." In 1847, the increasing use of slaves caused the remaining free laborers to go out on strike, until they were threatened with prosecution for forming an illegal combination. After this protest failed, Anderson vowed that he would show his workers that they could not dictate his labor policies: he refused to re-employ any of the strikers. Thereafter, as Anderson noted, Tredegar used "almost exclusively slave labor except as the Boss men. This enables me, of course, to compete with other manufacturers." [43]

But it was upon the idea of bringing textile mills to the cotton fields that southern advocates of industrialization with slave labor pinned most of their hopes. In cotton factories women and children were needed most, and hence it was often argued that they would provide profitable employment for the least productive workers in agriculture. Though the majority of southern textile workers were free whites, and though some believed that this work ought to be reserved for them, a small number of slaves were nevertheless employed in southern mills.

Occasionally mill owners managed to work slaves and free whites together with a minimum of friction. A visitor found equal numbers of the two groups employed in a cotton factory near Athens, Georgia: "There is no difficulty among them on account of colour, the white girls working in the same room and at the same loom with the black girls; and boys of each colour, as well as men and women, working together without apparent repugnance or objection." [44] But even if some white workers would tolerate this, slaveowners ordinarily looked upon it as a dangerous practice.

The southern press gave full reports of cotton mills which used slave labor and ecstatic accounts of their success. A Pensacola newspaper cited the local Arcadia Cotton Factory, which employed only slaves, to prove that "with the native skill and ingenuity of mere labor — the labor of the hands — the negro is just as richly endowed as the white." The Saluda mill, near Columbia, South Carolina, operated on the "slave-labor, or anti free-soil system." The white managers testified to the "equal efficiency, and great superiority in many respects" of slaves over free workers.[45] During the 1830's and 1840's, a half dozen other cotton mills in South Carolina's Middle and Low Country employed bondsmen. Most other southern states could point to one or more mills which used this type of labor. To many observers the enterprises of Daniel Pratt at Prattsville, near Montgomery, Alabama, provided models for other Southerners to copy. Pratt worked slaves not only in his cotton mill but also in his cotton gin factory, iron foundry, sash and door factory, machine shop, and carriage and wagon shop.[46]

Actually, the ante-bellum South had relatively few cotton mills, and most of them were small enterprises manufacturing only the coarser grades of cloth. In 1860, the fifteen slave states together had only 198 mills each employing an average of 71 workers, whereas Massachusetts alone had 217 mills each employing an average of 177 workers. Many of the southern factories resembled the one owned by a small manufacturer in East Tennessee which contained only three hundred spindles operated by fourteen slave hands.[47]

Still, in these textile mills and in what little other industry existed in the Old South there was abundant evidence that slaves could be trained to be competent factory workers. The evidence was sufficient to raise serious doubts that slavery was tied to agriculture, as some defenders and some critics of the institution believed.

Each year, around the first of January, at southern crossroad stores, on the steps of county courthouses, and in every village and city, large crowds of participants and spectators gathered for "hiring day." At this time masters with bondsmen to spare and employers in search of labor bargained for the rental of slave property. Thus thousands of nonslaveholders managed temporarily to obtain the services of slaves and to enjoy the prestige of tenuous membership in the master class. Thus, too, many bondsmen found it their lot to labor for persons other than their owners. Hired slaves were most numerous in the Upper South; during the 1850's perhaps as many as fifteen thousand were hired out annually in Virginia alone. But slave-hiring was a common practice everywhere.[48]

In December and January southern newspapers were filled with the advertisements of those offering or seeking slaves to hire. Some of the transactions were negotiated privately, some by auctioneers who bid slaves off at public outcry, and some by "general agents" who handled this business for a commission. In Richmond, P. M. Tabb & Son, among many others, advertised that they attended "to the hiring out of negroes and collecting the hires" and promised to give "particular attention . . . through the year to negroes placed under their charge."[49]

Though slaves were occasionally hired for short terms, it was customary to hire them from January until the following Christmas. Written contracts specified the period of the hire, the kind of work in which the slaves were to be engaged, and the hirer's obligation to keep them well clothed. Usually an owner could spare only a few, but occasionally a single master offered as many as fifty and, rarely, as many as a hundred. Though most slaves were hired in the vicinity of their masters' residences, many were sent long distances from home. Hamilton Brown, of Wilkes County, North Carolina, hired out slaves in Virginia, Tennessee, and Georgia; and Jeremiah Morton, of Orange County, Virginia, hired out fifty-two of his Negroes through an agent in Mobile.[50]

A variety of circumstances contributed to this practice. If for some reason the owner was unable to use his slaves profitably, if he was in debt, or if he had a surplus of laborers, he might prefer hiring to selling them. Executors hired out slave property while estates were being settled. Sometimes lands and slaves together were rented to tenants. Heirs who inherited bondsmen for whom they had no employment put them up for hire. Many spinsters, widows, and orphans lived off the income of hired slaves who were handled for them by administrators. Masters often directed in their wills that slaves be hired out for the benefit of their heirs, or that cash be invested in slave property for this purpose. A widow in Missouri hired out most of her slaves, because she found it to be "a better business" than working them on her farm.[51] Occasionally a slaveowner endowed a church or a benevolent institution with slaves whose hire was to aid in its support.

In addition, urban masters often hired out the husbands or children of their female domestics. Both they and planters who had more domestics than they could use or afford disposed of them in this manner. It was also very common for urban and rural owners of skilled slaves to hire them to others at least part of the time. Planters hired their carpenters and blacksmiths to neighbors when they had no work for them and thus substantially augmented their incomes. A master sometimes hired a slave to a white artisan with the understanding that the slave was to be taught his skill. For example, a contract between a North Carolina master and a white blacksmith provided that the hirer was to work a slave "at the Forge during the whole time and learn him or cause him to be learned the arts and mysteries of the Black Smith's trade." [52]

A few Southerners bought slaves as business ventures with the intention of realizing profits solely through hiring them to others. Between 1846 and 1852, Bickerton Lyle Winston, of Hanover County, Virginia, purchased at least fifteen slaves for this purpose. Winston kept careful records of these investments, noting the purchase prices, the annual income from and expenses of each slave, and the net profit. The slaves Randal and Garland were his first speculations. Randal's record ended abruptly in 1853 with the terse notation: "Deduct medical and funeral expenses: $20." Four years later Winston recorded the fact that "Garland came to his end . . . by an explosion in the Black Heath Pits." [53] Some overseers pursued a similar course by investing in slaves whom they hired to their employers. A resident in Mississippi knew families "who possess not an acre of land, but own many slaves, [and] hire them out to different individuals; the wages constituting their only income, which is often very large." [54]

Farmers and planters frequently hired field-hands to neighbors for short periods of time. Cotton growers who finished their picking early contracted to help others pick their cotton for a fee. When a planter's crop was "in the grass" he tried to borrow hands from neighbors with the understanding that the labor would be repaid in the future. Small slaveholders sometimes made less formal agreements to help each other. A Virginia farmer lent his neighbor two mules and received in return "the labor of one man for the same time." [55] Many masters were generous in lending the labor of their slaves to friends.

The demand for hired slaves came from numerous groups. The shortage of free agricultural labor caused planters to look to this practice as a means of meeting their seasonal needs for additional workers. During the grinding season sugar growers hired hands from Creole farmers or from cotton planters after their crops were picked.[56] Small farmers who could not afford to buy slaves were well represented in the "hiring-day" crowds. Some landowners employed free Negroes, Indians, or poor whites, but they generally preferred to hire slaves when they were available.

The great majority of hired slaves, however, were employed by those who sought a supply of nonagricultural labor. Many urban families hired rather than owned their domestic servants. Advertisements such as these appeared in every southern newspaper: "Wanted immediately, a boy, from 14 to 19 years of age, to do house work. One that can be well recommended from his owner." "Wanted a Black or Colored Servant, to attend on a Gentleman and take care of a Horse." [57] Hotels and watering places hired most of their domestics; laundries, warehouses, shipyards, steamships, cotton presses, turpentine producers, mine operators, lumberers, and drayage companies all made considerable use of hired slaves. Free artisans seldom could afford to own bondsmen and therefore hired them instead. Even a free Negro cooper in Richmond for many years hired a slave assistant.[58]

In most cases southern railroad companies did not own the slaves they employed; rather, they recruited them by promising their owners generous compensation. Railroad builders obtained most of their hands in the neighborhood of their construction work, but they often bid for them in distant places. In 1836, the Alabama, Florida, and Georgia Railroad Company advertised for a hundred slaves in Maryland, Virginia, and North Carolina. The Florida Railroad Company, in 1857, announced that for the past two years it had been employing slaves from Virginia and the Carolinas and offered to give masters evidence "of the health, climate, and other points of interest connected with the country and work." [59]

An advertisement in a Kentucky newspaper for "twenty-five Negro Boys, from thirteen to fifteen years old, to work in a woolen factory" pointed to another source of the demand for hired slaves. Gristmills, sawmills, cotton factories, hemp factories, iron foundries, and tobacco factories used them extensively, especially the smaller enterprises with limited capital. In 1860, about half of the slave laborers in Virginia tobacco factories were hired.[60]

A small group of slaves obtained from their masters the privilege of "hiring their own time." These bondsmen enjoyed considerable freedom of movement and were permitted to find work for themselves. They were required to pay their masters a stipulated sum of money each year, but whatever they could earn above that amount was theirs to do with as they wished. Almost all of the slaves who hired their own time were skilled artisans; most of them were concentrated in the cities of the Upper South. Though this practice was illegal nearly everywhere and often denounced as dangerous, there were always a few slaves who somehow managed to work in this manner under the most nominal control of their owners.

By permitting a trusted slave artisan to hire his own time the master escaped the burden of feeding and clothing him and of finding employment for him. Then, as long as his slave kept out of trouble, the master's sole concern was getting his payments (which were almost the equivalent of a quitrent) at regular intervals. Frederick Douglass described the terms by which he hired his own time to work as a calker in the Baltimore shipyards: "I was to be allowed all my time; to make all bargains for work; to find my own employment, and to collect my own wages; and, in return for this liberty, I was required, or obliged, to pay . . . three dollars at the end of each week, and to board and clothe myself, and buy my own calking tools. A failure in any of these particulars would put an end to my privilege. This was a hard bargain." [61]

But whatever the terms, most slave artisans eagerly accepted this arrangement when it was offered to them. A Negro blacksmith in Virginia pleaded with his master for the privilege of hiring his own time: "I would . . . be much obliged to you if you would authorize me to open a shop in this county and carry it on. . . . I am satisfied that I can do well and that my profits will amount to a great deal more than any one would be willing to pay for my hire." [62]

This slave had his wish granted, but few others shared his good fortune. It was the lot of the ordinary bondsman to work under the close supervision of his master or of some employer who hired his services. For him bondage was not nominal. It was what it was intended to be: a systematic method of controlling and exploiting labor.

Mammy Harriet had nostalgic memories of slavery days: "Oh, no, we was nebber hurried. Marster nebber once said, 'Get up an' go to work,' an' no oberseer ebber said it, neither. Ef some on 'em did not git up when de odders went out to work, marster nebber said a word. Oh, no, we was nebber hurried." [63] Mammy Harriet had been a domestic at "Burleigh," the Hinds County, Mississippi, estate of Thomas S. Dabney. She related her story of slave life there to one of Dabney's daughters who wrote a loving volume about her father and his cotton plantation.

Another slave found life less leisurely on a plantation on the Red River in Louisiana: "The hands are required to be in the cotton field as soon as it is light in the morning, and, with the exception of ten or fifteen minutes, which is given them at noon to swallow their allowance of cold bacon, they are not permitted to be a moment idle until it is too dark to see, and when the moon is full, they often times labor till the middle of the night." Work did not end when the slaves left the fields. "Each one must attend to his respective chores. One feeds the mules, another the swine — another cuts the wood, and so forth; besides the packing [of cotton] is all done by candle light. Finally, at a late hour, they reach the quarters, sleepy and overcome with the long day's toil." [64] These were the bitter memories of Solomon Northup, a free Negro who had been kidnapped and held in bondage for twelve years. Northup described his experiences to a Northerner who helped him prepare his autobiography for publication.

Mammy Harriet's and Solomon Northup's disparate accounts of the work regimen imposed upon slaves suggest the difficulty of determining the truth from witnesses, Negro and white, whose candor was rarely uncompromised by internal emotions or external pressures. Did Dabney's allegedly unhurried field-hands (who somehow produced much cotton and one of whom once tried to kill the overseer) feel the same nostalgia for slavery days? How much was Northup's book influenced by his amanuensis and by the preconceptions of his potential northern readers?

And yet there is nothing in the narratives of either of these ex-slaves that renders them entirely implausible. The question of their complete accuracy is perhaps less important than the fact that both conditions actually did exist in the South. Distortion results from exaggerating the frequency of either condition or from dwelling upon one and ignoring the other.

No sweeping generalization about the amount of labor extracted from bondsmen could possibly be valid, even when they are classified by regions, or by occupations, or by the size of the holdings upon which they lived. For the personal factor transcended everything else. How hard the slaves were worked depended upon the demands of individual masters and their ability to enforce them. These demands were always more or less tempered by the inclination of most slaves to minimize their unpaid toil. Here was a clash of interests in which the master usually, but not always, enjoyed the advantage of superior weapons.

Not only must glib generalizations be avoided but a standard must be fixed by which the slave's burden of labor can be judged. Surely a slave was overworked when his toil impaired his health or endangered his life. Short of this extreme there are several useful standards upon which judgments can be based. If, for example, the quantity of labor were compared with the compensation the inevitable conclusion would be that most slaves were overworked. Also by present-day labor standards the demands generally made upon them were excessive. These, of course, were not the standards of the nineteenth century.

Another standard of comparison — though not an altogether satisfactory one — is the amount of work performed by contemporary free laborers in similar occupations. Independent farmers and artisans set their own pace and planned their work to fit their own convenience and interests, but they nevertheless often worked from dawn to dusk. Northern factory workers commonly labored twelve hours a day. This was arduous toil even for free laborers who enjoyed the advantages of greater incentives and compensation. Yet contemporaries did not think that slaves were overworked when their masters respected the normal standards of their day. Some slaveowners did respect them, and some did not.

Unquestionably there were slaves who escaped doing what was then regarded as a "good day's work," and there were masters who never demanded it of them. The aphorism that it took two slaves to help one to do nothing was not without its illustrations. After lands and slaves had remained in the hands of a single family for several generations, planters sometimes developed a patriarchal attitude toward their "people" and took pride in treating them indulgently. Such masters had lost the competitive spirit and the urge to increase their worldly possessions which had characterized their ancestors. To live gracefully on their declining estates, to smile tolerantly at the listless labor of their field-hands, and to be surrounded by a horde of pampered domestics were all parts of their code.

In Virginia, the easygoing manner of the patricians was proverbial. But Virginia had no monopoly of them; they were scattered throughout the South. Olmsted visited a South Carolina rice plantation where the tasks were light enough to enable reasonably industrious hands to leave the fields early in the afternoon. Slaves on several sea-island cotton plantations much of the time did not labor more than five or six hours a day.[65]

The production records of some of the small slaveholding farmers indicated that neither they nor their slaves exerted themselves unduly. These masters, especially when they lived in isolated areas, seemed content to produce little more than a bare subsistence. In addition, part of the town slaves who hired their own time took advantage of the opportunity to enjoy a maximum of leisure. The domestics of some wealthy urban families willingly helped to maintain the tradition that masters with social standing did not examine too closely into the quantity or efficiency of their work.

From these models proslavery writers drew their sentimental pictures of slave life. The specific cases they cited were often valid ones; their profound error was in generalizing from them. For this leisurely life was the experience of only a small fraction of the bondsmen. Whether they lived in the Upper South or Deep South, in rural or urban communities, on plantations or farms, the labor of the vast majority of slaves ranged from what was normally expected of free labor in that period to levels that were clearly excessive.

It would not be too much to say that masters usually demanded from their slaves a long day of hard work and managed by some means or other to get it. The evidence does not sustain the belief that free laborers generally worked longer hours and at a brisker pace than the unfree. During the months when crops were being cultivated or harvested the slaves commonly were in the fields fifteen or sixteen hours a day, including time allowed for meals and rest.[66] By ante-bellum standards this may not have been excessive, but it was not a light work routine by the standards of that or any other day.

In instructions to overseers, planters almost always cautioned against overwork, yet insisted that the hands be made to labor vigorously as many hours as there was daylight. Overseers who could not accomplish this were discharged. An Arkansas master described a work day that was in no sense unusual on the plantations of the Deep South: "We get up before day every morning and eat breakfast before day and have everybody at work before day dawns. I am never caught in bed after day light nor is any body else on the place, and we continue in the cotton fields when we can have fair weather till it is so dark we cant see to work, and this history of one day is the history of every day."[67]

Planters who contributed articles on the management of slaves to southern periodicals took this routine for granted. "It is expected," one of them wrote, "that servants should rise early enough to be at work by the time it is light. . . . While at work, they should be brisk. . . . I have no objection to their whistling or singing some lively tune, but no *drawling* tunes are allowed in the field, for their motions are almost certain to keep time with the music." [68] These planters had the businessman's interest in maximum production without injury to their capital.

The work schedule was not strikingly different on the plantations of the Upper South. Here too it was a common practice to regulate the hours of labor in accordance with the amount of daylight. A former slave on a Missouri tobacco and hemp plantation recalled that the field-hands began their work at half past four in the morning. Such rules were far more common on Virginia plantations than were the customs of languid patricians. An ex-slave in Hanover County, Virginia, remembered seeing slave women hurrying to their work in the early morning "with their shoes and stockings in their hands, and a petticoat wrapped over their shoulders, to dress in the field the best way they could." [69] The bulk of the Virginia planters were businessmen too.

Planters who were concerned about the physical condition of their slaves permitted them to rest at noon after eating their dinners in the fields. "In the Winter," advised one expert on slave management, "a hand may be pressed all day, but not so in Summer. . . . In May, from one and a half to two hours; in June, two and a half; in July and August, three hours rest [should be given] at noon." [70] Except for certain essential chores, Sunday work was uncommon but not unheard of if the crops required it. On Saturdays slaves were often permitted to quit the fields at noon. They were also given holidays, most commonly at Christmas and after the crops were laid by.

But a holiday was not always a time for rest and relaxation. Many planters encouraged their bondsmen to cultivate small crops during their "leisure" to provide some of their own food. Thus a North Carolina planter instructed his overseer: "As soon as you have laid by the crop give the people 2 days but . . . they must work their own crops." Another planter gave his slaves a "holiday to plant their potatoes," and another "holiday to get in their potatoes." James H. Hammond once wrote in disgust: "Holiday for the negroes who fenced in their gardens. Lazy devils they did nothing after 12 o'clock." In addition, slave women had to devote part of their time when they were not in the fields to washing clothes, cooking, and cleaning their cabins. An Alabama planter wrote: "I always give them half of each Saturday, and often the whole day, at which time . . . the women do their household work; therefore they are never idle." [71]

Planters avoided night work as much as they felt they could, but slaves rarely escaped it entirely. Night work was almost universal on sugar plantations during the grinding season, and on cotton plantations when the crop was being picked, ginned, and packed. A Mississippi planter did not hesitate to keep his hands hauling fodder until ten o'clock at night when the hours of daylight were not sufficient for his work schedule.[72]

Occasionally a planter hired free laborers for such heavy work as ditching in order to protect his slave property. But, contrary to the legend, this was not a common practice. Most planters used their own field-hands for ditching and for clearing new ground. Moreover, they often assigned slave women to this type of labor as well as to plowing. On one plantation Olmsted saw twenty women operating heavy plows with double teams: "They were superintended by a male negro driver, who carried a whip, which he frequently cracked at them, permitting no dawdling or delay at the turning." [73]

Among the smaller planters and slaveholding farmers there was generally no appreciable relaxation of this normal labor routine. Their production records, their diaries and farm journals, and the testimony of their slaves all suggest the same dawn-to-dusk regimen that prevailed on the large plantations.[74] This was also the experience of most slaves engaged in nonagricultural occupations. Everywhere, then, masters normally expected from their slaves, in accordance with the standards of their time, a full stint of labor from "day clean" to "first dark."

Some, however, demanded more than this. Continuously, or at least for long intervals, they drove their slaves at a pace that was bound, sooner or later, to injure their health. Such hard driving seldom occurred on the smaller plantations and farms or in urban centers; it was decidedly a phenomenon of the large plantations. Though the majority of planters did not sanction it, more of them tolerated excessively heavy labor routines than is generally realized. The records of the plantation regime clearly indicate that slaves were more frequently overworked by calloused tyrants than overindulged by mellowed patriarchs.

That a large number of southern bondsmen were worked severely during the colonial period is beyond dispute. The South Carolina code of 1740 charged that "many owners . . . do confine them so closely to hard labor, that they have not sufficient time for natural rest." [75] In the nineteenth century conditions seemed to have improved, especially in the older regions of the South. Unquestionably the ante-bellum planter who coveted a high rank in society responded to subtle pressures that others did not feel. The closing of the African slave trade and the steady rise of slave prices were additional restraining influences. "The time has been," wrote a planter in 1849, "that the farmer could kill up and wear out one Negro to buy another; but it is not so now. Negroes are too high in proportion to the price of cotton, and it behooves those who own them to make them last as long as possible." [76]

But neither public opinion nor high prices prevented some of the bondsmen from suffering physical breakdowns and early deaths because of overwork. The abolitionists never proved their claim that many sugar and cotton growers deliberately worked their slaves to death every seven years with the intention of replacing them from profits. Yet some of the great planters came close to accomplishing that result without designing it. In the "race for wealth" in which, according to one Louisiana planter, all were enlisted, few proprietors managed their estates according to the code of the patricians.[77] They were sometimes remarkably shortsighed in the use of their investments.

Irresponsible overseers, who had no permanent interest in slave property, were frequently blamed for the overworking of slaves. Since this was a common complaint, it is important to remember that nearly half of the slaves lived on plantations of the size that ordinarily employed overseers. But planters could not escape responsibility for these conditions simply because their written instructions usually prohibited excessive driving. For they often demanded crop yields that could be achieved by no other method.

Most overseers believed (with good reason) that their success was measured by how much they produced, and that merely having the slave force in good condition at the end of the year would not guarantee re-employment. A Mississippi overseer with sixteen years of experience confirmed this belief in defending his profession:

"When I came to Mississippi, I found that the overseer who could have the most cotton bales ready for market by Christmas, was considered best qualified for the business — consequently, every overseer gave his whole attention to cotton bales, to the exclusion of everything else." [78]

More than a few planters agreed that this was true. A committee of an Alabama agricultural society reported: "It is too commonly the case that masters look only to the yearly products of their farms, and praise or condemn their overseers by this standard alone, without ever once troubling themselves to inquire into the manner in which things are managed on their plantations, and whether he may have lost more in the diminished value of his slaves by over-work than he has gained by his large crop." This being the case, it was understandably of no consequence to the overseer that the old hands were "worked down" and the young ones "overstrained," that the "breeding women" miscarried, and that the "sucklers" lost their children. "So that he has the requisite number of cotton bags, all is overlooked; he is re-employed at an advanced salary, and his reputation increased." [79]

Some planters, unintentionally perhaps, gave overseers a special incentive for overworking slaves by making their compensation depend in part upon the amount they produced. Though this practice was repeatedly denounced in the ante-bellum period, many masters continued to follow it nevertheless. Cotton growers offered overseers bonuses of from one to five dollars for each bale above a specified minimum, or a higher salary if they produced a fixed quota. A Louisiana planter hired an overseer on a straight commission basis of $2.75 per bale of cotton and four cents per bushel of corn. A South Carolina rice planter gave his overseer ten per cent of the net proceeds. And a Virginian offered his overseer "the seventh part of the good grain, tobacco, cotton, and flax" that was harvested on his estate. "Soon as I hear [of] such a bargain," wrote a southern critic, "I fancy that the overseer, determined to save his salary, adopts the song of 'drive, drive, drive.' " [80]

Masters who hired their slaves to others also helped to create conditions favoring ruthless exploitation. The overworking of hired slaves by employers with only a temporary interest in their welfare was as notorious as the harsh practices of overseers. Slaves hired to mine owners or railroad contractors were fortunate if they were not driven to the point where their health was impaired. The same danger confronted slaves hired to sugar planters during the grinding season or to cotton planters at picking time. Few Southerners familiar with these conditions would have challenged the assertion made before a South Carolina court that hired slaves were "commonly treated more harshly . . . than those in possession of their owner[s]." [81]

But the master was as responsible for the conduct of those who hired his slaves as he was for the conduct of the overseers he employed. Overworked slaves were not always the innocent victims of forces beyond his control; there were remedies which he sometimes failed to apply. A stanch defender of slavery described a set of avaricious planters whom he labeled "Cotton Snobs," or "Southern Yankees." In their frantic quest for wealth, he wrote indignantly, the crack of the whip was heard early and late, until their bondsmen were "bowed to the ground with over-tasking and over-toil." [82] A southern physician who practiced on many cotton plantations complained, in 1847, that some masters still regarded "their sole interest to consist in large crops, leaving out of view altogether the value of negro property and its possible deterioration." During the economic depression of the 1840's, a planter accused certain cotton growers of trying to save themselves by increasing their cotton acreage and by driving their slaves harder, with the result that slaves broke down from overwork. An Alabama newspaper attributed conditions such as these to "avarice, the desire of growing rich." [83]

On the sugar plantations, during the months of the harvest, slaves were driven to the point of complete exhaustion. They were, in the normal routine, worked from sixteen to eighteen hours a day, seven days a week.[84] Cotton planters who boasted about making ten bales per hand were unconsciously testifying that their slaves were overworked. An overseer on an Arkansas plantation set his goal at twelve bales to the hand and indicated that this was what his employer desired. On a North Carolina plantation a temporary overseer assured the owner that he was a "hole hog man rain or shine" and boasted that the slaves had not been working like men but "like horses." "I'd rather be dead than be a nigger on one of these big plantations," a white Mississippian told Olmsted.[85]

Sooner or later excessive labor was bound to take its toll. In the heat of mid-summer, slaves who could not bear hard driving without sufficient rest at noon simply collapsed in the fields. In Mississippi a planter reported "numerous cases" of sunstroke in his neighborhood during a spell of extreme heat. His own slaves "gave out." On a Florida plantation a number of hands "fainted in the field" one hot August day. Even in Virginia hot weather and heavy labor caused "the death of many negroes in the harvest field." [86]

NOTES

1. Joseph H. Ingraham (ed.), *The Sunny South; or, The Southerner at Home* (Philadelphia, 1860), pp. 51–52.
2. Plantation Manual in James H. Hammond Papers.
3. Henry Watson, Jr., to his father, February 24, 1843 (copy), Henry Watson, Jr., Papers.
4. This is a generalized description obtained from the records of many slaveholders who grew cotton in widely scattered parts of the cotton belt.
5. J. Carlyle Sitterson, *Sugar Country: The Cane Sugar Industry in the South, 1753–1950* (Lexington, Kentucky, 1953), pp. 112–56.
6. Michael Gramling, a small planter in the Orangeburg District, who was still producing indigo as late as 1845 was a rare exception. Michael Gramling Ms. Record Book.
7. Duncan Clinch Heyward, *Seed from Madagascar* (Chapel Hill, 1937), pp. 27–44; J. H. Easterby (ed.), *The South Carolina Rice Plantation as Revealed in the Papers of Robert F. W. Allston* (Chicago, 1945), pp. 31–32; Phillips, *Life and Labor in the Old South*, pp. 115–18.
8. Joseph Clarke Robert, *The Tobacco Kingdom* (Durham, 1938), pp. 32–50.
9. James F. Hopkins, *A History of the Hemp Industry in Kentucky* (Lexington, Kentucky, 1951), pp. 24–30, 39–64; Harrison A. Trexler, *Slavery in Missouri, 1804–1865* (Baltimore, 1914), pp. 23–25.
10. *Compendium of the Seventh Census* (Washington, 1854), p. 94.
11. Kenneth M. Clark to Lewis Thompson, June 20, 1853, Lewis Thompson Papers.
12. Columbus Morrison Ms. Diary, entry for November 27, 1845; Rosser H. Taylor, *Slaveholding in North Carolina: An Economic View* (Chapel Hill, 1926), pp. 36–37.
13. Avery O. Craven, *Soil Exhaustion as a Factor in the Agricultural History of Virginia and Maryland* (Urbana, Illinois, 1926), pp. 122–61; Robert, *Tobacco Kingdom*, pp. 18–19.
14. *De Bow's Review*, X (1851), pp. 625–27.
15. Ralph B. Flanders, *Plantation Slavery in Georgia* (Chapel Hill, 1933), p. 158.
16. Records of sales in Lloyd Family Papers. See also Frederick Law Olmsted, *A Journey in the Seaboard Slave States* (New York, 1856), p. 10.
17. Shirley Plantation Ms. Farm Journal; John Walker Ms. Diary.
18. Pettigrew Family Papers; Bennett H. Wall. "Ebenezer Pettigrew. An Economic Study of an Ante-Bellum Planter" (unpublished doctoral dissertation, University of North Carolina, 1946), *passim; Farmer's Journal*, I (1852), p. 147.
19. Sitterson, *Sugar Country*, pp. 50–51.
20. This information about small slaveholders was derived from a study of their production records in representative counties throughout the South as reported in the manuscript census returns for 1860.
21. *Southern Agriculturist*, VI (1833), p. 576.

22. Sellers, *Slavery in Alabama*, p. 67; Hammond Diary, entry for May 16, 1838.
23. These are generalized figures from a survey of many plantation records. See also *De Bow's Review, II* (1846), pp. 134, 138; *X* (1851), p. 625; Sydnor, *Slavery in Mississippi*, pp. 13–14; Gray, *History of Agriculture, II*, pp. 707–708; Sitterson, *Sugar Country*, pp. 127–28; Robert, *Tobacco Kingdom*, p. 18.
24. Olmsted, *Back Country*, p. 47; *id., Seaboard*, p. 433; *Southern Agriculturist, VI* (1833), pp. 571–73; Sydnor, *Slavery in Mississippi*, pp. 18–20; Sellers, *Slavery in Alabama*, p. 66.
25. [Joseph H. Ingraham], *The South-West. By a Yankee* (New York, 1835), *II*, p. 126; Charles S. Davis, *The Cotton Kingdom in Alabama* (Montgomery, 1939), p. 58.
26. Thomas Affleck, *The Cotton Plantation Record and Account Book* (Louisville and New Orleans, 1847–).
27. Gustavus A. Henry to his wife, December 3, 1846, Gustavus A. Henry Papers; Herbert A. Kellar (ed.), *Solon Robinson, Pioneer and Agriculturist* (Indianapolis, 1936), *II*, p. 203.
28. William H. Russell, *My Diary North and South* (Boston, 1863), p. 273.
29. Ingraham (ed.), *Sunny South*, pp. 179–81.
30. Henry Watson, Jr., to Theodore Watson, March 3, 1831, Watson Papers; Olmsted, *Seaboard*, pp. 18–19.
31. Solomon Northup, *Twelve Years a Slave* (Buffalo, 1853), pp. 178–79.
32. Gustavus A. Henry to his wife, December 12, 1848, Henry Papers; John Nevitt Ms. Plantation Journal; William S. Pettigrew to James C. Johnston, January 24, 1856, Pettigrew Family Papers; Olmsted, *Seaboard*, pp. 153–55.
33. Olmsted, *Seaboard*, pp. 339–42; Guion G. Johnson, *Ante-Bellum North Carolina* (Chapel Hill, 1937), pp. 487–88.
34. Fredrika Bremer, *The Homes of the New World* (New York, 1853), *II*, p. 174.
35. Joe Gray Taylor, "Negro Slavery in Louisiana" (unpublished doctoral dissertation, Louisiana State University, 1951), pp. 43–44, 115–17; Raleigh *North Carolina Standard*, June 6, 1855; August 13, 1859; Horace S. Fulkerson, *Random Recollections of Early Days in Mississippi*, (Vicksburg, 1885), pp. 130–31.
36. Richmond *Enquirer*, August 2, 1836; Sellers, *Slavery in Alabama*, pp. 200–220; Flanders, *Plantation Slavery in Georgia*, pp. 197–98; Taylor, "Negro Slavery in Louisiana," pp. 112–13.
37. [Ingraham], *South-West, II*, p. 249.
38. Quoted in Flanders, *Plantation Slavery in Georgia*, p. 47. See also Leonard P. Stavisky, "Negro Craftsmanship in Early America," *American Historical Review, IV* (1949), pp. 315–25.
39. *De Bow's Review, VIII* (1850), p. 76; *IX* (1850), pp. 432–33.
40. Hopkins, *Hemp Industry*, pp. 135–37; J. Winston Coleman, Jr., *Slavery Times in Kentucky* (Chapel Hill, 1940), pp. 81–82.
41. Robert, *Tobacco Kingdom*, pp. 197–203; Alexander MacKay, *The Western World; or Travels in the United States in 1846–47* (London, 1849), *II*, p. 74.
42. Coleman, *Slavery Times in Kentucky*, p. 64; Robert E. Corlew, "Some Aspects of Slavery in Dickson County," *Tennessee Historical Quarterly, X* (1951), pp. 226–29.
43. Kathleen Bruce, *Virginia Iron Manufacture in the Slave Era* (New York, 1931), pp. 231–38.
44. James S. Buckingham, *The Slave States of America* (London, [1842]), *II*, p. 112.
45. Pensacola *Gazette*, April 8, 1848; *De Bow's Review, IX* (1850), pp. 432–33.
46. E. M. Lander, Jr., "Slave Labor in South Carolina Cotton Mills," *Journal of Negro History, XXXVIII* (1953), pp. 161–73; Charles H. Wesley, *Negro Labor in the United States, 1850–1925* (New York, 1927), pp. 15–20; *American Cotton Planter and Soil of the South, I* (1857), pp. 156–57.
47. William B. Lenoir to William Lenoir, May 18, 1833, Lenoir Family Papers.
48. Frederic Bancroft, *Slave-Trading in the Old South* (Baltimore, 1931), pp. 404–405.
49. Richmond *Enquirer*, January 1, 1850; Bancroft, *Slave-Trading*, p. 149.
50. Hamilton Brown Papers; Memorandum dated December 15, 1860, in Morton-Halsey Papers.
51. S. F. Lenoir to her sisters, November 18, 1851, Lenoir Family Papers; Bancroft, *Slave-Trading*, pp. 145–47.
52. Contract between William Frew and R. S. Young, dated December 30, 1853, in Burton-Young Papers.
53. Rickerton Lyle Winston Ms. Slave Account Book.
54. [Ingraham], *South-West, II*, pp. 251–52.
55. Edmund Ruffin, Jr., Farm Journal, entry for September 7, 1843.
56. Sitterson, *Sugar Country*, pp. 61–62; Taylor, "Negro Slavery in Louisiana," p. 94.
57. Charleston *Courier*, August 16, 1852.
58. Copies of letters to "James Sims a Colored man," in Walker Diary.
59. Richmond *Enquirer*, August 8, 1836; Wilmington (N.C.) *Journal*, December 28, 1857.
60. Lexington *Kentucky Statesman*, December 26, 1854; Robert, *Tobacco Kingdom*, p. 198.
61. Frederick Douglass, *My Bondage and My Freedom* (New York, 1855), p. 328.
62. Charles White to Hamilton Brown, December 20, 1832, Hamilton Brown Papers.
63. Susan Dabney Smedes, *Memorials of a Southern Planter* (Baltimore, 1887), p. 57.
64. Northup, *Twelve Years a Slave*, pp. 166–68.
65. Olmsted, *Seaboard*, pp. 431–36; Guion G. Johnson, *A Social History of the Sea Islands* (Chapel Hill, 1930), pp. 124–25; E. Merton Coulter, *Thomas Spalding of Sapelo* (Baton Rouge, 1940), p. 85.

66. Gray, *History of Agriculture, I*, pp. 556–57.
67. Gustavus A. Henry to his wife, November 27, 1860, Henry Papers.
68. *Southern Cultivator, VIII* (1850), p. 163.
69. William W. Brown, *Narrative of William W. Brown, a Fugitive Slave* (Boston, 1847), p. 14; Olmsted, *Seaboard*, p. 109; *De Bow's Review, XIV* (1853), pp. 176–78; Benjamin Drew, *The Refugee: or the Narratives of Fugitive Slaves in Canada* (Boston, 1856), p. 162.
70. *Southern Cultivator, VIII* (1850), p. 163.
71. Henry K. Burgwyn to Arthur Souter, August 6, 1843, Henry King Burgwyn Papers; John C. Jenkins Diary, entries for November 15, 1845; April 22, 1854; Hammond Diary, entry for May 12, 1832; *De Bow's Review, XIII* (1852), pp. 193–94.
72. Jenkins Diary, entry for August 7, 1843.
73. Olmsted, *Back Country*, p. 81; Sydnor, *Slavery in Mississippi*, p. 12.
74. See, for example, Marston Papers; Torbert Plantation Diary; *De Bow's Review, XI* (1851), pp. 369–72; Drew, *Refugee*; Douglass, *My Bondage*, p. 215; Trexler, *Slavery in Missouri*, pp. 97–98.
75. Hurd, *Law of Freedom and Bondage, I*, p. 307; Flanders, *Plantation Slavery in Georgia*, p. 42.
76. *Southern Cultivator, VII* (1849), p. 69.
77. Kenneth M. Clark to Lewis Thompson, December 29, 1859, Thompson Papers.
78. *American Cotton Planter and Soil of the South, II* (1858), pp. 112–13.
79. *American Farmer, II* (1846), p. 78; *Southern Cultivator, II* (1844), pp. 97, 107.
80. *North Carolina Farmer, I* (1845), pp. 122–23. Agreements of this kind with overseers are in the records of numerous planters.
81. Catterall, *Judicial Cases, II*, p. 374.
82. Hundley, *Social Relations*, pp. 132, 187–88.
83. *De Bow's Review, I* (1846), pp. 434–36; *III* (1847), p. 419; Selma *Free Press*, quoted in Tuscaloosa *Independent Monitor*, July 14, 1846.
84. This is apparent from the records of sugar planters. See also Sitterson, *Sugar Country*, pp. 133–36; Olmsted, *Seaboard*, pp. 650, 667–68.
85. P. Weeks to James Sheppard, September 20, 1854, James Sheppard Papers; Doctrine Davenport to Ebenezer Pettigrew, April 24, 1836, Pettigrew Family Papers; Olmsted, *Back Country*, pp. 55–57, 202.
86. Jenkins Diary, entries for August 9, 1844; July 7, 1846; June 30, 1854; Ulrich B. Phillips and James D. Glunt (eds.), *Florida Plantation Records from the Papers of George Noble Jones* (St. Louis, 1927), p. 90; John B. Garrett Ms. Farm Journal, entry for July 19, 1830.

Ante-Bellum Reform

In the history of all nations, periods of change alternate with periods of relative stability. This generalization seems to hold true particularly in the realm of ideas and values. The years between 1815 and 1860 were just such an era of intellectual and ideological ferment in the United States, a period marked by a willingness to think everything, propose everything, try everything.

Though related to the momentous romantic revolution of sensibility that influenced every aspect of art, thought, politics, and perception in the Western world, it developed distinctive qualities in the United States. American society as a whole was more fluid and open, of course, than European. Political democracy was matched by a kind of intellectual democracy that made the ordinary American extraordinarily receptive to new ideas and new social nostrums. New thoughts, new proposals, new speculations were not confined to a small elite, but were shared by a large middle element of the population. The profoundly religious bent of the American people also gave the romantic revolution its unique cast in the United States. In pious Protestant America, the romantic sensibility was to take the form of an intense zeal for improving men and institutions. At times, it appeared to contemporaries that every man wanted to remake religion, society, the economy, the government, or the world as a whole.

Humanitarian reform was not uniformly diffused throughout the country. It was centered in the North, and within that section it flourished most exuberantly in New England and in areas where Yankees resided in large numbers, such as western New York and the Western Reserve of Ohio. It scarcely penetrated the South. That section, by the early years of the nineteenth century, had begun to diverge culturally and intellectually from the rest of the country. At the heart of this growing gap was slavery, an institution that not only affronted the earlier values of the Enlightenment, but even more, was incompatible with the romantic spirit. The reformers singled out slavery as one of their chief targets. This in itself was enough to convince southerners that reform and speculative social thought were dangerous to the whole fragile structure of slave society and to make them declared enemies of northern "isms." By 1860, romantic reform had helped to create two fairly distinct and antagonistic societies within the political limits of the United States.

FOR FURTHER READING:

FILLER, LOUIS. *The Crusade Against Slavery.* New York: Harper & Row, Publishers, Torchbooks, 1963.*
SMITH, TIMOTHY L. *Revivalism and Social Reform: American Protestantism on the Eve of the Civil War.* New York: Harper & Row, Publishers, Torchbooks, 1965.*
TYLER, ALICE FELT. *Freedom's Ferment: Phases of American Social History from the Colonial Period to the Outbreak of the Civil War.* New York: Harper & Row, Publishers, Torchbooks, 1962.*

Asterisk denotes paperback edition.

Romantic Reform in America, 1815–1865   JOHN L. THOMAS

Confronted by the bewildering variety of projects for regenerating American society, Emerson concluded his survey of humanitarian reform in 1844 with the observation that "the Church, or religious party, is falling away from the Church nominal, and . . . appearing in temperance and nonresistance societies; in movements of abolitionists and of socialists . . . of seekers, of all the soul of the soldiery of dissent." Common to all these planners and prophets, he noted, was the conviction of an "infinite worthiness" in man and the belief that reform simply meant removing "impediments" to natural perfection.[1]

Emerson was defining, both as participant and observer, a romantic revolution which T. E. Hulme once described as "spilt religion."[2] A romantic faith in perfectibility, originally confined by religious institutions, overflows these barriers and spreads across the surface of society, seeping into politics and culture. Perfectibility — the essentially religious notion of the individual as a "reservoir" of possibilities — fosters a revolutionary assurance "that if you can so rearrange society by the destruction of oppressive order then these possibilities will have a chance and you will get Progress." Hulme had in mind the destructive forces of the French Revolution, but his phrase is also a particularly accurate description of the surge of social reform which swept across Emerson's America in the three decades before the Civil War. Out of a seemingly conservative religious revival there flowed a spate of perfectionist ideas for the improvement and rearrangement of American society. Rising rapidly in the years after 1830, the flood of social reform reached its crest at midcentury only to be checked by political crisis and the counterforces of the Civil War. Reform after the Civil War, though still concerned with individual perfectibility, proceeded from new and different assumptions as to the nature of individualism and its preservation in an urban industrial society. Romantic reform ended with the Civil War and an intellectual counterrevolution which discredited the concept of the irreducible self and eventually redirected reform energies.

Romantic reform in America traced its origins to a religious impulse which was both politically and socially conservative. With the consolidation of independence and the arrival of democratic politics the new nineteenth-century generation of American churchmen faced a seeming crisis. Egalitarianism and rising demands for church disestablishment suddenly appeared to threaten an inherited Christian order and along with it the preferred status of the clergy. Lyman Beecher spoke the fears of more than one of the clerical party when he warned that Americans were fast becoming "another people." When the attempted alliance between sound religion and correct politics failed to prevent disestablishment or improve waning Federalist fortunes at the polls, the evangelicals, assuming a defensive posture, organized voluntary benevolent associations to strengthen the Christian character of Americans and save the country from infidelity and ruin. Between 1815 and 1830 nearly a dozen moral reform societies were established to counter the threats to social equilibrium posed by irreligious democrats. Their intense religious concern could be read in the

---

Source: John L. Thomas, "Romantic Reform in America, 1815–1865," *American Quarterly*, vol. 17 (1965), pp. 658–681.

titles of the benevolent societies which the evangelicals founded: the American Bible Society, the American Sunday School Union, the American Home Missionary Society, the American Tract Society. By the time of the election of Andrew Jackson the benevolent associations formed a vast if loosely coordinated network of conservative reform enterprises staffed with clergy and wealthy laymen who served as self-appointed guardians of American morals.[3]

The clerical diagnosticians had little difficulty in identifying the symptoms of democratic disease. Infidelity flourished on the frontier and licentiousness bred openly in seaboard cities; intemperance sapped the strength of American workingmen and the saving word was denied their children. Soon atheism would destroy the vital organs of the republic unless drastic moral therapy prevented. The evangelicals' prescription followed logically from their diagnosis: large doses of morality injected into the body politic under the supervision of Christian stewards. No more Sunday mails or pleasure excursions, no more grog-shops or profane pleasures, no family without a Bible and no community without a minister of the gospel. Accepting for the moment their political liabilities, the moral reformers relied on the homeopathic strategy of fighting democratic excess with democratic remedies. The Tract Society set up three separate printing presses which cranked out hundreds of thousands of pamphlets for mass distribution. The Home Missionary Society subsidized seminarians in carrying religion into the backcountry. The Temperance Union staged popular conventions; the Peace Society sponsored public debates; the Bible Society hired hundreds of agents to spread its propaganda.

The initial thrust of religious reform, then, was moral rather than social, preventive rather than curative. Nominally rejecting politics and parties, the evangelicals looked to a general reformation of the American character achieved through a revival of piety and morals in the individual. By probing his conscience, by convincing him of his sinful ways and converting him to right conduct they hoped to engineer a Christian revolution which would leave the foundations of the social order undisturbed. The realization of their dream of a nonpolitical "Christian party" in America would ensure a one-party system open to moral talent and the natural superiority of Christian leadership. Until their work was completed, the evangelicals stood ready as servants of the Lord to manage their huge reformational apparatus in behalf of order and sobriety.

But the moral reformers inherited a theological revolution which in undermining their conservative defenses completely reversed their expectations for a Christian America. The transformation of American theology in the first quarter of the nineteenth century released the very forces of romantic perfectionism that conservatives most feared. This religious revolution advanced along three major fronts: first, the concentrated anti-theocratic assault of Robert Owen and his secular utopian followers, attacks purportedly atheistic and environmentalist but in reality Christian in spirit and perfectionist in method; second, the revolt of liberal theology beginning with Unitarianism and culminating in transcendentalism; third, the containment operation of the "new divinity" in adapting orthodoxy to the criticism of liberal dissent. The central fact in the romantic reorientation of American theology was the rejection of determinism. Salvation, however, variously defined, lay open to everyone. Sin was voluntary; men were not helpless and depraved by nature but free agents and potential powers for good. Sin could be reduced to the selfish preferences of individuals, and social evils, in turn, to collective sins which, once acknowledged, could be rooted out. Perfectionism spread rapidly across the whole spectrum of American Protestantism as different denominations and sects elaborated their own versions of salvation. If man was a truly free agent, then his improvement became a matter of immediate consequence. The progress of the country suddenly seemed to depend upon the regeneration of the individual and the contagion of example.

As it spread, perfectionism swept across denominational barriers and penetrated even secular thought. Perfection was presented as Christian striving for holiness in the "new heart" sermons of Charles Grandison Finney and as an immediately attainable goal in the come-outer prophecies of John Humphrey Noyes. It was described as an escape from outworn dogma by Robert Owen and as the final union of the soul with nature by Emerson. The important fact for most Americans in the first half of the nineteenth century was that it was readily available. A romantic religious faith had changed an Enlightenment doctrine of progress into a dynamic principle of reform.

For the Founding Fathers' belief in perfectibility had been wholly compatible with a pessimistic appraisal of the present state of mankind. Progress, in the view of John Adams or James Madison, resulted from the planned operation of mechanical checks within the framework of government which balanced conflicting selfish interests and neutralized private passions. Thus a properly constructed governmental machine might achieve by artifact what men, left to their own devices, could not — gradual improvement of social institutions and a measure of progress. Perfectionism, on the contrary, as an optative mood demanded total commitment and immediate action. A latent revolutionary force lay in its demand for immediate reform and its promise to release the new American from the restraints of institutions and precedent. In appealing to the liberated individual, perfectionism reinforced the Jacksonian attack on institutions, whether a "Monster Bank" or a secret Masonic order, entrenched monopolies or the Catholic Church. But in emphasizing the unfettered will as the proper vehicle for reform it provided a millenarian alternative to Jacksonian politics. Since social evils were simply individual acts of selfishness compounded, and since Americans could attempt the perfect society any time they were so inclined, it followed that the duty of the true reformer consisted in educating them and making them models of good behavior. As the sum of individual sins social wrong would disappear when enough people had been converted and rededicated to right conduct. Deep and lasting reform, therefore, meant an educational crusade based on the assumption that when a sufficient number of individual Americans had seen the light, they would automatically solve the country's social problems. Thus formulated, perfectionist reform offered a program of mass conversion achieved through educational rather than political means. In the opinion of the romantic reformers the regeneration of American society began, not in legislative enactments or political maniuplation, but in a calculated appeal to the American urge for individual self-improvement.

Perfectionism radically altered the moral reform movement by shattering the benevolent societies themselves. Typical of these organizations was the American Peace Society founded in 1828 as a forum for clerical discussions of the gospel of peace. Its founders, hoping to turn American attention from the pursuit of wealth to the prevention of war, debated the question of defensive war, constructed hypothetical leagues of amity, and in a general way sought to direct American foreign policy into pacific channels. Perfectionism, however, soon split the Peace Society into warring factions as radical nonresistants, led by the Christian perfectionist Henry C. Wright, denounced all use of force and demanded the instant creation of an American society modeled on the precepts of Jesus. Not only war but all governmental coercion fell under the ban of the nonresistants who refused military service and political office along with the right to vote. After a series of skirmishes the nonresistants seceded in 1838 to form their own New England Non-Resistant Society; and by 1840 the institutional strength of the peace movement had been completely broken.

The same power of perfectionism disrupted the temperance movement. The founders of the temperance crusade had considered their reform an integral part of the program of moral stewardship and had directed their campaign against "ardent spirits" which could be banished "by a correct and efficient public sentiment." Until 1833 there was no general agreement on a pledge of total abstinence: some local societies required it, others did not. At the first national convention held in that year, however, the radical advocates of temperance, following their perfectionist proclivities, demanded a pledge of total abstinence and hurried on to denounce the liquor traffic as "morally wrong." Soon both the national society and local and state auxiliaries were split between moderates content to preach to the consumer and radicals bent on extending moral suasion to public pressure on the seller. After 1836 the national movement disintegrated into scattered local societies which attempted with no uniform program and no permanent success to establish a coldwater America.

By far the most profound change wrought by perfectionism was the sudden emergence of abolition. The American Colonization Society, founded in 1817 as another key agency in the moral reform complex, aimed at strengthening republican institutions by deporting an inferior and therefore undesirable Negro population. The cooperation of Southerners hoping to strengthen the institution of slavery gave Northern colonizationists pause, but they succeeded in repressing their doubts until a perfectionist ethic totally discredited their program. The abolitionist pioneers were former colonizationists who took sin and redemption seriously and insisted that slavery constituted a flat denial of perfectibility to both Negroes and whites. They found in immediate emancipation a perfectionist formula for casting off the guilt of slavery and bringing the Negro to Christian freedom. Destroying slavery, the abolitionists argued, depended first of all on recognizing it as sin; and to this recognition they bent their efforts. Their method was direct and intensely personal. Slaveholding they considered a deliberate flouting of the divine will for which there was no remedy but repentance. Since slavery was sustained by a system of interlocking personal sins, their task was to teach Americans to stop sinning. "We shall send forth agents to lift up the voice of remonstrance, of warning, of entreaty, and of rebuke," the Declaration of Sentiments of the American Anti-Slavery Society announced. Agents, tracts, petitions and conventions — all the techniques of the moral reformers — were brought to bear on the consciences of Americans to convince them of their sin.

From the beginning, then, the abolitionists mounted a moral crusade rather than an engine of limited reform. For seven years, from 1833 to 1840, their society functioned as a loosely coordinated enterprise — a national directory of antislavery opinion. Perfectionist individualism made effective organization difficult and often impossible. Antislavery delegates from state and local societies gathered at annual conventions to frame denunciatory resolutions, listen to endless rounds of speeches and go through the motions of electing officers. Nominal leadership but very little power was vested in a self-perpetuating executive committee. Until its disruption in 1840 the national society was riddled with controversy as moderates, disillusioned by the failure of moral suasion, gradually turned to politics, and ultras, equally disenchanted by public hostility, abandoned American institutions altogether. Faced with the resistance of Northern churches and state legislatures, the perfectionists, led by William Lloyd Garrison, deserted politics for the principle of secession. The come-outer abolitionists, who eventually took for their motto "No Union with Slaveholders," sought an alternative to politics in the command to cast off church and state for a holy fraternity which would convert the nation by the power of example. The American Anti-Slavery Society quickly succumbed to the strain of conflicting philosophies and warring personalities. In 1840 the Garrisonians seized control of the society and drove their moderate opponents out. Thereafter neither ultras nor moderates were able to maintain an effective national organization.

Thus romantic perfectionism altered the course of the reform enterprise by appealing directly to the individual conscience. Its power stemmed from a millennial expectation which proved too powerful a moral explosive for the reform agencies. In one way or another almost all of the benevolent societies felt the force of perfectionism. Moderates, attempting political solutions, scored temporary gains only to receive sharp setbacks. Local option laws passed one year were repealed the next. Despite repeated attempts the Sunday School Union failed to secure permanent adoption of its texts in the public schools. The Liberty Party succeeded only in electing a Democratic president in 1844. Generally, direct political action failed to furnish reformers with the moral leverage they believed necessary to perfect American society. The conviction spread accordingly that politicians and legislators, as Albert Brisbane put it, were engaged in "superficial controversies and quarrels, which lead to no practical results." [4] Political results, a growing number of social reformers were convinced, would be forthcoming only when the reformation of society at large had been accomplished through education and example.

The immediate effects of perfectionism, therefore, were felt outside politics in humanitarian reforms. With its confidence in the liberated individual perfectionism tended to be anti-institutional and exclusivist; but at the same time it posited an ideal society in which this same individual could discover his power for good and exploit it. Such a society would tolerate neither poverty nor suffering; it would contain no condemned classes or deprived citizens, no criminals or forgotten men. Impressed with the necessity for saving these neglected elements of American society, the humanitarian reformers in the years after 1830 undertook a huge rescue operation.

Almost to a man the humanitarians came from moral reform backgrounds. Samuel Gridley Howe was a product of Old Colony religious zeal and a Baptist education at Brown; Thomas Gallaudet, a graduate of Andover and an ordained minister; Dorothea Dix, a daughter of an itinerant Methodist minister, school mistress and Sunday school teacher-turned-reformer, E. M. P. Wells, founder of the reform school, a pastor of a Congregational church in Boston. Louis Dwight, the prison reformer, had been trained for the ministry at Yale and began his reform career as a traveling agent for the American Tract Society. Robert Hartley, for thirty years the secretary of the New York Association for Improving the Condition of the Poor, started as a tract distributor and temperance lecturer. Charles Loring Brace served as a missionary on Blackwell's Island before founding the Children's Aid Society.

In each of these cases of conversion to humanitarian reform there was a dramatic disclosure of deprivation and suffering which did not tally with preconceived notions of perfectibility — Dorothea Dix's discovery of the conditions in the Charlestown reformatory, Robert Hartley's inspection of contaminated milk in New York slums, Samuel Gridley Howe's chance conversation with Dr. Fisher in Boston. Something very much like a conversion experience seems to have forged the decisions of the humanitarians to take up their causes, a kind of revelation which furnished them with a ready-made role outside politics and opened a new career with which they could become completely identified. With the sudden transference of a vague perfectionist faith in self-improvement to urgent social problems there emerged a new type of professional reformer whose whole life became identified with the reform process.

Such, for example, was the conversion of Dorothea Dix from a lonely and afflicted schoolteacher who composed meditational studies of the life of Jesus into "D. L. Dix," the militant advocate of the helpless and forgotten. In a very real sense Miss Dix's crusade for better treatment of the insane and the criminal was one long self-imposed subjection to suffering. Her reports, which recorded cases of unbelievable mistreatment, completed a kind of purgative rite in which she assumed the burden of innocent suffering and passed it on as guilt to the American people. The source of her extraordinary energy lay in just this repeated submission of herself to human misery until she felt qualified to speak out against it. Both an exhausting schedule and the almost daily renewal of scenes of suffering seemed to give her new energies for playing her romantic reform role in an effective and intensely personal way. Intense but not flexible: there was little room for exchange and growth in the mood of atonement with which she approached her work. Nor was her peculiarly personal identification with the victims of American indifference easily matched in reform circles. Where other reformers like the abolitionists often made abstract pleas for "bleeding humanity" and "suffering millions," hers was the real thing — a perfectionist fervor which strengthened her will at the cost of psychological isolation. Throughout her career she preferred to work alone, deploring the tendency to multiply reform agencies and ignoring those that existed either because she disagreed with their principles, as in the case of Louis Dwight's Boston Prison Discipline Society, or because she chose the more direct method of personal appeal. In all her work, even the unhappy and frustrating last years as superintendent of nurses in the Union Army, she saw herself as a solitary spokesman for the deprived and personal healer of the suffering.

Another reform role supplied by perfectionism was Bronson Alcott's educator-prophet, the "true reformer" who "studied man as he is from the hand of the Creator, and not as he is made by the errors of the world." Convinced that the self sprang from divine origins in nature, Alcott naturally concluded that children were more susceptible to good than people imagined and set out to develop a method for uncovering that goodness. With the power to shape personality the teacher, Alcott was sure, held the key to illimitable progress and the eventual regeneration of the world. The teacher might literally make society over by teaching men as children to discover their own divine natures. Thus true education for Alcott consisted of the process of self-discovery guided by the educator-prophet. He sharply criticized his contemporaries for their fatal mistake of imposing partial and therefore false standards on their charges. Shades of the prison house obscured the child's search for perfection, and character was lost forever. "Instead of following it in the path pointed out by its Maker, instead of learning by observation, and guiding it in that path; we unthinkingly attempt to shape its course to our particular wishes. . . ."[5]

To help children avoid the traps set by their elders Alcott based his whole system on the cultivation of self-awareness through self-examination. His pupils kept journals in which they scrutinized their behavior and analyzed their motives. Ethical problems were the subject of frequent and earnest debate at the Temple School as the children were urged to discover the hidden springs of perfectibility in themselves. No mechanical methods of rote learning could bring on the moment of revelation; each child was unique and would find himself in his own way. The real meaning of education as reform, Alcott realized, came with an increased social sense that resulted from individual self-discovery. As the creator of social personality Alcott's teacher was bound by no external rules of pedagogy: as the primary social reformer he had to cast off "the shackles of form, of mode, and ceremony" in order to play the required roles in the educational process.

Alcott's modernity lay principally in his concept of the interchangeability of roles — both teacher and pupils acquired self-knowledge in an exciting give-and-take. Thus defined, education became a way of life, a continuing process through which individuals learned to obey the laws of their own natures and in so doing to discover the laws of the good society. This identification of individual development with true social unity was crucial for Alcott, as for the other perfectionist communitarians, because it provided the bridge over which they passed from self to society. The keystone in Alcott's construction was supplied by the individual conscience which connected with the "common conscience" of mankind. This fundamental identity, he was convinced, could be demonstrated by the learning process itself which he defined as "sympathy and imitation, the moral action of the teacher upon the children, of the children upon him, and each other." He saw in the school, therefore, a model of the good community where self-discovery led to a social exchange culminating in the recognition of universal dependency and brotherhood. The ideal society — the society he hoped to create — was one in which individuals could be totally free to follow their own natures because such pursuit would inevitably end in social harmony. For Alcott the community was the product rather than the creator of the good life.

Fruitlands, Alcott's attempt to apply the lessons of the Temple School on a larger scale, was designed to prove that perfectionist educational reform affected the "economies of life." In this realization lay the real import of Alcott's reform ideas; for education, seen as a way of life, meant the communitarian experiment as an educative model. Pushed to its limits, the perfectionist assault on institutions logically ended in the attempt to make new and better societies as examples for Americans to follow. Communitarianism, as Alcott envisioned it, was the social extension of his perfectionist belief in education as an alternative to politics.

In the case of other humanitarian reformers like Samuel Gridley Howe, perfectionism determined even more precisely both the role and intellectual content of their proposals. Howe's ideal of the good society seems to have derived from his experiences in Greece where, during his last year, he promoted a communitarian plan for resettling exiles on the Gulf of Corinth. With government support he established his colony, "Washingtonia," on two thousand acres of arable land, selected the colonists himself, brought cattle and tools, managed its business affairs, and supervised a Lancastrian school. By his own admission these were the happiest days of his life:

"I laboured here day & night in season & out; & was governor, legislator, clerk, constable, & everything but patriarch." [6] When the government withdrew its support and brigands overran the colony, Howe was forced to abandon the project and return home. Still, the idea of an entire community under the care of a "patriarch" shouldering its collective burden and absorbing all its dependents in a cooperative life continued to dominate the "Doctor's" reform thinking and to determine his methods.

The ethical imperatives in Howe's philosophy of reform remained constant. "Humanity demands that every creature in human shape should command our respect; we should recognise as a brother every being upon whom God has stamped the human impress." Progress he likened to the American road. Christian individualism required that each man walk separately and at his own pace, but "the rear should not be left too far behind . . . none should be allowed to perish in their helplessness . . . the strong should help the weak, so that the whole should advance as a band of brethren." It was the duty of society itself to care for its disabled or mentally deficient members rather than to shut them up in asylums which were "offsprings of a low order of feeling." "The more I reflect upon the subject the more I see objections in principle and practice to asylums," he once wrote to a fellow-reformer. "What right have we to pack off the poor, the old, the blind into asylums? They are of us, our brothers, our sisters — they belong in families. . . ." [7]

In Howe's ideal society, then, the handicapped, criminals and defectives would not be walled off but accepted as part of the community and perfected by constant contact with it. Two years of experimenting with education for the feeble-minded convinced him that even "idiots" could be redeemed from what he called spiritual death. "How far they can be elevated, and to what extent they may be educated, can only be shown by the experience of the future," he admitted in his report to the Massachusetts legislature but predicted confidently that "each succeeding year will show even more progress than any preceding one." [8] He always acted on his conviction that "we shall avail ourselves of special institutions less and the common schools more" and never stopped hoping that eventually all blind children after proper training might be returned to families and public schools for their real education. He also opposed the establishment of reformatories with the argument that they only collected the refractory and vicious and made them worse. Nature mingled the defective in common families, he insisted, and any departure from her standards stunted moral growth. He took as his model for reform the Belgian town of Geel where mentally ill patients were boarded at public expense with private families and allowed maximum freedom. As soon as the building funds were available he introduced the cottage system at Perkins, a plan he also wanted to apply to reformatories. No artificial and unnatural institution could replace the family which Howe considered the primary agency in the perfection of the individual.

Howe shared his bias against institutions and a preference for the family unit with other humanitarian reformers like Robert Hartley and Charles Loring Brace. Hartley's "friendly visitors" were dispatched to New York's poor with instructions to bring the gospel of self-help home to every member of the family. Agents of the AICP dispensed advice and improving literature along with the coal and groceries. Only gradually did the organization incorporate "incidental labors" — legislative programs for housing reform, health regulations and child labor — into its system of reform. Hartley's real hope for the new urban poor lay in their removal to the country where a bootstrap operation might lift them to sufficiency and selfhood. "Escape then from the city," he told them, " — for escape is your only recourse against the terrible ills of beggary; and the further you go, the better." [9] In Hartley's formula the perfectionist doctrine of the salvation of the individual combined with the conservative appeal of the safety-valve.

A pronounced hostility to cities also marked the program of Charles Loring Brace's Children's Aid Society, the central feature of which was the plan for relocating children of the "squalid poor" on upstate New York farms for "moral disinfection." The Society's placement service resettled thousands of slum children in the years before the Civil War in the belief that a proper family environment and a rural setting would release the naturally good tendencies in young people so that under the supervision of independent and hard-working farmers they would save themselves. [10]

There was thus a high nostalgic content in the plans of humanitarians who emphasized pastoral virtues and the perfectionist values inherent in country living. Their celebration of the restorative powers of nature followed logically from their assumption that the perfected individual — the truly free American — could be created only by the reunification of mental and physical labor. The rural life, it was assumed, could revive and sustain the unified sensibility threatened by the city. A second assumption concerned the importance of the family as the primary unit in the reconstruction of society. As the great debate among social reformers proceeded it centered on the question of the limits to which the natural family could be extended. Could an entire society, as the more radical communitarians argued, be reorganized as one huge family? Or were there natural boundaries necessary for preserving order and morality? On the whole, the more conservative humanitarians agreed with Howe in rejecting those communal plans which, like Fourier's, stemmed from too high an estimate of "the capacity of mankind for family affections." [11]

That intensive education held the key to illimitable progress, however, few humanitarian reformers denied. They were strengthened in their certainty by the absolutes inherited from moral reform. Thus Howe, for example, considered his work a "new field" of "practical religion." The mental defective, he was convinced, was the product of sin — both the sin of the parents and the sin of society in allowing the offspring to languish in mental and moral darkness. Yet the social evils incident to sin were not inevitable; they were not "inherent in the very constitution of man" but the "chastisements sent by a loving Father to bring his children to obedience to his beneficent laws." [12] These laws — infinite perfectibility and social responsibility — reinforced each other in the truly progressive society. The present condition of the dependent classes in America was proof of "the immense space through which society has yet to advance before it even approaches the perfection of civilization which is attainable." [13] Education, both the thorough training of the deprived and the larger education of American society to its obligations, would meet the moral challenge.

The perfectionist uses of education as an alternative to political reform were most thoroughly explored by Horace Mann. Mann's initial investment in public school education was dictated by his fear that American democracy, lacking institutional checks and restraints, was fast degenerating into "the spectacle of gladiatorial contests" conducted at the expense of the people. Could laws save American society? Mann thought not.

> With us, the very idea of legislation is reversed. Once, the law prescribed the actions and shaped the wills of the multitude; here the wills of the multitude prescribe and shape the

law . . . now when the law is weak, the passions of the multitude have gathered irresistible strength, it is fallacious and insane to look for security in the moral force of law. Government and law . . . will here be moulded into the similitude of the public mind. . . . [14]

In offering public school education as the only effective countervailing force in a democracy Mann seemingly was giving vent to a conservative dread of unregulated change in a society where, as he admitted, the momentum of hereditary opinion was spent. Where there was no "surgical code of laws" reason, conscience and benevolence would have to be provided by education. "The whole mass of mind must be instructed in regard to its comprehensive and enduring interests." In a republican government, however, compulsion was theoretically undesirable and practically unavailable. People could not be driven up a "dark avenue" even though it were the right one. Mann, like his evangelical predecessors, found his solution in an educational crusade.

> Let the intelligent visit the ignorant, day by day, as the oculist visits the blind mind, and detaches the scales from his eyes, until the living sense leaps to light. . . . Let the love of beautiful reason, the admonitions of conscience, the sense of religious responsibility, be plied, in mingled tenderness and earnestness, until the obdurate and dark mass of avarice and ignorance and prejudice shall be dissipated by their blended light and heat. [15]

Here in Mann's rhetorical recasting was what appeared to be the old evangelical prescription for tempering democratic excess. The chief problem admittedly was avoiding the "disturbing forces of party and sect and faction and clan." To make sure that education remained nonpartisan the common schools should teach on the *"exhibitory"* method, "by an actual exhibition of the principle we would inculcate."

Insofar as the exhibitory method operated to regulate or direct public opinion, it was conservative. But implicit in Mann's theory was a commitment to perfectionism which gradually altered his aims until in the twelfth and final report education emerges as a near-utopian device for making American politics simple, clean and, eventually, superfluous. In the Twelfth Report Mann noted that although a public school system might someday guarantee "sufficiency, comfort, competence" to every American, as yet "imperfect practice" had not matched "perfect theory." Then in an extended analysis of social trends which foreshadowed Henry George's classification he singled out "poverty" and "profusion" as the two most disturbing facts in American development. "With every generation, fortunes increase on the one hand, and some new privation is added to poverty on the other. We are verging toward those extremes of opulence and penury, each of which unhumanizes the mind." [16] A new feudalism threatened; and unless a drastic remedy was discovered, the "hideous evils" of unequal distribution of wealth would cause class war.

Mann's alternative to class conflict proved to be nothing less than universal education based on the exhibitory model of the common school. Diffusion of education, he pointed out, meant wiping out class lines and with them the possibility of conflict. As the great equalizer of condition it would supply the balance-wheel in the society of the future. Lest his readers confuse his suggestions with the fantasies of communitarians Mann hastened to point out that education would perfect society through the individual by creating new private resources. Given full play in a democracy, education gave each man the "independence and the means by which he can resist the selfishness of other men."

Once Mann had established education as an alternative to political action, it remained to uncover its utopian possibilities. By enlarging the "cultivated class" it would widen the area of social feelings — "if this education should be universal and complete, it would do more than all things else to obliterate factitious distinctions in society." Political reformers and revolutionaries based their schemes on the false assumption that the amount of wealth in America was fixed by fraud and force, and that the few were rich because the many were poor. By demanding a redistribution of wealth by legislative fiat they overlooked the power of education to obviate political action through the creation of new and immense sources of wealth.

Thus in Mann's theory as in the programs of the other humanitarians the perfection of the individual through education guaranteed illimitable progress. The constantly expanding powers of the free individual ensured the steady improvement of society until the educative process finally achieved a harmonious, self-regulating community. "And will not the community that gains its wealth in this way . . . be a model and a pattern for nations, a type of excellence to be admired and followed by the world?" The fate of free society, Mann concluded, depended upon the conversion of individuals from puppets and automatons to thinking men who were aware of the strength of the irreducible self and determined to foster it in others.

As romantic perfectionism spread across Jacksonian society it acquired an unofficial and only partly acceptable philosophy in the "systematic subjectivism" of transcendental theory.[17] Transcendentalism, as its official historian noted, claimed for all men what a more restrictive Christian perfectionism extended only to the redeemed. Seen in this light, self-culture — Emerson's "perfect unfolding of our individual nature" — appeared as a secular amplification of the doctrine of personal holiness. In the transcendentalist definition, true reform proceeded from the individual and worked outward through the family, the neighborhood and ultimately into the social and political life of the community. The transcendentalist, Frothingham noted in retrospect, "was less a reformer of human circumstances than a regenerator of the human spirit. . . . With movements that did not start from this primary assumption of individual dignity, and come back to that as their goal, he had nothing to do."[18] Emerson's followers, like the moral reformers and the humanitarians, looked to individuals rather than to institutions, to "high heroic example" rather than to political programs. The Brook-Farmer John Sullivan Dwight summed up their position when he protested that "men are anterior to systems. Great doctrines are not the origins, but the product of great lives."[19]

Accordingly the transcendentalists considered institutions — parties, churches, organizations — so many arbitrarily constructed barriers on the road to self-culture. They were lonely men, Emerson admitted, who repelled influences. "They are not good citizens; not good members of society. . . ."[20] A longing for solitude led them out of society, Emerson to the woods where he found no Jacksonian placards on the trees, Thoreau to his reclusive leadership of a majority of one. Accepting for the most part Emerson's dictum that one man was a counterpoise to a city, the transcendentalists turned inward to examine the divine self and find there the material with which to rebuild society. They wanted to avoid at all costs the mistake of their Jacksonian contemporaries who in order to be useful accommodated themselves to institutions without realizing the resultant loss of power and integrity.

The most immediate effect of perfectionism on the transcendentalists, as on the humanitarians, was the development of a set of concepts which, in stressing reform by example, opened up new roles for the alienated intellectual. In the first place, self-culture accounted for their ambivalence toward reform politics. It was not simply Emerson's reluctance to raise the siege on his hencoop that kept him apart, but a genuine confusion as to the proper role for the reformer. If government was simply a "job" and American society the senseless competition of the marketplace, how could the transcendentalist accept either as working premises? The transcendentalist difficulty in coming to terms with democratic politics could be read in Emerson's confused remark that of the two parties contending for the presidency in 1840 one had the better principles, the other the better men. Driven by their profound distaste for manipulation and chicanery, many of Emerson's followers took on the role of a prophet standing aloof from elections, campaigns and party caucuses and dispensing wisdom (often in oblique Emersonian terminology) out of the vast private resources of the self. In this sense transcendentalism, like Christian perfectionism, represented a distinct break with the prevailing Jacksonian views of democratic leadership and the politics of compromise and adjustment.

One of the more appealing versions of the transcendental role was the hero or genius to whom everything was permitted, as Emerson said, because "genius is the character of illimitable freedom." The heroes of the world, Margaret Fuller announced, were the true theocratic kings: "The hearts of men make music at their approach; the mind of the age is like the historian of their passing; and only men of destiny like themselves shall be permitted to write their eulogies, or fill their vacancies." [21] Margaret Fuller herself spent her transcendentalist years stalking the American hero, which she somehow confused with Emerson, before she joined the Roman Revolution in 1849 and discovered the authentic article in the mystic nationalist Mazzini.

Carlyle complained to Emerson of the "perilous altitudes" to which the transcendentalists' search for the hero led them. Despite his own penchant for hero-worship he came away from reading the *Dial* "with a kind of shudder." In their pursuit of the self-contained hero they seemed to separate themselves from "this same cotton-spinning, dollar-hunting, canting and shrieking, very wretched generation of ours." [22] The transcendentalists, however, were not trying to escape the Jacksonian world of fact, only to find a foothold for their perfectionist individualism in it. They sought a way of implementing their ideas of self-culture without corrupting them with the false values of materialism. They saw a day coming when parties and politicians would be obsolescent. By the 1850s Walt Whitman thought that day had already arrived and that America had outgrown parties.

> What right has any one political party, no matter which, to wield the American government? No right at all . . . and every American young man must have sense enough to comprehend this. I have said the old parties are defunct; but there remains of them empty flesh, putrid mouths, mumbling and speaking the tones of these conventions, the politicians standing back in shadow, telling lies, trying to delude and frighten the people. . . .[23]

Whitman's romantic alternative was a "love of comrades" cementing an American brotherhood and upholding a redeemer president.

A somewhat similar faith in the mystical fraternity informed Theodore Parker's plan for spiritual revolution. Like the other perfectionists, Parker began by reducing society to its basic components — individuals, the "monads" or "primitive atoms" of the social order — and judged it by its tendency to promote or inhibit individualism. "Destroy the individuality of those atoms . . . all is gone. To mar the atoms is to mar the mass. To preserve itself, therefore, society is to preserve the individuality of the individual." [24] In Parker's theology perfectionist Christianity and transcendental method merged to form a loving brotherhood united by the capacity to apprehend primary truths directly. A shared sense of the divinity of individual man held society together; without it no true community was possible. Looking around him at ante-bellum America, Parker found only the wrong kind of individualism, the kind that said, "I am as good as you, so get out of my way." The right kind, the individualism whose motto was "You are as good as I, and let us help one another," [25] was to be the work of Parker's spiritual revolution. He explained the method of revolution as one of "*intellectual, moral* and *religious* education — everywhere and for all men." Until universal education had done its work Parker had little hope for political stability in the United States. He called instead for a new "party" to be formed in society at large, a party built on the idea that "God still inspires men as much as ever; that he is immanent in spirit as in space." Such a party required no church, tradition or scripture. "It believes God is near the soul as matter to the sense. . . . It calls God father and mother, not king; Jesus, brother, not redeemer, heaven home, religion nature." [26]

Parker believed that this "philosophical party in politics," as he called it, was already at work in the 1850s on a code of universal laws from which to deduce specific legislation "so that each statute in the code shall represent a fact in the universe, a point of thought in God; so . . . that legislation shall be divine in the same sense that a true system of astronomy be divine." Parker's holy band represented the full fruition of the perfectionist idea of a "Christian party" in America, a party of no strict political or sectarian definition, but a true reform movement, apostolic in its beginnings but growing with the truths it preached until it encompassed all Americans in a huge brotherhood of divine average men. Party members, unlike time-serving Whigs and Democrats, followed ideas and intuitions rather than prejudice and precedent, and these ideas led them to question authority, oppose legal injustice and tear down rotten institutions. The philosophical party was not to be bound by accepted notions of political conduct or traditional attitudes toward law. When unjust laws interpose barriers to progress, reformers must demolish them.

So Parker himself reasoned when he organized the Vigilance Committee in Boston to defeat the Fugitive Slave Law. His reasoning epitomized perfectionist logic: every man may safely trust his conscience, properly informed, because it is the repository for divine truth. When men learn to trust their consciences and act on them, they naturally encourage others to do the same with the certainty that they will reach the same conclusions. Individual conscience thus creates a social conscience and a collective will to right action. Concerted right action means moral revolution. The fact that moral revolution, in its turn, might mean political revolt was a risk Parker and his perfectionist followers were willing to take.

Both transcendentalism and perfectionist moral reform, then, were marked by an individualist fervor that was disruptive of American institutions. Both made heavy moral demands on church and state; and when neither proved equal to the task of supporting their intensely personal demands, the transcendentalists and the moral reformers became increasingly alienated. The perfectionist temperament bred a come-outer spirit. An insistence on individual moral accountability and direct appeal to the irreducible self, the faith in self-reliance and distrust of compromise, and a substitution of universal education for partial reform measures, all meant that normal political and institutional reform channels were closed to the perfectionists. Alternate routes to the millennium had to be found. One of these was discovered by a new leadership which made reform a branch of prophecy. Another was opened by the idea of a universal reawakening of the great god self. But there was a third possibility, also deeply involved with the educational process, an attempt to build the experimental community as a reform model. With an increasing number of reformers after 1840 perfectionist anti-institutionalism led to heavy investments in the communitarian movement.

The attraction that drew the perfectionists to communitarianism came from their conviction that the good society should be simple. Since American society was both complicated and corrupt, it was necessary to come out from it; but at the same time the challenge of the simple life had to be met. Once the true principles of social life had been discovered they had to be applied, some way found to harness individual perfectibility to a social engine. This urge to form the good community, as John Humphrey Noyes experienced it himself and perceived it in other reformers, provided the connection between perfectionism and communitarianism, or, as Noyes put it, between "Revivalism" and "Socialism." Perfectionist energies directed initially against institutions were diverted to the creation of small self-contained communities as educational models. In New England two come-outer abolitionists, Adin Ballou and George Benson, founded cooperative societies at Hopedale and Northampton, while a third Garrisonian lieutenant, John Collins, settled his followers on a farm in Skaneateles, New York. Brook Farm, Fruitlands and the North American Phalanx at Redbank acquired notoriety in their own day; but equally significant, both in terms of origins and personnel, were the experiments at Raritan Bay under the guidance of Marcus Spring, the Marlboro Association in Ohio, the Prairie Home Community of former Hicksite Quakers, and the Swedenborgian Brocton Community. In these and other experimental communities could be seen the various guises of perfectionism.

Communitarianism promised drastic social reform without violence. Artificiality and corruption could not be wiped out by partial improvements and piecemeal measures but demanded a total change which, as Robert Owen once explained, "could make an immediate, and almost instantaneous, revolution in the minds and manners of society in which it shall be introduced." Communitarians agreed in rejecting class struggle which set interest against interest instead of uniting them through association. "Whoever will examine the question of social ameliorations," Albert Brisbane argued in support of Fourier, "must be convinced that *the gradual perfecting of Civilization* is useless as a remedy for present social evils, and that the only effectual means of doing away with indigence, idleness and the dislike for labor is to do away with civilization itself, and organize Association . . . in its place."[27] Like the redemptive moment in conversion or the experience of self-discovery in transcendentalist thought, the communitarian ideal pointed to a sharp break with existing society and a commitment to root-and-branch reform. On the other hand, the community was seen as a controlled experiment in which profound but peaceful change might be effected without disturbing the larger social order. Massive change, according to communitarian theory, could also be gradual and harmonious if determined by the model.

Perfectionist religious and moral reform shaded into communitarianism, in the case of a number of social reformers, with the recognition that the conversion of the individual was a necessary preparation for and logically required communal experimentation. Such was John Humphrey Noyes' observation that in the years after

1815 "the line of socialistic excitement lies parallel with the line of religious Revivals. . . . The Revivalists had for their one great idea the regeneration of the soul. The great idea of the Socialists was the regeneration of society, which is the soul's environment. These ideas belong together and are the complements of each other." [28] So it seemed to Noyes' colleagues in the communitarian movement. The course from extreme individualism to communitarianism can be traced in George Ripley's decision to found Brook Farm. Trying to win Emerson to his new cause, he explained that his own personal tastes and habits would have led him away from plans and projects. "I have a passion for being independent of the world, and of every man in it. This I could do easily on the estate which is now offered. . . . I should have a city of God, on a small scale of my own. . . . But I feel bound to sacrifice this private feeling, in the hope of the great social good." That good Ripley had no difficulty in defining in perfectionist terms:

> . . . to insure a more natural union between intellectual and manual labor than now exists; to combine the thinker and the worker, as far as possible, in the same individual; to guarantee the highest mental freedom, by providing all with labor, adapted to their tastes and talents, and securing to them the fruits of their industry; to do away with the necessity of menial services, by opening the benefits of education and the profits of labor to all; and thus to prepare a society of liberal, intelligent, and cultivated persons, whose relations with each other would permit a more simple and wholesome life, than can be led amidst the pressure of our competitive institutions. [29]

However varied their actual experiences with social planning, all the communitarians echoed Ripley's call for translating perfectionism into concerted action and adapting the ethics of individualism to larger social units. Just as the moral reformers appealed to right conduct and conscience in individuals the communitarians sought to erect models of a collective conscience to educate Americans. Seen in this light, the communitarian faith in the model was simply an extension of the belief in individual perfectibility. Even the sense of urgency characterizing moral reform was carried over into the communities where a millennial expectation flourished. The time to launch their projects, the social planners believed, was the immediate present when habits and attitudes were still fluid, before entrenched institutions had hardened the American heart and closed the American mind. To wait for a full quota of useful members or an adequate supply of funds might be to miss the single chance to make the country perfect. The whole future of America seemed to them to hinge on the fate of their enterprises.

Some of the projects were joint-stock corporations betraying a middle-class origin; others were strictly communistic. Some, like the Shaker communities, were pietistic and rigid; others, like Oneida and Hopedale, open and frankly experimental. Communitarians took a lively interest in each others' projects and often joined one or another of them for a season before moving on to try utopia on their own. The division between religious and secular attempts was by no means absolute: both types of communities advertised an essentially religious brand of perfectionism. Nor was economic organization always an accurate means of distinguishing the various experiments, most of which were subjected to periodic constitutional overhauling and frequent readjustment, now in the direction of social controls and now toward relaxation of those controls in favor of individual initiative.

The most striking characteristic of the communitarian movement was not its apparent diversity but the fundamental similarity of educational purpose. The common denominator, or "main idea" Noyes correctly identified as *"the enlargement of home — the extension of family union beyond the little man-and-wife circle to large corporations."*[30] Communities as different as Fruitlands and Hopedale, Brook Farm and Northampton, Owenite villages and Fournier phalanstaeries were all, in one way or another, attempting to expand and apply self-culture to groups. Thus the problem for radical communitarians was to solve the conflict between the family and society. In commenting on the failure of the Brook Farmers to achieve a real community, Charles Lane, Alcott's associate at Fruitlands, identified what he considered the basic social question of the day — "whether the existence of the marital family is compatible with that of the universal family, which the term 'Community' signifies."[31] A few of the communitarians, recognizing this conflict, attempted to solve it by changing or destroying the institution of marriage. For the most part, the perfectionist communitarians shied away from any such radical alteration of the family structure and instead sought a law of association by which the apparently antagonistic claims of private and universal love could be harmonized. Once this law was known and explained, they believed, then the perfect society was possible — a self-adjusting mechanism constructed in accordance with their recently discovered law of human nature.

Inevitably communitarianism developed a "science of society," either the elaborate social mathematics of Fourier or the constitutional mechanics of native American perfectionists. The appeal of the blueprint grew overwhelming: in one way or another almost all the communitarians succumbed to the myth of the mathematically precise arrangement, searching for the perfect number or the exact size, plotting the precise disposition of working forces and living space, and combining these estimates in a formula which would ensure perfect concord. The appeal of Fourierism stemmed from its promise to reconcile productive industry with "passional attractions." "Could this be done," John Sullivan Dwight announced, "the word 'necessity' would acquire an altogether new and pleasanter meaning; the outward necessity and the inward prompting for every human being would be one and identical, and his life a living harmony."[32] Association fostered true individuality which, in turn, guaranteed collective accord. In an intricate calculation involving ascending and descending wings and a central point of social balance where attractions equalled destinies the converts to Fourierism contrived a utopian alternative to politics. The phalanx represented a self-perpetuating system for neutralizing conflict and ensuring perfection. The power factor — politics — had been dropped out; attraction alone provided the stimulants necessary to production and progress. Here in the mathematical model was the culmination of the "peaceful revolution" which was to transform America.

The communitarian experiments in effect were anti-institutional institutions. In abandoning political and religious institutions the communitarians were driven to create perfect societies of their own which conformed to their perfectionist definition of the free individual. Their communities veered erratically between the poles of anarchism and collectivism as they hunted feverishly for a way of eliminating friction without employing coercion, sure that once they had found it, they could apply it in a federation of model societies throughout the country. In a limited sense, perhaps, their plans constituted an escape from urban complexity and the loneliness of alienation. But beneath the nostalgia there lay a vital reform impulse and a driving determination to make American society over through the power of education.

The immediate causes of the collapse of the communities ranged from loss of funds and mismanagement to declining interest and disillusionment with imperfect human material. Behind these apparent reasons, however, stood the real cause in the person of the perfectionist self, Margaret Fuller's "mountainous me," that proved too powerful a disruptive force for even the anti-institutional institutions it had created. It was the perfectionist ego which allowed the communitarian reformers to be almost wholly nonselective in recruiting their membership and to put their trust in the operation of an atomistic general will. Constitution-making and paper bonds, as it turned out, were not enough to unite divine egoists in a satisfactory system for the free expression of the personality. Perfectionist individualism did not make the consociate family. The result by the 1850s was a profound disillusionment with the principle of association which, significantly, coincided with the political crisis over slavery. Adin Ballou, his experiment at Hopedale in shambles, summarized the perfectionist mood of despair when he added that "few people are near enough right in heart, head and habits to live in close social intimacy." [33] Another way would have to be found to carry divine principles into social arrangements, one that took proper account of the individual.

The collapse of the communitarian movement in the 1850s left a vacuum in social reform which was filled by the slavery crisis. At first their failure to consolidate alternative social and educational institutions threw the reformers back on their old perfectionist individualism for support. It was hardly fortuitous that Garrison, Mann, Thoreau, Howe, Parker, Channing, Ripley and Emerson himself responded to John Brown's raid with a defense of the liberated conscience. But slavery, as a denial of freedom and individual responsibility, had to be destroyed by institutional forces which could be made to sustain these values. The antislavery cause during the secession crisis and throughout the Civil War offered reformers an escape from alienation by providing a new identity with the very political institutions which they had so vigorously assailed.

The effects of the Civil War as an intellectual counterrevolution were felt both in a revival of institutions and a renewal of an organic theory of society. The war brought with it a widespread reaction against the seeming sentimentality and illusions of perfectionism. It saw the establishment of new organizations like the Sanitary and the Christian Commissions run on principles of efficiency and professionalism totally alien to perfectionist methods. Accompanying the wartime revival of institutions was a theological reorientation directed by Horace Bushnell and other conservative churchmen whose longstanding opposition to perfectionism seemed justified by the war. The extreme individualism of the ante-bellum reformers was swallowed up in a Northern war effort that made private conscience less important than saving the Union. Some of the abolitionists actually substituted national unity for freedom for the slave as the primary war aim. Those reformers who contributed to the war effort through the Sanitary Commission or the Christian Commission found a new sense of order and efficiency indispensable. Older perfectionists, like Dorothea Dix, unable to adjust to new demands, found their usefulness drastically confined. Young Emersonians returned from combat convinced that professionalism, discipline and subordination, dubious virtues by perfectionist standards, were essential in a healthy society. A new emphasis on leadership and performance was replacing the benevolent amateurism of the perfectionists.

Popular education and ethical agitation continued to hold the post-war stage, but the setting for them had changed. The three principal theorists of social reform in post-war industrial America — Henry George, Henry Demarest Lloyd and Edward Bellamy — denounced class conflict, minimized the importance of purely political reform, and, like their perfectionist precursors, called for moral revolution. The moral revolution which they demanded, however, was not the work of individuals in whom social responsibility developed as a by-product of self-discovery but the ethical revival of an entire society made possible by the natural development of social forces. Their organic view of society required new theories of personality and new concepts of role-playing, definitions which appeared variously in George's law of integration, Lloyd's religion of love, and Bellamy's economy of happiness. And whereas Nemesis in the perfectionist imagination had assumed the shape of personal guilt and estrangement from a pre-established divine order, for the post-war reformers it took on the social dimensions of a terrifying relapse into barbarism. Finally, the attitudes of the reformers toward individualism itself began to change as Darwinism with the aid of a false analogy twisted the pre-war doctrine of self-reliance into a weapon against reform. It was to protest against a Darwinian psychology of individual isolation that Lloyd wrote his final chapter of *Wealth Against Commonwealth*, declaring that the regeneration of the individual was only a half-truth and that "the reorganization of the society which he makes and which makes him is the other half."

> We can become individual only by submitting to be bound to others. We extend our freedom only by finding new laws to obey. . . . The isolated man is a mere rudiment of an individual. But he who has become citizen, neighbor, friend, brother, son, husband, father, fellow-member, in one is just so many times individualized.[34]

Lloyd's plea for a new individualism could also be read as an obituary for perfectionist romantic reform.

NOTES

1. Ralph Waldo Emerson, "The New England Reformers," *Works* (Centenary ed.), *III*, 251; "Man the Reformer," Works, *I*, 248–49.
2. T. E. Hulme, "Romanticism and Classicism," *Speculations: Essays on Humanism and the Philosophy of Art,* ed. Herbert Read (London, 1924), reprinted in *Critiques and Essays in Criticism, 1920–1948,* ed. Robert Wooster Stallman (New York, 1949), pp. 3–16.
3. For discussions of evangelical reform see John R. Bodo, *The Protestant Clergy and Public Issues, 1812–1848* (Princeton, 1954) and Clifford S. Griffin, *Their Brothers' Keepers* (New Brunswick, N. J., 1960).
4. Albert Brisbane, *Social Destiny of Man: or, Association and Reorganization of Industry* (Philadelphia, 1840), introduction, p. vi.
5. For a careful analysis of Alcott's educational theories see Dorothy McCuskey, *Bronson Alcott, Teacher* (New York, 1940), particularly pp. 25–40 from which these quotations are taken.
6. Letter from Howe to Horace Mann, 1857, quoted in Harold Schwartz, *Samuel Gridley Howe* (Cambridge, 1956), p. 37.
7. Letter from Howe to William Chapin, 1857, quoted in Laura E. Richards, *Letters and Journals of Samuel Gridley Howe* (2 vols.; New York, 1909), *II*, 48.
8. Second Report of the Commissioners on Idiocy to the Massachusetts Legislature (1849), quoted in Richards, *Howe, II,* 214.
9. New York A.I.C.P., *The Mistake* (New York, 1850), p. 4, quoted in Robert H. Bremner, *From the Depths: the Discovery of Poverty in the United States* (New York, 1956), p. 38.
10. Brace's views are set forth in his *The Dangerous Classes of New York and Twenty Years Among Them* (New York, 1872). For a brief treatment of his relation to the moral reform movement see Bremner, *From the Depths,* chap. iii.
11. Letter from Howe to Charles Sumner, Apr. 8, 1847, quoted in Richards, *Howe, II,* 255–56.
12. First Report of the Commissioners on Idiocy (1848), quoted in Richards, *Howe, II,* 210–11.
13. *Ibid.,* pp. 210–11.
14. Horace Mann, "The Necessity of Education in a Republican Government," *Lectures on Education* (Boston, 1845), pp. 152, 158.
15. "An Historical View of Education; Showing Its Dignity and Its Degradation," *Lectures on Education,* pp. 260, 262.

16. This quotation and the ones from Mann that follow are taken from the central section of the *Twelfth Report* entitled "Intellectual Education as a Means of Removing Poverty, and Securing Abundance," Mary Peabody Mann, *Life of Horace Mann* (4 vols.; Boston, 1891), *IV*, 245–68. See also the perceptive comments on Mann in Rush Welter, *Popular Education and Democratic Thought in America* (New York, 1962), pp. 97–102, from which I have drawn.
17. The phrase is Santayana's in "The Genteel Tradition in American Philosophy." For an analysis of the anti-institutional aspects of transcendentalism and reform see Stanley Elkins, *Slavery* (Chicago, 1959), chap. iii.
18. Octavius Brooks Frothingham, *Transcendentalism in New England* (Harper Torchbooks ed.: New York, 1959), p. 155.
19. John Sullivan Dwight as quoted in Frothingham, *Transcendentalism,* p. 147.
20. "The Transcendentalist," *Works, I*, 347–48.
21. Such was her description of Lamennais and Beranger as quoted in Mason Wade, *Margaret Fuller* (New York, 1940), 195.
22. Quoted in Wade, *Margaret Fuller,* pp. 88–89.
23. Walt Whitman, "The Eighteenth Presidency," an essay unpublished in Whitman's lifetime, in *Walt Whitman's Workshop,* ed. Clifton Joseph Furness (Cambridge, 1928), pp. 104–5.
24. Quoted in Daniel Aaron, *Men of Good Hope* (Oxford paperback ed.: New York, 1961), p. 35.
25. Theodore Parker, "The Political Destination of America and the Signs of the Times" (1848) excerpted in *The Transcendentalists,* ed. Perry Miller (Anchor ed.: Garden City, N. Y., 1957), p. 357.
26. Quoted in R. W. B. Lewis, *The American Adam* (Chicago, 1955), p. 182.
27. Albert Brisbane, *Social Destiny of Man,* p. 286, quoted in Arthur Eugene Bestor, *Backwoods Utopias: The Sectarian and Owenite Phases of Communitarian Socialism in America: 1663–1829* (Philadelphia, 1950), p. 9.
28. John Humphrey Noyes, *History of American Socialism* (Philadelphia, 1870), p. 26.
29. Letter from Ripley to Ralph Waldo Emerson, Nov. 9, 1840, in *Autobiography of Brook Farm,* ed. Henry W. Sams (Englewood Cliffs, N. J., 1958), pp. 5–8.
30. Noyes, *American Socialisms,* p. 23.
31. Charles Lane, "Brook Farm," *Dial, IV* (Jan. 1844), 351–57, reprinted in Sams, *Brook Farm,* pp. 87–92.
32. John Sullivan Dwight, "Association in its Connection with Education," a lecture delivered before the New England Fourier Society, in Boston, Feb. 29, 1844. Excerpted in Sams, *Brook Farm,* pp. 104–5.
33. Letter from Ballou to Theodore Weld, Dec. 23, 1856, quoted in Benjamin P. Thomas, *Theodore Weld: Crusader for Freedom* (New Brunswick, N. J., 1950), p. 229.
34. Henry Demarest Lloyd, *Wealth Against Commonwealth* (Spectrum paperback ed.: Englewood Cliffs, N. J., 1963), pp. 174, 178.

Ante-Bellum Expansionism

Related to the romantic impulse of the pre-Civil War years, though quite different in its appeal and its political consequences, was the notion of a continental American destiny. It is no doubt granted to all large nations to conceive of a special destiny for themselves that seems brash, self-assertive and uncomfortable to their neighbors. At various times, other countries have avowed their "missions" — to "civilize the world," to "take up the white man's burden," to "encourage worldwide social revolution." The American version of this impulse in the early nineteenth century was "manifest destiny": the right even the duty of the United States to encompass the whole of the continent and indeed the hemisphere and to bring the blessings of abundance and a free society to all its inhabitants.

This doctrine was not only self-assertive, it was also self-serving. As Frederick Merk shows in the following selection, agrarian and commercial acquisitiveness were elements of manifest destiny. This doctrine was also arrogant, for at its center was the implied superiority of American institutions to all others. It was also, inevitably, hypocritical. Men have always clothed their desire for national wealth and power in fine-sounding, morally unimpeachable pronouncements. But Americans especially, from that day to this, have found it peculiarly necessary to deny realities to themselves.

At the same time, however, many Americans sincerely believed in the superiority of their society to that of their neighbors. Much of this was chauvinism, no doubt, and we have little patience with it today, but in a world characterized by stark social and economic inequalities, by religious bigotry, illiteracy, and political tyranny, Americans had valid reasons to think that incorporation into the United States would confer real and substantial blessings on the inhabitants of neighboring lands. It was to be clearly understood that these lands would become equal partners in the American union and that their people would enjoy the full rights of American citizens.

Professor Merk's essay examines the intellectual roots of manifest destiny as it emerged in the 1830s and 1840s and shows how it was used to justify the acquisition of Texas, California, and Oregon. He notes the concentration of manifest destiny sentiment largely in the North, but also suggests that southerners were not proof against it. Most historians would ascribe more expansionist feeling to the South than he does, however. Indeed, they have held that the one important intellectual current shared by the sections after 1830 was the notion of an American continental destiny.

FOR FURTHER READING:

GRAEBNER, NORMAN. *Empire on the Pacific.* New York: Ronald Press Co., 1955.*
PRATT, JULIUS. *Expansionists of 1812.* Magnolia, Mass.: Peter Smith, 1957.*
WEINBERG, ALBERT K. *Manifest Destiny: A Study of Nationalist Expansionism in American History.* Chicago: Quadrangle Books, 1963.*

Asterisk denotes paperback edition.

Manifest Destiny   FREDERICK MERK

In the mid-1840's a form of expansionism novel in name, appeal, and theory made its appearance in the United States. It was "Manifest Destiny." The term was not wholly new. Phrases like it had been used before, but this precise combination of words was novel and right for a mood, and it became part of the language.[1] It meant expansion, prearranged by Heaven, over an area not clearly defined. In some minds it meant expansion over the region to the Pacific; in others, over the North American continent; in others, over the hemisphere. Its appeal to the public, whatever the sense, was greater than its counterpart had been in the days of Adams's vision. It attracted enough persons by the mid-1840's to constitute a movement. Its theory was more idealistic than Adams's had been. It was less acquisitive, more an opportunity for neighboring peoples to reach self-realization. It meant opportunity to gain admission to the American Union. Any neighboring peoples, established in self-government by compact or by successful revolution, would be permitted to apply. If properly qualified, they would be admitted. Some — the Mexican, for example — might have to undergo schooling for a time in the meaning and methods of freedom before they were let in.[2] A century might be necessary to complete the structure of the great American nation of the future. Any hurried admission to the temple of freedom would be unwise; any forced admission would be a contradiction in terms, unthinkable, revolting.[3] But a duty lay on the people of the United States to admit all qualified applicants freely. The doors to the temple must be wide open to peoples who were panting for freedom. Any shrinking from admitting them, out of selfish disinclination to share with others the blessings of American freedom, would be disgraceful. If it grew out of fear of the consequences, "we should meekly take the badge of dishonor and pin it to our front." [4]

The architecture of the temple of freedom was ideal for accommodating neighboring peoples. Its dominant feature was federalism, which left control of local affairs — such as slavery — to the states, and entrusted to the central government control over only such extra-local functions as foreign affairs, interstate and foreign commerce, coinage, and taxation for federal purposes. Federalism permitted a spreading of the domain of the Union almost indefinitely without any danger that a central tyranny would emerge such as had disfigured the Roman and the British empires. Already in the era following the War of 1812 the excellence of this basic principle of the Constitution for purposes of territorial expansion was apparent to such nationalists as Adams and John C. Calhoun.

The safeguards of the original Constitution in assuring freedom to peoples entering the temple had been reinforced by constitutional interpretation. Madison's and Jefferson's Virginia and Kentucky Resolutions of 1798, the South Carolina Exposition of 1828, and the Fort Hill Letter of 1832 of the mature Calhoun had been especially helpful.[5] These gave complete guarantees of safety to any neighbors of the United States who were contemplating entrance into the temple. They showed the Constitution to be a compact. Under it the parties to the compact — the states —

Source: Frederick Merk, *Manifest Destiny and Mission in American History* (New York: Alfred A. Knopf, 1963), chap. 2, "Manifest Destiny," pp. 24–60.

reserve all governmental powers not delegated to the Union. If any dispute should arise over the reserved powers, and no satisfactory solution to it should emerge from the courts, the people of the separate states would be the final judges of what they had reserved. They would possess the right even to leave the Union if necessary to preserve their freedom.[6] The peoples possessing these rights were not only the original thirteen but all that subsequently entered the Union. States' rights was a protective mantle that wrapped itself about any people entering the temple. Such was the attractive form in which expounders of Manifest Destiny presented it to the public in the mid-1840's.

Expounders appeared in the press, in Congress, and on the hustings. In the press one of the most influential was John L. O'Sullivan. He was the theoretician of the doctrine. He was a mixture of visionary, literary artist, scholar, adventurer, and politician. Born of American parents in Europe in 1813, he took his early schooling in French and English schools and, in 1831, received an A.B. degree with distinction from Columbia College and an M.A. a few years later. He was read in the law and practiced it intermittently in New York City. In 1837 he was co-founder of the *Democratic Review* and, in 1844, co-founder, with Samuel J. Tilden, of the *New York Morning News*. He edited both until 1846. His *Democratic Review* was a literary journal, Democratic in complexion, and contributed to by major writers — Hawthorne, Poe, Whittier, Alexander H. Everett, and others. He was a major contributor himself. He was author of the potent phrase "Manifest Destiny," coined in an editorial on the Texas issue in the *Democratic Review* for July and August 1845. He was described by Julian Hawthorne as "one of the most charming companions in the world . . . always full of grand and world-embracing schemes, which seemed to him, and which he made to appear to others, vastly practicable and alluring; but which invariably miscarried by reason of some oversight which had escaped notice for the very reason that it was so fundamental a one." He became in 1846 a regent of the University of New York. At the same time he was active in filibustering adventures to Cuba which led to his arrest and trial. In Polk circles he stood well, and in the Pierce administration became American minister to Portugal. During the Civil War he became publicly a Confederate sympathizer and exiled himself in England. After the war he returned to New York City, where he remained in obscurity until his death in 1895.[7]

But some members of Congress were more adept at giving succinct formulation to principles of Manifest Destiny. They were at their best in connection with the admission of Texas into the Union. An Illinois congressman, John Wentworth, for example, spoke on the eve of the adoption of the joint resolution of annexation:

> Many of this body would live to hear the sound from the Speaker's chair, "the gentleman from Texas." He wanted them also to hear "the gentleman from Oregon." He would even go further, and have "the gentleman from Nova Scotia, the gentleman from Canada, the gentleman from Cuba, the gentleman from Mexico, aye, even the gentleman from Patagonia." He did not believe the God of Heaven, when he crowned the American arms with success [in the Revolutionary War], designed that the original States should be the only abode of liberty on earth. On the contrary, he only designed them as the great center from which civilization, religion, and liberty should radiate and radiate until the whole continent shall bask in their blessing.[8]

The same ideas were expressed in Congress a few days later by a fellow Illinoisan,

Stephen A. Douglas, who sought to make evident that he was really a moderate in the matter.

> He would blot out the lines on the map which now marked our national boundaries on this continent, and make the area of liberty as broad as the continent itself. He would not suffer petty rival republics to grow up here, engendering jealousy at each other, and interfering with each other's domestic affairs, and continually endangering their peace. He did not wish to go beyond the great ocean — beyond those boundaries which the God of nature had marked out.[9]

Another formulation was by Andrew Kennedy, of Indiana, speaking in the House early in 1846 in the debate on the Oregon issue.

> Go to the West and see a young man with his mate of eighteen; and [after] a lapse of thirty years, visit him again, and instead of two, you will find twenty-two. That is what I call the American multiplication table. We are now twenty millions strong; and how long, under this process of multiplication, will it take to cover the continent with our posterity, from the Isthmus of Darien to Behring's straits?[10]

Daniel S. Dickinson, of New York, gave the Senate, early in 1848, when the terms of peace with Mexico were under consideration, the same general formulation:

> But the tide of emigration and the course of empire have since been westward. Cities and towns have sprung up upon the shores of the Pacific. . . . Nor have we yet fulfilled the destiny allotted to us. New territory is spread out for us to subdue and fertilize; new races are presented for us to civilize, educate and absorb; new triumphs for us to achieve for the cause of freedom. North America presents to the eye one great geographical system . . . ; it is soon to become the commercial center of the world. And the period is by no means remote, when man . . . yielding to . . . laws more potent than those which prescribe artificial boundaries, will ordain that it [North America] shall be united . . . in one political system, and that, a free, confederated, self-governed Republic.[11]

A free, confederated, self-governed republic on a continental scale — this was Manifest Destiny. It was republicanism resting on a base of confederated states. Republicanism by definition meant freedom. It meant government by the people, or, rather, by the people's representatives popularly elected. It meant more. It was government of a classless society, as contrasted with that in a monarchy, which was dominated by an arrogant aristocracy and headed by a hereditary king. It meant, moreover, freedom from established churches headed by monarchs. Under American Republicanism religious denominations were equals. Among equals the most worthy were, perhaps, the Protestant denominations — at least this was the view of much of rural America. But in the larger cities, especially those with a growing Irish and German population, Roman Catholicism was given its due by editors of Democratic journals. Religious freedom was stressed as a feature of the American Arcadia increasingly as California and Mexico (which were Catholic) came within range of expansionist hopes. Journalistic emphasis on equality of religions was attractive especially to readers with memories of the disabilities suffered by themselves or their forebears in a Europe where kings fixed the religion of their subjects.

Democracy was another element in American freedom emphasized in the 1840's more than earlier. Democracy meant many things. It meant political democracy, with wide suffrage, frequent elections, and a hoped-for limit of presidential tenure to a single term. It also meant economic democracy, especially democracy of land ownership, which, in turn, meant ease of land acquisition. Low price of land, prospective pre-emption of government land under the act of 1841, were referred to happily; free homesteads, as urged by George H. Evans in the *Working Man's Advocate,* seemed in prospect. By contrast was described, with indignation, the shocking state of affairs in Europe, where land was engrossed by landlords, where people were excluded from possession, where famine was endemic. The chief evil of Europe, the *Democratic Review* pointed out, the blight which especially "oppresses England and destroys Ireland, is the exclusion of the people from the soil. England, with a population larger than our Union, has but thirty-two thousand proprietors of the soil. That which constitutes the strength of the Union, the wealth and independence of the people, is the boundless expanse of territory laid open to their possession." [12] This was rapidly being overrun by needy settlers. Business democracy, also, was stressed, the absence particularly of legalized monopolies. Free trade was glorified, especially when the Walker Tariff of 1846 had been achieved. Thus an admission as a state to the American Union was admission to a temple whose furnishings were steadily being made more attractive.

An especial value, promised to people admitted to the temple, was the beneficial use, with American help, of their natural resources. The use made by European monarchs of the resources of the wilderness was a negation of the kindly intentions of Providence. In the case of the Oregon Country, the contrast was pointed out by Adams in upholding the American claim to 54° 40′:

> We claim that country — for what? To make the wilderness blossom as the rose, to establish laws, to increase, multiply, and subdue the earth, which we are commanded to do by the first behest of God Almighty. . . . She [England] claims to keep it open for navigation, for her hunters to hunt wild beasts; and of course she claims for the benefit of the wild beasts as well as of the savage nations. There is the difference between our claims.[13]

Mexico's failure to improve California, a land of Eden, was attributed to an incompetent local bureaucracy, degenerating into a state of anarchy, and to a slothful population. The same was true of the agricultural and mining potentialities of Mexico proper. If those areas were brought into the American confederation, the people would be taught the value of their blessings and trained to develop them for the good of mankind.[14]

For lands in dispute with a foreign state, as the Oregon Country was, the theme was stressed that a true title is acquired only by actual occupation. Occupation was the moral force which should, and would, move territory into the American orbit. This was graphically phrased by O'Sullivan in the *New York Morning News,* at the end of 1845, in an editorial headed "The True Title." According to O'Sullivan, the legal title of the United States to all Oregon is perfect, but:

> Away, away with all these cobweb tissues of rights of discovery, exploration, settlement, contiguity, etc. . . . [The American claim] is by the right of our manifest destiny to overspread and to possess the whole of the continent which Providence has given us for the development of the great experiment of liberty and federative self government entrusted to us. It is a right such as that of the tree to the space of air and earth suitable for the full expansion of its principle and destiny of growth — such as that of the stream to the channel required for the still accumulating volume of its flow. It is in our future far more than in our past, or in the past history of Spanish exploration or French colonial rights, that our True Title is to be found. [American population is growing at a mighty pace. In little more than a lifetime it will number three hundred million souls.] Oregon can never

be to [England] or for her, any thing but a mere hunting ground for furs and peltries. . . . Nor can she ever colonize it with any sort of transplanted population of her own. It is far too remote and too ungenial for any such purpose. . . . In our hands . . . it must fast fill in with a population destined to establish within the life of the existing generation, a noble young empire of the Pacific, vying in all the elements of greatness with that already overspreading the Atlantic and the great Mississippi valley.[15]

A "noble young empire" of Oregon, vying with the United States for greatness, would be outside the United States in the beginning, of course. But needless to say, in its own good time, it would present itself at the portals of the temple.

By enlargement of the boundaries of Arcadia, room would be made for the oppressed of the Old World, as well as for the blest of the New. A refuge would be created for those fleeing the tyrannies of monarchical Europe. An Alabama congressman expressed that view early in 1845, in urging the annexation of Texas in terms differing from those of hundreds of others only in being more poetic.

Long may our country prove itself the asylum of the oppressed. Let its institutions and its people be extended far and wide, and when the waters of despotism shall have inundated other portions of the globe, and the votary of liberty be compelled to betake himself to his ark, let this government be the Ararat on which it shall rest.[16]

The extent to which the land of refuge for the oppressed should be enlarged occasioned little debate. The Republic would be, and should be, extended to its natural boundaries. Natural boundaries were a concept as old as the nation itself. Definitions had changed, however, from generation to generation. The natural boundaries at the west had been, in the closing years of the American Revolution, the Mississippi. In 1803 they had become, for Jeffersonians, the Rocky Mountains. In the 1840's they had become, for those who had vision, the Pacific Ocean; and for many, the continent, indeed, the hemisphere. Whatever the natural boundaries, they ought to be wide enough to ensure peace. If petty rival republics were allowed to grow up in North America, they not only would engender, as Douglas pointed out, "jealousies at each other" and interferences with each other's domestic affairs — with questions of slavery, for instance — but would offer tempting opportunities to European despots to create divisions in the New World and to harass the republican institutions of the United States. If natural limits were accepted as boundaries for the confederacy, the people of the continent would be at peace.

One other text was part of the gospel of Manifest Destiny — the duty of the United States to regenerate backward peoples of the continent. This was a concept tardy in arriving. It acquired importance only when Mexico moved, in the mid-1840's, into the focus of American expansionism. Regeneration had not been part of the thinking of the American government in dealing with the red man of the wilderness. The Indian was a heathen whose land title passed, according to canon well established, to the Christian prince and his heirs who had discovered or conquered him. Natives retained only rights of occupancy in their lands. Numbering but a few hundred thousand in the latitudes of the United States, they were provided for by concentration on reservations. Even Jefferson was content to dispose of them thus. Federalists preferred to deal with them, and with the scatterings of French and Spanish elements among them, simply by keeping their skirts clear of them. The "Gallo-Hispano-Indian *omnium gatherum* of savages and adventurers" was something respectable elements in the East did not wish to get near to. But Mexico — there was a problem. Eight million human beings, rooted in soil of their own, covered by a veneer of civilization, and professing the Christian religion! This was a problem the magnitude of which O'Sullivan recognized. Racial homogeneity of the Anglo-American stock had seemed to him an element of strength in his doctrine. It had permitted him to differentiate expansionism of the American sort from that of the Old World, where the process had always involved domination by one state over aliens of another. But O'Sullivan did not despair of Mexico's future. Someday, a century hence perhaps, her people would, by patterning themselves on the model of the United States, have advanced sufficiently to come rapping for admission at the door of the Union with a good chance of being admitted. However, a few months after the penning of that hopeful augury came the outbreak of the Mexican War, which sent Manifest Destiny on a new tack.[17]

A doctrine is significant in politics in proportion to the degree of its acceptance. Acceptance in the case of Manifest Destiny is an unknown quantity. It has never even been estimated. The attraction of such a concept to a national public is not easy to measure, since ordinary gauges of measurement are not usable. No vote was ever taken on it. Votes cast in the presidential elections of 1844 and 1848 are of little use, for they were directed to bundles of issues rather than to one. The votes cast on issues of expansionism in Congress are, likewise, unrevealing, since they were directed to issues that were short of continentalism. If a measurement is to be made of the response of the American public to the vision of continentalism, a special gauge must be devised.

Such a gauge must have as part of its mechanism a roster of journals that preached Manifest Destiny. The purpose of the roster is to locate centers of concentration of such journals. These centers are likely to be centers of believers in the doctrine. Readers of a journal do not always approve of its doctrines, to be sure. But it is a safe assumption that where continentalism was expounded by editors numerous, persistent, and eloquent, its believers were numerous also. In party affiliation, journals of Manifest Destiny views were Democratic. Organs of the Polk administration were strongly represented among them. On the North Atlantic seaboard all the important dailies which were nominally independent in politics but Democratically inclined were exponents of Manifest Destiny, and vociferous in their advocacy of it. Only a portion, however, of the Democratic press in any section adhered to such doctrines, and a part bitterly opposed them. In Whig journals, continentalism was opposed, even denounced, by virtually all. This reflected a well-marked position of the party.

Supplemental to the press gauge is the congressional gauge. This consists of speeches delivered by Manifest Destiny politicians in Congress and on the hustings. By their temper and number the speeches reveal the regions in which the doctrine was popular. By combining what was said by politicians with what was printed by editors in the sections it is possible to estimate, with a rough approximation to truth, the location, the numerical strength, and the devotion of the disciples of the doctrine in the nation.

The Northeastern and Northwestern sections of the nation were, in particular, areas of concentration of journals that advocated Manifest Destiny. New York City had the greatest concentration of them in the nation. Here the leading philosopher of the faith, John L. O'Sullivan, presided over two of its organs, the *New York Morning News* and the *Democratic Review*. Here operated also the great penny newspapers — the *New York Herald*, with James Gordon Bennett as editor, and the New York *Sun*, edited by Moses Y. Beach. These two papers each made claim to the distinction of having the greatest circulation among all dailies in the United States. The *Sun* had an offspring, the *True Sun*, which preached Manifest Destiny. Another crusader was the editor of the *Daily Plebeian*, Levi D. Slamm. He was a crusader by turn in many causes, Locofocoism, labor-unionism, Dorrism, and expansionism. In no cause was he more vehement than in expansionism. But he was deficient in business sense, and his papers failed. In 1845 the New York *Daily Globe* was set up for him to edit in the interests of Robert J. Walker, the ultra-expansionist among politicians.[18] The *New York Evening Post* was partial to Manifest Destiny, but its editor, William Cullen Bryant, was an independent as a Democrat and opposed the extension of slavery. The New York *Journal of Commerce* was in an independent class; it was moderately expansionist, especially in regard to California and New Mexico. The *Brooklyn Eagle* was of like outlook. These were outstanding journals of the metropolitan area and all were teachers of the faith in some degree.

In Massachusetts, in staid Boston, the *Bay State Democrat*, the organ of the historian and politician George Bancroft, was devoted to Manifest Destiny. So was the *Boston Times*, which took over the *Bay State Democrat*. In Connecticut the Hartford *Times* and in New Hampshire the *New Hampshire Patriot and State Gazette* were highly expansionist.

In upper New York the Albany *Argus* and the *Atlas* were believers. In Ohio the *Ohio Statesman*, edited by the redoubtable Samuel Medary, of Columbus, was conspicuous in championing the cause. The *Cincinnati Daily Enquirer* was of the same views. In Indiana the *Indiana State Sentinel* was a preacher. In Illinois the *Chicago Democrat*, Wentworth's organ, and at Springfield the widely read *Illinois State Register*, were vociferous crusaders. Illinoisans were the western cousins of New Yorkers in enthusiasm for the cause. Illinois was the most expansionist, probably, of the Middle Western states. States bordering the South in the West repeated this pattern of allegiance by loyal Democratic editors to expansionism. But throughout the North and West there were Democratic editors of weak faith with qualms about the setting up of slavery in the new acquisitions, especially in Texas, and who, in the Mexican War years, became supporters of the Wilmot proviso.

Distinct differences existed between New York papers and those of the Middle West. The New York ones were purer in doctrine, more ready to wait as long as might be necessary for states which were good prospects to enter the Union. They were moderate on the Oregon question; they were willing to settle that issue by compromise at the line of 49°. Why fight for all of Oregon when all of British North America would ultimately enter the portals of the Union?[19] This may have been a response to pacifist voices in the commercial world. Slamm, however, one of the most ardent of the faith, would have no truck with compromise. On hearing a rumor in February 1846 of a compromise at 49°, he declared in a tone of authority that the administration had too much regard for the honor and wishes of the American people to yield to the arrogant pretensions of Great Britain. He believed it a "duty of our government to *seek* rather than *evade* a war with that power."[20]

Belligerence on the Oregon issue was normally a Western Democratic characteristic. The *Illinois State Register*, for instance, declared in May 1845: "Nothing would please the people of the entire West half so well as a war with England; and, for our part, we think enough has been done by Parliament, and said by Sir Robert [Peel] to justify Congress in declaring war against that country forthwith. . . . We are all for War! War!" [21] In Congress the Democratic spokesmen of the Middle West expressed the same relish for war. In the House, Andrew Kennedy, of Indiana, denied, in the Oregon debate early in 1846, that he was for war, but "Shall we pause in our career, or retrace our steps because the British lion has chosen to place himself in our path? Had our blood already become so pale that we should tremble at the roar of the King of beasts? We will not go out of our way to seek a conflict with him; but if he crosses our path, and refuses to move at a peaceful command, he will run his nose in the talons of the American eagle, and his blood will spout as from a harpooned whale." [22]

Notoriously bellicose were Michigan's congressional spokesmen on the Oregon issue. Lewis Cass, in the Senate, was, in particular, war-hawkish, or at least he seemed so to the East. And in the House, John S. Chipman, a few days after the Kennedy speech, drew attention to himself by declaring:

> He would pledge himself . . . Michigan alone would take Canada in ninety days; and if that would not do, they would give it up, and take it in ninety days again. The Government of the United States had only to give the frontier people leave to take Canada. If conflict should come between republican and monarchical systems he would be glad to see it in his day.[23]

Toward Mexico, Western exponents of Manifest Destiny were more combative, also, than Eastern. They were less inclined to wait while Mexico considered entering the temple of freedom; more inclined to drag her in, or, at least, some of her possessions.[24] Restless spirits were dreaming of sacking the Halls of the Montezumas before relations with Mexico were even at the point of clash. Still, those south of the National Road took a less hopeful view of the possibility of regenerating colored races. They viewed even free Negroes residing among them with distaste and suspicion. They wrote into the codes of Ohio, Indiana, and Illinois the so called "Black Laws," limiting the rights of Negroes, including mulattoes, to establish residence and restricting their movements as residents.[25]

The South was the section least attracted to the full implications of the doctrine of Manifest Destiny. It certainly was not much interested in annexing all of Oregon or the frozen reaches of British North America. It was interested, at least its Democrats were, in Texas and the sparsely inhabited parts of Mexico west of Texas. It was deeply divided during the Mexican War, however, over the issue of absorbing the whole of Mexico. The South tended to be, as will appear, parochial in attitude toward Manifest Destiny and to be very color-conscious as well.

Some Southern papers, however, did have expansionist views. The Baltimore *Sun*, a penny sheet with a big circulation, was one of them. The Washington *Globe* of Francis P. Blair, and its successor, the *Daily Union*, edited by the veteran Thomas Ritchie, were others. But the *Sun* was primarily devoted to news gathering and to circulation, and the Washington dailies just named were administration organs.

Whigs objected to continent-wide expansion. Almost without exception they opposed immediate annexation of Texas, though Southern Whigs generally would have liked it in time. They opposed, also, an All-Oregon program. Among New England Whigs a peaceful acquisition of the harbor of San Francisco seemed desirable, but any aggressive pressures on Mexico seemed reprehensible. Whigs tended to approve Jefferson's concept of sister republics bordering the United States. Webster would have favored an independent status for Oregon. Henry Clay declared, in his famous "Raleigh" Letter, that if Canada won independence from England, she should, for the indefinite future, maintain only a sisterly relationship with the United States.[26] John Tyler, in one of his moods, declared, in his annual message to Congress in December 1843:

> Under the influence of our free system of government new republics are destined to spring up at no distant day on the shores of the Pacific similar in policy and in feelings to those existing on this side of the Rocky Mountains and giving a wider and more extensive spread to the principles of civil and religious liberty.[27]

Whigs, as a party, were fearful of spreading out too widely. They adhered to the philosophy of concentration of national authority in a limited area, as contrasted with the Democratic philosophy of dispersion of authority over wide spaces. Webster best expressed this mood in advice he gave his followers in 1844, in which he repeated the admonition of an ancient Spartan to his people on the issue of expansion: "You have a Sparta, embellish it!" [28]

Outside politics some few intellectuals among Americans were attracted to Manifest Destiny as a widener of horizons of opportunity. Ralph Waldo Emerson was one of these, as revealed in his essay "The Young American" and in his journals. William Cullen Bryant was another, though objecting, because of his opposition to slavery, to annexing Texas or much of Mexico. He did, however, reluctantly and belatedly, throw his influence, in the election of 1844, to Polk. Walt Whitman, as editor of the *Brooklyn Eagle*, was an enthusiast for expansion. But his enthusiasm declined as a result of the conflict over the Wilmot proviso, and he resigned from the paper in 1847. George Bancroft, the historian, was consistently an expansionist. Alexander H. Everett, editor for a time of the *North American Review*, was notable as a preacher of Manifest Destiny. So was Charles J. Ingersoll, littérateur and politician from Pennsylvania and, also, Lieutenant Matthew F. Maury, oceanographer and writer on naval problems, who expressed such views under a transparent pseudonym. These names will appear again in the course of this narrative.

In every section of the Union, and at every level of intelligence, believers in the doctrine of Manifest Destiny were thus found. They differed widely in their definitions of the scope of the doctrine and in their enthusiasm for its separate parts. Those who were confirmed continentalists were still few in number in the early 1840's, though more numerous than they had been in the War Hawk days of 1812. Though still deemed sadly wrongheaded and unreliable prophets of the future, they were no longer considered a lunatic fringe.

The date at which the doctrine emerged as a force to be reckoned with in politics is important to ascertain. It serves as a means of identification. It can be ascertained only approximately, for many facets were present in this complex phenomenon and some of them came into prominence sooner than others. Some editorial voices proclaiming the full doctrine were heard already during the campaign of 1844. They were voices crying in the wilderness.[29] The date when the full chorus proclaimed the doctrine came after the election, as late even as the closing months of the Tyler administration. It came after the annexation of Texas had emerged as a good prospect in politics.

A good prospect in politics is a major stimulant to effort. It is especially so after a long period of frustration. The campaign for the annexation of Texas has been marked by frustration ever since the Texans had made their wishes for union evident in the Jackson administration. They had been turned away again and again.

The issue had become dormant until Tyler reawakened it in 1843. He had drawn up a treaty of annexation with the Texans in 1844. Whether he had done this to save the province from falling into British hands, or to create an issue for purposes of re-election, was then, and still is, a debated matter. The issue was likely to create discord between sections, and between parties. Ratification of a Texas treaty would require a two-thirds Senate majority. In the hope of obtaining it Tyler and his Secretary of State, Calhoun, resorted to the "foreign devil" game, so the opposition charged. In the documents accompanying the treaty they maintained that Great Britain was plotting to reduce Texas to the status of a satellite, that she planned to abolitionize the Republic, that she aimed thus to destroy the slave structure of Southern society, and that the only means of defeating her plot was to annex Texas forthwith.[30]

The treaty, so defended, had encountered hostility in the Senate. It had been opposed by Northern Whigs on slavery grounds; by Southern, on grounds, among others, of the competition of Texan soils with the worn-out cotton and sugar soils of the South. The authors of the treaty were disliked, not only by Whigs but also by Van Burenites among the Democrats. Benton *ipso facto* opposed anything bearing the Tyler or Calhoun imprint. Early in the debate he blasted the treaty and the documentary defenses of it in a blistering three-day speech. He pointed out that a boundary dispute with Mexico involving a 2,000-mile stretch lay implicit in the treaty in the form of a Texan claim to territory up to the Rio Grande. Large parts of four Mexican provinces adjacent to Texas, including Santa Fe, the capital city of New Mexico, were brought in question by the Texan claim, and would, if the treaty were ratified, be transferred to the United States. The Tyler government, in forwarding the treaty, made no attempt, he said, to justify the boundary. It proposed merely to negotiate a new treaty with Mexico after a ratification. Would such a procedure be tried, Benton thundered, if the administration were annexing a revolted Canadian province? The answer was: "No! Sooner would they nip the forked lighting with their naked fingers." If such a procedure with Britain was inconceivable, why with Mexico? "Because Great Britain is powerful and Mexico is weak."

The alleged British plot was analyzed by Benton. It was, he said, "a pretext," a cover for the purposes of Tyler and Calhoun, a rumor of "imaginary designs," a "raw-head and bloody-bones," a "cry of wolf where there was no wolf." Four solemn disavowals had been made by Lord Aberdeen, the British Secretary of Foreign Affairs, of any design to interfere with slavery in Texas, or of any intent to convert Texas into a dependency, or of any plan "to acquire any dominent influence in Texas, or to have any kind of connexion with her except the fair and open trade and commerce which she has with all other nations." Dispatches of Edward Everett from London were read into the record to substantiate these disavowals. The charge of "plot," Benton thought, was discrediting to our government, insulting to England, and damaging to the United States in that it turned upon us the accusing eyes of the civilized world. The speech was read throughout the nation. Its impact was not diminished by the fact that Benton had a constituency overwhelmingly desirous of annexing Texas, that he was, or claimed to be, the earliest advocate in the nation of a legitimately acquired Texas, and that he was, when occasion required, himself capable of twisting the lion's tail a bit.[31]

The fight had spread beyond the closed doors of the Senate. A copy of the treaty and of its accompanying documents was leaked to the press by a senator of the Van

Buren school. The Senate debates were, thereupon, ordered to be made public. Letters from Van Buren and Clay were published declaring their opposition to immediate annexation. The editor of the Washington *Globe,* Francis P. Blair, declared the treaty had been framed and documented with a view to being defeated and to uniting the Southern Democracy in a Calhoun secession movement.[32] The national convention of the Democrats met. It ignored both Tyler and Van Buren, and nominated Polk for the presidency. The Senate administered a heavy defeat to the treaty. The issue was thrown into the presidential campaign of 1844.

In the campaign the Democratic party and its candidate pledged themselves to immediate annexation of Texas. They won, but only by a bare plurality in the election. Annexationists considered the election a mandate, however, for action at once. In the lame-duck session of Congress, which convened in December 1844, they brought a joint resolution of annexation before both houses. A counter measure was offered by Benton in December, proposing diplomatic negotiations, prior to annexation, between the United States, Texas, and Mexico, for a friendly adjustment of the boundary. The basis of the adjustment was to be a line running parallel to the Nueces in the desert prairie just west of the river, which Benton privately declared was Jackson's idea of the true boundary. The line was to continue along the highlands dividing the headwaters of the Rio Grande and the Mississippi to the 42nd parallel. If Mexico refused to negotiate on such a basis, then her consent could be dispensed with.[33]

After the election the factions among the Democrats had stronger incentives to agree on a Texas settlement than before. Tyler had been disposed of. So, in a sense, had Van Buren, and even Calhoun. Texas, after all, was desirable as an addition to the Union. In the course of the election Benton had received warning of the eagerness of his constituents for Texas. His fraternizing with Whigs, to the extent of supplying them ammunition to use against Tyler and Calhoun, was dangerous. In January 1845 he expressed in the Senate his approval of a set of resolutions which his state legislature had adopted, favoring annexation, with the understanding that the boundary would be left to "future" negotiation with Mexico.[34] Early in February he became still more tractable. In place of his precise December plan he offered a proposal authorizing the President (he had Polk in mind) to arrange with Texas for annexation.[35]

The Senate was the scene of the final battle. Lines were drawn there upon an annexation resolution adopted by the House late in January. The House resolution provided that the territory "properly included within and rightfully belonging to . . . Texas" may be erected into a state and admitted thus to the United States.[36] A Senate majority to pass it was not in sight, in the opinion of Walker. Therefore, when the debate ended, he moved an amendment to widen the resolution's base. The amendment provided that the President could select, for annexation purposes, either the House resolution or a new Texas negotiation. Walker hoped by means of the amendment to attract Benton's swing vote. An anti-Texan Whig moved that Benton's December resolution, which was favorable to Mexico, be adopted as a substitute for the Walker proposal. In making that motion he casually expressed the hope that Benton would not kill his own child. Benton's immediate answer was: "I'll kill it stone dead." He voted for the Walker proposal, which was adopted, as was presently the amended joint resolution, by a margin of 27 to 25.[37] The House readily approved the Walker modification and the resulting resolution went to the President.

The intention of Congress was that the incoming President would be the one to make a choice between the alternatives. By virtually everyone the outgoing President was thought disqualified, as a matter of courtesy, from acting. But Tyler was eager to act. He had been persuaded by Calhoun that the need for action was so compelling as to forbid delay for even as much as a few hours. He acted, choosing the initial House preference — immediate annexation. On the night of March 3 he sent directives to the American chargé in Texas to arrange immediate annexation. This was the situation when Polk assumed office the next day.

Polk was less impressed than Tyler had been with the need for instant action. He believed, moreover, he still had the right to the final word. He wanted advice from the Cabinet as to what the word should be. As the Cabinet was not yet formed, Polk sent a notice to Texas enjoining proceedings under the Tyler directive. On March 10 he met his Cabinet and they acted on the issue. They advised approval of Tyler's proceedings. Accordingly, a new directive, confirming Tyler's, was sent, offering immediate annexation to the Texan government. Andrew J. Donelson, a nephew of Andrew Jackson, was the American chargé. He found that the President of Texas and Sam Houston, the former President, were in favor of a new negotiation with the American government. They believed more favorable admission terms were obtainable. Further delay was the result. But sentiment in Texas was overwhelmingly in favor of immediate annexation; Donelson was an adroit diplomat, and Andrew Jackson exerted his great influence with Houston for immediate action. The result was that the Texan Congress and a Texan Convention were successively summoned. The Texan Congress voted unanimously for immediate annexation, and the Convention (on July 4) voted overwhelmingly for it, there being only one dissenting voice. A popular referendum confirmed these decisions, and all that remained was approval, by Washington, of the Texan constitution when Congress convened in December.

It was then, when frustrations were passing, that Douglas proclaimed he would blot out the lines on the map which marked the national boundaries, and make the area of liberty as broad as the continent itself. Then O'Sullivan wrote: "Yes, more, more, more! . . . till our national destiny is fulfilled and . . . the whole boundless continent is ours." [38] And Bennett wrote in the *New York Herald,* to the horror of the London *Times:*

> The patriotic impulses of the United States have been awakened to fresh and greatly augmented vigor and enthusiasm of action. . . . The minds of men have been awakened to a clear conviction of the destiny of this great nation of freemen. No longer bounded by those limits which nature had in the eye of those of little faith [in] the last generation, assigned to the dominion of republicanism on this continent, the pioneers of Anglo-Saxon civilization and Anglo-Saxon free institutions, now seek distant territories, stretching even to the shores of the Pacific; and the arms of the republic, it is clear to all men of sober discernment, must soon embrace the whole hemisphere, from the icy wilderness of the North to the most prolific regions of the smiling and prolific South.[39]

Texas was a perfect example of how Manifest Destiny would work, a pattern to be copied by the remainder of the continent. Prior to American occupation it had been a raw wilderness, rich in resources, but unused, or misused. American settlers had converted it into a smiling society of homes. Its people, by compact, had formed a state and had applied to the Union for admission. They had persisted, despite rebuffs, in applying, and at last had succeeded. Here was a plan, favored by God, for North America.

Several days after the adoption of the joint resolution of annexation, the New York *Sun* felt it must put to rest a bogy which had been frightening Whigs. The bogy was that expansionism would produce an unwieldy Union, a Union likely to collapse of its own weight, as Rome had done, in the process of empire building. Such a view, said the *Sun*, was un-American — circulated by the British party in America. It had no basis whatsoever. What had the provinces of Rome, with their hundred tongues, ruled by military force, in common with the sovereign and self-governing states of the American Union, all of one thought, language, and blood, and linked together by cordial fraternal ties in one happy family? No parallel to such moral greatness existed in history. "The energies of a people really free, governed by Christian institutions, have in them something of divine omnipotence." The Union was not too extensive. It had already doubled its original territory, and with it the number of the original states, but it had doubled its strength, also, in the process. The natural boundaries of the republic were the Atlantic and the Pacific, and the Arctic Ocean on the north and the Isthmus of Darien on the south. "Who shall say there is not room at the family altar for another sister like Texas, and in the fullness of time for many daughters from the shores of the Pacific." [40]

One of the daughters from the shores of the Pacific, expected at the altar soon, was Oregon. This was a region O'Sullivan had declared the United States had a perfect title to, a title that would be improved, however, by occupation. It was being so improved. American pioneers were flowing into the Willamette Valley, a restless crest on an advancing wave of population. Oregon society was maturing. Already in 1843 American settlers at Champoeg had adopted a compact of government. They, and their countrymen in the East, hoped the compact would be a prelude to admission to the Union. The Baltimore *Sun* was confident it would be. Oregonians "are sure to come home at last." [41] The *Sun* gave no thought to settlers of British origin, some of whom hoped that either an independent republic of the Pacific or a union with Great Britain would emerge from a compact — at least for the region north of the Columbia. The London *Times* and the *New York Herald* observed a "family resemblance" between what was happening in Oregon and what had happened in Texas. The *Times* bemoaned it; the *Herald* exulted over it. The pattern, according to the *Times*, was repeating itself in California. Its sameness was monotonous, but it was the sameness of a deep and determined policy. It was a law of "American progress." It would go on indefinitely unless "something," which the *Times* did not like to name, occurred to interrupt its progress.[42] The *New York Herald* believed Oregon would move not only as Texas had, but much more quickly; it was connected with all the political movements in the United States, and any administration which attempted to impede its course would be quickly deposed.[43]

In California, the inner valley was already virtually in American possession. Its coastal cities contained many Yankee merchants of affluence and growing influence. Letters from them and from other settlers describing the province as God's paradise were appearing in American newspapers in growing numbers. Editors, commenting on the letters, advised readers to "go West." The *New York Herald* cited the added attraction of California heiresses, who were beautiful and virtuous.[44] Early in 1845 a revolt of native Californians against a Mexican governor — one of a series — succeeded. The news was in the American press by the summer. To editors of journals preaching Manifest Destiny, it carried an obvious moral, which they pointed out for the less alert: independence for California, as soon as its American population had reached the right size, and after that — the Texas pattern.[45]

New Mexico seemed to have a similar future. Santa Fe, its capital, was an old center of American trade. Its population was believed to look with favor on the United States. The look was returned with longing by expansionist editors. Even Texas, while yet a babe among nations, had taken notice of the charms of New Mexico. Its curious Santa Fe expedition of 1841, a half-military, half-commercial venture launched by President Lamar, was to have swung the province into the Texan orbit. But the expedition was mismanaged, and landed its luckless participants in Mexican jails. When the Mexican Congress, after the American joint resolution annexing Texas had passed, ordered non-intercourse with the United States, the Albany *Atlas* commented: "There will be one result . . . her commercial intercourse with this country will cease, but the exportation of provinces to the United States, provided the Texas sample suits us in price and quality, will soon supply the place of its staples."[46] Some American editors thought that Yucatán also was qualified for admission to the Union,[47] and, indeed, the whole of Mexico.

The two Canadas were thought to be predisposed to a union with the United States. They had recently shown a rebellious mood to Great Britain. Sidney Breese, of Illinois, had assured the Senate early in 1844 that they favored republicanism.[48] In the same year, Levi Woodbury, soon to be a justice of the United States Supreme Court, speaking in the Senate, predicted that they would eventually be annexed peacefully.[49] The *Bay State Democrat,* of Boston, considered Canadian possessions less a chaplet of roses on the brow of Queen Victoria than a crown of thorns.[50] Some expansionist editors predicted, after the annexation of Texas, that Canadians would shortly "become ashamed of their state of slavery, and, casting off the yoke of England, set up for themselves." Others felt that they still needed southerly breezes to warm them to republicanism.[51] But O'Sullivan raised the right question in the summer of 1845, when news came of action by Texas on the annexation resolution. He raised the question of priority. "Texas, we repeat, is secure; and so now, as the Razor Strop Man says, 'Who's the next customer?' Shall it be California or Canada?"[52]

Among the statesmen who lent glamour to Manifest Destiny in the mid-1840's was the hero of the Democrats, Andrew Jackson. He was in declining health but was still actively guiding events from the Hermitage at Nashville and did so until his death on June 8, 1845. He sent repeated letters in the years preceding his death to friends urging the annexation of Texas and the occupation of Oregon, and these were usually promptly transmitted to the press. Jackson urged annexation to insure the national safety and interest and to checkmate the machinations of the British. The death of the Old Hero was followed by a welling up of emotion among the Democrats and a renewed determination to carry out his wishes. As important as his personality in stimulating Manifest Destiny were the ideals of democracy he stood for, the new authority of the masses — especially of the urban masses — in national politics, and the improved techniques of mass propaganda, which had become the property of both parties after his rise to the presidency.

Of major importance in the growth of Manifest Destiny were technological changes, including those that transformed transportation and communication. The steam engine had come into its own in river, ocean, and land travel. From distant territories to the center of government travel time by water had been sensationally reduced. On land railroads had proved themselves practical. But even more remarkable than the actual achievements of these agencies in contracting space was the stimulus given to the expansion of thought. In the mid-1840's projects to build transcontinental railroads to the Pacific by northern, central, and southern routes were on the lips of all. Asa Whitney's project of a line from Lake Michigan to the mouth of the Columbia or to Puget Sound was but one of such plans under public discussion. No doubt was entertained that all these plans would be realized. Railroads would, in the near future, bind the Pacific, the Mississippi Valley, and the Great Lakes in one iron clasp. They would bring congressmen from the Northwest coast to Washington in less time than it had taken those who had come from the Ohio a few years before. The success of Morse's magnetic telegraph fired the public imagination. It drew from President Tyler the awed exclamation: "What hath God wrought!" The immediate expansionist reply was: proof of the feasibility of Manifest Destiny. Electricity and steam had annihilated space and time as limitations on God's will. "The magnetic telegraph," the exuberant O'Sullivan wrote in the summer of 1845, "will enable the editors of the 'San Francisco Union,' the 'Astoria Evening Post,' or the 'Nootka Morning News' to set up in type the first half of the President's Inaugural before the echoes of the latter half shall have died away beneath the lofty porch of the Capitol, as spoken from his lips." [53]

Another force in the growth of Manifest Destiny was a vague, uneasy sense, in some quarters, of an insufficiency of good land. It was a new note in the national life. The old note had been confidence that the Republic's territorial resources were boundless. Jefferson had expressed it in his Inaugural Address. He had assured the nation (bounded still by the Mississippi) that it possessed "a chosen country, with room enough for our descendants to the thousandth and thousandth generation." [54] He was perhaps giving reassurance, merely, as to his purposes in the presidency. More likely he was voicing a national mood. But by 1845 western settlement was at the great bend of the Missouri. Beyond lay serried rows of Indian reservations, and farther west, semi-aridity. The plains and the intermountain plateaus were conceived of by many as the "Great American Desert." Travel across them to Santa Fe and to the Oregon Country had not entirely dispelled this illusion. Proposals to import Bactrian camels for travel there had appeared in the press. In the 1850's the Army experimented with several varieties of camels in western Texas. The prairies of the Middle West seemed — to Southerners at least — not very promising. They would not even give sustenance to trees. Yet a vast surplus of arable land would be needed if a refuge was to be kept open for the oppressed of the world.[55] The answer to the need was obvious. It was given by O'Sullivan: "Yes, more, more, more! . . . till our national destiny is fulfilled and . . . the whole boundless continent is ours." [56]

A boundless continent was expected to be attractive to the commercial and manufacturing classes. It would give them new markets. On this ground they were counted on to lend support to expansionist programs. In 1837 Jackson counseled the Texan representative, who was seeking admission of his people to the Union, to induce his government to claim California and especially the harbor of San Francisco, for it was Jackson's belief that this would make Texas palatable to New England and New York merchants.[57] Webster longed for San Francisco. He considered it worth twenty times all of Texas. In 1844 the Cushing treaty opened five new Chinese treaty ports to American commerce, and thus made the Pacific harbors more valuable to the business classes. In the final debates on the annexation of Texas, expansionists plied the commercial world with statistics showing the extent and value of the prospective trade with Texas.

Economic distress was another factor in the upsurge of Manifest Destiny. A succession of crises — in 1837, 1839, 1841 — had crippled business and had been followed by four years of national prostration. The economy in nearly all its phases had fallen to depths not plumbed again until the mid-1890's. Cotton sank in price to an all-time low in 1844. The price of corn and hogs — the measure of the well-being of the Middle West — was, in 1843, at the disastrous level it had dropped to in 1822, and the upturn was slow to come. The depression was registered in the flight of defeated farmers to Oregon and California and in restless dreaming about the Halls of the Montezumas.[58] Voters in the election of 1844 attributed what had happened to a Whig administration and withheld crucial votes from Clay. Polk won votes he might otherwise not have had. Travail, nation-wide, was a characteristic of the era of the early 1840's. So was a nation-wide agitation for reform — reform of every kind, political, social, and spiritual. This was the era of the "roaring forties." Manifest Destiny was one of the reforms — perhaps the most important.

Youth was necessary for effective reform. It was needed to shake off the shackles of the past, to get the nation going again, to move to new frontiers. Youth had vision, generous idealism, the high enthusiasm demanded by the times. The hands of graybeards and of Hunkers were tied by expediency, by patronage of office, by corruption and crass materialism. The Hunkers, in any case, were associates of stockjobbers and money-changers and Whigs who should be driven out of the temple.

The *Boston Times,* near the end of 1844, observed:

> The spirit of Young America . . . will not be satisfied with what has been attained, but plumes its young wings for a higher and more glorious flight. The hopes of America, the hopes of Humanity must rest on this spirit. . . . The steam is up, the young overpowering spirit of the Country will press onward. It would be as easy to stay the swelling of the ocean with a grain of sand upon its shore, as to stop the advancement of this truly democratic and omnipotent spirit of the age.[59]

The *United States Journal* in Washington observed in the spring of 1845:

> There is a new spirit abroad in the land, young, restless, vigorous and omnipotent. It manifested itself in infancy at the Baltimore Convention. It was felt in boyhood in the triumphant election of James K. Polk; and in manhood it will be still more strongly felt in the future administration of public affairs in this country. . . . It sprang from the warm sympathies and high hopes of youthful life, and will dare to take antiquity by the beard, and tear the cloak from hoary-headed hypocrisy. Too young to be corrupt . . . it is Young America, awakened to a sense of her own intellectual greatness by her soaring spirit. It stands in strength, the voice of the majority. . . . It demands the immediate annexation of Texas at any and every hazard. It will plant its right foot upon the northern verge of Oregon, and its left upon the Atlantic crag, and waving the stars and the stripes in the face of the once proud Mistress of the Ocean, bid her, if she dare, "Cry havoc, and let slip the dogs of war." [60]

Young America, in answer to the voice, appeared in Congress. It likewise manned the press. It came to Congress — more particularly from the Middle West — proclaiming that Texas and 54° 40' were first installments merely of continentalism. Its spokesmen included such statesmen as Wentworth, aged 30; Douglas, 32; Edward Hannegan, 38; William Allen, 42; Sidney Breese, 45; Andrew Kennedy, 35. In the press its representatives were hardly more bent with years. In 1845, John L. O'Sullivan was 32; Levi D. Slamm, 33; William M. Swain, 36; James Gordon Bennett, 50; Samuel Medary, 44. Thomas Ritchie was 67. He was described by approving Democrats as "venerable"; by Whigs, as senile. Walt Whitman restored the average to the right level; he was 26.

One youth Young America called to office was James K. Polk. He was slightly overage. When he entered the White House, he was 49. He was the youngest President, until then, to appear there. He had been, in the campaign, confidently introduced to voters as "Young Hickory." On his election his jubilant followers emphasized the "Young" in the title as much as the "Hickory." He was advised to follow Old Hickory in his program: to take a strong position on foreign issues, to arouse "a degree of excitement amongst the popular masses similar to that which had supported and sustained General Jackson in his first term," and to reorganize the party to make it a Polk Democracy, as the General had made it a Jackson Democracy. He was told that Van Buren's type of leadership, which had cast a spell of timidity over the preceding eight years, would no longer do. As for the Hunkers, they were curtly advised to jump aboard.[61]

Youth was responsible, doubtless, for such characteristics of Manifest Destiny as its grandeur and scope, and for the moral exaltation with which it was set forth. But another force may also account for these results — the geography of the western country itself. A geographic explanation of Manifest Destiny was attractively offered by the Albany *Argus:*

> It is frequently asked why are those western people so peculiarly colossal in their notions of things and the prospects of our nation. Does not this inspiration spring from their extraordinary country? Their mighty rivers, their vast sea-like lakes, their noble and boundless prairies, and their magnificent forests afford objects which fill the mind to its utmost capacity and dilate the heart with greatness. To live in such a splendid country . . . expands a man's views of everything in this world. . . . Here everything is to be done — schools are to be established, governments instituted. . . . These things fill their lives with great enterprises, perilous risks and dazzling rewards.[62]

But a doctrine needs more than a set of favorable conditions to propel it into orbit. It needs means of dissemination to keep it in the air, and in this respect the doctrine of Manifest Destiny was well served. It was disseminated by the agencies of mass propaganda, of which the press was the most important. The press in the era of the mid-1840's reached a degree of effectiveness never known before. This was partly an outcome of improvements in communications, but principally of the development of the high-speed printing press. This press, in turn, was the creation of a number of inventors and firms, but especially of Richard M. Hoe, of the famous New York manufacturing firm of Hoe and Company. His machine, a revolving-cylinder press, was tested at the plant of the Philadelphia *Public Ledger* in 1846, and proved successful. It had a running capacity of 8,000 papers an hour. The next year a yet speedier double-cylinder press was in operation; it was capable of throwing off 10,000 papers an hour. Such presses transformed the printing plants of the great Eastern dailies and engendered astonishment and envy in newspapermen of the rural press.[63]

Accompanying this development came advances in the methods of news gathering. Telegraph lines were extended. Gaps in the lines were bridged by the use of railroads, packet steamships, pony express, and carrier pigeon. Organization to facilitate the gathering and dissemination of news was effected. Journalism, in these respects, came of age. The leaders of these enterprises were the giants of the penny press — Bennett, Beach, and Benjamin H. Day, of New York City; William M. Swain, of the Philadelphia *Public Ledger*; and Arunah S. Abell, of the Baltimore *Sun*. These men were interested in reaching the city masses and in drawing the profits of mass operation.

The penny press employed sensationalism to achieve these ends — especially the papers of Bennett and Day. For general news, nothing was more sensational or exhilarating than the soul-stirring doctrine of Manifest Destiny. For local news, Bennett and Day exploited police-court stories and stories of human interest and society scandal. Tastes in New York City were earthy, much more so than in Boston or Philadelphia or Baltimore. Whig papers commented sourly on the unpleasant contrast, in the New York papers, between heaven-scented editorials on such themes as Manifest Destiny and the smelly local items presented alongside. Editors of the Bennett type and those of the Whig type, such as Horace Greeley, were at opposite poles of journalism. Bennett supported causes that paid, was inclined to be flippant, irresponsible, chauvinistic; Greeley was high-toned, deeply interested in the uplift of mankind, in schemes for social reorganization, in the anti-slavery and peace causes. Yet Greeley was obliged to increase the price of the *Daily Tribune* to two cents in the year after its founding in 1841.

In politics the penny press was independent. By roaming over areas of interest to the masses, it increased its income from circulation and advertising so that it did not need the uncertain revenues paid to party organs in the form of printing patronage. It was the chief purveyor of Manifest Destiny to the nation. More persistently than even the organs of the Polk administration it spread the doctrine. And its influence extended deep into the interior, where its exciting and well-written editorials were copied widely by journals of lesser rank. Manifest Destiny was a product, thus, of many forces, and the vigor with which it was disseminated was a product of others almost as numerous and powerful.

But a single force is credited in some writings with having generated Manifest Destiny — nationalism in an invigorated form, dating from the early 1840's.[64] This view has been suggested rather than carefully developed or defended. It is out of accord with the temper of the era. The era was that of Tyler and Polk, which exhibited little nationalism, at least in terms of any definition Clay would have approved. It defeated efforts to resurrect a United States Bank. It insisted, instead, on an Independent Treasury. It accepted the burgeoning of state banking, and it approved the Walker tariff of 1846. It rejected the principle of federal aid for internal improvements. It left internal improvements to the states and to private enterprise. In the field of constitutional interpretation it upheld the Taney court, which had moments of nationalism but was not the Marshall court. If the test of nationalism be public sentiment, the era was marked by sectionalism — sectionalism emerging from such issues of expansionism as Texas, 54° 40', and the Mexican War.

A nationalist explanation fits ill, also, into the ideas of Manifest Destiny held by the theorist O'Sullivan. In the *Democratic Review* of September 1844, O'Sullivan wrote an article entitled "True Theory and Philosophy of our System of Government." It was a simplification of Calhoun's "South Carolina Exposition" and of the "Fort Hill Letter," and was one of the most cogent brief defenses of states' rights and state interposition ever written. Its conclusion was:

> Each new State or people who may be associated with us, to the extent of their common interests and feelings, and to that extent only, would increase the strength and extend the

beneficence of our institutions. The differences in national sentiment and interest, and the peculiarities in national genius, which are inevitable in so large a confederacy, would then cease to present formidable difficulties, for they are left to their own free development under the single restriction of not interfering with the equal rights of their neighbors, or coming into collision with others. How magnificent in conception! How beneficent in practice is this system, which associates nations in one great family compact, without destroying the social identity, or improperly constraining the individual genius of any; and cements into elements of strength and civilization those very sources of difference which have heretofore destroyed the peace of mankind! [65]

The harmonies flowing from a blending of states' rights and Manifest Destiny were described rapturously by other writers of the day, including all the editors of the Democratically-inclined penny press. A successor of O'Sullivan on the *Democratic Review* wrote that the constitutional principle under which authority over general matters is delegated to the nation, and authority over all others is reserved to the states, is more than human wisdom — it is "an emanation from Providence." [66]

Polk, in his Inaugural Address, gave formal approval to the contribution of states' rights to expansionism. The Union, he pointed out, is a growing confederacy of "independent" states. The states have increased in number from thirteen to twenty-eight. Two have been admitted to the Union within the past week. New communities and states — especially Texas — are seeking to come under its aegis. In an earlier day some held the opinion that our system could not operate successfully over an extended territory. Serious objections were made even to such extensions as the Louisiana Purchase. The objections have been shown not to have been well grounded. As our boundaries have expanded and our population has grown, our system has acquired additional strength. Indeed, it would probably be in greater danger of being overthrown if our present population were confined to the narrow bounds of the original thirteen states. Our system may be safely extended to the utmost bounds of our present limits. Indeed, as these are extended, the bonds of union, far from being weakened, will become stronger.

Our population, Polk continued, has increased from three to twenty millions. Multitudes from the Old World are flocking to our shores to participate in our blessings. In this republican land of freedom all distinctions of birth and rank have been abolished. All citizens, native or adopted, are considered equal. Church and state are separate, freedom of religion is guaranteed, freedom of trade is maintained, peace is assured among the American states. If the Confederacy expands it will bring these blessings to other areas and to other millions. On such errands it should be clothed, the President made clear, in the garments of states' rights.[67]

But a special variety of nationalism — resentment in the nation over interference by Europe in the affairs of Texas — is credited in some accounts with having generated Manifest Destiny. British interference, particularly, is alleged, and its aim is said to have been to induce Texas to abolish slavery, to preserve a nominal independence, but actually to take the status of a satellite of England. Intriguing of this sort was a repeated expansionist charge in the campaign for immediate annexation of Texas, and the thesis that Manifest Destiny was a product of it has plausibility.

Yet a resentment, nation-wide, over alleged intriguing of this kind would have had to be apparent well before the summer of 1845, when Texas was voting to enter the Union, if the thesis has real validity. Nothing approaching that state of feeling appeared in the press or in Congress. Charges of British meddling with slavery in Texas were prominent in 1844, in the Senate fight over the ratification of the Tyler-

Calhoun treaty. They were denounced at once by Benton and other Van Burenites as a fraud, as a cry of wolf where there was no wolf. They seemed no less a political trick to Whigs. The overwhelming rejection of the treaty by the Senate suggests no nation-wide acceptance of the charges.

In American politics the game of unmasking the foreign devil was no novelty. It was as old as the formation of national parties. It included efforts by each party to implicate the other in the plots of European states to harass the United States. In the era of Tyler and Polk, Whigs were dubbed the "pro-British party" by most Democrats. They were called, for variety, "blue-light Federalists," which meant a continuation of the treasonable relations their ancestors had maintained with the British before and during the War of 1812. Whigs and independents were accustomed to discount such charges.

The period of the Texas crisis was the foreground of the presidential election of 1844. It was filled with the extravagances of party campaigning, of the venom among Democrats, of factional infighting, and of bitterness produced in the sections by a clash over slavery. That a national spirit so strong and unified as to generate Manifest Destiny could have emerged from such a composite of disharmonies is inconceivable. The forces that produced Manifest Destiny were domestic for the most part. They were ample in number to account for Manifest Destiny, and among them one was undoubtedly powerful — the strong taste of expansionists for the doctrine of states' rights.

NOTES

1. Julius W. Pratt: "John L. O'Sullivan and Manifest Destiny," *New York History, XIV* (1933), 213.
2. *Democratic Review* (New York), *XVII* (October 1845), 243–8.
3. The admission of Texas was considered a pattern which would be followed in all future cases. It was not aggression, as zealous Britishers maintained; it was the opposite. This was made clear in the *New York Morning News* in an editorial on October 13, 1845:

    It is looked upon as aggression, and all the bad and odious features which the habits of thought of Europeans associate with aggressive deeds, are attributed to it. . . . But what has Belgium, Silesia, Poland or Bengal in common with Texas? It is surely not necessary to insist that acquisitions of territory in America, even if accomplished by force of arms, are not to be viewed in the same light as the invasions and conquests of the States of the old world. No American aggression can stab the patriot to the heart, nerve the arm of a Kosciusko, or point the declamation of a Burke; our way lies, not over trampled nations, but through desert wastes, to be brought by our industry and energy within the domain of art and civilization. We are contiguous to a vast portion of the globe, untrodden save by the savage and the beast, and we are conscious of our power to render it tributary to man. This is a position which must give existence to a public law, the axioms of which a Pufendorf or Vattel had no occasion to discuss. So far as the disposition to disregard mere conventional claims is taken into account, the acquisition of Texas, commencing with the earliest settlements under Austin down to the last conclusive act, may be admitted at once, to be aggressive. But what then? It has been laid down and acted upon, that the solitudes of America are the property of the immigrant children of Europe and their offspring. Not only has this been said and reiterated, but it is actually, although perhaps, not heretofore dwelt upon with sufficient distinctness, the basis of public law in America. Public sentiment with us repudiates possession without use, and this sentiment is gradually acquiring the force of established public law. It has sent our adventurous pioneers to the plains of Texas, will carry them to the Rio del Norte, and even that boundary, purely nominal and conventional as it is, will not stay them on their march to the Pacific, the limit which nature has provided. In like manner it will come to pass that the confederated democracies of the Anglo American race will give this great continent as an inheritance to man. Rapacity and spoliation cannot be the features of this magnificent enterprise, not perhaps, because we are above and beyond the influence of such views, but because circumstances do not admit of their operation. We take from no man; the reverse rather — we give to man. This national policy, necessity or destiny, we know to be just and beneficent, and we can, therefore, afford to scorn the invective and imputations of rival nations. With the valleys of the Rocky Mountains converted into pastures and sheep-folds, we may with propriety turn to the world and ask, whom have we injured?

Other striking expressions of such views are in the New York *Sun,* May 30, 1845, and the Washington *Globe,* April 28, 1845. Senator Levi Woodbury had the same views; *Cong. Globe,* 28 Cong., 2 Sess., App. 233 (February 17, 1845).

4. *New York Morning News,* November 15, 1845. For the conception that it was selfish to withhold the blessings of freedom from other peoples, see *Kendall's Expositor, IV,* Nos. 10 and 11 (May 21, 1844), 167–72; *New York Morning News,* December 1, 1845; *Illinois State Register,* December 10, 1847.
5. Richard K. Crallé (ed.): *Works of John C. Calhoun* (6 vols., New York, 1853–5), *VI,* 1, 59.
6. *Democratic Review, XIV* (April 1844), 423; *XV* (September 1844), 219; *XXI* (October 1847), 285; Washington *Union,* October 7, 1845; *New York Morning News,* November 29, December 27, 1845; *New York Herald,* September 23, 1845.
7. Pratt: "John L. O'Sullivan and Manifest Destiny"; Julian Hawthorne, *Nathaniel Hawthorne and His Wife* (2 vols., Boston, 1885), *I,* 160; *New York Morning News,* December 1, 1845.
8. *Cong. Globe,* 28 Cong., 2 Sess., 200 (January 27, 1845).
9. Ibid., 227 (January 31, 1845).
10. Ibid., 29 Cong., 1 Sess., 180 (January 10, 1846).
11. Ibid., 30 Cong., 1 Sess., App. 86–7 (January 12, 1848).
12. *Democratic Review, XXI* (October 1847), 291–2. Pre-emption and the prospects of graduation and donation in the future were all discussed as part of the image of land democracy in the United States. Examples of such discussion are Washington *Union,* October 23, 1845; *New York Morning News,* June 13, 1846; *Illinois State Register,* October 1, 1847; *Cong. Globe,* 30 Cong., 1 Sess., App. 128 (January 19, 1848).
13. *Cong. Globe,* 29 Cong., 1 Sess., 342 (February 9, 1846).
14. Hartford *Times,* July 24, 1845.
15. *New York Morning News,* December 27, 1845.
16. *Cong. Globe,* 28 Cong., 2 Sess., App. 43 (January 3, 1845).
17. The augury is in the *Democratic Review, XVII* (October 1845), 243–8. In a lead editorial in the *New York Morning News,* on October 13, 1845, O'Sullivan wrote:

    The records of the past, teeming as they are with instructive lessons, fail to convey an adequate idea of what will be the history of this Republic. We are not merely to possess and occupy an unequalled extent of territory, or to extend our laws and institutions over a countless population, for the territory, though vast, will be compact, and what is of still greater value, the population will be homogeneous. This latter element of power and stability has heretofore been wanting to all great empires. Those which have passed away, were all, without exception, composed of dissimilar and hostile materials, and the same may be said of the great European monarchies of the present day. The glittering diadem of England must fade, the colossus of Russia must crumble, but who can foresee the decline of American freedom.

18. When the New York *Globe* folded in 1846, Slamm was humanely taken care of by appointment to the Navy. He was made purser on a war vessel by George Bancroft, who knew a good Democrat when he saw one. Slamm got the job despite a warning that a "man who is not able to take care of his own family and property is not fit to be entrusted with the property of others." He remained happily in service as a purser until his death in 1862. James Lee to James K. Polk, June 10, 1845, George Bancroft Papers, Massachusetts Historical Society.
19. The *New York Morning News,* for example, on June 5, 1845, admitted that early offers by the United States of partition at the line of 49° had somewhat compromised the thesis of 54° 40'. This weakness in the *News* was associated by indignant Western editors with rumors of weakness in Buchanan. See also ibid., November 15, 1845. The West was chided for its belligerency in the *Democratic Review, XVII* (1845), 248. See also *New York Herald,* November 15, 1845, and *New York Sun,* March 2, 1846.
20. New York *Globe,* February 18, 1846.
21. *Illinois State Register,* May 9, 1845.
22. *Cong. Globe,* 29 Cong., 1 Sess., 180 (January 10, 1846).
23. Ibid., 207 (January 14, 1846).
24. Detroit *Free Press,* August 29, 1845.
25. The Mexican race seemed to Westerners "but little removed above the negro"; *Illinois State Register,* December 27, 1844. See also Edgar A. Holt: *Party Politics in Ohio, 1840–1850* (Columbus, 1931), passim.
26. *Niles' Register, LXVI* (1844), 152–3.
27. James D. Richardson (comp.): *Messages and Papers of the Presidents* (11 vols., Washington, 1905), *IV,* 258.
28. *Writings and Speeches of Daniel Webster* (18 vols., Boston, 1903), *XVI,* 423.
29. Detroit *Free Press,* September 9, 1844; *Illinois State Register,* December 27, 1844; *Cong. Globe,* 28 Cong., 2 Sess., App. 105 (January 10, 1845).
30. Frederick Merk: "Safety Valve Thesis and Texan Annexation," *M.V.H.R., XLIX* (1962–3), No. 3.
31. *Cong. Globe,* 28 Cong., 1 Sess., App. 474 ff. (May 16, 18, 20, 1844). Another speech was made by Benton on June 12, 1844. It is consolidated here, for reasons of brevity, with the first (ibid., 570). Clay believed there was "not the smallest foundation for the charge that Great Britain has a design to

establish a colony in Texas"; Mrs. Chapman Coleman (ed.): *Life of John J. Crittenden* (Philadelphia, 1871), 209. The charge of a plot by Great Britain was deemed a fraud by the Tennessee Whig Spencer Jarnagan. A charge of that sort struck a chord that "always vibrates to the touch"; *National Whig,* May 21, 1847.
32. Washington *Globe,* May 27, 1844.
33. *Cong. Globe,* 28 Cong., 2 Sess., 19 (December 11, 1844).
34. Ibid, 154 (January 20, 1845).
35. Ibid., 244 (February 5, 1845).
36. Ibid., 129, 193 (January 13, 25, 1845).
37. Ibid., 359–62 (February 27, 1845).
38. *New York Morning News,* February 7, 1845. The title of the editorial was "More! More! More!" The fullest development of the theme of the Texan pattern is *Democratic Review, XVII* (July–August 1845), 5–10; (October 1845), 243–8.
39. *New York Herald,* September 25, 1845; London *Times,* October 21, 1845.
40. New York *Sun,* March 7, 1845.
41. Baltimore *Sun,* June 4, 1845. On August 21, 1845, the editor recommended that the Oregon issue be left to "settlement." He thought that "the independence of today would, *à la Texas,* resolve itself into the annexation of tomorrow."
42. London *Times,* October 1, December 15, 1845.
43. *New York Herald,* October 1, 1845.
44. Ibid., September 30, 1845. The *New York Herald* was filled with letters from and about California. "Ho! for California" was the word.
45. *New York Morning News,* December 16, 1845.
46. Albany *Atlas* (weekly, *hereafter abbreviated* w.), April 24, 1845.
47. New York *Sun,* March 11, 1846; *New York Herald,* September 17, 1845; *New York Morning News,* July 2, 1846.
48. *Cong. Globe,* 28 Cong., 1 Sess., 330 (February 27, 1844). A brief account of American designs on Canada in the late 1830's is Ephraim D. Adams: *Power of Ideals in American History* (New Haven, 1913), 74–9.
49. Ibid., 28 Cong., 1 Sess., App. 767 (June 4, 1844).
50. *Bay State Democrat,* February 22, 1844; also Detroit *Free Press,* January 18, 1845.
51. *New York Morning News,* July 14, 1845; *New York Herald,* November 30, 1845.
52. *New York Morning News,* July 7, 1845.
53. *Democratic Review, XVII* (July–August 1845), 9.
54. Richardson (comp.): *Messages and Papers, I,* 323.
55. On December 28, 1844, the Baltimore *Sun* wrote: "As a commercial nation, we must lay our hand upon the Pacific Coast of this continent, else the time is not far distant when we shall, notwithstanding our 'broad acres,' find ourselves 'cabin'd, cribb'd, confined.' "
56. *New York Morning News,* February 7, 1845.
57. Frederick Merk: "The Oregon Question in the Webster-Ashburton Negotiations," *M.V.H.R., XLIII* (1956–7), 398.
58. *New York Morning News,* August 28, 1845.
59. *Boston Times,* December 11, 1844.
60. *United States Journal* (semi-weekly, *hereafter abbreviated* s.w.), May 3, 1845. The *Journal* was edited by Theophilus Fisk, a champion of various causes. He was successively a left-wing Jacksonian, a hard-money man, an anti-clerical, a Calhounist, defender of slavery, ultra-expansionist, and Polkist. He never prospered in journalism, and ended his days as a writer of religious tracts. "Young America" was a term used interchangeably with "Young Democracy." The history of the term is sketched in James T. Adams (ed.): *Dictionary of American History* (6 vols., New York, 1940), *V,* 509. Fisk got some editorial ribbing from Whigs for his exuberant image of a young, flag-waving giant bestriding the continent from northern Oregon to the Atlantic crag. Whigs were dismayed at the quantity of broadcloth needed for the pantaloons of the young man. *Louisville Journal* (w.), May 14, 1845; *United States Journal* (s.w.), June 6, 1845.
61. *New York Herald,* September 16, November 8, 1845.
62. Albany *Argus,* July 26, 1845.
63. New Orleans *Picayune,* July 30, 1847; Baltimore *Sun,* September 9, 1847; *New Hampshire Patriot,* April 6, 1848.
64. Weinberg: *Manifest Destiny,* 101, 108 ff.; Adams: *Power of Ideals,* 66 ff.; John D. P. Fuller: *Movement for the Acquisition of All Mexico* (Baltimore, 1936), 38; Jesse S. Reeves: *American Diplomacy under Tyler and Polk* (Baltimore, 1907), 58.
65. *Democratic Review, XV* (September 1844), 219–32, 320.
66. Ibid., *XXI* (October, 1847), 285. See also *Kendall's Expositor, IV,* Nos. 10 and 11 (May 21, 1844).
67. Richardson (comp.): *Messages and Papers, IV,* 375. The two new states referred to by the President were Florida and Iowa. For Tyler on the states' rights theme see ibid., *IV,* 335–6; for George Bancroft, a campaign speech reported in *New Hampshire Patriot,* June 13, 1844.

The Causes of the Civil War

Scarcely anyone today would deny that in some final sense slavery was responsible for the Civil War. The South and the North disagreed over other matters besides slavery. The two sections often argued over economic issues, such as the tariff and western lands. They also differed in their cultural and social values. But it was the presence of slavery in one section and the absence of it in the other that ultimately led to the South's secession and the Civil War.

But while it is important to recognize this fact, it is, by itself, insufficient to explain how the war came about. Slavery had always existed in America. Why did it generate such intense sectional conflict after 1815, and why should that conflict prove to be particularly irreconcilable in 1860–61? A necessary component of the slavery controversy was the sectionalizing of the institution. Slavery was legally recognized in all parts of the American colonies. During the Revolution and the years immediately following, it was gradually abolished north of the Mason-Dixon Line. The Northwest Ordinance of 1787 further excluded it from the area north of the Ohio River and west of Pennsylvania, while to the south of this region the expansion of cotton culture opened vast new areas for the spread of plantation slavery.

Had the territorial extent of the nation been stabilized at this point, it is possible that there would have been no Civil War. But the country continued to grow by purchase, as in the case of the vast Louisiana territory, and by war, as in the case of the Mexican Cession. With each addition to the settled area, the issue of slavery extension arose anew. The question might have been settled peaceably as in the past, however, had slavery not come to seem increasingly immoral and anachronistic to northerners. The process by which this occurred is described in the following selection by Arthur Bestor. By the 1840s many Americans in the free North were convinced that slavery was a moral blight and inconsistent with a progressive, democratic society, while many Americans in the slave South believed their happiness and prosperity depended on it.

This conflict of interests and values could not have easily been reconciled under any circumstances. But according to Arthur Bestor, it would not have taken the form of civil war had it not been for the special constitutional structure of the United States. Because of the ambiguities of the federal compact called the Constitution, honest men could disagree over the relative power of the states and the federal government. Particularly uncertain was the power of Congress in new territories as against the people of those territories and as against established states. Few men denied the right of the states to either uphold or abolish slavery within their own bounds. The question was rather what to do with the vast West, and, who should do whatever was to be done — Congress, the first settlers in the territories, or the people living there at the time the area was admitted as a state?

Had the question not continually recurred after 1846, the nation might have settled it without bloodshed. Unfortunately, western state-making was a constant problem in these years, and the continual need to redefine the powers of federal, state, and territorial governments regarding slavery kept the sectional controversy at a fever pitch. It ended in the tragedy of the Civil War. Obviously behind the constitutional and legalistic arguments were other, more fundamental, elements of sectional disagreement and distrust, but Arthur Bestor makes a good case for the role of the American constitutional structure in bringing on the conflagration.

FOR FURTHER READING:

CRAVEN, AVERY. *The Coming of the Civil War.* Chicago: University of Chicago Press, 1966.*
PRESSLY, THOMAS. *Americans Interpret Their Civil War.* New York: The Macmillan Company, Free Press, 1965.*
STAMPP, KENNETH M. *And the War Came.* Chicago: University of Chicago Press, 1964.*

Asterisk denotes paperback edition.

The American Civil War as a Constitutional Crisis ARTHUR BESTOR

Within the span of a single generation — during the thirty-odd years that began with the annexation of Texas in 1845 and ended with the withdrawal of the last Union troops from the South in 1877 — the United States underwent a succession of constitutional crises more severe and menacing than any before or since. From 1845 on, for some fifteen years, a constitutional dispute over the expansion of slavery into the western territories grew increasingly tense until a paralysis of normal constitutional functioning set in. Abruptly, in 1860–1861, this particular constitutional crisis was transformed into another: namely, that of secession. Though the new crisis was intimately linked with the old, its constitutional character was fundamentally different. The question of how the Constitution ought to operate as a piece of working machinery was superseded by the question of whether it might and should be dismantled. A showdown had come, and the four-year convulsion of Civil War ensued. Then, when hostilities ended in 1865, there came not the hoped for dawn of peace, but instead a third great constitutional struggle over Reconstruction, which lasted a dozen years and proved as harsh and divisive as any cold war in history. When the nation finally emerged from three decades of corrosive strife, no observer could miss the profound alterations that its institutions had undergone. Into the prodigious vortex of crisis and war every current of American life had ultimately been drawn.

So all-devouring was the conflict and so momentous its effects, that to characterize it (as I have done) as a series of constitutional crises will seem to many readers an almost irresponsible use of language, a grotesque belittling of the issues. Powerful economic forces, it will be pointed out, were pitted against one another in the struggle. Profound moral perplexities were generated by the existence of slavery, and the attacks upon it had social and psychological repercussions of incredible

---

Source: Arthur Bestor, "The American Civil War as a Constitutional Crisis," *American Historical Review,* vol. 69 (1964), pp. 327–352.

complexity. The various questions at issue penetrated into the arena of politics, shattering established parties and making or breaking the public careers of national and local leaders. Ought so massive a conflict to be discussed in terms of so rarified an abstraction as constitutional theory?

To ask such a question, however, is to mistake the character of constitutional crises in general. When or why or how should they arise if not in a context of social, economic, and ideological upheaval? A constitution, after all, is nothing other than the aggregate of laws, traditions, and understandings — in other words, the complex of institutions and procedures — by which a nation brings to political and legal decision the substantive conflicts engendered by changes in all the varied aspects of its societal life. In normal times, to be sure, routine and recurrent questions of public policy are not thought of as constitutional questions. Alternative policies are discussed in terms of their wisdom or desirability. Conflicts are resolved by the ordinary operation of familiar constitutional machinery. A decision is reached that is essentially a political decision, measuring, in some rough way, the political strength of the forces that are backing or opposing some particular program of action, a program that both sides concede to be constitutionally possible, though not necessarily prudent or desirable.

When controversies begin to cut deep, however, the constitutional legitimacy of a given course of action is likely to be challenged. Questions of policy give place to questions of power; questions of wisdom to questions of legality. Attention shifts to the Constitution itself, for the fate of each particular policy has come to hinge upon the interpretation given to the fundamental law. In debating these constitutional questions, men are not evading the substantive issues. They are facing them in precisely the manner that the situation now requires. A constitutional dispute has been superadded to the controversies already present.

Should the conflict become so intense as to test the adequacy of existing mechanisms to handle it at all, then it mounts to the level of a constitutional crisis. Indeed the capability of producing a constitutional crisis is an ultimate measure of the intensity of the substantive conflicts themselves. If, in the end, the situation explodes into violence, then the catastrophe is necessarily a constitutional one, for its very essence is the failure and the threatened destruction of the constitutional framework itself.

The secession crisis of 1860-1861 was obviously an event of this kind. It was a constitutional catastrophe in the most direct sense, for it resulted in a civil war that destroyed, albeit temporarily, the fabric of the Union.

There is, however, another sense — subtler, but perhaps more significant — in which the American Civil War may be characterized as a constitutional crisis. To put the matter succinctly, the very form that the conflict finally took was determined by the pre-existing form of the constitutional system. The way the opposing forces were arrayed against each other in war was a consequence of the way the Constitution had operated to array them in peace. Because the Union could be, and frequently had been, viewed as no more than a compact among sovereign states, the dissolution of the compact was a conceivable thing. It was constitutional theorizing, carried on from the very birth of the Republic, which made secession the ultimate recourse of any group that considered its vital interests threatened.

Since the American system was a federal one, secession, when it finally occurred, put the secessionists into immediate possession of fully organized governments, capable of acting as no *ad hoc* insurrectionary regime could possibly have acted.

Though sometimes described as a "rebellion" and sometimes as a "Civil War," the American conflict was, in a strict sense, neither. It was a war between pre-existing political entities. But it was not (to use a third description) a "War between the States," for in war the states did not act severally. Instead, the war was waged between two federations of these states: one the historic Union, the other a Confederacy that, though newly created, was shaped by the same constitutional tradition as its opponent. In short, only the pre-existing structure of the American Constitution can explain the actual configuration even of the war itself.

The *configurative* role that constitutional issues played is the point of crucial importance. When discussed in their own terms and for their own sakes, constitutional questions are admittedly theoretical questions. One may indeed say (borrowing a phrase that even academicians perfidiously employ) that they are academic questions. Only by becoming involved with other (and in a sense more "substantive") issues, do they become highly charged. But when they do become so involved, constitutional questions turn out to be momentous ones, for every theoretical premise draws after it a train of practical consequences. Abstract though constitutional issues may be, they exert a powerful shaping effect upon the course that events will in actuality take. They give a particular direction to forces already at work. They impose upon the conflict as a whole a unique, and an otherwise inexplicable, pattern or configuration.

To speak of a configuration of forces in history is to rule out, as essentially meaningless, many kinds of questions that are popularly supposed to be both answerable and important. In particular, it rules out as futile any effort to decide which one of the various forces at work in a given historical situation was "*the* most important cause" of the events that followed, or "*the* decisive factor" in bringing them about, or "*the* crucial issue" involved. The reason is simple. The steady operation of a single force, unopposed and uninterrupted, would result in a development so continuous as to be, in the most literal sense, eventless. To produce an event, one force must impinge upon at least one other. The event is the consequence of their interaction. Historical explanation is, of necessity, an explanation of such interactions.

If interaction is the crucial matter, then it is absurd to think of assigning to any factor in history an intrinsic or absolute weight, independent of its context. In the study of history, the context is all-important. Each individual factor derives its significance from the position it occupies in a complex structure of interrelationships. The fundamental historical problem, in short, is not to measure the relative weight of various causal elements, but instead to discover the pattern of their interaction with one another.[1]

A cogent illustration of this particular point is afforded by the controversy over slavery, which played so significant a role in the crisis with which this paper deals. Powerful emotions, pro and con, were aroused by the very existence of slavery. Powerful economic interests were involved with the fate of the institution. Nevertheless, differences of opinion, violent though they were, cannot, by themselves, account for the peculiar configuration of events that historically occurred. The forces unleashed by the slavery controversy were essentially indeterminate; that is to say, they could lead to any number of different outcomes, ranging from simple legislative emancipation to bloody servile insurrection. In the British West Indies the former occurred; in Haiti, the latter. In the United States, by contrast with both, events took an exceedingly complicated course. The crisis can be said to have commenced with a fifteen-year dispute not over slavery itself, but over its expansion into the territories.

It eventuated in a four-year war that was avowedly fought not over the issue of slavery, but over the question of the legal perpetuity of the Union. The slavery controversy, isolated from all other issues, cannot begin to explain why events followed so complex and devious a course. On the other hand, though other factors must be taken into account in explaining the configuration of events, these other factors, isolated from those connected with slavery, cannot explain why tensions mounted so high as to reach the breaking point of war.

No single factor, whatever its nature, can account for the distinctive form that the mid-nineteenth-century American crisis assumed. Several forces converged, producing a unique configuration. Men were debating a variety of issues simultaneously, and their various arguments intertwined. Each conflict tended to intensify the others, and not only to intensify them but also to alter and deflect them in complicated ways. The crisis was born of interaction.

The nature of these various converging conflicts is abundantly clear. They are spread at length upon the historical record. Documents, to be sure, are not always to be taken at face value; there are occasions when it is legitimate to read between the lines. Nevertheless, the documentary record is the foundation upon which historical knowledge rests. It can be explained, but it cannot be explained away, as many writers on the causes of the Civil War attempt to do. Most current myths, indeed, depend on such wholesale dismissals of evidence. Southern apologetics took form as early as 1868 when Alexander H. Stephens unblinkingly asserted that "this whole subject of Slavery, so-called . . . was, to the Seceding States, but a drop in the ocean compared with . . . other considerations," [2] by which he meant considerations of constitutional principle. The dogma of economic determinism can be sustained only by dismissing, as did Charles and Mary Beard in 1927, not merely that part of the record which Stephens rejected but also the part he accepted. Having decided, like Stephens, that "the institution of slavery was not the fundamental issue," the Beards went on to assert that constitutional issues likewise "were minor factors in the grand dispute." [3]

When the historical record is as vast as the one produced by the mid-nineteenth-century American crisis — when arguments were so wearisomely repeated by such multitudes of men — it is sheer fantasy to assume that the issues discussed were not the real issues. The arguments of the period were public ones, addressed to contemporaries and designed to influence their actions. If these had not touched upon genuine issues, they would hardly have been so often reiterated. Had other lines of argument possessed a more compelling force, they would certainly have been employed.

The only tenable assumption, one that would require an overwhelming mass of contrary evidence to rebut, is that men and women knew perfectly well what they were quarreling about. And what do we find? They argued about economic measures — the tariff, the banking system, and the Homestead Act — for the obvious reason that economic interests of their own were at stake. They argued about slavery because they considered the issues it raised to be vital ones — vital to those who adhered to the ideal of a free society and vital to those who feared to disturb the *status quo*. They argued about the territories because they felt a deep concern for the kind of social order that would grow up there. They argued about the Constitution because they accepted its obligations (whatever they considered them to be) as binding.

These are the data with which the historian must reckon. Four issues were mentioned in the preceding paragraph: the issue of economic policy, the issue of slavery, the issue of the territories, and the issue of constitutional interpretation. At the very least, the historian must take all these into account. Other factors there indubitably were. To trace the interaction of these four, however, will perhaps suffice to reveal the underlying pattern of the crisis and to make clear how one of these factors, the constitutional issue, exerted a configurative effect that cannot possibly be ignored.

Conflicts over economic policy are endemic in modern societies. They formed a recurrent element in nineteenth-century American political conflict. To disregard them would be an even greater folly than to assume that they determined, by themselves, the entire course of events. Between a plantation economy dependent upon the sale of staples to a world market and an economy in which commerce, finance, and manufacturing were rapidly advancing, the points of conflict were numerous, real, and important. At issue were such matters as banks and corporations, tariffs, internal improvements, land grants to railroads, and free homesteads to settlers. In a general way, the line of division on matters of economic policy tended, at mid-century, to coincide with the line of division on the question of slavery. To the extent that it did so (and it did so far less clearly than many economic determinists assume), the economic conflict added its weight to the divisive forces at work in 1860-1861.

More significant, perhaps, was another and different sort of relationship between the persistent economic conflict and the rapidly mounting crisis before the Civil War. To put the matter briefly, the constitutional theories that came to be applied with such disruptive effects to the slavery dispute had been developed, in the first instance, largely in connection with strictly economic issues. Thus the doctrine of strict construction was pitted against the doctrine of loose construction as early as 1791, when Alexander Hamilton originated the proposal for a central bank. And the doctrine of nullification was worked out with ingenious thoroughness in 1832 as a weapon against the protective tariff. Whatever crises these doctrines precipitated proved to be relatively minor ones so long as the doctrines were applied to purely economic issues. Within this realm, compromise always turned out to be possible. The explosive force of irreconcilable constitutional theories became apparent only when the latter were brought to bear upon the dispute over slavery.

Inherent in the slavery controversy itself (the second factor with which we must reckon) were certain elements that made compromise and accommodation vastly more difficult than in the realm of economic policy. To be sure, slavery itself had its economic aspect. It was, among other things, a labor system. The economic life of many regions rested upon it. The economic interests that would be affected by any tampering with the institution were powerful interests, and they made their influence felt.

Nevertheless, it was the noneconomic aspect of slavery that made the issues it engendered so inflammatory. As Ulrich B. Phillips puts it, "Slavery was instituted not merely to provide control of labor but also as a system of racial adjustment and social order." The word "adjustment" is an obvious euphemism; elsewhere Phillips speaks frankly of "race control." The effort to maintain that control, he maintains, has been "the central theme of Southern history." The factor that has made the South "a land with a unity despite its diversity," Phillips concludes, is "a common resolve indomitably maintained — that it shall be and remain a white man's country."[4]

It was this indomitable resolve — say rather, this imperious demand — that lay at the heart of the slavery controversy, as it lies at the heart of the struggle over civil rights today. To put the matter bluntly, the demand was that of a master race for a completely free hand to deal as it might choose with its own subject population. The word "sovereignty" was constantly on the lips of southern politicians. The concept they were invoking was one that Blackstone had defined as "supreme, irresistible, absolute, uncontrolled authority." [5] This was the kind of authority that slaveholders exercised over their chattels. What they were insisting on, in the political realm, was that the same species of power should be recognized as belonging to the slaveholding states when dealing with their racial minorities. "State Sovereignty" was, in essence, the slaveowner's authority writ large.

If slavery had been a static system, confined geographically to the areas where the institution was an inheritance from earlier days, then the demand of the slaveholding states for unrestricted, "sovereign" power to deal with it was a demand to which the majority of Americans would probably have reconciled themselves for a long time. In 1861, at any rate, even Lincoln and the Republicans were prepared to support an ironclad guarantee that the Constitution would never be amended in such a way as to interfere with the institution within the slaveholding states. An irrepealable amendment to that effect passed both houses of Congress by the necessary two-thirds vote during the week before Lincoln's inauguration.[6] The incoming President announced that he had "no objection" to the pending amendment,[7] and three states (two of them free) actually gave their ratifications in 1861 and 1862.[8] If the problems created by slavery had actually been, as slaveowners so vehemently maintained, of a sort that the slaveholding states were perfectly capable of handling by themselves, then the security offered by this measure might well have been deemed absolute.

As the historical record shows, however, the proposed amendment never came close to meeting the demands of the proslavery forces. These demands, and the crisis they produced, stemmed directly from the fact that slavery was *not* a static and local institution; it was a prodigiously expanding one. By 1860 the census revealed that more than half the slaves in the nation were held in bondage *outside* the boundaries of the thirteen states that had composed the original Union.[9] The expansion of slavery meant that hundreds of thousands of slaves were being carried beyond the territorial jurisdictions of the states under whose laws they had originally been held in servitude. Even to reach another slaveholding state, they presumably entered that stream of "Commerce . . . among the several States," which the Constitution gave Congress a power "to regulate." [10] If they were carried to United States territories that had not yet been made states, their presence there raised questions about the source and validity of the law that kept them in bondage.

Territorial expansion, the third factor in our catalogue, was thus a crucial element in the pattern of interaction that produced the crisis. The timing of the latter, indeed, indicates clearly the role that expansion played. Slavery had existed in English-speaking America for two centuries without producing any paralyzing convulsion. The institution had been brought to an end in the original states of the East and North by unspectacular exercises of legislative or judicial authority. Federal ordinances barring slavery from the Old Northwest had operated effectually yet inconspicuously since 1787. At many other points federal authority had dealt with slavery, outlawing the foreign slave trade on the one hand and providing for the return of fugitive slaves on the other. Prior to the 1840's constitutional challenges to its authority in these matters had been few and unimportant. Indeed, the one true crisis of the period, that of 1819–1821 over Missouri, was rooted in expansionism, precisely as the later one was to be. The nation was awaking to the fact that slavery had pushed its way northward and westward into the virgin lands of the Louisiana Purchase. Only when limits were drawn for it across the whole national domain did the crisis subside.

Suddenly, in the election of 1844, the question of territorial expansion came to the fore again. Events moved rapidly. Within the space of precisely a decade, between the beginning of 1845 and the end of 1854, four successive annexations added a million and a quarter square miles to the area under undisputed American sovereignty.[11] Expansion itself was explosive; its interaction with the smoldering controversy over slavery made the latter issue explosive also.

The annexation of Texas in 1845, the war with Mexico that followed, and the conquests in the Southwest which that war brought about gave to the campaign against slavery a new and unprecedented urgency. Within living memory the plains along the Gulf of Mexico had been inundated by the westward-moving tide of slavery. Alabama and Mississippi, to say nothing of Arkansas and Missouri, furnished startling proof of how quickly and ineradicably the institution could establish itself throughout great new regions. Particularly telling was the example of Texas. There slavery had been carried by American settlers to nominally free soil beyond the boundaries of the United States; yet in the end the area itself was being incorporated in the Union. To guard against any possible repetition of these developments, antislavery forces reacted to the outbreak of the Mexican War by introducing and supporting the Wilmot Proviso. Originally designed to apply simply to territory that might be acquired from Mexico, it was quickly changed into an all-encompassing prohibition: "That there shall be neither slavery nor involuntary servitide in any territory on the continent of America which shall hereafter be acquired by or annexed to the United States . . . in any . . . manner whatever." [12] The steadfast refusal of the Senate to accept the proviso did not kill it, for the prospect of continuing expansion kept the doctrine alive and made it the rallying point of antislavery sentiment until the Civil War.

This prospect of continuing expansion is sometimes forgotten by historians who regard the issue of slavery in the territories as somehow bafflingly unreal. Since 1854, it is true, no contiguous territory has actually been added to the "continental" United States. No one in the later 1850's, however, could know that this was to be the historic fact. There were ample reasons to expect otherwise. A strong faction had worked for the annexation of the whole of Mexico in 1848. Filibustering expeditions in the Caribbean and Central America were sporadic from 1849 to 1860. As if to spell out the implications of these moves, the notorious Ostend Manifesto of 1854 had announced (over the signatures of three American envoys, including a future President) that the United States could not "permit Cuba to be Africanized" (in plainer language, could not allow the slaves in Cuba to become free of white domination and control), and had defiantly proclaimed that if Spain should refuse to sell the island, "then, by every law, human and divine, we shall be justified in wresting it from Spain if we possess the power." [13] This was "higher law" doctrine with a vengeance.

Behind the intransigent refusal of the Republicans in 1860–1861 to accept any sort of compromise on the territorial question lay these all too recent developments. Lincoln's letters during the interval between his election and his inauguration contained pointed allusions to filibustering and to Cuba.[14] And his most explicit instructions on policy, written on February 1, 1861, to William H. Seward, soon to take office as his Secretary of State, were adamant against any further extension of slavery in any manner:

> I say now . . . as I have all the while said, that on the territorial question — that is, the question of extending slavery under the national auspices — I am inflexible. I am for no compromise which *assists* or *permits* the extension of the institution on soil owned by the nation. And any trick by which the nation is to acquire territory, and then allow some local authority to spread slavery over it, is as obnoxious as any other.

The obnoxious "trick" that Lincoln feared was, of course, the acceptance of Stephen A. Douglas' doctrine of popular sovereignty. The supreme importance that Lincoln attached to the territorial issue was underlined by the final paragraph of his letter, wherein he discussed four other issues on which antislavery feeling ran high: the Fugitive Slave Act, the existence of slavery in the national capital, the domestic slave trade, and the slave code that the territorial legislature of New Mexico had enacted in 1859. Concerning these matters, Lincoln wrote Seward:

> As to fugitive slaves, District of Columbia, slave trade among the slave states, and whatever springs of necessity from the fact that the institution is amongst us, I care but little, so that what is done be comely, and not altogether outrageous. Nor do I care much about New-Mexico, if further extension were hedged against.[15]

The issues raised by territorial expansion were, however, not merely prospective ones. Expansion was a present fact, and from 1845 onward its problems were immediate ones. Population was moving so rapidly into various parts of the newly acquired West, most spectacularly into California, that the establishment of civil governments within the region could hardly be postponed. Accordingly, within the single decade already delimited (that is, from the beginning of 1845 until the end of 1854), state or territorial forms of government were actually provided for every remaining part of the national domain, except the relatively small enclave known as the Indian Territory (now Oklahoma). The result was an actual doubling of the area of the United States within which organized civil governments existed.[16] This process of political creation occurred not only in the new acquisitions, but it also covered vast areas, previously acquired, that had been left unorganized, notably the northern part of the old Louisiana Purchase. There, in 1854, the new territories of Kansas and Nebraska suddenly appeared on the map. With equal suddenness these new names appeared in the newspapers, connected with ominous events.

The process of territorial organization brought into the very center of the crisis a fourth factor, the last in our original catalogue, namely, the constitutional one. The organization of new territories and the admission of new states were, after all, elements in a constitution-making process. Territorial expansion drastically changed the character of the dispute over slavery by entangling it with the constitutional problem of devising forms of government for the rapidly settling West. Slavery at last became, in the most direct and immediate sense, a constitutional question, and thus a question capable of disrupting the Union. It did so by assuming the form of a question about the power of Congress to legislate for the territories.

This brings us face to face with the central paradox in the pre-Civil War crisis. Slavery was being attacked in places where it did not, in present actuality, exist. The slaves, close to four million of them, were in the states, yet responsible leaders of the antislavery party pledged themselves not to interfere with them there.[17] In the territories, where the prohibition of slavery was being so intransigently demanded and so belligerently resisted, there had never been more than a handful of slaves during the long period of crisis. Consider the bare statistics. The census of 1860, taken just before the final descent into Civil War, showed far fewer than a hundred slaves in all the territories,[18] despite the abrogation of restrictions by the Kansas-Nebraska Act and the Dred Scott decision. Especially revealing was the situation in Kansas. Though blood had been spilled over the introduction of slavery into that territory, there were actually only 627 colored persons, slave or free, within its boundaries on the eve of its admission to statehood (January 29, 1861). The same situation obtained throughout the West. In 1846, at the time the Wilmot Proviso was introduced, the Union had comprised twenty-eight states. By the outbreak of the Civil War, more than two and a third million persons were to be found in the western areas beyond the boundaries of these older twenty-eight states, yet among them were only 7,687 Negroes, free or slave.[19] There was much truth in the wry observation of a contemporary: "The whole controversy over the Territories . . . related to an imaginary negro in an impossible place." [20]

The paradox was undeniable, and many historians treat it as evidence of a growing retreat from reality. Thus James G. Randall writes that the "larger phases of the slavery question . . . seemed to recede as the controversies of the fifties developed." In other words, "while the struggle sharpened it also narrowed." The attention of the country was "diverted from the fundamentals of slavery in its moral, economic, and social aspects," and instead "became concentrated upon the collateral problem as to what Congress should do with respect to slavery in the territories." Hence "it was this narrow phase of the slavery question which became, or seemed, central in the succession of political events which actually produced the Civil War." As Randall sees it, the struggle "centered upon a political issue which lent itself to slogan making rather than to political analysis." [21]

Slogan making, to be sure, is an important adjunct of political propaganda, and slogans can easily blind men to the relatively minor character of the tangible interests actually at stake. Nevertheless, a much more profound force was at work, shaping the crisis in this peculiar way. This configurative force was the constitutional system itself. The indirectness of the attack upon slavery, that is to say, the attack upon it in the territories, where it was merely a future possibility, instead of in the states, where the institution existed in force, was the unmistakable consequence of certain structural features of the American Constitution itself.

A centralized national state could have employed a number of different methods of dealing with the question of slavery. Against most of these, the American Constitution interposed a barrier that was both insuperable and respected.[22] By blocking every form of frontal attack, it compelled the adoption of a strategy so indirect as to appear on the surface almost timid and equivocal.[23] In effect, the strategy adopted was a strategy of "containment." Lincoln traced it to the founding fathers themselves. They had, he asserted, put into effect a twofold policy with respect to slavery: "restricting it from the new Territories where it had not gone, and legislating to cut off its source by the abrogation of the slave trade." Taken together, these amounted to "putting the seal of legislation against its spread." The second part of their policy was still in effect, but the first, said Lincoln, had been irresponsibly set aside. To restore it was his avowed object:

> I believe if we could arrest the spread [of slavery] and place it where Washington, and Jefferson, and Madison placed it, it would be in the course of ultimate extinction, and

the public mind would, as for eighty years past, believe that it was in the course of ultimate extinction. The crisis would be past.[24]

Whether or not slavery could have been brought to an end in this manner is a totally unanswerable question, but it requires no answer. The historical fact is that the defenders of slavery regarded the policy of containment as so dangerous to their interests that they interpreted it as signifying "that a war must be waged against slavery until it shall cease throughout the United States."[25] On the other hand, the opponents of slavery took an uncompromising stand in favor of this particular policy because it was the only one that the Constitution appeared to leave open. To retreat from it would be to accept as inevitable what Lincoln called "the perpetuity and nationalization of slavery."[26]

To understand the shaping effect of the Constitution upon the crisis, one must take seriously not only the ambiguities that contemporaries discovered in it, but also the features that all alike considered settled. The latter point is often neglected. Where constitutional understandings were clear and unambiguous, responsible leaders on both sides accepted without serious question the limitations imposed by the federal system. The most striking illustration has already been given. Antislavery leaders were willing to have written into the Constitution an absolute and perpetual ban upon congressional interference with slavery inside the slaveholding states. They were willing to do so because, as Lincoln said, they considered "such a provision to now be implied constitutional law," which might without objection be "made express, and irrevocable."[27]

Equally firm was the constitutional understanding that Congress had full power to suppress the foreign slave trade. On the eve of secession, to be sure, a few fire-eaters proposed a resumption of the importation of slaves. The true index of southern opinion, however, is the fact the Constitution of the Confederate States outlawed the foreign trade in terms far more explicit than any found in the Constitution of the United States.[28]

Far more surprising, to a modern student, is a third constitutional understanding that somehow held firm throughout the crisis. The Constitution grants Congress an unquestioned power "To regulate Commerce with foreign Nations, and among the several States, and with the Indian Tribes."[29] Employing this power, Congress had outlawed the foreign slave trade in 1808, with the general acquiescence that we have just noted. To anyone familiar with twentieth-century American constitutional law, the commerce clause would seem to furnish an obvious weapon for use against the domestic slave trade as well. Since the 1890's the power of Congress to regulate interstate commerce has been directed successively against lotteries, prostitution, child labor, and innumerable other social evils that are observed to propagate themselves through the channels of interstate commerce.

The suppression of the domestic slave trade, moreover, would have struck a far more telling blow at slavery than any that could possibly have been delivered in the territories. Only the unhampered transportation and sale of slaves from the older seaboard regions can account for the creation of the black belt that stretched westward through the new Gulf States. By 1840 there were already as many slaves in Alabama and Mississippi together, as in Virginia. During the twenty years that followed, the number of slaves in the two Gulf States almost doubled, while the number of slaves in Virginia remained almost stationary.[30]

The migration of slaveholding families with the slaves they already possessed can account for only part of this change. The domestic slave trader was a key figure in the process. His operations, moreover, had the indirect effect of pouring money back into older slaveholding states like Virginia, where slavery as an economic system had seemed, in the days of the Revolution, on the verge of bankruptcy. Furthermore, a direct attack upon the domestic slave trade might well have aroused less emotional resentment than the attack actually made upon the migration of slaveholders to the territories, for the slave trader was a universally reprobated figure, the object not only of antislavery invective but even of southern distrust and aversion.

No serious and sustained effort, however, was ever made to employ against the domestic slave trade the power of Congress to regulate interstate commerce. The idea was suggested, to be sure, but it never received significant support from responsible political leaders or from public opinion. No party platform of the entire period, not even the comprehensive, detailed, and defiant one offered by the Liberty party of 1844, contained a clear-cut proposal for using the commerce power to suppress the interstate traffic in slaves. Public opinion seems to have accepted as virtually axiomatic the constitutional principle that Henry Clay (who was, after all, no strict constructionist) phrased as follows in the set of resolutions from which the Compromise of 1850 ultimately grew:

> *Resolved,* That Congress has no power to prohibit or obstruct the trade in slaves between the slaveholding States; but that the admission or exclusion of slaves brought from one into another of them, depends exclusively upon their own particular laws.[31]

Careful students of constitutional history have long been at pains to point out that the broad interpretation that John Marshall gave to the commerce clause in 1824 in the notable case of *Gibbons* v. *Ogden*[32] represented a strengthening of federal power in only one of its two possible dimensions. The decision upheld the power of Congress to sweep aside every obstruction to the free flow of interstate commerce. Not until the end of the nineteenth century, however, did the commerce power begin to be used extensively for the purpose of regulation in the modern sense, that is to say, restrictive regulation. The concept of a "federal police power," derived from the commerce clause, received its first clear-cut endorsement from the Supreme Court in the Lottery Case,[33] decided in 1903. These facts are well known. Few scholars, however, have called attention to the dramatic illustration of the difference between nineteenth- and twentieth-century views of the Constitution that is afforded by the fact that the commerce clause was never seriously invoked in connection with the slavery dispute. This same fact illustrates another point as well: how averse to innovation in constitutional matters the antislavery forces actually were, despite allegations to the contrary by their opponents.

Various other constitutional understandings weathered the crisis without particular difficulty, but to catalogue them is needless. The essential point has been made. The clearly stated provisions of the Constitution were accepted as binding. So also were at least two constitutional principles that rested upon no specific written text, but were firmly ingrained in public opinion: the plenary authority of the slaveholding states over the institution within their boundaries and the immunity of the domestic slave trade to federal interference.

In the Constitution as it stood, however, there were certain ambiguities and certain gaps. These pricked out, as on a geological map, the fault line along which earthquakes were likely to occur, should internal stresses build up to the danger point.

Several such points clustered about the fugitive slave clause of the Constitution.[34] Clear enough was the principle that slaves might not secure their freedom by absconding into the free states. Three vital questions, however, were left without a clear answer. In the first place, did responsibility for returning the slaves to their masters rest with the states or the federal government? As early as 1842, the Supreme Court, in a divided opinion, placed responsibility upon the latter.[35] This decision brought to the fore a second question. How far might the free states go in refusing cooperation and even impeding the process of rendition? The so-called "personal liberty laws" of various northern states probed this particular constitutional question. Even South Carolina, originator of the doctrine of nullification, saw no inconsistency in its wrathful denunciation of these enactments, "which either nullify the Acts of Congress or render useless any attempt to execute them."[36] A third question arose in connection with the measures adopted by Congress to carry out the constitutional provision, notably the revised Fugitive Slave Act of 1850. Were the methods of enforcement prescribed by federal statute consistent with the procedural guarantees and underlying spirit of the Bill of Rights? From the twentieth-century viewpoint, this was perhaps the most profound of all the constitutional issues raised by the slavery dispute. It amounted to a direct confrontation between the philosophy of freedom and the incompatible philosophy of slavery. Important and disturbing though the issues were, the mandate of the fugitive slave clause was sufficiently clear and direct to restrain all but the most extreme leaders from outright repudiation of it.[37]

Of all the ambiguities in the written Constitution, therefore, the most portentous proved in fact to be the ones that lurked in the clause dealing with territory: "The Congress shall have Power to dispose of and make all needful Rules and Regulations respecting the Territory or other Property belonging to the United States."[38] At first glance the provision seems clear enough, but questions were possible about its meaning. Eventually they were raised, and when raised they turned out to have so direct a bearing upon the problem of slavery that they would not down. What did the Constitution mean by mingling both "Territory" and "other Property," and speaking first of the power "to dispose of" such property? Was Congress in reality given a power to govern, or merely a proprietor's right to make regulations for the orderly management of the real estate he expected eventually to sell? If it were a power to govern, did it extend to all the subjects on which a full-fledged state was authorized to legislate? Did it therefore endow Congress with powers that were not federal powers at all but municipal ones, normally reserved to the states? In particular, did it bestow upon Congress, where the territories were concerned, a police power competent to deal with domestic relations and institutions like slavery?

This chain of seemingly trivial questions, it will be observed, led inexorably to the gravest question of the day: the future of slavery in an impetuously expanding nation. On many matters the decisions made by territorial governments might be regarded as unimportant, for the territorial stage was temporary and transitional. With respect to slavery, however, the initial decision was obviously a crucial one. A single article of the Ordinance of 1787 had eventuated in the admission of one free state after another in the Old Northwest. The omission of a comparable article from other territorial enactments had cleared the way for the growth of a black belt of slavery from Alabama through Arkansas. An identical conclusion was drawn by both sides. The power to decide the question of slavery for the territories was the power to determine the future of slavery itself.

In whose hands, then, had the Constitution placed the power of decision with respect to slavery in the territories? This was, in the last analysis, the constitutional question that split the Union. To it, three mutually irreconcilable answers were offered.

The first answer was certainly the most straightforward. The territories were part of the "Property belonging to the United States." The Constitution gave Congress power to "make all needful Rules and Regulations" respecting them. Only a definite provision of the Constitution, either limiting this power of specifying exceptions to it, could destroy the comprehensiveness of the grant. No such limitations or exceptions were stated. Therefore, Congress was fully authorized by the Constitution to prohibit slavery in any or all of the territories, or to permit its spread thereto, as that body, in exercise of normal legislative discretion, might decide.

This was the straightforward answer; it was also the traditional answer. The Continental Congress had given that answer in the Ordinance of 1787, and the first Congress under the Constitution had ratified it. For half a century thereafter the precedents accumulated, including the precedent of the Missouri Compromise of 1820. Only in the 1840's were these precedents challenged.

Because this was the traditional answer, it was (by definition, if you like) the conservative answer. When the breaking point was finally reached in 1860–1861 and four identifiable conflicting groups offered four constitutional doctrines, two of them accepted this general answer, but each gave it a peculiar twist.

Among the four political factions of 1860, the least well-organized was the group that can properly be described as the genuine conservatives. Their vehicle in the election of 1860 was the Constitutional Union party, and a rattletrap vehicle it certainly was. In a very real sense, however, they were the heirs of the old Whig party and particularly of the ideas of Henry Clay. Deeply ingrained was the instinct for compromise. They accepted the view just stated, that the power of decision with respect to slavery in a particular territory belonged to Congress. But they insisted that one additional understanding, hallowed by tradition, should likewise be considered constitutionally binding. In actually organizing the earlier territories, Congress had customarily balanced the prohibition of slavery in one area by the erection elsewhere of a territory wherein slaveholding would be permitted. To conservatives, this was more than a precedent; it was a constitutional principle. When, on December 18, 1860, the venerable John J. Crittenden offered to the Senate the resolutions summing up the conservative answer to the crisis, he was not in reality offering a new plan of compromise. He was, in effect, proposing to write into the Constitution itself the understandings that had governed politics in earlier, less crisis-ridden times. The heart of his plan was the re-establishment of the old Missouri Compromise line, dividing free territories from slave.[39] An irrepealable amendment was to change this from a principle of policy into a mandate of constitutional law.

That Congress was empowered to decide the question of slavery for the territories was the view not only of the conservatives, but also of the Republicans. The arguments of the two parties were identical, up to a point; indeed, up to the point just discussed. Though territories in the past had been apportioned between freedom and slavery, the Republicans refused to consider this policy as anything more than a policy, capable of being altered at any time. The Wilmot Proviso of 1846 announced, in effect, that the time had come to abandon the policy. Radical though the proviso may have been in a political sense, it was hardly so in a constitutional sense. The existence of a congressional power is the basic constitutional question.

In arguing for the existence of such a power over slavery in the territories, the Republicans took the same ground as the conservatives. In refusing to permit mere precedent to hamper the discretion of Congress in the *use* of that power, they broke with the conservatives. But the distinction they made between power and discretion, that is, between constitutional law and political policy, was neither radical nor unsound.

One innovation did find a place in antisalvery, and hence in Republican, constitutional doctrine. Though precedent alone ought not to hamper the discretion of Congress, specific provisions of the Constitution could, and in Republican eyes did, limit and control that discretion. With respect to congressional action on slavery in the territories, so the antislavery forces maintained, the due process clause of the Fifth Amendment constituted such an express limitation. "Our Republican fathers," said the first national platform of the new party in 1856, "ordained that no person shall be deprived of life, liberty, or property, without due process of law." To establish slavery in the territories "by positive legislation" would violate this guarantee. Accordingly the Constitution itself operated to "deny the authority of Congress, of a Territorial Legislation [*sic*], of any individual, or association of individuals, to give legal existence to Slavery in any Territory of the United States." [40] The Free Soil platform of 1848 had summed the argument up in an aphorism: "Congress has no more power to make a SLAVE than to make a KING; no more power to institute or establish SLAVERY, than to institute or establish a MONARCHY." [41] As a doctrine of constitutional law, the result was this: the federal government had full authority over the territories, but so far as slavery was concerned, Congress might exercise this authority in only one way, by prohibiting the institution there.

The conservatives and the Republicans took the constitutional system as it stood, a combination of written text and historical precedent, and evolved their variant doctrines therefrom. By contrast, the two other factions of 1860 — the northern Democrats under Stephen A. Douglas, and the southern Democrats whose senatorial leader was Jefferson Davis and whose presidential candidate was John C. Breckinridge — appealed primarily to constitutional theories above and beyond the written document and the precedents. If slogans are meaningfully applied, these two factions (each in its own way) were the ones who, in 1860, appealed to a "higher law."

For Douglas, this higher law was the indefeasible right of every community to decide for itself the social institutions it would accept and establish. "Territorial Sovereignty" (a more precise label than "popular sovereignty") meant that this right of decision on slavery belonged to the settlers in a new territory fully as much as to the people of a full-fledged state. At bottom the argument was one from analogy. The Constitution assigned responsibility for national affairs and interstate relations to the federal government; authority over matters of purely local and domestic concern were reserved to the states. So far as this division of power was concerned, Douglas argued, a territory stood on the same footing as a state. It might not yet have sufficient population to entitle it to a vote in Congress, but its people were entitled to self-government from the moment they were "organized into political communities." Douglas took his stand on what he regarded as a fundamental principle of American political philosophy: "that the people of every separate political community (dependent colonies, Provinces, and Territories as well as sovereign States) have an inalienable right to govern themselves in respect to their internal polity." [42]

Having thus virtually erased the constitutional distinction between a territory and a state — a distinction that was vital (as we shall see) to the state sovereignty interpretation — Douglas proceeded to deal with the argument that since a territorial government was a creation of Congress, the powers it exercised were delegated ones, which Congress itself was free to limit, to overrule, or even to exercise through direct legislation of its own. He met the argument with an ingenious distinction. "Congress," he wrote, "may institute governments for the Territories," and, having done so, may "invest them with powers which Congress does not possess and can not exercise under the Constitution." He continued: "The powers which Congress may thus *confer* but can not *exercise,* are such as relate to the domestic affairs and internal polity of the Territory." [43] Their source is not to be sought in any provision of the written Constitution, certainly not in the so-called territorial clause,[44] but in the underlying principle of self-government.

Though Douglas insisted that the doctrine of popular sovereignty embodied "the ideas and principles of the fathers of the Revolution," his appeal to history was vitiated by special pleading. In his most elaborate review of the precedents (the article in *Harper's Magazine* from which quotations have already been taken), he passed over in silence the Northwest Ordinance of 1787, with its clear-cut congressional ban on slavery.[45] Douglas chose instead to dwell at length upon the "Jeffersonian Plan of government for the Territories," embodied in the Ordinance of 1784.[46] This plan, it is true, treated the territories as virtually equal with the member states of the Union, and thus supported (as against subsequent enactments) Douglas' plea for the largest measure of local self-government. When, however, Douglas went on to imply that the "Jeffersonian Plan" precluded, in principle, any congressional interference with slavery in the territories, he was guilty of outright misrepresentation. Jefferson's original draft (still extant in his own hand) included a forthright prohibition of slavery in all the territories.[47] The Continental Congress, it is true, refused at the time to adopt this particular provision, a fact that Douglas mentioned,[48] but there is no evidence whatever to show that they believed they lacked the power to do so. Three years later, the same body exercised this very power by unanimous vote of the eight states present.[49]

Disingenuousness reached its peak in Douglas' assertion that the Ordinance of 1784 "stood on the statute book unrepealed and irrepealable . . . when, on the 14th day of May, 1787, the Federal Convention assembled at Philadelphia and proceeded to form the Constitution under which we now live." [50] Unrepealed the ordinance still was, and likewise unimplemented, but irrepealable it was not. Sixty days later, on July 13, 1787, Congress repealed it outright and substituted in its place the Northwest Ordinance,[51] which Douglas chose not to discuss.

Despite these lapses, Douglas was, in truth, basing his doctrine upon one undeniably important element in the historic tradition of American political philosophy. In 1860 he was the only thoroughgoing advocate of local self-determination and local autonomy. He could justly maintain that he was upholding this particular aspect of the constitutional tradition not only against the conservatives and the Republicans, but also (and most emphatically) against the southern wing of his own party, which bitterly repudiated the whole notion of local self-government, when it meant that the people of a territory might exclude slavery from their midst.

This brings us to the fourth of the parties that contested the election of 1860, and to the third and last of the answers that were given to the question of where the Constitution placed the power to deal with slavery in the territories.

At first glance there would appear to be only two possible answers. Either the power of decision lay with the federal government, to which the territories had been ceded or by which they had been acquired; or else the decision rested with the people of the territories, by virtue of some inherent right of self-government. Neither answer, however, was acceptable to the proslavery forces. By the later 1850's they were committed to a third doctrine, state sovereignty.

The theory of state sovereignty takes on a deceptive appearance of simplicity in most historical accounts. This is because it is usually examined only in the context of the secession crisis. In that situation the corollaries drawn from the theory of state sovereignty were, in fact, exceedingly simple. If the Union was simply a compact among states that retained their ultimate sovereignty, then one or more of them could legally and peacefully withdraw from it, for reasons which they, as sovereigns, might judge sufficient. Often overlooked is the fact that secession itself was responsible for reducing the argument over state sovereignty to such simple terms. The right to secede was only one among many corollaries of the complex and intricate doctrine of the sovereignty of the states. In the winter and spring of 1860–1861, this particular corollary, naked and alone, became the issue on which events turned. Earlier applications of the doctrine became irrelevant. As they dropped from view, they were more or less forgotten. The theory of state sovereignty came to be regarded simply as a theory that had to do with the perpetuity of the Union.

The simplicity of the theory is, however, an illusion. The illusion is a consequence of reading history backward. The proslavery constitutional argument with respect to slavery in the territories cannot possibly be understood if the fifteen years of debate prior to 1860 are regarded simply as a dress rehearsal for secession. When applied to the question of slavery, state sovereignty was a positive doctrine, a doctrine of power, specifically, a doctrine designed to place in the hands of the slaveholding states a power sufficient to uphold slavery and promote its expansion *within* the Union. Secession might be an ultimate recourse, but secession offered no answer whatever to the problems of power that were of vital concern to the slaveholding states so long as they remained in the Union and used the Constitution as a piece of working machinery.

As a theory of how the Constitution should operate, as distinguished from a theory of how it might be dismantled, state sovereignty gave its own distinctive answer to the question of where the authority lay to deal with matters involving slavery in the territories. All such authority, the theory insisted, resided in the sovereign states. But how, one may well ask, was such authority to be exercised? The answer was ingenious. The laws that maintained slavery — which were, of course, the laws of the slaveholding states — must be given extraterritorial or extrajurisdictional effect.[52] In other words, the laws that established a property in slaves were to be respected, and if necessary enforced, by the federal government, acting as agent for its principals, the sovereign states of the Union.

At the very beginning of the controversy, on January 15, 1847, five months after the introduction of the Wilmot Proviso, Robert Barnwell Rhett of South Carolina showed how that measure could be countered, and proslavery demands supported, by an appeal to the *mystique* of the sovereignty of the several states:

> Their sovereignty, unalienated and unimpaired . . . , exists in all its plenitude over our territories; as much so, as within the limits of the States themselves. . . . The only effect, and probably the only object of their reserved sovereignty, is, that it secures to each State the right to enter the territories with her citizens, and settle and occupy them with their property — with whatever is recognised as property by each State. The ingress of the citizen, is the ingress of his sovereign, who is bound to protect him in his settlement.[53]

Nine years later the doctrine had become the dominent one in proslavery thinking, and on January 24, 1856, Robert Toombs of Georgia summed it up succinctly: "Congress has no power to limit, restrain, or in any manner to impair slavery: but, on the contrary, it is bound to protect and maintain it in the States where it exists, and wherever its flag floats, and its jurisdiction is paramount." [54] In effect, the laws of slavery were to become an integral part of the laws of the Union, so far as the territories were concerned.

Four irreconcilable constitutional doctrines were presented to the American people in 1860. There was no consensus, and the stage was set for civil war. The issues in which the long controversy culminated were abstruse. They concerned a seemingly minor detail of the constitutional system. The arguments that supported the various positions were intricate and theoretical. But the abstractness of constitutional issues has nothing to do, one way or the other, with the role they may happen to play at a moment of crisis. The sole question is the load that events have laid upon them. Thanks to the structure of the American constitutional system itself, the abstruse issue of slavery in the territories was required to carry the burden of well-nigh all the emotional drives, well-nigh all the political economic tensions, and well-nigh all the moral perplexities that resulted from the existence in the United States of an archaic system of labor and an intolerable policy of racial subjection. To change the metaphor, the constitutional question of legislative authority over the territories became, so to speak, the narrow channel through which surged the torrent of ideas and interests and anxieties that flooded down from every drenched hillside upon which the storm cloud of slavery discharged its poisoned rain.

NOTES

1. A contrary view is advanced by Sidney Hook: "The validity of the historian's findings will . . . depend upon his ability to discover a method of roughly measuring the relative strength of the various factors present." (Social Science Research Council, Bulletin 54, *Theory and Practice in Historical Study: A Report of the Committee on Historiography* [New York, 1946], 113.) Hook, writing as a philosopher, insists that his criterion is part of the "pattern of inquiry which makes a historical account scientific." (*Ibid.,* 112.) But, as another philosopher, Ernest Nagel, points out, "the natural sciences do not appear to require the imputation of relative importance to the causal variables that occur in their explanations." On the contrary, "if a phenomenon occurs only when certain conditions are realized, all these conditions are equally essential, and no one of them can intelligibly be regarded as more basic than the others." (Ernest Nagel, "Some Issues in the Logic of Historical Analysis," *Scientific Monthly,* LXXIV [Mar. 1952], 162–69, esp. 167.)
2. Alexander H. Stephens, *A Constitutional View of the Late War between the States* (2 vols., Philadelphia, 1868–70), *I,* 542.
3. Charles A. and Mary R. Beard, *The Rise of American Civilization* (2 vols., New York, 1927), *II,* 40, 42.
4. Ulrich B. Phillips, *The Course of the South to Secession,* ed. E. Merton Coulter (New York, 1939), 152.
5. William Blackstone, *Commentaries on the Laws of England* (4 vols., Oxford, Eng., 1765–69), *I,* 49.
6. Joint Resolution to Amend the Constitution, Mar. 2, 1861, 12 US Statutes at Large 251. It passed the House by a vote of 133 to 65 on February 28, 1861, and the Senate by a vote of 24 to 12 on the night of March 3–4, 1861. Technically, the sitting of March 2, 1861, was still in progress in the Senate, hence the date attached to the joint resolution as officially published. (*Congressional Globe,* 36 Cong., 2 sess., 1285, 1403 [Feb. 28, Mar. 2, 1861].)
7. First inaugural address, Mar. 4, 1861, *The Collected Works of Abraham Lincoln,* ed. Roy P. Basler *et al.* (9 vols., New Brunswick, N.J., 1953–55), *IV,* 270.
8. Ohio on May 13, 1861, Maryland on Jan. 10, 1862, Illinois on Feb. 14, 1862. (Herman V. Ames, *The Proposed Amendments to the Constitution of the United States during the First Century of Its History, Annual Report, American Historical Association, 1896* [2 vols., Washington, D.C., 1897], *II,* 363.)
9. Of the 3,953,760 slaves in the United States in 1860, 2,174,996 were held in the 9 states of Kentucky, Tennessee, Florida, Alabama, Mississippi, Missouri, Arkansas, Louisiana, and Texas. (US, Ninth Census [1870], Vol. I, *The Statistics of the Population* [Washington, D.C., 1872], 3–8 [a corrected recompilation of previous census figures].)

10. US Constitution, Art. I, Sec. 8 [clause 3].
11. The area of so-called "continental" United States (exclusive of Alaska as well as of Hawaii) is officially put at 3,022,387 square miles. It attained this size in 1854. More than two-fifths of this area, that is, 1,234,381 square miles, is conventionally regarded as having been acquired through the annexation of Texas by joint resolution in 1845, the partition of the Oregon country by agreement with Great Britain in 1846, the cessions from Mexico by the treaty ending the Mexican War in 1848, and the additional territory acquired from the latter country by the Gadsden Purchase of 1853–1854. The conventional reckoning (which disregards all the complex questions created by prior American claims) is given in US Bureau of the Census, *Historical Statistics of the United States, Colonial Times to 1957: A Statistical Abstract Supplement* (Washington, D.C., 1960), 236.
12. This was the form in which the proviso was adopted by the House on February 15, 1847. (*Congressional Globe*, 29 Cong., 2 sess., 424–25 [Feb. 15, 1847].) In its original form, as moved by David Wilmot of Pennsylvania on August 8, 1846, and adopted by the House the same day, it spoke only of "the acquisition of any territory from the Republic of Mexico." (*Ibid.*, 29 Cong., 1 sess., 1217 [Aug. 8, 1846].)
13. Ostend Manifesto (actually dated at Aix-la-Chapelle), Oct. 18, 1854, *The Ostend Conference, &c.* (*House Executive Documents*, 33 Cong., 2 sess., *X*, No. 93), 131. Though the Secretary of State, William L. Marcy, was forced by public opinion to repudiate the manifesto, James Buchanan was helped to the presidency in 1857 by the fact that his signature was on it.
14. *Collected Works of Lincoln*, ed. Basler *et al.*, *IV*, 154, 155, 172. It should be noted that Stephen A. Douglas, in his third debate with Lincoln, at Jonesboro, Illinois, on September 15, 1858, declared in forthright language that the doctrine of popular sovereignty ought to apply "when we get Cuba" and "when it becomes necessary to acquire any portion of Mexico or Canada, or of this continent or the adjoining islands." (*Ibid.*, *III*, 115.) The word was "when," not "if."
15. Lincoln to Seward, Feb. 1, 1861, *ibid.*, *IV*, 183.
16. At the beginning of 1845 the United States comprised approximately 1,788,000 square miles (exclusive of its claims in the Oregon country). Of this total, 945,000 square miles were within the boundaries of the 26 full-fledged states of the Union; another 329,000 square miles belonged to organized territories; and the remaining 514,000 square miles were without organized civil governments. At the end of 1854 the total area had increased to approximately 3,022,000 square miles, of which 1,542,000 lay within the 31 states that were now members of the Union (Florida, Texas, Iowa, Wisconsin, and California having been admitted during the decade); another 1,410,000 square miles belonged to organized territories; and only 70,000 square miles remained in the unorganized Indian Territory. Boundaries are shown in Charles O. Paullin and John K. Wright, *Atlas of the Historical Geography of the United States* (Washington, D.C., 1932), plates 63A and 63B (for the situation in 1845), plates 63B, 64A, and 64C (for 1854).
17. In his first inaugural, Lincoln reiterated a statement he had made earlier in his debates with Douglas: "I have no purpose, directly or indirectly, to interfere with the institution of slavery in the States where it exists. I believe I have no lawful right to do so, and I have no inclination to do so." (*Collected Works of Lincoln*, ed. Basler *et al.*, *IV*, 263.) The statement was originally made in the debate at Ottawa, Illinois, August 21, 1858. (*Ibid.*, *III*, 16; see also the discussion of the proposed constitutional amendment of Mar. 2, 1861, above, notes 6–8.)
18. US, Eighth Census (1860), *Preliminary Report on the Eighth Census, 1860* (Washington, D.C., 1862), 131; confirmed in the final report, *Population of the United States in 1860* (Washington, D.C., 1864), 598–99. Slaves were recorded in only three territories: fifteen in Nebraska, twenty-nine in Utah, and two in Kansas; a total of forty-six. Certain unofficial preliminary reports gave slightly higher figures: ten slaves in Nebraska, twenty-nine in Utah, twenty-four in New Mexico, and none in Kansas; a total of sixty-three. (*American Annual Cyclopaedia, 1861* [New York, 1862], 696.) It should be noted that the census figures for 1860 were tabulated in terms of civil divisions as they existed early in 1861. Thus Kansas was listed as a state, though it was not admitted until January 29, 1861, and statistics were presented for the territories of Colorado, Dakota, and Nevada, though these were organized only in February and March 1861.
19. Census figures for the six states admitted from 1846 to 1861, inclusive (Iowa, Wisconsin, California, Minnesota, Oregon, and Kansas), and for the seven organized territories enumerated in the census of 1860 (Colorado, Dakota, Nebraska, Navada, New Mexico, Utah, and Washington) showed an aggregate of 2,305,096 white persons, 7,641 free persons of color, and 46 slaves; making a total (including also "civilized Indians" and "Asiatics") of 2,382,677 persons. (Eighth Census [1860], *Population*, 598–99.) Ironically enough, the aborigines in the Indian Territory held in slavery almost as many Negroes as were to be found, slave or free, in the entire area just specified. (Eighth Census [1860], *Preliminary Report*, 136.) This special tabulation for the Indian Territory (not incorporated in the regular census tables) showed 65,680 Indians, 1,988 white persons, 404 free colored persons, and 7,369 slaves.
20. James G. Blaine, *Twenty Years of Congress* (2 vols., Norwich, Conn., 1884), *I*, 272, quoting an unnamed "representative from the South."
21. James G. Randall, *The Civil War and Reconstruction* (Boston, 1937), 114–15. In a later work, Randall

described the issue of slavery in the territories, when debated by Lincoln and Douglas in 1858, as "a talking point rather than a matter for governmental action, a campaign appeal rather than a guide for legislation." (*Lincoln the President* [4 vols., New York, 1945–55], *I*, 125.)

22. As I have written elsewhere: "The fact that the controversy of 1846–1860 turned on the extension of slavery to the territories (and, to a lesser extent, on the fugitive-slave law) showed that antislavery leaders, far from flouting the Constitution, were showing it a punctilious respect. Had they been disposed, as their opponents alleged, to ride roughshod over constitutional imitations, they would hardly have bothered with the question of the territories or the question of fugitive slaves." (Arthur Bestor, "State Sovereignty and Slavery," *Journal of the Illinois State Historical Society, LIV* [Summer 1961], 127.)
23. The failure of the Republicans to mount a frontal attack upon slavery in the slaveholding states seemed to the Beards sufficient reason for treating the attack upon slavery as hardly more than a sham battle. Secession, they argued, was the southern planters' "response to the victory of a tariff and homestead party that proposed nothing more dangerous to slavery itself than the mere exclusion of the institution from the territories." (Beard, *Rise of American Civilization, II*, 37, see also 39–40.)
24. First debate with Douglas, Ottawa, Ill., Aug. 21, 1858, *Collected Works of Lincoln*, ed. Basler *et al., III*, 18 (italics of the original not reproduced here).
25. "Declaration of the Immediate Causes which Induce and Justify the Secession of South Carolina from the Federal Union," Dec. 24, 1860, *Journal of the Convention of the People of South Carolina, Held in 1860, 1861 and 1862* (Columbia, S. C., 1862), 465.
26. *Collected Works of Lincoln*, ed. Basler *et al., III*, 18.
27. First inaugural, Mar. 4, 1861, *ibid., IV*, 270; see also above, notes 6–8.
28. In the US Constitution the only reference to the slave trade is in a provision suspending until 1808 the power of Congress to prohibit "the Migration or Importation" of slaves. (Art. I, Sec. 9 [clause 1].) The power itself derives from the commerce clause (Art. I, Sec. 8 [clause 3]), and Congress is not required to use it. By contrast, the Confederate Constitution not only announced that the foreign slave trade "is hereby forbidden," but also went on to *require* its Congress to pass the necessary enforcement laws. (Constitution of the Confederate States, Art. I, Sec. 9 [clause 1]; text in Jefferson Davis, *The Rise and Fall of the Confederate Government* [2 vols., New York, 1881], *I*, 657.)
29. US Constitution, Art. I, Sec. 8 [clause3].
30. In 1840 there were 448,743 slaves in Alabama and Mississippi, as against 448,987 in Virginia. In 1860 there were 871,711 slaves in the two Gulf States, as against only 490,865 in Virginia. During the same twenty years there was a net increase of 365,911 in the white population of the two Gulf States, and a net increase of 306,331 in the white population of Virginia. (US, Ninth Census [1870], *I, Population*, 3–8.)
31. Last of the eight resolutions introduced in the Senate by Henry Clay, *Congressional Globe*, 31 Cong., 1 sess., 246 (Jan. 29, 1850). According to Clay himself, the resolution proposed no new legislation, but merely asserted "a truth, established by the highest authority of law in this country." He expected, he said, "one universal acquiescence." (*Ibid.*)
32. 9 Wheaton *1* (1824).
33. *Champion* v. *Ames,* 188 US Reports 321 (1903).
34. US Constitution, Art. IV, Sec. 2 [clause 3].
35. *Prigg* v. *Pennsylvania,* 16 Peters 539 (1842).
36. South Carolina, "Declaration," Dec. 24, 1860, *Journal of the Convention,* 464.
37. In 1844, to be sure, the Liberty party solemnly repudiated this specific obligation: "We hereby give it to be distinctly understood, by this nation and the world, that, as abolitionists, . . . we owe it to the Sovereign Ruler of the Universe, as a proof of our allegiance to Him, in all our civil relations and offices, whether as private citizens, or as public functionaries sworn to support the Constitution of the United States, to regard and to treat the [fugitive slave clause] of that instrument . . . as utterly null and void, and consequently as forming no part of the Constitution of the United States, whenever we are called upon, or sworn, to support it." (*National Party Platforms, 1840–1956*, ed. Kirk H. Porter and Donald B. Johnson [Urbana, Ill., 1956], 8.) Lincoln, on the other hand, solemnly reminded the nation in his first inaugural that public officials "swear their support to the whole Constitution — to this provision as much as to any other." (*Collected Works of Lincoln,* ed. Basler *et al., IV*, 263.)
38. US Constitution, Art. IV, Sec. 3 [clause 2].
39. *Congressional Globe*, 36 Cong., 2 sess., 114 (Dec. 18, 1860).
40. *National Party Platforms,* ed. Porter and Johnson, 27. This argument from the due process clause went back at least as far as the Liberty party platform of 1844. (*Ibid.,* 5.) It was reiterated in every national platform of an antislavery party thereafter: in 1848 by the Free Soil party, in 1852 by the Free Democrats, and in 1856 and 1860 by the Republicans. (*Ibid.,* 13, 18, 27, 32.)
41. *Ibid.,* 13. Repeated in the Free Democratic platform of 1852. (*Ibid.,* 18.)
42. Stephen A. Douglas, "The Dividing Line between Federal and Local Authority: Popular Sovereignty in the Territories," *Harper's Magazine, XIX* (Sept. 1859), 519–37, esp. 526.
43. *Ibid.,* 520–21.
44. Douglas insisted that this clause referred "exclusively to property in contradistinction to persons and communities." (*Ibid.,* 528.)

45. He likewise ignored all subsequent enactments of the same sort, save to register agreement with the dictum of the Supreme Court, announced in the Dred Scott opinion, that the Missouri Compromise had always been unconstitutional. (*Ibid.*, 530.)
46. *Ibid.*, 525–26.
47. Report to Congress, Mar. 1, 1784, and revised report, Mar. 22, 1784, *The Papers of Thomas Jefferson*, ed. Julian P. Boyd *et al.* (16 vols., Princeton, N. J., 1950–), *VI*, 604, 608.
48. Douglas, "Federal and Local Authority," 526. The antislavery provision came to a vote in the Continental Congress on April 19, 1784, under a rule requiring the favorable vote of the majority of the states for adoption. Six states voted in favor of the provision, only three against it. One state was divided. Another state could not be counted, because a quorum of the delegation was not present, but the single delegate on the floor voted "Aye." (*Journals of the Continental Congress,* ed. Worthington C. Ford *et al.* [34 vols., Washington, D.C., 1904–37], *XXVI,* 247.)
49. *Ibid., XXXII,* 343. This was the vote on July 13, 1787, adopting the Ordinance of 1787 with its antislavery article; only one member voted against the ordinance. There is no evidence of opposition to the antislavery article itself, which was added as an amendment in the course of the preceding debate.
50. Douglas, "Federal and Local Authority," 526.
51. *Journals of the Continental Congress,* ed. Ford *et al., XXXII,* 343. As if anticipating Douglas' contention that the earlier ordinance was "irrepealable," the Congress that had adopted it not only repealed it, but declared it "null and void."
52. These terms were suggested, and their propriety defended, in my article, "State Sovereignty and Slavery," 128–31, 147.
53. *Congressional Globe,* 29 Cong., 2 sess., Appendix, 246 (Jan. 15, 1847).
54. Speech in Boston, reprinted in an appendix to Stephens, *Constitutional View, I,* 625–47, esp. 625.

Lincoln and the Civil War

The sectional crisis that culminated in the Civil War elevated Abraham Lincoln to prominence. Lincoln was an enigma to many of his contemporaries, and he is an enigma to us today. On the one hand, he is America's secular saint; but he was also an opportunistic politician. He was the defender of the common man; but he was also a lawyer for the powerful Illinois Central Railroad. He was the Great Emancipator; but he was a southerner by birth with many of the racial prejudices of that section's poor white class. He was a rock of strength for the Union; but his own youth was full of uncertainties and self-doubts.

Much of our fascination with Lincoln grows out of these ambiguities in his career and personality. It also grows out of the drama of the Civil War. No event in our history has exerted the same allure as this great crisis of the Union. The very survival of the nation was at stake, and every twist and turn of events seems portentous. Even the intricacies of national finance, or military logistics, or diplomatic negotiations — historical details that often seem arid and tedious for other periods of time — take on a special interest for the Civil War. The man who stood at the helm in this American *Iliad* inevitably becomes a figure larger than life.

It is difficult sometimes to get behind this image to the man himself and to the realities of his achievements. One of the most successful attempts in brief compass is the following essay by Professor David Donald. Donald is obviously aware of Lincoln's greatness, but he also recognizes that part of this, indeed an essential prerequisite to it, was his ability to manipulate the political levers. Lincoln, in a word, was not only a "statesman," he was also that much-maligned figure in our political mythology, a clever politician. Part of that astuteness was his success in creating, even among his contemporaries, the illusion of simplicity, guilelessness, and utter sincerity. It is clear that some of the difficulties we experience in perceiving the real man we can blame on the careful work of Abraham Lincoln himself.

FOR FURTHER READING:

CURRENT, RICHARD N. *Lincoln and the First Shot.* Philadelphia: J. B. Lippincott Company, 1963.*
NEVINS, ALLAN. *The War for the Union.* 2 vols. New York: Charles Scribners' Sons, 1959, 1960.*
THOMAS, BENJAMIN. *Abraham Lincoln: A Biography.* New York: Random House, Modern Library, 1968.*

Asterisk denotes paperback edition.

A. Lincoln, Politician   DAVID DONALD

The statesmanship of Abraham Lincoln is so widely recognized as to require no defense. But it is not always realized that Lincoln's opportunities for statesmanship were made possible by his accomplishments as a politician. Perhaps it is too cynical to say that a statesman is a politician who succeeds in getting himself elected President. Still, but for his election in 1860, Lincoln's name would appear in our history books as that of a minor Illinois politician who unsuccessfuly debated with Stephen A. Douglas. And had the President been defeated in 1864, he would be written off as one of the great failures of the American political system — the man who let his country drift into civil war, presided aimlessly over a graft-ridden administration, conducted an incompetent and ineffectual attempt to subjugate the Southern states, and after four years was returned by the people to the obscurity that he so richly deserved.

Lincoln's fame, then, was made possible by his success as a politician, yet in many of the techniques used by present-day political leaders he was singularly ineffectual. He never succeeded in selling himself — to the press, to the politicians, or to the people. To a public-relations expert, the Lincoln story would seem a gift from heaven. Like a skillful organist playing upon the keyboard of popular emotion, he could pull out the sentimental tremolo for Lincoln's humble origins, for his hardscrabble Kentucky and Indiana childhood, for his Illinois rise from rags to respectability. A good publicity man would emphasize Lincoln's sense of humor (but, as a recent campaign has demonstrated, he should not overemphasize it), his down-to-earth folksiness, his sympathy for the oppressed. Appealing to the traditional American love of a fighter, especially an underdog, he could capitalize upon the virulent assaults of Lincoln's political enemies. The whole campaign, if managed by a Batten, Barton, Durstine & Osborn agent, should have been as appealing, as saccharine, as successful as the famous 1952 television appearance of our current Vice President.

In Lincoln's case, however, astonishingly little use was made of these sure-fire appeals — and when they were used, they backfired. The President said that he was a man of humble origins — and his opponents declared that, as Southern poor white trash, he was still cowed by the slaveholders and afraid of vigorously prosecuting the war. Lincoln stressed his sense of humor — and even his supporters protested: "... I do wish Abraham would tell fewer dirty stories." Mrs. Lincoln regularly visited the wounded in Washington's hospitals — and hostile newspapers hinted that she was really passing along military secrets to the Confederates.

Lincoln never succeeded in making his own case clear. He had no sounding-board. While Congressmen orated in the Capitol, the President sat gagged in the White House. In the 1860's, convention had it that a President must pretend not to be a politician. After wirepulling for a lifetime to secure the nomination, the successful candidate must be surprised when a committee from his party officially notified him that he was the lucky man. In the campaign that followed, he was supposed to sit indifferently at home, pretending to be a Cincinnatus at the plow, while his fellow citizens, unsolicited, offered him the highest post in the land. And, once in the Executive Mansion, he was to be muffled and dumb.

Source: David Donald, *Lincoln Reconsidered* (New York: Random House, Vintage Books, 1956), chap. 4, "A. Lincoln, Politician," pp. 57–84.

Like most self-made men, Abraham Lincoln was very conventional, and he never challenged the rules of the political game. A strict view of the proprieties prevented President Lincoln from going directly to the people. Although he had made his fame as a public speaker, he never once addressed the Congress in person, but, following Jefferson's example, submitted written messages that dreary clerks droned out to apathetic legislators. Rarely after 1861 did Lincoln make any speeches or public pronouncements. "In my present position," he told a Maryland crowd in 1862, "it is hardly proper for me to make speeches." Later, as candidate for re-election, Lincoln still further limited his utterances. "I do not really think," he said in June 1864, "it is proper in my position for me to make a political speech. . . ." ". . . I believe it is not customary for one holding the office, and being a candidate for re-election, to do so. . . ." During the four years of civil war, the people could hear every strident and raucous voice in America, but not the voice of their President.

The President's negative attitude discouraged support from the press. Although he gave a number of informal interviews, Lincoln held no press conference; reporters were still not considered quite respectable, certainly not worthy of private audience with the President. Newspapermen go where there is news. When a Washington correspondent found the White House well dry, he turned naturally to those running streams of gossip and complaint and criticism and intrigue, the Congressmen, whose anti-Lincoln pronouncements all too often agreed with the prejudices of his editor. Most of the leading American newspapers were anti-Lincoln in 1860, and they remained anti-Lincoln till April 15, 1865, when they suddenly discovered that the President had been the greatest man in the world. There were some notable exceptions, of course — the Springfield *Republican* and the New York *Times*, for example — but even these were handicapped by Lincoln's negative attitude toward the press. As one editor complained: ". . . it is our great desire to sustain the President, and we deplore the opportunity he has let go by, to sustain himself."

But most newspapers had no desire whatever to sustain the President, and they berated Lincoln with virulent obscenity that makes even the anti-Roosevelt campaigns of our own day seem mild. The sixteenth President was abused in the newspapers as "a slang-whanging stump speaker," a "half-witted usurper," a "mole-eyed" monster with "soul . . . of leather," "the present turtle at the head of the government," "the head ghoul at Washington."

President Lincoln was no more successful with the politicians than with the press. One of the saddest aspects of Civil War history is the sorry failure of Lincoln's appeals for bipartisan support. The Copperheads, outright antiwar Democrats, he could not hope to win, but the enormous mass of the Democratic party was as loyal to the Union as the President himself. On all crucial issues Lincoln was closer to George B. McClellan or Horatio Seymour than to many members of his own party. "In this time of national peril," Lincoln kept saying to such War Democrats, he hoped to meet them "upon a level one step higher than any party platform." He did not expect them to endorse every measure of a Republican regime, but he did wish that " 'the Government' [might] be supported though the administration may not in every case wisely act." So earnestly did he desire the support of an energetic War Democrat like Governor Seymour of New York that in 1862 he sent him a message: if the Governor would help "wheel the Democratic party into line, put down rebellion, and preserve the government," Lincoln said, "I shall cheerfully make way for him as my successor."

Such hopes for bipartisan co-operation were blighted at birth. Governor Seymour regarded Lincoln's offer as a trap, and he spent most of his term in Albany denouncing the corruption and the arbitrary methods of the Lincoln administration. Far from co-operating, Democratic politicians took out time to compare Lincoln with the "original gorilla," a baboon, and a long-armed ape; the more scurrilous elements of the opposition party suggested that the President suffered from unmentionable diseases or that he had Negro blood in his veins.

If the President's failure with the Democrats was to be expected in a country with a vigorous two-party tradition, his inability to influence leaders of his own party was a more serious weakness. In Washington, reported Richard Henry Dana, author of *Two Years before the Mast*, "the most striking thing is the absence of personal loyalty to the President. It does not exist. He has no admirers, no enthusiastic supporters, none to bet on his head." Republican critics openly announced that Lincoln was "unfit," a "political coward," a "dictator," "timid and ignorant," "pitiable," "too slow," a man of "no education," "shattered, dazed, utterly foolish." "He is ignorant, self-willed, & is surrounded by men some of whom are almost as ignorant as himself," historian George Bancroft declared. Republican editor Murat Halstead thought Lincoln "an awful, woeful ass," and a correspondent of the Chicago *Tribune* said that "Buchanan seems to have been a granite pillar compared to the 'Good natured man' without any spinal column. . . ." Republican Senator James W. Grimes of Iowa felt that Lincoln's "entire administration has been a disgrace from the very beginning to every one who had any thing to do with bringing it into power."

From the beginning the President and his own party leaders in Congress were often at loggerheads. Radicals and Conservatives, former Whigs and ex-Democrats, Easterners and Westerners, all viewed Lincoln with suspicion. Such a situation is, of course, fairly normal in American politics. As our major parties consist of conflicting interest groups bound together by political expediency rather than by ideology, a President is bound constantly to disappoint nine tenths of the voters who elected him. But in Lincoln's case the situation was more serious because he seemed unable to build up any personally loyal following. Nearly every important Republican leader — Chase, Sumner, Greeley, Stevens, Wade, Davis, Chandler, Browning, Grimes, Weed — doubted the advisability of a second term for Lincoln. When a Pennsylvania editor visited the Capitol in 1864 and asked to meet some Congressmen who favored the President's renomination, old Thad Stevens stumped over to Representative Isaac N. Arnold of Illinois, announcing: "Here is a man who wants to find a Lincoln member of Congress. You are the only one I know and I have come over to introduce my friend to you."

A failure with the press and the politicians, Lincoln is said by sentimentalists to have won the favor of the common people. This stereotype, so comforting to those who like to believe in the democratic dogma, started with Lincoln himself. When Congressmen and editors erupted in a frenzy of anti-Lincoln fury, the President liked to reflect that the "politicians" could not "transfer the people, the honest though misguided masses" to their course of opposition. Lincoln felt that he understood the mind of the masses. Day after day he greeted the throngs of visitors, petitioners, and office-seekers who besieged him in the White House, and he claimed that these "public-opinion baths" helped him sense the popular will. In return for his sympathy, the President felt, he received popular support. His private secretary, John Hay, echoed Lincoln's belief: "The people know what they want and will have it" — namely, a re-election of the President in 1864.

In fact, though, the evidence for Lincoln's enormous popular appeal during the war is sketchy and unreliable. One could quote, for instance, Congressman Lewis D. Campbell's opinion of the 1864 election: "Nothing but the undying attachment of our people to the Union has saved us from terrible disaster. Mr. Lincolns popularity had nothing to do with it. . . ." More convincing, however, than such impressionistic evidence are the actual election returns. Lincoln was a minority President in 1861. His party lost control of the crucial states of New York, Pennsylvania, Ohio, Indiana, and Illinois in the off-year elections of 1862. And in 1864 — when all the Southern states were out of the Union and, of course, not voting — Northerners, given a chance to demonstrate their alleged enthusiastic support for the President, cast forty-five percent of their ballots against Lincoln and for a Democratic platform that called both his administration and the war for the Union failures. A change of only eighty-three thousand votes — two per cent of the toal — could have meant Lincoln's defeat.

Although Lincoln failed to win the press, the politicians, and the people, he was nevertheless a successful politician. He kept himself and his party in power. He was the first President since Andrew Jackson to win re-election, and his administration began an unbroken twenty-four years of Republican control of the Presidency.

The secret of Lincoln's success is simple: he was an astute and dextrous operator of the political machine. Such a verdict at first seems almost preposterous, for one thinks of Lincoln's humility, so great as to cause his opponents to call him a "Uriah Heep"; of his frankness, which brought him the epithet "Honest Abe"; of his well-known aversion for what he termed the "details of how we get along." Lincoln carefully built up this public image of himself as a babe in the Washington wilderness. To a squabbling group of Pennsylvania party leaders he said ingenuously: "You know I never was a contriver; I don't know much about how things are done in politics. . . ."

Before breaking into tears of sympathy for this innocent among thieves, it is well to review Lincoln's pre-Presidential career. When elected President, he had been in active politics for twenty-six years; politics was his life. "He was an exceedingly ambitious man," his Springfield law partner wrote, "a man totally swallowed up in his ambitions. . . ." "Rouse Mr. Lincoln's peculiar nature in a point where he deeply felt — say in his ambitions — his general greed for office . . . then Mr. Lincoln preferred Abm Lincoln to anybody else." But during his long career in Illinois politics Lincoln had never been chosen to major office by the people of his state; state legislator and one-term member of Congress he was, but never Senator — though he twice tried unsuccessfully — and never governor. Lack of appeal at the polls did not, however, prevent him from becoming the master wirepuller who operated the state political organization first of the Whig party and, after its decay, that of the Republicans. Behind that façade of humble directness and folksy humor, Lincoln was moving steadily toward his object; by 1860 he had maneuvered himself into a position where he controlled the party machinery, platform, and candidates of one of the pivotal states in the Union. A Chicago lawyer who had known Lincoln intimately for three decades summarized these pre-presidential years: "One great public mistake . . . generally received and acquiesced in, is that he is considered by the people of this country as a frank, guileless, and unsophisticated man. There never was a greater mistake. . . . He handled and moved men remotely as we do pieces upon a chess-board."

Lincoln's Illinois record was merely finger exercises to the display of political virtuosity he was to exhibit in the White House. He brought to the Executive office an understanding of the value of secrecy. So close did Lincoln keep his ideas, it can be said that no one of his associates understood him. Herndon concluded that this man was "a profound mystery — an enigma — a sphinx — a riddle . . . incommunicative — silent — reticent — secretive — having profound policies — and well laid — deeply studied plans." Nobody had his complete confidence. His loyal Secretary of the Navy was kept as much in the dark about Lincoln's views as the veriest outsider. "Of the policy of the administration, if there be one," Welles complained, "I am not advised beyond what is published and known to all." Lincoln moved toward his objectives with muffled oars. After ninety years historians are still arguing whether Lincoln arranged for Andrew Johnson to be nominated as his vice-presidential running-mate in 1864. Impressive and suggestive evidence can be cited to show that the President picked the Tennessean — or that he favored someone else entirely.

Lincoln's renowned sense of humor was related to his passion for secrecy. Again and again self-important delegations would descend upon the White House, deliver themselves of ponderous utterances upon pressing issues of the war, and demand point-blank what the President proposed to do about their problems. Lincoln could say much in few words when he chose, but he could also say nothing at great length when it was expedient. His petitioners' request, he would say, reminded him of "a little story," which he would proceed to tell in great detail, accompanied by mimicry and gestures, by hearty slapping of the thigh, by uproarious laughter at the end — at which time he would usher out his callers, baffled and confused by the smoke-screen of good humor, with their questions still unanswered.

Akin to Lincoln's gift for secrecy was his talent for passivity. When he arrived in Washington, he was faced by a crisis not of his own making. Fort Sumter, provocatively located in the harbor of Charleston, the very hotbed of secession, had to be reinforced or evacuated. Reinforcement would be interpreted, not merely by the Confederates but also by large peace-loving elements at the North, as an aggressive act of war; withdrawal would appear to other Northerners a cowardly retreat on the part of a spineless administration. Lincoln considered both alternatives. Characteristically, he sought clear-cut written opinions from his Cabinet advisers on the course to follow — but left his own ideas unrecorded. Characteristically, the whole episode is muffled in a fog of confusion which has produced an interesting argument among later historians. But characteristically, too, Lincoln's final decision was neither to reinforce nor to withdraw; he would merely send food and supplies to the beleaguered Sumter garrison and sit back and wait. His passivity paid off. Confederate hotheads were unable to wait so long as the cool-blooded Northern President, and they fired the first shot at Sumter. To Lincoln's support all elements of Northern society now rallied. "At the darkest moment in the history of the republic," Ralph Waldo Emerson wrote, "when it looked as if the nation would be dismembered, pulverized into its original elements, the attack on Fort Sumter crystallized the North into a unit, and the hope of mankind was saved."

Repeatedly, throughout the war, Lincoln's passive policy worked politically. Because any action would offend somebody, he took as few actions as possible. Outright abolitionists demanded that he use his wartime powers to emancipate the Negroes. Border-state politicians insisted that he protect their peculiar institutions. Lincoln needed the support of both groups; therefore, he did nothing — or, rather, he proposed to colonize the Negroes in Central America, which was as near to nothing as he could come — and awaited events. After two years of hostilities, many even in the South came to see that slavery was doomed, and all the important segments of Northern opinion were brought to support emancipation as a wartime necessity. Only then did Lincoln issue the Emancipation Proclamation.

Along with secrecy and passivity, Lincoln brought to his office an extraordinarily frank pragmatism — some might call it opportunism. Often while in the White House he repeated an anecdote that seemed to have a special meaning for him — how the Irishman who had forsworn liquor told the bartender that he was not averse to having a spot added to his lemonade, "so long as it's unbeknownst to me." Again and again the President showed himself an imitator of his Irish hero. When the Pennsylvania miners broke out in open rebellion against the operation of the draft law in their section, worried Harrisburg officials inquired whether Lincoln would send troops to execute the law. Entrusting nothing to paper, Lincoln sent a confidential messenger to A. K. McClure, the aide of the Pennsylvania governor: "Say to McClure that I am very desirous to have the laws fully executed, but it might be well, in an extreme emergency, to be content with the appearance of executing the laws; I think McClure will understand." McClure did understand, and he made no more than a feeble effort to subdue the miners' revolt, but let the agitation die out of its own accord. Thus, the Lincoln administration won the credit both for preserving the peace and for enforcing the draft.

Lincoln enjoyed a similar pragmatic relationship with his unpleasant and irritable Secretary of War, Edwin M. Stanton. There was a sort of tacit division of labor between these two dissimilar men. Lincoln himself explained the system: ". . . I want to oblige everybody when I can; and Stanton and I have an understanding that if I send an order to him which cannot be consistently granted, he is to refuse it. This he sometimes does." The President then had the pleasant and politically rewarding opportunity of recommending promotions, endorsing pension applications, pardoning deserters, and saving sleeping sentinels, and Stanton, who was something of a sadist, took equal pleasure in refusing the promotions, ignoring the petitions, and executing the delinquent soldiers. While the Secretary received the blame for all the harsh and unpopular acts that war makes necessary, the President acquired a useful reputation for sympathy and generosity.

Valuable as were these negative traits of secrecy, passivity, and pragmatism, Lincoln understood that it was not policies or principles which would cause Congressmen to support his direction of the war. To mobilize votes in Congress, the Head of State must be a practicing Party Leader. Lincoln was a political realist, and he worked with the tools he had at hand. He understood that in a democratic, federal government like ours, patronage is the one sure way of binding local political bosses to the person and principles of the President, and for this reason he used and approved the spoils system.

Lincoln's entire administration was characterized by astute handling of the patronage. Even in picking his Cabinet, he took leaders from all factions of his own party, giving all groups hope but no group dominance. The result was that Cabinet members were so suspicious of each other that they hardly had time to be jealous of the President. It was not efficient administration, for the Secretary of State met with the President privately — to regale him, enemies said, with vulgar stories; the Secretary of War would not discuss his plans in Cabinet meeting because he thought —

with some justice — that his colleagues could not be trusted with secrets; and the Secretary of the Treasury finally refused to attend the "so-called" Cabinet meetings at all. Of all these men, outstanding political leaders in 1860, not one ever became President; in Lincoln's Cabinet they ate one another up.

Even without such competition, a Cabinet officer found his political activity necessarily curbed. The fading of Salmon P. Chase's presidential hopes provides an illuminating insight into Lincoln's use of the appointing power. Self-confident, upright, and able, Chase thought that he had deserved the Republican nomination in 1860, and from the first the Secretary of the Treasury looked upon Lincoln as a well-meaning incompetent. He never saw reason to alter his view. Chase was not a modest man; he was sure of his ability and his integrity, sure that he would make an admirable President. As a senator said: "Chase is a good man, but his theology is unsound. He thinks there is a fourth person in the Trinity" — namely, himself.

The day he became Secretary of the Treasury, Chase began scheming for the 1864 nomination, but he found himself hampered by his ambiguous position in the Cabinet. If his financial planning went wrong, he received the blame; but whenever he achieved a success, in the issue of greenbacks or the sale of bonds, the credit went to the Lincoln administration, not to Chase alone. He converted his numerous Treasury agents into a tightly organized and highly active Chase-for-President league, but as long as he remained in the Cabinet, he could not openly announce his presidential aspirations. To relieve himself from embarrassment, to go into outright opposition to Lincoln, Chase needed to get out of the Cabinet, but an unprovoked resignation would be political suicide, a cowardly evasion of his duties. All through 1863 and 1864, then, Chase wriggled and squirmed. Time after time he cooked up little quarrels over patronage, squabbles over alleged slights, and the like, so that he would have an excuse for resigning. Every time Lincoln blandly yielded the point in dispute and refused to accept Chase's withdrawal. But in June 1864, just after the Republican national convention at Baltimore had renominated Lincoln, Chase once again tried his obstructionist tactics that had worked so well in the past, and he threatened to resign from the Cabinet. This time, to his vast chagrin, it was different, and Lincoln accepted his withdrawal. Now that the race was over, Chase was free to run.

If patronage could close a Cabinet member's mouth, it could open the lips of an editor. James Gordon Bennett, the sinful and unscrupulous editor of the New York *Herald,* was one of the most powerful newspapermen of his day. Spiced with sex and scandal, the *Herald* had the largest circulation of any American newspaper, and it was a potent agency in shaping public opinion. Bennett had opposed Lincoln in 1860, and throughout the war he kept up a criticism that was all the more painful to Lincoln because it was well informed and witty. In 1864 Bennett hoped that Grant would run for President, and he also flirted capriciously with the Democratic nominee, General McClellan. For Lincoln he had no use.

> President Lincoln [read a typical *Herald* editorial] is a joke incarnated. His election was a very sorry joke. The idea that such a man as he should be President of such a country as this is a very ridiculous joke. . . . His inaugural address was a joke, since it was full of promises which he has never performed. His Cabinet is and always has been a standing joke. All his State papers are jokes. . . . His title of "Honest" is a satirical joke. . . . His intrigues to secure a renomination and the hopes he appears to entertain of a re-election are, however, the most laughable jokes of all.

The vote in New York was going to be close, and Lincoln needed the *Herald*'s support. Emissaries went up from Washington to interview the canny Scottish editor and ascertain his price. Bennett's terms were high. "The fact is B. wants attention," Lincoln's agent reported. "He wants recognition — & I think it will pay." A newspaperman before he was anything else, Bennett promised to give the administration's views "a thorough exposition in the columns of the Herald," provided Lincoln and his advisers "would occasionally confidentially make known to him [their] plans." Then, too, the editor, who was barred from polite New York society because of his flagrant immorality and was generally considered "too pitchy to touch," had a hankering for social respectability. When Lincoln's agents approached him, the editor "asked plumply, 'Will I be a welcome visitor at the White House if I support Mr. Lincoln?'" The answer was unequivocally affirmative, and, as proof of his good faith, the President promised to the totally unqualified Bennett an appointment as minister to France. Bennett did not want to go abroad, for he was too busy with his paper, but he did want the social recognition that such an offer implied; he wanted to be able to refuse. The bargain was complete, and the *Herald* abandoned its criticism of the President.

As a practical politician, Lincoln understood that election victories required more than the support of Cabinet officers or newspaper editors. Like a famous New York politician, he knew that "Parties are not built up by deportment, or by ladies' magazines, or gush." In the United States, party machinery is more important than public opinion, and patronage more influential than principles. In recent years American liberal historians, scorning the sordid realities of political life, have pictured Lincoln as somehow above the vulgar party apparatus that elected him, unconcerned with the greasy machinery of party caucuses, conventions, nominations, and patronage. This idea is the political equivalent of the doctrine of the immaculate conception. Lincoln himself would have been astonished at it. Politics was his life, and he was a regular party man. Long before he became President, Lincoln said that "the man who is of neither party is not, and cannot be, of any consequence" in American life. As Chief Executive, he was a party President, and he proudly claimed that his had "distributed to its party friends as nearly all the civil patronage as any administration ever did."

Lincoln believed in party regularity. In 1864 there was much discontent in New York with Representative Roscoe Conkling, a Radical Republican who sought reelection, and more moderate party members threatened to bolt the ticket. Conkling was no personal friend of Lincoln's. Boasting the "finest torso" in American political life, he used to descend upon the harried inmate of the White House and, with his wilting contempt, "his haughty disdain, his grandiloquent swell, his majestic, supereminent, turkey-gobbler strut," proceed to lecture the President on how to conduct the war. But Conkling in 1864 was the regular nominee of the New York Republican Party, and the President wrote a public letter to aid him:

> . . . I am for the regular nominee in all cases; . . . and no one could be more satisfactory to me as the nominee in that District, than Mr. Conkling. I do not mean to say that there [are] not others as good as he is in the District; but I think I know him to be at least good enough.

Lincoln made the politicos pay for his support. They could vote against administration bills and they could grumble in Capitol cloakrooms about presidential "imbecility," but he expected them to support his renomination. Those who refused were cut off from patronage and promotion. When Senator Samuel C. Pomeroy of Kansas tried to organize the Chase boom in 1864, every patronage plum in his state was snatched from his greedy hands. After a few months of dignified hostility, Pomeroy sidled up to the White House and begged forgiveness. But Lincoln, who could be so forgiving to sleeping sentinels and deserting soldiers, had no mercy for defecting politicians, and Pomeroy went hungry.

Using the sure goad of patronage, Lincoln's agents early in 1864 began lining up delegates to the Republican national convention. Before the other presidential hopefuls knew that the round-up had begun, Lincoln had corralled enough votes to insure his renomination. The work of the Lincoln men in a state like New Hampshire is instructive. Dignified Salmon P. Chase was making eyes toward this state where he had been born, but while he was still flirting at a gentlemanly distance, New Hampshire eloped with Lincoln. Shrewd Lincoln agents, dispensing patronage to the faithful and threats of punishment to the disobedient, moved in on the state convention at Concord in January 1864 and rushed through a resolution calling for Lincoln's renomination. They permitted New Hampshire Republicans to mention their native son, Chase, in the state platform — but only in order to urge that he clean up the corruption in his Treasury Department.

Everywhere it was the same — Connecticut, Pennsylvania, New York, and even Chase's own Ohio. From state after state Chase's friends protested: "I have never seen such an exhibition of office holders in any convention before." But, packed or not, these conventions chose the delegates to the national assembly at Baltimore. By March Lincoln's renomination was assured, and, with poor grace, Chase was compelled to withdraw from a hopeless contest.

Patronage had helped defeat Lincoln's enemies within the Republican party, and patronage would help defeat the Democratic nominee, George B. McClellan. No one knows how much money the Republicans spent in the 1864 campaign — indeed, no one knows how much either major party has spent in any campaign — but it is certain that a large part of the sum came from assessments levied upon Federal officeholders. A man who received a job from Lincoln might expect to contribute regularly ten per cent of his income to the Republican campaign chest; some gave much more. Henry J. Raymond, chairman of the Republican National Committee, planned systematically to levy upon war contractors, customs officers, and navy-yard employees. When the upright Secretary of the Navy protested this proposal "to take the organization of the navy yard into their keeping, to name the Commandant, to remove the Naval Constructor, to change the regulations, and make the yard a party machine for the benefit of party, and to employ men to elect candidates instead of building ships," Raymond summoned him into the President's office in the White House and gave the Secretary a little lecture on the political facts of life, with Lincoln silently approving each word.

In the long run, though, it took not merely delegates and money but votes to carry the election. During the summer of 1864 the war was going badly. "I am a beaten man," Lincoln said in August, "unless we can have some great victory." As late as October he calculated that he would carry the electoral college by only six votes — three of them from the barren desert of Nevada, which Lincoln leaders in Congress had providently admitted to the Union precisely for such an emergency.

Although propriety prevented him from campaigning, the President personally concerned himself with the turn-out of Republican voters in key states like Indiana, Ohio, Pennsylvania, and New York. Seeing that the Northwestern states were going to show a closely balanced vote, Lincoln wrote in September to General Sherman, whose army was in a tight spot in Georgia: "Any thing you can safely do to let [your] soldiers, or any part of them, go home to vote at the State election, will be greatly in point." Although he added: "This is, in no sense, an order," Lincoln was clearly giving a directive, and it was one that Sherman promptly obeyed. The Republicans carried the Northwest by narrow majorities.

In the East, too, the soldier vote was crucial. Pennsylvania Republicans, fearing defeat, persuaded the President to furlough thousands of soldiers just in time to return home and vote. When the ballots were counted, Lincoln had carried the state by only twenty thousand and would have lost it entirely but for the army. In New York the soldier influence on the election was somewhat different. There, allegedly to prevent rioting, daredevil Republican General Benjamin F. Butler was put in charge of Federal troops and, over the protests of New York officials, he stationed plainclothesmen at the polling-places and had four regiments of troops waiting on ferryboats, ready to "land and march double quick across the island" — just in case there were Democratic disturbances. Some years later, reviewing his career, Butler denied that he had earned his military laurels in the Louisiana campaign. ". . . I do not claim," he said modestly, "to be the hero of New Orleans. Farragut has that high honor; but I do claim to be the hero of New York city in the election of 1864, when they had an honest election, the only one before or since." A Democrat might question the "honesty" of the proceedings, but, under the protection of Federal bayonets, New York went Republican by seven thousand votes.

November 8 was a "rainy, steamy and dark" night in Washington, but politicians gathered in the War Department to await the telegraphic election returns. Most of the visitors were tense, but Abraham Lincoln was relaxed, "most agreeable and genial all the evening." At a little midnight supper he "went awkwardly and hospitably to work shoveling out the fried oysters" to others, and more than once he was reminded of a little story. A mishap to one of the guests brought to mind an anecdote about wrestling which began: "For such an awkward fellow, I am pretty sure-footed. It used to take a pretty dextrous man to throw me." His political management of the Civil War demonstrated that Abraham Lincoln was still sure-footed. By dominating his party, securing a renomination, and winning re-election, a superb politician had gained the opportunity of becoming a superb statesman.

Constitutional Reconstruction

Lee surrendered to Grant at Appomattox on April 9, 1865. In the following few weeks, the last remaining Confederate forces also laid down their arms. The great conflagration was over.

Immense problems remained. An immediate one was how to restore the political relationship between the former Confederate states and the Union. Most northerners rejected the idea that the southern states should be readmitted without penalties. Loyal men had poured out their blood and wealth for four grim years to put down what they insisted was an unjustified rebellion against the most benevolent government on earth. Was it conceivable that all would be forgiven?

To many Unionists certain conditions to readmission seemed essential. Southern leaders, many of whom had been federal officials, had violated their oaths of office in going with the Confederacy. Such traitors could not be allowed to represent the South in a reunited nation. And what about slavery and emancipation? Should not the South be compelled to formally acknowledge the end of slavery and to provide some protection for the newly freed blacks? The Confederate debt seemed a potential problem. It was unendurable for northerners to allow the restored states to pay any part of this debt.

Even before the fighting ended, Lincoln had begun to devise a plan for readmitting the seceded states. His "ten percent plan" of 1864 provided for an easy return of these states. Congress, jealous of its own prerogatives and more intent on punishing traitors, balked at Lincoln's scheme, and in the Wade-Davis Bill of 1864 proposed its own reconstruction blueprint. Lincoln's veto, followed by his assassination, placed the problem squarely in the lap of his successor Vice-President Andrew Johnson. Johnson was not the ideal leader of a nation divided between North and South. He was a southerner by birth, and though he detested secession and despised the planter elite, he possessed all the Negrophobic racial attitudes of the poor white class from which he came. He was also a Democrat with a Republican Congress. Moreover, he was touchy and easily flattered. His sensitivity would embitter his relations with Congress; his susceptibility to flattery would make him succumb to the blandishments of prominent ex-Confederates.

But if the clash of personalities, principles, and jurisdictions contributed to the growing strife between conservatives and radicals, so did the intransigence of the South. Though defeated in battle, southerners were can History-Volume I—0341 concede the need to change in any significant way. In the months following Appomattox, until Congress convened in December 1865, the white South was allowed free reign, under Johnson's lenient reconstruction plan, to put its own house in order. During that time, southern legislatures enacted the Black Codes. These laws, designed to regularize and regulate the new status of freedmen, virtually consigned them to peonage. These same Johnson-plan reconstruction governments selected congressional delegations, often composed of prominent ex-Confederates. Both actions were provocative to northerners who wanted contrition, not self-assertion, from the defeated South.

The beginnings of the confrontation of men and issues are described in the following thoughtful analysis of W. R. Brock, an Englishman, who is able to see the events of Reconstruction with a fresh eye.

FOR FURTHER READING:

Cox, LaWanda and John. *Politics, Principle and Prejudice, 1865–1866: Dilemma of Reconstruction America.* New York: Atheneum Publishers, 1969.*

Donald, David. *The Politics of Reconstruction, 1863–1867.* Baton Rouge: Louisiana University Press, 1968.*

McKitrick, Eric. *Andrew Johnson and Reconstruction.* Chicago: University of Chicago Press, 1960.*

Asterisk denotes paperback edition.

Policies and Possibilities   W. R. BROCK

Three questions lay at the heart of the Reconstruction controversy: who was to control the South, who was to govern the nation, and what was the status of the negro? Like many simple questions they demanded intricate answers and it was an error of Northern opinion to expect easy ones. In May 1865 Sam Wilkinson, of the firm of Jay Cooke, gave a picture of Northern opinion distilled from the reports of some 4,000 loan agents. "The feeling is now general," he wrote, "that the war must be prosecuted until the Rebels lay down their arms and submit to the Government. To the poor deluded soldier in the ranks, pardon — if repentant. To the leaders and their accomplices in Treason, the justice that is due to *Traitors!!* No peace until it can be made a permanent peace — and the feeling is, that peace cannot be permanent with Slavery in the country." This statement was typical of much Northern opinion, and its various elements were to recur again and again with countless variations. Submission and a return to allegiance was the first requisite, and once the Southern armies had laid down their arms this was not difficult to obtain. Indeed the willingness of Southerners to take an oath of allegiance to the United States as the price of amnesty became a source of embarrassment to Northerners who concluded that the formal oath of loyalty was being taken by large numbers who remained at heart enemies of the United States. Allegiance as a legal concept was not enough, but how could it be defined in such a way that it would include those who were loyal at heart and exclude all others? This question was to plague and weaken every Northern plan of Reconstruction. A possible escape from the dilemma seemed to be indicated by Wilkinson's second point, for it might be possible to achieve a workable solution by distinguishing between the mass of the Southern people and their leaders. The North had evolved a convenient theory that the real will of the Southern people had always been in favour of the Union and against se-

---

Source: W. R. Brock, *An American Crisis: Congress and Reconstruction,* 1865–1867 (New York: Harper & Row, Publishers, 1963), chap. 2, "Policies and Possibilities," pp. 15–48.

cession, but that they had fallen under the selfish domination of their aristocratic leaders. There might be ardent secessionists among the men in the ranks, and there might be true Unionists among the leaders, but they did not form the majorities in their respective classes; though some of the wicked might flourish and some of the innocent might suffer, discrimination by class might be the most equitable way of distinguishing the secessionist goats from the deluded sheep. This argument made it necessary to define a leader and here the difficulties began. Every plan of Reconstruction proposed by the two Presidents and by Congress included some scheme for discriminating against Confederate leaders, but the proposals ranged from a narrow schedule which would penalize only those who had held high executive or military rank and members of legislatures to the exclusion of all who had supported the Confederacy. The more far-reaching the proposal for penalization the more difficult it became to provide for law and order in the South, and the more restricted the discrimination the more likely was the South to fall into "disloyal" hands.

The difficulties in devising a programme for penalizing the leaders of secession did not alter the invincible repugnance of Northerners to the idea that Confederate leaders should resume their places of authority in the nation. This was indeed one of the pivots upon which the crisis of Reconstruction turned, and it was one of the common strands which bound together the diverse elements of the Republican party.

The problem was complicated by the myth of Southern Unionism. The favourite belief that many, perhaps the majority, of those fighting for the Confederacy were "deluded" and not true secessionists was supplemented by a persistent conviction that there were large numbers of faithful Unionists in the South, suppressed and persecuted during the war, but ready to step forward and assume the lead. Again it was a common feature in all plans of Reconstruction that power should be transferred to this hard core of real Unionists. Lincoln's ten-per-cent plan implemented this idea, and so, for that matter, did Andrew Johnson while war governor of Tennessee. This transference of power might be effected in Tennessee and Arkansas, where considerable districts had remained Unionist during the war, and might just work in Louisiana if the Unionists could capture the commercial interests of New Orleans; elsewhere in the South it was unlikely to succeed because the Unionists were scattered and drawn from the least educated portions of the population. And even if the Unionists could be placed in power by the authority of the national government they were unlikely to win from former Confederates that degree of respect and consent without which government would be impossible. Was it better to entrust civil government to a despised minority with the support of Federal troops, or to allow the suspect majority to resume or continue the functions of civil government, or to continue unqualified military rule until loyalty had grown deeper roots in the South? And if the South was held in tutelage was this more likely to lead to reconciliation through a change of heart or to permanent alienation? Again the simple expectation led into a bewildering maze of speculation.

The myth of Southern Unionism was but one aspect of Northern ignorance about Southern society. One way or another Northerners had accumulated a good deal of information about the South but much of it came through partisan channels. The pictures drawn by abolitionists, by wartime propaganda, and by genuine Southern loyalists, were unlikely to present the whole truth about the society or the men whom they condemned. A great many Northerners, including some of the politicians, had been in the South as soldiers, but the impressions gathered by armies of occupation are notoriously unreliable as sources of information about conquered peoples. Northern journalists and writers who went South after the war visited it as alien territory — to discover the facts which reinforced preconceived notions about the Southern character — and saw a demoralized and partially ruined society in which it was difficult to distinguish between the effects of war and the consequences of defects in the social system. For most of the time, therefore, Northerners were not only feeling in the dark but in a darkness which they had been taught to despise and attributed to slavery and "aristocracy." Northern congressmen had, however, their own sources of information and during the winter of 1865–6 their desks were being piled high with letters from the South which spoke of secessionism revived, of Unionists ostracized or even persecuted, of negroes denied their rights as free men, and of a bitterness which seemed incompatible with formal professions of allegiance to the United States.

Of all Republican propositions the easiest to state was the obligation to end slavery, and it was not difficult to demonstrate that this was not fulfilled with the formal act of abolition. If the negro was no longer a slave he had still to be made a citizen, and this carried Northern aims into the heart of Southern society. As Carl Schurz observed in his report on the South which President Johnson commissioned and rejected: "The General Government of the republic has, by proclaiming the emancipation of the slaves, commenced a great revolution in the South, but has as yet not completed it. Only the negative part of it is accomplished. The slaves are emancipated in point of form, but free labor has not yet been put in the place of slavery in point of fact. And now, in the midst of this critical period of transition, the power which originated the revolution is expected to turn over its whole future development to another power which from the beginning was hostile to it and has never yet entered into its spirit, leaving the class in whose favor it was made completely without power to protect itself and to take an influential part in that development." In course of time President Johnson was to evolve a theory of Reconstruction by which the whole of congressional policy was the outcome of a Radical conspiracy to force negro suffrage upon the South, and modern writers have added to this a corollary that the motive behind negro suffrage was the wish to fasten the economic domination of the North upon the South. In a sense the Johnson theory was true because abolitionists saw negro suffrage as a necessary element in Reconstruction, but on no point did they find it harder to convince the bulk of the Republican party. Even among the Radicals there was hesitation, and rank and file Republican politicians showed no eagerness to commit themselves. At the close of the war the Republicans could be divided into three main groups: those who carried on with varying degrees of sincerity and enthusiasm the abolitionist quest for racial equality, those who believed in the biological inferiority of the negro and were conscious of the dislike of the negro among their constituents especially in the Midwest, and those who believed in racial equality as an abstract proposition but thought that any attempt to give the negro all the rights of citizens was inexpedient and premature. Most members of the party were, however, able to subscribe to the general proposition that the rights of the negro must be protected against his former masters. Like other simple statements this concealed a multitude of snags and difficulties.

What were the rights which ought to be protected? The majority of Republicans, shirking the difficulties of full equality under the law, attempted to compromise by distinctions between the various kinds of right. There were, ran the theory most popular among moderate Republicans, three kinds of right — civil, political and social. The first ought to be secured to all citizens, the second lay within the discretionary power of State legislatures, and the third — being mainly affected by the private decisions of individuals — was beyond the reach of any law. Civil rights were confined to equal status in courts of law and equal protection outside; political rights included suffrage and the laws for such matters as public transport and public education; social rights were those which individuals could freely accord to or withhold from their fellow citizens when receiving them into their homes, giving them equal participation in business or equal status as labour, or welcoming them into private associations or private schools. Some Republicans could make and adhere to these distinctions to their own satisfaction; others were troubled from the start by the illogicality of declaring that a man was an equal citizen while allowing "political" and social discrimination against him; Radicals such as Sumner and Thaddeus Stevens believed from the start that equal right was an indivisible concept though the latter was prepared to temporize in order to gain a point. Behind the theory of equal right, however subdivided, was a further and major difficulty, for the protection of negro rights was an implicit recognition of his inferiority in society. The Radical answer was that this inferiority was an artificial condition imposed by the slavery, and that once the negro was armed with the rights of a citizen he would raise himself to economic and educational equality; others were not so sure. It was an act of faith to believe in the unproven assumptions of racial equality, and circumstances alone could produce the admission that they were worth a trial. Opportunism brought more men to an acceptance of equal rights than faith in the principle, but it would be an error to discredit the cause because some men came to support it because they believed that it was necessary before they believed that it was right. Few great movements of reform would not be open to the same accusation.

The many variations upon the Republican attitude were in sharp contrast to the theory of State rights. The key doctrine was that the States were indestructible and retained under all circumstances rights which were guaranteed to them under the Constitution. These rights could be changed only by an amendment to the Constitution, and an extreme version of the State rights theory could maintain that even an amendment was unconstitutional if it subtracted from the essential reserved rights of States. Paradoxically the upholders of State rights seized avidly upon the equally mystical doctrine that the Union was indissoluble. Secession was void and must be treated as a nullity; individuals had renounced their allegiance to the United States and had gone into rebellion, but the States could not do this as the war had been fought to prove, and it followed that once individuals had ceased their resistance to lawful authority the rights of States, which were a part of that authority, were resumed without alteration or diminution. The only Reconstruction which was necessary and lawful was for the people in the States to choose a new government and this government would then have exactly the same rights in the Union as loyal States and neither the President nor Congress could impose any conditions which were not already in the Constitution. This theory had a superficial logic for a people accustomed to believe that law was superior to events, but a close examination of its arguments will show an even deeper confusion than that which existed on the Republican side. It pretended that events which were legally void had never happened. It confused the State as a geographical entity, as a government, and as a community of people, and assumed that when the government and people had fought the United States there remained some quality inherent in the land of a State which was different from the will of its people. It failed to recognize that the initiative in remaking the States had to come from somewhere, and that in most of the Southern States there was no effective authority save the occupying armies of the national government. It imagined that a legalistic theory could compel a government with the power to act to acquiesce in chaos or in what its supporters believed to be wrong.

There was moreover one entering wedge which weakened the State rights position, and which appeared to have great force. Emancipation had automatically terminated the provision of the Constitution under which slaves counted as three-fifths of a man in making the count upon which congressional representation was based. If the law took its course without amendment the Southern States, when restored, would find themselves with a handsomely increased congressional apportionment. At the same time it was evident that, if left to themselves, no Southern States would give the vote to any negroes. It could be argued that the Northern States counted unnaturalized foreigners for the purpose of apportionment, but there was a difference between counting those who would probably become qualified voters before the next census and counting those who were considered by their States to be permanently debarred from the suffrage. Calculations varied but it seemed that the South might expect between twelve and twenty additional seats in the House of Representatives, and therefore in the electoral colleges, because of abolition. This was a prospect which even sympathetic Northerners were disposed to regard with alarm.

In point of fact no plan of Reconstruction accepted the State rights theory as its starting-point. Lincoln ignored it and attempted to deal with things as they were. Johnson ignored it when he imposed his own conditions on the South, but invoked it to prevent the Republicans from imposing their conditions. Yet in a sense State rights did lie at the end of every Reconstruction road, for sooner or later the Southern States must be back in the Union with the same rights as all other States. Johnson believed that this must come soon; Radicals believed that it must be delayed until a revolution had been consummated in the South; but both accepted the eventual equality of all States in the Union. This gave a particular flavour to the great debate over Reconstruction because everyone knew that the Southerners must return to Congress (and perhaps with Northern Democrats to control the national government) and that even if they remained there as an isolated group they would have the power to resist amendments to the Constitution. If Republicans could see this danger only too clearly, the sad fragment of the once invincible Democratic party looked eagerly to the promised land; the future of both parties was at stake, and this gave an added bitterness and a frantic urgency to the debates over Reconstruction. The constitutional deduction for Republicans was that any programme which they enacted must be enshrined in amendments to the Constitution and not left at the mercy of future congressional majorities, and thus moderates were driven towards constitutional changes which might otherwise have alarmed them. Whatever policy was agreed would also have to be enacted before the Southerners returned, because future Congresses might be unwilling or unable to pass the necessary laws. The main casualty was any programme of staged development which might lead the negroes from their depressed condition towards full citizenship.

This is the background for the various Reconstruction policies from Lincoln to the Reconstruction Acts. In his Proclamation of 8 December 1863 Lincoln offered a full pardon to all who had participated in the rebellion on condition that they would take an oath of allegiance to the United States and undertake to observe all presidential proclamations respecting slaves. This general amnesty was qualified by a long list of exceptions which excluded from its provisions all who had held positions of authority under the Confederacy or left offices under the United States to join the rebellion. When the loyal portion of the State, so defined, amounted to ten per cent of the votes cast in 1860, this minority could then set up a government which would be recognized by the President as the lawful government of the State. The President would not object to laws affecting the freedmen which "shall recognize and declare their permanent freedom, provide for their education, and which may yet be consistent as a temporary arrangement with their present condition as a laboring, landless, and homeless class." Critics noticed in this the lack of any specific requirement that the freedmen should be given civil rights (though it was recognized that it was difficult to be more precise so long as emancipation depended solely upon a proclamation issued under the war power), and they were disturbed by the President's deliberate sanction to the continuance of pre-war State constitutions and legal codes which had included discriminatory treatment of free negroes. The most striking fact about this ten-per-cent plan was, however, its role in war strategy. In the midst of a war it was extremely useful to set up, in secessionist States, governments which could claim to be loyal; puppet Unionist administrations could give a show of legality to Northern rule in occupied areas, might serve to attract waverers back into the Union fold, and would encourage Unionists still under Confederate rule. These arguments were, however, no longer applicable once the South had surrendered. If the ten-per-cent governments acted as magnets to attract the support of lapsed or defeated Confederates their future might be assured, but they were far more likely to be treated as governments dependent upon Federal arms and composed of discreditable men who had abandoned the cause in the hour of need. Thaddeus Stevens made a cogent criticism of the ten-per-cent plan, as a means of Reconstruction, when he said that "the idea that the loyal citizens, though few, *are the State*, and in State municipalities may overrule and govern the disloyal millions, I have not been able to comprehend. . . . When the doctrine that the *quality* and not the *number* of voters is to decide the right to govern, then we no longer have a Republic but the worst form of despotism. The saints are the salt of the earth, but the 'salt of the earth' do not carry elections and make governments and presidents."

The Wade-Davis Bill of July 1864 is usually contrasted sharply with Lincoln's plan, though Lincoln described himself as "fully satisfied with the system for restoration contained in the bill as one very proper plan for the loyal people of any State choosing to adopt it," and was prepared "to give the Executive aid and assistance to any such people. . . ." Lincoln vetoed the bill because he did not wish to be committed to any one scheme of Reconstruction and because it included a clause emancipating the slaves in the Confederate States which he thought must be done by constitutional amendment. The Wade-Davis plan operated in three stages. The first required an oath to support the Constitution of the United States, and when a majority of white males in a State had taken this oath the next stage of Reconstruction could begin. In the second stage a convention was to be elected by loyal white male citizens who could take the "iron clad" oath of 2 July 1862 which excluded all who had given any aid or support to the rebellion; this convention was to make a Constitution which would exclude from voting for the State legislature or governor all persons who had held "any office, civil or military, except offices merely ministerial, and military offices below the grade of colonel, state or confederate, under the usurping power," to abolish slavery and to repudiate debt incurred under the Confederacy. This Constitution was then to be ratified by a majority of the legal voters as already defined. The third stage was the recognition by the United States (i.e. by President and Congress) of the State government as republican in form. It was specifically stated that the State should then be re-admitted to representation in Congress, but the right of Congress to accept or reject individual senators or representatives was tacitly assumed. The laws of the State, other than slave codes, in force before the rebellion would remain in force except that "the laws for the trial and punishment of white persons shall extend to all persons" and the qualification for jurors should be same as that for voters. The bill then emancipated slaves in the rebel States and imposed penalties upon persons who restrained the liberty of freedmen with the intention of reducing them to involuntary servitude or labour. Looked at in reverse this procedure meant that in taking an oath of allegiance to the United States the majority of former Confederates would give assent to the remaking of the State by the Unionists, to the emancipation of the slaves, to civil rights for the freedmen, and to congressional control over the process of Reconstruction. Once the process of Reconstruction was complete all white males, with the exception of the disqualified classes, would be able to vote though nothing would prevent the convention from imposing restrictions beyond those which were mandatory in the bill.

It was expected that the process laid down in the Wade-Davis Bill would be a slow one, and in no Southern State would the white majority surrender constitution-making power to the Unionists so long as a hope of Confederate victory or of a negotiated peace remained. In the eyes of many Republicans this delay was a merit of the bill. "These States," said Wade, "must remain under military dominion, but I hope with all the equities that can be extended to a people thus unfortunate, until such time as they manifest to the people of the United States that they are able to govern themselves properly and subject to the laws of the General Government. . . . The only sensible plan is to leave these communities until in some way we can have at least reasonable evidence to show that a majority of them are loyal, and in a condition to maintain a free republican government of their own." "Reasonable evidence" would be a willingness on the part of the majority to assent to the procedure laid down by the Wade-Davis Bill. The Bill would have prevented the institution of puppet ten-per-cent governments during the war, but it might not have worked too badly when defeat persuaded a majority of Southerners to agree to any conditions as the price of a return to normal political relations within the Union. It would also have satisfied the Northern demand for the exclusion from public life of the Confederate leaders and for a guarantee of negro civil rights. It did not introduce Negro suffrage which was the ultimate abomination in Southern eyes. The least which can be said of the Wade-Davis Bill is that it would have been better than no plan at all which was what the United States had when Lincoln was assassinated and the war ended.

Lincoln was like a good poker player who had kept his hand concealed, and it will never be known whether it contained a straight flush or a single pair. His last public utterance gave little away, and he had confided in none of his cabinet ministers. The last public address was concerned largely with the question of Louisiana, which had established the most stable of the ten-per-cent governments. Lincoln did not give an unequivocal undertaking to support that government; "as to sustaining it," he said, "my promise is out . . . but, as bad promises are better broken than kept, I shall treat this as a bad promise and break it, whenever I shall be convinced that keeping it is adverse to the public interest; but I have not yet been so convinced." This might be taken as a veiled threat to the Louisiana government that it would have to conform to the wishes of the President in order to keep his support. He seemed then to admit that the Louisiana government was not all that might be desired, but argued that it was probably better to keep it in being as the twelve thousand voters who had supported its constitution would be better encouraged than repelled and demoralized. "We encourage the hearts and nerve the arms of twelve thousand to adhere to their work, and argue for it, and proselyte for it, and fight for it, and feed it, and grow it, and ripen it to a complete success." Whatever the present deficiencies of the Louisiana government it was the best which could be obtained, and might prove to be the nucleus around which the State could re-form as a loyal and acceptable member of the Union. Lincoln's advice was therefore purely empirical, devoted largely to the affairs of one problem child which had advanced a small way along the road to Reconstruction, and offered no solution for those States in which even a ten-per-cent government still lay beyond the range of practical politics. It is untrue to say that Lincoln had a "plan" of Reconstruction; he had certainly announced no method of dealing with the new situation created by the collapse of the South.

In this new situation two plans, poles apart, were to emerge. There was a Radical plan, associated particularly with Thaddeus Stevens, and a conservative plan which was put into operation by President Johnson. Stevens wanted to give the former Confederate States Territorial status without any statement of the conditions under which they would be readmitted to the Union. This would have had some advantages. The status of a Territory was familiar to law and opinion in the United States, it would give to the Territories lacal self-government with their own legislatures, but with governors and officials appointed by the President with the consent of the Senate, while reserving to Congress power to make general laws affecting them. It provided a procedure by which the Territories would submit their constitutions to Congress when applying for statehood. There is no doubt that Stevens intended the period of Territorial status to be employed to reconstruct Southern society; he intended to destroy the power of the Southern ruling class by imposing political disabilities, by confiscating their estates, and by distributing their land among the freedmen to provide the economic basis for a free negro peasantry. Stevens did not favour immediate negro suffrage because he believed that in their present condition the freedmen would fall under the influence of their former masters, but when they had been made economically secure he expected them to be given the vote and assume a Jeffersonian role as cultivators of the soil and bulwarks of political virtue. "This is not a 'white man's Government,' " he said, "this is a man's Government; the Government of all men alike." He did not expect any but white men to be elected to office for "long ages to come" because "the prejudices engendered by slavery would not soon permit merit to be preferred to color. But suffrage would still be beneficial to the weaker races. In a country where political division will always exist, their power joined with just white men, would greatly modify, if it did not entirely prevent, the injustice of majorities." Reconstruction in the South would thus create a new political interest which would act as a safeguard for the Union and a pillar of support for the party of the Union. The plan proposed by Stevens had the advantage of letting everyone know where they stood; its disadvantage was that it had not the slightest chance of being enacted.

President Johnson succeeded at a moment which could hardly have been more awkward. As the news of the surrender of the remaining Southern forces came in he had to make decisions which would affect the whole future of the United States, and he had to do so with all the handicaps of inexperience in an atmosphere charged with emotion. The first decision was whether to call Congress into special session to consider the problems of the peace. It is known that Lincoln had not intended to anticipate the normal session of Congress in December 1865, but it was probably a mistake for Johnson not to do so. Lincoln had behind him a triumphant re-election, he was closely acquainted with leading men of all shades of opinion in the Union party, and he had spent the whole of his political life in the climate of opinion of the Northern and Midwestern States; he knew from experience and political instinct what was or was not possible and he knew how to defeat ardent friends without making enemies. Johnson was an accidental President; everyone knew that he could not have reached even the Vice-Presidency except on the Lincoln ticket. His personal prestige had suffered from his unfortunate lapse during the inauguration. He was a Southern Unionist and had very little idea of the way in which the Northern mind worked. He was not on familiar terms with leading men in the Republican party. It was therefore urgently necessary for him to establish the kind of relation with Congress which is necessary for a successful President; it was necessary for him to know Congress and for Congress to know him and if he intended to continue the wartime ascendancy of the Presidency the way to do so was by understanding the coordinate branch of government and not by appearing to slight it. Failing an early call to Congress Johnson should have made an effort to impress his views upon congressional leaders and to hear their views in return, for these were men who would ultimately come to sit in judgment upon his policy. Yet though several congressional leaders called upon Johnson most of them found the experience singularly unsatisfying and Johnson himself made no overtures towards the men who, whatever their merits or demerits, were the chief movers among the representatives of the people.

At his succession to the Presidency the career of Andrew Johnson formed one of the great success stories of American history. From humble origins in a small country town and handicapped by early illiteracy he had made his way to the supreme position in the United States. His great assets had been honesty, fixity of purpose, and a command of the kind of oratory which was so popular with rural American audiences. Lacking subtlety he met attacks by attacking vigorously himself. He had become the spokesman of the small farmers of Tennessee in their running fight with the large planters who dominated the Mississippi valley in the State, and epitomized the aspirations of Jacksonian democracy in the West. At the outbreak of the Civil War he had earned fame as the only Southern senator to oppose secession (though he was as bitter against abolitionists as against secessionists), and in the war years he became the most distinguished representative of the elusive Southern Unionists and thus a key figure in the nation. This won him the vice-presidential nomination in 1864 at a time when it was particularly important to prevent the slave States in the Union from going sour on the war effort. Before that he had been a severe and successful governor of occupied Tennessee, introducing emancipation, and standing no nonsense from former Confederates. In spite of his Democratic antecedents his war record led him well into the fold of the Union party and it seemed that there was little to distinguish him from many Republicans. Indeed the Radicals rather than the moderates took comfort from the fierceness of his denunciations of Southern traitors. As President he was to prove a good administrator (much better than the somewhat casual Lincoln) and he had a natural dignity which made him a much more impressive figure than such predecessors as Pierce and Buchanan. He earned the respect and loyalty of the majority of those who worked closely with him in the administration, and there can be little doubt that in happier times he would have made a successful President.

Yet with all his qualities Johnson had limitations which were to be disastrous for his own policies. General Richard Taylor, son of the former President, who saw a good deal of him during the period of controversey, found "that he always postponed action, and was of an obstinate, suspicious temper. Like a badger, one had to dig him out of his hole; and he was ever in one except when on the hustings addressing a crowd. . . . He had acquired much knowledge of the principles of government, and made himself a fluent speaker, but could not rise above the level of the class in which he was born and to which he always appealed. He well understood the few subjects laboriously studied, and affected to despise other knowledge, while suspicious that those possessing such would take advantage of him. . . . Compelled to fight his way up from obscurity, he had contracted a dislike of those more favoured of fortune, whom he was in the habit of calling 'the slave aristocracy,' and became incapable of giving his confidence to any one, even to those on whose assistance he relied in a contest . . . with Congress." These comments may be discounted as those of a Southern gentleman and old Whig but the points made are corroborated too frequently to be dismissed: initial indecision, followed by a decision which was then adhered to with great obstinacy, a kind of defensive arrogance towards those who were better endowed by birth or nature, a fear of betraying his thoughts, and a confirmed reluctance to take counsel with those who might give him unwelcome advice, were all characteristics which unfitted him for the delicate tasks which the President was called upon to perform. Men who went to see him on business often found him apparently receptive and went away with the impression that they had made their points; when they discovered, from his later actions, that they might never have spoken, they were apt to conclude that they had been intentionally deceived.

Johnson hoped to surprise the country, and to win over public opinion, by the striking success of his Southern policy. Unable to admit that he had ever been wrong, he treated all criticism as betrayal or as the work of a malignant and frustrated minority. His perseverance in a policy which was obviously running into difficulties has often been described as "courageous"; but his was not a courage illuminated by understanding, and never for one moment would he consider an escape from the lonely rock upon which his own logic had stranded him. This loneliness is perhaps the most evident symptom of Johnson's personal tragedy. With an invalid wife and a drunken son, working enormously long hours at his desk, and seeing the world as a succession of faces which appeared before him for brief interviews, he created the self-portrait of a man of the people who could interpret their wishes without listening to what they were saying. This withdrawal from the real world of politics became disastrous when the people whose wishes would decide policy were those of the Northern and Midwestern States whose opinions Johnson never had understood and never would.

During the five weeks after he became President Johnson reached the decision from which he never afterwards withdrew, and on 29 May 1865 he issued a Proclamation of Amnesty and a Proclamation on North Carolina which was to be the model for others issued to all those Southern States which had not already set up governments under the Lincoln plan. The amnesty promised a pardon to all those who would take an oath of allegiance to the United States and of obedience to the proclamations affecting the emancipation of slaves. A very long list of exceptions to the general amnesty included all those already made by Lincoln and added men with taxable property of over $20,000 who had taken part in the rebellion; but these drastic exclusions from pardon (and thus from public life and a valid title to property) were qualified by a promise that special application could be made for pardon by all members of the excepted classes and "such clemency will be liberally extended as may be consistent with the facts of the case and with the peace and dignity of the United States." The Proclamation on North Carolina laid the constitutional foundations for the President's action by stating his duty to take care that the laws be faithfully executed and inferring that it therefore became necessary and proper for him to carry out and enforce the obligation of the United States to secure to the States a republican government. The claim to act without the participation of Congress was sound in logic but weak in application: the President might be bound to enforce the law but he was operating in a new situation in which the supreme legislature of the United States had been given no opportunity to say what the law should be. The proclamation went on to appoint a provisional governor "whose duty it shall be, at the earliest practicable period, to prescribe such rules and regulations as may be necessary and proper for convening a convention composed of delegates to be chosen by that portion of the people . . . who are loyal to the United States, and no others." Loyalty was defined as willingness to take the oath prescribed in the amnesty proclamation. This convention was to draw up a new Constitution and either it or the new legislature "will prescribe the qualification of electors and the eligibility of persons to hold office under the constitution and laws of the State — a power the several States composing the Federal Union have rightfully exercised from the origin of the Government to the present time."

The Reconstruction proclamations came like a tonic to the demoralized South. The mass of the people were unconditionally pardoned, and their leaders were led to expect a favourable consideration if they made personal application for presidential pardons. All except the unpardoned could take part in Reconstruction if they took a simple oath to the United States, which was no more than a recognition of the situation following Southern defeat. The vital power of fixing the qualifications for office and suffrage was specifically given to the States, and the claim of Congress to exclude leaders of the rebellion from State office or to alter the suffrage was denied. The whole process was unencumbered with conditions, and though Johnson was later to insist upon ratification of the Thirteenth Amendment abolishing slavery and repudiation of the Confederate debt, and to suggest limited negro suffrage, he did so only when Southern hopes of "home rule" had so far revived that they felt able to reject advice or to accept it on conditions. The hope which dawned for the majority of Southerners with Johnson's proclamations was a mortal blow to Southern Unionists. They had enjoyed a brief spell of influence so long as it seemed that they might be given a special role to play in remaking the Southern States and their subsequent plight is epitomized in the frantic plea to Ben Butler of a humble loyalist, who claimed to have broken through the lines at Richmond to bring intelligence to the Northern armies: "I am out of employment and get nothing to do. The rebels won't employ me because I went to the Yankees, and I went to Gen. Terry but he had nothing to give me to do; all the positions he had to fill were filled, and most of them by rebels — young men who served in the rebel army. My most noble Patron, I tell you such treatment is almost enough to make a man curse his Government." At the end of the year, when Johnson had issued pardons in profusion, another reported a conspiracy amongst ex-Confederate soldiers in Louisiana to renew the struggle for secession or at least to prescribe Union men. "All this is nonsense you may say in the North, but it is death or ruin to the Union men of the South. And what is the real cause of all this new Southern movement? In our opinion, it is the too early granted pardons to them. No one is punished as the law directs. The sovereignty of the law is not enforced — no it is made a perfect nullity. The rebels are courted and flattered instead of reproved."

Southern exuberance was the natural consequence of restored hope and unexpected freedom of action, but they used their opportunities with a singular lack of wisdom. They should have realized that the final word on their readmission would lie with Congress, and wisdom would have counseled a cautious respect for Northern opinion. One difficulty was that their only channel of communication with the North was through the President. Few Northern newspapers circulated in the South except the New York *World* which was emphatically pro-Southern, and it was said that even Federal officials found it impossible to obtain newspapers such as *Tribune* and other influential Northern papers. Southerners believed that the President was on their side, and they may have seen him as a new Andrew Jackson come to judgment, who would overawe Congress and force through his policy. They overlooked the fact that while Jackson had stood upon the strong ground of popular support in the North and West Johnson represented nobody. Johnson himself was singularly hesitant in the advice which he offered and did not exploit to the full the enormous influence which he could have exerted upon Southern actions. Even his famous telegram to Governor Sharkey advising the extension of suffrage to negroes on some literacy or property test was offered as a tentative suggestion on grounds of expediency because it "would completely disarm the adversary." His pardons seemed often to follow rather than to anticipate Southern movements and were given not infrequently to those who had already been chosen for office; nor does he seem to have used the pardon as an instrument by which men of influence could be bound to the national government.

Under these circumstances, the people of the South followed their natural preferences and chose for State offices the respected leaders of the Confederacy. More discretion might have been expected in the choice of senators and representatives for Congress, but the delegations which presented themselves at Washington in December — and included several Confederate congressmen and members of State legislatures under the Confederacy, four generals and five colonels of the Confederate army, and Alexander H. Stephens sometime Vice-President of the Confederate States — seemed to epitomize in Northern eyes the unchastened spirit of rebellion. More grievous and provocative was the passage by the new Southern legislatures of "black codes" for the emancipated negroes. That some form of regulation was necessary could hardly be denied though the States might have been justified in leaving responsibility for the time being to the Federal Freedmen's Bureau. The Southern States did give formal recognition to the legal rights acquired with freedom, allowing negroes the right to hold property, to sue and be sued, to make contracts and to marry, but in some States the conferment of these rights was accompanied by apprenticeship and vagrancy laws which made it clear that the negroes were to be treated as a subordinate caste assigned to labour. The code of Mississippi laid down that labour contracts should be in writing and that "every civil officer shall, and every person may, arrest and carry back to his or her legal employer any freedman, free negro or mulatto who shall have quit the service of his or her employer before the expiration of his or her term of service without good cause." Louisiana laid down conditions of labour and added, "Bad work shall not be allowed. Failing to obey reasonable orders, neglect of duty, and leaving home without permission will be deemed disobedience; impudence, swearing, or indecent language to or in the presence of the employer, his family or agent, or quarreling and fighting with one another will be deemed disobedience. . . . All difficulties arising between the employers and laborers . . . shall be settled by the former; if not satisfactory to the laborers, an appeal may be had to the nearest Justice of the Peace and two freeholders, citizens, one of the said citizens to be selected by the employer and the other by the laborer." Mississippi had an elaborate apprenticeship law under which negroes under the age of eighteen who were orphans or whose parents had not the means or will to support them were apprenticed to employers; the law laid down conditions for humane treatment and for teaching those under fifteen to read and write, but any apprentice could be ordered to return to his or her master by any justice of the peace and severe penalties were provided for not doing so. Negroes over the age of eighteen without lawful employment or business, and all white persons "usually associating" with them, were deemed vagrants and subject to heavy fines. It was an old Southern belief that the negro would not work without compulsion and it was reasonable to maintain that coercion was necessary to revive the Southern economy, but a system under which negroes were forced to make labour contracts under the penalties of the vagrancy laws, then held strictly to the conditions of service — with grievances determined by employers in the first instance and then by white officials whose interests were likely to be those of the employing class — was not free labour as understood in the North. If the codes did not re-enact slavery they might well make the condition of the negro worse in some respects than it had been under slavery, for the machinery of the State was now brought in to enforce obligations which had hitherto been the responsibility of the master. "This arbitrary and inhuman act," said the Radical Henry Wilson of the code of Mississippi, "makes the freedmen the slaves of society, and it is far better to be the slave of one man than to be the slave of arbitrary law." Exaggeration was to be expected from Radical critics, but no one aware of the sensitivity of Northern opinion to the negro question could have expected approval. What was perhaps more shocking than anything else was the assumption that the negro was condemned by nature to a dependent status; as the compiler of a collection of South Carolina laws remarked, "These two great classes, then, are distinctly marked by the impress of nature. They are races separate and distinct: the one the highest and noblest type of humanity, the other the lowest and most degraded." He believed that to mingle the social and political existence of the classes more closely "would surely be one of the highest exhibitions of treason to the race."

President Johnson himself was probably unhappy about the trend of events in the South, and Gideon Welles, who of all the Cabinet was nearest to him in temperament and opinion, wrote in his diary on 1 August 1865, "The tone of sentiment and action of people of the South is injudicious and indiscreet in many respects. I know not if there is any remedy, but if not, other and more serious disasters await them, and us also perhaps, for if we are one people, dissension and wrong affect the whole." Johnson, however, regarded the indiscretions of Southerners as irritating but irrelevant to the main issue of Reconstruction. Fundamentally he agreed with them about the place of the negro in society, though sufficiently humane not to close the door of opportunity to those who could deserve it. The strong expressions of gratitude which he was receiving from the South convinced him that he was on the right lines in overcoming as rapidly as possible the feelings of resentment and hatred in the South. Nor was he without support in the North from quarters in which a man of his antecedents was least likely to expect it. Merchants in the Eastern cities tended to favour a policy which would lead to an early resumption of normal commercial relations, and on 20 October Adam Badeau wrote to E. B. Washburn, "Everywhere I hear warm commendation of Mr Johnson's policy; in New York as well as at Washington — just as at Galena, all the sober substantial men seemed to support him. The attempt of foolish impractical men to foist their notions upon the country has met with no success, so far as I can judge." The comment was not without significance for Adam Badeau was secretary to General Grant who was susceptible to the opinions of sober substantial men. By the middle of December Johnson had on his desk a concise report from the General himself on conditions in the South in which he said that "the citizens of the Southern States are anxious to return to self-government, within the Union, as soon as possible; that whilst reconstructing they want and require protection from the government; that they are in earnest in wishing to do what they think is required by the government, not humiliating them as citizens, and that if such a course were pointed out they would pursue it in good faith." Warmed by the gratitude of Southerners, supported by his Cabinet, Johnson believed that his policy of restoration was a success, that its opponents were troublemakers and hollow men, and that Congress would respond to the arguments of the first annual message which he had commissioned George Bancroft to cast in literary form. Beyond Congress were the people of the Northern and Western States, a shadowy entity conceived perhaps as a vastly enlarged audience of Tennessee farmers who had always been so responsive to his oratory.

There were, however, indications of dissent which Johnson might have taken more seriously. There was for instance the report of Carl Schurz which reached him before the meeting of Congress. Schurz was the most distinguished of German Americans; a refugee from Germany inspired by the liberalism of the mid-century he had seen in the Republican party an American version of the universal movement for freedom; he had had much to do with winning Midwestern Germans from their Democratic affiliations, and had gone on to a distinguished career in the army reaching the rank of Major-General. He had made no secret of his Radical leanings, and he was therefore surprised to receive in July a request from the President accompanied "with many flattering assurances of his confidence in my character and judgment" to undertake a tour in the South and to report upon conditions. By his own account he told the President that "so far as I was then informed, I considered the reconstruction policy ill-advised and fraught with great danger, but that if my observations should show this view to be erroneous, no pride of opinion would prevent me from saying so." The President repeated his expressions of confidence and sent him on his way. Schurz was not a rich man and he was receiving only nominal pay for his mission; with something less than complete discretion he allowed some Northern friends to pay the premium on a life insurance and during his tour contributed anonymous articles to Northern newspapers on conditions in the South. The real cause of his offence to Johnson was, however, a well-meant effort to interfere in a dispute between Governor Sharkey of Mississippi and General Slocum, commanding the Federal troops, in which the latter attempted to stop the arming of the State militia. Johnson sustained Sharkey and rebuked both Slocum and Schurz. It was probably this incident (in which most fair-minded men would admit that the President was wrong) which convinced Johnson that Schurz was intriguing against him. Whatever the explanation Schurz received on his return the coldest possible reception from the President, who informed him that there was no need for him to submit a report. Schurz nevertheless wrote one, though it is doubtful whether Johnson read it and because of its Radical authorship it has been largely ignored by historians. This neglect has been unfortunate for the report was the work of a humane and unusually intelligent man who had immersed himself for six months in the problems of the South.

Schurz was able to appreciate the tragedy of the South and left it "troubled by great anxiety." "No fair-minded man could have had my experiences in the Southern country without conceiving and cherishing a profound and warm sympathetic feeling for the Southern people, white as well as black." He respected the gallantry of the South though lamenting that it had been "wasted upon a hopeless cause — the cause of slavery — which, while held sacred by the white people of the South, was abhorred by the moral sense and enlightened opinion of the century." He wasted no words in pointless accusations of treason, but emphasized the magnitude of the Southern crisis: "Now the South found precipated upon it a problem of tremendous moment and perplexing difficulty — the problem of abruptly transforming a social organism based upon slave labor into a free labor society." Southerners, true to their traditions, tried to avoid the implications of abolition, and attempted to combine a professed willingness to accept the results of the war with a true purpose which was "to use the power of the State Governments, legislative and executive, to reduce the freedom of the negroes to a minimum and to revive so much of the old slave code as was thought necessary to make the blacks work for the whites." These were the facts of the case as he saw them, and the true remedy was not to indulge in frantic denunciations of the Southerners but to take action if a different result was desired. On the vital question of Southern loyalty his report was illuminating and his separation of Southern leaders into various groups demonstrated how easy it was to draw different conclusions according to one's Southern company: first there were men, mostly of mature age and experience — planters, merchants and professional men — who "have a clear perception of the irreversible changes produced by the war, and honestly endeavour to accommodate themselves to the new order of things" (these were the men with whom Grant talked on his brief visit, and in this class one might also include some of the Confederate military leaders); then there were those who wanted at all costs to restore their States to influence in the Union and would make any concession which did not threaten their own control at home — these were mainly the professional politicians and all were strong supporters of Johnson and bitter opponents of the Freedmen's Bureau; the third group was composed of the irreconcilables, mainly young men who continued to talk of eventual Southern independence and were actively suppressing negroes and Unionists, but of whom many had taken the oath of allegiance and worked temporarily with the politicians; finally there was the mass of the people "whose intellects are weak, but whose prejudices and impulses are strong." Reviewing the whole problem he believed that there were great dangers in "home rule" without national protection for negroes and Unionists, nor did he believe that danger threatened the blacks alone for there was no knowing what savage impulses might not be released if the promise of negro freedom remained unfulfilled.

Throughout the summer and autumn the storm clouds gathered on the Radical front. A few days after the North Carolina Proclamation Sumner was writing to Ben Wade asking whether he could give him "any comfort with regard to the policy of the President. *He has missed a golden opportunity,* and is entailing upon the country trouble, controversy and expense. *He cannot prevent the triumph of the cause.* This is certain. But he may delay it." In July Ben Butler was telling one correspondent that he still had faith in the President's "integrity and desire to do right" and that he expected him to change his policy when he saw it to be wrong, but was writing to Wade that "all is wrong. We are losing the just results of this four years struggle." Wade told the President frankly that "the policy he was pursuing with regard to reconstruction was filling many of our best friends with alarm" and that he ought to add some Radical representation to his Cabinet, but thought that his advice would be ignored. He then wrote to Sumner that "all appears gloomy. The President is pursuing, and I believe is resolved to pursue a course in regard to reconstruction that can result in nothing but consigning the great Union, or Republican party, bound hand and foot, to the tender mercies of the rebels we have so lately conquered in the field and their copperhead allies in the north. . . . We have in truth already lost the whole moral effect of our victories over the rebellion and the golden opportunity for humiliating and destroying the influence of the Southern aristocracy has gone forever." In October the influential though erratic Wendell Phillips was saying the same thing to Butler: "It seems to me that the Administration is handing us over, bound hand and foot, into the power of the rebels." He added that "the Administration needs to be defied or overawed by such an exhibition of popular sentiment as you and Sumner and one or two others could easily start. To be effectual this should be attempted before Congress meets."

To men who believed that Reconstruction must be drastic to be just the future seemed bleak, for the majority of the Republican party might be swayed to an easy acceptance of Johnson's restoration.

Ben Butler wrote to Henry Wilson, with a copy to Thaddeus Stevens, suggesting a preamble to a Reconstruction Act which would declare the negroes entitled to the rights of citizens, and that Congress, acting upon the second section of the Thirteenth Amendment, should declare void all discriminatory State legislation, and adding that "the whole preamble seems to be necessary in order to hold the weak kneed brethren of the Republican party, who are troubled upon the question whether the States are in or out of the Union will be carried by the claim that they ought to vote to admit some States so as to have ratified the Constitutional Amendment by the requisite majority." He hoped to force the wavering majority to commit themselves "to give life and effect to the Constitutional Amendment and in favor of liberty and equal rights not raising however any question of the rights of suffrage." But it is difficult to demonstrate a Radical plot in the rising tide of disquiet in the Northern Press, and the most disturbing influence was emanating not from Radical quarters but from the South itself with its choice of Confederate leaders, its black codes, its reviving arrogance, its open contempt for the moralistic ideas of the North, and its clear determination to rescue as much as possible from the past. Most alarming of all was Johnson's apparent tolerance of these things, and his failure to indicate that the South was not going to have everything its own way.

At the end of November the mild-mannered Schuyler Colfax, speaker designate of the new Congress, came to town and made a little speech which attracted considerable notice. He praised the President warmly, but warned against haste. He did not think that Congress ought to be in a hurry about the admission of Southerners. He was not satisfied with Southern behaviour because the States had quibbled about ratifying the abolition amendment, about repudiating their debts and about nullifying secession, because of their hostility to Unionists and because they had not made proper laws for the freedmen. The government had given the slave his freedom and meant to maintain it. He did not, however, believe that these doubts meant a rupture with the President and thought that "the executive and legislative departments of government, when they compare views together, will cordially co-operate in this great work before us all, and so act that the foundations of our Union, wisely and patriotically reconstructed, shall be eternal as the ages, with a hearty acceptance by the South of the new situation." This speech — with its temperate statement of Northern doubts, its expressed willingness to work with the President and its belief in harmony with justice — was widely welcomed in the North. The speech did, however, indicate that Congressional leaders intended to take the initiative and this was sheer Radicalism to a man who believed that "restoration" was complete. Johnson did not expect to alter or enlarge his policy to comprehend Northern anxieties which were, he was convinced, the work of a few troublemakers. He was, however, about to meet Northern opinion in the form of a Congress chosen at the same election as that which had raised him to the Vice-Presidency, and the meeting was to prove a shock for both.

Some Radicals wished to scrap the whole presidential plan, but a majority in the party were ready and willing to allow the President credit for his work in restoring the normal machinery of government and to believe that he would readily accept the additional "guarantees" proposed by Congress. These guarantees were aimed to protect the Union against its enemies and the negro against those who would deprive him of civil rights. According to temperament or interest men stressed one danger or one remedy more than another. Roscoe Conkling said later that the one binding tie amongst all Republicans was a conviction "that the destinies of the nation should never be yielded up to men whose hands and faces are dripping with the blood of murder" and Schuyler Colfax had written privately to a friend, "I remember very well that last day I was in Congress, they were fighting us and killing our soldiers, and had their members in the Rebel Congress. It would be rather pleasant for them to take their seats the first day of the next session; but I am a little too old fogyish for that. I want to be very certain that a majority of their voters are — not merely whipped back into the Union, as they say — but heartily devoted to the Union and ready to fight with us against all its enemies at home and abroad, now and in the future." Other Republicans saw negro rights as the dominant and binding issue. "The Union party are agreed," said Senator Stewart (who wanted a general amnesty), "that all men are entitled to life, liberty and the pursuit of happiness, and they will endorse any reasonable means to secure these inalienable rights to every American citizen. . . . The President's plan of restoration was unsatisfactory because it ignored the rights and excluded from constitutional liberty four million loyal citizens guilty of no offence but fidelity to the Government . . . because it placed the State government of the South in the hands of the very men who plunged the country into war for secession, and the extension of slavery, and because it admitted into Congress an increased representation of the disloyal elements of the rebellion." Nearly all Republicans felt the force of one or other of these criticisms, and even Henry J. Raymond, who clung to the President long after other Republicans had abandoned him, and who wished to accept the restoration of the Southern States as suggested by him, wished also to "provide by law for giving to the freedmen of the South all rights of citizens in courts of law and elsewhere," to exclude from Federal office "the leading actors in the conspiracy which led to the rebellion," to make such amendments to the Constitution as might seem appropriate, and to use troops to prevent the overthrow of Southern governments which were Republican in form.

Public opinion in the North had been bewildered by the course of events, and there was no clear determination as the year 1865 drew to its close upon the policy which should be followed. But in a negative sense there was a growing consensus of opinion that not enough had been done. Anyone could have predicted that Radical attacks would be made, but the new factor in the situation was the response which they aroused. Many moderate Republicans were sincerely anxious for a generous peace and were likely to be extremely cautious of any commitments on the racial problem, but even they felt that further guarantees were necessary. Thaddeus Stevens declared that the Southern States ought "never to be recognised as capable of acting in the Union, or being counted as valid States, until the Constitution shall have been so amended as to make it what its framers intended; and so as to secure perpetual ascendancy to the party of the Union; and so as to render our republican government firm and stable for ever." Though expressed by the sternest of Radicals this assertion united rather than divided the party. Equal rights in the Constitution and perpetual union proved to be the two hinges upon which congressional policy turned, and the doom of Johnson's policy lay in the discovery that the party could be united upon the need for certain "guarantees" which he had failed to provide.

The Republican concensus was as yet limited in scope and it did not extend to any advanced propositions about racial equality. For many Republicans the sticking-point was the question of suffrage. A good many were prepared to see the vote given to negroes with property and education, and even the Democrat Reverdy Johnson was ready to admit that many of the negroes were "capable of as much and as high a civilization as the white race" and that if protected by the paramount authority of the Constitution "they will ere long become valuable citizens of the country." But there was a long gap between this kind of statement and a commitment to immediate and unqualified suffrage. On the one hand many Republicans were aware of the racial prejudice in their own constituencies — several Northern States excluded negroes from the suffrage and were to reaffirm this during the Reconstruction controversy — and on the other some Republicans were alarmed by the idea of indiscriminate suffrage extended to the illiterates of either race. Privately Horace Greeley proposed that the suffrage should be given to all who had voted prior to 1861 and to such others "as shall have read understandingly the Constitution of the United States, and have paid a State tax during the year preceding."

Though no agreement on negro suffrage was likely in the immediate future, the case for it was being made. Speaking for the negro to the annual meeting of the Massachusetts Anti-Slavery Society in 1865 in a lecture called "What the Black Man Wants" Frederick Douglass explained that they wanted suffrage "because it is our *right* first of all. No class of men can, without insulting their own nature, be content with any deprivation of their rights. We want it again as a means of educating our race. . . . Again I want the elective franchise, for one, as a colored man, because ours is a peculiar government, based upon a peculiar idea, and that idea is universal suffrage. If I were in a monarchical government, where the few bore rule and the many were subject, there would be no special stigma resting upon me, because I did not exercise the elective franchise." He concluded that if the negro "knows as much when sober as an Irishman knows when he is drunk, he knows enough to vote, on good American principles." The abstract case for negro suffrage was, however, being powerfully reinforced by a purely political argument. In March 1865 Sumner, whose sincerity in the cause of racial equality cannot be doubted, was writing to Bright that without negro votes "we cannot establish stable government in the rebel States . . . without them the enemy will reappear, and under forms of law take possession of the governments, choose magistrates and officers, and in alliance with the Northern democracy, put us all in peril again." It could also be argued that negro suffrage must be the keystone for any policy of guarantees and when Congress met, the Radical George Boutwell argued that restoration without negro suffrage "opens the way to the destruction of this government from which there is no escape" while rights without suffrage were illusory for "with the right of voting everything that a man ought to have or enjoy of civil rights comes to him. Without the right to vote he is secure in nothing." Thus stood the question of negro suffrage at the end of the year 1865: with strong advocates, encountering many doubts, drawing upon the stock of traditional American beliefs, and provided with arguments arising from the political situation and increasing in cogency as men pondered upon the future distribution of power in the United States. For those who believed that negro suffrage in the South would be a disaster the best tactics would have been to settle with the moderate Republican majority before they were forced to choose between the negro vote and the abandonment of what they deemed to be essential. Such would have been the wisdom of political calculation, but in times of stress politicians are, perhaps, no more likely than other men to calculate correctly. Johnson, his supporters, and the South were set upon the surest road to colour-blind democracy but they remained oblivious of the direction in which they were heading and adhered instead to their belief that "restoration" could be achieved without "guarantees."

Black Reconstruction in the South

Resuming full partnership within the Union was one half of the reconstruction process after 1865. The other half was reconstructing southern society to accommodate the changes the war had produced. Part of this was purely physical. Much of the upper South had been a battleground for the contending armies and had been devastated. Where Sherman's army had swung through Georgia and the Carolinas, it had created a blackened swath of destruction. Substantial towns like Columbia and Atlanta had been almost totally burned out. The South's railroads and factories had either been destroyed or had worn out from excessive use and poor maintenance. Financial loss was added to physical damage. Millions of dollars of paper assets were swept away with the bankruptcy of the Confederate government and the collapse of the banks.

More serious was the social disruption produced by emancipation and the end of slavery. As has often been noted, Lincoln's Emancipation Proclamation of 1863, applying as it did only to regions of the South out of reach of federal power, did not itself free a single slave. But Union armies did, in vast numbers, and by the time of Confederate surrender in April 1865, slavery was dead. This event profoundly disturbed the South's social and economic arrangements. Four million former slaves, without previous experience as citizens or as breadwinners, were suddenly told that they were on their own. The Freedmen's Bureau, it is true, attempted to provide some economic help and guidance for ex-slaves, but it was spasmodic, inconsistent, short-lived, and, as we would say today, underfunded. Political help came from so-called scalawags, southerners who embraced the new order, and carpetbaggers, northerners who came south to take advantage of it. Moved by both civic spirit and avarice, these white men helped organize the freedmen politically within the ranks of the Republican party. Joining with talented black leaders, these white radicals succeeded in modernizing and liberalizing the constitutions of the former Confederate states and in providing expanded social services and educational opportunities for all southerners, white and black.

But though the ex-slave was now a citizen, he was also still part of the labor force, and a part that was largely unskilled and illiterate. Could the blacks be reintegrated into the southern economy as free men without massive economic disruption? Slavery had done little to prepare them for the market economy the nation endorsed, and many white men were fearful that, under the new regime, ex-slaves would not be willing to work, and the southern economy would stagnate.

Interwoven with this was the social issue: Would the blacks become a wage-earning proletariat, or would they be encouraged to become owners of property? Prevailing Jeffersonian values hallowed the yeoman and the family farm, and held that both the political and economic health of society demanded that there be a large class of small landholders. The recent Homestead Act had embodied this Jeffersonian ideal, but the lands to which it applied were largely in the Northwest, far removed from the South and from the cotton culture that the ex-slaves knew best.

Given these circumstances, it would have surely been wise for the federal government to have provided land for the freedmen. A number of prominent Radicals saw this clearly and sought to redistribute the land of prominent Confederates among them. Some land actually passed to ex-slaves through the efforts of the Freedmen's Bureau. But on the whole, little was done by Congress to create a black yeomanry. In the following essay, Joel Williamson discusses the actual economic readjustments that occurred in one southern state, South Carolina, in the absence of federal guidance.

FOR FURTHER READING:

DuBois, William E. B. *Black Reconstruction in America, 1860–1880.* New York: Atheneum Publishers, 1969.*
Stampp, Kenneth M. *The Era of Reconstruction, 1865–1867.* New York: Random House, Vintage Books, 1965.*
Wharton, Vernon Lane. *The Negro in Mississippi, 1865–1890.* Harper & Row, Publishers, Torchbooks, 1965.*

Asterisk denotes paperback edition.

New Patterns in Economics

JOEL WILLIAMSON

Before the end of Reconstruction, the Negro in South Carolina found that the pattern of his employment was already well defined. In agriculture, he belonged to one or more of four distinct groups. Either he rented the land upon which he worked, labored for wages, sold his supervisory skills as a foreman or a manager, or owned his own land.

In the first days of freedom, the Negro agrarian usually found himself in one of the first two categories. His desire to rent land was strong and persistent. He was also averse to working for wages and, especially, to working in gangs under direct supervision. David Golightly Harris, visiting Spartanburg village on January 4, 1866, observed: "The negroes all seem disposed to rent land, & but few are willing to hire by the day, month or year." Occasionally, the desire to rent became a mania. "I am about renting some land on the aint (Aunt) Juriy Hemphill place to Bek, Smith Sam & Peggy," wrote a Chester County planter in November, 1869. "They have hardly corn for Bread & will make nothing but are rent Crazy & must be gratified."

In the first years after manumission, renting was poor economics for most freedmen. Few had the managerial experience, and fewer still had the capital necessary to succeed as independent renters. Moreover, the late 1860's was a period of agricultural depression. Landowners were aware of these problems and, in addition to their aversion to renting land to Negroes for social and political reasons, they op-

---

Source: Joel Williamson, *After Slavery: The Negro in South Carolina During Reconstruction, 1861–1877* (Chapel Hill: University of North Carolina Press, 1965), chap. 5, "New Patterns in Economics," pp. 126–163.

posed the practice as economically unsound. "Negroes will not do to rely upon as croppers," journalized David Harris in the spring of 1869. "They will not [look] far enough ahead to do any good." As buildings, fences, ditches, and lands deteriorated under the neglect of successive tenants, resistance to renting to either blacks or whites became stronger among landowners. In the spring of 1868, Harris recorded a complaint frequently heard: "I have no little trouble to get my renters to do such work [maintenance], & have almost determined never to rent again. I sometimes think that if I can [not] hire hands to work my land as I want it done, it shall not be worked at all."

Possibly, the Negro renter made his choice against the clear dictates of agrarian economy because he wanted to free himself from the pattern of life he had known as a slave. As a wage laborer, he would have continued to live in the plantation village and to work in gangs under the eye of the white man. As a renter, he labored independently and lived with his family upon his own farm, having either moved a cabin from the plantation village or, as frequently happened, having built a new one upon his plot of earth.

Statistically, the "rent crazy" Negroes often had their way. A generation after emancipation, 37 per cent of the Negro farmers in the state were renters, a large majority occupying plots of less than fifty acres. Indeed, renting became the usual form of land tenure in the upcountry. For instance, of thirty-four Negro farmers who testified on the subject before a Congressional committee in the spring of 1871, twenty-one were renters, eight were wage laborers, and five owned their own land. Further, renting existed in considerable degree in every part of the state. "The negroes who cultivated cotton, as a general rule, rented land from their former masters," reported one native several decades later.

Negro renters paid their landlords in a variety of ways, but, generally, the method of payment belonged to one of two broad categories. In South Carolina in 1880, about one-quarter of the farm operators of both races compensated landlords with a share of the crop. Renting land for a share of the proceeds tended particularly to pervade those areas where cotton was grown; and, even after the return of prosperity, many planters (or landowners) continued to adhere to the system, deeming it more profitable than slavery. This was especially true in the upcountry. "In the upper counties the negroes work better and the masters treat them fairly, so that in some cases farms are still worked on shares with a profit to both parties," reported a Northern correspondent in 1874.

The proportion of the crop paid for the use of land normally varied from one-half to three-quarters, depending largely on the goods and animals that the landlord supplied in addition to the land. The share arrangement was thus capable of endless variety and complexity. For instance, in Edgefield District in 1866, Alfred rented a certain acreage from his late master for one-third the expected crop. However, for the cultivation of another plot, Alfred was to get a tenth of the gross yield in payment for his services as stockminder, then the owner was to have a third of the remainder as rent, and the last two-thirds was to go to Alfred as wages.

In 1880, slightly less than a quarter of the farm operators in South Carolina were renters who paid their landlords a fixed-cash rental. Like share-renting, the term fixed-cash renting covered a wide variety of methods of payment. A common device was the payment of the rent by a specific quantity of a given crop. Thus, in St. Paul's Parish, Colleton District, in December, 1865, "Miles (a Freedman of Colour) and Alfred E. Stokes of the same place" agreed to rent sixteen acres of land from

Charles H. Rice for the coming season. The rental was to be paid in November, 1866, and consisted of sixty-four bushels of corn and a third of the "peace and fodder that may be made." Frequently, Negro renters paid a money rental for their land. For instance, a planter near Adams Run filled his plantation with renters at five dollars per acre, whereas another planter in St. Andrews Parish, in 1872, had difficulty finding renters at three dollars an acre. Occasionally, labor was given in total or partial payment of rent. In Spartanburg County, David G. Harris recorded the terms of a contract with a Negro renter for 1869: "Prince morris has built a house[,] garden[,] cut a ditch & cleared an small field. He gives me Sim's [his son's] labour this year for this land."

To meet the needs of the renter, the landlord, the crop, and of the land itself, rental arrangements often assumed a bewildering complexity as various methods of sharing and paying produce, cash, and labor were combined to provide a satisfactory rental. In 1871 in Colleton County, seven renters (two of whom may have been white) agreed to six different arrangements with the same landowner. Benjamin Kelley agreed to pay the owner a fourth share which was to be used by Kelley himself to improve the house on his rented plot. A pair of renters agreed to work a mule for the owner on a given field and to pay the owner a half of the yield from this field in addition to the fourth due from their main plot. Didemus Allen agreed to farm four acres and to pay the owner two bushels of corn per acre and a fourth of all else he grew. Jerry Smith, a Negro, agreed to pay on Christmas Day, 1871, $12.00 plus a fourth of the produce from a twenty-acre plot that he was allowed to use. In the following year, Jerry contracted with the owner to set up ten thousand turpentine boxes on his land and to divide the profits of the enterprise evenly.

Contrary to the general impression, the plantations of South Carolina did not at the end of the war immediately crumble into many small parts. Indeed, probably most plantations continued to be worked, on a reduced scale, as integral units using wage labor. In the rice districts, fragmentation was impossible since the production of that crop required dikes, ditches, and flood gates which could only be constructed and maintained by a number of laborers organized under a well-financed management. Although few rice plantations were restored to full productivity during Reconstruction, many of these were operated as units. On the other hand, many cotton plantations were indeed divided into small farms and operated under the rental system. Even in the cotton areas, however, some plantations continued to be operated as units for some time after the war, and many planters who rented portions of their lands to others frequently retained large "home places" which they managed themselves.

Employers placed restrictions upon Negro wage laborers that were much more onerous than those imposed upon renters by landlords. The amount, the time, and, frequently, the quality of the wage hand's labor were closely prescribed in his contract, and any delinquency in his performance was severely penalized by fines. In the early years of Reconstruction, the task — the unit of labor used in the slave period — was widely utilized. Ideally, a task was an amount of work which an adult Negro of average abilities could do well in a day's time. The contract signed by thirty-six wage laborers on the Peter B. Bacot plantation in Darlington District in 1867 was typical: "The said servants agreed to perform the daily tasks hitherto usually allotted on said plantation, to wit: 125 to 150 rails; cutting grain 3 to 6 acres; ditching & banking 300 to 600 feet; hoeing cotton 70 to 300 rows an acre long; corn 4000 to 6000 hills. In all cases where tasks cannot be assessed, they agree to labor diligently ten hours a day." While the task system of measuring labor tended to persist in the rice areas, elsewhere there was a general trend toward substituting a given number of hours of labor per day. Ten hours daily was the usual requirement, beginning at or shortly after sunrise and ending at sunset, with greater and lesser periods of freedom allowed for the noon meal as the days lengthened and shortened. Often, attempts were made to control the quality of labor by including in contracts provisions binding Negroes to work "as heretofore," or to "the faithful discharge of his duties as an industrious farm labourer doing whatever he is directed to do . . ." The fine for "absence, refusal or neglect" was everywhere fifty cents for each day lost, and illness gave no exemption from the penalty. Absence from the plantation without leave was subject to fine at the rate of two dollars a day. Persistent absence or misbehavior was punishable by expulsion from the plantation and forfeiture of any claim to wages at the end of the year.

Contracts also included a host of minor regulations designed to enhance the efficiency of the laborer. Typically, the laborer was "not to leave the premises during work hours without the consent of the Proprietor or his Agent," and "not to bring visitors without permission." On some plantations, laborers were committed to observe silence in their cabins after nine o'clock in the evening, "to bring no ardent spirits at any time upon the plantation," and not to have private livestock or pets or to converse with one another in the fields. Often, the laborers as a group were required to supply from their numbers a foreman, a nurse when sickness occurred, a stockminder, and a watchman for the harvested crop. Employers also sought to use the contract to enforce a proper demeanor upon their Negro employees. Thus, laborers were often bound to "perfect obedience," promptness, diligence and respectful conduct," or "to conduct themselves faithfully, honestly & civilly," or to be "peaceable, orderly and pleasant," or "reliable and respectful and to mind all directions," or "to be kind and respectful to Employer and Agent," or to "treat the Employer with due respect." Disrespectful behavior, evidenced by "impudence, swearing; or indecent and unseemly language," was often punishable by fines. Finally, the laborer was invariably bound to pay for the loss or injury of tools and animals either through neglect or by his willful act.

In return for his toil, the agricultural laborer was paid by combinations of goods, services, and cash. In the early postwar years, most received at the end of the season a share of the crop, commonly a third of the gross yield. As with share-renting, the proportion taken by the employer depended largely on the degree to which he maintained his employees. In 1869, an upcountry editor averred that contracts usually granted the laborer a third of the crop in lieu of wages. However, he added, if the employer fed the laborer a weekly ration of four pounds of meat and one peck of meal with small allowances of coffee, salt, sugar, and lesser items, the share granted was a fourth. Share-wage arrangements were often very complicated. For example, on the MacFarland plantation in Chesterfield District, in 1866, twenty-five Negro workers agreed to share evenly with the landowner the net profit of the year after a fourth of the cotton crop or seven bales, whichever was less, was deducted for rent and the overseer's wages and other expenses had been paid.

Neither the share nor the specific amount of money the laborers received for their share was the ultimate measure of the individual's wages. On virtually every plantation, wage laborers contracted as a group, and the share which they earned collectively was divided among them in proportion to the working capacity of each as agreed upon in the contract itself. Thus, a full hand was paid a certain amount, while three-quarter, half, and quarter hands received proportionately less. In addition, employers promised "to furnish each family with quarters on his plantation & a garden plot and the privilege of getting firewood from some portion of the premises indicated by the Employer . . ." Also, laborers were sometimes allowed an "outside crop." A. H. Boykin, in Kershaw County, in 1875, permitted his dozen workers to cultivate as much land as "each thinks he can work every other saturday . . ." Further, he promised to let each employee keep "one cow & one hog," not unusual concessions ten years after emancipation. Occasionally, special allowances were made for family chores. On Dean Hall plantation on the lower Cooper River, in 1866, the contract provided that "only half a day's work on Saturdays will be required of female employees who are heads of families." Employers usually agreed to advance goods and services to their employees, the costs of which were deducted from their share at the end of the season. Whether a part of the contract or not, most employers were forced to supply rations to their employees to enable them to finish the season. In addition, they often advanced other items: tobacco, salt, molasses, blankets, overcoats, shoes, taxes, medical care, and even, with striking frequency, preachers' salaries, coffins, and grave sites. Sometimes, too, the laboring force was required to pay a fraction of the cost of fertilizer, insurance, bagging, and rope — all of which were advanced in the same manner by the employer.

Although it was true that many impoverished planters had no other resort in the early postwar years when cash was scarce, there are indications that many planters and laborers deliberately elected, at first, to use the share system. "I found very few [planters] — not more than one or two, who were offering monthly wages," wrote the owner of extensive lands on the Cooper River in February, 1866. "All on the Cooper River as far as I could learn were offering a share in the crops whether from a want of ability to pay wages &c or because they believed an interest in the crop would secure a more steady course of labor and prevent stealage, I know not, perhaps both." Many Negro workers, themselves, preferred shares to cash wages. "The negroes will not contract for wages," reported a lowcountry planter in the winter of 1866. In the fall of the same year, the majority of a large meeting of Negro laborers gathered in Sumter rejected a suggestion to change to cash wages, clinging "to their preference for a moiety of the crops." One planter thought the Negroes preferred goods to money because they feared: "Maybe it git lak Confeddick money."

Nevertheless, the great majority of planters shifted to money wages within the first few years after the war. Even in 1867, the number of planters paying cash wages, either entirely or partly, greatly increased. A cotton planter on Cooper River who ran "ten steady plows & more as the necesity [sic] calls for them and 30 hoe hands" wrote to a friend in the spring of 1867 that "We pay money for our labour half cash at the End of Each month." A Northern correspondent reported in that year that the few Sea Island planters who could afford it had shifted to monthly wages; and another, writing in 1874, asserted that the share system had been "entirely abandoned" in the lowcountry a year or two after the war and that most planters "now pay their hands monthly wages."

A preference for cash wages also spread among Negro laborers. In June, 1874, a planter on the Combahee River reported that "The negroes now work for money & I have to send out & pick them up where I can get them, & am obliged to take what I can get in order to get along." Such was still the case in the following winter: "Uncle Hawk is here with some hands that know how to work & will work here all the week, they work for money, exclusively, & don't draw from the Commissary." As described earlier, the Combahee Riots in 1876 were partly caused by the desire of Negro laborers for payment of their wages in cash.

Definitions of the amount of labor demanded of an employee who worked for cash and the manner in which his wages were paid varied widely. On the whole, however, both were much less complicated than share agreements, and the parties concerned often dispensed entirely with formal, written contracts. A Combahee planter described one of his arrangements in 1875: "I have hired John Barnwell to Plow & attend to the mules at $5.00 per month, & give him 2 lbs meat & a package of flour per week . . ." In the early postwar years, planters, suspicious of the constancy of Negro labor, were prone to withhold a portion of their employees' wages until the crop was harvested. In Newberry District, in 1866, for instance, an employer contracted to retain half the wages due his employees until "after summer work begins," and the other half until the end of the year to insure "faithful performance." By the end of Reconstruction, however, most wage laborers were paid daily, weekly, or monthly, had contracted with their employers individually rather than collectively, and had taken a giant step away from the organizational forms of slavery.

Cash wages were also paid for part-time labor. Employees working on shares were paid cash for extra work. For instance, in 1867, the owner of Dirleton plantation on the Pee Dee contracted to pay fifty cents per day in wages to those share-laborers who would do "plantation work," particularly "carpenter work," beyond the terms of their contract. Extra labor, on and off the plantation, was hired "to get the crop out of the grass," or to assist in its harvesting. Gathering in the cotton crop was a usual occasion for hiring additional laborers, and the standard rate of fifty cents per hundred pounds of cotton picked soon became the fixed wage. In the lowcountry, many Negroes owning or renting small plots worked as day laborers whenever they could. In 1868, the Reverend John Cornish was breakfasting with John Jenkins at Gardenia Hall near Adams Run when "quite a gang of negroes came up the avenue with their hoes in hand, looking for work — John sent them into his cotton field — gives them 20cts a task — if very hard 25cts. In this way John is cultivating 30 odd acres of cotton this year — has but one hand constantly employed, & that is his plough man — "

In the Sea Islands generally, and on some rice plantations on the Cooper River, the payment of wages by a combination of land allotments and cash called the "two-day system" came to be widely practiced. As applied to cotton on the Sea Islands, the system involved the laborer's giving two days of work a week (usually Monday and Tuesday) during the ten-month working season in return for quarters, fuel, and five to seven acres of land to work as he wished. Additional labor performed for the planter was paid for in cash at the rate of fifty cents a day or task. "Laborers prefer this system," asserted an agricultural expert in 1882. The system was also applied to rice culture. Gabriel Manigault, having just completed the 1876 season on Rice Hope on the Cooper River, urged his brother Louis, who had had an unsuccessful year in rice on a Georgia Sea Island, to exchange land for two days' labor a week and to hire workers for two more, thereby cutting his cash expenses from $5,000 to $3,000 a year and avoiding "the paying of wages at every step." The "two-day system," too, was capable of infinite variation. In 1868, for instance, rice planters near Adams Run were said to give two and a half acres of rice land, two pounds of bacon, and four quarts of corn in exchange for three days of labor each week. Here again, possibly, the preference of the Negro worker for the "two-day system" marked his desire for greater independence in economic pursuits.

A third class of Negro agricultural worker emerged under the title of "foreman," or, less frequently, "agent" or "manager." Functionally, the foreman was the all too familiar "driver" of the slave period trading under a new label. Francis Pickens inadvertently recognized this fact when he drafted his first contract to employ his ex-slaves as free laborers. In that document he, at first, bound his workers "to obey faithfully the Overseer or Driver." Having second thoughts, he crossed out the word "Driver" and substituted "Agent." The primary function of the foreman (as that of the driver had been) was the day-to-day assignment of tasks to individual laborers and seeing that they were properly done. Unlike the driver, however, the foreman did not carry a whip as his badge of office, and his demeanor was often in sharp contrast with that of the driver. In 1868, the mistress of El Dorado, a lowcountry plantation, noted this development with disgust. "The work here consists in going out at 9 & hoeing in a very leisurely manner till 12 — when they disappear for the day," she reported. "The 'foreman' escorts the women with an air of gallantry — & Mary P. one day heard him saying in the most courteous manner — 'Hide your grass, ladies, hide your grass.' " Further, the foreman frequently assumed the obligations of a full field hand, laboring alongside his charges and, thus, becoming more of a leader among equals than a superior. Contracts typically bound all hands to obey the foreman equally with the owner, and occasionally, foremen possessed the power to discharge "disrespectful and idle or unfaithful" employees. Foremen were doubtless numerous because plantations which continued to be farmed as a unit invariably relied upon the services of at least one member of this class.

The foreman sometimes earned only as much as a full hand, sometimes more. In 1866, H. L. Pinckney made James, an ex-slave who had not been a driver, foreman over some thirty-three field hands on his Sumter District plantation. For his trouble, James seems to have received only a full hand's share of the crop. Two years later, Pinckney broke his force into three groups of which James, Mitchell (another Negro), and the owner himself were the leaders. James and Mitchell, apparently, received only the shares due full hands. Francis Pickens, in contrast, was very liberal in compensating his foremen. In 1866, he agreed to pay Jacob, who had been one of his drivers in the slave period, $100 at the end of the year and to keep him and his five dependents "in the old fashion." Comparatively, two years later, Pickens employed a "field labourer" for the year at $60 and maintenance.

Largely out of the ranks of the foremen, there arose a higher level of agricultural supervisors who might be described collectively as the "managerial class." Managers differed from foremen in that their primary concern was with yearly, rather than daily, operations, though they usually performed both functions. In essence, the manager substituted for the absentee owner. He planned the crops, scheduled the various phases of cultivation and harvesting, executed the schedules, kept the records, attended to the health, welfare, and efficiency of the laboring force, and prepared, shipped, and frequently marketed the finished product. The manager might also do field work, but he was clearly more than a field hand. He was the fully authorized agent of the owner, filling an office which before the war was dominated by whites. Frequently, the manager received a special share of the profits from the owner. Occasionally, he became the lessee of the plantation and operated it for his own profit and, thus, passed into the entrepreneurial class where he competed directly with white men.

The Negro manager in action was personified by Adam R. Deas. He had been born a slave, the son of Robert, a driver on The Grove, a rice plantation near Adams Run belonging to John Berkeley Grimball. In July, 1863, during an inland raid conducted by Union gunboats and a portion of the First South Carolina Volunteers, he fled to the Union lines along with the entire Negro population of The Grove, including his father, his mother Amy, and his grandmother Sally. Like so many refugee families, they pre-empted a plot on Edisto Island in the spring of 1865 and remained there through 1866. In the spring of 1866, however, Robert contracted with Grimball to serve as caretaker of The Grove and an adjacent rice plantation, Pinebury, which was also owned by Grimball. In return, Robert was allowed to farm whatever portion of land he chose with a mule provided by Grimball. Adam's mother and grandmother, however, elected to remain on Edisto, partly because they had already begun a crop.

Through 1868, Grimball attempted unsuccessfully to resume profitable operations on his two rice plantations. In 1865 and 1866, he and his son, Arthur, were unable to induce their ex-slaves to return from their Edisto homes. In 1867, Robert persuaded a few Negroes to plant rice on The Grove, paying a third of the produce as a rental. Since Grimball did not provide seed rice and advances, some of these laborers had to earn expenses by working on neighboring plantations and the yield was both late and scanty. In 1868, Pinebury, the buildings of which had been razed and the fields neglected since 1863, was taken up by a Negro manager named Henry Jenkins with the same unsatisfactory results.

In November, 1868, Grimball sent for Adam Deas. Deas, in a letter written in his clear, squarish script, promised to come to Grimball in Charleston within a week. "I was at the Grove on Thursday afternoon," he wrote, catching a scene. "The people are all busy thrashing & I met my father cleaning out the house, expecting you up. I hope the family are all well." In Charleston, early in December, he called on Grimball and agreed to act as the owner's agent in restoring Pinebury to productivity. What happened to Pinebury during the next eleven years was adequate testimony to Deas's worth as a manager. On December 5, Adam returned to the country and on December 9 he wrote: "The time being so Short I was out from 6 oclock this morning up [to] 10½ oclock to night, the Place being in Such bad order & no Building. It is ahard Task for me to gat any one, but up to this date the 9th, I have the Promise of 15 hands who Expect to move Right on the Plantation." On December 21, while laborers were searching for places for the coming year, he again reported to Grimball: "Everybody & my Self are Standing quite Still at present Waiting for Jan . . . So you must allow me a little Chance, I cant go to Work With a Rush, because I have no money." In concluding, he advised Grimball to take any offer for the lease of The Grove which he might receive.

In January, 1869, Deas mustered a score of rice hands on Pinebury and by early February was hard at work. Apparently, however, he had located his family on the Gibbes' plantation, near Willtown, perhaps because there were no buildings remaining on Pinebury. ". . . I was down to the Plantation Purty Much all this Week, and We are trying to do the Best We Can," he informed Grimball. "Just now the men are Busy Building & preparing Some Where to Put their Provision & Seed Rice." He rejected Grimball's idea of transferring some Pinebury acreage to the Grove. "I don't think Sir that you aught to take a way any of the Pinebury land to Put with the Grove because If We Should not be able to Plant all of It this Season We will Want It to put in order this Summer for the next Season and I am trying to get the Place full up." Several days later, Deas wrote that nothing had been done on the Grove for the coming season. On April 1, while some planters were still seeking laborers, he reported: "We are trying to Push things through in the Best Way We Can We have one Square under water & in a day or 2 We Will have 2 more." By the end of June, the crop was planted. "We have Planted 74 acres of Rice & 50 acres of Corn. We are Now trying to Keep the Grass out of What is Planted." During 1869, Deas acted as Grimball's "agent and nominal leasee" for Pinebury. The payment for his services was a fifth of Berkeley's rental fee of five bushels of rice for each acre of rice land planted and one bushel of rice for each acre of high ground cultivated. On October 26, Deas's commission produced $142.92 in cash.

In 1870, Deas worked on Pinebury under the same terms, but a better yield on increased acreage raised his income to $233.74. In 1871, he received $243.84 for his portion of the crop. In July, 1871, Deas journeyed to Charleston where he signed a three-year contract with Grimball to "cash" rent Pinebury himself for 1000 bushels of rice a year. Hardly had Deas returned to Pinebury when the area was lashed by a hurricane. Nevertheless, by September 3, he reported that the laboring force was hard at work and would soon repair the damage to flood gates, dikes, ditches, and the crop. In 1872, Deas actually leased Pinebury for himself, generously agreeing to pay Grimball the rental which the owner would have received under the previous system only if the plantation were under maximum cultivation. Deas, apparently, intended to profit by using the two-day system to pay his laborers, a system which Grimball had steadfastly refused to utilize. Deas's income from Pinebury in 1872 was about $800, roughly half the salary of a South Carolina circuit judge. By some means Grimball broke the three-year lease, and, in 1873, Deas agreed to manage Pinebury for two-thirds of the yield of 105 acres of rice to be planted. Grimball's share of the crop sold for $946 and Deas's for twice that amount. Deducting $600 in expenses, Deas's income for the year was approximately $1300. Thus, Deas, for the first time, derived a higher income from managing Pinebury than its owner received as a rental.

Grimball was unhappy with the contract for 1873. Even in April, 1873, he had pressed Deas to plant more than the 105 acres stipulated in the agreement. However, a scarcity of laborers prevented further expansion. On June 30, Grimball met Deas in the Charleston office of their marketing agent, Ingraham, and told him he would only agree to share equally both expenses and profits in 1874. In August, Grimball thought that Deas was unwilling to agree to these terms, "says he has made nothing by planting," and complained that even the present terms were too high. Deas was to write his decision. Ultimately, Deas offered Grimball a cash rental of $1200, due on December 1, 1874, and Grimball accepted. The rent was no longer fixed by the acreage planted, and Deas expanded to the fullest the area under cultivation. Perhaps with the benefit of information from the marketing agent, Grimball estimated that Deas's sales grossed $4975 in the year 1874. If this were true, after deducting the expense of planting the increased acreage, Deas's income for the year was about $3,000, a handsome figure in view of the fact that the governor of South Carolina earned only $3,500 during the same period. Grimball agreed to a cash rental in 1875 also, and Deas's profits were probably similar to those of 1874.

Again unhappy with the terms of the contract, Grimball offered, in the summer of 1875, to rent Pinebury to Deas in 1876 for either $1625 in cash or one-third of the net profits. Finally, they agreed to plant at least 150 acres in rice, and the owner was to get a third of the net profits. However, a poor crop and poorer prices produced only about $900 for Grimball and twice as much for Deas. In 1877, they agreed to share both expenses and profits equally. At the end of the year, Grimball resolved to offer Deas a straight 10 per cent commission on profits to act as his manager. It is not clear whether Deas accepted or not, but he did remain in control of Pinebury in 1878 and 1879.

Finally, on December 20, 1879, in a letter addressed to John Berkeley Grimball at 19 Lynch Street, Charleston, Deas severed his connection with Pinebury and gave the owner some parting advice: "It is true I don't expect to plant pinebury next year but things there are moving too slowly. Other planters are moving and you should too, otherwise you allow the hands to Scatter off And it is so much trouble to Get them together again. I know that you dont like to Commence your work until January, but you throw things to far back why Sir you ought [to] be Ploughing now, Giving the Lands to the Rain and Frost." Unfortunately for Pinebury, Grimball did not take Deas's advice. At the end of the year, he gave management of the plantation to his son Lewis, a physician and druggist who had been singularly and repeatedly unsuccessful in his profession. Grimball, himself, remained in Charleston, visiting old friends and being visited, presiding over sessions of the Charleston Library Society, ordering books for the Library, and writing over and over again ever-diminishing lists of the ill-paying stocks and bonds of his and his wife's estates.

A similar story could be told of Bacchus Bryan, a Negro who managed five other hands in planting rice, cotton, and provision crops on a plantation in the vicinity of Adams Run. From 1866 through 1876, Bacchus agreed with the owner, Reverend John Cornish, each year to pay half the yield in return for the use of the land and the advance of supplies. Bacchus's profits were much less spectacular than those of Adam Deas but were probably nearer those of the average manager. For instance, in 1869, Bacchus's share of the cotton crop sold for about $160, and this probably constituted nearly the whole of his cash income for the year.

The Negro manager was a persistent figure in post-Reconstruction South Carolina. In 1888, a Northerner returning to the Sea Islands twenty-five years after he had first come there as a teacher, found that Cuffee, who had been a foreman on one of the plantations, was managing a stock farm for a Northern firm. In 1900, however, there were only 180 farm managers among the 85,000 Negro farm operators in South Carolina, and probably most of these were less like the entrepreneurs Adam Deas and Bacchus Bryan than the salaried Cuffee.

"We all know that the colored people want land," cried the carpetbag delegate from Barnwell District to the members of the Constitutional Convention which assembled in Charleston in January, 1868. "Night and day they think and dream of it. It is their all in all." The speaker hardly exaggerated; yet, at that time, relatively few Negroes had entered the class of agricultural landholders. Some free Negroes had owned land (and, indeed, slaves) before the war, a negligible number had been given lands by their late masters after emancipation, and some two thousand had secured titles to lands on the Sea Islands. But, in view of the desires of Negro agrarians, these were, after all, mere tokens. Under the circumstances, it is hardly surprising that Negro agriculturalists simply shifted the focus of their expectations from the federal to the state government, and that local Republican leaders, mindful of where their strength lay, were anxious to accommodate them.

Doubtless, many Negro voters would have favored confiscation. "I know how hard it was to beat down that idea," declared a Massachusetts man on the floor of the Constitutional Convention. "It has been in their minds that government would some day present them with their old homes and old farms. There is no gentleman on this floor from the country who does not know how much he has had to contend with when he has had to oppose that desire which has been uppermost in the hearts of the people." A few of the most radical of Republican leaders endorsed confiscation. A scalawag delegate to the organizing convention of the Republican party, held in May, 1867, was "perfectly disgusted with the negroes, that they advocate confiscation of lands . . ."; and as late as the campaign of 1870, the scalawag boss of Laurens County was vigorously preaching confiscation with the result, one resident observed, that "none of the men want to work, all looking forward to next month when they expect to get land & houses." White anxiety concerning confiscation was partially justified, but much of the furor was generated by an overly timorous white community. In Spartanburg, in November, 1867, a prospective purchaser of a plot of land was too cautious when he reneged because he was "afraid of confiscation." Furthermore, there were Conservative politicians who were not above promoting and playing upon the anxieties of their friends. "Knowing that the Radicals had scared the Southern people with *Confiscation* by Congress, from the path of honor and patriotism, I thought I would scare them back again with *Confiscation* by the negroes," B. F. Perry wrote to one of his supporters in the spring of 1867. "You have lived long enough in the world . . . to know that most persons are influenced more by their *fears* than by their honor," concluded that gentleman of highly vaunted democratic reputation.

Confiscation met with the early, persistent, and successful opposition of the main body of Republican leadership. In the convention of the party in July, 1867, the idea was not even formally introduced; in the field, campaigners subsequently adopted the same attitude; and the Constitutional Convention of 1868 with the full assent of its Negro delegates pointedly asserted that "The only manner by which any land can be obtained by the landless will be to purchase it." Two years later, in a political meeting at Christ Church, native Negro A. J. Ransier was still answering the charge that Republicans had offered Negroes forty acres and a mule. "We had never," he declared, "promised any such thing, but on the contrary advised the people to buy lands by saving their money, and not to expect confiscation or the possession of lands that were not theirs, nor ours to give them . . ."

To some extent, Republicans rejected confiscation as inexpedient — that is, that titles conferred might be impermanent, that Congress might disallow such a measure, or that whites might be driven to violence. Primarily, however, they refused confiscation because they felt it was contrary to the natural laws of economic morality; it would be useless, they argued, even pernicious, to legislate against the fiats of classical economics. "The sooner the public mind is disabused of that impression, the sooner every man knows that to acquire land he must earn it," declared W. J. Whipper, a Northern-born Negro delegate, to the convention, "the sooner he feels the Government has no lands to dispose of or to give him the better. Do what is necessary to protect the laborer in his labor and you will effect the greatest possible good."

Republican leaders were strong in their rejection of confiscation, but by no means did they abandon the use of political power to achieve the popular goal of a division of large landed estates among their supporters. Ultimately, they settled upon two complementary but separate programs. One of these involved the purchase of lands by the state for division and resale to actual settlers. By the spring of 1869, acting upon an ordinance of the Constitutional Convention, the Republican legislature had created a Land Commission which was to purchase, by the issue of bonds guaranteed by the state, lands at public sales and "otherwise." Under a land commissioner these acquisitions were to be surveyed, divided into smaller tracts, and sold to settlers at the purchase price. The settler would pay taxes on the land and 7 per cent interest yearly on the principal of the loan. One half the plot was to be under cultivation within three years, at which time payments on the purchase price would begin and would extend over such period as the legislature directed.

Almost from its inception the land program was hamstrung by political involvement. At least some Radical politicians thought that the partisan purposes of the relocation scheme were as important as the economic goals. In October, 1869, for instance, a leading Republican concurred in a statement by the land commissioner that party interest dictated "That in the upper counties it is necessary to purchase large tracts, so that colonies may be planted of sufficient strength to help, & protect each other, and to be the nucleas [sic] of education &c &c &c. . . . We must draw the union people to points where they will be a power & mutual supporters." In addition, the office of land commissioner, itself, soon became a political pawn. The first incumbent was Charles P. Leslie, an aging, erratic, unscrupulous New Yorker who was given the office, it was said, to compensate him for losing the United States marshalship which he really wanted. Whatever talents Leslie may have possessed were turned immediately to filling his own pockets, an occupation at which he was very adept. Using $200,000 in bonds authorized by the legislature, Leslie began to buy land at a rapid rate.

A very few purchases were well made at sheriff's sales, from the executors of estates, and by conscientious agents with an eye for a bargain. For instance, Henry E. Hayne, an ex-sergeant of the First South Carolina, acting as Leslie's agent in Marion County, arranged to buy 1734 acres of land for $1,500. The tract contained, by Hayne's report, 200 acres of "good swamp land, a splendid range for cattle &c and good corn and grain land. The balance is good upland, a large portion of woodland. There is good water on the place, several good buildings." The tract was then rented for $100 yearly, suggesting that the offered price was reasonable. But more to the point: "A number of citizens are prepared to purchase small tracts of this property from the State."

Unfortunately, most purchases were made by men less reliable than Hayne. In Darlington County, Leslie's agent bought lands at a sheriff's sale supposedly for the land agency. He later changed the titles to indicate that he had bought them on his own account and then re-sold the land to the state at twice the price he had paid. Throughout the life of the commission, a suspiciously large number of purchases were made from men directly involved in Republican politics — including Governor Scott, himself.

The secretary of state, Francis L. Cardozo, a Negro, had never approved of the choice of Leslie as land commissioner and soon refused to participate as a member of the advisory board. As rumors of fraud and mismanagement in the Land Commission began to circulate, Cardozo and other Negro leaders — including Rainey, Whipper, Elliott, Ransier, and Nash — moved to force Leslie out of his post. Dominant in the legislature in the winter of 1870, these men refused to pass a proposed bill authorizing the issuance of an additional $500,000 in bonds for the use of the commission. Leslie and others were very anxious to win the new issue because they had already overspent the amount initially authorized. It was arranged, finally, that Leslie would resign and the legislature would sanction the new issue. According to the subsequent testimony of N. G. Parker, treasurer of the state until 1872, Leslie demanded and got $25,000 in return for his resignation and the surrender of his one-twelfth share in the Greenville and Columbia Railroad. To raise this money, Parker arranged the fraudulent purchase by the commission of some 27,000 acres (one portion of which was appropriately known as "Hell Hole Swamp") for about $119,000 nominally, but actually for much less. D. H. Chamberlain, then attorney-general, discovered that the title to one of these tracts was faulty and that Parker and his associates were aware of the fault. However, he did not expose his findings.

One of the demands of the Negro legislators was the appointment of a Negro as land commissioner. The stipulation was met, but the choice was unfortunate, falling upon R. C. De Large, a native Charlestonian, still young in 1870 and very ambitious politically. Parker later asserted that De Large was Scott's choice and that the latter arranged his appointment so that De Large could steal enough money to unseat scalawag Congressman C. C. Bowen of Charleston, Scott's most bitter personal and political enemy. True or not, De Large was in fact immediately caught up in a year-long, vitriolic campaign against Bowen from which he emerged victorious. During De Large's absence, the scalawag comptroller-general, apparently, took the lead in administering the land program. Again, most purchases were made at exorbitant prices through the agency of or directly from officers of the state, and by 1871 the funds of the commission were exhausted. They were never renewed, but the quality of lands purchased during De Large's tenure did improve somewhat. The improvement may have resulted from the closer scrutiny to which Cardozo and Chamberlain subjected prospective transactions. Since Cardozo, as secretary of state, had to record purchases and Chamberlain, as attorney-general, was responsible for the legitimacy of titles, each man was in a position to block suspicious transactions. During the De Large period, interested parties were, apparently, willing to solicit their approval for purchases and the degree of control which they exercised was considerable.

Criticism within the Republican party during the spring and summer of 1870 forced many officials to defend their connections with purchases made by the commission. Chafing under charges that professional politicians were obstructing the efficient administration of the land program, an aroused legislature ordered the land commissioner to report immediately, formed a joint committee to investigate the program, and passed legislation clarifying the conditions of settlement on state lands. Ultimately, the legislature assigned the duties of the land commissioner to the secretary of state, and, thus, Cardozo, himself, assumed responsibility for the program. A very able administrator, Cardozo quickly systematized the haphazardly kept records of the office, ascertained the location of the one hundred thousand acres in twenty-three counties which belonged to the state, investigated the degree to which these lands were settled, and arranged to receive regular payments from the settlers. In April, 1872, the advisory board permitted the commissioner to base the price of lots (those already sold, as well as those remaining unsold) upon their actual value rather than the price which the state had paid for them. Immediately, a wave of additional settlers moved onto state lands. On one state-owned plantation on St.

John's Island, for instance, fifteen lots which had lain barren for two years were promptly settled by Negro families.

Henry E. Hayne, who succeeded Cardozo as secretary of state in 1872, continued the good work. He improved the administration of the program still more by appointing a single agent, J. E. Green, to replace the many county agents. Green familiarized himself with each tract, encouraged settlement, and made collections. In 1874, Hayne reported that the administration of the program under the new system cost only 8 per cent of collections, whereas before expenses had often exceeded revenues. On one occasion, when settlers were about to be evicted from their Darlington County plots because of a fault in the title purchased by the state, Hayne used the resources of the commission to correct the deficiency. The humane policy of the state was further revealed in February, 1874, when the legislature, following a poor farming season in some areas and a money scarcity which generally prevailed after the panic of 1873, authorized the commissioner to postpone payments in cases where subsistence was endangered.

Strangely enough, although they did not buy new lands to perpetuate the program, the Redeemers continued and improved still further the administration of the Land Commission. Through litigation they added about 1300 acres to the program, the only addition made after 1870. Further, they refunded taxes paid by settlers before titles were granted, it being customary for titleholders to pay tax claims against real estate, in this case the state itself. In November, 1877, about 47,000 acres or one-half of the state's lands remained unsettled. The Redeemers reduced prices on unsold plots, surveyed tracts more suitably, allowed occupants to reduce the size of their farms to adjust to their ability to pay, and passed on the lands of those unable to pay to other settlers.

The end result was that by the late 1880's nearly all the state's lands had been disposed of to actual settlers; and by the early 1890's approximately 2,000 families had obtained titles to farms through the agency of the Land Commission.

Perhaps the most effective scheme of land redistribution implemented by Republicans in South Carolina was also the most subtle. In its earliest form, it was conceived as a heavy tax on unused land. This tax was expected to force owners of such lands either to bear the burden of the tax from their other resources, to put the land under cultivation and thus employ laborers or renters, or to allow the land to be sold either to the state for resale or directly to private parties. As it matured, the basic concept expanded. Not only would unused lands be heavily taxed, but all property, real and personal, used and unused, would be so burdened. Thus, all capital would be forced into full productivity, or, in essence, would be confiscated and sold. One anticipated result of the program was that a large quantity of land would be offered for sale at prices that the landless could afford to pay. Also, heavy taxation would support a prospective expansion of public services rendered by the state: internal improvements; care for the insane, orphans, and indigents; a modern penitentiary; a streamlined and efficient judiciary; and, most important, a system of public education from primary to university levels. Heavy taxation, then, was the core of the Republican program in Reconstruction South Carolina. It was a program designed to give its supporters land, educational opportunity, and other benefits that would imbue them with a spirit of loyalty to the party and insure its continuance in power.

From its birth, the Republican party in South Carolina consciously and deliberately advocated land division through taxation. "We must drive them to the wall by taxation," cried one carpetbagger to a Republican convention in the summer of 1867. While the convention was more circumspect in its choice of words, its resolution on the subject was commonly interpreted as an endorsement of a tax program which, as one Negro delegate observed, "would force owners of large tracts of waste lands to sell and give us a chance." As the campaign for the Constitutional Convention of 1868 proceeded, the tax program supplanted confiscation in popularity. Such a program, one observer noted, would be as effective as confiscation, "and yet avoid the strenuous opposition that any scheme of general land pillaging would infallibly meet with in the North." Perhaps, with this criticism in mind, the Convention itself decided to tax all real and personal property at a single, uniform rate based upon actual values. This amendment did not mean that the party had deserted the tax program. The carpetbag delegate who was soon to become the treasurer of South Carolina put the case succinctly:

> Taxes are always (at least in hard times) a burden, will be assessed yearly upon all lands, and they must be paid. The expenses of the State (constantly increasing, will be a continual drag upon those who attempt to carry on large landed estates with a small amount of money,) will alone force sufficient lands upon the market at all times to meet the wants of all the landless. This Convention will cost the State quite a large sum of money. A legislature will soon assemble, and that will cost money. Education, once limited, is to be general, and that will be expensive; and, to keep up with the age, it is fair to presume that the State tax will be greater next year than this, and increase yearly; this will be felt, and will be the stimulus to many for owning less land, and cause them to see the necessity for disposing of their surplus.

The Convention adopted other measures which were to supplement the tax program. It requested and obtained from the military authorities a stay law — or rather order — designed to delay forced sales of lands to allow the landless an opportunity to accumulate capital and the tax program time to depress land prices. Once the agriculturalist had acquired a small holding, the Convention sought to protect him against the direct effects of forced sales in civil actions by a constitutional provision that exempted from such sales a homestead worth $1000 and personal property worth $500. A suggested corollary to the tax program would have required state officers to subdivide all tracts sold for taxes into plots of 160 acres or less. This proposal met with the sympathy of the Convention, but the majority ultimately decided that no satisfactory defense could be made against monied men buying as many plots as they chose.

Once in power on the state level, Republicans hastened to carry out the tax program. The burden of taxation was shifted from mercantile interests to landed property, and the total tax bill increased rapidly to astounding heights. During Reconstruction, the amount of taxes levied and collected every year was well over a million dollars; before 1860 it had always been considerably less, and, during the Orr regime, had been only about $600,000 — less than one dollar each for every man, woman, and child in the state.

Some Republican politicians contended that the state tax rate in South Carolina was no more than in some Northern states. Such, indeed, was the case, but the whole story of taxation in South Carolina was not told by the *state tax rate*. Actually, the rate was kept deliberately low, but other variables in the tax equation were manipulated to raise the tax bill ever higher. In addition to the state levy, each county taxed its property owners for the administration of regular county affairs and for special purposes such as new buildings and roads. Furthermore, the school tax was often quoted separately. Thus, E. Gelzer, in Abbeville County in 1871, paid a state tax of only $59.64; but, at the same time, he paid a $25.56 county tax and an $8.52 school tax. Property owners residing in towns and cities paid municipal taxes as well. Census returns indicate that Carolinians paid $2,800,000 in state and local taxes in 1870, an enormous sum by prewar standards. Of this amount, $1,600,000, including the school tax, went to Columbia, while almost half was consumed locally.

A second variable in the tax equation was the value placed on property for tax purposes. Before the advent of the Republican regime, the tendency was to undervalue property in assessing it for tax purposes; after, the tendency was drastically reversed. This weapon for increasing taxes was sharpened by the authority given to the governor to appoint and remove assessors within each county and by the creation of a State Board of Equalization with power to decrease or increase (two- or threefold if it wished) the assessment of a given county. There was abundant evidence that this power was abused during the first six years of Republican rule. A meeting of Conservative white leaders in Columbia in 1871 admitted that the state tax rate (about 1 per cent at that time) was not excessive but complained that assessments were unduly high. Wide fluctuations in the total of assessments between 1869 and 1873 show clearly that this power was freely used. For instance, in 1870, the figure was placed at $184,000,000. In the hard election year of 1872, it was reduced to $146,000,000, only to be raised again after the election. Even some Republicans deprecated such blatant unfairness. Martin R. Delany, the former major, stated in 1871 that lands were often sold at one-half to one-fourth of the assessed value. "Land in South Carolina is greatly depreciated," he declared, "while taxes have become proportionately higher." "Taxes are enormous," exclaimed a Northern businessman residing in Charleston, voicing a fact all too well known among his landowning Carolina contemporaries.

Astonishing as the tax bill was in the aggregate, it was even more astounding to the individual taxpayer. In May, 1871, a Chester County planter lamented: "I have paid $400.00 Dollars of Tax this year & expect to pay about $300.00 in the fall making $700 in all. before the war my Tax was from 30 to 50 Dollars. Where does the money go?" By January 6, 1873, he had paid $365 in taxes for that year and would have to pay another large tax bill before the year ended. "I can go to some other place (say Augusta) & live comfortably on my Tax," he asserted.

Republican reform Governor Daniel H. Chamberlain, who held office from November, 1874, until he was ousted by Hampton in April, 1877, made a determined and partly successful attempt to reduce the tax burden. In this he was ably assisted by Secretary of the Treasury Francis L. Cardozo. In 1874, Chamberlain recommended to the legislature an across-the-board reduction in expenditures and, soon thereafter, executed a re-assessment of taxable property throughout the state which very nearly equalized assessed and market values. When the legislature passed a tax bill in the spring that exceeded his recommendations, Chamberlain courageously vetoed it, and in the legislative session of 1875–1876 he succeeded in reducing the rate of taxation from 13 to 11 mils.

Chamberlain won much praise and considerable support from the native white community for his efforts, but other circumstances were operating in the fall of 1875 to turn the tide of taxpayer sentiment against him. In the counties and cities where corruptionists remained entrenched, local tax rates were largely beyond the control of the governor. In spite of Chamberlain's reforms, these drove the total tax bill for their areas to great heights. In heavily agricultural Kershaw County, yearly taxes (county and education, as well as state) amounted to about 2 per cent of the total value of taxable property. Taxpayers, under such circumstances, were hardly impressed with the fact that Chamberlain had saved them from a 2.2 per cent levy. One upcountry editor queried, "Does this mean reform or confiscation?" Even in counties under native white control, where local levies had been kept at a consistent minimum, Chamberlain's moderate gains were more than offset by the decline in cotton profits and the increase in food costs which began in the fall of 1875. "Our crops are poorer, the prices range much lower than for years past, while flour and bacon are higher," complained an Anderson County editor early in December. When he learned that the tax rate for his county was to be about 1.5 per cent he cried, "Thus our worst fears are realized."

The results of the Republican tax program were everything that its authors anticipated — and more. Vast quantities of land were forfeited to the state every year, and others passed under the hammer to satisfy judgments rendered in civil suits. When the Republicans took office, the state held only about 23,000 acres of land forfeited for taxes. This figure dwindled into insignificance as tax foreclosures by the Radical government proceeded. In the early 1870's, the local press, particularly in the middle and lower counties, abounded in advertisements of tax sales. During the state fiscal year which ended October 31, 1873, officials reported 270,000 acres of land as forfeited for about $21,000 in taxes; and in the following year the figure rose to more than 500,000 acres. Interestingly, the twelve counties in which the most land was forfeited were precisely those dozen counties in which the proportion of Negro to white voters was highest.

White landowners in the lower counties were convinced that Republican tax collectors were, indeed, conspiring to "drive them to the wall." One Georgetown plantation owner complained in the spring of 1869 that the county tax collector had told him he did not know how much his tax would be or when it would be determined. "The scallawags and capt Baggers would no doubt like right well to see my place advertised and sold for taxes," he surmised. "I trust they will not be gratified." John Berkeley Grimball could have added that confiscation by hook was fully as possible as by crook. In the spring of 1873, he was surprised to see that Pinebury, which Adam Deas was operating, was up for sale within two weeks for delinquent taxes. Hasty inquiry revealed that his tax payment had gone astray and much ado at the county seat eventually brought rectification. In January of the following year, when the tax collector visited Charleston for the convenience of residents owning land in Colleton County, Grimball proceeded to the appointed place prepared to pay his dues, only to find that the collector had fled to avoid meeting a rival claimant to his office. For some days, he tried to locate the elusive collector, always arriving just after the tax agent had departed, pursued by his rival. Finally, he succeeded in passing the duty to the post office by resorting to the use of registered mail.

In the fall of 1875, as agricultural profits declined and the price of foods increased, economic distress began to spread into the white counties. In 1873, no land had been forfeited for taxes in Anderson County, and, in 1874, only two acres were lost to the state. In December, 1875, however, the editor of the local newspaper noted that "a very large amount of property was sold" at the monthly sheriff's sales for the execution of tax and civil judgments against property.

The losses of property owners were not entirely reckoned in the number of acres forfeited. Obviously, all labored under the burden of paying unusually high taxes on lands which had never yielded so little income. J. B. Grimball paid state and local taxes on Pinebury amounting to $119.36 in 1873 and $136.08 in 1874. During the same period, he received about $1200 yearly by leasing the plantation to Adam Deas. Thus, the tax on the property amounted to about 10 and 11 per cent of the gross income in 1873 and 1874 respectively, and, in terms of productivity, these were banner years for Pinebury. Taxpayers were also distressed by the extremes to which they were forced to save their lands from the sheriff. The widow of the most prominent Know-Nothing leader in ante-bellum South Carolina complained to a friend in 1874: "Having six pieces of property not yielding me one dollar, and those demons after taking my Plantation from me, have this year levied 50 per cent Taxes which I have had to sell Silver to pay." Similarly, in 1872, a Charlestonian, noting that the ownership of a plantation "will *cost* me a good deal" during the year, complained: "I don't think you cd get any attempt at resistance in any part of the Old State to an immediate Confiscation of all the property of the whites if the so called Legislature ordered it."

The price of land in South Carolina was depressed after the war and continued to decline until 1868. Even after prosperity returned, prices remained relatively low. In some measure, this was a result of the uncertain political situation; but, more particularly, it was the fruit of the Republican tax program. In 1870, one upcountry farmer painted the picture rather deftly:

> Our country is in a bad condition. Negroes have every thing in their own hands, and do as they please. The Legislature is radical out and out. All or nearly all of our County officers are negroes. The consequence is that lands and every other kind of property is taxed so high that they have decline twenty five percent in value since last fall. Every little negro in the county is now going to school and the public pays for it. There is a negro school near Billy Turners, with over fifty schollars and lands principally are taxed to pay for them. This is a hell of a fix but we cant help it, and the best policy is to conform as far as possible to circumstance . . .

It is evident that many Negroes took advantage of these conditions to acquire lands by purchase. Unfortunately, no census of Negro farm owners was taken in South Carolina before 1890, but in that year 13,075 Negro farmers owned farms of some size. Since only about 4,000 Negroes obtained lands through government agencies, roughly 9,000 Negro farmers must have bought farms through their own efforts during the generation that followed emancipation. A large portion of these realized their desire for land during the eight years of Republican rule. In 1870, Reuben Tomlinson, a Northern missionary who came to the Sea Islands during the war and remained to become a Bureau educator and a state legislator, declared on the floor of the House of Representatives that "If we could get together the statistics of the laboring men who have during the past year become land owners through their own exertions and industry, we would be perfectly astounded." Random evidence seems to bear out this assumption, for one cannot travel far into contemporary writings without encountering numerous incidental references to the sale of land to Negroes.

It is improbable that many Negroes acquired land through cooperative purchases, but on at least two occasions, Negroes formed associations for the purchase of lands. In January, 1868, in the low country, F. L. Cardozo described one such operation to his colleagues in the Constitutional Convention: "About one hundred poor colored men of Charleston met together and formed themselves into a Charleston Land Company. They subscribed for a number of shares at $10 per share, one dollar payable monthly. They have been meeting for a year. Yesterday they purchased 600 acres of land for $6,600 that would have sold for $25,000 or $50,000 in better times. They would not have been able to buy it had not the owner through necessity been compelled to sell." In 1872, a similar group acquired a 750-acre estate on Edisto Island.

The Negro generally paid his poll tax and his one- or two-dollar levy on personal property cheerfully, but once he had acquired lands, he was subject to the same adverse effects of the Republican tax program as his white neighbors. Contrary to the design of the politicians, small holders suffered equally with large. In 1874, a Northern traveler visited the home of a Negro farmer who had bought his land two years previously with two hundred hard-saved dollars. "Now the cabin has fallen into decay, the rain and wind come through great cracks in the walls of the one cheerless room, the man and his wife are in rags, and the children run wild about the parched and stony fields, clothed very much as they were when they first saw the light. Negro voters are not exempt from the visits of the tax gatherer, and it is almost certain that the poor fellow's place will, with many others, be forfeited to the State at the next sale for delinquent taxes." It is hardly surprising that Negro property owners were observed in one lowcountry community in January, 1877, paying taxes for the support of the Hampton government while a Republican still sat in the governor's office.

Native white resistance to the aggressive tax program of the Republicans was at first tentative and cautious. There was, after all, no assurance that Republican rule through Negro voters would ever end and an imprudent resistance might close doors which could never be re-opened. Nevertheless, almost as soon as the first Republican tax bills reached the taxpayers a quiet desperation crept into Conservative politics. "Negro laws will ruin any people," an upcountry farmer advised his brother during the summer of 1869, "those that was not broke by the old debts will be by tax my tax was 57 dollars & 30 cents. I have paid but how long I can do so I dont no but we still hope for better times we think in the year 1870 we will be able to change the law making power . . ." In 1870, native whites looked anxiously to the polls and placed their trust in a "Reform" Republican candidate for governor. "If the Radicals gain the day what is to become of us, I don't see how we can stay in the country," a Laurens resident wrote to her son on the eve of the elections "for our taxes will be increased, and we will be under the very heels of the Radicals." The election was lost and taxes rose as expected. Among John Berkeley Grimball's papers there is an artifact, a clipping from a March, 1871, issue of a Charleston paper. What Grimball saved was an article which concluded with the sentence: "This is a TAXATION which is tantamount to CONFISCATION." Several weeks later, an upcountry woman wrote to her cousin: "I have nothing of a political nature to communicate that would interest you, — nothing much talked of these days except Taxation & the Ku Klux."

It was characteristic of the native white community that their anxiety should lead to meetings and that meetings should soon assume some state-wide organization. The state-wide conference took place in May, 1871, under the name of the Taxpayers' Convention. Even though the convention included Negroes, carpetbaggers, and scalawags, as well as rising young professional politicians within the ranks of the Conservatives, it was dominated by the prewar aristocracy — men such as Chesnut, Kershaw, Aldrich, Trenholm, Porter, Trescot, Bonham, and Hagood. Indeed, it was generally conceded that no comparably distinguished body of men had met in the state since the Secession Convention. Nevertheless, the leadership remained cautious. The debates were temperate, no Republican officeholder was personally impugned, and the resolutions were innocuous: it was in essence a whitewash of the Republican regime.

The Moses administration (1872–1874) brought still higher taxes and consequent agitation among the whites. ". . . our tax this year is full one third higher than last year and it looks to me like that it will finally result in confiscation of the land by Taxation," wrote a Laurens planter in February, 1873. The whites called another Taxpayers' Convention for February, 1874. "Things are blue enough here & the taxation is practically confiscation," wrote a resident of Georgetown in January, "I trust there may be some good in the Taxpayer's [sic] Convention *this time.*" The desperation of the whites rapidly became less quiet, particularly as they began to read signs outside the state which suggested that Negro rule might not be perpetual. The tone of the convention of 1874 was radically different from that of 1871. An impressive delegation of gentlemen from the convention journeyed to Washington where they formally presented to both Grant and the House of Representatives a vigorous indictment of the Republican regime in South Carolina. "It has been openly avowed by prominent members of the Legislature," the memorial of the convention declared, "that taxes should be increased to a point which will compel the sale of the great body of the land, and take it away from the former owners." Perhaps the most important result of the convention was the legacy of organization which it left to the white community. Largely under the leadership of the "Bourbons," local Tax Unions were formed which were to function as the watchdogs of persons in office. These organizations were very active in the 1874 campaign and in supporting the reform programs of the Chamberlain administration. In the fall of 1875, however, the Tax Union rapidly lost ground to more radical elements among the native whites and, by 1876, had virtually ceased to exist.

During 1876, native whites stymied the Republican tax program by extra-legal means. In the fall of 1876, they refused to pay taxes to the Chamberlain government which claimed victory in the November elections while they voluntarily paid 10 per cent of the previous year's levy to the Hampton government. By general concert, native whites also refused to buy lands being sold for taxes. In December, 1876, in Charleston County numerous parcels of land had been forfeited for some $200,000 in taxes and costs, but not one single purchaser could be found for any of these. Once firmly in power, the Redeemers hastened to restore forfeited lands to the tax books and allow delinquents generous limits within which to repair their deficiencies.

Although the great mass of Negroes in Reconstruction South Carolina earned their living through agricultural pursuits, others worked as domestics, as skilled or unskilled laborers, and as business and professional men.

With the exception of agriculture, the domestic class was by far the most numerous economic group. These found employment in various capacities in the homes of the whites. Negro men became butlers, valets, coachmen, gardeners, and handy men. Negro women became housemaids, personal maids, cooks, laundresses, nurses, and serving girls. As described earlier, a general reduction in household staffs occurred immediately after the war. As Reconstruction progressed, further reductions ensued. Typical was the H. L. Pinckney plantation near Statesburg, in Sumter District, in June, 1866, where a unique arrangement prevailed in which ten domestics — two cooks, two houseboys, a house servant, a gardener, a nurse, a housemaid, a washer, and "Louisia — (little)" — were included with thirty-nine agricultural workers in a contract by which all would receive a third of the crop. By 1868, the total work force had been reduced to sixteen, only three of whom were domestics.

In relations with his employer, the Negro domestic experienced grievances similar to those felt by his agrarian contemporaries. His responses, too, were much the same. In a sense, however, he was freer to express his dissatisfaction since desertion — the ultimate reply to unsatisfactory conditions — could follow the daily or weekly payday and he need not forfeit or await the division of a crop. Occasionally, individual domestics revealed a persistent reluctance to remain with any single employer very long. In 1872, in Charleston a Negro cook told her employer that she was leaving the household, not because she was dissatisfied with her position but "because, ma'am, it look like old time to stay too long in one place." However, like their brothers in agriculture, most Negro servants adjusted to the new order during the first years of Reconstruction and established rather permanent relations with a single employer. For instance, in 1870, a lady residing in a large household in the village of Chicora wrote: "We have only made one change in our domestic arrangements since you left [a year previously] & that is in the outdoor department, the indoor servants are all with us still & we go on so smoothly & comfortably that I hope it will be long before we have to make any change."

A glimpse into the life of a servant girl working in one of the Campbell households in Charleston in 1868 is preserved in a letter from her to her aunt in Camden. The girl, Celia Johnson, was a member of a "free" Negro family living in Camden and had come to Charleston as a servant. To her aunt's invitation to visit Camden, she replied that she would like to, but it was too "hard to get away from Mrs. Campbell, and hard to get money." Not all of Celia's life was drudgery. "I spent last Sunday night with sister Mary Stewart, and went to a meetin to the African church. We heard a blind man preacher and had good times." But, there was work to be done. "Excuse this short letter as I am very busy ironing," she concluded. "All the way I will get to go home is to promise to come back in October. If I don't I will make hard feelings . . . I have been sleeping upstairs so long that you will have [to] get me an upstairs room when I get there. I don't know how to sleep down stairs."

In slavery, large numbers of Negroes had performed relatively unskilled labor in the lumbering and turpentine industries and in construction, particularly railroad construction. In freedom, many laborers continued the occupations which they had learned as slaves and these were joined by freedmen who had never before had an opportunity to leave the fields. Frequently, the choice was made even more attractive by the prospect of higher and certain wages in industry. In 1873, a resident of the once rice-rich county of Georgetown noted the growing profitability of the production of naval stores and commented: "The turpentine interest being very lucrative, controls a great deal of labor & the Rice fields suffer thereby." The war, itself, promoted the growth of the laboring population outside of agriculture. During and after the war, hundreds of Negro laborers found employment in the Quartermaster and Engineering departments of the army and in the Freedmen's Bureau. The dislocations of the war and of the months immediately following left large numbers of

Negroes in Charleston and in the towns and villages of the interior. These often earned a subsistence by working as stevedores, street cleaners, yardkeepers, porters, draymen, messengers, and at other unskilled jobs. The repair of war-worn and torn rail lines and a boom in the construction of new lines gave at least temporary employment to several thousand Negro laborers. Many others found jobs in a new and fantastically profitable industry — the mining of phosphates for processing into fertilizers. Some of the rock was dug from tidewater river beds by giant dredges, but large deposits lay on or near the surface of the land. These "land deposits" were mined with pick and shovel, wielded by Negroes under the supervision of white foremen. "A common laborer will raise a ton a day, for which he is paid $1.76," wrote an agricultural expert in 1882. "The product of the land rock is about 100,000 tons a year." Negroes struggling to retain their small farms in the Sea Islands during the hard years following emancipation must have viewed the rise of the phosphate industry as providential.

Many of the free Negroes of Charleston had long earned their living as artisans. A month after their liberation, the Negro tradesmen of the city participated in a parade, described earlier, which indicated the diversity of their occupations and the solidity of their organization. Free Negroes in other centers of population followed much the same pattern on minor scales. Further, emancipation freed numerous slaves who had been trained in the trades, particularly in those connected with plantation maintenance. Thus, literally thousands of more or less proficient blacksmiths, carpenters, wheelrights, masons, plasterers, millers, mechanics, and engineers (who had operated steam engines supplying power to rice threshers, cotton gins, sawmills, and flour mills) became "free" economic agents.

Many of these, of course, were only partially trained for their occupations, and many combined the practice of their trade with other pursuits (e.g., farming) in order to support themselves. Still, a few Negro tradesmen attained eminence as artists in their work. The Noisette family in Charleston, for instance, was nationally praised for the products of their nursery and the elder Noisette gained a creditable reputation as botanist. Ben Williams, a Negro shoemaker in Columbia, was awarded a premium in November, 1869, "for the second best lot of shoes" exhibited at the annual fair of the State Agricultural and Mechanical Society.

In Reconstruction South Carolina, Negroes tended to withdraw or abstain from entering certain trades, leaving them entirely to whites. "The well wishers of the negro race see with regret that they seem to have little inclination to take to mechanical pursuits," reported a Northern journalist from Charleston in 1870. ". . . it is a rare thing to find a negro adopting the trade of blacksmith, or carpenter, or any other requiring skilled labor." This particular gentleman was apparently suffering from myopia induced by the fact that he did not, in truth, wish very well for the Negro race, but he did glimpse a part of a large trend among tradesmen. The results of this retirement of the Negro tradesman is evident in the business directory of the state published in 1880. In the entire state, it listed no Negroes among the cigar-makers, coopers, or coppersmiths, and only one Negro dyer and cleaner was polled. Furthermore, outside of Charleston there were no Negroes listed as tailors, dressmakers, tinners, upholsterers, wheelwrights, or builders and repairmen; in Charleston about half of the tradesmen engaged in each specialty were Negroes. Although the evidence is by no means conclusive, for obviously many Negro tradesmen continued to serve white customers, there was also a trend toward Negro tradesmen serving Negro customers exclusively. In Spartanburg District, in the winter of 1867,

David Golightly Harris probably touched a deep reason for this tendency. Vexed at the inefficiency of the white man he had chosen to run his flour mill, he had reached the point of exasperation. "I have an idea of puting Paschal to the mill," he wrote. "But some say a negro will drive all the customers away. . . . Everything is a botheration." Charleston, again, was perhaps exceptional in this respect.

Probably most Negro tradesmen worked independently and a few worked for established white employers, but many were also businessmen in that they kept shops in which their goods or services were sold. In addition to those in the trades, a large number of Negroes engaged in small enterprises, such as the flourishing trade in supplying firewood to Charleston from the neighboring islands. More typical of small Negro-owned businesses, perhaps, were those of Beverly Nash who operated a produce stand in Columbia in 1867 and later opened a coal and wood yard, and of Samuel Nuckles, a political refugee from Union County, who, in 1871, operated a drayage wagon in the same city. Occasionally, Negroes embarked upon large-scale undertakings in business. For instance, in the spring of 1866, "The Star Spangled Banner Association" led by Tom Long, a veteran of the First South, raised $20,000 by $15 to $100 subscriptions with which they opened a store at Beaufort and acquired a steamer to operate along the coast under the captaincy of Robert Smalls. During the Republican ascendency, Negro politicians participated in ventures darkened in greater or lesser degree by partisan shadows. Thus, F. L. Cardozo and J. H. Rainey were two of the twelve stockholders in the Greenville and Columbia Railroad Company and, with several other Negro leaders, charter members of the Columbia Street-Railway Company. However, the most striking successes in business were made by individuals in private life who gradually accumulated capital and expanded the scope of their operations. John Thorne, who had apparently led in a cooperative land purchase on Edisto Island in 1872, ten years later owned 250 acres of land on the island, "an extensive store and storehouse," and a comfortable residence. "He also runs a gin-house with six gins, and last year ginned out upwards of 400 bags of cotton of 300 pounds each, for which work he received four cents per pound. He advanced largely to several colored planters, and is worth from $15,000 to $20,000."

Although not numerous, the Negro professional class was very influential during and after Reconstruction. Ministers, politicians, and lawyers led the professions, while teachers and medical doctors formed a rather weak second rank, both in popular influence and economic importance.